Commodities

FINANCIAL MARKETS AND INVESTMENTS SERIES
H. Kent Baker and Greg Filbeck, Series Editors

Portfolio Theory and Management
Edited by H. Kent Baker and Greg Filbeck

Public Real Estate Markets and Investments
Edited by H. Kent Baker and Peter Chinloy

Private Real Estate Markets and Investments
Edited by H. Kent Baker and Peter Chinloy

Investment Risk Management
Edited by H. Kent Baker and Greg Filbeck

Private Equity: Opportunities and Risks
Edited by H. Kent Baker, Greg Filbeck, and Halil Kiymaz

Mutual Funds and Exchange-Traded Funds: Building Blocks to Wealth
Edited by H. Kent Baker, Greg Filbeck, and Halil Kiymaz

Financial Behavior: Players, Services, Products, and Markets
Edited by H. Kent Baker, Greg Filbeck, and Victor Ricciardi

Hedge Funds: Structure, Strategies, and Performance
Edited by H. Kent Baker and Greg Filbeck

Commodities

MARKETS, PERFORMANCE, AND STRATEGIES

EDITED BY

H. KENT BAKER

GREG FILBECK

and

JEFFREY H. HARRIS

OXFORD
UNIVERSITY PRESS

OXFORD
UNIVERSITY PRESS

Oxford University Press is a department of the University of Oxford. It furthers the University's objective of excellence in research, scholarship, and education by publishing worldwide. Oxford is a registered trade mark of Oxford University Press in the UK and certain other countries.

Published in the United States of America by Oxford University Press
198 Madison Avenue, New York, NY 10016, United States of America.

Library of Congress Cataloging-in-Publication Data
Names: Baker, H. Kent (Harold Kent), 1944– author. | Filbeck, Greg, author. |
Harris, Jeffrey H., 1964– author.
Title: Commodities : markets, performance, and strategies / H. Kent Baker,
Greg Filbeck, Jeffrey H. Harris.
Description: New York, NY : Oxford University Press, [2018] | Includes index.
Identifiers: LCCN 2017034125 | ISBN 9780190656010 (hardcover : alk. paper) |
ISBN 9780190656034 (epub)
Subjects: LCSH: Commodity exchanges. | Investments.
Classification: LCC HG6046 .B3227 2018 | DDC 332.63/28—dc23
LC record available at https://lccn.loc.gov/2017034125

Dedication

We dedicate this book to the late James T. Moser Jr., who was an Executive-in-Residence at American University's Kogod School of Business and faculty program director for the Master in Finance program. Before joining American University, Professor. Moser worked as senior director at the Chicago Mercantile Exchange, an economic advisor and research officer at the Federal Reserve Bank of Chicago for 14 years, and deputy chief economist at the Commodity Futures Trading Commission for six years. He also taught at the University of Kentucky, Michigan State University, Illinois Institute of Technology, University of Illinois at Champaign–Urbana, Louisiana Tech University, and University of Maryland at College Park, among others. His research focused on the contribution of derivatives to the real economy, the arrangements private markets make to resolve problems arising from the use of derivatives, and the proper role of government in regulating derivatives activity.

Contents

Figures

Tables

Acknowledgments

There's a lot more to publishing a book than writing it and slapping a cover on it.
—Vince Flynn

Publishing an edited book involves many people, and everyone plays an important part. We greatly appreciate the contributions of all involved with this project, and we want to highlight several groups and individuals. First, we thank the helpful comments of those who reviewed our book proposal and ultimately helped us craft a better end product.

Second, we gratefully acknowledge our chapter authors, who contributed their expertise and talents to provide a comprehensive view of the world of commodities. Although writing a book chapter often is a more difficult and time-consuming task than originally anticipated, the authors persevered. We worked closely with each author in the editing process to bring out the best of each chapter. We have also tried to create a common voice to the topics while retaining the individuality of approaches among the expert authors involved.

Third, we thank our partners at Oxford University Press, who performed in the same highly professional manner that they have throughout the Financial Markets and Investments Series. Special thanks go to David Pervin (Senior Editor), Rajakumari Ganessin (Project Manager), Richard Isomaki (Copyeditor), and Claudie Peterfreund (Indexer), but others played important roles in this book project.

Fourth, we appreciate the research support provided by our respective institutions—the Kogod School of Business at American University and the Behrend College at Penn State Erie. Finally, our families provided encouragement and support for which we are very appreciative: Linda and Rory Baker; Mickey, Judy, Janis, Aaron, Kyle, and Grant Filbeck; Andy, Alex, Kelly, and Emma Harris and Kirsten Anderson.

About the Editors

H. Kent Baker, CFA, CMA, is University Professor of Finance in the Kogod School of Business at American University. Professor Baker is the author or editor of 28 books, including *Investment Traps Exposed: Navigating Investor Mistakes and Behavioral Biases, Investor Behavior: The Psychology of Financial Planning and Investing, Behavioral Finance: Investors, Corporations, and Markets, Portfolio Theory and Management, Survey Research in Corporate Finance,* and *Understanding Financial Management: A Practical Guide*. As one of the most prolific finance academics, he has published more than 170 peer-reviewed articles in such outlets as the *Journal of Finance, Journal of Financial and Quantitative Analysis, Financial Management, Financial Analysts Journal, Journal of Portfolio Management,* and *Harvard Business Review*. He has consulting and training experience with more than 100 organizations. Professor Baker holds a BSBA from Georgetown University; MEd, MBA, and DBA degrees from the University of Maryland; and an MA, MS, and two PhDs from American University.

Greg Filbeck, CFA, FRM, CAIA, CIPM, PRM, holds the Samuel P. Black III Professor of Finance and Risk Management at Penn State Erie, the Behrend College, and serves as the Director for the Black School of Business. He formerly served as Senior Vice President of Kaplan Schweser and held academic appointments at Miami University and the University of Toledo, where he served as the Associate Director of the Center for Family Business. Professor Filbeck is an author or editor of eight books and has published more than 90 refereed academic journal articles in the *Financial Analysts Journal, Financial Review,* and *Journal of Business Finance & Accounting*, among others. Professor Filbeck holds and conducts training worldwide for candidates for the CFA, FRM™, and CAIA® designations. Professor Filbeck holds a BS from Murray State University, an MS from Penn State University, and a DBA from the University of Kentucky.

Jeffrey H. Harris is the Director and Chief Economist, Division of Economic and Risk Analysis, at the U.S. Securities and Exchange Commission. He also holds the Gary Cohn Goldman Sachs Endowed Chair in Finance at the Kogod School of Business at American University. He recently served as Chief Economist at the U.S. Commodity Futures Trading Commission (CFTC), and formerly as a Visiting Academic at NASDAQ and the U.S. Securities and Exchange Commission. He has held faculty appointments at Syracuse, Southern Methodist, Delaware, Notre Dame, and Ohio State. He has testified about commodity markets before Congress, the CFTC, and the European Commission.

His research appears in the *Energy Journal, Financial Management, Journal of Finance, Journal of Financial and Quantitative Analysis, Journal of Financial Economics, Journal of Futures Markets*, and *Review of Financial Studies*, among others. Professor Harris received his BA in physics and an MBA from the University of Iowa, and a PhD in finance from The Ohio State University.

About the Contributors

Ramesh Adhikari is an Assistant Professor of Finance at Humboldt State University. Before joining the faculty at Humboldt State, he worked at Tribhuvan University in Nepal and served at the central bank of Nepal. He received multiple outstanding graduate student awards from both Tribhuvan University and the University of New Orleans. He was also a research fellow at Osaka Sangyo University in Japan. His research interests are in empirical asset pricing, corporate finance, commodities, portfolio management, and risk management. He received a BA in mathematics with a minor in economics from Tribhuvan University of Nepal, an MA in economics from California State University, Sacramento, and an MS and PhD in financial economics from the University of New Orleans.

Azizah Aljohani is a master's student in e-business at the University of Ottawa. She has conducted scholarly research on the role of social media and more recently on volatility clustering of virtual currencies. She received several government scholarships and awards based on her academic achievements. She holds a bachelor's degree in administrative sciences from King Saud University, Saudi Arabia.

Thomas Barkley, CFA, FRM, CAIA, is a Professor of Finance Practice at the Whitman School of Management, Syracuse University, and is also the director of the MS in finance program. His teaching and research interests are in corporate finance and derivatives. He previously worked for Enron (Research Group) and the Risk Analytics Group at Florida Power & Light. In both cases, his work included pricing exotic options and structuring products for use in the energy markets. Other experience includes retail banking in the United Kingdom, teaching high-school mathematics in the Bahamas, and general management of a family-run publishing company. He received an MBA from Thunderbird, the American Graduate School of International Management, and a PhD in finance from the University of Florida.

Claudio Boido is a Professor of Financial Markets and Alternative Investments at the School of Economics University of Siena. He also teaches investments at the LUISS School of Business and Management in Rome. Professor Boido has published several books, including *Mercati, Strumenti Finanziari, Investimenti Alternativi* (*Financial Markets and Alternative Assets*) and *Il trasferimento alternativo dei rischi e la finanza strutturata di parte assicurativa* (*Alternative Risk Transfer and Structured Finance and Insurance*). He has also published in the *ICFAI Journal of Behavioural Finance, ICFAI University Journal of Derivative Markets, ICFAI University Journal of Financial Risk Management, Journal of Financial Management, Markets and Institutions,* and *Financial Assets and Investing.* Professor Boido has served as a reviewer for *Quantitative Finance* (Routledge), *Rivista Bancaria Minerva Bancaria,* and *Economic Notes: Review of Banking Finance and Monetary Economics.* He has been a member of the board in Real Estate Funds and a consultant in derivative contracts for Italian courts.

Gustavo Camilo is an Associate at Cornerstone Research, an economic and financial consulting firm. He previously was a researcher at the Monetary Programming and Economic Studies Department of the Central Bank of the Dominican Republic, where he created big-data models to assist in the development of monetary policy decisions. Dr. Camilo has taught macroeconomics and econometrics at the undergraduate level. He holds a PhD in economics from the University of Pennsylvania, where he specialized in corporate finance, macroeconomics, and development economics with a focus on China and cycles in product markets.

Pattanaporn Chatjuthamard is an Associate Professor of Finance at Sasin Graduate Institute of Business Administration of Chulalongkorn University, Bangkok, Thailand. Before joining the faculty at Sasin, she was an assistant professor at Texas A&M International University in Laredo, Texas. She was also a Visiting Professor at Levin Graduate Institute, the University at Buffalo. Her primary research interests include corporate finance, corporate governance, and international financial markets. She has published in leading scholarly and professional journals including the *Journal of Financial Intermediation, Journal of Corporate Finance, Journal of Banking and Finance, Journal of Financial Research, Journal of Business Ethics,* and *International Review of Economics and Finance.* Professor Chatjuthamard received a PhD in finance from the University of Wisconsin–Milwaukee.

Frankie Ho-Chi Chau is an Associate Professor of Finance at the Durham University Business School, University of Durham, United Kingdom. Professor Chau's research focuses on behavioral economics and finance, derivative securities, and international financial management. He has published in the *Journal of Business Finance & Accounting, International Review of Financial Analysis, Economic Modelling,* and *Journal of International Financial Markets, Institutions & Money,* among others. He is a recipient of the best-paper award at the Spring Conference of the Multinational Finance Society (MFS) held in Cyprus in April 2016. He has also written book chapters on the role of commodity futures in strategic asset allocation and international finance topics, which appeared in *Alternative Investments: Instruments, Performance, Benchmarks, and Strategies* and *China's Role in Global Economic Recovery.* Professor Chau received a PhD in finance from Durham University.

Lamia Chourou is an Assistant Professor of Accounting at the Telfer School of Management, University of Ottawa. She holds the Chartered Professional Accountant (CPA) Ontario Fellowship. Her research focuses on capital markets, particularly fair value accounting, corporate governance, earnings management, and executive compensation. She has published in such journals as the *Canadian Journal of Administrative Sciences, Journal of Multinational Financial Management, Quarterly*

Journal of Finance and Accounting, and *Canadian Investment Review*. She was previously a Teaching Fellow at Queen's School of Business and Assistant Professor at the University of Sousse. She holds a PhD in financial accounting from the Smith School of Business, Queen's University, and a PhD in finance from the University of Tunis.

Janko Cizel is an Associate at Cornerstone Research. His research covers a broad range of topics in credit risk, financial regulation, financial stability, and early-warning systems. He worked as a researcher at various policy institutions, including the International Monetary Fund (Financial Crisis Division, Monetary and Capital Markets Department), European Central Bank (Fiscal Policy Division), Dutch Central Bank (Financial Stability Division), and European Commission (Joint Research Center in Ispra, Italy). His recent policy assignments include evaluation of macro-prudential policies, development of early-warning indicators for sovereign distress, and analysis of Basel risk weights. Dr. Cizel holds a PhD in finance from Tinbergen Institute and Vrije Universiteit Amsterdam.

Xu Dai is a Senior Researcher in the Jilin Research Center of Rural Finance, and an Associate Professor and postgraduate supervisor at the School of Finance in Jilin University of Finance and Economics. She worked in one of the well-known, big-four state banks, Industrial and Commercial Bank of China, for more than eight years before returning to the university. Her primary research interests include international finance, commercial banking, rural finance, internet finance, and corporate finance. China Finance Press published her authoritative scholarly book entitled *The Study on the Capitalization of Chinese Foreign Reserves*. She has also coauthored two textbooks in international finance and published many articles in Chinese journals. Professor Dai was also a Visiting Scholar at the Australian Charles Sturt University. She received both her master's degree and PhD in finance from Jilin University.

Rataporn Deesomsak is an Assistant Professor of Finance at the Durham University Business School, University of Durham, United Kingdom. Professor Deesomsak's research interests are primarily in empirical corporate finance, specifically in the areas of capital structure, debt maturity, dividend policy, and cash-holding decisions. Her work has appeared in the *Journal of Multinational Financial Management, International Review of Financial Analysis, Journal of International Financial Markets, Institutions & Money*, among others. She is a recipient of the best-paper award at the Spring Conference of the Multinational Finance Society (MFS) held in Cyprus in April 2016. Professor Deesomsak received a PhD in economics and finance from Durham University.

Xiaohu Deng is Assistant Professor of Finance in the Tasmanian School of Business and Economics at University of Tasmania in Australia. He previously served on the faculty at Ohio University. Professor Deng's research focuses on corporate finance and short selling. He received an undergraduate degree in management from Wuhan University (China), an MS in quantitative finance from Hofstra University, and a PhD from the University of Memphis.

Erik Devos is the JP Morgan Chase Professor in Business Administration and Professor of Finance at the College of Business Administration of the University of Texas El Paso. He previously taught at Ohio University and Binghamton University (SUNY). He has published in finance and accounting journals such as *Review of Financial Studies, Journal of Accounting and Economics, Journal of Corporate Finance, Financial Management,* and *Journal of Banking and Finance.* He has also published in real estate journals such as *Real Estate Economics, Journal of Real Estate Economics and Finance,* and *Journal of Real Estate Research.* Professor Devos serves as an associate editor for the *Financial Review.* He received a master's degree in financial economics from Erasmus University in Rotterdam and a PhD in finance from Binghamton University (SUNY).

Joseph Eagleeye is a principal of the consulting firm Quartile Risk, LLC, as well as cofounder of Premia Capital Management. He codeveloped the Premia Research Bancor Index, which is a smart commodity-oriented beta. Previously, Mr. Eagleeye was a senior derivatives strategist at Putnam Investments. While at Putnam, he researched, back-tested, and implemented systematic, relative-value derivative strategies as well as comanaging Putnam's institutional commodity program. He was also a senior consultant for Merrill Lynch Investment Management in the Risk Management Group. where he advised on benchmark construction, hedging strategies, index replication strategies, portfolio construction, performance attribution, and risk management. Before joining Putnam Investments, Mr. Eagleeye developed programmed trading applications for Morgan Stanley's Equity Division. He is a member of the Editorial Advisory Board of the *Global Commodities Applied Research Digest* and is also the coeditor of *Intelligent Commodity Investing.* Mr. Eagleeye holds a BS in applied mathematics from Yale University and an MBA from the University of California at Berkeley.

Aaron Filbeck, CFA, CAIA, is an Investment Analyst at The Joseph Group Capital Management, a registered investment advisor, in Columbus, Ohio. As a key member of the firm's investment committee, he is responsible for investment research and portfolio construction initiatives including asset allocation recommendations, fund manager due diligence and selection, and fundamental research for individual equity securities. He earned a BS in finance from Pennsylvania State University, where he served as President and Chief Investment Strategist of The Intrieri Family Student Managed Fund.

Raymond P. H. Fishe is the Patricia A. and George W. Wellde, Jr. Distinguished Professor of Finance at the University of Richmond. He was previously Professor of Economics and Finance at the University of Miami, Senior Academic Fellow at the U.S. Securities and Exchange Commission, and Consultant at the Commodity Futures Trading Commission. He has published articles in the *American Economic Review, Journal of Finance, Journal of Financial Economics, Journal of Financial Markets, Journal of Financial and Quantitative Analysis, Journal of Futures Markets, Journal of Money, Credit and Banking, Review of Economics and Statistics, Journal of Econometrics,* and other journals in finance and economics. He received a PhD from the University of Florida.

Michael S. Haigh is Managing Director and Global Head of Commodities Research for Société Générale in New York City. From 2013 to 2017, SG CIB was voted the Best Overall in Commodity Research in both *risk* and *energy risk.* Previously, Dr. Haigh was Global Head of Commodities Research at Standard Chartered Bank, Managing Director at K2 Advisors LLC, Managing Director and U.S. Head of Commodities Research and Strategy at Société Générale, and Associate Chief Economist at the U.S. Commodity Futures Trading Commission. Formerly, he was a tenured Associate Professor of

Economics at the University of Maryland and he has taught derivative courses at NYU Stern, Johns Hopkins, and George Washington University. He has published numerous papers in leading journals including the *Journal of Finance, Journal of Business, Journal of Futures Markets,* and *Journal of Applied Econometrics.* He holds a PhD in economics with a minor in statistics from North Carolina State University.

Richard Heckinger is a member of the Working Group on Financial Markets at the Federal Reserve Bank of Chicago. Mr. Heckinger was formerly Vice President and Senior Policy Advisor, Financial Markets Group, at the Federal Reserve Bank of Chicago. He started his career in financial markets at the Chicago Board Options Exchange in 1973, and has held positions in trading, exchange operations, project management, clearing, risk management, product development and marketing. In the 1990s, he was Chief Operating Officer of the Stock Exchange of Hong Kong, and subsequently Chief Executive of the Hong Kong Securities Clearing Corporation. Mr. Heckinger is the Contributing Editor of the *Central Banking Journal* and is also an Associate Editor of *Journal of Financial Market Infrastructures.* He also serves as an Editorial Advisory Board member of the *Global Commodities Applied Research Digest.* He has a BA in mathematics and a MPhil in economics from the London School of Economics

Hunter M. Holzhauer is the UC Foundation Assistant Professor of Finance at the University of Tennessee, Chattanooga. Professor Holzhauer has taught various graduate and undergraduate classes, including corporate finance, investments, behavioral finance, portfolio management, and derivatives. His financial industry experience includes positions as a credit analyst with Colonial Bank and a financial planner and fixed-income portfolio manager with AmSouth Bank. Professor Holzhauer has published a dozen papers on such topics as alternative investments, socially responsible investing, risk management, and behavioral finance. His research has been published in several academic journals including multiple papers with the *Journal of Investing* and *Journal of Applied Finance.* He has also written several chapters on investment subjects, including mutual funds, risk management, and hedge funds. He received a BS in business administration and bio-psychology from Birmingham-Southern College, an MBA from Mississippi State University, and a PhD from the University of Alabama.

Florian Ielpo is Head of Macro Research at Unigestion in Geneva, Switzerland. He is also an associate researcher at the Centre d'Economie de la Sorbonne, University of Paris 1. Dr. Ielpo has worked for 15 years in the asset management industry first as an economist and then as a fixed income portfolio manager. He teaches a commodity finance class at the 272 Master at Dauphine University in Paris, France and has coauthored a book on *Economics of Commodities.* He has published in such journals as the *Journal of Economic Dynamics and Control, Quantitative Finance,* and *Journal of Forecasting.* He graduated from the Ecole Normale Supérieure de Cachan (ENS) and the Ecole Nationale de la Statistique et de l'Administration Economique (ENSAE).

Halil Kiymaz, CFA, is Bank of America Professor of Finance at Rollins College, Crummer Graduate School of Business. Professor Kiymaz maintains an extensive research agenda and has published more than 70 articles in scholarly and practitioner journals. He also coedited four books: *The Art of Capital Restructuring: Creating Shareholder Value through Mergers and Acquisition* (Wiley & Sons, Inc. 2011), *Market*

Microstructure in Emerging and Developed Markets (Wiley & Sons, Inc. 2013), *Private Equity: Opportunities and Risks* (Oxford University Press, 2015), and *Mutual Funds and Exchange-Traded Funds: Building Blocks to Wealth* (Oxford University Press, 2016). His research has appeared in the *Journal of Banking and Finance, Financial Review, Global Finance Journal, Journal of Applied Finance, Journal of Economics and Finance, Review of Financial Economics,* and *Quarterly Journal of Business and Economics,* among others. He is the former president of the Academy of Financial Services and finance editor of *International Journal of Emerging Markets.* Professor Kiymaz received an MBA, MA, and PhD from the University of New Orleans.

Timothy A. Krause is an Assistant Professor and the Director of the Intrieri Family Student Managed Fund at the Black School of Business at Penn State Behrend. He previously was in the financial services industry for 20 years as an investments professional at Bank of America, BNP Paribas, Vector Capital Markets, and Zecco Trading (now part of TradeKing). He previously taught undergraduate and MBA finance courses at the University of Texas at San Antonio, Pepperdine University, and St. Edward's University. His research and teaching interests include investments, derivatives, risk management, financial institutions, market microstructure, and general financial markets. He has published in the *Review of Quantitative Finance and Accounting, Journal of Derivatives, Applied Financial Economics, International Review of Economics and Finance, Journal of Asset Management,* and *International Journal of Accounting and Information Management.* He received a BA in government/economics, an MBA in finance from Georgetown University, and a PhD in finance from the University of Texas at San Antonio.

Donald F. Larson is a development economist and founder of the International Institute for Development and Environmental Studies. He also holds a courtesy faculty position at William and Mary's Institute for the Theory and Practice of International Relations. He has written on a range of topics with a focus on rural development, natural resource management, food security, carbon markets, and trade. He has authored or coedited six books, and has published in a diverse range of scholarly journals, including the *Journal of Development Economics, Journal of Environmental Economics and Management, Annales d'Economie et Statistique, Journal of Futures Markets,* and *World Bank Economic Review.* He has worked with governments on policy issues in Africa, Asia, Europe, the Caribbean, Latin America, and the South Pacific. Dr. Larson was also part of a World Bank team that launched the first climate-finance fund, the Prototype Carbon Fund, in 1999. He has a PhD in agricultural and resource economics from the University of Maryland, and also holds degrees in economics from Virginia Tech and the College of William and Mary.

Greg Leonard heads Cornerstone Research's energy and commodities practice. He has more than 15 years of consulting experience in litigation and regulatory proceedings involving energy, commodities, finance, and antitrust. In the energy and commodity markets, Dr. Leonard has extensive experience in analyzing market manipulation claims, analyzing trading patterns and strategies, valuing trading businesses and portfolios, valuing alleged breaches of contract, evaluating risk management practices, and analyzing the price impacts of alleged wrongful conduct. On behalf of clients, he has appeared before the enforcement staffs of the Commodity Futures Trading

Commission, Federal Energy Regulatory Commission, Federal Bureau of Investigation, and Department of Justice. Dr. Leonard received a PhD in economics from University of Rochester.

Mingwei (Max) Liang is an independent financial consultant and former research assistant at Frank G. Zarb School of Business, Hofstra University. Mr. Liang worked as a credit risk analyst intern in the enterprise risk management department at a multinational utility company, analyzing counterparty creditworthiness and managing credit exposure. He also has experience in both the hedge fund and venture capital industries. As a research assistant, he collaborated with faculty on multiple research projects about corporate finance, fixed income, derivatives, and risk management. Mr. Liang has dual undergraduate degrees in international trade and economics and in German from Shandong University, and graduated with distinction with both an MS in finance and an MS in quantitative finance from Hofstra University.

Jerry W. Markham is a Professor of Law at the Florida International University in Miami. He was previously a Professor of Law at the University of North Carolina at Chapel Hill and taught as an Adjunct Professor at the Georgetown Law Center in Washington, DC. Professor Markham earlier served as chief counsel, Division of Enforcement, U.S. Commodity Futures Trading Commission; secretary and counsel, Chicago Board Options Exchange, Inc.; attorney, Securities and Exchange Commission; and was a partner in the international law firm of Rogers & Wells (now Clifford Chance). He has published numerous articles and books including a six-volume *Financial History of the United States*. He is the chairman of Markham Consulting Inc., which provides consulting and expert witness testimony on financial market issues, and serves on the board of directors of Nomura Derivative Products, Inc., a swap dealer.

Christopher Milliken, CFA, is an industry professional and Vice President of Hennion & Walsh Asset Management's Portfolio Management Program. Hennion & Walsh Asset Management is a Registered Investment Advisory firm that uses exchange-traded funds to construct investment strategies. Mr. Milliken works under the chief investment officer and conducts research on capital markets and asset allocation strategy while overseeing the sales and trading desk. He received a BS in business administration with a focus in finance from Marist College.

Scott Mixon is Associate Director of the Office of the Chief Economist at the U.S. Commodity Futures Trading Commission. His research has been published in leading outlets including the *Journal of Derivatives*, *Journal of Economic History*, and *Journal of Financial Economics*. Before joining the Commission, Dr. Mixon was an alternative investments strategist and fund of hedge funds portfolio manager for Lyxor Asset Management, a subsidiary of Société Générale. He was previously part of Bates White Economic Consulting's Antitrust Practice. He began his career at UBS as a quantitative and derivatives strategist. Dr. Mixon received a PhD in economics from Duke University.

Nicole Moran is a Senior Manager at Cornerstone Research. She provides financial and economic analysis in complex commercial litigation and regulatory proceedings. She supports experts in preparing for deposition and trial testimony. Her experience spans several industries, including energy, agriculture, foreign exchange, consumer lending, and electronics. Dr. Moran's case experience includes arbitration, regulatory investigations, market manipulation, antitrust, consumer finance, and financial institutions. Her emphasis is on derivative markets for both exchange-traded and over-the-counter products that involve trading activity and evaluation of market design that affect market participant behavior. Before joining Cornerstone Research, Dr. Moran was a research economist at the U.S. Commodity Futures Trading Commission, where she conducted statistical and econometric analyses on derivative markets and agricultural futures. Her research has been published in leading journals, including the *Journal of Futures* and the *Journal of Agricultural and Applied Economics*. Dr. Moran received a PhD from the University of Illinois.

Ehsan Nikbakht, CFA, FRM, is a Professor of Finance in the Frank G. Zarb School of Business at Hofstra University and previously served as department chair and Associate Dean. He served on the Advisory Board of the International Association of Financial Engineers and Chair of Derivatives Committee of the New York Society of Security Analysts. Professor Nikbakht currently serves on the editorial board of the *Global Finance Journal*. He authored *Finance*, published by Barron's, and *Foreign Loans and Economic Performance*. Professor Nikbakht received a BA from the Tehran School of Business, an MBA from the Iran Center for Management Studies, and a DBA in finance from the George Washington University.

John R. Nofsinger is the William H. Seward Endowed Chair in International Finance at the College of Business and Public Policy at the University of Alaska, Anchorage. He is one of the world's leading experts in behavioral finance. He has authored/coauthored 10 finance trade books, textbooks, and scholarly books that have been translated into 11 languages. Professor Nofsinger is a prolific scholar who has published more than 50 articles in peer-reviewed journals, including prestigious scholarly journals such as the *Journal of Finance* and *Journal of Financial and Quantitative Analysis* and practitioner journals including the *Financial Analysts Journal* and *Journal of Wealth Management*. He is often quoted in the financial media, including the *Wall Street Journal, Financial Times, Fortune, Business Week, Smart Money, Money Magazine*, the *Washington Post, Bloomberg, Nightly Business Report* (NBR), and CNBC, and other media from The Dolans to TheStreet.com. Professor Nofsinger received a PhD in finance from Washington State University.

Chanel O'Neill has more than 15 years of experience conducting economic analysis for complex business litigation and regulatory matters at Cornerstone Research. She specializes in cases involving securities and commodities, including antitrust issues that arise in those markets. She has led projects addressing alleged price fixing and market manipulation of commodity spot and futures products, including spoofing and collusion allegations. She has led teams valuing commodity futures, forwards, and options as well as modeling valuation scenarios for commodity businesses, including oil fields, refineries, utilities, and coal transport. She has coordinated analysis of financial institution trading models and practices for internal investigations.

Seow Eng Ong, CFA, is Professor of Real Estate at the National University of Singapore. His research interests include real estate investment trusts, securitized real estate, auctions, housing finance, and affordability, and real estate innovations. Professor

Eng has substantial work experience in REITs, investment and portfolio management, derivative analysis and property valuation during his stints with the Inland Revenue Authority, Government of Singapore Investment Corporation, and Overseas Union Bank. He was an independent director of Cambridge Industrial Trust, a REIT listed on the Singapore Exchange. He holds a Master in Business and a PhD in finance from Indiana University.

Michael A. Penick has worked for the U.S. Commodity Futures Trading Commission (CFTC) since 1991 and for its Office of the Chief Economist since 2002. He has been involved in numerous CFTC rulemakings related to futures exchanges, swaps trading, and market manipulation. He has also worked with the Division of Enforcement on numerous manipulation investigations in the energy markets, including Amaranth and Enron. He created and maintains the CFTC History pages on the CFTC website. Before 2002, he reviewed new futures contracts and rule amendments for the CFTC's Product Review Branch. Previously, he was a member of the Chicago Board of Trade, where he traded options on Treasury bond futures and stock index futures and a stock market analyst for a market maker firm on the Chicago Board Options Exchange. He received a BA in mathematical methods in the social sciences and economics from Northwestern University and an MA in economics from Stanford University.

Dianna Preece CFA, is a Professor of Finance at the University of Louisville. She provides consulting and training to banking associations including the American Bankers Association and the Kentucky Bankers Association as well as for Schweser, a division of Kaplan. Professor Preece has published in the *Journal of Banking and Finance* and *Financial Review,* has co-authored two practitioner books on investments, and has written book chapters on topics ranging from hedge fund performance to the future of private equity. She received a BS and MBA from Marshall University and a DBA from the University of Kentucky.

Kyle J. Putnam is an Assistant Professor of Finance in the Business Department at Linfield College. Before joining the faculty at Linfield, he worked at the University of Houston–Downtown as an Assistant Professor. His research interests are in commodities, investments, portfolio management, financial institutions, and international finance. While in graduate school, he received several teaching awards as an undergraduate and MBA teaching assistant. Professor Putnam received a BA in finance and economics (summa cum laude) from George Fox University and an MS and PhD in financial economics from the University of New Orleans.

Lynn Riggs has worked for the U.S. Commodity Futures Trading Commission (CFTC) since 2011 and for its Office of the Chief Economist since 2015. She has worked extensively with the Large Trader Reporting data for both swaps and futures to examine trading activity in both markets. She has also been involved in various CFTC rulemakings related to swaps data reporting and swaps trading. Before 2011, she worked for the U.S. Census Bureau and the U.S. Centers for Disease Control. She received a PhD in economics from the University of Wisconsin–Milwaukee.

Samir Saadi is an Associate Professor of Finance at Telfer School of Management, University of Ottawa. He was a Visiting Scholar at New York University and a Visiting

Researcher at INSEAD. He has published more than 30 academic papers in such journals as *Financial Management, Journal of Corporate Finance, Journal of Banking and Finance, Contemporary Accounting Research,* and *Journal of Business Ethics.* He is the recipient of best-paper awards and various scholarships and awards. He was invited by the Standing Senate Committee on Banking, Trade, and Commerce (Government of Canada) as an expert witness to testify on the highly debated issue of digital currencies. His input made a major impact on the committee's final recommendations to the government of Canada as evidenced by the report published by this committee in 2015. He holds a PhD in financial economics from Smith School of Business, Queen's University.

Neil C. Schofield is the Managing Director of Financial Markets Training Ltd and a Visiting Fellow at the University of Reading ICMA center. Previously, he was global head of Financial Markets training at Barclays Capital from 2001 to 2008. Mr. Schofield started his career as an internal auditor at Chase Manhattan Bank but also conducted numerous internal and external training seminars for the Bank of England and the Federal Reserve System. He has authored three books: *Commodity Derivatives: Markets and Applications, Trading the Fixed Income, Inflation and Credit Markets,* and *Equity Derivatives: Institutional Applications.* Mr. Schofield holds a BSc in economics from Loughborough University and an MBA from Manchester Business School. He was elected as a Fellow of the IFS School of Finance.

Koray D. Simsek is an Associate Professor of Finance at Rollins College Crummer Graduate School of Business. Before joining Rollins, he taught at Sabanci University and EDHEC Business School. His research focuses on investments, risk management, and derivatives markets and has appeared in *Operations Research, Journal of Portfolio Management, Quantitative Finance, Journal of Investment Management,* and *International Review of Economics and Finance.* He has served as a consultant or a trainer for various companies and organizations in asset management, banking, energy, and financial technology industries in France, Turkey, and the United States. He holds a PhD in operations research and financial engineering from Princeton University.

Kamal Smimou is an Associate Professor of Finance at the Faculty of Business, University of Ontario Institute of Technology. Professor Smimou's consulting and research interests primarily focus on the application of theoretical models and empirical studies in portfolio theory and asset pricing, commodity markets, international finance, emerging markets finance, market microstructure, and within the cross-disciplinary area of finance and ethics. He has published in such journals as *Emerging Markets Review, Journal of Alternative Investments, International Review of Financial Analysis,* and *European Journal of Operational Research.* He received the 2016 Emerald Literati Network Award for Excellence for his published article in the *International Journal of Emerging Markets* and the 2010 Competitive Paper Award of the Financial Education Association. He teaches portfolio and investment strategies, international finance, financial management, derivative securities, and personal finance in undergraduate and graduate programs. Professor Smimou received a PhD from the University of Manitoba.

Aaron D. Smith is a Professor of Agricultural and Resource Economics at the University of California, Davis, where he has been since 2001. He was previously a contractor at the U.S. Commodity Futures Trading Commission. He has published his research in the

Review of Economics and Statistics, Journal of Econometrics, Journal of Financial Markets, Journal of Futures Markets, Journal of Applied Econometrics, American Journal of Agricultural Economics, and other academic journals. His research has won the Quality of Research Discovery Award from the Agricultural and Applied Economics Association (twice), the Outstanding American Journal of Agricultural Economics Article Award, and the Quality of Research Discovery Award from the European Association of Agricultural Economists. He received a PhD from the University of California, San Diego.

Andrew C. Spieler, CFA, CAIA, FRM, is a Professor of Finance in the Frank G. Zarb School of Business at Hofstra University. He has published papers in *Real Estate Economics, Journal of Real Estate Finance and Economics, Journal of Real Estate Portfolio Management, Global Finance Journal, Journal of Applied Finance*, and other journals. He served as Chair of the Derivatives Committee at the New York Society of Securities Analysts. Professor Spieler also serves as Co-director of the annual real estate conference sponsored by the Wilbur F. Breslin Center for Real Estate Studies. He received undergraduate degrees in mathematics and economics from Binghamton University (SUNY), an MS in finance from Indiana University, and an MBA and PhD from Binghamton University (SUNY).

Kelsey Syvrud is an Associate at Cornerstone Research. Before her career in consulting, she served as Visiting Assistant Professor of Finance at the Muma College of Business, University of South Florida, where she currently serves as an adjunct instructor. Dr. Syvrud's research focuses on international corporate finance, politics, law and finance, contract procurement, and entrepreneurship. She has published in the *Journal of International Business Studies*. As a doctoral candidate, Dr. Syvrud was selected to participate in the George Washington University's Summer Doctoral Institute on Institutions, the State and Development in International Business. Dr. Syvrud received a PhD from Florida State University.

Hilary Till is a principal of Premia Research LLC, which designs investment indices that are calculated by S&P Dow Jones Indices. Before joining Premia, Ms. Till was the Chief of Derivatives Strategies at Putnam Investments and a Quantitative Analyst at the Harvard Management Company. She is a member of the North American Advisory Board of the London School of Economics, the Contributing Editor of the *Global Commodities Applied Research Digest*, a publication of the J.P. Morgan Center for Commodities at the University of Colorado Denver Business School, a Research Associate at the EDHEC-Risk Institute, and the Co-editor of *Intelligent Commodity Investing*. Ms. Till is also a member of the Federal Reserve Bank of Chicago's Working Group on Financial Markets. She has a BA with general honors in statistics from the University of Chicago and a MSc in statistics from the London School of Economics.

Desmond Tsang, CFA, CPA, is an Associate Professor of Accounting in the Desautels Faculty of Management at McGill University. He began his career in auditing at Deloitte and Touche in Hong Kong and later worked as an economist at the Ontario Ministry of Finance in Canada. Subsequently, he pursued a PhD in real estate and accounting at the University of California at Berkeley. His research in real estate specializes in real estate investment trusts, performance measurement, corporate governance, and international real estate. His research in accounting includes earnings management, IFRS, and financial reporting fraud. Professor Tsang has published in top journals such as *Review of Accounting Studies, Real Estate Economics, Journal of Real Estate Research*, and *Journal of Real Estate Finance and Economics*. He has presented his research at conferences and has received several best-paper awards. In 2015, he received the Aareal Award of Excellence in Real Estate Research.

Paul Zurek is a Principal at Cornerstone Research. He advises clients in commercial litigation and regulatory matters and serves as an expert witness in legal and regulatory proceedings. His engagements involve valuations of companies, pricing of complex financial derivatives, and issues regarding market microstructure and risk management. He taught finance and economics to students and executives in the United States, Europe, and Asia. Before joining Cornerstone, he worked as a mergers and acquisitions investment banker. Dr. Zurek holds a PhD in finance from the Wharton School at the University of Pennsylvania, where his research focused on asset pricing.

Abbreviations

ADF	augmented Dicker-Fuller
ADPI	American Dairy Products Institute
AF	African
AIG	American International Group
ALJ	administrative law judge
AMA	Alternative Marketing Arrangement
AMF	Autorité des marchés financiers, Quebec
AMRC	Agricultural Marketing Resource Center
AMS	Agricultural Marketing Service
AP	associated person
AR	autoregressive
ASX	Australian Securities Exchange
ATM	at-the-money
ATS	Automated Trading System
AUM	assets under management
BCOM	Bloomberg Commodity Index
B/D	broker-dealer
BEPS	Base Erosion and Profit Sharing
BFGS	Broyden–Fletcher–Goldfarb–Shanno
BHC	bank holding company
BIS	Bank for International Settlements
BoE	Bank of England
BRIC	Brazil, Russia, India, and China
BRL	Brazilian real
Btu	British thermal units
CAPM	capital asset pricing model
CAD	Canadian dollar
CBOE	Chicago Board Options Exchange
CBOT	Chicago Board of Trade
CCC-GARCH	Constant Conditional Correlation generalized autoregressive conditional heteroscedasticity
CCP	central counterparty
CDS	credit default swap

CEA	Commodity Exchange Act
CEO	chief executive officer
CFMA	Commodity Futures Modernization Act
CFTC	Commodity Futures Trading Commission
CISDM	Center for International Securities and Derivatives Markets
CIT	commodity index trader
CIT-HF	commodity index trade and hedge fund
CLN	commodity-linked note
CMCI	Constant Maturity Commodity Index
CME	Chicago Mercantile Exchange
CMF	commodity mutual fund
COMEX	New York Commodity Exchange
COT	Commitments of Traders
CPA	certified public accountant
CPI	consumer price index
CPO	commodity pool operator
CRB	Commodity Research Bureau
CRSP MF database	Center for Research in Security Prices at the University of Chicago Bias-Free U.S. Mutual Fund Database
CRU	CRU International Ltd.
CTA	commodity trading advisor
CTF	commodity trading firm
CTR III	Corporate Tax Reform III
CVaR	conditional VaR
CVSI	Commodity Volatility Spillover Index
DBC	PowerShares DB Commodity Index Tracking Fund
DBIQ	Deutsche Bank Index Quant
DCC	dynamic conditional correlation
DCE	Dalian Commodity Exchange
DCM	designated contract market
DCO	derivatives clearing organization
DCR	Division of Clearing and Risk
DF-GLS	Dickey-Fuller Generalized Least Squares
DGL	PowerShares DB Gold Fund
DJIA	Dow Jones Industrial Average Index
DJ-UBSCI	Dow Jones-UBS Commodity Index
DMO	Division of Market Oversight
DOE	Division of Enforcement
DOJ	Department of Justice
DSIO	Division of Swap Dealer and Intermediary Oversight
DTB	Deutsche Terminbörse
DTN	Data Transmission Network
DY	Diebold and Yilmaz
EAFE	Europe/Anstralasia/Far East
ECB	European Central Bank
ECM	exempt commercial market

ECP	eligible contract participant
EFET	European Federation of Energy Traders
EFP	Exchange of Futures for Physical
EFRP	exchange for related position
EGARCH	exponential generalized autoregressive conditional heteroscedastic
EIA	Energy Information Administration
EITI	Extractive Industries Transparency Initiative
EM	emerging market
EMBI	emerging markets bond index
EMIR	European Market Infrastructure Regulation
EPA	Environmental Protection Agency
ERS	Economic Research Service
EST	Eastern Standard Time
ETC	commodity exchange-traded fund *or* exchange-traded commodity
ETF	exchange-traded fund
ETN	exchange-traded note
ETP	exchange-traded product
EU	European Union
EWMA	exponentially weighted moving averages
FAO	Food and Agricultural Organization
FAOSTAT	Food and Agriculture Organization Corporate Statistical Database
FAS	Foreign Agricultural Service
FCM	futures commission merchant
FDIC	Federal Deposit Insurance Corporation
FDM	Forex Dealer Member
FERC	Federal Energy Regulatory Commission
FHC	financial holding company
FINRA	Financial Industry Regulatory Authority
FMIA	Financial Markets Infrastructure Act
FOB	free on board
FSOC	Financial Stability Oversight Council
FTC	Federal Trade Commission
FTPA	Futures Trading Practices Act
FTSE NAREIT	Financial Times Stock Index National Association of Real Estate Investment Trusts
FX	foreign exchange
GABI	Global Advisors Bitcoin Investment Funds
GARCH	generalized autoregressive conditional heteroskedasticity
GARP	Global Association of Risk Professionals
GCCA	Global Cold Chain Alliance
GDP	gross domestic product
GDV	Gesamtverband der Deutschen Versicherungswirtschaft
GEM	Global Economic Monitor
GFA	Grain Futures Act
GFC	global financial crisis
GLD	SPDR Gold Trust

GSCI	*formerly* Goldman Sachs Commodity Index
GVT	government
HAC	heteroskedasticity autocorrelation consistent
HFT	high frequency trader
HRS	hard red spring
HRW	hard red winter
HY	high yield
IAU	iShares Gold Trust ETF
IB	introducing broker
ICAC	International Cotton Advisory Committee
ICCO	International Cocoa Organization
ICE	Intercontinental Exchange
ICO	International Coffee Organization
IG	investment grade
IMF	International Monetary Fund
IOS	International Organization for Standardization
IOSCO	International Organization of Securities Commissions
IPE	International Petroleum Exchange
IR	information ratio
IRS	interest rate swapInternal Revenue Service
ISD	Investment Services Directive
ISDA	International Swaps and Derivatives Association
ISIS	Islamic State of Iraq and Syria
ISO	International Organization for Standardization
IT	information technology
ITM	in-the-money
ITRI	Industrial Technology Research Institute
JFSC	Jersey Financial Services Commission
JVB	Jarque-Bera
KMPG	Klynveld Peat Marwick Goerdeler
KPPS	Koop, Pesaran, and Potter (1996) and Pesaran and Shin (1998)
LA	Latin American
LB	Ljung-Box
LBMA	London Bullion Market Association
LIFFE	London International Financial Futures Exchange
LLC	Limited Liability Company
LLS	Louisiana light sweet
LME	London Metals Exchange
LMEX	LME index
LNG	liquefied natural gas
LOOP	Louisiana Offshore Oil Port
LPPM	London Platinum and Palladium Market
LSOC	legally separate operationally comingled
LTRS	Large Trader Reporting System
LVaR	Liquidity-adjusted Value at Risk
MA	moving average

MCX	Multi Commodity Exchange of India
MENA	Middle East and North Africa
MF	mutual fund
MiFID	Markets in Financial Instruments Directive
MT	metric ton
MTA	minimum transfer amount
MLA	myopic loss aversion
MLCX	Merrill Lynch Commodity Index eXtra
MLM	Mount Lucas Management
MM	million
MPT	modern portfolio theory
MSB	Money Service Business
MSBSP	major security-based swap participant
MSCI	Morgan Stanley Capital International
MSCI EAFE	Morgan Stanley Capital International Europe, Australasia and Far East
MSP	major swap participant
MT	metric ton
MTM	mark-to-market
MUV	Manufacturers Unit Value
MXN	Mexican peso
NAESB	North American Energy Standards Board
NASD	National Association of Securities Dealers
NASS	National Agricultural Statistics Service
NAV	net asset value
NBBO	National Best Bid and Offer
NCA	National Crime Agency
NCCA	National Cotton Council of America
NDM	nonfat dry milk
NFA	National Futures Association
NGL	natural gas liquid
NGO	nongovernmental organization
NOK	Norwegian kroner
NQCI	NASDAQ Commodity Benchmark Index
NYDFS	New York Department of Financial Services
NYM	New York Mercantile Exchange
NYMEX	New York Mercantile Exchange
OA	order anticipation
OCE	Office of the Chief Economist
ODT	Office of Data and Technology
OGC	Office of General Counsel
OPEC	Organization of Petroleum Exporting Countries
OTC	over-the-counter
OTM	out-of-the-money
PaR	Profit at Risk
PCA	principal component analysis
PMI	Purchasing Manager's Index

PP	Phillips-Perron
PRA	price reporting agency
PRIMA	Professional Risk Managers' International Association
PSI	Permanent Subcommittee on Investigations
PTFS	primitive trend-following strategy
PWC	PricewaterhouseCoopers, LLP
REMIT	Regulation on Market Integrity and Transparency
RIC	Registered Investment Company
RMB	Renminbi
RBOB	reformulated gasoline blendstock
RBS	Royal Bank of Scotland
REIT	real estate investment trust
RFED	retail foreign exchange dealer
RTM	repo to maturity
SAA	strategic asset allocation
SDCI	SummerHaven Dynamic Commodity Index
SDR	Swap Data Repository
SE	Special Emerging
SEC	Securities and Exchange Commission
SEF	swap execution facility
SFA	Securities and Futures Act
SGE	Shanghai Gold Exchange
SGEI	International Board subsidiary of SGE
SGX	Singapore Exchange
SHCP	Secretaría de Hacienda y Crédito Público
SHFE	Shanghai Futures Exchange
SIPC	Securities Investor Protection Corporation
SMO	smart order routing
SPDR	S&P Depository Receipt
SRB	Strategic Reserve Bureau
SRO	self-regulatory organization
SRW	soft red winter
SUCDEN	Sucres et Denrées
TAA	tactical asset allocation
TAIEX	Taiwan Stock Exchange Capitalization Weighted Stock Index
TC/RC	treatment and refining charge
TED spread	spread between treasury yields and Eurodollar interest rates
TOCOM	Tokyo Commodity Exchange
TRACE	Trade Reporting And Compliance Engine
TSI	The Steel Index
UBS	Union Bank of Switzerland
UBTI	Unrelated Business Taxable Income
ULSD	ultra-low sulfur diesel
UN	United Nations
U.S. CPI-U	Consumer Price Index for All Urban Consumers
UNCR	Uniform Net Capital Rule

USD	U.S. dollars
USDA	U.S. Department of Agriculture
USDX	U.S. Dollar Index
USGS	U.S. Geological Survey
USO	United States Oil Fund
VC	virtual currency
VaR	value at risk
VAR	vector autoregression
VAT	value-added tax
VIX	volatility index
WASDE	World Agricultural Supply and Demand Estimates
WDI	World Development Indicators
WFE/IOMA	World Federation of Exchanges and International Options Market Association
WO	Whistleblower Office
WPM	whole powdered milk
WTI	West Texas Intermediate
WTO	World Trade Organization

Commodities

Part One

BACKGROUND

1

Commodities

An Overview

H. KENT BAKER
University Professor of Finance, Kogod School of Business, American University

GREG FILBECK
Samuel P. Black III Professor of Finance and Risk Management
Director, Black School of Business, Penn State Erie, The Behrend College

JEFFREY H. HARRIS
Gary D. Cohn Goldman Sachs Chair in Finance, Kogod School of Business, American University

Introduction

Commodities tend to zig when the equity markets zag.
—Jim Rogers (2013)

Dating from the ancient use of goods and assets, including sheep, goats, pigs, and other items, as commodity money, individuals have sought ways as early as the 1500s B.C. to standardize and trade commodities for delivery in a manner that would be smooth and predictable. Rice futures traded in China as long as 2,000 to 2,500 years ago. Although the origin of the term "commodity" is French (*commodité*, meaning benefit or profit) and dates back to the 1400s, the first futures pricing in commodities originated in the late 1500s based on advanced pricing by Spain and Portugal of spices from the newly opened India routes. The first modern organized futures exchange began in 1710 at the Dojima Rice Exchange in Osaka, Japan, where merchants stored rice in warehouses for future use (West 2000). In the United States, futures trading started in the middle of the nineteenth century in the grain markets at the Chicago Board of Trade (CBOT)—the oldest established commodities house.

Commodities can be traded directly (as real-time trades) or indirectly (e.g., futures, options, and exchange-traded funds [ETFs]). Most individual commodities are traded in the form of futures, in which the trading is not based on the commodity itself but rather on a contract to buy or sell it for a certain price by a stated date in the future. The motivation for such trading is based on either price speculation or hedging. Speculators take positions in futures contracts for the purpose of trying to recognize a gain before closing out their position before the delivery (ending) date of the contract. Hedgers use futures contracts to lock in a future price at which they can buy or sell. This practice carries a potential for losses from market fluctuations, but for investors who are willing to ride out possibly substantial market volatility, commodity exposure offers the opportunity to reap high rewards. Positions can be long or short depending on the market outlook or hedging needs.

Commodity futures and options are highly leveraged and are traded in terms of contract sizes, instead of in terms of shares such as with stocks. Also, investors can buy and sell positions whenever the markets are open.

COMMODITY PERFORMANCE: BENEFITS AND RISKS

In his seminal paper on portfolio theory, Markowitz (1952) develops a diversification strategy that seeks to combine, in a portfolio, assets with returns that are less than perfectly positively correlated, in an effort to lower portfolio risk (variance) without sacrificing return. Alternative investments, including real estate, private equity, hedge funds, and commodities, have the potential to provide diversification within a traditional portfolio. Kat (2007) offers four considerations when adding an alternative asset class: (1) the expected return of the asset class, (2) the variation of the returns around its mean, as well as the higher moments of the return distribution, (3) the correlation with traditional assets in the existing portfolio, and (4) the liquidity of the asset class, as well as any fees.

Evidence on the ability of commodity exposure to enhance returns is mixed. Bodie and Rosansky (1980) and Gorton and Rouwenhorst (2006) find stock-like historical returns for unleveraged commodity futures indices. Conversely, Erb and Harvey (2006), Kat (2007), and Kat and Oomen (2007) find limited evidence of time-persistent risk premiums for single commodities. As Erb and Harvey (2006) and Gorton and Rouwenhorst (2006) show, most commodity return distributions are positively skewed and leptokurtic, implying the existence of high extreme risks. Commodity returns exhibit a low or even negative correlation with nonrelated commodities permitting the structuring of a well-diversified commodity portfolio.

Additionally, commodities serve as an inflation hedge due to their generally positive correlation with inflation. They exhibit a correlation of close to zero with bonds and equity (Bodie and Rosansky 1980; Georgiev 2006; Gorton and Rouwenhorst 2006). Fabozzi, Fuess, and Kaiser (2007) contend that a commodity futures index serves as a proxy for asset class commodities. The S&P GSCI Commodity Index is often included in the mixed-asset portfolio optimization as total return indices best replicate an investment in a diversified commodity portfolio. The liquidity of this investable index is generally high. Furthermore, the fees for those passive products are low.

COMMODITY INVESTMENT STRATEGIES

Various ways are available to invest in commodities through different types of financial instruments, including (1) direct investments in the physical goods, (2) indirect investment in stocks of natural resource companies, (3) commodities mutual funds and ETFs, and (4) derivative contracts such as futures.

Direct Investments

When investors decide to buy physical goods, they follow a direct approach. This approach provides the purest exposure to the commodity's price, but involves a cost. When investors buy commodities, they need to understand the quality of the goods and the problems that can exist if that quality is lacking. Another problem is the presence of different costs relating to storage, insurance, and cash opportunity costs. These costs affect the management of the physical good. As a result of the disadvantages of direct investment, investors typically prefer to indirectly assume a position in commodity markets to avoid the problems linked to the management of physical goods.

Stock of Natural Resource Companies

The most common way to indirectly invest in commodities is to purchase stocks in companies whose core business depends on different commodities and various sector or geographical markets. When investors select equities, they must consider two different kinds of risk: systematic (nondiversifiable) and specific (diversifiable). If they invest in commodity-related equities, their objective is to earn a positive return given an increase in the value of the commodity. In each case, the return depends not only on the commodity but also on the performance of the stock market. Investors must consider which indirect exposure they want to add: a domestic large-cap company, a small-cap company, or a start-up company. Their decision adds other components of risk related to the selected company (specific risk) as well as the overall market (systematic risk) that could reduce the earnings linked to the choice of a specific, physical commodity on the market. One potential problem is that the return can have the opposite sign of the commodity return.

Commodity Mutual Funds and ETFs

Mutual funds investing in commodities give their investors exposure to this asset class. Commodity ETFs are investment vehicles for investors and traders who need to hedge risk or want to gain exposure to physical goods such as agriculture products, energy resources, and precious metals. These contracts represent the commodity and track the performance of a particular product. For investors who are looking to commodities for simple hedging and diversification purposes, a commodity ETF offers an appropriate vehicle. It is also an appropriate vehicle if the investor is seeking to gain exposure to commodities because of current long-term trends in the market.

Commodity Futures

The main commodity-trading groups also include currencies, energies, food and fiber, grains, interest rates, meats, metals, and stock indices. The commodity futures market includes items such as corn, gold, heating oil, lumber, pork bellies, silver, wheat, and many other commodities. For traders and those investors who require a smaller margin of safety, futures are probably the better vehicle. Futures carry greater volatility and hence greater potential for losses and gains, but disciplined traders or investors can credibly use futures to their benefit.

Futures contracts allow investment in a commodity without being forced to deliver and store the commodities. At the maturity of the contract, investors can choose to close the position with an opposite position or to roll the contracts forward (i.e., sell the expiring contract and simultaneously buy the next contract). The management of a futures contract position requires posting *margin* (an initial deposit in money or securities) to cover any daily fluctuations in the value of the position. Contract values are adjusted daily (called *mark-to-market*) to account for gains and losses. Alternatively, investors can use option contracts on commodities to protect against adverse price movements or to gain exposure in commodities. The management of these positions is complicated because of both the volatility of commodities and the complexity of option pricing.

Outlook for Commodity Performance

Although forecasting any security price is difficult, doing so for commodities is especially complex. The forecasts made are aligned with commodities' expected supply and demand. The World Bank (2016) observes that commodities prices have begun to rebound after their five-year decline through January 2016. Energy prices remain the dominant driver for the commodity sector's performance, comprising 56.24 percent of the S&P GSCI Commodity Index for 2017 (S&P Dow Jones Indices 2016). With the lifting of sanctions, Iran is likely to ramp up oil production, resulting in substantial increases in volume of oil and natural gas if the country attracts the necessary investment and technology to leverage its substantial reserves. According to the World Bank (2016), the prospects for oversupply of oil diminished in the last half of 2016 with prices expected to increase by 22.2 percent during 2016–2017.

Over the long run, commodities have given investors a positive real rate of return. The main risk to investors and traders in terms of their expectations of real returns on commodities would be in not understanding that commodities are a volatile asset class. Prices will not go up in a straight line; some periods will have negative returns. Worah (2011) writes that the commodities with the best opportunities for gain have two characteristics in common: (1) they are geared to global growth and (2) supply constraints exist. In contrast to stock prices, which are based on the market's long-term assessment of a firm's discounted cash flows, commodity prices are dictated by demand-supply dynamics, which are often more short term in nature.

Purpose and Scope

The purpose of this scholarly book is to provide an objective look into the dynamic world of commodities. It examines commodity markets around the world and the role of commodities as investments, including risk management, and also provides a synthesis of relevant research on commodities. *Commodities: Markets, Performance, and Strategies* provides important insights about such topics as commodity markets, competing forces shaping these commodity markets, trading strategies, performance and measurement, and trends and future prospects. This book provides an in-depth understanding about commodities from experts in this field, both practitioners and academics, from around the world.

Today, commodities continue to play an important role as an alternative asset class. In fact, commodities still fascinate both market participants and observers. During the past decade, commodity markets have undergone many changes and developments. For example, the financial crisis of 2007–2008 created a period characterized by large price movement and volatility. During the aftermath of this crisis, a push toward regulatory reforms occurred that was intended to increase efficiency and security within commodity markets. This book not only takes readers through the core topics and issues of commodities but also dispels common myths and examines the latest trends, issues, and developments.

Discussion of commodities research permeates the book. The coverage extends from discussing basic concepts and their application to increasingly intricate and real-world situations. For instance, the book addresses the question: Should investors include commodities in their portfolios? Thus, this volume spans the gamut from theoretical to practical, while attempting to offer a useful balance of detailed and user-friendly coverage. It provides both a broad survey of the field and in-depth presentations of specific areas within this field of study. In summary, this book provides a fresh look at this intriguing but often complex subject.

Distinguishing Features

The distinguishing features of *Commodities: Markets, Performance, and Strategies* are:

- The book skillfully blends the contributions of a wide array of scholars and practitioners into a single review of some of the most important topics in this area. The diverse backgrounds of the contributors ensure different perspectives and a rich interplay of ideas.
- The book reflects the latest trends and research involving commodities in a global context and discusses controversial issues as well as trends and the future outlook.
- The book emphasizes empirical evidence involving commodities and presents the results of studies in a straightforward manner understandable to a wide array of readers.
- Chapters contain discussion questions to help to reinforce key concepts, accompanied by guideline answers. This feature should be especially useful to faculty and students using the book in classes.

Intended Audience

The practical and comprehensive nature of this book should be of interest to a broad audience. For example, investors can use this book to provide guidance in helping them navigate through the key areas involving investing in commodities. For academics, the book provides the basis for gaining a better understanding about various aspects of commodities and as a springboard for future research. They can also use the book as a stand-alone or supplementary resource for advanced undergraduate or graduate courses in commodities. Others including researchers, policymakers, students, and libraries, should find this book suitable as a reference. Thus, *Commodities: Markets, Performance, and Strategies* should be essential reading for anyone who desires a better understanding of commodities.

Structure of the Book

The remaining 27 chapters are divided into six parts. A brief overview of each chapter follows.

PART ONE: BACKGROUND

Besides Chapter 1, this part consists of five chapters. These chapters examine a wide array of topics including the economics of commodities and commodity markets, commodity exchanges and regulation, behavioral aspects of commodity markets, commodity derivatives, and fundamentals and commodity prices.

Chapter 2: The Economics of Commodities and Commodity Markets (Florian Ielpo)

This chapter covers the economic fundamentals of commodity markets (i.e., what shapes the evolution of the price of raw materials) in three steps. First, it covers the theories explaining why the futures curve can be upward or downward sloping, an essential element for commodity-producing companies. The evolution of inventories and hedging pressures are the two dominant sources of explanation. Second, the chapter reviews the fundamentals of commodity spot prices: technologies, supply, demand, and speculation. Production costs draw the long-term evolution of prices, but demand and supply shocks can trigger substantial variations in commodity prices. Third, the chapter presents how commodity prices interact with the business cycle. Commodities are influenced by the world activity but can also have a material impact on it.

Chapter 3: Commodity Exchanges and Regulation (Jerry W. Markham)

The U.S. Commodity Futures Trading Commission (CFTC) intensively regulates commodity futures, options, and swaps pursuant to the provisions of the Commodity Exchange Act of 1936. The Securities and Exchange Commission (SEC) and federal banking agencies also have some jurisdiction over derivative financial instruments. This chapter describes the CFTC regulations, including registration requirements for designated contract markets, clearinghouses, and various swap market participants. It also describes the financial responsibility requirements imposed on futures commission merchants and safeguards for customer funds in the futures markets. Additionally, the chapter addresses prohibitions against misleading sales activities, deceptive trading practices, and price manipulations. Finally, it reviews the role of the SEC and bank regulators in regulating financial derivative contracts, particularly securities derivatives and foreign currency exchange transactions.

Chapter 4: Behavioral Aspects of Commodity Markets (John R. Nofsinger, Pattanaporn Chatjuthamard, and Xu Dai)

Are behavioral biases prevalent in commodities and futures markets? Although retail equity investors display many psychological biases, more sophisticated investors exhibit fewer biases. The market makers, traders (locals), speculators, hedgers, and institutions of the commodities and futures markets tend to be professional participants, and thus less prone to behavioral biases. Nevertheless, the fast-paced action of these markets is an environment that fosters behavioral errors. This chapter reviews the literature on the pervasiveness of prospect theory behavior and other biases in these markets. Strong evidence indicates that market participants exhibit loss aversion, the impact of reference points, the disposition effect, and overconfidence. They also engage in positive feedback trading and momentum investing. Lastly, the chapter reviews risk taking and behavioral biases by the type of market participant, particularly focusing on market makers, floor traders, clearing members, and the public.

Chapter 5: Commodity Derivatives (Neil C. Schofield)

Like most asset classes, commodity derivatives consist of the traditional building blocks: forwards, futures, swaps, and options. This chapter discusses the main features of each of these products but within an investment context. For example, the coverage focuses on using exchange-traded futures to compile investment indices. The section on swaps examines the total return variant of the classic "fixed for floating" structures. Because the fundamentals of derivatives are generally well documented, this chapter highlights the instances in which commodities differ from traditional financial assets. The chapter includes some popular investment structures to illustrate the use of these instruments.

Chapter 6: Fundamentals and Commodity Prices (Michael S. Haigh)

Commodity markets occasionally co-move with the broader macro markets for reasons beyond their own fundamentally driven physical characteristics. This chapter focuses on two related avenues to look beyond the fundamentals of counting barrels, tonnes, bushels, or molecules. The first section uses a principal component analysis to disentangle how fundamentals versus nonfundamentals drive commodity prices and focuses on the crude oil market. The results are intuitive and allow isolating the extent to which supply and demand matter to price changes experienced in the market. Furthermore, the results enable understanding whether the diversification benefits of commodity markets exist in almost real time. Second, given the ability to segment fundamentally driven commodities from others, the chapter then focuses on how much supply or demand factors contribute to the fundamental variation in prices. The analysis reveals that, in the oil market, supply concerns drive prices during geopolitical tensions, while demand concerns dominate during economic crises.

PART TWO: PHYSICAL COMMODITIES

This section focuses on physical commodities, including agricultural, energy, livestock, and metals. More recently, the definition of commodities has expanded to include financial products, such as foreign currencies and indexes, but this part does not examine financial commodities.

Chapter 7: Physical Commodities (Erik Devos, Seow Eng-Ong, and Andrew C. Spieler)

Unlike other financial assets, commodities have a physical component that introduces additional complexities for valuation and hedging. Physical commodities are broadly classified into agricultural, energy, livestock, and metals with each having unique characteristics. Still, commodities of the same type are subject to varying degrees of quality. Commodity investments typically use futures contracts, as opposed to spot transactions. Most futures transactions are closed before expiration, and physical delivery is infrequent. The futures price is rarely equal to the spot price, and the intertemporal difference is related to the carrying costs and benefits of possessing the underlying commodity. Carrying costs include transportation, insurance, storage, and opportunity costs, while benefits are reflected in convenience yield and lease rate. Speculators seek to profit from discrepancies between markets over time. Manufacturers and end users are more likely to conduct hedging transactions, while large-scale financial institutions are more likely to conduct speculative positions.

Chapter 8: Agricultural (Nicole Moran and Kelsey Syvrud)

Society relies on agricultural commodities (grains and oilseeds, dairy, and softs) to feed and clothe the world's population. These commodities also play an important role in both the economy and financial markets. Unlike other commodities, agricultural commodities have unique characteristics that may include seasonality, perishability, and production dependent on weather conditions. Further, these products are an important part of international trade and are crucial in providing food security to ensure a stable supply of food worldwide. Financial investments within the agriculture industry have increased over the last several decades due in part to the commercialization of food production, introduction of agricultural commodity index funds, and increased investment in futures markets. This chapter introduces the major agricultural products, discusses price determinants and how to invest in agriculture, and highlights the differences between agricultural commodities and other commodities.

Chapter 9: Energy (Michael A. Penick and Lynn Riggs)

This chapter discusses the development and structure of energy cash and futures markets, along with current regulatory issues. It begins with a discussion of common features of energy markets and then discusses the energy markets with actively traded benchmark futures contracts as well as the development of over-the-counter (OTC) derivatives that can be used by end users in conjunction with futures contracts to refine their hedges. The chapter concludes with a discussion of the effects of derivatives market regulation, including hedging and speculation in energy markets, position limits, and the "futurization" of OTC derivatives that were formerly structured as swaps.

Chapter 10: Livestock (Xiaohu Deng, Andrew C. Spieler, and Desmond Tsang)

The exponential population growth rate is increasingly straining the supply of food and resources. Meat is a key component in the diet of many global cultures. The increase in demand for meat has shifted production from small farms and ranches to large corporate livestock production facilities. The complexity of the livestock industry and production processes has increased the need to manage the financial risk associated with raising the various types of livestock, such as feeder cattle, live cattle, and lean hogs, and the processing, packaging, and distribution of livestock products. The Chicago Mercantile Exchange (CME) has created an array of financial futures and options to assist livestock producers and processors with their price risk management needs.

Chapter 11: Metals (Greg Leonard and Chanel O'Neill)

Metals and metal products have long been traded on commodity markets. Trading in futures and options, as well as forwards, swaps, and other derivatives, is available for about a dozen metals. Traditionally, metals have been divided into precious metals and base metals, used in industrial applications. Today the precious metals silver, platinum, and palladium are also primarily used in industrial applications, while gold is still primarily used as a store of value. CME Group exchanges and the London Metal Exchange are the best-known exchanges for metals derivatives trading. In recent years, trading volumes in all metals on exchanges in China have increased tremendously, and these exchanges have begun to contribute to global price discovery. Steel has the largest production of the base metals, but on-exchange trading of steel and its precursor, iron ore, has become important only in the last few years, with trading focused in China.

PART THREE: METHODS TO INVEST IN COMMODITIES

The three chapters in this part examine different methods of investing in commodities. These chapters focus on commodity trading advisors (CTAs) and managed futures, commodity ETFs, and commodity mutual funds.

Chapter 12: Commodity Trading Advisors and Managed Futures (Koray D. Simsek and Halil Kiymaz)

Managed futures strategies provide investors with a dynamic exposure to commodities. Among other ways of investing in them, CTAs have become synonymous with this asset class, as they provide professional money management services using derivatives markets in either a pooled or an individual setting. Most managed futures strategies display trend-following and momentum-type systematic trading features, which result in adopting a long-short portfolio approach. This chapter explains the characteristics and the growth of this commodity-investing industry and provides an extensive literature review. Much of the literature finds that managed futures investing through CTAs provides excellent diversification benefits and performs well, especially in crisis times. Conversely, the nonuniformity of the databases and indices used in these studies suffer from several biases. Some recent studies that directly address these shortcomings question the performance persistence of CTAs after fees.

Chapter 13: Commodity Exchange-Traded Funds (Christopher Milliken, Ehsan Nikbakht, and Andrew C. Spieler)

Commodity exchange-traded funds (ETCs), which debuted in 2004, enable investors to access an asset class previously difficult or expensive to access. Although a small segment of the overall exchange-traded fund (ETF) universe, ETCs have grown in popularity with both speculators and investors looking for long-term portfolio diversification. Examples of the types of commodities that are now accessible through ETCs include gold, oil, and agricultural. The literature on ETCs is limited, but academic and industry work have centered on using futures contracts to replicate the performance of the underlying commodities spot price as well as the effect additional capital has had on the integrity of the futures market. This chapter covers this topic by reviewing the growth, investment strategies, and regulatory structure of ETCs as well as the underlying effects these funds have had on the underlying markets with which they engage.

Chapter 14: Commodity Mutual Funds (Gustavo Camilo, Janko Cizel, and Paul Zurek)

The chapter describes the main institutional features of commodity mutual funds such as active management, the assets in which these funds invest, the process through which shares are bought and sold, the fees borne by investors, as well as the risks associated with investing in the funds. It also examines trends in fund flows and the correlations to commodity returns. Correlations to commodity returns are positive but lower than those of commodity exchange-traded funds that invest directly in underlying commodities, as opposed to commodity mutual funds, which invest largely in equities. Lastly, the chapter examines data on fees and net-of-expense commodity mutual fund performance between 1996 and 2016. The data show a decline in fund expense ratios over time, with the exception of large funds, negative average risk-adjusted performance using a four-factor model, and evidence consistent with a lack of persistence in fund returns over the sample period.

PART FOUR: PERFORMANCE OF COMMODITIES

This part consists of four chapters covering topics related to commodity performance. These chapters focus on pricing of futures contracts, return characteristics of commodities, issues in benchmarking commodity performance, and volatility transmission across commodity futures markets.

Chapter 15: Pricing of Futures Contracts (Timothy A. Krause)

This chapter examines the relation between futures prices relative to the spot price of the underlying asset. Basic futures pricing is characterized by the convergence of futures and spot prices during the delivery period just before contract expiration. However, "no arbitrage" arguments that dictate the fair value of futures contracts largely determine pricing relations before expiration. Although the cost of carry model in its various forms largely determines futures prices before expiration, the chapter presents alternative explanations. Related commodity futures complexes exhibit mean-reverting behavior, as seen in commodity spread markets and other interrelated commodities. Energy commodity futures prices can be somewhat accurately modeled as a generalized autoregressive conditional heteroskedastic (GARCH) process, although whether these models provide economically significant excess returns is uncertain.

Chapter 16: Return Characteristics of Commodities (Dianna Preece)

The role of commodities in a diversified portfolio has been the subject of research and debate since the late 1970s. Investors can hold the physical commodity or use derivatives such as futures contracts to access commodity exposure. Institutional investors primarily gain exposure to commodities via futures contracts. Commodity futures returns are comprised of a collateral return, a spot return, and a roll return. Research dating back to the late 1970s suggests that commodities should be included in diversified portfolios because they act as an inflation hedge, are portfolio diversifiers due to negative correlation with stocks and bonds, and potentially offer returns and volatility comparable to equities. Commodity performance has been generally weaker in the years after the financial crisis of 2007–2008. Many studies find that the correlation of commodity returns with stocks and bonds increases during periods of financial stress.

Chapter 17: Issues in Benchmarking Commodity Performance (Aaron Filbeck)

Commodity investments have continued to gain traction in diversified portfolios since the 1990s. Historically low correlations relative to traditional asset classes, different fundamental drivers, and investor demand for alternative sources of return have brought commodity investments forward as a solution that provides overall portfolio diversification while maintaining similar long-term return streams. A large inflow of institutional investors and noncommercial traders has increased demand and lowered barriers to entry. Many of these investors simply want exposure to commodities as an asset class, often investing in index funds or ETFs. In some cases, investors assume that the underlying commodity indexes that these investment vehicles track represent appropriate benchmarks for asset class performance. In reality, many different commodity indexes are available making benchmarking asset class performance more difficult.

Chapter 18: Volatility Transmission across Commodity Futures Markets (Frankie Ho-Chi Chau and Rataporn Deesomsak)

The recent sharp movements in crude oil prices and their impact on other commodities have renewed interest in the assessment of dynamic interactions between commodity futures markets. This chapter examines this important topic by investigating the intensity and direction of volatility transmission across three major classes of commodities including agricultural products (corn, coffee, and soybeans), energy (crude oil and gas), and metals (copper, gold, and silver). Overall, the evidence suggests that important volatility episodes and fluctuations exist across major commodity markets; the total cross-market spillovers are limited until the onset of the financial crisis of 2007–2008. As the crisis intensified, so too did the commodity volatility spillovers with substantial stress carrying over from the energy and metal markets to others. These findings are important in understanding the level and transmission mechanism of risk across commodity futures markets and are relevant to regulators in formulating effective policies to tackle excessive volatility, particularly during turbulent periods.

PART FIVE: STRATEGIES AND PORTFOLIO MANAGEMENT

This part consists of four chapters covering topics related to commodity-related strategies and their impact on portfolio performance. These topics include commodities in international and emerging markets; commodity-trading strategies, common mistakes, and catastrophic blowups; asset allocation strategies and commodities; and food prices and food prices volatility, including strategies for extending the reach of risk markets.

Chapter 19: Commodities in International and Emerging Markets (Kamal Smimou)

This chapter seeks to elucidate the relations of U.S.-listed global commodity futures, the business cycle, and stocks and bonds of emerging markets. It shows that global investors poised to benefit from investing in emerging market securities can concurrently learn from and better understand the dynamic intermarket relations when establishing such trading strategies. Investment in emerging markets can enhance the performance and sturdiness of an equity or bond portfolio strategy. Evidence lends support to the conjecture that a subtle contemporaneous and occasionally trailing effect exerted by the movement of global commodities on the business cycle exists. Global commodities also affect equity and bond market dynamics. The evidence also reveals differences in terms of economic significance and magnitude among selected emerging nations and across various commodities.

Chapter 20: Commodity Trading Strategies, Common Mistakes, and Catastrophic Blowups (Hilary Till, Joseph Eagleeye, and Richard Heckinger)

Becoming an expert in the commodity markets has traditionally required a novice to seek an apprenticeship at an established commodity firm. This chapter provides an alternative approach. This reasonably comprehensive tour of the always dynamic and frequently opaque commodity markets includes views on (1) commodity trading strategies, (2) common mistakes, and (3) catastrophic blowups. The specific commodity trading strategies covered are trend-following and calendar spreads. The common mistakes that the chapter includes are (1) targeting returns rather than risk metrics, (2) establishing inappropriate trade sizing, and (3) failing to fully appreciate the psychological discipline required for trading. The chapter also provides case studies on the catastrophic derivatives blowups at both Amaranth and MF Global.

Chapter 21: Asset Allocation Strategies and Commodities (Claudio Boido)

As a result of the financial crisis of 2007–2008 and subsequent central banking decisions, the asset management industry changed its asset allocation choices. Asset managers are focusing their attention on the search for new asset classes by taking advantage of new opportunities to capture risk premia with the aim of exceeding the returns given by traditional investments, including traded equities, fixed income securities, and cash. By doing so, they are trying to improve the selection of alternative assets such as commodities that sometimes have relatively low correlations with traditional assets. The chapter begins by describing the principles of asset allocation, distinguishing between passive and active asset allocation, and also focusing on beta and alternative beta. It then concentrates on how investors can gain exposure to commodities through different investment vehicles and strategies.

Chapter 22: Food Prices and Food Price Volatility (Donald F. Larson)

This chapter examines food prices between 1900 and 2015. Despite growing populations, rising incomes, new technologies, globalization, and the emergence of commodities as an asset class, no trends are evident in food price levels or volatility. Still, food prices have averaged higher since 2010 than during recent decades, harming the poor and raising fears that agricultural productivity growth has slowed. Since 1900, food prices have consistently been more volatile than the prices of manufactured goods and most other commodity groups. This relation drives terms-of-trade volatility, which slows economic growth. At the farm level, price volatility impedes investment and technology adoption, and encourages low-income livelihood strategies. Past policies to manage food prices have not worked, and governments have shifted to policies aimed at mitigating the consequences of high and volatile food prices. By extending the reach of risk markets, warehouse receipt systems, index insurance, and contract farming can be successful policy components.

PART SIX: ISSUES INVOLVING COMMODITIES

This final part contains six chapters covering various issues involving commodities. These issues are high frequency trading of commodities, energy risk management, financialization of commodity markets, virtual currencies as commodities, research issues in commodities and commodity derivatives, and the future of commodity markets and investments.

Chapter 23: High Frequency Trading of Commodities (Raymond P. H. Fishe and Aaron D. Smith)

Electronic platforms and high frequency traders (HFTs) have changed the nature of trading. Like equity markets, commodity markets have experienced an influx of algorithmic traders and a decline in "pit" or open outcry trading. Regulatory efforts to understand the effects of HFTs and to offer prudent guidelines or new rules are in their infancy. An overall hesitancy exists because academic studies have produced diverse results on liquidity, volatility, and market quality. This survey focuses on high frequency trading research in commodity derivative markets, documenting basic results and extracting inferences when warranted. Evidence indicates that HFTs act as market makers and that their speed advantage has lowered transaction costs, generally during normal markets. Although not entirely conclusive, evidence also suggests that HFTs may exacerbate volatility by withdrawing liquidity in times of market stress such as during "flash" crashes.

Chapter 24: Energy Risk Management (Thomas Barkley, Mingwei (Max) Liang, and Andrew C. Spieler)

The backdrop of the rapid growth of worldwide energy consumption and increasing concerns about global energy sustainability and environment protection, as well as an increasing uncertainty of commodity prices, require energy companies to use derivatives to hedge against risks related to energy trading. Over time, this situation has led to a more important role for energy risk management as part of a company's core business operation. This chapter discusses the primary financial instruments used in the energy sector and risk management for energy companies. It reviews the application of several important quantitative methodologies, including value at risk and its variant risk metrics, to measure market risk. The chapter also examines credit risk measures and credit risk migration. Lastly, it discusses liquidity risk, operational risk, and legal risk. Overall, the chapter focuses more on the risk the commodity producer/deliverer faces than on the end user.

Chapter 25: Financialization of Commodity Markets (Kyle J. Putnam and Ramesh Adhikari)

In the early 2000s, financial investors began pouring billions of dollars into the commodity futures markets, seeking the unique investment benefits of this distinct asset class. This "financialization" process has called into question the fundamental risk and return properties of commodity futures as evidence has emerged favoring the idea that the massive increase in investor flows caused a rise in futures prices, volatility, and intra- and intermarket return correlations. However, a contrarian line of research contends that the effects of the new "speculative" capital on the futures markets are unsubstantiated and the increased participation of financial investors poses little consequence to the economics of the marketplace. This latter line of literature maintains that the investment benefits of commodity futures have not been diminished and that fundamental factors and business cycle variations can explain the observed changes in commodity price behavior.

Chapter 26: Virtual Currencies as Commodities (Lamia Chourou, Samir Saadi, and Azizah Aljohani)

The rapid advancement in encryption and network computing gave birth to new tools and products that have influenced the local and global economy alike. One recent and notable example is the emergence of virtual currencies, also known as cryptocurrencies or digital currencies. Virtual currencies, such as Bitcoin, introduced a fundamental transformation that affected the way goods, services, and assets are exchanged. As a result of its distributed ledgers based on blockchain, cryptocurrencies not only offer some unique advantages to the economy, investors, and consumers, but also pose considerable risks to users and challenges for regulators when fitting the new technology into the old legal framework. This chapter offers a nontechnical discussion of several aspects and features of virtual currencies and a glimpse at what the future may hold for these decentralized currencies.

Chapter 27: Research Issues in Commodities and Commodity Derivatives (Scott Mixon)

Commodity derivatives allow hedgers to smooth wealth across different states of the world and provide a direct link between financial markets and the real economy. This chapter describes recent research related to core concepts for these products: hedging behavior, the provision of liquidity in commodity markets, and the financialization debate related to the recent inflow of institutional investments into commodities. Intermediation activity in these markets has evolved in recent years. Modern commodity markets now incorporate extensive intermediation by swap dealers to facilitate over-the-counter swap dealing activity and execute the associated hedging activity linking swap and futures markets. The emergence of highly computerized, automated trading and the trend toward liquidity provision by commercial firms are intermediation issues that require better understanding. The chapter also provides insights into the types of topics faced by researchers who consider policy-related issues.

Chapter 28: Future of Commodity Markets and Investments (Hunter M. Holzhauer)

This chapter begins with a breakdown of recent growth trends for the overall commodities market. However, the long-term future of the market will heavily depend on three pressing issues: excess supply, increased regulations, and algorithmic trading. The section on excess supply explores how traders are changing strategies to adjust to the current imbalance between supply and demand, especially in the steel industry, and how that imbalance might change in the future based on global population trends and climate change concerns. The next section examines several regulatory trends, including the dramatic exodus of some investment banks from certain segments of the commodities market followed by a section focusing on how algorithmic trading is influencing how commodities are traded. A discussion of potential scenarios for the commodities market follows. The chapter concludes by examining a few ways in which the market and commodity traders may both survive and even thrive in the future.

Summary and Conclusions

The investment landscape involving commodities continues to expand in terms of opportunities and purposes within a portfolio context. *Commodities: Markets, Performance, and Strategies* attempts to integrate the most recent research to assist investment professionals, financial experts, and individual investors in learning about the latest developments in commodity markets. It endeavors to interweave the contributions of both scholars and practitioners into an authoritative synthesis of important but selective topics. This book covers a wide array of topics, including the background of commodities, types of physical commodities, methods to invest in commodities, performance of commodities, strategies and how they fit into portfolio management, and their current and future state in the industry. Commodities represent an important alternative investment and merit consideration in some portfolios.

References

Bodie, Zvi, and Victor I. Rosansky. 1980. "Risk and Returns in Commodity Futures." *Financial Analysts Journal* 36:3, 27–39.

Erb, Claude B., and Campbell R. Harvey. 2006. "The Strategic and Tactical Value of Commodity Futures." *Financial Analysts Journal* 62:2, 69–97.

Fabozzi, Frank J., Roland Fuess, and Dieter Kaiser. 2007. "A Primer on Commodity Investing." In Frank Fabozzi, Roland Füss, and Dieter Kaiser (eds.), *The Handbook of Commodity Investing*, 3–37. Hoboken, NJ: John Wiley and Sons, Inc.

Georgiev, Georgi. 2006. "The Benefits of Commodity Investment: 2006 Update." Working Paper, Center for International Securities and Derivatives, Isenberg School of Management, University of Massachusetts, Amherst.

Gorton, Gary B., and Geert K. Rouwenhorst. 2006. "Facts and Fantasies about Commodity Futures." *Financial Analysts Journal* 62:2, 47–68.

Kat, Harry M. 2007. "How to Evaluate a New Diversifier with 10 Simple Questions." *Journal of Private Wealth Management* 9:4, 29–36.

Kat, Harry M., and Roel C. A. Oomen. 2007. "What Every Investor Should Know about Commodities, Part II: Multivariate Return Analysis." *Journal of Investment Management* 5:3, 1–25.

Markowitz, Harry. 1952. "Portfolio Selection." *Journal of Finance* 7:1, 77–91.

Rogers, Jim. 2013. "Commodities Tend to Zig When the Equity Markets Zag." Jim Rogers Blog. November 6. Available at http://jimrogers1.blogspot.com/2013/11/jim-rogers-commodities-tend-to-zig-when.html.

S & P Dow Jones Indices. 2016. "Review of 2017 S&P GSCI® Index Rebalancing." October 6. Available at http://us.spindices.com/documents/index-news-and-announcements/20161006-sp-gsci-rebalance-advisory-panel.pdf?force_download=true.

West, Mark D. 2000. "Private Ordering at the World's First Futures Exchange." *Michigan Law Review* 98:8, 2574–2615.

Worah, Mihir P. 2011. "Economic Outlook: Higher Commodity Prices and the End of Economic Growth without Inflation." PIMCO. June. Available at http://www.pimco.com/EN/Insights/Pages/Higher-Commodity-Prices-and-the-End-of-Economic-Growth-Without-Inflation.aspx.

World Bank. 2016. "Commodity Markets Outlook." Available at http://pubdocs.worldbank.org/en/328921469543025388/CMO-July-2016-Full-Report.pdf.

2

The Economics of Commodities and Commodity Markets

FLORIAN IELPO
Head of Marco Research at Unigestion and Associate Researcher at Sorbonne University

Introduction

Commodity markets are financial markets that trade raw materials such as crude oil, copper, or soybeans. These markets have long attracted the attention of economists because their price evolutions reflect industrial demand for such products while also affecting the growth rate across a large spectrum of economies. A vast stream of research has tried to assess commodity market fundamentals (supply and demand characteristics) as much as their impact over gross domestic product (GDP) growth and inflation. This chapter provides an overview of the outcome of these various research efforts and highlights their essential conclusions.

Commodities are usually grouped into several sectors: energy, industrial metals, precious metals, and agricultural products. *Energy commodities* include different types of crude oils and their refinements, from gasoline to heating oil or cargo fuel. *Industrial metals* are those incorporated in the production of various types of goods such as copper or iron ore. *Precious metals* are so rare they have an intrinsic value, such as gold and silver, despite some being used for industrial purposes, such as palladium or platinum. Finally, *agricultural commodities* include all food-related products, including corn, wheat, and pork bellies.

Despite a perception that commodities operate as a single market, the factors driving the supply of these four types of commodities differ substantially. Each relies on different factors, such as weather conditions in the case of grains, and extraction technologies in the case of oil. Demand factors among commodities can also differ. For instance, the demand for industrial metals is intuitively connected to the level of industrial production, whereas the demand for gold often depends more on risk perceptions in financial markets or on the level of inflation. From this standpoint, the notion of "economics of commodity markets" makes little sense, as each sector is likely to respond to its own idiosyncratic factors.

Yet a certain level of common ground exists for each of these commodity markets, and the experience of the financial crisis of 2007–2008, also called the global financial crisis (GFC), helps in understanding the roots common to all of them. That is, global activity and trade played an important role both in the rise of commodity prices ahead of the GFC and in the collapse of commodity prices in the aftermath of the U.S. housing bubble bursting. This chapter aims to cast light on all these common phenomena while also highlighting the specific economic factors unique to individual commodity markets.

Investing in commodity markets has become increasingly popular in the investment industry, notably since the publication of Erb and Harvey (2006) and Gorton and Rouwenhorst (2006). Both contributions highlight the interest of investing in commodity markets and point out the historically low correlation between commodities and traditional markets such as equities and bonds. The diversification benefits and, for some markets, the risk premium that they embed made commodity markets attractive investment opportunities. Therefore, the variation in commodity prices relies not only on physical supply and demand, but also on speculation. So far, very limited evidence shows that future-based speculation affects the price of commodities, but the existing empirical evidence on speculation remains worthy of review. The GFC demonstrated that the celebrated low correlation with traditional markets was not robust, as most commodity markets became strongly correlated to equities during the 2008 market crash. Here again researchers aimed to answer whether speculation was at work or whether a global demand shock affected many raw material markets. Beyond the correlation question, exploring the existence of a risk premium is also an essential exercise. Stock and bond markets have historically rewarded risk-taking investors with dividends and coupons, respectively, serving as a reasonable source of returns. Commodities do not deliver any revenue per se. Hence, their risk premium—should it exist—needs to come from somewhere else.

Investors usually gain exposure to commodities using futures. Thus, assessing commodity futures performance requires disentangling spot returns from the contribution of futures. *Spot returns* are the returns obtained from holding physical commodities today, while *commodity futures* are financial assets that commit their buyers and sellers to delivering a commodity at a given price in the future. As the future date comes closer, future prices converge toward spot prices. This convergence contributes to the performance of the position. The spread between future prices and spot prices defines the commodity future slope. Because the slope of the future curve drives part of their performance through the convergence between future and spot prices, this issue has historically attracted much attention from academia. Although stock index futures display an upward-sloping term structure, commodity term structures can have either positive or negative slopes, depending on their economic fundamentals. An upward-sloping curve implies that commodity buyers will pay more for futures than for the spot commodity. If the spot price does not move until the futures expire, then the buyer will have lost a return proportional to the initial slope of the future curve. This phenomenon leads to a positive or negative premium coming from the simple roll of futures positions. Many investors who are unwilling to hold physical commodities buy futures with a given maturity and then sell them back a couple days before renewing their long future position with a more distant maturity future. Rolling such future positions therefore implies a rolling cost. Then the fundamentals of supply and demand in the underlying physical commodity also need to be envisaged in determining whether spot prices reflect demand, supply, technological change, or speculation.

Lastly, commodities are a key ingredient to the world economy. The 1979 and 1981 oil price shocks showed that the economic backdrop influences commodities, but commodities also influence global growth and inflation. The end of this chapter offers a digest of key findings on this issue.

Given the wide spectrum of existing commodities, this chapter focuses on four commodities representing different sectors. Oil prices are used as a proxy for the energy sector; copper as a proxy for industrial metals; gold as a proxy for precious metals; and corn as a proxy for the agricultural sector.

The chapter is organized as follows. The first section discusses the theory and empirical evidence of the term structure of futures, followed by an investigation of the connection among demand, supply, speculation, and physical commodity prices. The final section focuses on the impact of commodity price movements on growth and inflation,

Fundamentals of the Slope of Commodity Futures

A substantial portion of commodity trading involves using futures contracts. These financial derivatives commit the seller to deliver a certain quantity of an asset—here raw materials—to a buyer at a predefined price called the *strike price* and at a certain delivery date called the *maturity date*. Once purchased, the buyer can disengage from the transaction by selling the futures contract to another potential buyer at the prevailing market price. By contrast, an option allows the buyer to decide whether to make the purchase at the maturity date. For each commodity, a large number of potential future maturity dates exist, and the traded price for each maturity date forms a full *term structure*. Term structures are very familiar to bond markets participants, as interest rates are a function of the maturity of bonds, among other factors. In the case of bonds, longer-term rates are connected to shorter-term rates through expectations. If market participants agree that the one-year bond rate should be 1 percent, and that in one year this very same rate should be 2 percent, then seen from today, the two-year rate should be about 1.5 percent. This relation reflects the fact that the rate should be close to the average between 1 and 2 percent in order to prevent arbitrage opportunities.

In the case of commodities, such a term structure also exists. But while the bond market term structure phenomenon is well understood, the commodity future term structure remains a subject of debate. The debate, involving noted economists such as Nicholas Kaldor and John Maynard Keynes, has spread over nearly 100 years, but recently researchers appear to be moving toward a more uniform view with robust models of the commodity world. What explains the term structure of commodity prices? How can the term structure slope upward or downward in different markets and in different time periods? This section explains the origins of this debate and the nature of the resolving argument.

As a starting point, Equation 2.1 shows the calculation of the basis.

$$\frac{S_t - F_{t,T}}{F_{t,T}} \times \frac{365}{T-t}. \tag{2.1}$$

In Equation 2.1, S_t is the spot is price of the commodity and $F_{t,T}$ is the future price of the commodity at time t, with maturity T. The ratio between 365 and $T - t$ is an annualization factor.

This equation shows returns from buying a commodity future of maturity T and then holding it until the maturity date, assuming that the current spot price does not change. Suppose the future price is $101 and the spot price is $100 today. If the spot price is still $100 one year later, then the investor would have lost 1 percent, which is the cost of knowing in advance the price at which she would buy this commodity, the cost of *convenience*. The industry usually refers to this return as the *basis* or the *roll yield*. When buying futures to eventually sell them at maturity, the roll yield is what the investor yields to the futures seller if market prices fail to move. When the basis is positive for a given commodity market, this market is said to be in *backwardation* (i.e., the term structure of futures is downward sloping). *Contango* is just the opposite of backwardation. When the basis is negative, the market is in contango (i.e., its future curve is upward sloping). In the case of a contango market, the basis is negative because the futures price is more than the spot price. Thus, the roll yield is positive in backwarded markets and negative in contangoed markets.

Setting the price at which to sell a commodity in the future is very convenient to commodity producers. Therefore, producers should accept lower future prices than spot prices, inducing risk-averse commodity buyers to enter into a future deal. For such a case, the hedging demand of producers should lead to a downward-sloping futures term structure. When commodity producers accumulate raw material stocks, they have a net "long" position in the commodity. By selling futures contracts, producers net out part of their long exposure: a typical hedge drives future prices lower than current prices. This theory has been named the theory of "normal backwardation" after the contribution of Keynes (1930) and Hicks (1939) and implies that commodity futures market term structures should be downward sloping. Intuitively, the higher the commodity inventories, the more positive the basis across maturities. As commodity producer long positions increase, their hedging needs increase, creating additional negative pressures on futures prices. On the contrary, when producers stock-out, future prices should converge toward spot prices as the need to hedge dissipates. The main predictions of this theory are that the commodity basis should be positive and commodity markets should be backwardated.

Unfortunately, empirical evidence shows that this theoretical relation is only partially accurate. Figure 2.1 displays the time series of the basis associated with four different commodities: oil, copper, gold, and corn—one for each type of commodity. Obviously, between 1990 and 2016 the basis is positive for some commodities, but not for all, and is commonly negative. The oil and the corn markets have had long periods of backwardation, but gold has rarely been backwardated. Although the oil market has been backwardated for most of this period, oil has recently been in contango,

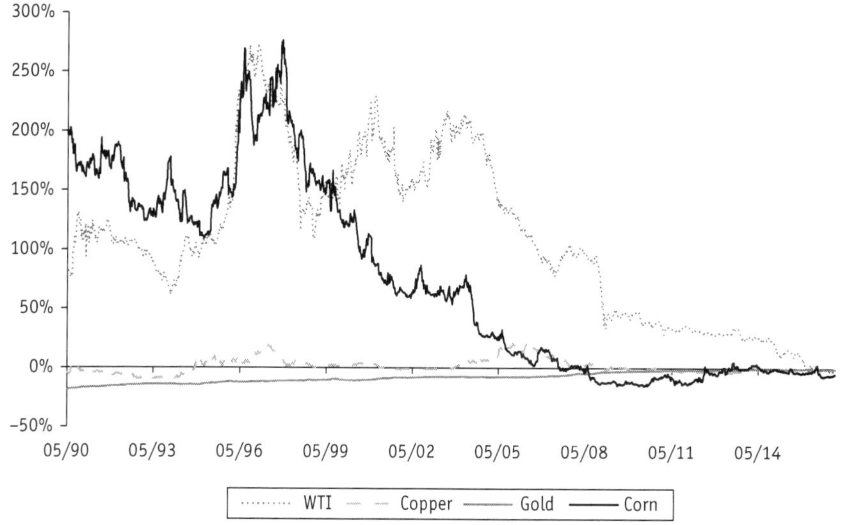

Figure 2.1 Time-Series Evolution of the Basis for Four Commodities
This figure shows the time series of the basis for four commodities—oil (WTI), cooper, gold, and corn, as defined in Equation 2.1. Source: Bloomberg and author's calculations.

which is unusual from historical standards. Lastly, the copper market switches from backwardation to contango depending on the sub-period.

Table 2.1 presents statistics comparing the net total futures position with each market's basis for the four markets considered in this chapter. Net total futures are the sum of the reported long and short futures positions for commercial and non-commercial (also known as speculative) market participants. When this number is positive, the market is net long on the commodity with more buyers than sellers; when negative, the market is net short with more sellers than buyers. In the case of oil, throughout the sample period, the market was net short with a positive basis, but this relation is the only case for which the theory works well. In the case of corn, for example, the basis is positive, but the market had a tendency to be net long. Lastly, in the case of copper, the market was on average net short with a zero basis. Clearly, the data reject the permanent backwardation hypothesis, suggesting the need for another explanation.

An alternative theory is the *theory of storage* originating from Kaldor (1939) and Working (1949). Storage plays an important role for producers to hedge their natural long spot positions. How do inventories and the basis interact? In the theory of normal backwardation, large commodity stockpiles generate substantial hedging pressures, and therefore a backwarded market, as producers worry about substantial exposure to price variations. However, holding inventories of commodities enables supplies to meet uncertain demand. The implicit benefit in holding inventories is known as the *convenience yield*. This benefit is an increasing function of inventory levels. As inventories grow, their marginal benefit progressively diminishes so that the marginal

Table 2.1 **Hedging Pressures (Net Combined Position on Futures Markets, Quantity of Contracts) versus Commodity Basis between 1995 and 2016**

	Oil	*Copper*	*Gold*	*Corn*
Median position	−1,307	−2,200	−22,861	75,138
Maximum position	39,109	13,141	15,080	320,890
Minimum position	−55,635	−16,446	−60,944	−511,205
Frequency of net short position	54%	63%	90%	6%
Median commodity basis	105.6%	−0.3%	−7.7%	62.2%
Maximum commodity basis	272.1%	22.3%	−0.3%	276.0%
Minimum commodity basis	−3.1%	−10.6%	−18.5%	−15.1%
Frequency of backwarded markets	97%	47%	0%	69%

Note: This table shows the median, maximum, and minimum net position of futures on four markets: oil, copper, gold, and corn. It compares each market's net position to historical figures for the basis of various markets. A *net position* is the difference between the long and the short total positions.

Source: Bloomberg.

benefit is a decreasing function of inventory stocks. What creates convenience can progressively create inconvenience as the cost of storing inventories reduces the value of holding stocks. Therefore, this theory predicts that the slope of the futures' curve should depend on the difference between the convenience yield (i.e., the implicit return coming from holding stocks to meet the demand) and storage costs. In its simplest version, increasing inventory levels should lead to increasing convenience yields and therefore to an upward-sloping futures curve. A more refined version says that the basis is a decreasing function of inventories. As inventories grow, the basis decreases, potentially up to the point where the term structure turns to contango.

Figures 2.2, 2.3, 2.4, and 2.5 compare the inventory levels of oil, copper, gold, and corn to the basis of each of these markets, respectively. The inverse relation between each is obvious from these figures, except for gold. For the other three commodities, the "quality" of the fit varies depending on the data. The increase in the oil inventories that started in 2003 likely explains a substantial portion of the collapse in the oil basis, turning it from positive to negative. Still, the theory is imperfect. Not every increase in the inventory level is followed by a decrease in the basis. Therefore, other factors such as seasonality, structural changes in production technologies, or even in producers should be considered. These additional factors are beyond the scope of this chapter and lie at the frontier of current economic research.

Gold is a special case among commodities given that most commodities are used as an input in some production process. Although gold is used for some processes, gold buyers from the industrial sector are commonly outnumbered by speculative

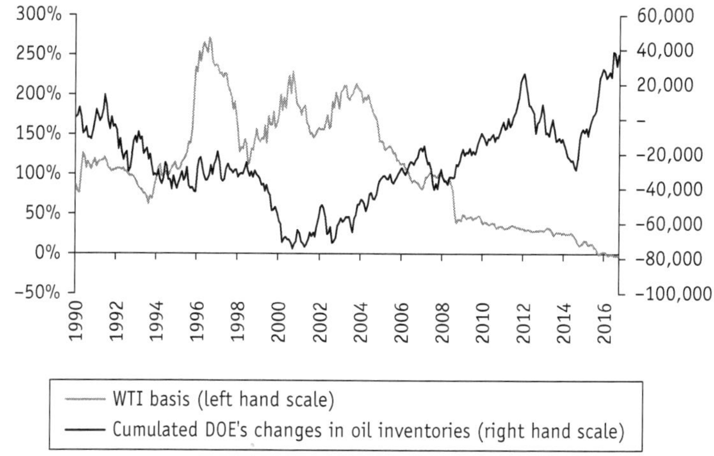

Figure 2.2 Oil Prices (WTI) versus Inventories between 1990 and 2016
This figure compares the price on the oil (WTI) to the cumulated level of oil inventories. Source: Bloomberg.

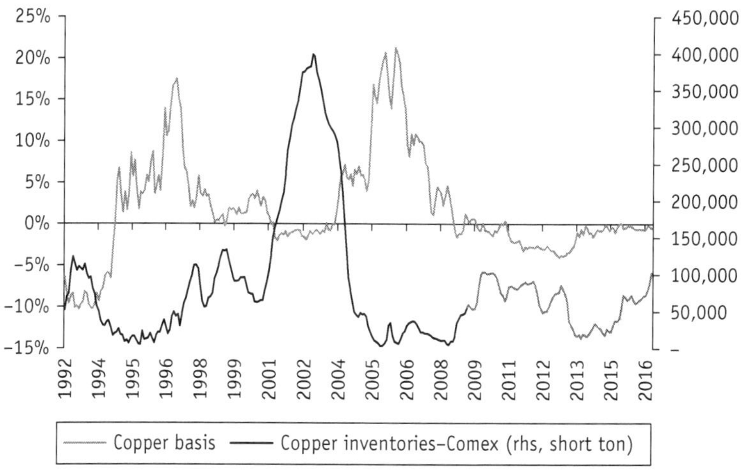

Figure 2.3 Copper Prices versus Inventories between 1992 and 2016
This figure compares the price of copper to the cumulated level of copper inventories. Source: Bloomberg.

buyers. That is, some view gold as a "safe haven" or as an inflation hedge. These beliefs shape a substantial portion of the gold market. Gold cannot be modeled as the rest of the commodities (Gorton, Hayashi, and Rouwenhorst 2013), and its fundamentals are unusual compared to other commodity markets.

Beyond these descriptive statistics, many empirical studies attempt to test both theories with greater emphasis on the theory of storage. Brennan (1991) and Pindyck

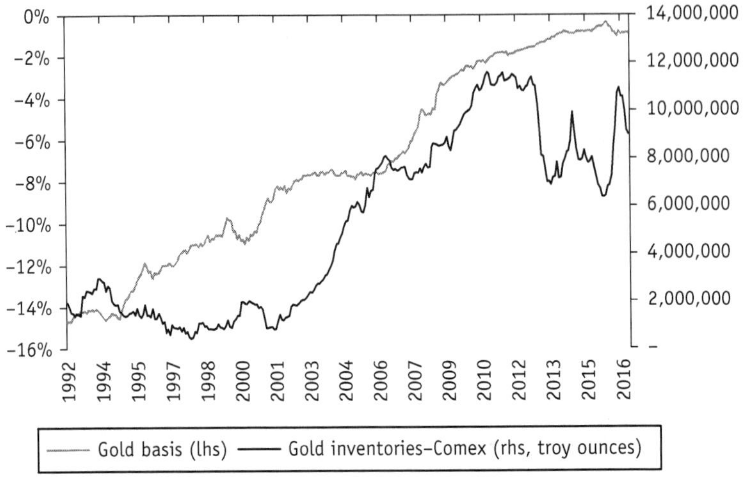

Figure 2.4 Gold Prices versus Inventories between 1992 and 2016
This figure compares the price of gold to the cumulated level of gold inventories. Source: Bloomberg.

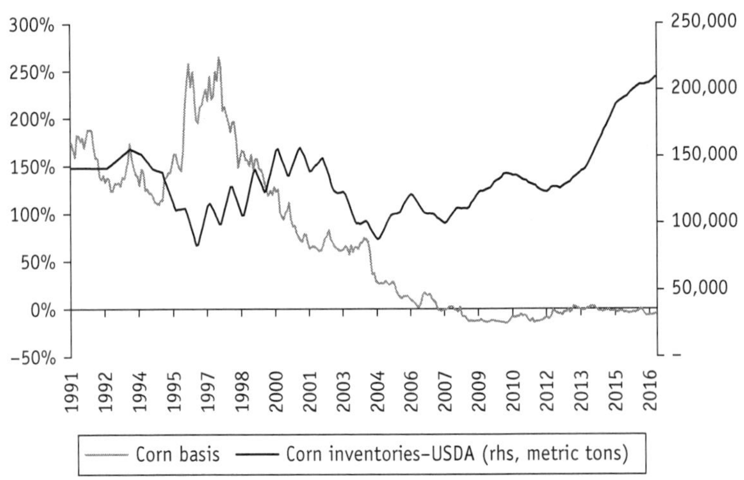

Figure 2.5 Corn Prices versus Inventories between 1992 and 2016
This figure compares the price of corn to the cumulated level of corn inventories. Source: Bloomberg.

(1994) find that the basis is a decreasing function of inventories and displays a convex connection. That is, the basis decreases less and less as inventories increase. Their conclusions hold for various metals and other selected commodities. More recently, Dincerler, Khoker, and Simin (2005) and Carbonez, Nguyen, and Sercu (2009) extend these results for other types of commodities such as energy (e.g., crude oil and gas) and agricultural products (e.g., wheat, corn, and oats), using samples covering various time periods. Stoll (1979) and Hirshleifer (1989) provide recent formulations of the theory of normal backwardation.

Various researchers attempt to test this theory. Rouwenhorst and Tang (2012) provide a review of one of the key predictions of the theory. Because hedgers are expected to overpower risk-averse speculators, a commodity risk premium should exist. Systematically holding futures until a few days before their maturity should deliver a positive risk premium to speculators assuming that the underlying spot price does not move sufficiently. As Rouwenhorst and Tang show, most of the evidence at the individual commodity level rejects this prediction. The authors rely on an extension in terms of the spectrum of commodity markets and conclude that empirical support for the theory of normal backwardation is weak.

Gorton et al. (2013) find similar results involving hedging pressures and the commodity risk premium. According to Rouwenhorst and Tang (2012), the empirical findings supporting the theory of storage are stronger than for the normal backwardation theory. Inventories and the basis seem to be inversely related, while the basis and expected returns have also been historically positively related. The quest to understand the factor driving the scale and size of commodity bases could help explain why commodities deliver a risk premium. The connection between inventory levels and commodity risk premiums holds for most of the 31 commodity futures investigated by Gorton et al. This evidence could help end more than 100-year debate around the origin of the commodity basis. The basis is positively related to the commodity risk premium. Given the inverse relation between inventories and the commodity basis, the commodity risk premium declines as inventories grow.

Economic Fundamentals to Commodity Spot Price Variations

The basis is only a part of the commodity risk premium. Another part is the time-series variation in the underlying spot price. When buying a commodity future at time t with a maturity T and then selling this contract back a couple days before the expiry of the future, the return on this financial operation is shown in Equation 2.2:

$$\begin{aligned}\text{Total return} &= \frac{\text{Spot price at time T}}{\text{Future price at time t}} - 1 \\ &= \underbrace{\frac{\text{Spot price at time T}}{\text{Spot price at time t}}}_{\text{1+Spot price return}} \times \underbrace{\frac{\text{Spot price at time t}}{\text{Future price at time t}}}_{\text{Pro-rated commodity basis}} - 1. \end{aligned} \tag{2.2}$$

Equation 2.2 clearly shows the origin of the return on commodities. One part of the return is the basis and the other part is the time-series variation in the spot price. This section now focuses on the fundamentals of the first part of the right-hand side of this equation: the dynamics of the spot price.

Four factors usually affect this part of commodity returns: technology, demand, supply, and speculation. Technology is usually seen as affecting both the production cost and storage cost of commodities. Technology is probably the most important driver of commodity prices because it determines which commodity producer can be profitable and which cannot. Commodity prices cannot stay below their production cost for an extended period: if the weakest players are wiped out, supply will become scarce and prices will increase until production becomes profitable again. Similarly, a commodity market cannot remain above its production cost for long, as higher prices incentivize increased production, which then leads to downward price pressure. Various researchers discuss this mean-reverting behavior of commodity prices around what sets their long-term trend (Laughton and Jacoby 1993, 1995; Cortazar and Schwartz 1994; Dixit and Pindyck 1994; Smith and McCardle 1998; Schwartz and Smith 2000).

Determining actual production costs for a given commodity is extraordinarily difficult because limited information on costs is available. First, various producers often use different technologies. Oil is probably the most common example. Crude oil can be extracted onshore or offshore, from "sand oil" in Canada or from "shale oil" technology in the United States. The costs of extraction from each source differ and evolve differentially over time. For example, the technologies that underpin the production of shale oil have changed considerably between 2013 and 2017, forced by collapsing oil prices and taking advantage of accumulated production experience. Collapsing commodity prices can drive technological improvements, while high prices can lead to higher average production costs as efficiency becomes less important over such periods.

Before moving to the supply and demand mechanics, the Prebisch and Singer theory must be discussed. In two different works exploring why emerging countries had difficulties exiting impoverished conditions, Prebisch (1950) and Singer (1950) formulate a prediction about the course of commodity prices. A large portion of emerging countries are commodity producers, and their economic conditions therefore depend on commodity prices. The Prebisch and Singer theory unfolds as follows. Because commodities are *basic goods* (i.e., goods that are closely related to the most basic consumer needs), commodity demand is barely sensitive to an increase in the average consumer's income. That lack of sensitivity applies especially to agricultural goods and to a lesser extent to industrial metals and energy.

Moreover, Prebisch and Singer anticipate an increased supply on commodity markets, as technological improvements progress. Both factors—the inelastic demand of commodities to increased revenues and the expected increase in commodity production—likely create long-term negative pressures on raw materials prices. Therefore, both authors predict a long-term drop in commodity prices.

A revised version of their theory relies on "real prices" instead of headline market prices: the natural increase in consumer goods could lead to an impression of higher prices, whereas when deflated by inflation (real prices), commodity prices would still trend downward. On average, using long-term data sets, the theory's support is mixed. Harvey, Kellard, Madsen, and Wohar (2010) present four centuries of evidence showing that fewer than 50 percent of the commodity markets investigated show significant downward price trends over their history. This conclusion is consistent with the mixed finding about the existence of a *commodity risk premium* (i.e., a systematic reward to holding commodity risk over the long run). If such a negative price trend exists in commodities, then a commodity risk premium should not exist, which would imply rising prices over the long run.

Gorton and Rouwenhorst (2006) find that a diversified portfolio of commodities between 1959 and 2004 would have delivered about a 14 percent return of which 10 percentage points come from the basis, which was positive over the period. The remaining four percentage points are well proportioned to the 12 percent of volatility of the underlying portfolio. When performing such computations commodity by commodity, average returns over time are mixed, as in the price trend analysis mentioned earlier.

The most striking example is oil. Oil prices in 2004 and slightly later show positive long-term trends. The end of the sample shows much higher values than at the beginning. In 2016, oil prices dropped to $20 and even lower in real price terms, annihilating the positive long-term trend. Tests of the existence of a long-term trend are both market and period specific. Figure 2.6 shows the time series of the price of oil, copper, gold, and corn. All of these time series illustrate a divergence between commodities and over their own history. Not only does the price of each commodity seem to exhibit positive or negative trends over sub-periods, but trends also differ across commodities.

Several other attempts to explain the long-run dynamics of commodities are worth mentioning. For example, using a century of data, Pindyck (1999) finds that the long-term evolution of various prices formed a U-shape. Pindyck and Rotemberg (1988)

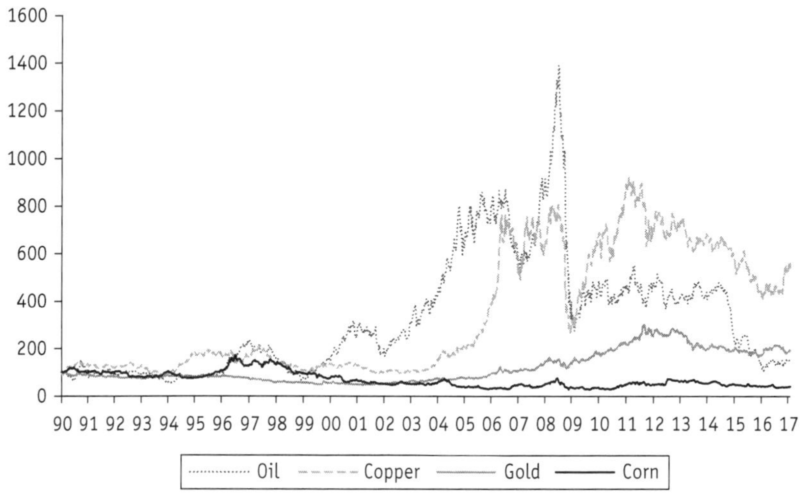

Figure 2.6 Cumulated Performance of Oil, Copper, Gold, and Corn between 1990 and 2017

This figure compares the movement of the spot price of four commodities: oil, copper, gold, and corn. Their respective prices have been rebased to 100 in 1990 for the sake of comparison. Source: Bloomberg.

find that the price of commodities shows surprisingly higher than expected co-movements between each other over the long run. This finding is unexpected because oil and corn should not be highly related given the fact that they meet different kinds of demand. Nonetheless, a "herding" pattern seems to exist in commodity markets with traders partially treating all commodities the same way in their portfolios.

Supply affects commodity prices through the cost of production and storage. Supply has its own temporary shocks that can have a substantial impact on the price of raw materials. A key element of commodities is also their scarcity because they come in a limited supply. An episode of constrained production and/or inventories can push prices sharply higher. For example, the constraint on the oil production by the Organization of Petroleum Exporting Countries (OPEC) in the 1970s led to large increases in oil prices. By contrast, large increases in oil supplies can create negative pressures on prices. The increase in U.S. oil production from shale oil contributed to the decrease in crude oil prices between 2015 and 2016.

A temporary change in the expected scarcity of a natural resource can have a major impact on prices. Pindyck (1994) analyzes how inventory levels interact with market prices, finding that inventories play a different role depending on whether prices are low or high from smoothing production to avoiding stock-outs. Scarcity can also be thought of as a contributor to the volatility of commodity prices. Periods of extreme scarcity in the oil market can be matched with periods of heightened volatility. Here, empirical evidence delivers contradictory results. Pindyck (2004) fails to find that inventory levels in the oil markets drives volatility. Symeonidis, Prokopczuk, Brooks, and Lazar (2012) find that commodity price volatility is negatively correlated to inventory levels across a broad spectrum of commodities. Geman and Nguyen (2005) reach a similar conclusion.

Finally, demand is another fundamental to oil price movement. By "demand," the literature often refers to "excess demand," meaning that the growth in the world GDP is higher or lower than usual, resulting in increased or decreased demand in commodities. Summarizing the findings in the literature, Jacks and Stuermer (2015) list demand shocks as a generally important contributor to price variations, echoing the essential message in Kilian (2009) for the oil market. Jensen, Johnson, and Mercer (2002) find that the returns on commodities tend to be stronger over tightening monetary policy conditions (i.e., when the Federal Reserve (Fed) raises its target short-term rate in order to slow down the U.S. economy). Frankel (2006) discovers a dependency between the demand-related monetary policy stance of the Fed and commodity markets: low rates can be matched with periods of subdued commodity returns. Gorton and Rouwenhorst (2006) find that rising commodity prices tend to appear at the end of the growth cycle and over the early stage of U.S. recessions. Nguyen and Sercu (2010) affirm that both tighter monetary policy periods and late cycle periods can be matched with abnormally high returns on commodities. Finally, Chevallier, Gatumel, and Ielpo (2014) find that commodity prices react significantly to growth-related economic news. They also report that the returns on various commodity indices outperform those of equities over late cycle periods.

The last potential driver to commodity prices is speculation. Since Erb and Harvey (2006) and Gorton and Rouwenhorst (2006), institutional investors started taking increased interest in adding commodities to portfolios because commodities are very heterogeneous and weakly related to equities and bonds. For example, commodities have considerable appeal to pension funds in terms of diversification. From this moment onward, the investing community took a greater interest in investing in commodity markets. Since the mid-2000s, suspicion rose that these "index speculators" buying futures for diversification without aiming at getting the underlying product delivered created positive correlations between commodity returns and equity returns. Chevallier and Ielpo (2013) and Chevallier et al. (2014) find that the impact of economic news on commodity markets rose in 2008. Still, much difficulty exists in determining whether this increased sensitivity to economic news reflects the "financialization" of commodities or simply reflects the GFC, which significantly diminished the demand for commodities.

Beyond this question lie the age-old questions of how and whether speculation affects commodity markets. Here again, the conclusions reached in the academic literature are mixed. For example, Singleton (2013) shows that investor flows had a significant impact on oil prices. Investor flow data track where money as a flow is actually invested, measuring investor willingness to buy more or less of certain assets, beyond simple price fluctuations. Flows also affect the steepness of the oil futures price curve if increased access from speculators has a tendency to compress the slope of the futures term structure. Hamilton and Wu (2014) find that the slope of the oil futures curve is flatter since 2005 and that this evolution can be partially attributed to the increased role of index fund investing. On the contrary, Knittel and Pindyck (2016) propose a simplified model of supply, demand, and storage. They find that speculation has had a limited impact on oil prices since 2004, validating the conclusions of Fattouh, Kilian, and Mahdeva (2013), Kilian and Lee (2014), and Kilian and Murphy (2014). So far, studies focusing on price movements fail to find a significant effect of speculation on commodity prices, whereas those estimating flows data sometimes find an impact of speculation. To date, this debate has not reached a conclusion.

Influence of Commodities on the Economic Cycle

The final discussion point in this chapter concerns the interaction between commodity cycles and the economic cycle. The connection between commodity prices and demand is related to this topic and has been explored extensively in the academic literature on oil markets. Through a conversation extending over 15 years, two scholars—James Hamilton and Lutz Kilian—have explored how supply and demand affect oil prices, economic growth, and inflation. The case made for crude oil can also be extended to other commodities, but oil has gathered the most attention from academia.

The original issue discussed in Hamilton (2003) examines how increasing and decreasing oil prices affect U.S. GDP. On the demand side, wages are slower to rise and adapt to the inflationary environment. A rise in oil prices leads to lower purchasing power and therefore lower employment. On the supply side, an oil shock—like a drop in the production level—is usually seen as lowering productivity. Hamilton acknowledges that most studies prior to 2003 assume that this connection is negative and linear: negative because an increase in oil prices can trigger to a recession and linear because a rise in oil prices triggers a recession, while a substantial decrease should create more growth. Lower oil prices would indeed imply that consumers have additional disposable income to spend more on filling their tanks, while considering the purchase of a bigger car depends on expectations of future oil prices. Evidence shows that surges in oil prices contribute negatively to economic growth. Depending on estimates, a 10 percent surge in oil prices leads to a 1.5 percent decrease in real GDP. However, very limited evidence exists for dropping oil prices leading to stronger growth. For example, while oil prices dropped 70 percent during 2014 and 2015, U.S. GDP growth struggled to exceed to 2 percent annually.

Hamilton (2003) shows that the economic response to oil prices can be asymmetric. That is, the economy reacts more strongly to rising prices than to dropping oil prices. Figure 2.7 corroborates this idea.

To further explore this asymmetric response, a first step is to analyze the origin of oil shocks. Demand and supply shocks in oil markets have very different impacts on the economy. Until 2008, the literature generally focused on the supply side of the oil equation. The oil supply shocks of 1973 and 1979 were major contributors to the slowdown of the world economy. Similarly, the start of the Gulf War is marked by a spike in oil prices, as shown in Figure 2.8. An initial explanation was that constrained supply by exogenous factors (i.e., factors such as geopolitical crises) led to higher oil prices. However, a different theory emerged in the aftermath of the 2008 oil price shock.

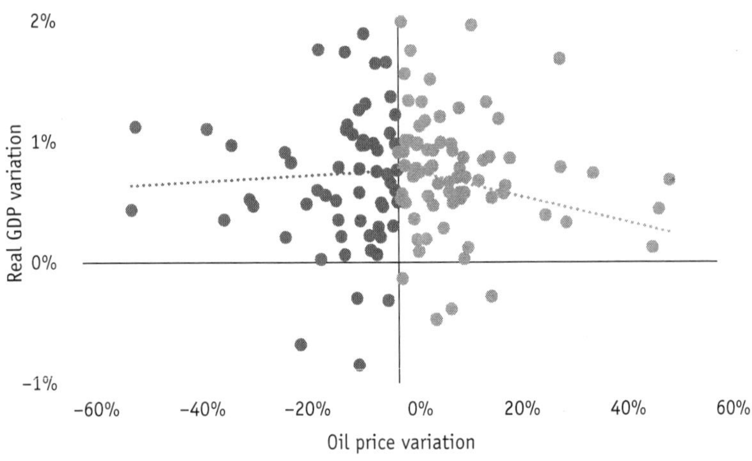

Figure 2.7 Oil Price Variations (WTI) versus the Change in the U.S. Gross Domestic Product

This figure shows the scatterplot of the returns on oil prices against the real GDP growth in the United States and illustrates the shape of the empirical relation. The dark gray dots are for negative returns on oil prices, while the light gray ones are for positive oil price variations. Source: Fred database.

Figure 2.8 Oil Prices (WTI) Evolution between 1969 and 2017
This figure shows the historical evolution of the spot price of the WTI between 1969 and 2017. Source: Fred database.

According to Hamilton (2009, p. 1), "Whereas previous oil price shocks were primarily caused by physical disruptions of supply, the price run-up of 2007–08 was caused by strong demand confronting stagnating world production." Until the beginning of 2000, the dominant explanation for oil shocks and oil volatility spikes had been on the supply side, and the demand part of the equation had been neglected. Hamilton points to the importance of accelerating world demand to explain oil price shocks, emphasizing that these shocks are likely to trigger recessions.

Kilian (2009, 2014) proposes a different interpretation. His works decompose oil shocks into three sources: supply shocks, global commodity demand shocks, and oil market demand shocks. Oil market demand shocks express a higher precautionary demand associated with concerns about future oil supply shortfalls. This key concept is essential to the results found in various Kilian studies. According to his estimates, 75 percent of historical oil price shocks have been demand driven. Kilian (2014) reviews historical price shocks—those previously regarded as supply shocks—such as the 1973 Yom Kippur War, the 1973–1974 Arab oil embargo, and the late 1980s Iran-Iraq War. He shows that the shock timing is often not contemporaneous to the timing of the supply-side disruption. The 1990–1991 Gulf War is the perfect example of a supply-side shock. It resulted in a short-lived shock on prices with other fundamentals eventually taking hold as shown in Figure 2.6. For each of these presumably supply shocks, Kilian presents evidence that demand was actually at work as well and that each shock included a mixture of the previously listed three factors, with demand dominating supply. This debate is still ongoing. Other analyses should eventually help to disentangle demand from supply shocks on commodity markets.

Accompanying Kilian's (2014) decomposition is the idea that the composition of each shock affects GDP growth differentially. A supply shock leads to a temporary decrease in GDP. Global demand shocks first lead to an improvement in GDP as global demand sustains economic activity. This positive effect eventually dissipates, leading to recessionary pressures over the longer term. Lastly, the oil-market-specific demand shocks are only recessionary. According to Kilian's estimates, the more recent oil shocks primarily reflect global demand-driven shocks. Their surprising inability to have triggered a recession is explained by their very nature. On the contrary, Hamilton (2009) sees a reflection of an oil shock in the 2008 crisis. Interestingly, Kilian's mixture of shocks helps to explain the asymmetric relation between GDP growth and oil prices. Negative oil shocks usually intervene over periods of negative global demand shocks. Alone, the reduction in oil prices cannot offset the rise in recessionary forces. However, in periods of rising oil prices such as in the United States during 2014 and 2015, an oil market demand shock can undermine GDP growth.

Summary and Conclusions

Commodities have attracted much attention in both the world of commodity trading and academia. The debates previously discussed are largely unresolved. For example, most view the theory of storage as the dominant explanation to the existence of a term structure of commodity futures. The recent rise in inventories between 2014 and 2016 is consistent with the decline of the basis, making the theory of storage the best current candidate. Regarding the dynamics of commodity spot price, many still debate the respective roles and importance of technologies, demand, and supply. Although many view the role of speculation as negligible, more evidence is needed to reach a conclusion. Although the asymmetric impact of commodities on growth is now better understood, the Hamilton-Kilian debate still continues.

Discussion Questions

1. Discuss two common explanations for the term structure of commodity prices.
2. Explain the relation between the commodity basis and the expected returns on commodities.
3. Identify the main drivers of spot returns of commodities.
4. Discuss the typical effects of an oil price shock.

References

Brennan, Michael J. 1991. "The Price of Convenience and the Valuation of Commodity Contingent Claims." In Diderik Lund and Bernt Oeksendal (eds.), *Stochastic Models and Options Value*, 22-71. Amsterdam: Elsevier Science Publications.

Carbonez, Katelijne A. E., Van Thi Tuong Nguyen, and Piet Sercu. 2009. "Do Inventories Really Yield a Convenience? An Empirical Analysis of the Risk-adjusted Spread." SSRN Working Paper 1344391. Available at https://ssrn.com/abstract=1344391.

Chevallier, Julien, Mathieu Gatumel, and Florian Ielpo. 2014. "Commodity Markets through the Business Cycle." *Quantitative Finance* 14:9, 1597–1618.

Chevallier, Julien, and Florian Ielpo. 2013. *The Economics of Commodity Markets*. Hoboken, NJ: John Wiley & Sons, Inc.

Cortazar, Gonzalo, and Eduardo S. Schwartz. 1994. "The Valuation of Commodity Contingent Claims." *Journal of Derivatives* 1:4, 27–39.

Dincerler, Cantekin, Zeigham Khoker, and Timothy Simin. 2005. "An Empirical Analysis of Commodity Convenience Yields." SSRN Working Paper 748884. Available at https://ssrn.com/abstract=748884.

Dixit, Avinash K., and Robert S. Pindyck. 1994. *Investment under Uncertainty*. Princeton, NJ: Princeton University Press.

Erb, Claude B., and Campbell R. Harvey. 2006. "The Strategic and Tactical Value of Commodity Futures." *Financial Analysts Journal* 62:2, 69–97.

Fattouh, Bassam, Lutz Kilian, and Lavan Mahadeva. 2013. "The Role of Speculation in Oil Markets: What Have We Learned So Far?" *Energy Journal* 34:3, 7-33.

Frankel, Jeffrey A. 2006. "The Effect of Monetary Policy on Real Commodity Prices." National Bureau of Economic Research Working Paper No. 12713.

Geman, Hélyette, and Vu-Nhat Nguyen. 2005. "Soybean Inventory and Forward Curve Dynamics." *Management Science* 51:7, 1076–1091.

Gorton, Gary B., Fumio Hayashi, and K. Geert Rouwenhorst. 2013. "The Fundamentals of Commodity Futures Returns." *Review of Finance* 17:1, 35–105.

Gorton, Gary B., and K. Geert Rouwenhorst. 2006. "Facts and Fantasies about Commodity Futures." *Financial Analysts Journal* 62:2, 47–68.

Hamilton, James D. 2003. "What Is an Oil Shock?" *Journal of Econometrics* 113:2, 363–398.

Hamilton, James D. 2009. "Causes and Consequences of the Oil Shock of 2007–08." *Brookings Papers on Economic Activity*. Available at http://econweb.ucsd.edu/~jhamilto/Hamilton_oil_shock_08.pdf.

Hamilton, James D., and Jing Cynthia Wu. 2014. "Risk Premia in Crude Oil Futures Prices." *Journal of International Money and Finance* 42:C, 9–37.

Harvey, David I., Neil M. Kellard, Jakob B. Madsen, and Mark E. Wohar. 2010. "The Prebisch-Singer Hypothesis: Four Centuries of Evidence." *Review of Economics and Statistics* 92:2, 367–377.

Hicks, John R. 1939. *Value and Capital*. Oxford: Oxford University Press.

Hirshleifer, David. 1989. "Determinants of Hedging and Risk Premia in Commodity Futures Markets." *Journal of Financial and Quantitative Analysis* 24:3, 313-331.

Jacks, David, and Martin Stuermer. 2015. "What Drives Commodity Prices in the Long Run?" Bank of Canada Working Paper. Available at http://www.bankofcanada.ca/wp-content/uploads/2015/05/what-drives-commodity-prices-long-run-stuemer.pdf.

Jensen, Gerald R., Robert R. Johnson, and Jeffrey M. Mercer. 2002. "Tactical Asset Allocation and Commodity Futures." *Journal of Portfolio Management* 28:4, 100–111.

Kaldor, Nicholas 1939. "Speculation and Economic Stability." *Review of Economic Studies* 7:1, 1–27.

Keynes, John Maynard. 1930. *Treatise on Money*. Volume 2. London: Macmillan.

Kilian, Lutz. 2009. "Not All Oil Price Shocks Are Alike: Disentangling Demand and Supply Shocks in the Crude Oil Market." *American Economic Review* 99:3, 1053–1069.

Kilian, Lutz. 2014. "Oil Price Shocks: Causes and Consequences." *Annual Review of Resource Economics* 6:1, 133–154.

Kilian, Lutz, and Thomas K. Lee. 2014. "Quantifying the Speculative Component in the Real Price of Oil: The Role of Global Oil Inventories." *Journal of International Money and Finance* 42:April, 71–87.

Kilian, Lutz, and Dan P. Murphy. 2014. "The Role of Inventories and Speculative Trading in the Global Market for Crude Oil." *Journal of Applied Econometrics* 29:3, 454–478.

Knittel, Christopher R., and Robert S. Pindyck. 2016. *American Economic Journal: Macroeconomics* 8:2, 85–110.

Laughton, David G., and Henry D. Jacoby. 1993. "Reversion, Timing Options, and Long-term Decision-Making." *Financial Management* 22:3, 225–240.

Laughton, David G., and Henry D. Jacoby. 1995. "The Effects of Reversion on Commodity Projects of Different Length." In Lenos Trigeorgis (ed.), *Real Options in Capital Investments: Models, Strategies, and Applications*, 185–205. Westport, CT: Praeger Publisher.

Nguyen, Van Thi Tuong, and Piet Sercu. 2010. "Tactical Asset Allocation with Commodity Futures: Implications of Business Cycle and Monetary Policy." SSRN Working Paper 1695889. Available at https://ssrn.com/abstract=1695889.

Pindyck, Robert. S. 1994. "Inventories and the Short-Run Dynamics of Commodity Prices." *Rand Journal of Economics* 25:1, 141–159.

Pindyck, Robert S. 1999. "The Long-Run Evolution of Energy Prices." *Energy Journal* 20:2, 1–27.

Pindyck, Robert S. 2004. "Volatility and Commodity Price Dynamics." *Journal of Futures Markets* 24:11, 1029–1047.

Pindyck, Robert S., and Julio J. Rotemberg. 1988. "The Excess Co-movement of Commodity Prices." *Economic Journal* 100:403, 1173–1189.

Prebisch, Raul 1950. *The Economic Development of Latin America and Its Principal Problems*. UN document no. E/CN.12/89/Rev.1. Lake Success, NY: United Nations.

Rouwenhorst, K. Geert, and Ke Tang. 2012. "Commodity Investing." *Annual Review of Financial Economics* 4:1, 447–467.

Schwartz, Eduardo, and James E. Smith. 2000. "Short-Term Variations and Long-Term Dynamics in Commodity Prices." *Management Science* 46:7, 893–911.

Singer, Hans W. 1950. "The Distribution of Gains between Investing and Borrowing Countries." In Sir Alec Cairncross and Mohinder Pur (eds.), *The Strategy of International Development: Essays in the Economics of Backwardness*, 58-66. London: Palgrave Macmillan.

Singleton, Kenneth. 2013. "Investor Flows and the 2008 Boom/Bust in Oil Prices." *Management Science* 60:2, 300--318.

Smith, James E., and Kevin F. McCardle. 1998. "Valuing Oil Properties: Integrating Option Pricing and Decision Analysis Approaches." *Operations Research* 46:2, 198–217.

Stoll, Hans R. 1979. "Commodity Futures and Spot Price Determination and Hedging in Capital Market Equilibrium." *Journal of Financial and Quantitative Analysis* 14:4, 873-894.

Symeonidis, Lazaros, Marcel Prokopczuk, Chris Brooks, and Emese Lazar. 2012. "Futures Basis, Inventory and Commodity Price Volatility: An Empirical Analysis." *Economic Modelling* 29:6, 2651–2663.

Working, Holbrook 1949. "The Theory of Price of Storage." *American Economic Review* 39:6, 1254–1262.

3

Commodity Exchanges and Regulation

JERRY W. MARKHAM
Professor of Law, Florida International University

Introduction

Commodity exchanges serve a vital role in the economy. They provide a centralized marketplace in which commodity producers can sell their commodities to those who want to use them for manufacturing or consumption. Regulating the trading of commodities poses various challenges. The purpose of this chapter is to describe the structure of derivative markets and the role of the professionals who participate in those markets. This chapter also provides an overall description of the regulations imposed by the federal government on the trading of derivatives. Those regulations include prohibitions against fraud and manipulation; the imposition of supervision requirements; and the requirement of specified disclosures to customers of trading risks. This chapter further addresses margin requirements for customers that are designed to prevent or limit shortfalls in the event of a customer default, and it describes requirements for the segregation of customer funds and net capital standards for firms holding customer accounts.

Evolution of Commodity Exchanges and Regulation

The use and development of derivative contracts have been traced back to antiquity, but modern futures exchanges did not develop in the United States until just before the Civil War (Markham 1987). The Board of Trade of the City of Chicago, founded in 1848, became the center for such trading. Futures trading also appeared in New York and other cities during the nineteenth century.

The first attempt at regulating futures trading occurred during the Civil War, when the Union government banned trading in gold futures. That ban was imposed because some thought speculation in gold futures and options was undercutting the value of the Greenback dollars that were used to fund the Union war effort. That legislation proved to be unworkable and was repealed only two weeks after its passage.

Following the Civil War, many raised concern about the frequent manipulation of commodity prices through futures trading on the commodity exchanges. So-called "bucket shops" were another problem. These operations were simply betting parlors for taking bets on commodity price fluctuations. The bucket operators frequently absconded with customer funds when the bets turned against those operators.

Legislators introduced numerous bills in Congress to address these concerns, but none passed until 1921. Congress then passed a statute that imposed a prohibitive tax on futures contracts executed on venues other than boards of trade licensed by the federal government. The courts held that legislation to be an unconstitutional use of federal taxing powers. However, Congress reenacted virtually the same statute in 1922 under the Commerce Clause, which the Supreme Court later upheld. That legislation, the Grain Futures Act of 1922 (GFA) required the futures exchanges to register under the GFA as "contract markets." The GFA also proscribed commodity price manipulations, but this prohibition applied only to a few specified ("enumerated") agricultural commodities on which futures were traded.

The GFA proved to be ineffective in stopping price manipulations and was replaced by the Commodity Exchange Act of 1936 (CEA). The CEA expanded the scope of federal regulation over futures trading. Among other things, futures commission merchants (FCMs) were subject to regulation, customer funds had to be held in specially segregated accounts, and sales solicitation fraud was prohibited.

Like its predecessor, the CEA proved to be ineffective in preventing market abuses. The CEA also focused only narrowly on a small number of "enumerated" agricultural products. The CEA had to be amended whenever other commodities became the subject of futures trading.

Congress was unable to keep up with the pace of industry expansion, and the CEA did not regulate many futures contracts. This dichotomy created a two-tier system of "regulated" and "unregulated" contracts. The CEA suffered from other flaws, including being administered by a small bureau in the Agriculture Department that lacked the resources to deal with a rapidly expanding industry. Congress sought to correct these flaws through a broad-scale amendment of the CEA by the Commodity Futures Trading Commission Act of 1974 (CFTC Act). The CFTC Act created the Commodity Futures Trading Commission (CFTC).

CFTC Jurisdiction over Futures and Options

The CFTC Act dropped the practice of regulating only commodities enumerated in the CEA. Instead, Congress gave the CFTC exclusive jurisdiction over all commodity futures and options trading. This change removed the need to amend the CEA when futures trading expanded to include new commodities. Still, this grant of exclusive jurisdiction proved to be problematic. After enactment of the CFTC Act, futures trading spread quickly from contracts whose underlying commodities were agricultural commodities to futures on financial products such as Treasury securities and stock indexes. Indeed, in just a few years following enactment of the CFTC Act, futures trading on financials dominated the industry.

The assignment of exclusive jurisdiction to the CFTC on all futures, agricultural and financial, touched off a long-running war between the CFTC and the Securities and Exchange Commission (SEC). The SEC believed that derivative contracts on securities should be subjected to its regulation. Indeed, in 1973, the year before the enactment of the CFTC Act, the SEC began regulating options on equity stocks. Although the SEC retained that authority after enactment of the CFTC Act, it sought to expand its jurisdiction to include all derivatives on all securities.

After the SEC lost some high-profile court battles over the reach of the CFTC's exclusive jurisdiction, it reached an agreement with the CFTC over their respective jurisdictions. This agreement, known as the Shad-Johnson Accord in reference to the chairmen of the two agencies who negotiated the agreement, was enacted into law by the Futures Trading Act of 1982. Under that statute, the SEC was given jurisdiction over options traded on national securities exchanges and on options on securities traded in the over-the-counter (OTC) market. The SEC was granted jurisdiction over options traded on stock indexes, while the CFTC had jurisdiction over futures on stock indexes. Congress also allowed the CFTC to regulate options on futures contracts where the underlying is a security index. Further amendments to the CEA gave the CFTC and SEC shared jurisdiction over futures traded on a single stock.

CFTC Organization

The CFTC is a five-member federal agency whose members are appointed for five-year terms by the president with the advice and consent of the Senate. No more than three members of the CFTC may be in the same political party at any one time. The CFTC is headquartered in Washington, DC, but it also has branch offices in New York, Chicago, and Kansas City.

The CFTC has a staff that administers the CEA on a day-to-day basis. That staff is organized into various divisions and offices. Those units have jurisdiction over particular areas subject to regulation.

CFTC DIVISION OF ENFORCEMENT

The CFTC's Division of Enforcement (DOE) is responsible for investigating and conducting civil prosecutions of violations of the CEA and CFTC rules. Criminal violations are referred to the Department of Justice (DOJ) for prosecution.

The CFTC may authorize the DOE to subpoena documents and require sworn investigative testimony from witnesses. Such subpoenas are enforceable through actions brought in a federal district court. Failure to comply with a court order requiring compliance with a CFTC subpoena may result in contempt-of-court proceedings.

Following an investigation, the DOE may seek authority from the CFTC to file an administrative proceeding before a CFTC administrative law judge (ALJ). The ALJ may impose administrative sanctions that include requiring restitution of customer funds, civil monetary penalties, suspensions or revocation of a professional's registration with the CFTC, and suspension or revocation of trading privileges.

The DOE also may, with CFTFC authorization, seek injunctive relief in a federal district court to stop ongoing violations. The CFTC may also seek ancillary relief from the court, including appointment of a receiver, an order freezing assets, directing restitution and disgorgement of unlawful proceeds, and the imposition of civil monetary penalties.

OTHER CFTC DIVISIONS

The CFTC's Division of Market Oversight (DMO) is responsible for the day-to-day oversight of the futures markets. That oversight includes commodity exchanges, other trade execution facilities, and swaps data repositories. The DMO conducts commodity market surveillance for the purposes of detecting abusive trading practices and price manipulations.

The CFTC's Division of Clearing and Risk (DCR) oversees clearing organizations, clearing brokers, swap dealers, major swap participants, and large traders. The DCR seeks to maintain the financial integrity of those market participants in order to prevent defaults that could pose a systemic market risk. In carrying out that oversight, the DCR conducts risk assessment and surveillance of market participants. The DCR also reviews applications for clearinghouse registration. Additionally, the DCR advises the CFTC on which swaps should be cleared and should be allowed to trade without clearing through a central counterparty.

The CFTC's Division of Swap Dealer and Intermediary Oversight (DSIO) oversees compliance with regulations governing swaps trading. The DSIO's oversight includes business conduct standards and compliance with CFTC-imposed capital requirements for swap dealers and margin requirements.

CFTC OFFICES

Besides its divisions, the CFTC staff includes various specialized offices including the following:

- *Office of Executive Director.* This office is responsible for allocating CFTC staff resources. It also implements management and administrative policy, and measures CFTC staff program performance.
- *Office of General Counsel (OGC).* This office acts as the CFTC's lawyer. OGC advises the CFTC on legal issues affecting the agency and represents the agency in actions brought against the CFTC or staff. OGC also represents the CFTC in appellate cases involving the agency or its programs and bankruptcy cases involving CFTC registrants.
- *Office of the Chief Economist (OCE).* This office provides economic analysis and advice to the CFTC. The OCE also conducts research on economic policy issues affecting the agency and cost-benefit studies of proposed CFTC regulations.
- *Office of Data and Technology (ODT).* The ODT provides technology and data management support for the CFTC's market and financial regulatory programs. ODT is, in effect, the CFTC's information technology (IT) department.
- *Whistleblower Office (WO).* This office receives whistleblower complaints. It oversees payment of monetary incentives to individuals who report violations of the CEA that lead to a successful enforcement action. Additionally, the WO is

responsible for both ensuring the confidentiality of whistleblower complaints and preventing retaliation against them.

Exchange and Clearinghouse Regulation

A central part of the regulatory structure of the CEA is the requirement that futures exchanges register with the CFTC as a "designated contract market" (DCM). Exchange clearinghouses must also register with the CFTC as "derivatives clearing organizations" (DCOs). The CFTC regulates these registrants under separate sets of regulations.

DCM REGULATION

The CEA and CFTC regulations require DCMs to act as self-regulatory organizations (SROs) (Johnson and Hazen 2004). This means that DCMs must police the conduct of their members to prevent and detect abuses. The theory of self-regulation is that the commodity exchanges or other industry organizations should be responsible in the first instance for preventing abusive conduct by their members. Meeting this responsibility reduces the need for taxpayer-funded regulation.

DCMs must comply with several CEA specified "core principles." These principles include the responsibility for detecting violations and enforcing the DCM's rules, preventing market disruptions, ensuring that trading is competitive, and creating systems safeguards against operational risks. The CFTC's Division of Market Oversight is responsible for determining whether DCMs are complying with these core principles and whether abusive trading is occurring.

Historically, DCMs operated trading floors where exchange members gathered to trade through an open outcry competitive process. Today, that form of trading is nearing extinction. Instead, computer algorithms on DCM electronic trading platforms match most transactions.

High-frequency traders (HFTs) who use algorithms to generate orders rapidly, most of which are quickly canceled, dominate trading on DCMs. The CFTC is considering regulations to govern these traders, including a possible requirement that the HFTs disclose their trading algorithms to the agency.

Contrary to securities markets, in which market makers must quote a continuous two-sided market at a spread between the bid and ask prices, thus providing liquidity to other traders, the commodity exchanges impose no such market-making obligations on futures traders. However, futures trades may be given monetary incentives by DCMs to act as liquidity providers.

DERIVATIVES CLEARING ORGANIZATION REGULATION

Another critical part of the futures industry is the DCO (Filler and Markham 2014). A DCO acts as a counterparty to both the buyer and seller of a futures contract. This intercession allows the parties to rely on the credit of the DCO instead of that of the party on the opposite side of the trade. This guarantee function is essential to the efficient operation of the futures markets. Indeed, the Financial Stability Oversight Council (FSOC) has designated DCOs as systemically important financial institutions. The Dodd-Frank Wall Street Reform and Consumer Protection Act of 2010 (Dodd-Frank Act) created the FSOC to provide special supervision over such systemically important institutions.

Like DCMs, DCOs must adhere to specified core principles in carrying out their activities. These principles include maintaining adequate financial, operational, and managerial resources, adequate and appropriate risk management capabilities, standards and procedures to protect member and participant funds, adequate and appropriate systems safeguards, emergency procedures, and a plan for disaster recovery.

"Clearing firm" members who are responsible for the financial performance of their non-member customers clear customer accounts. This responsibility means that, if a customer defaults, the clearing member is responsible for any deficit. If a clearing member defaults, safeguards are in place to protect the DCO from loss, including assessments against other clearing firms and safety funds that may be tapped to meet deficits.

Exchange-set margin requirements further protect the financial integrity of the DCO. Customers trading commodity futures are required by contract markets to "post" margin to protect the DCO from a default by the customer. Margin posted by a commodities futures customer thus constitutes a good faith deposit of money to help ensure that the customer performs its obligations.

In the first instance, "initial" margin is required to be posted for each futures contract when it is initially executed. This amount is expressed as a small portion of the notional value of the futures contract. Initial margin is based on an assessment of the potential amount that a commodity price might change before a commodity broker can liquidate the account of a defaulting customer.

Besides initial margin, "variation" margin payments are required to be posted by customers when their account value drops below an exchange-set "maintenance margin" level. *Variation margin* is an additional deposit of money required to reflect losses incurred by a customer from adverse price changes on open commodity futures positions.

Variation margin requirements are computed through a "mark to market" system. That is, the market value of the commodity is computed daily to determine if its value has changed. The purchaser or seller experiencing a loss is required to post an additional amount equivalent to that loss, often called a "margin call." Conversely, if a customer is experiencing a gain, that amount is credited to the customer's account.

National Futures Association

The National Futures Association (NFA) is another SRO for the commodity futures and options industry and for retail OTC foreign currency (forex) and commodity swaps. The NFA's counterpart in the securities industry is the Financial Industry Regulatory Authority (FINRA). NFA membership or association is mandatory for commodity industry professionals.

The NFA is responsible under the CEA for the registration of persons and organizations doing business as futures professionals. The NFA screens applicants to determine their fitness to engage in business as commodity derivative professionals. In 2016, more than 4,000 firms and 57,000 associated persons were registered with the NFA.

The NFA does not operate any exchange but has rules that seek to maintain the financial integrity of its member firms and to prevent abusive practices. Among other things, NFA rules govern sales practices, disclosures to customers of risks and fees, and abusive trading practices. An NFA rule also requires FCMs to "know your customer," which means that FCMs must obtain information about the financial sophistication of customers and their trading goals.

NFA rules further govern recordkeeping requirements, financial reporting, and minimum capital requirements for member firms. The NFA conducts periodic examinations of its member firms to monitor their financial condition. It requires daily electronic confirmation of the amount of customer segregated funds required to be held at banks and other depositories.

In its capacity as an SRO, the NFA is authorized to bring disciplinary actions against members and their associated persons. It issues warning letters for minor rule violations and initiates more serious cases by the filing of a formal complaint. The NFA, and DCMs acting as SROs, may impose penalties when they find violations, including expulsion or suspension of NFA membership and participation in the industry as a registered professional, censure, and fines of a maximum $250,000 per violation. Respondents in such proceedings are entitled to a fair and orderly process of adjudication. This includes notice of the charges and a hearing before an SRO committee. Appeals from committee decisions are usually first made to higher levels of the SRO's governing body. Appeals by respondents from the final SRO disciplinary sanctions are made to the CFTC, which may hear such appeals in its discretion. Appeals may be made from the CFTC's decision on an SRO-imposed sanction to an appropriate federal court.

Futures Commission Merchants

The analogue of a securities broker-dealer in the futures markets is the "futures commission merchant" (FCM) (Filler and Markham 2014). A person trading commodity contracts on a contract market must use the services of a CFTC-registered FCM or of a registered "introducing broker" (IB). The FCM or IB acts as the customers' broker. An IB may solicit customer orders but is not allowed to handle customer funds. An FCM is permitted to solicit customer orders and to handle customer funds. The FCM is often a "clearing member," meaning that it can carry customer accounts with a DCO.

The "associated persons" (APs) of the FCM or IB are also required to register with the CFTC. An *associated person* is any salesperson or a person who supervises salespersons. The AP registration requirements apply to all persons in the supervisory chain-of-command even if they do not directly supervise the solicitations of orders, customers, or funds.

CFTC rules impose a supervision requirement on FCMs. FCMs are also subject to extensive recordkeeping and reporting requirements. For example, FCMs must file monthly and annual financial reports with the CFTC and NFA. A certified public accountant (CPA) must certify the annual financial report as being in conformance with generally accepted accounting principles and CFTC requirements.

FCMs are subject to CFTC net capital requirements, which require FCMs to have sufficient liquid assets on hand to meet customer obligations. This net capital further ensures that FCMs have a sufficient financial commitment to their business. The net capital requirement helps protects against FCM insolvencies.

Another customer protection measure is that customer funds held in CEA-regulated accounts be maintained in segregation in specially designated accounts maintained at specified depositories, usually a bank. No Securities Investor Protection Corporation (SIPC) or Federal Deposit Insurance Corporation (FDIC) insurance is available for CEA-regulated accounts. Instead, futures customers are dependent on this CEA segregation requirement to protect their funds in the event of bankruptcy. Special provisions in the bankruptcy code apply to the liquidation of FCMs and give priority for customer funds segregated under the CEA. In the last several years, failures of large FCMs have occurred. Some of those failures resulted in shortfalls in customer segregated accounts, not all of which were recovered in bankruptcy proceedings.

FCMs are required to compute on a daily basis the total amount of customer funds required to be held in segregated accounts and the amount of the FCM's residual interest in those funds. FCMs must notify the CFTC and NFA if funds and securities held in segregated accounts are less than the required amount. FCMs may invest customers' segregated funds in securities authorized by CFTC rules, including U.S. Treasury securities. FCMs can keep the interest payments from such investments.

CFTC rules require FCMs to provide customers with a written risk disclosure statement before they trade. Among other things, this document advises commodity futures customers of the fact that they may lose more than their initial margin deposit and that commodity futures contracts are highly leveraged. Customers are further advised that their funds are not covered by government insurance. Customers are required to sign an acknowledgment that they understand these risks before trading.

Commodity Pool Operators and Commodity Trading Advisors

The CFTC Act regulates entities called "commodity pool operators" (CPOs) and "commodity trading advisors" (CTAs). CPOs and CTAs and their associated persons must register with the CFTC.

A *CPO* is simply a pool of investor funds that are traded by the fund operator in commodity futures or commodity options. The commodity pool is often described as the analogue to mutual funds in the securities industry. CPOs typically operate their commodity pools as hedge funds. Like other hedge funds, commodity pools are highly leveraged, which means they can be very profitable. However, that leverage also means that a CPO can quickly incur large losses.

A *CTA* provides trading advice to persons trading commodity futures or commodity options, which clients can accept or reject. CTAs may also be given discretionary authority to trade client accounts without seeking prior client authorization for each trade.

CFTC rules require CTAs and CPOs to provide their clients with a brochure, which, among other things, must contain a risk disclosure statement describing the risks of loss from the instruments traded by the CPO or upon which advice is given by the CTA. Additionally, the risk disclosure statement must describe the fees that may be charged by the CTA or CPO.

CPOs and CTAs are also required to provide disclosures setting forth their prior performance results (i.e., their past track record in advising customers or directing investments in a commodity pool or through a discretionary account). CFTC rules impose advertising restrictions on CPOs and CTAs, including required disclosures for hypothetical trading results.

Anti-fraud Protections

The CEA and CFTC rules contain several anti-fraud prohibitions applicable to products subject to their regulation (Markham 2016). The CEA prohibition against fraud in connection with futures trading is somewhat convoluted in its wording, but the courts have interpreted it to have wide application.

In order to prove a violation, the courts and CFTC have held that the actor has the requisite scienter (i.e., intent). That is, the actor must be at least "reckless" in engaging in conduct that misleads others. Misrepresentations must also be shown to be "material" (i.e., a reasonable investor would consider the information to be important in making an investment decision).

Fraud claims under the CEA anti-fraud provision for commodity futures include downplaying or misrepresenting the risks of trading and unrealistic profit predictions. This prohibition also applies to unauthorized trading in a customer's account. Unauthorized trading was previously one of the most common violations of the CEA because voice brokers, who had an incentive to seek commissions through unauthorized customer trades, entered orders manually. However, the growth of electronic trading has much reduced such claims. Customers trading on electronic trading platforms may enter the orders themselves and can monitor their accounts more closely.

Another fraud claim under the CEA involves a practice called "churning." *Churning* occurs when the AP of an FCM controls a customer account and the AP engages in excessive trading in the account to generate commissions.

CFTC rules contain separate anti-fraud prohibitions for commodity options and retail foreign currency transactions. The language of these rules varies from the CEA prohibition for commodity futures but still contains many of the same elements.

Another anti-fraud prohibition in the CEA is addressed to CPOs and CTAs. Claims under that statutory prohibition often include charges of misrepresenting the expertise of traders, the success of trading programs, and the failure to disclose that trading results for a trading program are only hypothetical.

The CEA and CFTC rules do not prohibit insider trading, a charge that is common in the securities industry. Indeed, the CEA contains provisions stating that its anti-fraud prohibitions do not require disclosure of nonpublic information about the commodity being traded. Nevertheless, trading on "misappropriated information" (i.e., stolen information) is prohibited. Trading or disclosing nonpublic information to others is prohibited for CFTC commissioners and their employees, personnel of SROs, as well as employees and members of Congress and judicial employees.

Secondary Liability

Liability may lie in CFTC enforcement actions for violations of the CEA and CFTC rules for persons directly engaging in violations. Secondary liability may be imposed on other actors under the doctrines of *respondeat superior*, "aiding and abetting," failing to "supervise," or situations in which the party is a "controlling" person.

RESPONDEAT SUPERIOR LIABILITY

Respondeat superior liability is imposed by the CEA on principals, such as an FCM, for the acts of their agents (i.e., APs). This statutory liability is simply an extension of the common-law rule that makes employers responsible for the acts of their employees.

The theory behind the doctrine of *respondeat superior* is that the principal set the AP in motion and should bear the responsibility for losses inflicted by the employee on innocent third parties. This liability attaches even if the principal did not approve of or direct the violation by the AP. However, to establish liability under this doctrine, evidence must show that the AP was acting within the scope of her or his employment.

SUPERVISORY LIABILITY

As previously noted, CFTC rules require that registrants have a system in place for diligently supervising their APs. Such a supervisory system must be reasonably designed to prevent and detect violations of the CEA and CFTC rules. This supervision requirement has two elements: (1) a system of procedures and controls that are reasonably designed to detect and prevent violations of CFTC rules; and (2) the diligent application of those procedures and controls.

CFTC rules generally give each FCM the discretion to determine how this supervisory requirement is to be carried out. Nevertheless, some CFTC rules may mandate supervisory requirements, such as the appointment of a chief compliance officer.

The CFTC imposed duty of supervision rests initially with the chief executive officer (CEO) of a registrant. However, those officers may delegate that duty to subordinates and often do so. In large FCMs, this delegation of duty may extend through several layers of supervisors and into branch offices.

AIDING AND ABETTING LIABILITY

Secondary liability for aiding and abetting a violation is present when a person willfully aids or abets the commission of a violation by another person. Such liability typically applies for violators of criminal laws as well as civilly under the CEA.

Aiding and abetting is present when a person acts in combination or concert with another person who commits a violation. Such liability also lies when the aider and abettor willfully caused an act to be done or provided substantial assistance to a party committing a violation. Evidence must also show that the accused had the specific intent to aid or abet a violation. In such cases, the aider and abettor may be held responsible for such violation as a principal.

CONTROLLING PERSON LIABILITY

Controlling person liability occurs in CFTC enforcement actions in which a person directly or indirectly controls another person who has violated the CEA or CFTC rules. This provision in the CEA seeks to impose liability on persons who control a corporation or other business entity and allow or direct violations by others. The CFTC has the burden of proving that the controlling person did not act in good faith or knowingly induced, directly or indirectly, the act or acts constituting the violation. Controlling person liability is unavailable in private actions seeking damages.

Customer Remedies

Three forums are available for customers damaged by violations of the CEA or CFTC rules to seek recompense: (1) arbitration, (2) an action in federal court, and (3) a reparations proceeding before the CFTC. Each of these forums has both advantages and disadvantages.

ARBITRATION

Arbitration is a matter of contract. Instead of a judge and jury, persons appointed by an arbitration forum selected by the parties decide arbitrations privately. Arbitration is typically the fastest and least expensive method for seeking and obtaining damages.

Arbitration proceedings are generally less formal than court proceedings, which reduces costs for the parties. Because judicial review of an arbitration award is extremely limited, this process reduces costs and speeds up the entry of a final decision. This limitation also means that, even where an error exists by the arbitrators concerning applicable law or facts, the court will not correct such errors.

CFTC rules regulate the form of customer agreements that contain pre-dispute arbitration clauses. The CFTC's rules seek to ensure that customers of registrants enter into such provisions voluntarily.

The NFA provides an arbitration and mediation forum for the resolution of customer complaints against commodity professionals who are members of the NFA. However, the parties may agree on an alternative arbitration forum.

FEDERAL COURT ACTIONS

A private right of action is available in federal court under the CEA to persons directly damaged by fraudulent activities or commodity futures price manipulations. The CEA sets a two-year statute of limitations for bringing such actions.

Federal court actions under the CEA provide several advantages, including the right to a jury trial, broad discovery, and multiple levels of judicial review. Because of these features, federal court actions tend to be more prolonged and expensive than arbitration proceedings. The many motions that are typically filed in federal court, availability of broad discovery through documents and depositions, and judicial review can prolong these proceedings for years.

CFTC REPARATIONS

CFTC reparation proceedings are a somewhat unique method for resolving customer claims. Instead of a court or arbitrators, reparations are conducted before the CFTC. Reparation proceedings are limited to claims made against CFTC registrants for violations of the CEA or CFTC rules.

No jury trial is available in reparations. Rather, such actions are conducted before a CFTC hearing officer. These hearings vary in formality depending on the size of the claim. Reparations decisions by hearing officers may be appealed first to the CFTC and then to a court of appeals.

CFTC reparations proceedings offer the advantages of having decision-makers who are familiar with CEA and CFTC rule requirements and industry practices. Still, the process can also be very slow. Discovery in reparation proceedings may not be as broad as that available in federal court proceedings. Expense is also of concern because reparations proceedings can involve extended delays and appeals that increase the costs and duration of the proceedings.

Trading Abuses

The CEA prohibits various trading abuses that involve "fictitious" transactions. A *fictitious transaction* is one that is structured to eliminate market risk and to evade market competition (Markham 2016). One common form of fictitious transaction is a *wash sale*, which involves a buy and sell order in the same futures contract by the same person or group with the intent that the orders offset each other. The trader has no real market risk in such a transaction, and the trade only serves to give a false appearance of bona fide market activity. Wash sales and other fictitious transactions should be distinguished from *scalping*, which involves quick in-and-out trades that are intended to limit market risk, but not to eliminate such risk entirely. Most electronic trading platforms now have "wash blocker" algorithms that prevent scalpers and other traders from accidentally or intentionally entering wash trades.

The Dodd-Frank Act added additional prohibitions against abusive trading practices such as violating the bids and offers of other participants. This practice is now curbed on electronic trading platforms by exchange matching engines. The Dodd-Frank Act also prohibits orders that demonstrate an intentional or reckless disregard for the orderly execution of trades during the closing period of trading on an exchange. Such conduct is usually engaged in order to affect exchange closing prices. This abusive practice seeks to create an artificial price on an exchange that is used as a benchmark price to value OTC or other contracts.

Another provision of the Dodd-Frank Act prohibits orders that are of the character of *spoofing*, which is bidding or offering with the intent to cancel the bid or offer before execution. This provision is somewhat problematic in application because the vast majority of orders (i.e., 90 percent or more) on electronic markets are canceled before execution, oftentimes within milliseconds of initial entry.

Manipulation

The original CEA contained prohibitions against commodity price "manipulation" and false price reports. This prohibition was problematic because the CEA did not define what constitutes manipulation. In the absence of a statutory definition, the courts and the CFTC have held that four elements are needed to prove manipulation: (1) the existence of an "artificial price," (2) the ability to cause the artificial price, (3) a showing that the party in fact caused the artificial price, and (4) the intent to create the artificial price (Markham 2014a).

These elements are very difficult to prove, as illustrated by the fact that, although the CFTC has obtained numerous settlements in manipulation cases, it has won only one adjudicated case in its 40-year history. Especially difficult to prove are the intent and artificial price elements because evidence must show that the actor had the specific intent to create an artificial price. Price artificiality also is difficult to prove because many market elements affect price. Economic experts often disagree over whether a trader's actions caused a price movement and whether the movement was the result of bona fide supply and demand.

Claims that electricity prices in the California market had been manipulated through OTC derivatives in 2000–2001 resulted in administrative actions against violators by the CFTC and by the Federal Energy Regulatory Commission (FERC). Congress later granted FERC and the Federal Trade Commission (FTC) additional anti-manipulation authority after the occurrence of further energy price increases and claims of manipulation. An anti-fraud provision in the Securities Exchange Act of 1934 (1934 Act), which the SEC has used for many years to prosecute manipulation as well as fraud, served as a model for those provisions.

The Dodd-Frank Act added an additional manipulation prohibition to the CEA in 2010 that was also modeled after the 1934 Act. How much, if any, that this provision will lessen the CFTC's burden in proving whether manipulation has occurred is unclear. The principal difference between the old and new CEA anti-manipulation authority is the scienter requirement. The courts have held that "recklessness" suffices for proving intent under the 1934 Act, while specific intent is required under the old CEA provision. Nevertheless, the reckless standard is still a very high scienter requirement.

Traditionally, the most common commodity price manipulations involved the misuse of market power in so-called "corners" and "squeezes." A *corner* occurs in which a party buys all available supplies of a commodity in order to dictate prices to purchasers. Those purchasers are forced to pay an artificial price to obtain the commodity for their operations or to deliver on a futures contract. In a *squeeze*, the manipulating party acquires control of a substantial amount, but not all, of the available supplies for a particular commodity. The resulting shortage of supply allows the manipulating party to "squeeze" prices higher. The corner and squeeze are "market power" manipulations employed by large traders.

Another form of manipulation involves "rigged sales" that are conducted at artificial prices. *Rigged sales* are usually short-term manipulations that are for the purpose of reducing margin requirements or artificially creating a benchmark price used as a reference to price separate transactions.

Still another form of price manipulation is conducted by using false reports of OTC volume or pricing. For example, energy trading firms settled numerous CFTC cases charging that they made artificial price and volume reports to commercial reporting services that those and other traders used to value their positions. Some energy-trading firms were also charged with making false volume reports to those reporting services in order to present the false appearance that they were large market makers. This false reporting of volume sought to induce other traders to trade with the manipulator.

Swaps and Other OTC Instruments

Beginning in the 1970s, much innovation occurred in the development of derivative transactions that involve financial instruments. In 1973, the Chicago Board of Trade opened the Chicago Board Options Exchange, Inc. (CBOE). The CBOE traded options on equity securities. Regulatory jurisdiction over its activities fell to the SEC by default, as the result of the then very narrow reach of the CEA.

Further innovation in the development of OTC derivatives occurred after enactment of the CFTC Act. Many of these new instruments had elements of commodity options and futures regulated by the CFTC and securities transactions regulated by the SEC. Of particular interest were swaps that began trading in 1981 and grew into a $4 trillion market within a decade. These instruments were not traded on regulated exchanges. Rather, AAA-rated swap dealers who guaranteed their performance arranged swaps. An industry standard master agreement that created by the International Swap Dealers Association (later renamed as the International Swaps and Derivatives Association) (ISDA) generally governed the terms of these swaps.

The CFTC issued a policy statement in 1989 that asserted that commercial swap transactions were not subject to the CEA provisions that require futures contracts to be traded through a DCM. To clarify the authority of the CFTC to issue that interpretation, the Futures Trading Practices Act of 1992 (FTPA) authorized the CFTC to exclude swaps and OTC energy derivatives from regulation under the CEA. The CFTC used that authority to exempted swap transactions in which the parties were "eligible swap participants" that included natural persons with a net worth in excess of $5 million or assets totaling $10 million.

The Commodity Futures Modernization Act of 2000 (CFMA) further deregulated swap transactions by allowing them to be traded on "exempt commercial markets" (ECMs). Access to ECMs was limited to large commercial traders. This exemption resulted in the development of a large centralized market in swaps operated by the Intercontinental Exchange (ICE) headquartered in Atlanta, Georgia.

Swaps Regulation

The unregulated swaps market caused much concern during the financial crisis of 2007-2008. In particular, credit default swaps created problems that caused massive losses at the American International Group Inc. (AIG). AIG was a systemically significant insurance company with more than $1 trillion in assets and operations in more than 130 countries. The federal government provided $182 billion in financial assistance to bail AIG out during the crisis period.

AIG's collapse and other problems led to including provisions in the Dodd-Frank Act that regulated swaps and other OTC derivative instruments. The Dodd-Frank Act created new categories of regulated entities, including commodity-based "swap dealers," "security-based swap dealers," "major swap participants," "major security-based swap participants," and "swap data repositories." The Dodd-Frank Act requires most swaps to be cleared through an exchange clearinghouse or other central counterparty (CCP).

Jurisdiction over swaps was divided by the Dodd-Frank Act among the SEC, CFTC, and bank regulators. The CFTC was given jurisdiction over "swaps" when the underlying is a commodity. The SEC has jurisdiction over *security-based swaps,* which are swaps that have a security as the underlying. The SEC and CFTC have joint jurisdiction over *mixed swaps,* which are swaps that have elements of both swaps and securities-based swaps. Bank regulators were given jurisdiction over swap transactions by banking institutions.

The CFTC and SEC engaged in joint rulemaking to define the swaps that are subject to their respective jurisdictions. Swaps were broadly defined to include traditional "plain vanilla" swaps, such as a fixed for floating interest rate swap. Also included in the definition of swaps were the following: interest rate floors, caps, and collars; cross-currency rate swaps; basis swaps; total return swaps; equity index swaps; equity swaps; debt index swaps; debt swaps; credit spreads; credit default swaps; credit swaps; weather swaps; energy swaps, metal swaps; agricultural, and emissions swaps. The definition of a swap excluded state regulated insurance products and forward contracts.

The Dodd-Frank Act created a four-part statutory definition of the terms commodity "swap dealer" and "securities-based swap dealer." They include persons holding themselves out as a dealer in swaps or security-based swaps; making a market in swaps or security-based swaps; regularly entering into swaps or security-based swaps with counterparties as an ordinary course of business for one's own account;

or engaging in any swap that causes the person to be commonly known in the trade as a dealer or market maker in swaps or security-based swaps.

The Dodd-Frank Act prohibits persons that are not "eligible contract participants" (ECPs) from engaging in CFTC- or SEC-regulated swaps except through a DCM or a national securities exchange. ECP status includes individuals having aggregate amounts invested on a discretionary basis in excess of $10 million, or $5 million that is used to manage risks.

Dodd-Frank requires registration of "major swap participants" (MSPs) and "major security-based swap participants" (MSBSPs). Such registrants are generally subject to the same statutory requirements that apply to swap dealers and security-based swap dealers. MSPs and MSBSPs are entities that are not swap dealers or security-based swap dealers, and who meet any of the following three statutory tests: (1) persons who maintain substantial swap positions; (2) persons whose outstanding swaps have substantial counterparty exposure that could have serious adverse effects on the financial stability of the U.S. banking system or financial markets; or (3) highly leveraged financial entities that are not subject to capital requirements of a federal banking regulator agency.

The CFTC and SEC have adopted business conduct rules for swaps registrants. The CFTC business conduct rules impose a "suitability" obligation on swap dealers and MSPs (i.e., recommendations to potential counterparties by swap dealers and MSPs to engage in swap transactions must be suitable for the customer receiving the recommendation). Swap dealers and MSPs must have a reasonable basis to believe that the counterparty receiving the recommendation is capable of independently evaluating the risks related to the particular swap or trading strategy recommended. The CFTC has not imposed such a suitability requirement on FCMs making recommendations to customers trading futures or commodity options. However, the SEC has traditionally applied a suitability requirement on firms registered with it as broker-dealers.

The CFTC and SEC business conduct swap rules require swap dealers, MSPs, and MSBSPs to communicate with counterparties in a fair and balanced manner that is based on principles of fair dealing and good faith. These rules prohibit such actions as providing exaggerated or unwarranted forecasts and profit claims. Forecasts and profit predictions must be balanced by a disclosure of potential risks and loss.

The CFTC business conduct rules require that swap dealers and MPSs make risk disclosures to counterparties and provide trade confirmations. These entities must describe the degree of the complexity of their swap and the nature of any leverage in the transaction. They must also disclose liquidity risks and lack of price transparency.

Unlike for CFTC regulated futures and options, the CFTC declined to adopt a standardized risk disclosure form for swaps. The CFTC concluded that standardized disclosures would be inappropriate for swaps because those transactions are often of a "bespoke" nature, rather than standardized, as is the case for exchange-traded futures and options.

The CFTC and SEC swap rules impose supervisory requirements on swap dealers and major swap participants. These rules also require registrants to have a chief compliance officer who must prepare and certify an annual report that assesses the registrant's compliance efforts. The rules further require creating and enforcing risk management procedures; monitoring of position limits; and establishing business continuity and disaster recovery plans. SEC rules impose conflict-of-interest requirements that require "firewalls" between research units and trading desks and between clearing and trading operations.

Foreign Currency Derivatives Regulation

Foreign currency (forex) derivatives are the subject of regulations separate from those for commodity futures, options, and swaps (Markham 2014b). The development of this separate regulation was the result of a provision contained in the CFTC Act, which stated that the CEA did not govern transactions in foreign currency. That provision, the so-called "Treasury amendment" was added to the CEA to exclude the interbank currency market from CFTC regulation. The Treasury amendment exclusion was thought to be appropriate because large banks that were already the subject of regulation by the banking agencies maintained the interbank currency market.

Unscrupulous firms that fraudulently sold forex derivatives to unsophisticated retail customers (retail forex) exploited the Treasury amendment. Those retail forex dealers often failed or misappropriated customer funds. To stop those operations, the CFTC sought to limit the reach of the Treasury amendment to derivative transactions in foreign currency by large institutions. The Supreme Court rejected that limitation.

Congress thereafter amended the CEA to shut down the firms engaged in retail forex fraud. Those firms then exploited another loophole in the CEA that excluded "cash" transactions from regulation. Although Congress made further amendments to the CEA to deal with that problem, retail forex fraud continued. The Dodd-Frank Act then sought to comprehensively regulate retail forex firms. The Dodd-Frank Act allocated jurisdiction over retail forex transactions among the SEC, CFTC, and the federal banking agencies. These regulators prohibited retail forex transactions unless conducted in accordance with the rules of one of those regulators.

The CFTC rules for retail forex derivatives apply to dealers offering off-exchange forex transactions that are unregulated by the SEC or the banking regulators. A firm offering retail off-exchange forex transactions to retail customers, which excludes ECPs because they are not considered to be retail forex customers, is required to register with the CFTC as a retail foreign exchange dealer (RFED). FCMs are excluded from that registration requirement if their business is primarily exchange-traded commodity futures or options. Both RFEDs and FCMs dealing in OTC forex transactions are subject to a net capital requirement of $20 million, plus a surcharge of 5 percent where their exposure to retail forex customer positions exceeds $10 million.

CFTC rules impose supervision requirements on RFEDs including the appointment of a chief compliance officer. RFEDs are required to ensure that they are setting fair and objective settlement prices for retail forex trades. Customers must also be warned that they have no control over the settlement prices set by their RFED.

The CFTC prohibits RFEDs from executing orders on behalf of customers unless specifically authorized to do so. Another CFTC rule prohibits RFEDs from guaranteeing retail forex customers against losses from their forex transactions. Such guarantees can jeopardize the financial stability of a firm and cause losses to other customers when the firm fails.

The NFA has also adopted rules governing RFEDs and FCMs engaging in retail forex derivative transactions. These entities must register with the NFA as "Forex Dealer Members" (FDMs). Among other things, NFA rules impose supervision requirements on FDMs. FDMs must also observe high standards of commercial honor and just and equitable principles of trade in their retail forex transactions.

The SEC rule for retail forex governs transactions conducted by registered broker-dealers. The SEC rule requires retail forex transactions to be conducted in accordance with the SEC's other rules and those of FINRA. This rule had a sunset provision that required the SEC to determine by 2016 whether additional rules are needed. FINRA rules require members dealing in retail forex derivatives to conduct that business in accordance with the rules of the NFA, an unusual form of cross-market regulation in the United States.

The Federal Reserve Board, Office of the Controller of the Currency, and FDIC adopted rules governing retail forex transactions engaged in by banks regulated by those agencies. Among other things, banks must provide notification to their regulator before engaging in the retail forex business. Those rules contain requirements for disclosures to customers, recordkeeping, and capital and margin standards. The prescribed risk disclosures that must be made to retail forex customers include the percentage of customers experiencing losses and those with profitable positions. The rules of the banking regulators further prohibit fraud by banks in their retail forex business.

Summary and Conclusions

The regulation of derivatives trading has spread from very limited regulation by a small bureau in the Department of Agriculture to broad and complex regulations adopted by a host of federal agencies, including the CFTC, SEC, FERC, FTC, and banking regulators. The SROs, including DCMs, the NFA, and FINRA, supply another level of regulation.

This chapter examined the role of derivative market professionals, including FCMs, IBs, APs, CTAs, CPOs, swap dealers, MSPs, MBSPs, FDMs, and RFEDs. The goal of this chapter is to provide an overall description of the regulations imposed on these entities. Those regulations have business conduct elements, including prohibitions against fraud and manipulation and supervision requirements. Disclosures to customers of trading risks are also required and recordkeeping standards are imposed. These regulations further address margin requirements for customers to prevent or limit shortfalls upon a customer default, segregation of customer funds, and net capital standards for firms holding customer accounts.

Discussion Questions

1. Explain the roles of DCMs, DCOs, FCMs, IBs, APs, CTAs, CPOs, swap dealers, MSPs, MBSPs, FDMs, and RFEDs.
2. Explain the differences between a CPO and a CTA.
3. Discuss how customer funds are protected in bankruptcy if a FCM fails.
4. Discuss how margin requirements are calculated for futures contracts.
5. Describe how jurisdiction is allocated among the SEC, CFTC, and bank regulators over swaps and retail forex derivatives.

References

Filler, Ronald H., and Jerry W. Markham. 2014. *Regulation of Derivative Financial Instruments (Swaps, Options and Futures): Cases and Materials*. St. Paul, MN: West Academic Publishing.

Johnson, Philip McBride, and Thomas Lee Hazen. 2004. *Derivatives Regulation*. 3 vols. Frederick, MD: Aspen Publishers.

Markham, Jerry W. 1987. *The History of Commodity Futures Trading and Its Regulation*. New York, NY: Praeger Press.

Markham, Jerry W. 2014a. *Law Enforcement and the History of Financial Market Manipulation*. Armonk, NY: M. E. Sharpe.

Markham, Jerry W. 2014b. *Regulation of Swap and Other Over-the-Counter Derivative Contracts*. Securities Practice Portfolio Series No. 263. Arlington, VA: Bloomberg/BNA.

Markham, Jerry W. 2016. *Commodities Regulation: Fraud, Manipulation & Other Claims*. Eagan, MN: West, Thomson, Reuters.

4

Behavioral Aspects of Commodity Markets

JOHN R. NOFSINGER
Professor and William H. Seward Endowed Chair in International Finance,
University of Alaska Anchorage

PATTANAPORN CHATJUTHAMARD
Associate Professor of Finance, Chulalongkorn University

XU DAI
Associate Professor of Finance, Jilin University of Finance and Economics

Introduction

The trading activity in futures markets is large compared with the size of physical production. The increase in commodity derivatives trading comes from investors, hedgers, traders, and speculators. The behavior of these participants has the potential to impact markets, prices, and investment success. The initial work in behavioral finance emphasized the effect of investor biases, emotions, and cognitive errors in financial markets, which are inconsistent with the traditional view of investor rationality. More recently, research has identified behavioral influences on derivative traders in predominantly professionally traded markets such as oil, gold, and foreign exchange. With the increased recognition that the same behavioral biases can affect professional traders that affect individual investors, the need to understand these biases becomes increasingly important.

Speculation and the seemingly irrational behavior of market participants have attracted the notice of scholars, the media, and the public. Why do market participants depart from the rational standard of traditional expected utility theory? Many concepts are available in the finance literature to analyze the behavior of individual and institutional investors. More specifically, behavioral finance introduces different psychological biases caused by cognitive processes. These biases have their place and purpose in allowing a person to function, but they also often lead to erroneous investment decisions. In addition, when a bias exists across many market participants, the overall market can be affected, leading to panics and bubbles. Commodity investors, hedgers, traders, and speculators have a vested interest in understanding behavioral finance, not only to capitalize on commodity market fluctuations but also to be more aware of their own decision-making processes.

The rest of this chapter has the following organization. The next section describes the behavioral biases, with commodity and futures markets examples. The following section discusses the behavioral role in risk attitudes and trading strategies. The chapter then examines the different types of market participants to understand the role of information and skill in the context of their roles in the marketplace. The final section provides a summary and conclusions.

Behavioral Finance in Commodity Markets

Shefrin (2006) identifies three categories of psychological phenomenon: biases, heuristics, and framing effects. In the biases category, he includes overconfidence and excessive optimism, confirmation bias, and illusion of control. The heuristics are representativeness, availability, anchoring, and affect (or emotion). For framing effects, he includes loss aversion and prospect theory. According to behavioral finance, having many participants suffer from the same psychological bias can affect the equity market (Coval and Shumway 2005). Their impact is often called *noise trader risk* (DeLong, Shleifer, Summers, and Waldmann 1990b). This situation is also true for commodities markets. For example, Coakley, Dollery, and Kellard (2011) argue noise trader risk influences the pricing of 17 futures contracts in agriculture, metals, stock index, and exchange rates on U.S. futures markets. Cummins, Dowling, and Lucey (2015) examine the non-ferrous metals markets on the London Metal Exchange and report a behavioral influence for copper, aluminum, lead, and aluminium alloy.

PSYCHOLOGICAL PRINCIPLES

Barberis and Thaler (2005) describe the irrational behavior of professional investors. They discuss ambiguity aversion, overconfidence, and prospect theory to explain insufficient and naive diversification, excessive trading, and irrationalities in selling and seemingly irrational selling and buying decisions. *Ambiguity aversion* refers to the distaste people feel for events in which the probability distribution is uncertain. *Overconfidence* refers to people who generally consider themselves as being above average in their abilities (Yates 1990). They also overestimate the precision of their knowledge relative to others. Overconfidence results in excess trading, which results in trading costs that reduce profits and an attention to markets that enhance other psychological biases. For example, many traders believe they can consistently time the market, but overwhelming evidence indicates otherwise. Many grain producers may be overconfident (Mattos, Garcia, and Pennings 2008) in that they expect prices greater than those reflected in the futures markets and place little weight in the tails of the returns distribution. An outcome of overconfidence may explain their underuse of futures markets for hedging price risk.

Kahneman and Tversky's (1979) Nobel Prize–winning prospect theory has become one of the most important concepts in analyzing the psychological behavior of market participants in today's investment world. First, prospect theory suggests people express a different degree of emotion toward gains than toward losses. Individuals are more stressed by prospective losses, which create more stress to individuals than equal gains create happiness. Thus, people may behave oddly to avoid taking a loss. A second aspect of prospect theory is loss aversion, which is behavior noticed by scholars and became a foundational observation in the development of prospect theory. It indicates another reason investors might choose to hold their losers and sell their winners—they may believe that today's losers may soon outperform today's winners. Investors often make the mistake of chasing market action by investing in stocks or funds that garner the most attention. Third, reference points become very important in decision-making as investors use them to frame the context, which ultimately determines whether they view themselves as experiencing a loss or a gain. People become attached to salient references points. Consider the commodities examples by Narayan, Narayan, and Popp (2011) and Bharati, Crain, and Kaminski (2012), who investigate price clustering in oil futures and NYMEX oil contracts. They find significant evidence of clustering in these contracts around whole dollar amounts. These price points become reference points that influence trader psychology and thus drive behavior.

Disposition Effect

Prospect theory leads to investors avoiding the pain of regret from taking a loss. This fear leads to them holding onto losing positions. Alternatively, investors seek the feeling of pride when selling a winning position, which leads to selling winners too soon. Shefrin and Statman (1985) termed this tendency the *disposition effect* because investors are predisposed to hold their losers too long and sell their winners too soon. Evidence by Odean (1998) shows stock investors with discount brokerage accounts hold their losing positions too long. These positions continue to underperform the market. Additionally, delaying the sale of a loser postpones the allowable tax loss deduction. Investors also sell their winning positions too quickly, as those stocks continue to outperform the market after being sold. Selling a winner incurs a tax liability. Barberis and Xiong (2009) illustrate that realized gains and losses predict the disposition effect, whereas annual gains and losses do not. For derivative markets, Choe and Eom (2009) examine the realization of gains and losses in the Korean stock index futures market. Using a unique database, they show strong evidence of the disposition effect and explain it in terms of investor characteristics. They find that individual investors are much more susceptible to the disposition effect than are institutional and foreign investors. In addition, higher trader sophistication and experience tend to reduce the disposition effect.

Loss-Aversion Theory

One important implication of prospect theory is that people care about changes in wealth more than wealth itself and care more about avoiding losses than making gains. Individuals prone to loss aversion tend to be more sensitive to wealth losses than to wealth gains but are less sensitive to additional losses when the loss is large. Thaler, Tversky, Kahneman, and Schwartz (1997) provide consistent support for loss aversion through experimental studies. As Odean (1998) shows, investors in the stock market are reluctant to realize losses. Locke and Mann (2005) find that professional floor traders hold their losses longer than their gains, but this is not a costly behavior.

Lien (2001) studies the effect of loss aversion on the futures trading behavior of a short hedger using a modified, constant-absolute-risk aversion utility function and modifying the functional form to incorporate loss aversion. Comparing the optimal futures positions under each of the two utility functions, Lien shows that the impact of loss aversion depends on the contract's relative price. Specifically, loss aversion leads to less active trading when the hedger is very risk-averse and loss-averse under backwardation pricing. However, when the price exhibits contango, loss aversion leads to more active trading.

Using 1995 transactions data from the Chicago Mercantile Exchange (CME), Locke and Mann (2009) re-examine loss-related trader behavior in the context of the broader literature, investigating reference dependence preferences. Specifically, they examine the impact of morning gains and losses on afternoon trading behavior by professional future traders. Locke and Mann report increased afternoon trading and risk-taking by traders with morning losses, which supports both a daily income target and loss aversion hypotheses. However, they find no evidence of costly loss aversion behavior in terms of reduced trading performance or irrational prices after morning losses.

Mattos et al. (2008) examine the effect of loss aversion and risk aversion for a soybean producer using the futures market to hedge price risk. They develop distributions for soybean cash and futures price changes to simulate the producer's operational hedging decision for a relevant range of parameter values. First, loss and risk aversion only have an impact in efficient markets. Second, in a static context, loss aversion has a relatively small impact on hedge ratios for all parameter values, while risk aversion only becomes relevant for a limited range of risk coefficients, resulting in implausible speculative behavior in the futures market and a long position in the cash market. Therefore, prior outcomes affecting risk attitudes have the most influence on hedging behavior.

Nolte and Voev (2011) investigate the disposition effect and loss-aversion behavior in groups of small retail investors, big institutional traders, and professional traders in the foreign exchange market. Wealthier investors who are more likely to trade with a portfolio strategy are more prone to the disposition effect at the portfolio level instead of the single-position profit/loss level. They also confirm that investors who face a higher than normal risk exposure trade more cautiously, which is a sign of risk-averse behavior and more careful risk management.

Reference Points

People are attracted to whole number prices, which can lead to price clustering in some markets. Many studies explain the relation between price clustering and its impact on bid-ask spreads in both equity and future markets, such as Barclay (1997), Bessembinder (1997), and Chung, Kim, and Kitsabunnarat (2005). Traditional research usually asserts that psychological factors should mainly influence the investment decisions made by small equity investors. However, reference points also appear to influence participants in the more sophisticated markets of foreign exchange

(Westerhoff 2003; Mitchell and Izan 2006), gold (Aggarwal and Lucey 2007), and energy (Dowling, Cummins, and Lucey 2016).

Emotions

The layperson's initial reaction to behavioral finance is that it is about fear and greed. Although behavioral finance primarily focuses on psychological biases, emotions can also play a role. Psychological biases tend to affect financial decisions when people have stronger emotional reactions. For example, Lo, Repin, and Steenbarger (2005) conduct an experiment with 80 day traders and find that those who exhibit more intense emotional responses stimuli also exhibit significantly worse trading performance.

Researchers have tested the impact of emotions on stock returns through correlation studies between weather and market returns. Sunshine makes people happy and more inclined to buy stocks; sad people are more critical of stock investments. Hirshleifer and Shumway (2003) examine the daily stock market returns in 26 cities around the world and find a positive correlation with the degree of sunshine that day. Do weather-related emotions affect the commodities and futures markets? Limpaphayom, Locke, and Sarajoti (2007) provide direct evidence on the effect of local weather on investor behavior. Their examination of both wind and sunshine in Chicago shows that floor traders buy on relatively calm days and earn less income on days with higher wind strength.

Trading Strategies

This section describes the role of behavioral biases in risk-taking and trading strategies. Specifically, people are considered to be risk averse. However, people can change their level of risk aversion and even become risk seeking depending on their situation. In addition, commodities and futures participants often engage in positive feedback trading in an attempt to capture momentum in returns.

RISK-TAKING STRATEGY

The literature on behavioral finance has long emphasized the relation between prior gains or losses and subsequent risk-taking behavior. Thaler and Johnson (1990) show the "house money effect" occurs when people are more likely to take risks after prior gains. Conversely, they also note that prior losses lead to risk-seeking behavior in situations in which future outcomes offer an opportunity to break even. Heath, Huddart, and Mark (1999) study the relation between prior profits and subsequent risk-taking behavior in employee stock option plans. They find that employees exercise their options after prior stock price increases, especially at the one-month interval. The employees also seem to use the prior maximum stock price as an important reference point and tend to exercise options once that price is exceeded. The relation between risk-taking and prior gains/losses differs across various types of market participants, such as retail investors (Odean 1998), traders (Frino, Johnstone, and Zheng 2004;

Locke and Mann 2005), fund managers (O'Connell and Teo 2009), and foreign institutions (Grinblatt and Keloharju 2001).

Huang and Chan (2014) conduct a detailed analysis of the trading behavior of three types of participants in the context of Taiwan's futures market. They determine the relation between afternoon risk-taking and different magnitudes of morning gains or losses for active individual investors, foreign institutions, and futures proprietary firms. Regarding active individual investors, both gains and losses positively affect subsequent trading risk. Specifically, Huang and Chan show a tendency toward the break-even effect when facing morning losses, no matter whether those losses are large or small. Only large morning gains stimulate the house money effect. Foreign institutions only show a tendency toward the house money effect for small morning gains. Futures proprietary firms only show a tendency toward the break-even effect for large morning losses.

A common belief is that institutional investors are more sophisticated than are individual investors. The additional risk-seeking behaviors of both foreign institutions and futures proprietary firms do not have significant effects on market volatility and liquidity. Only risk-seeking behaviors of active individual investors facing large morning losses affect both market volatility and liquidity. Frino, Grant, and Johnstone (2008) also observe evidence consistent with the house money effect in the trades executed by professional futures traders (locals) on the Sydney Futures Exchange. Liu, Tsai, Wang, and Zhu (2010) use the complete order and trade record of leading traders at the Taiwan Stock Exchange (TAIEX) option market to document greater risk-taking after morning profits and less risk-taking after morning losses for market makers. They also note that studying how the reference point is determined is important because that can frame the magnitude of losses and gains.

POSITIVE FEEDBACK TRADING

Positive feedback trading, also known as trend chasing, involves buying securities after price increases and selling after price decreases. As in the case of the NASDAQ stock bubble of the late 1990s, positive feedback traders can push prices away from fundamental values. Furthermore, DeLong et al. (1990b, 1991) theoretically and empirically show that rational speculators do not fully eliminate, and can even amplify, the effect of positive feedback trading on asset prices.

Many positive feedback trading studies examine this subject at the market level. DeLong, Shleifer, Summers, and Waldmann (1990a) show that investors often follow positive feedback trading strategies, even rational speculators amplify the effect of such strategies on asset prices. Sentana and Wadhwani (1992) confirm the consistency of the relation between volatility and return autocorrelations with positive feedback trading. Nofsinger and Sias (1999) posit that positive feedback trading drives, at least in part, changes in portfolio holdings of individual and institutional investors observed at monthly, quarterly, and annual intervals. Antoniou, Koutmos, and Pericli (2005) show that positive feedback trading increased in the stock markets of six developed nations after the introduction of stock index futures in these markets. Daníelsson and Love (2006) find positive feedback trading at the one- and five-minute frequency in the spot USD/EUR foreign exchange market.

Kurov (2008) examines how recent price changes affect the order flow of traders in index futures markets. He shows that index futures traders use positive feedback trading strategies. Kurov also finds a positive relation between the intensity of the positive feedback trading and investor sentiment. This result suggests that positive feedback trading consists, at least in part, of sentiment-driven noise trading. Consistent with the noise-trading hypothesis, Kurov finds that order flow contains less information in periods of bullish sentiment and a strong negative relation between the variance of intraday pricing errors and investor sentiment measures. This latter finding implies that sentiment-driven trading increases market liquidity, helping to stabilize temporary price fluctuations.

Lastly, Tokic (2011) investigates the 2008 oil price bubble. He contends that institutional investors can impose limits to arbitrage, especially in financial crisis when the demand for commodities is especially strong. Tokic concludes that during this time commercial hedgers engaged in positive feedback trading and thus contributed to the bubble by bidding prices higher.

MOMENTUM STRATEGIES

The predictability of stock prices based on past returns is a subject of increased attention. However, most of the literature on momentum focuses on low-frequency daily or monthly data in stock markets and it does not consider high-frequency data or futures markets. Less evidence is available on the predictability of intraday returns in stock and futures markets. In one notable exception, Chen (2013) provides evidence for the predictive power of the beginning of day (open-to-period) returns for the returns of the balance of the trading day using intraday data of Taiwan Stock Index Futures between 2001 and 2006. The empirical results show that the open-to-period return strategy is profitable, even when considering transaction costs and using different index futures contracts and cash index. Thus, the open-to-period cumulative returns contain valuable information for predicting future returns over the day. If traders want to trade futures without facing immediate losses, they can either follow this strategy for the rest of the day, or at least refrain from taking an opposite position until the close. When the first five-minute index return momentum turns bullish (bearish), positive feedback institutional traders may increase (decrease) their net positions and this can lead to the persistence of price momentum.

Dewally, Ederington, and Fernando (2013) provide new evidence on the major theories of commodity futures pricing. They use unique proprietary data on individual traders in three energy futures markets derived from the Commodity Futures Trading Commission's Large Trader Reporting System, consisting of 350 contracts for crude oil, 250 for heating oil, and 150 for gasoline. They classify each trader into 11 trader categories: (1) refiners, (2) independent producers, (3) pipelines and marketers, (4) large energy consumers, (5) commercial banks, (6) energy traders, (7) hedge funds, (8) households, (9) investment banks and dealers, (10) market makers, and (11) an unclassified group. They find that momentum in commodity futures markets is due largely to hedging pressure. Dewally et al. find no evidence that traders profit by holding long futures positions with positive short-run momentum or short positions with negative short-run momentum, after controlling for hedging pressure and storage variables.

Trading by Type of Market Participant

The information structure and the characteristics of market participants, such as differences in risk-taking, trading strategy, incentives, or skill, systematically influence individuals' investment decisions, as well as trading profitability. Dewally et al. (2013) reject the possibility that different profits by different commodities traders are due to luck. Even though some individual traders have an informational or skill advantage, no evidence exists that other trader types, such as hedge funds, have better information or skills than other types. Such evidence indicates that trading profits generated by speculators and hedge funds are compensation from the risk absorption and liquidity they provide to hedgers.

Using the Madhavan and Smidt (1991) model, Lyons (1995) finds support for both information and inventory effects in the pricing of a foreign exchange (FX) dealer using 1992 data. The dealer increases his spread with trade size to protect against private information, and adjusts the midpoint in the spread (quote shading) to induce trades in a preferred direction to adjust inventory. However, Bjønnes and Rime (2005) study the behavior of four interbank spot foreign exchange dealers using data in 1998 and they find no support for the information and inventory effects. The reasons for these conflicts are differences in trading styles among the dealers, and the change in the trading environment caused by the introduction of electronic brokers. Additionally, the dealer tracked by Lyons may have been playing an interdealer risk-sharing role. Adopting the indicator model suggested by Huang and Stoll (1997), Bjønnes and Rime show that private information is indeed important in the FX market. Interestingly, they find strong evidence of mean reversion for all four dealers, and the median half-lives of the inventories range from less than one to 15 minutes.

To be more specific on trader groups, which may or may not have informational or skill advantages, it is worthwhile to look more thoroughly into the types of traders and compare their trading skills and information set to understand their behavior better in the commodity markets. The types of market participants examined are the market makers, floor traders who trade for other exchange members, clearing members such as financial institutions trading for their own account, and the public (e.g., individual speculators, managed funds, and small hedgers). The following section provides a review of the empirical evidence of their prior investment outcomes and their subsequent trading strategy.

MARKET MAKERS

According to Coval and Shumway (2005), market makers engage in greater risk-taking after prior losses to try to break even, and experience a reduction in risk exposure after prior gains to stay ahead. This finding is consistent with the notion that investors try to avoid a sure loss. Locke and Mann (2005) show a similar effect determined by professional futures traders at the CME during 1995. Frino et al. (2008) contend that the value function of Kahneman and Tversky (1979) builds on the understanding that human decision-makers react disparately to gains and losses. Accordingly, both a house money effect and break-even effect can occur at the same time because traders exhibit symmetric risk-taking behavior with respect to gains and losses. Kaustia (2010) suggests that different levels of past performance affect the propensity to sell a stock.

Although much literature focuses on the relation between market structure and execution costs in specialist and dealer markets, researcher pay relatively little attention to the open outcry structure of futures exchanges. The dynamic movement of competing market makers in and out of the futures pit, the lack of firm bid-ask quote, and the open outcry of customer orders suggest that effective CME customer trading costs may differ substantially from the NYSE and NASDAQ. Ferguson and Mann (2001) examine the customer execution spreads (trading costs) based on the comparison between execution spread and the quoted bid-ask spread, also studied by Locke and Venkatesh (1997), by analyzing the audit trail order flow data for both locals and off-exchange customers provided by the Commodity Futures Trading Commission (CFTC). They conclude that CME market makers are active, rather than strictly passive, traders. Order flow information is likely available to skilled traders. This conclusion suggests that negative spreads may result from market makers offering price improvement to some of their customers to facilitate trading on their informational advantage. Kuserk and Locke (1996) examine the positions and trades of market makers on days in which pork belly futures prices hit price limits. The market makers do not seem to fully anticipate the price moves and hold positions when the price limits are hit, unlike on non-limit days. Thus, market makers mostly react to the order flow instead of predicted prices.

FLOOR TRADERS TRADING FOR OTHER EXCHANGE MEMBERS

Most floor-traded securities exchanges provide a special class of trader, called the *active informed local trader,* with direct access to the trading floor. They can trade on their own account. Several studies have analyzed data for U.S. futures markets and quantify total profits earned by local traders. Silber (1984) analyzes complete trade data for a single local trader and extrapolates that traders in general may have some sort of information advantage allowing them to predict and trade on order-flow related information. The profits earned by locals represent their reward for providing liquidity and/or trading on order flow-related information.

To provide evidence on their economic role, Frino, Jarnecic, and Feletto (2010) use unique data of floor trading on the Sydney Futures Exchange to describe how locals in the floor-traded futures markets derive income. The authors decompose the profits earned by locals into two components: reward for providing liquidity and position-taking profit. As for the position-taking profit component, they find a relation between the ability of locals to earn positive position-taking profit and their presence on the trading floor, by comparing their local income on the floor and screen-traded markets. Their evidence shows that locals on the trading floor make large position-taking profits, which show a positive relation to short-term order-flow related to information such as trading frequency and volatility. However, those profits also show a negative association with the presence of exogenous information, local liquidity profits, and the length of locals' inventory cycle. As for the liquidity profit component, locals on the floor play a more complicated role than is traditionally outlined in the futures market literature. Specifically, locals are not only suppliers of liquidity, but also appear to be willing to demand liquidity and sacrifice their liquidity profit to realize position-taking profits. Thus, they are net liquidity suppliers who may actively trade when in the possession of information related to future price volatility.

As for the behavioral traits of futures floor traders conducting proprietary trading during volatile market conditions, two contradictory research statements are available. The traditional view is that professional floor traders should be profitable in their proprietary trading even during volatile market conditions. Unlike equity market makers, futures floor traders do not have an obligation to make a market; thus, perceived profitability ought to be the prime motive for proprietary trading (Silber 1984; Kuserk and Locke 1996; Manaster and Mann 1996). A more recent perspective is that professional floor traders also suffer a performance reduction during volatile markets. Even the most seasoned futures floor traders succumb to significant psychophysical biases during high-volatility periods. For example, professional floor traders in many futures markets worldwide succumb to the disposition effect (Lo and Repin 2002; Coval and Shumway 2005; Haigh and List 2005; Locke and Mann 2005).

To examine the profitability of proprietary trading under different market conditions, Chen (2008) uses the transaction data of every proprietary floor trader in four futures contracts traded on the CME in 1995, which provide a complete and robust picture of the true landscape of performance by proprietary traders. This study finds a large dispersion in the behavior of floor traders in their proprietary trading. Specifically, only a small group of elite traders enjoy profits. Conversely, proprietary traders will increase their trading volume if market volatility increases, while their trading performance will depend on the degree of market volatility. The proprietary trading performance is better during intermediate volatile market days, but generally not higher during the most volatile market days than during the least volatile market days.

Frino et al. (2004) compare the behavior of professional floor traders with small off-floor traders and test the extent to which loss riding by professional traders is due to their informational advantages relative to off-floor traders. They use a sample of professional futures traders (locals) on the Sydney Futures Exchange, as well as a sample of matched nonlocal traders. After controlling for potential differences in trader characteristics, comparisons reveal a stronger disposition effect among locals than non-local traders. This difference may not be completely due to a behavioral bias. The frequency with which the losing positions held by locals become profitable is greater than that of the less well informed, but otherwise matched, non-locals. Even though they cannot reject the hypothesis that behavioral biases reinforce the disposition effect, their evidence supports the proposition that an inclination to ride losses among professional futures traders is at least in part a product of rational informed trading.

INSTITUTIONAL INSTITUTIONS, INDIVIDUAL SPECULATORS, MANAGED FUNDS, AND SMALL HEDGERS

Benartzi and Thaler (1995) combines two behavioral concepts—Kahneman and Tversky's (1979) loss aversion and Thaler's (1985) mental accounting—to provide a theoretical foundation for the observed equity premium puzzle. Only a few experimental studies have tested Benartzi and Thaler's myopic loss aversion (MLA) theory. This theory involves a situation in which investors exhibit preoccupation with the negative effects of losses in comparison to an equivalent amount of gains and take a very short-term view on an investment. A criticism of these experiments is that any inferences are based on observing the behavior of undergraduate students. However, Haigh and List (2005) use undergraduate students and recruit 54 professional futures and options pit traders from the Chicago Board of Trade to explore MLA. They find that the professional futures traders show more myopic loss aversion than less experienced decision-makers (undergraduate students).

Indeed, O'Connell and Teo (2009) suggest that whether a person succumbs to a behavioral bias is sensitive to investor type. Retail investors (Odean 1998; Dhar and Zhu 2006) and professional investors (Frino et al. 2004; Locke and Mann 2005) ride their losses, quickly cash out their gains, and are thus prone to the disposition effect. Chevalier and Ellison (1997) suggest that fund managers motivated by career or reputation concerns tend to increase risk-taking after a period of poor performance and reduce risk after a period of good performance. By contrast, O'Connell and Teo (2009) suggest that fund managers aggressively control risks after losses and mildly increase risks after gains. Their result is consistent with dynamic loss aversion (Barberis, Huang, and Santo 2001).

A common belief is that institutional investors or professional traders are more sophisticated than are individuals. Locke and Mann (2005) contend that individuals display irrational behavior and that disciplined market professionals can minimize potential behavioral influences. Likewise, Grinblatt and Keloharju (2001) investigate the disposition effect and find significant differences in trading styles between Finnish individual investors and foreign institutions. Choe and Eom (2009) investigate the Korean futures market and find that individuals are much more prone to the disposition effect than institutional and foreign investors. Chou, Yen, and Wang (2010) find this same pattern in Taiwan's futures markets.

Summary and Conclusions

The primary participants in the commodities and futures markets are professionals. Do these sophisticated market makers, traders, speculators, hedgers, and institutions exhibit the same behavioral biases as retail investors? The current review of the literature illustrates that many of the psychological biases are prevalent in the commodities and futures markets. Prospect theory describes the cognitive processes that often lead to behavior that deviates from traditional expected utility theory. Prospect theory suggests people are more stressed by prospective losses than they are pleased from equal gains. Thus, they are loss averse. Traditional expected utility theory focuses on risk aversion. Given the high-risk nature of the commodities and futures markets, participants often exhibit risk-averse behavior. However, the literature suggests that participants also exhibit loss aversion. An important difference between risk aversion and loss aversion occurs when an investor holds a losing position. In loss aversion, that investor is willing to become risk seeking to resolve the loss and break even. That is, investors may be willing to accept gambles that they normally would not take if they can break even. This behavior is called the *break-even effect*, and futures market participants exhibit risk seeking in that situation. In addition to loss aversion, an extension is that investors hold their losers too long and sell their winners too soon, called the *disposition effect*. The disposition effect appears to be pervasive in the commodities and futures markets. Lastly, prospect theory relies on reference points that help a decision-maker frame the context and magnitudes of losses and gains. Activity around whole numbers in the futures markets suggests that salient reference points play an important role.

This review also identifies the pervasive use of positive feedback trading and momentum investing. *Positive feedback trading* is the purchase (sale) of long (short) positions after price increases (declines). The literature shows that this occurs, especially in short time intervals, measured in minutes, and probably relates to market sentiment. The expectation is to benefit from price momentum, which is a closely related strategy.

Discussion Questions

1. Discuss how futures markets participants might exhibit psychological biases.
2. Explain how loss aversion differs from risk aversion and who is likely to exhibit loss aversion.
3. Explain the disposition effect and indicate who in the commodities and futures markets exhibits this effect.
4. Define positive feedback trading and how it might affect futures markets.

References

Aggarwal, Raj, and Brian M. Lucey. 2007. "Psychological Barriers in Gold Prices?" *Review of Financial Economics* 16:2, 217–230.

Antoniou, Antonios, Gregory Koutmos, and Andreas Pericli. 2005. "Index Futures and Positive Feedback Trading: Evidence from Major Stock Exchanges." *Journal of Empirical Finance* 12:2, 219–238.

Barberis, Nicholas, Ming Huang, and Tano Santos. 2001. "Prospect Theory and Asset Prices." *Quarterly Journal of Economics* 116:1, 1–53.

Barberis, Nicholas, and Richard H. Thaler. 2005. "A Survey of Behavioral Finance." In Richard H. Thaler (ed.), *Advances in Behavioral Finance*, volume 2, 1–75. Princeton, NJ: Princeton University Press.

Barberis, Nicholas, and Wei Xiong. 2009. "What Drives the Disposition Effect? An Analysis of a Long-Standing Preference-Based Explanation." *Journal of Finance* 64:2, 751–784.

Barclay, Michael J. 1997. "Bid-Ask Spreads and the Avoidance of Odd-Eighth Quotes on NASDAQ: An Examination of Exchange Listings." *Journal of Financial Economics* 45:1, 35–60.

Benartzi, Shlomo, and Richard Thaler. 1995. "Myopic Loss Aversion and the Equity Premium Puzzle." *Quarterly Journal of Economics* 110:1, 73–92.

Bessembinder, Hendrik. 1997. "The Degree of Price Resolution and Equity Trading Costs." *Journal of Financial Economics* 45:1, 9–34.

Bharati, Rakesh, Susan J. Crain, and Vincent Kaminski. 2012. "Clustering in Crude Oil Prices and the Target Pricing Zone Hypothesis." *Energy Economics* 34:4, 1115–1123.

Bjønnes, Geir Høidal, and Dagfinn Rime. 2005. "Dealer Behavior and Trading Systems in Foreign Exchange Markets." *Journal of Financial Economics* 75:3, 571–605.

Chen, Chun-nan. 2013. "The Predictability of Opening Returns for the Returns of the Trading Day: Evidence from Taiwan Futures Market." *International Review of Economics & Finance* 25:C, 272–281.

Chen, Haiwei. 2008. "Market Conditions and Profitability of Proprietary Trading by Futures Floor Traders: Performance Persistence or Mutation under Stress." *Journal of Trading* 3:4, 14–23.

Chevalier, Judith, and Ellison G. Glenn. 1997. "Risk Taking by Mutual Funds as a Response to Incentives." *Journal of Political Economy* 105:6, 1167–1200.

Choe, Hyuk., and Yunsung Eom. 2009. "The Disposition Effect and Investment Performance in the Futures Market." *Journal of Futures Markets* 29:6, 496–522.

Chou, Robin K., George H. K. Wang, and Yun-Yi Wang. 2010. "Patterns and Consequences of the Disposition Effect." The 18th Conference on the Theories and Practices of Securities and Financial Markets, National Sun Yat-Sen University, Taiwan.

Chung, Kee H., Kenneth A. Kim, and Kitsabunnarat Pattanaporn. 2005. "Liquidity and Quote Clustering in a Market with Multiple Tick Sizes." *Journal of Financial Research* 28:2, 177–195.

Coakley, Jerry, Jian Dollery, and Neil Kellard. 2011. "Long Memory and Structural Breaks in Commodity Futures Markets." *Journal of Futures Markets* 31:11, 1076–1113.

Coval, Joshua D., and Tyler Shumway. 2005. "Do Behavioral Biases Affect Prices?" *Journal of Finance* 60:1, 1–34.

Cummins, Mark, Michael Dowling, and Brian M. Lucey. 2015. "Behavioral Influences in Non-ferrous Metals Prices." *Resources Policy* 45, 9–22.

Daníelsson, Jón, and Ryan Love. 2006. "Feedback Trading." *International Journal of Finance & Economics* 11:1, 35–53.

DeLong, J. Bradford, Andrei Shleifer, Lawrence H. Summers, and Robert J. Waldmann. 1990a. "Positive Feedback Investment Strategies and Destabilizing Rational Speculation." *Journal of Finance* 45:2, 379–395.

DeLong, J. Bradford, Andrei Shleifer, Lawrence H. Summers, and Robert J. Waldmann. 1990b. "Noise Trader Risk in Financial Markets." *Journal of Political Economy* 98:4, 703–738.

DeLong, J. Bradford, Andrei Shleifer, Lawrence H. Summers, and Robert J. Waldmann. 1991. "The Survival of Noise Traders in Financial Markets." *Journal of Business* 64:1, 1–20.

Dewally, Michaël, Louis H. Ederington, and Chitru S. Fernando. 2013. "Determinants of Trader Profits in Commodity Futures Markets." *Review of Financial Studies* 26:10, 2648–2683.

Dhar, Ravi, and Ning Zhu. 2006. "Up Close and Personal: Investor Sophistication and the Disposition Effect." *Management Science* 52:5, 726–740.

Dowling, Michael, Mark Cummins, and Brian M. Lucey. 2016. "Psychological Barriers in Oil Futures Markets." *Energy Economics* 53, 293–304.

Ferguson, Michael F., and Steven C. Mann. 2001. "Execution Costs and Their Intraday Variation in Futures Markets." *Journal of Business* 74:1, 125–160.

Frino, Alex, Joel Grant, and David Johnstone. 2008. "The House Money Effect and Local Traders on the Sydney Futures Exchange." *Pacific-Basin Finance Journal* 16:1, 8–25.
Frino, Alex, Elvis Jarnecic, and Roger Feletto. 2010. "Local Trader Profitability in Futures Markets: Liquidity and Position Taking Profits." *Journal of Futures Markets* 30:1, 1–24.
Frino, Alex, David Johnstone, and Hui Zheng. 2004. "The Propensity for Local Traders in Futures Markets to Ride Losses: Evidence of Irrational or Rational Behavior?" *Journal of Banking & Finance* 28:2, 353–372.
Grinblatt, Mark, and Matti Keloharju. 2001. "What Makes Investors Trade?" *Journal of Finance* 56:2, 589–616.
Haigh, Michael S., and John A. List. 2005. "Do Professional Traders Exhibit Myopic Loss Aversion? An Experimental Analysis." *Journal of Finance* 60:1, 523–534.
Heath, Chip, Steven Huddart, and Mark Lang. 1999. "Psychological Factors and Stock Option Exercise." *Quarterly Journal of Economics* 114:2, 601–627.
Hirshleifer, David, and Tyler Shumway. 2003. "Good Day Sunshine: Stock Returns and the Weather." *Journal of Finance* 58:3, 1009–1032.
Huang, Roger D., and Hans R. Stoll. 1997. "The Components of the Bid-Ask Spread: A General Approach." *Review of Financial Studies* 10:4, 995–1034.
Huang, Yu Chuan, and Shu Hui Chan. 2014. "The House Money and Break-Even Effects for Different Types of Traders: Evidence from Taiwan Futures Markets." *Pacific-Basin Finance Journal* 26, 1–13.
Kahneman, Daniel, and Amos Tversky. 1979. "Prospect Theory: An Analysis of Decision under Risk." *Econometrica* 47:2, 263–292.
Kaustia, Markku. 2010. "Prospect Theory and the Disposition Effect." *Journal of Financial and Quantitative Analysis* 45:3, 791–812.
Kurov, Alexander. 2008. "Investor Sentiment, Trading Behavior and Informational Efficiency in Index Futures Markets." *Financial Review* 43:1, 107–127.
Kuserk, Gregory J., and Peter R. Locke. 1996. "Market Making with Price Limits." *Journal of Futures Markets* 16:6, 677–696.
Lien, Donald. 2001. "A Note on Loss Aversion and Futures Hedging." *Journal of Futures Markets* 21:7, 681–692.
Limpaphayom, Piman, Peter R. Locke, and Pattarake Sarajoti. 2007. "Gone with the Wind: Chicago's Weather and Futures Trading." *Review of Futures Markets* 16:1, 55–73
Liu, Yu-Jane, Chih-Ling Tsai, Ming-Chun Wang, and Ning Zhu. 2010. "Prior Consequences and Subsequent Risk Taking: New Field Evidence from the Taiwan Futures Exchange." *Management Science* 56:4, 606–620.
Lo, Andrew W., and Dmitry V. Repin. 2002. "The Psychophysiology of Real-Time Financial Risk Processing." *Journal of Cognitive Neuroscience* 14:3, 323–339.
Lo, Andrew W., Dmitry V. Repin, and Brett N. Steenbarger. 2005. "Fear and Greed in Financial Markets: A Clinical Study of Day-Traders." *American Economic Review* 95:2, 352–359.
Locke, Peter R., and Steven C. Mann. 2005. "Professional Trader Discipline and Trade Disposition." *Journal of Financial Economics* 72:2, 401–444.
Locke, Peter R., and Steven C. Mann. 2009. "Daily Income Target Effects: Evidence from a Large Sample of Professional Commodities Traders." *Journal of Financial Markets* 12:4, 814–831.
Locke, Peter R., and P. C. Venkatesh. 1997. "Futures Market Transaction Costs." *Journal of Futures Markets* 17:2, 2229–2245.
Lyons, Richard K. 1995. "Tests of Microstructural Hypotheses in the Foreign Exchange Market." *Journal of Financial Economics* 39:2–3, 321–351.
Madhavan, Ananth, and Smidt Seymour. 1991. "A Bayesian Model of Intraday Specialist Pricing." *Journal of Financial Economics* 30:1, 99–134.
Manaster, Steven, and Steven C. Mann. 1996. "Life in the Pits: Competitive Market Making and Inventory Control." *Review of Financial Studies* 9:3, 953–975.
Mattos, Fabio, Philip Garcia, and Joost M. E. Pennings. 2008. "Probability Weighting and Loss Aversion in Futures Hedging." *Journal of Financial Markets* 11:4, 433–452.

Mitchell, Jason, and H. Y. Izan. 2006. "Clustering and Psychological Barriers in Exchange Rates." *Journal of International Financial Markets, Institutions and Money* 16:4, 318–344.

Narayan, Kumar P., Seema Narayan, and Stephan Popp. 2011. "Investigating Price Clustering in the Oil Futures Market." *Applied Energy* 88:1, 397–402.

Nofsinger, John R., and Richard W. Sias. 1999. "Herding and Feedback Trading by Institutional and Individual Investors." *Journal of Finance* 54:6, 2263–2295.

Nolte, Ingmar, and Valeri Voev. 2011. "Trading Dynamics in the Foreign Exchange Market: A Latent Factor Panel Intensity Approach." *Journal of Financial Econometrics* 9:4, 685–716.

O'Connell, Paul G. J., and Melvyn Teo. 2009. "Institutional Investors, Past Performance, and Dynamic Loss Aversion." *Journal of Financial and Quantitative Analysis* 44:1, 155–188.

Odean, Terrance. 1998. "Are Investors Reluctant to Realize Their Losses?" *Journal of Finance* 53:5, 1775–1798.

Sentana, Enrique, and Sushil Wadhwani. 1992. "Feedback Traders and Stock Return Autocorrelations: Evidence from a Century of Daily Data." *Economic Journal* 102:411, 415–425.

Shefrin, Hersh. 2006. *Behavioral Corporate Finance*. New York: McGraw-Hill.

Shefrin, Hersh, and Meir Statman. 1985. "The Disposition to Sell Winners Too Early and Ride Losers Too Long: Theory and Evidence." *Journal of Finance* 40:3, 777–790.

Silber, William. L. 1984. "Marketmaker Behavior in an Auction Market: An Analysis of Scalpers in Futures Markets." *Journal of Finance* 39:4, 937–953.

Thaler, Richard H. 1985. "Mental Accounting and Consumer Choice." *Marketing Science* 4:3, 199–214.

Thaler, Richard H., and Eric J. Johnson. 1990. "Gambling with the House Money and Trying to Break Even: The Effects of Prior Outcomes on Risky Choice." *Management Science* 36:6, 643–660.

Thaler, Richard H., Amos Tversky, Daniel Kahneman, and Alan Schwartz. 1997. "The Effect of Myopia and Loss Aversion on Risk Taking: An Experimental Test." *Quarterly Journal of Economics* 112:2, 647–661.

Tokic, Damir. 2011. "Rational Destabilizing Speculation, Positive Feedback Trading, and the Oil Bubble of 2008." *Energy Policy* 39:4, 2051–2061.

Westerhoff, Frank. 2003. "Anchoring and Psychological Barriers in Foreign Exchange Markets." *Journal of Behavioral Finance* 4:2, 65–70.

Yates, J. Frank. 1990. *Judgment and Decision Making*. Englewood Cliffs, NJ: Prentice-Hall.

5

Commodity Derivatives

NEIL C. SCHOFIELD
Managing Director, Financial Markets Training Limited and Visiting Fellow, Reading University

Introduction

This chapter covers the derivative building blocks of commodity investing. It focuses on the characteristics and applications of the product rather than valuing the product. In late 2016, commodity investment assets under management (AUM) amounted to $245 billion (Barclays Bank 2016). These investments comprise precious metals ($129 billion), energy ($63 billion), agriculture ($37 billion), and base metals ($17 billion).

Within the wholesale markets, investors seek exposure to commodities using three main structures: (1) total return swaps, (2) exchange-traded products (ETPs), which incorporate exchange-traded funds (ETFs), notes (ETNs), and commodities (ETCs), and (3) over-the-counter (OTC) structured products. So investment structures are not necessarily created using the actual physical commodity. Although instances occur in which the physical assets back the product, the exposure could also be created using derivatives.

The chapter begins by introducing commodity indices and then explores exchange-traded futures, total return swaps, and option products. The options section considers both vanilla and exotic options as well as three popular structured products. A summary and conclusions section follows.

Commodity Indices

Indices are one of the central themes of commodity investing, as they are referenced extensively by the different types of commodity investment product, such as total return swaps. Traditionally, the most commonly referenced index is the S&P GSCI, formerly known as the Goldman Sachs Commodity Index. This index is categorized as a "beta" index in that it tracks "the market." An equivalent financial beta index would be similar to the S&P 500 index for equities. However, the S&P GSCI is not an index of physical commodities but rather an index of traded commodity futures, which means that it is an *investable index*. That is, market participants can replicate the index by trading in the underlying components per the index rules.

The S&P GSCI has 24 exchange-traded futures covering five major sectors: energy, industrial metals, precious metals, agriculture, and livestock. Not all of the futures have equal weight because the allocation to the index is based on world production. For 2016, energy futures had the largest weightings: Brent crude oil, 21.52 percent; WTI crude oil, 20.91 percent; gas oil, 6.83 percent; heating oil, 5.56 percent; RBOB gasoline, 5.50 percent; and natural gas, 3.23 percent (Standard and Poor's 2016).

The rationale behind the construction of the S&P GSCI is that it is designed to replicate the investor returns from a long, unleveraged futures position. To understand the implications of this strategy, consider the following simplified example. Suppose an asset manager wants to take a long exposure to crude oil. Because the asset manager does not want to own the physical commodity, he decides to buy the shortest dated future, which is trading at, say, \$47.79. Each future references 1,000 barrels and so the contract has an associated monetary value of \$477,900. The asset manager has an internal restriction that prevents him from taking leveraged positions and so must set aside a cash deposit of the same amount to support the futures position. For ease of illustration, this example ignores all forms of margin. This futures position generates the investor three sources of return:

- *Profit or loss from the futures price movement.* If the price of the future rises, the investor will profit, but will lose if the price falls. Confusingly, the return generated from futures price movement is sometimes referred to as "the spot return."
- *Profit or loss from "rolling" the futures position.* Because the investor is long a short-dated future, this position will eventually mature. An investor would roll a position if he wanted to maintain his exposure to the oil market but wanted to avoid taking physical delivery of the commodity. Rolling a futures contract involves selling a long position shortly before its maturity and immediately buying a longer-dated contract. If the future into which the investors are rolling is trading at a lower price, this would generate a profit. Conversely, if the longer-dated future is trading at a higher price, then the investor would suffer a loss. *Roll yield* is the profit or loss generated from rolling a position.
- *Interest on the cash deposit.* Because the investor has deposited money to remove the position's leverage, he can earn interest. The interest earned is assumed to be equal to the short-term U.S. Treasury bill rate.

Because the aim of the index is to replicate such a futures strategy, it is published in three forms: (1) spot return, (2) excess return (i.e., spot return +/− roll yield), and (3) total return, which is excess return plus interest on the cash deposit. The specific calculation of the index is involved and is outside the scope of this chapter, but one aspect should be noted. Adding the excess return and the interest on the cash deposit does not give a number equal to the published total return. The index calculation reflects both the interest earned on the cash deposit, which can be reinvested into the futures position, and the change in the monetary value of the futures position, which affects the size of the cash deposit. Subsets of the main index are also quoted. So an investor can potentially gain exposure to some components of the index such as precious metals or agriculture.

As the commodity markets have evolved, many banks have offered investors bespoke indices that are constructed in different ways often in an attempt to overcome what some perceive as weaknesses in the beta versions. These indices are generally referred to as *enhanced beta indices*. Some characteristics of these indices are as follows:

- *A different roll period.* Most beta indices publish the range of dates during which the futures that underpin the index are assumed to be rolled, such as from the fifth to the ninth of each month. If a large number of investors trade futures aiming to replicate the index returns, this situation could cause an imbalance between demand and supply. Bespoke indices attempt to identify roll periods where this distortion is less pronounced.
- *Changing the futures maturity.* Most beta indices are designed to track short-dated futures. Bespoke indices reference futures of different maturities in an attempt to offer better value.
- *Customized weightings.* Weightings can take many forms. The bespoke index could offer a portfolio of commodities that is not skewed toward a particular sector. Another technique is to allow the index to go both long and short the underlying futures.

Exchange-Traded Futures

A *futures contract* is one that fixes a price on the trade date that applies on the future settlement of the contract. Consider the following contract specification for Brent crude oil quoted on the Intercontinental Exchange (ICE) (2016). Oil prices are typically quoted on a "free on board" (FOB) basis, meaning at the price at the point of loading. For Brent crude oil, this price is applicable at Sullom Voe in the Shetland Islands. Suppose that the following (hypothetical) prices for the Brent future are observed in mid-July: October, \$47.79; November, \$48.28; December, \$48.95; January, \$49.46; February, \$49.92; and March, \$50.33. Table 5.1 shows the contract specification for Brent crude futures contract.

What do these prices indicate? Take the first price of \$47.79 for October delivery. If a participant were to buy this futures contract, he would be fixing the price in mid-July for delivery or cash settlement of 1,000 barrels of Brent crude oil in October of the same year. Note that the futures prices increase with respect to maturity, a situation called *contango*. If futures prices decline with respect to maturity, this relation would be described as a market in *backwardation*. Carry considerations normally drive contango prices. That is, if a consumer wants to fix the price today for future delivery, the supplier's costs determine the price. To avoid any price risk, the supplier

Table 5.1 **Contract Specification for Brent Crude Futures Contract**

Contract size	1,000 barrels
Currency	USD per barrel
Minimum price movement ("tick size")	$0.01
Expiration months	Up to 96 consecutive months
Expiration date	The last business day of the second month before the relevant contract month (e.g., the October contract month will expire on the last business day of August).
Delivery	The contract has a provision for either physical or cash settlement.

Note: This table illustrates the main characteristics of the Brent crude futures contract traded at ICE.

Source: Intercontinental Exchange (2016).

would buy the asset for immediate delivery and hold it until the required future date, incurring storage, insurance costs, and financing charges. Because the supplier is providing a service, these charges are passed onto the buyer. However, backwardated markets do occur and these tend to be caused by factors such as supply bottlenecks or disruptions, spikes in short-term demand, structural supply constraints, and storage difficulties. The traditional "no arbitrage" principles of asset valuation that commonly exist in the market for financial assets do not readily apply in commodities (Schofield 2007).

Some market participants distinguish between "normal backwardation" and "backwardation." *"Normal" backwardation* is used in the context of forward price formation and represents an alternative to the "no arbitrage" principles that are used to value financial contracts. One way to view a single forward commodity price is to describe it as the expected spot price less a risk premium. Suppose a producer of crude oil wants to sell for delivery in six months and believes that prices at that time will be $50. If the producer could source a refiner or trader for this sale who agreed with his price outlook, his counterpart would be unlikely to pay $50 because he would be taking the full price risk for no expected return (Greer 2005; Hull 2014). So the counterparty may feel that a fair forward price would be, say, $49; this is "normal" backwardation—where the observed forward price ($49) is less than the expected spot price ($50).

A feature of exchange-traded futures is the existence of a clearinghouse that is associated with an exchange. The clearinghouse's main role is to act as a counterpart to each side of the transaction. Once a transaction has been executed, the transaction between the original buyer and seller is novated into two separate deals in which the clearinghouse becomes the buyer to the seller and the seller to the buyer. This process is designed to remove risk of either of the original counterparties defaulting. However, the process simply transfers the risk of default to the clearinghouse. To mitigate the risk of either party defaulting, the clearinghouse requires that both buyer and seller deposit a small percentage of the monetary value of the contract. This deposit is termed the *initial margin* and is determined using an algorithm by the exchange. For ICE contracts, the initial margin is set to cover the expected cost of closing out a defaulting member's position in normal market conditions with a 99 percent confidence level.

Another clearinghouse role is the daily collection of profits and losses via the variation margin system. Suppose that an investor buys one October Brent crude oil future at a price of $47.79. Because each futures contract references 1,000 barrels of crude oil, the contract would have a monetary value of $477,900. Assuming a 5 percent initial margin, the equity position would be about $24,000. If the contract closes the day at a price of $47.80, then the investor's position is now valued at $478,000 and so he would receive $100 (i.e., $0.01 per 1,000 barrels).

If the futures contract is held to maturity, the delivery process depends on the chosen settlement method. For contracts that allow cash settlements, the process occurs the day after the last trading date based on an index of prices in the physical market compiled by the exchange. Recall that the October contract is settled on the first business day of September. On this final day, the settlement price published by the exchange is not based on physical deliveries for the first business day of September, as the physical market does not work in such a fashion. The convention in the Brent crude oil market is that delivery does not take place any earlier than 10 days after the trade date. This restriction is mainly due to the logistics of arranging for a crude tanker to be present at the delivery terminal. By design, the index used to settle the Brent future market represents the average price for physical oil in the OTC forward market for the relevant delivery month.

The other main oil futures contract included within the S&P GSCI references West Texas Intermediate (WTI or sometimes just TI), which is quoted on the Chicago Mercantile Exchange (CME). This contract is also quoted on an FOB basis and allows for physical delivery at a given location, which for this contract is in Cushing, Oklahoma. Each WTI futures contract also references 1,000 barrels, which if physically delivered will be done over the course of the delivery month.

Total Return Swaps

A *total return swap* is a swap agreement in which one party makes payments based on a set rate, either fixed or variable, while the other party makes payments based on the return of an underlying asset, including both the income it generates and any capital gains (Investopedia 2016). A total return swap allows an investor to take exposure to a wide variety of commodities without having to take physical delivery or manage a number of futures positions. To illustrate how a total return swap works, consider the following hypothetical term sheet:

Effective date	July 12, 2017
Termination date	July 12, 2018
Reference index	S&P GSCI total return index
Notional quantity	$100 million fixed
Fixed amount payer	Investor
Fixed amount	0.25 percent (notional quantity) (fee days / 365). Fee days refer to the number of calendar days in each payment month
Index amount payer	Bank
Index payment dates	Monthly
Index amount	On each payment date, the index amount payer pays to the floating amount payer the index amount for that payment date determined in accordance with Equation 5.1: $$Notional\,Quantity \times \left(\frac{Index_t}{Index_{t-1}} - 1 \right) \quad (5.1)$$ If the calculated index amount is a negative amount, then the floating amount payer pays to the index amount payer the absolute value of the negative amount so calculated.
Floating amount payer	Investor
Floating amount	On each payment date, the floating amount payer pays to the index amount payer the floating amount for that payment date determined in accordance with Equation 5.2: $$Notional \times \left[\prod_d \left(1 - \frac{91}{360} R_d \right)^{\left(\frac{-1}{91}\right)} - 1 \right] \quad (5.2)$$ where R_d is the 3-month Treasury bill rate.

Figure 5.1 provides a diagram of the transaction.

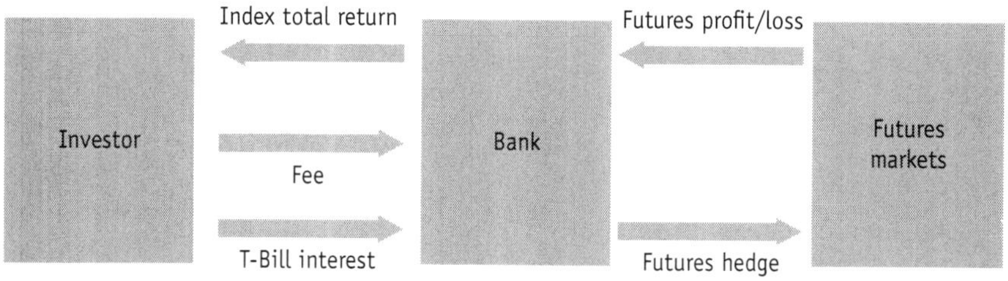

Figure 5.1 Total Return Commodity Index Swap
The left-hand side of this diagram illustrates the exchange of cash flows between an investor and a bank on a total return equity swap that references a commodity index. The right-hand side of the figure illustrates the hedging of the structure.

Based on the term sheet and Figure 5.1, a few key points can be made:

- The investor can choose between competing indices or sub-indices depending on his investment objectives.
- The notional amount in the example was fixed for the term of the transaction. Some swaps can be structured in such a way that their notional amount moves in line with movements in the index. So if in the first month the index were to increase, the notional amount in the following month would increase by the same percentage amount.
- If the swap is referencing a "long only" index such as the S&P GSCI, then the investor profits if the index rises over the period but is required to compensate the bank if the index falls in value. This potential loss is consistent with the profits and losses that a "long only" investor would experience.
- Many index swaps require the investor to pay a "fee" referred to in the previous term sheet as the fixed amount. This fee is based on the structuring bank having to trade futures in order to replicate the movement in the published index.
- In the example, the swap's structure enables the investor to receive the total return on the index. The swap can be structured to only pay the excess return. In this case, the only cash flow payable by the investor would be the fee component.
- The swap as illustrated has a monthly reset and payment feature. It could also be structured as a "bullet swap" in which only a single exchange of cash flows takes place at maturity.

To illustrate the mechanics of the product, consider the following hypothetical example based on the first exchange of cash flows.

Initial index value	2,200
Final index value	2,250
Days in the period	31
Treasury bill rate	Assumed to be constant at 0.5 percent annually

Index amount:

$$\$100 \text{ million} \times \frac{2{,}250}{2{,}200} - 1 = \$2{,}272{,}727$$

Floating amount:

$$\$100 \text{ million} \times \left[\left(\left(1 - \frac{91}{360} \times 0.5\% \right)^{\frac{-1}{91}} \right)^{31} - 1 \right] = \$43{,}092$$

Fixed amount:

$$\$100 \text{ million} \times 0.25\% \times \frac{31}{365} = \$21{,}233$$

Given that the index has increased, this amount is payable to the investor; the floating and fixed amounts are payable to the bank. Therefore, the net settlement is \$2,208,402 in favor of the investor.

Options

Within an investment context, commodity options are most commonly embedded within structured notes. These notes may exist in many different forms, including capital protected, yield enhancement, income structures, volatility structures, and hybrid notes.

OPTION FUNDAMENTALS

An option contract is essentially a forward/futures contract in disguise. Futures require the holder to either make or take delivery of the asset at a specified fixed price, which means that the holder cannot subsequently benefit if the price of the underlying asset moves in his favor. If a crude oil refiner bought an October future at \$47.79 and the price of oil drops before the contract's expiry, then the refiner remains committed to take delivery of the asset at this price. By the same token, the refiner is immunized against an increase in the asset's price. A *call option* is a substitute for a long forward/futures position with downside protection, whereas a *put option* is a substitute for a short forward/futures position with upside protection.

An *option* is a contract that allows the buyer the right but not the obligation to buy or sell an underlying asset. Thus, the option buyer has the right to do something and the option seller has the obligation to perform if required by the buyer.

A *call option* gives the holder the right but not the obligation to buy the underlying asset. A *put option* allows the buyer to sell the underlying. Selling a call option means that the seller must make delivery of the underlying asset if the buyer exercises the option. Selling a put requires the seller to take delivery of the underlying asset.

The buyer of the option pays a fee, called the *premium*, which is a sunk cost irrespective of whether the buyer exercises the option. The premium represents the maximum loss to the buyer and the maximum profit to the seller. The *strike* or *exercise price* is the price at which the two parties trade.

Figure 5.2 shows different profit and loss profiles for the four main option building blocks. To illustrate these payoffs, consider the following examples based on options that reference crude oil futures. Each of the options has a strike price of $50/barrel and a premium of $2/barrel. The buyer of a long call option will exercise the option if the futures price at the option's maturity is greater than the strike price. So if at maturity the futures price is, say, $60/barrel, the profit to the buyer will be $8/barrel; the profit is the difference between the strike and the final price of the future less the premium paid. Note that the buyer only breaks even once the price of the underlying has risen by at least $2/barrel such that his premium has been recouped. However, if the futures price ends up at $51/barrel, exercising the option would still make sense. If the buyer chose not to exercise, he would need to pay the prevailing futures price ($51/barrel) but would also have paid the $2/barrel premium, making the cost of

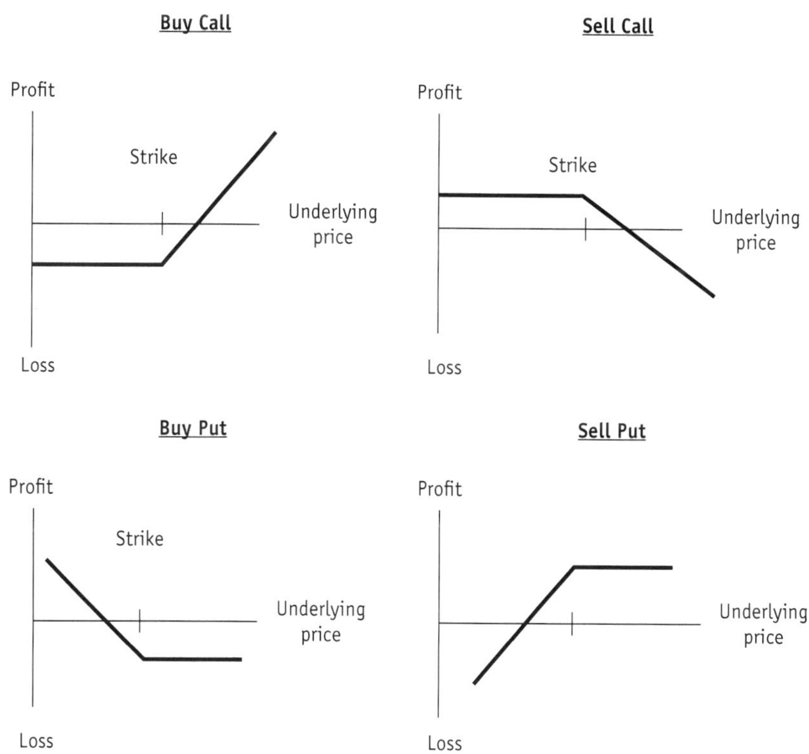

Figure 5.2 Expiry Option Payoff Profiles
The figure illustrates the profits or losses of the four option building blocks.

acquiring each future $53/barrel. If he exercised the option, the cost of taking delivery of the future is the strike plus the premium, which would be $52/barrel. If the futures price at the option's maturity is less than the strike price, the buyer would not exercise. If the price had fallen to $45/barrel it would make more sense to walk away from the option, forfeiting the premium and buying the future in the open market.

The sale of a call option is the mirror image of the purchase of the call. If the option buyer does not exercise, the seller retains the premium. If the price of the asset rises to $60/barrel and if the option seller has not hedged his position, he will be required to buy the underlying at this price in the market and then deliver it to the option buyer in return for receiving the strike price. This would result in a loss of $10/barrel less the premium received.

A similar logic could be applied to a put option. Here the option buyer makes money if the futures price falls. So, if the price falls to $45/barrel, the buyer would deliver futures and receive the strike price of $50/barrel, giving him a $5/barrel profit less the premium paid. If the price of oil rose to $60/barrel, the buyer would walk away from the option and sell the future at the prevailing market price. In this instance, the buyer's loss would be equal to the premium paid. Again, the seller's profile is the mirror image of the buyer. If the option is not exercised, the seller retains the premium, which represents his maximum profit. As the price of the asset falls, the seller's losses increase. So if the price moves to $45/barrel, the seller would pay the $50/barrel strike price to the buyer and then would sell the barrel he received at the prevailing market price losing $5/barrel less the premium he had initially received.

For buyers of traditional financial options, the profits are seen to be unlimited, while the losses are limited to the premium paid. Sellers of financial options have limited profits and unlimited losses (Natenberg 2015). However, this analysis disguises some subtleties. If an investor were to buy a put option on an equity security, his profits cannot be unlimited, as share prices cannot fall below zero. This situation is not the same for commodities, as negative prices have been observed in markets such as natural gas, power, and agricultural commodities (Schofield 2007). Negative prices could occur when overproduction of a commodity occurs and the price at which the market clears is negative.

The buyer can exercise an *American option* at any time during its life but can exercise a European option only at maturity. A *semi-American option*, also called a *Bermudan option*, incorporates features of both, as the buyer can only exercise it according to a pre-agreed schedule. Although some may disagree, the argument goes that Bermuda lies half way between the Americas and Europe and therefore a Bermudan option incorporates features of both markets.

The value of options is often expressed in terms of whether the position is likely to be exercised. For call options, an *in-the-money (ITM) option* occurs when the strike price is greater than the underlying price. An *out-of-the-money (OTM) option* occurs when the strike price is less than the underlying price. An *at-the-money (ATM) option* occurs when the strike price is equal to the underlying price.

Options can be settled physically or with cash. A *physically-settled option* trade is the exchange of the asset for cash. So a buyer of a call option delivers the cash value of the strike price and receives the underlying asset, while the buyer of a put delivers the asset and receives the strike price. A cash-settled transaction does not involve the movement of the asset but is economically equal to a physically-settled transaction. For a regular financial option, the cash settlement amounts will be:

- Value of a long call option: MAX (underlying price - strike, 0)
- Value of a long put option: MAX (strike - underlying price, 0)

where MAX means "the maximum of."

One distinguishing feature of some commodity options is that they do not reference a single price at settlement but an average of prices over some pre-agreed period. In this case, the settlement formulas are now:

- Value of a long call option: MAX (average of underlying price—strike, 0)
- Value of a long put option: MAX (strike—average underlying price, 0)

Not surprisingly, this variant is referred to as an average rate option or colloquially as an "Asian-style" option. The geographical reference has nothing to do with when the option can be exercised, as they are typically European in style. Market anecdotes suggest the use of the phrase "Asian" relates to the location where such options first became popular. Although Asian-style options are traded in other asset classes, anecdotally they are more popular in commodity markets.

OPTION PRICING: THE INTUITION

A detailed review of option pricing is outside the scope of this chapter. However, to understand its attraction within an investment context requires knowing some fundamental concepts. As a starting point, the magnitude of the premium can be viewed from two perspectives. Buyers pay a premium that reflects the amount they expect to receive; sellers charge a premium that covers the cost of hedging their exposures.

Some variant of the Black-Scholes-Merton model is the basis for valuing most European-style financial options. For example, using this model to assess the value of an equity option requires the following inputs: (1) spot price, (2) strike price, (3) time to expiry, (4) dividend yields, (5) funding costs, and (6) implied volatility.

Because European-style options cannot be exercised until maturity, they are valued relative to an equivalent underlying instrument, which is a forward contract. This process can be confusing given that the instrument is valued using a spot price. However, this type of option pricing model estimates the forward price implied by the carry parameters (i.e., dividend yields and funding costs) and then derives the option's value. For many commodity options, the underlying is a futures contract and so a popular approach to their valuation is the Black model for options on futures (Black 1976). A main attraction of the Black model is its simplicity because the observed forward or futures price replaces the spot and the carry parameters. Such replacement means that the inputs are (1) price of future, (2) strike price, (3) time to maturity, and (4) implied volatility of the future.

An option's implied volatility traditionally represents the volatility implied by an observed option price. Yet, this definition is an unsatisfactory because it suggests some degree of circularity—from where did the observed option price obtain its own implied volatility? Although many definitions exist, *implied volatility* is the market's expectation of how widely the underlying price is likely to fluctuate around the forward price. Formally, implied volatility is the expected standard deviation of the underlying price expressed as an annualized percentage. Indeed, traders often quote options in terms of implied volatility because it is the only unknown factor within the valuation framework.

As mentioned earlier, investors commonly use Asian-style options in commodity markets. Several models exist to value these types of options (Haug 2007) but a key characteristic is that the averaging process results in a lower premium than a non-averaging equivalent.

Capital Protected Structures

Capital protected notes were one of the earliest forms of structured product available to investors. To illustrate their mechanics, consider the following hypothetical term sheet:

Issuer	Bank
Issue size	$10 million
Note amount	$1,000 per note
Price per note	100 percent
Tenor	5 years
Principal protection	100 percent
Interest	None
Underlying metal	Aluminum
Participation rate	100 percent
Initial cash price of metal	$1,700
Payment at maturity	• If the final cash price of the metal is greater than the initial cash price, the investor earns $1,000 + supplemental return amount. • If the final cash price of the metal is less than or equal to the initial cash price, the investor receives $1,000.
Supplemental return	$1,000(participation rate)(metal percent change)
Metal percent change	(final cash price – initial cash price)/initial cash price

In this example, if the price of aluminum is below $1,700/ton in five years' time, then the investor receives the initial investment (i.e., $1,000). If the price of the metal had risen by 10 percent, then the investor receives the principal plus a return of 10 percent (i.e., $1,100). The note is constructed by allocating part of the investor's initial proceeds into a deposit that grows over the life of the transaction to generate the $1,000 protected amount. The investor then uses the balance of the proceeds to buy a call option on the underlying asset.

Arguably, the challenge for the structurer in this case is to make the participation rate as attractive as possible. An assumption is that after the requisite proportion of the initial proceeds has been diverted to the deposit component, sufficient cash remains to be able to afford such an option. The cost of this option affects the participation rate that can be offered by the structurer. In this example, the structurer has embedded an option with a notional amount of $1,000 that offers 100 percent participation. The lower the option premium, the more options the structurer can buy and so the greater the participation rate. These types of products are well-established in the equities world. Thus, several techniques are available to increase the participation rate by lowering the cost of the option (e.g., selecting an index with a higher dividend yield). However, some structuring techniques are unique to commodities that the structurer can use to increase the participation rate.

Shape of the Forward Curve

As previously noted, the commodities forward curve slopes either upward (contango) or downward (backwardation). In the example of the capital protected note, the return was measured from the initial cash price (i.e., the spot price) of the metal, which is the strike price of the option. Because the option is European in style, it takes its value from the five-year forward. If the market is in backwardation, the option becomes deeply out-of-the-money and is relatively inexpensive.

Term Structure of Implied Volatility

In option valuation, the greater the option's implied volatility, the greater is the cost of the option. Empirically, option volatilities display a term structure that tends to be inverted for commodities. The implication is that short-term options should be valued using a higher implied volatility than longer-dated options. The shape of this term structure reflects the fact that shorter-dated futures prices tend to be more volatile than longer-dated maturities. Within a capital protected structure, the longer-dated option embedded within the structure is valued using a lower implied volatility and as such the premium is relatively lower.

PATH-DEPENDENT OPTIONS

Barrier options are European-style options that incorporate an extra element of conditionality that influences the final payout. The extra condition is the addition of a price barrier, which if breached results in the option being activated or deactivated.

Some practitioners differentiate between regular and reverse barriers in order to describe the placement of the price barrier relative to the current spot price. Regular barrier options have an OTM barrier (i.e., the barrier is placed in a region where a conventional option would not be exercised). For call options, this barrier is below the spot price, but for put options the barrier is above the spot price. Reverse barriers have the barrier placed in the ITM region (i.e., the barrier is set above the spot price for a call option and below spot for a put option).

If the barrier is breached, the option is either activated ("knocked in") or deactivated ("knocked out"). Based on these scenarios, the market has adopted a shorthand way to describe the nature of the barrier option. As an example, a regular knock-in call option with the barrier set below the spot is termed a *down and in* (i.e., the spot price has to fall past the barrier for the option to be activated). These scenarios result in four basic permutations: (1) up and in, (2) up and out, (3) down and in, and (4) down and out. From these four building blocks, the option can then be either a call or a put, giving eight potential positions. Specifying whether the options would be bought or sold yields a total of 16 permutations.

Typically, one of the parties monitors the movement of the spot on an ongoing basis, which is why the option is referred to as being *path dependent*. The evolution of the spot price over the life of the transaction determines whether the option will be knocked in or out. Given some probability of either early deactivation or non-activation, the premium payable on the option is lower than a non-barrier equivalent. Haug (2007) provides a more detailed treatment of barrier option valuation.

The Reverse Convertible

A reverse convertible option is a common application of barrier options within commodity investing. Consider the following hypothetical term sheet:

Issuer	Bank
Investor	Client
Tenor	3 years
Currency	USD
Underlying	Brent crude oil
Barrier	80 percent of $Brent_{Initial}$
Enhanced coupon	5 percent with underlying rates at 1.5 percent
Redemption at maturity	If $Brent_{Final} / Brent_{Initial}$ > Barrier, investor earns 100 percent of the initial investment + coupon. Otherwise the investor earns 100 percent – Max (0, 100 percent – $Brent_{Final} / Brent_{Initial}$)

Here $Brent_{Final}$ = price of Brent at the note's maturity and $Brent_{Initial}$ = price of Brent at the start of the transaction. In this structure, the investor is long an interest-bearing deposit and short a cash-settled "down and in" barrier put option on a crude oil future.

To understand how this structure is engineered, consider the "at maturity" payoff scenario. Initially, the investor pays $1,000 to the issuer, which is placed on deposit to earn interest at the prevailing market rate (i.e., 1.5 percent). Because the investor is short an option, he also receives a premium, which is paid to the investor in the form of an enhanced coupon. If the price of crude oil is greater than the initial price established by the issuer, the put option is OTM and so is not exercised by the bank. Therefore, the investor receives his initial investment as well as the enhanced coupon, which is the interest earned on the investment plus the option premium.

If at maturity the price of crude oil has fallen, the amount received by the investor depends on whether the barrier has been breached. If the price of crude oil has fallen but the barrier has not been breached, the investor receives his initial investment plus the enhanced coupon. If the barrier is breached, the issuing bank exercises the put option and the investor's initial proceeds are unwound to finance the payout.

Although this situation means that the structure is not principal protected, the barrier option does afford the investor some degree of protection. The barrier option is only activated when the final price of the underlying is at 80 percent of the initial price level. So if $\text{Brent}_{\text{Initial}}$ were set at $50, then a barrier set at 80 percent would mean the put would have a strike of $50 but would only be activated if the price of the underlying hit $40. If the option is activated, then the issuer receives the difference between the strike price ("$\text{Brent}_{\text{Initial}}$") and the prevailing price of the underlying at maturity ("$\text{Brent}_{\text{Final}}$").

The monitoring of the barrier can be continuous (i.e., the put option is activated at any time when $40 trades) or can be set according to the terms of the issue (e.g., the put option is only activated if the price of crude oil is less than $40 at maturity). The barrier option offers the investor more protection given that a smaller likelihood of exercise exists; then the option premium is logically lower, reducing the enhanced coupon.

CORRELATION-DEPENDENT OPTIONS

So far the options analysis has only focused on the payoffs that result from the performance of single assets. Anecdotally, a substantial proportion of commodity investment structures reference the performance of multiple assets. This section covers two popular structures: basket options and outperformance options. Marroni and Perdomo (2014) provide further discussion of other multi-asset related structures.

The price associations between the assets influence the value of multi-asset options (Bouzoubaa and Osseiran 2010). As a result, the model input parameters needed to value the option now include price correlation. *Correlation* measures the strength and direction of a linear relation between two variables. Although a complete discussion on the valuation of correlation-dependent options is outside the scope of the chapter, Bouzoubaa and Osseiran (2010) and Schofield (2016) provide additional discussion.

Basket Options

A *basket option* allows an investor to hedge multiple underlying exposures with a single structure. Such options are of interest to asset managers who want to take exposure to a number of commodities without having to buy an option on each individual asset. Basket options tend to be cash-settled, as delivery of the multiple underlying assets can be time consuming and operationally difficult.

The payoff of a basket options is based on the premise that within a portfolio, asset prices never all rise and fall in tandem. That is, the correlations between the underlying assets in the basket work as a form of natural hedge. This assumption is based on the notion that the risk of a diversified portfolio of assets is less than the sum of the individual risks.

Suppose an investor decides to buy a three-month ATM, equally-weighted basket call option on both aluminum and copper. To construct a single basket option on both metals requires calculating the basket's initial market value. Assume that copper is trading at $4,900/ton while aluminum is trading at $1,700/ton:

$$\text{Strike} = \left[\left(50\,\text{percent} \times \$4{,}900\right) + \left(50\ \text{percent} \times \$1{,}700\right)\right]$$
$$= \$2{,}450 + \$850 = \$3{,}300$$

Given that the option is ATM, this value is also the option's strike price.

At maturity, assume that the underlying copper price rises to \$5,000 and the aluminum price rises to \$1,800. Consider first what the payoff to the investor would have been if they had bought a vanilla option on each asset. An ATM call on copper would have paid out \$100, as would a call on aluminum. To compare these payoffs to those of a basket option requires determining the "at expiry" market value of the basket, which similar to its initial value is a weighted average of the final expiry prices: = [(50 percent × \$5,000) + (50 percent × \$1,800)] = \$2,500 + \$900 = \$3,400.

The payoff of the basket option is the difference between the initial strike price (\$3,300) and the price of the basket (\$3,400) at maturity, which is \$100. The two vanilla call options would have paid out a total of \$200, while an equally-weighted basket paid out half this amount. In this example, both of the underlying commodity prices had increased. If, however, one had fallen, the final expiry price of the basket would have been pulled down, resulting in a lower basket payoff.

When valuing basket options, the investor needs to consider the correlation that exists between the underlying assets using principles of modern portfolio theory so the risk associated with a portfolio consisting of two assets is calculated as the weighted sum of the individual risks adjusted for their correlation. Provided that the assets in the portfolio are not perfectly positively correlated, the volatility of the portfolio will be less than the weighted sum of the volatilities of the assets that form that portfolio. Equation 5.3 shows the composite volatility for a two-asset portfolio.

$$\sigma_{basket} = \sqrt{(w^2_{x_1}\sigma^2_{x_1}) + (w^2_{x_2}\sigma^2_{x_2}) + 2(w_{x_1} w_{x_2} \rho_{x_1x_2} \sigma_{x_1} \sigma_{x_2})} \tag{5.3}$$

where:

$\sigma^2_{x_1}$ = Variance of asset 1
$\sigma^2_{x_2}$ = Variance of asset 2
$\rho_{x_1x_2}$ = Correlation between asset 1 and asset 2
σ_{x_1} = Volatility of asset 1
σ_{x_2} = Volatility of asset 2
w_{x_1} = Proportion of asset 1
w_{x_2} = Proportion of asset 2

The same formula can be used for multiple assets, except multiple correlations would need to be taken into account.

Using the previous values, a three-month ATM call option on each individual metal priced with a volatility of 20 percent would be \$195 (copper) + \$68 (aluminum) = \$263 (total). The value of an equally-weighted basket option with the same parameters but priced with a correlation of 0.50 would be \$118. Although in the previous payoff example the basket option paid off 50 percent less than the single call options, the premium is less than 50 percent of that of the combined single options, which reflects the impact of correlation. For basket options, a positive relation exists between the correlation input and the price of the option. If the metals are positively correlated, then the payoff on the basket option is likely to be greater and thus increases its cost.

Basket options are attractive from a structuring viewpoint because intra-commodity correlations tend to be relatively low. Although they are both industrial metals, copper and aluminum have very different demand and supply characteristics. Additionally, they are not perfectly positively correlated, which reduces the option's premium and increases the participation rate offered by the structurer. In this example, the underlying assets were both drawn from the commodities world. However, including any two assets, such as copper and equity, is possible. Although this would be termed a "hybrid" structure, it is nothing other than a basket option.

Outperformance Options

Investors can use an outperformance option to express a view on the relative performance of two assets, while not necessarily requiring any directional view. These options are most frequently quoted as call options (i.e., the return of asset "A" over asset "B"). Suppose an investor believes asset A will outperform asset B over some given period. Equation 5.4 shows the expiry payoff at a future time period (t), of an outperformance asset written on two assets, A and B.

$$\text{Notional amount} \times \text{MAX}\left(\frac{\text{Asset}_{A,t}}{\text{Asset}_{A,0}} - \frac{\text{Asset}_{B,t}}{\text{Asset}_{B,0}}, 0\right) \tag{5.4}$$

Consider a hypothetical example of an outperformance note referencing aluminum and gold.

Issuer	Bank
Issue size	\$10 million
Note amount	\$1,000 per note
Price per note	100 percent
Tenor	5 years
Principal protection	100 percent
Interest	None
Underlying metals	Aluminum and gold
Participation rate	230 percent
Initial cash price of metal	Aluminum \$1,700/ton and gold \$1,300/ounce
Payment at maturity	• If aluminum outperforms gold, the investor earns \$1,000 + supplemental return amount. • If gold outperforms aluminum, the investor receives \$1,000.
Supplemental return	\$1,000(participation rate)(relative outperformance of aluminum over gold)

The value of an outperformance option is dependent on the price correlation that exists between the underlying assets. This option exhibits negative correlation (i.e., a decrease in correlation increases the value of the option). This relation is somewhat intuitive because the payoff to the holder of an outperformance option is greatest when the prices of the two assets diverge.

Summary and Conclusions

The main structures used by investors to take exposure to commodities are exchange-traded products, total return swaps, and structured notes. Understanding the structure of each of these products requires being aware of the fundamentals of commodity derivatives. A key technique used in commodity investing is to structure a return that references some form of index. A popular index used for this purpose is the S&P GSCI, which references a portfolio of futures. The index replicates the returns that would be earned from a long-only, non-leveraged futures position. Commodity futures fix the price of a commodity for future delivery. The chapter focused on a crude oil future whose specification reflected the mechanics of the underlying market.

Total return swaps were arguably the earliest form of product and allow an investor exposure to create a synthetic long exposure to a commodity index such as the S&P GSCI.

Commodity investing uses different options, including vanilla options, average rate options, barrier options, and correlation-dependent options. Given that intra-commodity correlations tend to be low, correlation-dependent options tend to be relatively inexpensive and when embedded within structured products, they can offer attractive returns to investors.

Structured products offer a return to an investor that is difficult to replicate. They can take many different forms but anecdotally popular structures include those offering capital protection or yield enhancement with some risk to the principal.

Discussion Questions

1. Discuss the main features of a "beta" commodity index such as the S&P GSCI.
2. Identify and explain some features of commodity futures that differentiate them from traditional financial equivalents.
3. Explain how commodity structured notes differ from popular structures seen in other markets such as equities.
4. Identify the features of commodities structurers can exploit to increase the participation rate of a structured product.

References

Barclays Bank. 2016. "Allocating to Commodities Again." October.

Black, Fischer. 1976. "The Pricing of Commodity Contracts." *Journal of Financial Economics* 3:1–2, 167–179.

Bouzoubaa, Mohamed, and Adel Osseiran. 2010. *Exotic Options and Hybrids: A Guide to Structuring, Pricing and Trading*. Chichester, UK: John Wiley & Sons, Ltd.

Greer, Robert J. 2005. "Commodity Indexes for Real Returns." In Robert J. Greer (ed.), *Handbook of Inflation Hedging Investments*, 105–126. New York: McGraw-Hill.

Haug, Epsen Gaarder. 2007. *The Complete Guide to Option Pricing Formulas*. New York: McGraw-Hill.

Hull, John C. 2014. *Options, Futures and Other Derivatives*. 9th edition. London: Pearson.

Intercontinental Exchange. 2016. "Contract Specification for Brent Crude Oil Futures Contract." Available at http://www.theice.com.

Investopedia. 2016. "Total Return Swap." Available at http://www.investopedia.com/terms/t/totalreturnswap.asp?lgl=no-infinite.

Marroni, Leonardo, and Irene Perdomo. 2014. *Pricing and Hedging Financial Derivatives: A Guide for Practitioners*. Chichester, UK: John Wiley & Sons, Ltd.

Natenberg, Sheldon. 2015. *Option Volatility and Pricing: Advanced Trading Strategies and Techniques*. 2nd edition. New York McGraw-Hill.

Schofield, Neil C. 2007. *Commodity Derivatives: Markets and Applications*. Chichester, UK: John Wiley & Sons Ltd.

Schofield, Neil C. 2016. *Equity Derivatives: Corporate and Institutional Applications*. London: Palgrave Macmillan.

Standard and Poor's. 2016. "S&P GSCI Methodology." Available at http://us.spindices.com/index-family/commodities/sp-gsci.

6

Fundamentals and Commodity Prices

MICHAEL S. HAIGH
Managing Director, Societe Generale Corporate and Investment Bank

Introduction

In some commodity markets such as oil, "nonfundamental" information can move prices for years at a time. Knowing when these changes occur is critical for analyzing commodity prices and forecasting future price movements. For other commodity markets, such as the U.S. natural gas markets, fundamental factors such as weather patterns drive prices. This chapter presents a principal component analysis (PCA) to group assets into fundamental or non-fundamental categories. As commodity market participants grapple with demand uncertainty amid structural changes to commodity supplies, the analysis presents a useful and topical exercise for a deeper understanding of commodity markets. In fact, the chapter sheds light on historical periods that appear to show commodity market prices deviating from fundamental supply and demand factors. The results provide some context for exploring allegations that "financialization" or other non-fundamental factors affect commodity prices.

Forces Driving Oil Prices beyond Fundamentals

Typically, analysts of commodity markets believe that fundamental (supply and demand) information pertaining to each specific market drives commodity prices rather than financial factors. For example, increased demand for metals by China could drive copper prices because China consumes 50 percent of the world's copper. Given that Chile provides 35 percent of the world's copper production, mine outages in Chile could affect the supply of copper. For U.S. natural gas, demand shocks from extreme cold weather in the U.S. Northeast or supply shocks from shale production declines in the United States could drive price. For oil, increases in global gross domestic product (GDP) could drive demand, resulting in an increase in prices, or prices could rise as supply concerns arise due to geopolitical tensions. As commodities have become a financial asset and part of larger portfolios, prices could move beyond fundamentals. Disentangling these effects is the initial purpose of the first part of this chapter.

Before the late 1990s, commodity markets generally experienced excess capacity as innovations and new discoveries created greater supply. If the commodity markets experienced any kind of persistent supply-side shock that resulted in higher commodity prices and higher inflation, equity markets would drop. Hence, both a strong and negative relation existed between commodity markets and equity markets. By 2000, demand for commodities began to accelerate as China's economy started to show strong signs of expansion and underinvestment in the supply chain of commodities meant that the excess capacity was gradually absorbed. Moving forward to early 2008, the substantial underinvestment in commodity activities became strikingly clear as the credit crisis resulted in cancellations and suspensions of hundreds of different commodity projects. As such, starting around 2008, changes in the global economic outlook, changes in indicators such as the Purchasing Manager's Index (PMI) strength or weakness, changes in inflation expectations, and events such as quantitative easing and changes in the dollar value began to play a much more important role in commodity price changes.

Given the increased influence of non-fundamental information on commodity markets, this chapter quantifies the level of this influence across commodities and time. To rigorously assess the role of non-fundamentals over time, the chapter employs a PCA decomposing the covariance matrix of multiple variables such as financial indicators, volatilities, and groups of commodity returns. The origins of PCA can be traced to Pearson (1901), who explored ideas concerning an affine space that best fits a series of points, which measures fit as the sum of squared orthogonal distances from each point to the space. Hotelling (1933) later developed the concept.

PCA grew in popularity to become an important statistical tool used in almost all areas of quantitative finance. For example, portfolio managers use the methodology to allocate funds among different assets and assets classes. Interest rate structurers employ the technique to model the yield curve and analyze its changing shape. Rates and fixed income traders use the methodology to hedge portfolios. Equity traders use the algorithm to buy and sell stocks, and foreign exchange (FX) algorithmic traders use this method to generate price signals. Many other disciplines use PCA, from biology, physics, engineering, and economics to software development and Internet search engines. In the commodity space several researchers have employed PCA. Tolmasky and Hindanov (2002) apply PCA to value contingent claims in multi-commodity and seasonal markets (petroleum in particular). More recently, Nomikos and Pouliasis (2014) study the dependence structure between correlated petroleum forward curves using PCA. Their findings have important implications for energy trading and risk management, being particularly useful for predicting short-term spreads and the correlation matrix among traded contracts.

Using daily historical data, the analysis in this chapter determines the principal components of the covariance matrix (i.e., the way in which the asset price movements correlate in order of importance). The analysis includes the covariances of various commodities against a diversified basket of 23 assets across many different financial markets: volatility indexes (European Union and the United States), foreign exchange (dollar, yen, euro), carry trade (G10 and EM), bonds (spreads: 10Y GVT and inflation break evens), equities (eurozone; Brazil, Russia, India, and China, or

BRICs; European Union; United States; and emerging markets), credit (European Union and United States and IG versus HY).

Factors are estimated using the 23-member basket, which implies that each factor is a weighted average of the 23 assets with different weights for each factor. If all assets are independent but each exhibiting importance, analysis could conceivably recover 23 principal components. In reality, some assets co-move either positively or negatively, reducing the number of components.

The model returns three main explanatory factors that are highly stable over time. Although labeling the factors is an art, by observing the weights and relations within each factor, the three factors appear to represent a macro factor, a U.S. dollar factor, and a liquidity factor. The macro factor mainly captures the relation between global equities and volatility, while the dollar factor represents the relations between different currencies. The liquidity factor primarily represents interest rate differentials globally. Although the PCA model could be estimated daily using daily data, for computational ease, the chapter assigns the weights estimated by the PCA at the end of each year, applies those weights over the following year, and then re-estimates the PCA again one year later. The fixed yearly weights are multiplied by each of the 23 variables (prices) each day and summed. The price multiplied by the weight changes daily as the prices change but the weights remain constant throughout the year. The analysis then regresses a 40-day moving window of these factors against commodity prices. An analysis of variance, breaking out what proportion of the R^2 each factor explains, extracts how these non-fundamental factors influence commodity prices over time. The remaining unexplained variance is then attributed to market fundamentals and is simply calculated as $1 - R^2$. Depending on each commodity, the relative significance of each of the non-fundamental factors varies considerably, as does the influence on each of the factors combined. Moreover, very extreme events, such as the subprime crisis and the Lehman bankruptcy, have structurally altered the importance of each factor. In particular, the macro factor began to dominate other factors, and in the case of certain commodities even dominated fundamental influences. Before this extreme episode in history, the dollar factor primarily had the dominant influence among these factors.

Energy

Since the rise of shale oil, Brent oil has generally been regarded as the more global oil benchmark. Before September 2008, fundamentals with the dollar explained about 20 percent of Brent's oil price variance with macro accounting explaining the remaining 20 percent. However, starting in mid-September 2008, when Lehman Brothers declared bankruptcy, global growth concerns started to massively influence Brent's price formation, and the macro influence jumped to a staggering 55 percent of Brent's price formation. Fundamentals had taken a back seat to macro concerns. The job of an oil analyst who focused on counting barrels to forecast prices subsequently became extremely difficult.

As Figure 6.1 shows, as far back as the early 2000s, when commodities had not yet become regarded as a distinct asset class and were very physical in nature (i.e., derivative

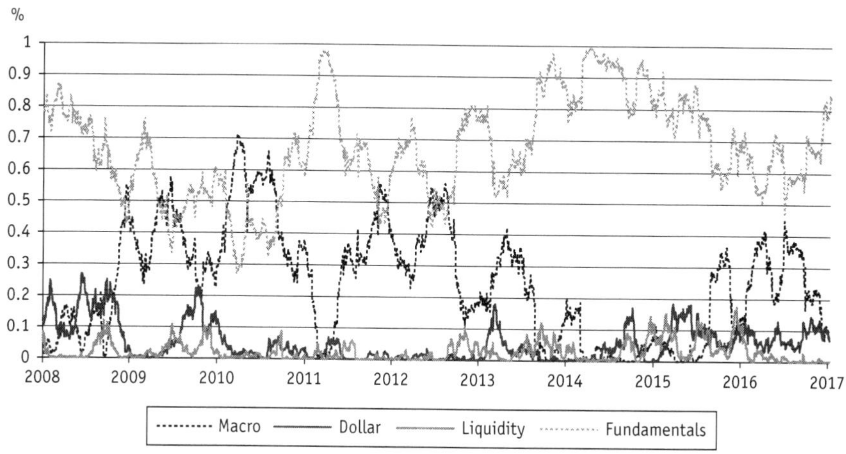

Figure 6.1 Portion of Brent Oil's Price Movement Explained by Fundamentals and Non-fundamentals

This figure shows that by September 2008 (Lehman bankruptcy) fundamental macroeconomic factors dominated oil's price variance. The euro crisis in 2011 had the same effect. By 2014, oil was a "deeply" fundamental market. Source: SG Cross Asset Research.

trading and investment in financial commodity products were extremely small on a relative basis), fundamentals explained about 90 percent of Brent oil price movements. The dollar and liquidity factors explained roughly 10 percent. The macro influence that started during and after the financial crisis of 2007–2008 dominated Brent's price variance, and the fundamentals became less related to oil as other elements dominated the Brent oil market. By 2011, fundamentals appeared to return to the forefront, but in August 2011 the euro crisis hit. Yet again, fundamentals took a backseat and the macro influence explained between 20 and 60 percent of the Brent oil price movements. In late 2013 and into 2014, Brent appeared to return to a more "normal" environment with fundamentals largely dominating and the dollar, at times, being the most significant influence on Brent's price formation (outside of true fundamentals).

To provide an extreme comparison/contrast in the energy space, the chapter also includes an analysis of U.S. natural gas markets. This market is a "contained" market with just a small amount of U.S. natural gas being imported/exported in and out of Canada and Mexico by pipeline or via liquefied natural gas (LNG) tankers. For the most part, the U.S. natural gas market is regional, dominated by weather patterns and not geopolitical risks or macro concerns. If the euro area sees a worsening economic environment, during the U.S. winter for example, no influence should exist on the U.S. demand for natural gas for heating.

As Figure 6.2 shows, given that the y-axis scale remains the same as Brent, the U.S. natural gas is a deeply fundamental market. The only prior episode where the macro factor becomes significant was in late 2008 during the financial crisis, but even during the financial crisis the macro factor explained only 10 to 15 percent of the natural gas price variance. In some ways, understanding the natural gas market is much

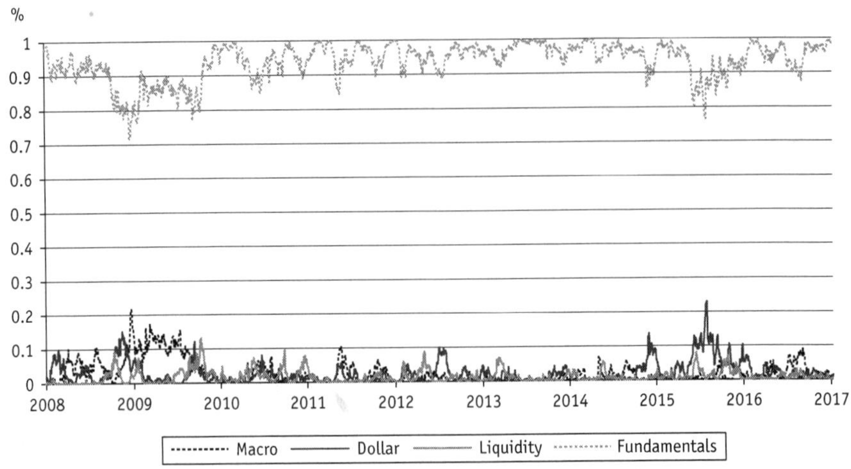

Figure 6.2 Proportion of U.S. Natural Gas Price Movement Explained by Fundamentals and Non-fundamentals
This figure shows that macroeconomic fundamentals explain almost 100 percent of natural gas price variability. The lowest fundamental explanatory power was 72 percent in late 2008. Source: SG Cross Asset Research.

easier than understanding the Brent oil market because the fundamentals almost always prevail in explaining the U.S. natural gas market.

Base Metals

Before the Lehman crisis, fundamentals dominated copper, such as Brent, but the dollar continued to have a major impact on its price formation. Figure 6.3 shows that the euro crisis of 2011 heavily influenced copper, similar to Brent. Fundamentals did not dominate the copper market until late 2013 or early 2014.

The China equity price collapse in August of 2015 meant copper's fundamental influence retreated slightly, but fundamentals appear to consistently drive copper's price variance. Generally speaking, only a major glitch in the global marketplace causes the copper market to deviate from fundamentals.

Precious Metals

The PCA highlights the fact that gold is a massive outlier among commodity markets. What might be considered non-fundamental factors for the commodity complex could easily be considered fundamental for gold. Changes in the U.S. dollar, expectations about inflation, and changes in interest rates often influence gold prices. Not

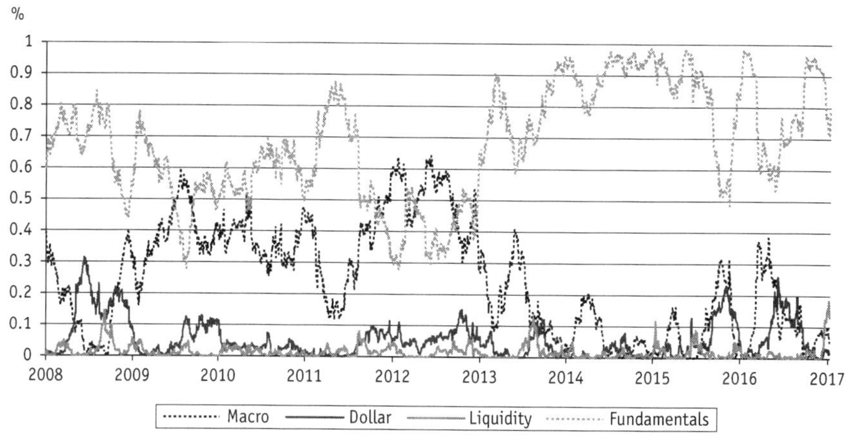

Figure 6.3 Proportion of Copper's Price Movement Explained by Fundamentals and Non-fundamentals
This figure shows that copper's price variance is explained mainly by fundamental macroeconomic influences since 2013. Source: SG Cross Asset Research.

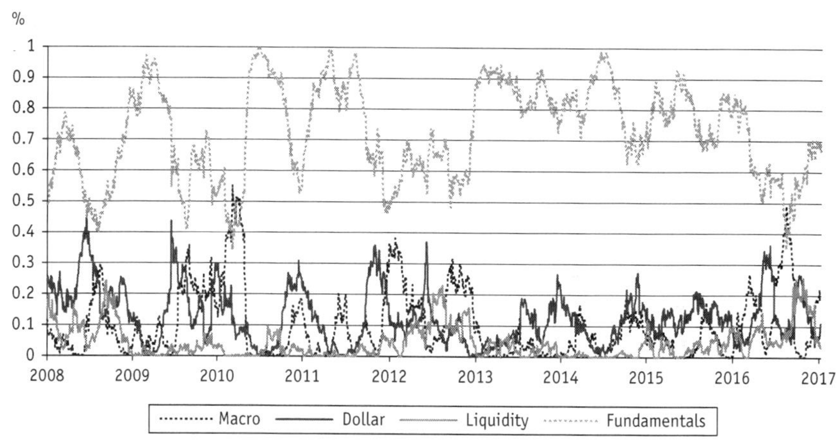

Figure 6.4 Proportion of Gold's Price Movement Explained by Fundamentals and Non-fundamentals
This figure shows that the U.S. dollar is the dominant driver beyond macroeconomic fundamentals, which makes gold unique among all commodities. Source: SG Cross Asset Research.

surprisingly, as Figure 6.4 shows, the PCA profile for gold looks extremely different for gold compared to other commodities.

As gold becomes a widely used store of value and competes with interest rates, the dollar often solely influences gold price changes. As such, all three components of the PCA analysis are significant throughout the study period. However, as with the remainder of the commodity complex, when major global interruptions occur such as the subprime crisis, euro crisis, or large Chinese equity market declines, the macro factor increases in terms of significance for gold market price changes.

Agriculture

The agricultural complex is similar to the natural gas market in that agriculture markets are somewhat isolated from the broader macro influence. With the exception of the subprime crisis and euro crisis, fundamentals drive the wheat markets, explaining more than 90 percent of its price variance, as shown in Figure 6.5.

Table 6.1 summarizes the recent explanatory power of the three factors for 22 commodity markets that comprise the Bloomberg Commodity Index (BCOM) during December 2016. The average shown at the bottom of the table is the equally weighted arithmetic average of the 22 markets. The average value differs from the BCOM value due to the weighting and correlation effects. As shown, the average percentage across all commodity markets is 87.13 percent fundamental, meaning that currently commodities can be considered a distinct asset class driven by its own characteristics. Unsurprisingly, the least fundamental market as of December 2016 is gold, with macro having a large influence on gold price changes. The most fundamentally driven commodity market is, also unsurprisingly, the U.S. natural gas with 99.61 percent of its price variance explained by supply and demand fundamentals. As a group, commodities appear to be trading on their own fundamentals, and, accordingly, the portfolio diversification benefits from commodities at the end of 2016 are clear.

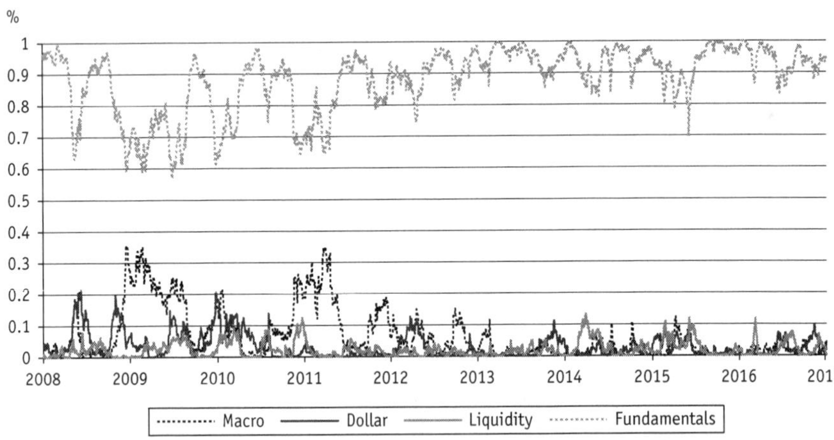

Figure 6.5 Proportion of Wheat's Price Movement Explained by Fundamentals and Non-fundamentals

This figure shows that wheat is independent from non-fundamental influences but at times is heavily influenced by fundamental macroeconomic factors. Source: SG Cross Asset Research.

Table 6.1 **PCA Analysis: December 2016**

Commodity	*Macro* %	*Dollar* %	*Liquidity* %	*Fundamental* %
WTI	11.88	9.07	0.15	78.90
Brent	10.94	9.41	0.24	79.41
Heating Oil	6.60	12.16	0.02	81.23
Gasoline	3.07	8.73	0.11	88.08
Gasoil	3.58	15.99	0.42	80.00
Natural Gas	0.37	0.00	0.02	99.61
Aluminium	2.99	1.77	4.47	90.76
Copper	9.43	3.08	15.54	71.94
Lead	2.86	4.03	5.86	87.25
Nickel	16.28	6.50	6.09	71.14
Zinc	4.77	3.37	10.86	81.00
Gold	19.32	5.13	5.69	69.85
Silver	4.20	14.51	0.52	80.78
Corn	0.60	6.07	0.01	93.32
Wheat	2.19	0.59	2.69	94.54
Soybeans	0.39	4.93	0.02	94.66
Cotton	0.01	0.88	0.00	99.10
Sugar	1.99	0.04	2.84	95.13
Coffee	0.18	0.22	3.66	95.94
Cocoa	11.25	0.42	0.19	88.15
Live Cattle	0.35	0.13	0.10	99.42
Lean Hogs	1.85	1.38	0.00	96.77
BCOM	**6.75**	**15.98**	**0.06**	**77.20**
Average	**5.23**	**4.93**	**2.70**	**87.13**

Note: This table shows the percentage of the price movement explained by macro (equity/volatility), dollar (safe versus nonsafe currencies), and liquidity (interest rate differentials) versus the percentage explained by commodity fundamentals by commodity.

Source: SG Cross Asset Research, January 2017, "Commodity Compass—A New Generation of RSI Indicator."

Fundamental Drivers of Oil Price Variance

As previously discussed, periods occur when oil prices move beyond fundamentals, but results from early 2016 display a strong fundamental influence in the oil markets. However, oil prices between 2013 and 2016 have been on a rollercoaster and physical players in oil are interested in knowing what is driving these rollercoaster patterns from a fundamental perspective. Between June 2014 and mid-March 2016, for instance, oil prices plummeted about 65 percent. This price drop is one of the three largest declines in oil prices since the 1970s. From March to June 2016, oil prices reversed direction and increased an astonishing 74 percent. As a result, a common question is: "What is driving the price movement and how much of the price decline was a result of oversupply versus weaker demand or, more recently, reduced supply or increased demand?" To address this question quantitatively, this section uses another PCA algorithm as discussed in the technical appendix to explain how much of the oil price variability comes from supply versus demand.

This analysis avoids using the typical fundamental data specific to commodity markets such as shipments, inventory changes, and published secondary data on demand because these characteristics are commonly measured infrequently, may only represent estimated data, and are usually revised, making real-time analysis impossible. Rather, the PCA technique uses more than 100 forward-looking asset prices on a daily basis that explain a large proportion of oil price movements. These prices include credit default swaps (CDSs), currencies, and global equities (the bulk of the data) that act as proxies for the supply and demand of crude oil. For example, the prices of exploration and production companies, oil drillers, oilfield services companies, CDSs, and currencies from oil-producing countries, including Mexico, Russia, and Brazil, each proxy for supply by sector. From a demand perspective, dozens of asset prices from various sectors, including utilities, chemicals, railways, marine, trucking, airlines, distribution, and retail serve as proxies. All forward-looking assets are standardized by dividing by a broad-based equity index (the S&P 500 index) in an attempt to remove the "beta" from the "oil" variables.

The inspiration from a methodology standpoint comes not just from client enquiries, but also from research produced by the Bank of England (BoE): "Oil is not as it seems: Expectations of future oil supply key to explaining drop in price" (Kindberg-Hanlon and Middeldorp 2015, p. 1). This research suggests three possible explanations for the fall in prices between 2014 and March 2016 and tests these theories. Moreover, the analysis breaks out what proportion comes from supply rather than demand. The BoE published this research in June 2015, shortly after the surge in Saudi and Iraqi oil output and before the lifting of oil sanctions against Iran in January 2016. Generally, this prior work made three observations:

1. The sharp increase in realized supply of oil was due to the ongoing U.S. shale oil production boom at the time and the recovery in Libyan production, which was temporary.
2. Future oil supply expectations would be high based on the November 2014 Saudi-led OPEC decision to abandon its swing supplier role and to not cut production.
3. Slower prospects for global demand would persist on the back of weaker global growth.

Given that oil markets seem to be largely fundamentally driven, as illustrated in the first section of this chapter, these fundamental observations appear sensible. Some economists suggest that the weaker outlook for oil demand (the third point listed here) has played an underappreciated role in affecting oil price changes. Indeed, the dramatic post–November 2014 decline in the oil price have largely been attributed to the decisions made at the OPEC meeting to continue the enormous supply overhang. In the background of these decisions has been the fact that major strides have been made to increase shale oil production in the United States. The supposition that this added supply would affect prices seems intuitive. The OPEC decision meant that the market itself (i.e., prices) would balance supply with weakening demand (rather than Saudi Arabian production in November 2014). In this regard, many market participants understood that the supply overhang would last longer without OPEC actively managing and restricting supply.

Since the publication of Kindberg-Hanlon and Middeldorp's (2015) research, OPEC reversed the decision to continue adding supply at a relatively constant rate. In November 2016, OPEC decided to intervene by managing (i.e., restricting supply). Importantly, since oil demand remained resilient through 2015 and 2016 and was expected to remain resilient, the market price changes would most likely remain focused on supply rather than demand. This focus is primarily due to the fact that despite intervening in the supply side, market observers will scrutinize OPEC and non-OPEC members for their compliance on supply cutbacks. Therefore, OPEC member country compliance on the supply side will be the focus of the market at least until OPEC changes policy. However, despite these facts, the original purpose of the BoE's research was to introduce a quantitative model that could separate the proportion of variance of oil prices into supply and demand components. Employing a partial least squares model using asset prices from hundreds of variables, the report illustrates that supply rather than demand explains the vast majority of the price decline from mid-2014 through early 2016.

The BoE report only used data since June 2014. This chapter employs a different methodology than the BoE, and goes back further in time to check the robustness of this approach. The underlying premise in the analysis is that changes in the prices of assets related to oil yields a forward-looking assessment of whether changes in the crude oil price have come from a change in supply, a change in demand, or both. The simple logic is that different asset prices react differently to oil demand and supply shocks. For example, if oil prices decline dramatically, the equity prices of utilities, railroads, marine merchants, and retail, for example, would react favorably. By contrast, the CDSs of producing countries, their currencies, exploration and production equities, and oilfield services equities would react negatively. These data are available daily and even in real time, providing a major advantage over using physical supply and demand data that are reported only infrequently, with a lag, and may subsequently be revised. In this analysis, the magnitude of the reaction for supply and demand proxies depends on whether the decline in prices came from oversupply or demand weakness. With demand weakness, demand variables would react negatively, as would supply. However, with oversupply, demand variables would react positively, whereas supply variables would not. The data employed include 119 financial time series along with the price of crude oil (WTI).

Figure 6.6 show the weightings as of March 2016 for the three factors that emerge from the analysis. The weightings are similar year after year, indicating that the PCA model is robust and fairly stable. The technical appendix provides for a complete explanation of the methodology. The first factor in the left-hand column relates to oil supply. As supply-sensitive equities do well when oil prices increase, the producer country currencies also rise (i.e., the U.S. dollar weakens with an opposite sign of the advancing equities). The exchange rates reflected include U.S. dollar / Mexican peso (USD/MXN), U.S. dollar / Canadian dollar (USD/CAD), U.S. dollar / Norwegian kroner (USD/NOK), and U.S. dollar / Brazilian real (USD/BRL). Meanwhile, the CDS prices of those countries fall (a positive). The CDSs used here are Brazil, Mexico, and Russia with only one CDS labeled due to spacing limitations.

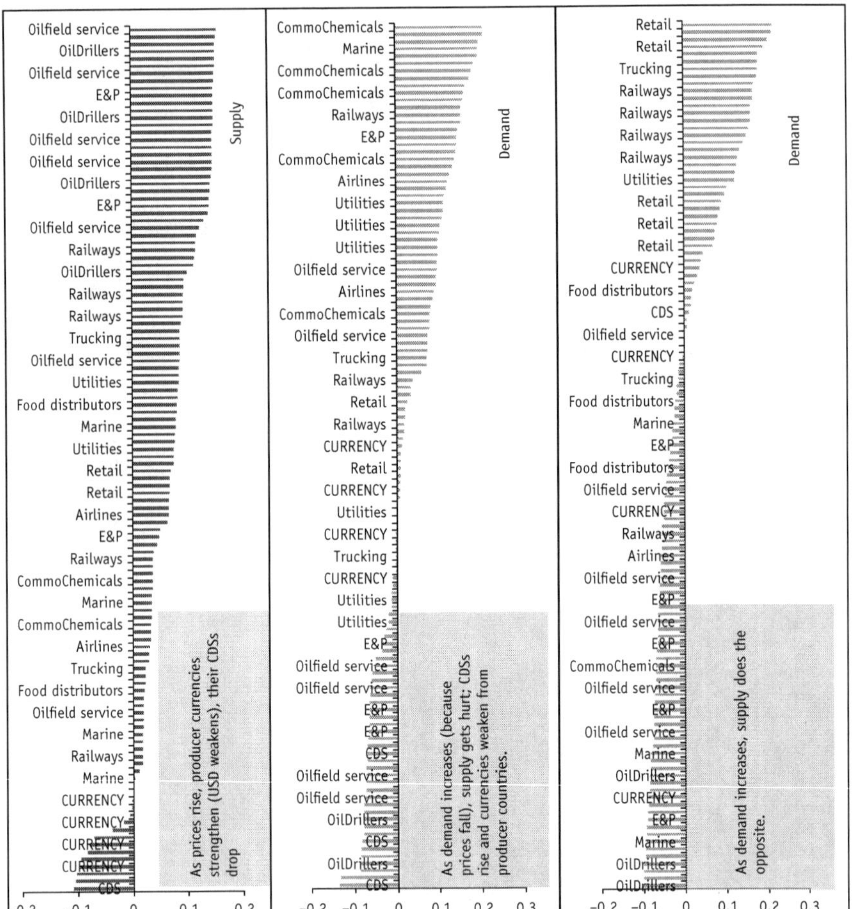

Figure 6.6 PCA Weightings of Factor 1 (Supply Dominated) and Factors 2 and 3 (Demand Dominated)
This figure shows the weightings in each factor of the different equity sectors within the supply and demand categories. Source: SG Cross Asset Research.

The second factor in the middle column relates to oil demand. With lower oil prices (demand does well), the factor has positive weightings, so the CDS of the producer countries would go in the opposite direction and appear with a negative sign. Intuitively, lower oil prices make oil-producing countries more vulnerable and hence their CDS rises. These countries include Brazil, Mexico, and Russia.

The third factor in the right-hand column also relates to oil demand. This factor is the least significant in terms of explanatory power, but is included because it is still significant. Examining this factor suggests that the weightings make sense as being related to demand. Equities in firms that rely on oil as an input increase with lower oil prices, but the equity of firms which supply oil decrease with lower prices. The analysis uses the fact that oil prices affect different companies in different ways, depending on whether the firms demand or supply oil, and assigns supply or demand labels based on this fact. Therefore, factor 1 is labeled supply; factor 2 is added to factor 3 and is labeled demand. Once this history of weightings on the supply and demand factors is compiled, the analysis couples these time-series results with changes in the price of crude oil.

The second stage of the analysis includes running regressions of supply and demand on the oil price changes, and deriving an R^2 statistic, which captures the proportion of oil price variability coming from supply and demand. The R^2 can be calculated and plotted daily by using a rolling regression model. The proportion of price movement that is not explained by either supply or demand (the white area in Figure 6.3) is the residual.

The results displayed in Figure 6.3 appear to be intuitively related to how the factors have reacted to events that would affect oil markets. As of early March 2016, about 65 percent of oil price variation resulted from supply and about 6 percent from demand. The remaining 29 percent indicates that something outside of the model is partially explaining oil's price variation. The fact that some unexplained variation remains after considering supply and demand factors is common in the original PCA algorithm described previously. In sum, observable supply and demand characteristics combined to explain about 71 percent of oil's price variation. Of the combined 71 percent supply and demand components, supply characteristics explain 91 percent of the total (65 percent divided by 71 percent).

Comparing these results to the other PCA algorithm which disentangles fundamentals from non-fundamentals, the new analysis (applied to March 2016) explains 11 percentage points more of the oil price variation—fundamentals previously explained about 60 percent of oil's price variation relative to the 71 percent explained in the March 2016 analysis. The original model uses completely different variables from the new supply and demand PCA algorithm. Thus, the fact that the new fundamentals of supply plus demand explain a similar percentage of oil price variation as explained by the original PCA approach is somewhat reassuring. Figure 6.7 also displays a few key events that have influenced oil markets since June 2014. The early June 2014 ISIS attack and takeover of Mosul and other areas of Iraq caused a brief but noticeable increase in supply's influence on the oil price due to market fears of a supply disruption. When such a disruption did not take place and the situation became clear that this would be a low-probability event, the increase in supply's influence quickly faded to zero by July 2014. U.S. imports of light sweet crude essentially ceased in

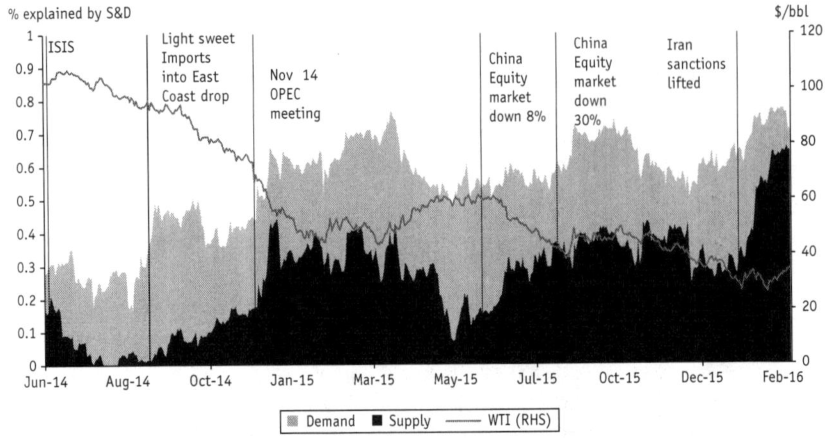

Figure 6.7 Proportion of Price Variation Explained by Supply and Demand and Recent Events That Have Moved or Potentially Moved Oil
The vertical black lines represent the point in time the event occurred. The gray and black areas represent the proportion of price variation explained by demand and supply, respectively. Source: Bloomberg, SG Cross Asset Research.

mid-2014 due to surging domestic light sweet shale oil supply. Consequently, the situation became increasingly clear that the United States had reached a tipping point in becoming as much a producer of light sweet crude oil as a consumer. Light sweet crude oil imports to the U.S. Gulf Coast had essentially ended much earlier, but light sweet imports to the U.S. Atlantic Coast continued declining for some months before dropping close to zero in the summer of 2014. As Figure 6.7 shows, the supply factor started to pick up in terms of explanatory power at this point.

Following along with further events, the OPEC meeting in November 2014 pushed supply much higher in terms of explanatory power. The two periods of sharp declines in Chinese equities in 2015 meant that the demand factor increased substantially, reflecting a fear of demand weakness, relative to supply. Subsequently, in January 2016, sanctions relief for Iran and the prospects of strong growth in Iranian production and exports pushed supply to the forefront of market participants' minds. At this time, the analysis reflects a dramatic growth in the importance and proportion of supply factors driving oil price variability. For a longer-term perspective on the analysis, the chapter concludes by estimating precisely the same PCA algorithm employed earlier using supply and demand factors going back to 2007. To highlight major oil market events, Figure 6.8 labels 12 separate historical events, indicated as Events A through L. A brief description of each appears next.

- Event A: The peak of the crude oil price at $147/bbl in July 2008. Concerns over demand destruction mean that demand explains about 40 percent of price variability compared with 20 percent related to supply.
- Event B: Lehman bankruptcy, September 2008. The market focused on demand destruction as the financial crisis causes sharply slower economic growth (i.e., the

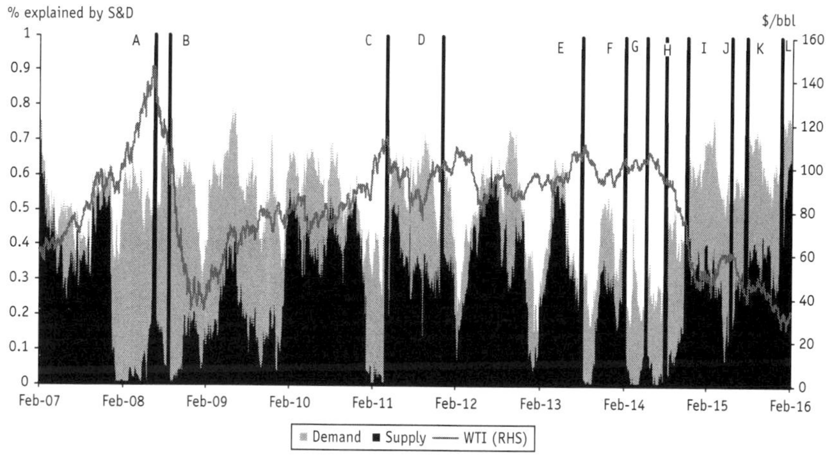

Figure 6.8 Proportion of Price Variation Explained by Supply and Demand and Historical Events
The vertical black lines represent the point in time the event occurred. The gray and black areas represent the proportion of price variation explained by demand and supply, respectively.

"Great Recession"). Supply has no bearing on price volatility during this period, while demand dominates, explaining 70 percent of the oil price variance.

- Event C: Libyan civil war, February 2011. Over the course of three months, Libyan oil production dropped from 1.6 million bbl/day to almost zero in May. Supply goes from explaining 0 percent of oil price variability in January 2011 to 50 percent one month later. The event line (C) denotes March 2011, when Libyan production had fallen to 450 thousand bbl/day.
- Event D: Potential closure of the Straits of Hormuz, December 2011–January 2012. Geopolitical tensions over the nuclear issue are high, accompanied by saber-rattling from both Iran and the West, and both conduct naval exercises. A supply disruption does not ultimately transpire, but supply concerns meant the supply component explanatory power rose from 25 percent to 35 percent.
- Event E: Syrian crisis, August 2013. For several weeks, the oil markets expect U.S.-led military action against Syria. Although Syria itself was not and is not a major source of supply, the concern was that violence might spill over to Iraq, which was and is a major oil producer and exporter. Although military action did not occur, prices surged and the oil market focused on possible demand destruction that might result from the crisis, including reduced air travel during wartime. Demand dominates during the period and supply takes a back seat.
- Event F: Ukraine crisis, February–March 2014. The crisis itself had much higher potential to affect natural gas flows than oil exports. Fear over demand weakness as a result of the conflict and few concerns over supply means supply explains zero percent of oil's price move during this episode.
- Event G: ISIS emerges in early June 2014. A brief but noticeable impact on the explanatory power of supply accompanies this episode.

- Event H: The United States backs out light sweet imports to the U.S. Atlantic Coast during the summer of 2014. As the market shifts its focus to this key fundamental development, supply explains 13 percent of oil's price variance in early August 2014, but grows to explain 40 percent by the month-end.
- Event I: OPEC meeting, November 2014. OPEC says that the market itself will be the supply-adjustment mechanism. The percentage of explanatory power from supply doubles, reflecting OPEC's active statements.
- Event J: China's equity markets drop 8 percent from April to June 2015. Demand picks up by five percentage points in terms of explanatory power, reflecting concerns about weak worldwide demand.
- Event K: China's equity markets decline by 30 percent by the end of August 2015. Demand increases in explanatory power by more than 15 percentage points, reflecting continued concerns about demand.
- Event L: Iranian sanctions lifted, January 2016. Supply explains a near-record level of oil's price variance.

Summary and Conclusions

This chapter has explored the role of nonfundamental information in helping to understand the market structure for oil and the relations between supply and demand factors to oil price volatility. The first part builds a PCA algorithm that focuses on how much of commodity price variance can be explained by fundamentals versus non-fundamentals. The results are intuitive with large global negative shocks resulting in many commodity markets becoming less fundamental, which is consistent with financialization of commodity markets having come into play, but does not prove it. Not surprisingly, this analysis highlights that some commodities are more fundamental than others, including the U.S. natural gas and the agriculture complexes. Commodities more exposed to macro shocks, such as oil and copper, are more likely to experience more frequent episodes of influence from the non-fundamental factors. In 2016, however, commodity markets can be described as deeply fundamental in nature, hence offering diversification benefits.

Given that oil fundamentals drive its price, the next question addressed in this chapter is how much of oil's price variance can be explained by demand and supply. This analysis employs more than 100 forward-looking asset prices that reflect these demand and supply components and applies a similar PCA algorithm. The results are intuitive because they match up well with and can be explained by numerous historical events. In fact, over time, these estimates suggest that supply factors rather than demand factors explain the vast majority of oil price volatility. Comparing the relative importance of the two fundamental factors yields the insight that supply explains more than 90 percent of price movements in February 2016. That percentage increased dramatically after January 2016 as Iran was granted oil sanctions relief, so supply from that country was expected to recover substantially. Additionally, production from OPEC excluding Iran remains high, driven by productive oil fields in Saudi Arabia and Iraq. U.S. output has been resilient, even if it is declining gradually in response to lower prices between 2014 and 2016. From March to July 2016, oil's price has risen dramatically and yet the proportion of oil's price variance is still explained mainly by supply rather than demand factors. This is especially true after OPEC decided at its November 30, 2016, meeting to re-enter the market and manage supply. The PCA analysis of determining what proportion of a commodity market's variance comes from supply rather than demand factors can easily be extended to other commodity markets using similar forward-looking equity prices, such as metals (mining) or the agriculture sector. This chapter marks a first step in applying this innovative technique toward analyzing the value of commodities for effective diversification in portfolios of stocks and bonds. In fact, the chapter sheds light on historical periods that appear to show commodity market prices deviating from fundamental supply and demand factors. The results show that different commodity markets respond to different fundamental factors over time. Moreover, within individual commodity markets the importance of fundamental factors also changes over time. These results demonstrate that any non-fundamental structural market changes such as "financialization" appear to have, at most, a relatively transitory impact on commodity prices with supply and demand fundamentals more commonly influencing prices over time.

Discussion Questions

1. Explain why commodities such as lean hogs or cotton are expected to be more fundamentally driven than commodities such as oil or copper.
2. Despite commodity markets being deeply fundamentally driven, explain what could reverse that relation.
3. Explain the meaning of the following statement: "The non-fundamentals for commodities are the fundamentals for gold."
4. Explain why using forward-looking equity prices to proxy supply and demand fundamentals are more appropriate than using fundamental data on supply and demand.
5. Explain why different asset prices react differently to oil demand and supply shocks.

Technical Appendix

The idea behind the supply/demand PCA tool is to find the $n < p$ best factors from a list of factors $(X_1, \ldots, X_n)$ (n is the number of factors input by the user) that most explain the variance of the set $(X_1, \ldots, X_p)$. For instance, the goal is to explain the movements in crude oil with 10 supply-demand factors but also keep the three factors that are explaining the most variance of the set. The approach is to run a PCA to select the three factors, and then run a regression using those factors against the crude oil price. A high R^2 means that a high correlation exists on the crude oil market (i.e., most of the variance of crude oil can be explained by the supply and demand factors). Otherwise, with a low R^2, factors beyond supply and demand drive most of crude oil's variance. Moreover, the analysis can separate the proportion of the R^2 that each factor explains. The factor weightings thus reflect the relative importance of demand and supply.

To perform this task mathematically requires diagonalizing the covariance (or correlation) matrix of the factors ($X_1, \ldots, X_n$) and ranking the eigenvalues and correspondingly the eigenvectors. The eigenvectors are the weights (i.e., multiplicators) that are applied to the data to get the PCA score. The next step is to run a regression on the factor portfolio (score) versus the crude oil price and to get the R^2 of the regression and separate the proportion of the R^2 that each factor explains.

The following are the steps in creating the algorithm.

- Retrieve the underlying forward-looking asset prices from Bloomberg and, depending on the data, keep the raw data, compute returns, or compute normalized daily data. The operations of "spread" or "ratio" can be input by the user to transform the raw data before conducting these operations. The next task is to attempt to remove beta from broad equity moves from most data by dividing by the S&P 500. Then, each year, run a PCA on a growing time window of one year, then two years, then three years (parameter "yearly growing") or a fixed time window on the previous year (parameter "yearly fixed") depending on the user. In this particular application, the chapter uses "yearly fixed".
- Diagonalize the covariance (or correlation) matrix depending on whether the user inputs COVAR or CORR) from the data, rank the (normalized) eigenvalues, and correspondingly rank the eigenvectors. Retain the first three factors and their weights (eigenvectors).
- Compute the score of the PCA by multiplying the returns of crude oil by the eigenvectors (weights) of each factor. For a given iteration, use the data up to that point to compute the weights.
- Regress the returns of crude oil (Y) on a moving window of k days, which is 40 days in this case, to better pinpoint actual events, against the
  - Returns of the first factor (score of the first factor).
  - Returns of the first two factors (score of the first and second factor). Continue for the third factor.
  - Returns of the first three factors (score of the first to third factor).
- Using the output, obtain the R^2 RSQ_1 (labeled Supply here).
- Obtain the R^2 RSQ_2 and calculate the difference RSQ_1–RSQ_2 (labeled $Demand_1$ here).
- Obtain the R^2 RSQ_3 and calculate the differences RSQ_3–RSQ_2 and RSQ_3–RSQ_1 (labeled $Demand_2$ here) and add RSQ_2 and RSQ_3 together and label this Demand.
- The residual is everything that is not explained by the R^2 values.

References

Hotelling, Harold. 1933. "Analysis of a Complex Statistical Variables into Principal Components." *Journal of Educational Psychology* 24:6, 417-441.

Kindberg-Hanlon, Gene, and Menno Middeldorp. 2015. "Oil Is Not as It Seems: Expectations of Future Oil Supply Key to Explaining Drop in Price." Bank of England, Bank Underground.

Available at https://bankunderground.co.uk/2015/06/26/oil-is-not-as-it-seems-expectations-of-future-oil-supply-key-to-explaining-drop-in-price/.

Nomikos, Nikos K., and Panos K. Pouliasis. 2014. "Petroleum Term Structure Dynamics and the Role of Regimes." *Journal of Futures Markets* 35:2, 163-185.

Pearson, Karl. 1901. "On Lines and Planes of Closest Fit to Systems of Points in Space." *Philosophical Magazine* Series 6 2:11, 559–572.

Tolmasky, Carlos, and Dmitry Hindanov. 2002. "Principal Component Analysis for Correlated Curves and Seasonal Commodities: The Case of the Petroleum Market." *Journal of Futures Markets* 22:11, 1019-1035.

SG Cross Asset Research. 2017. "Commodity Compass—A New Generation of RSI Indicator."

Part Two

PHYSICAL COMMODITIES

7

Physical Commodities

ERIK DEVOS
JPMorgan Chase Professor of Business Administration and Professor of Finance, College of Business Administration, University of Texas–El Paso

SEOW ENG ONG
Professor of Real Estate, School of Design and Environment, National University of Singapore

ANDREW C. SPIELER
Professor of Finance, Frank G. Zarb School of Business, Hofstra University

Introduction

Financial assets derive their value from specific contractual claims based on the underlying asset or process. For example, a bond is a financial asset that gives the owner—the lender—the contractual claim to the stream of coupons payments from the bond. A share of common equity grants the owner the right to a proportionate share of earnings, the right to vote, and a residual claim to assets in bankruptcy. Commodities possess a physical component, unlike the aforementioned securities. Each commodity requires unique methods of creation (e.g., wheat requires extraction; crude oil requires storage and transportation). Furthermore, the actual physical commodities of the same class are heterogeneous, falling somewhere on a spectrum of quality. In physical commodity markets, a trader can transact at the current spot price for immediate delivery, or enter into a trade via the derivative markets denoting a future commitment to buy or sell. Often, however, market participants close the underlying commodity position by reversing the original position. The resulting transaction is far more complex than other financial securities due to incorporating transportation, which presents logistical hurdles and additional constraints, storage, and other associated carrying costs contingent on the length of the investment period. As a result, retail investors are unlikely to directly invest in physical commodities due to the additional constraints, resorting to using derivatives or indirect investment vehicles such as a commodity exchange-traded fund (ETF). In turn, the exchange of physical commodities is left to firms whose operations revolve around the creation and use of commodities, including commodity producers, manufacturers, commodity trading firms (CTFs), and large financial institutions with the resources to physically trade commodities. These market participants, through conducting transactions in both the spot market and derivatives market, convey information about the levels of supply and demand, improve the price discovery of commodities, and ultimately establish the global physical commodities markets.

Commodities as Physical Assets

The term *commodity* is often associated with raw or in-process materials used by a wide array of entities, ranging from large manufacturers who transform commodities into other products to individuals who may consume the commodity either directly or indirectly through a manufactured good. The commodity markets, in turn, encompass all these products, as market participants attempt to buy and sell based on their operations. At a broad level, physical commodities can be divided into five sectors (agriculture, energy, livestock, industrial metals, and precious metals) as found in the NASDAQ Commodity Benchmark Index (NQCI) (NASDAQ 2012). Some of these sectors can be further subdivided into subsectors, such as the agricultural sector, which can be bifurcated into the grains, livestock, and soft commodities subsectors. Given the unique characteristics of each commodity type, market participants have to account for an array of peculiarities for each commodity type that influences the flow of global transactions, apart from the fundamental levels of supply and demand. Some peculiarities are commodity-specific such as storability and perishability, while others are market-specific such as the availability of storage and the methods of transportation to connect buyers and sellers. These factors extend to national government involvement around the world, with various government policies such as production subsidies, import and export quotas, and tariffs that can increase the transaction costs of trading.

Schnepf (2006) highlights key trends influencing the physical commodity markets and more specifically, those that fall within the agricultural sector. He posits that the main drivers of commodity prices are traditional supply and demand factors that are contingent on existing prices and proposed and expected bids within a respective market. Other factors are exogenous to the levels of demand in the physical market, such as crop failures, widespread disease, and crop production revisions. In particular, agricultural commodities are subject to seasonality within some geographic areas of production, and in some instances, production is limited to three-quarters of a year or less due to harsh winters in some regions. As a result, commodities originating from these areas experience inelastic supply and demand characteristics due to the substantial lead time required for production. The lead time generally entails months of nurturing and growth. Therefore, participants supplying agricultural products cannot quickly alter production in response to shortages or gluts. As a result, market prices then fluctuate as participants establish a new trading equilibrium. Additional factors that affect a commodity's price include the availability of substitutes, homogeneity, storability, transparency in the price formation process, and the ease of transportation between market participants. Such participants have access to multiple sources of information about the expectations of future prices and quantity through assumptions derived from the futures market for the respective commodity type, private news sources, and government agencies, such as the U.S. Department of Agriculture. For example, this agency releases monthly estimates for harvested acreage and yield for grains, oilseeds, and cotton through its National Agricultural Statistics Service (NASS), which market participants can use to forecast future levels of supply and expected prices.

For a trader wanting to buy or sell assorted commodities, three unique transformations for commodities must be kept in mind. These transactions entail transformations in space, time, and form of commodity types. Spatial transformation refers to the movement of commodities from areas of net production to areas of net consumption. Time transformation refers to the storage of commodities for future use to assist in smoothing the trends in production or consumption over time. The ability to store commodities helps to mitigate market volatility, which arises from factors including the seasonality of production, especially agricultural commodities, supply or demand shocks, and general economic patterns of both growth and recessionary periods. Form transformation describes the transformation of commodities into either manufactured products or production inputs for other commodity types, such as agricultural commodities being used as feed for livestock commodities (Pirrong 2014). These transformations take place at varying stages in the physical commodity life cycle: upstream (initial production or extractions), midstream (transportations and storage), and downstream (final manufacturing and general retail) stages. Regarding the varying stages of transformations, those buying or selling physical commodities focus on the price differentials between different stages of production, as pricing discrepancies may provide opportunities to profit for those with the means of completing the necessary transformations.

Super Cycles and Commodity Markets

Throughout history, many instances of commodity super cycles have occurred. These cycles are characterized by extended periods of increased demand and rising commodity prices in response to periods of high urbanization and industrialization of a single or multiple major economies. Heap (2005) analyzes the history of commodity demand and price levels and has identified recent commodity super cycles, such as the nineteenth-century industrial revolution of the United States, the post–World War II reconstruction of Europe, and the recent rapid growth in China. During these super cycles, increases in demand typically exceed the available supply, leading to larger annual growth of commodity prices over time as compared to prior periods. One example would be the trade of industrial metals (e.g., aluminum, nickel, zinc, and steel) between 1940 and 1980 in response to the reconstruction needs of Europe following World War II. Since 2000, copper has experienced explosive price growth, in line with China's extensive growth during the twentieth century and increased demand for the metal. For example, China contributed 112 and 78 percent to the year-over-year world consumption growth for 2002 and 2003, respectively (Heap 2005). The increasing commodity prices during these super cycles is the dominant trend, but smaller seasonal patterns and business cycle trends are also present, which result in fluctuating spot prices.

Cuddington and Jerrett (2008) find evidence supporting super cycles and their impact on abnormal growth for commodity prices. Their study consists of locating three super cycles, defined as expansion phases lasting from 10 to 35 years that fell in 1890-1911, 1930-1951, and 1962-1977, and analyzing the growth trends of the six base metals (i.e., aluminum, copper, lead, nickel, tin, and zinc) traded on the London Metal Exchange. They find large variations of 20 to 40 percent above or below prior long-term price growth rates during these times, accompanied by higher correlations between the trends of each industrial metal during the super cycle.

Erten and Ocampo (2012) find similar results analyzing historical commodity price growth during super cycles of 30 to 40 years. They identify three cycles, 1894-1932, 1932-1971, and 1971-1999, as well as a post-2000 cycle that is currently mid-cycle, all of which display the similar 20 to 40 percent abnormal price growth found in Cuddington and Jerrett (2008). The authors also find a tendency for declining growth of non-oil commodity prices in each super cycle, especially for agricultural products, with the lone exception being metal during the post-2000 cycle.

This long-run trend of declining commodity price growth supports the Prebisch-Singer hypothesis, which posits that over time, commodity prices incur a decreasing trend in growth relative to the manufactured products into which they are later transformed.

Harvey, Kellard, Madsen, and Wohar (2010) conduct a study of the price changes of 25 commodities between the seventeenth and twenty-first centuries. They find that 11 of the 25 commodities exhibit a trend of a long-run decline in price relative to manufactured products using the commodity, providing support for the hypothesis. According to Harvey et al., this trend may be explained by highly competitive markets, productivity differentials between manufacturers and commodity-producing markets, and oligopolistic rents being earned by manufacturers due to a concentrated market as opposed to commodity-producers earning zero economic profit due to competition. Also, Harvey et al. posit Sir W. A. Lewis's contention that poor countries experience lower real-wage growth due to the abundance of available labor at low wages, a downward pressure not shared by the labor supply within the manufacturing market.

Spot Market and Futures Market

The spot market, also known as the cash market, entails the purchase or sale between market participants of a quantity of a commodity for immediate delivery at the prevailing spot price as determined by the existing levels of supply and demand. Participants within the spot market can trade at varying steps within the value chain of a commodity, either in the primary or secondary form. Commodity types of the primary form entail resources that have been directly extracted or produced, and those of the secondary form entail commodities that have already been processed in some form. For example, within the energy sector, raw materials such as coal, crude oil, and natural gas can be considered primary form commodities, whereas diesel, gasoline, and liquefied natural gas are considered secondary form because they are the result of processing at a refinery (Trafigura 2016). When buying or selling either commodity type, those looking to profit from trading physical commodities operate in an environment of high-volume and low-margin transactions if they seek to capitalize on market mispricing, such as with price discrepancies between different geographical markets or between commodities at varying stages of processing. Depending on the means of production, they can also profit on short-term supply and demand shocks by leveraging current commodities through blending commodities to create new types, such as with various metals or oil types, to suit the needs of varying refinery production specifications.

In many instances, market participants do not rely solely on buying or selling commodities at the spot price, but rather incorporate a strategy integrating spot and derivative transactions such as by using futures contracts in an effort to mitigate the risk of price fluctuations over time. Transactions within the futures markets entail a buy or sell transaction of a specified quantity at a future date, clearly delineated within the contract. Futures contracts can be bought or sold at various maturities to help match almost any investment horizon of a market participant. Although both futures and spot transactions may entail the same transfer of commodities, the element of time causes different intertemporal prices between the current and futures spot prices. The futures contract's price can be either above or below the expected spot price of the commodity in the market at the time of the futures contract's maturity. These conditions are known as contango and backwardation, respectively.

The contango condition takes into account the presence of positive carrying costs, which reflect the costs associated with carrying a physical commodity from one period to another. Here, the market participant that is short, or has agreed to sell the commodity at a later date, on the futures contract is responsible for absorbing these costs, and in turn requires an additional premium as compensation. This premium normally does not exceed the future spot price plus the aggregate carrying costs. As a result, the participant long on the futures contract would essentially be buying storage when agreeing to pay the premium. The carrying cost would be the largest at the time of the futures contract's inception, all else equal. Over time, the futures contract price would decrease to ultimately converge with future spot price on the day of expiration as market participants capitalize on arbitrage between intertemporal prices within the market. For example, if the market were to misprice a futures contract by having the futures contract price above the expected spot price plus the aggregate carrying costs, a trader would simply sell a futures contract, purchase the commodity at the current spot price, hold the commodity, and pay the carrying costs until expiration to profit on the difference. Here, the trader can capitalize on the price discrepancy by pairing the investment in the physical asset with a sale of the futures contract. As numerous investors in the market conduct this trade and similar trades for other conditions, the intertemporal prices should align and arrive at a fairly-priced equilibrium between spot prices and futures contract prices.

Backwardation indicates the presence of negative, or inverse, carrying costs resulting in the futures contract price below the expected future spot price. Working (1948) posits that consideration of these negative charges as carrying charges may be misleading, and rather believes that these charges are the result of an implicit yield. Working suggests that holding a physical commodity provides a current "convenience" yield, which varies in relation to the type of commodity and the potential benefits it could offer to the owner that should be deducted from the positive cost of carry when determining the futures price. If the convenience yield exceeds the positive carrying costs, the net value is negative, resulting in a lower futures contract price. He posits that the convenience yield is contingent on the current level of supply of a commodity in the market, in which the marginal yield of additional supply decreases as supply increases. This relation is due to market participants' unwillingness to hold "surplus stocks" without the expectation of special returns to offset the additional carrying costs.

Weymar (1966) expands on the elements of the convenience yield, particularly for manufacturers and merchants. For companies that rely on commodities as inputs in production, sufficient supplies prevent plant closures and reduce the uncertainty about the cost of finished products relative to the levels of raw materials. For merchants, sufficient supplies provide the ability to sustain trading during most changing market conditions.

Pindyck (2001) posits one potential case of expected backwardation for a firm that owned rights to in-ground reserves of crude oil. This firm would possess a "real option"—similar to a call option of choosing whether to extract the commodity it owns to sell in the spot market. As price volatility increases, so does the firm's convenience yield since a price at which the extraction would be profitable may be reached and further price increases will lead to additional profits.

By pairing trades in the spot and futures markets, traders reduce the risk of price volatility between the present and future trading price of a commodity. However, in turn, they assume a new risk, basis risk, which is the risk that prices between spot transactions and the associated derivative contract deviate. In a perfect environment, a firm's basis risk would be negligible because paired trades seek to match the exact commodity type and quantity from the transaction in the spot market with the equivalent futures contracts. This perfect pairing, however, is not always possible because a firm may be unable to find a suitable liquid derivatives market for the underlying commodity. For example, airline companies seeking to hedge future jet fuel purchases often must resort to using heating oil and gasoline futures contracts to hedge fluctuating jet fuel prices. However, these alternative energy futures are imperfectly correlated with jet fuel, leaving the airline at risk of rising jet fuel prices that outpace the appreciation of the futures contracts used to hedge (Pindyck 2001).

Brooks, Lazar, Symeonidis, and Prokopczuk (2012) analyze the relations between commodity inventory levels and the shape of their respective interested-adjusted forward basis, or price difference between current spot prices and forward prices, at horizons between two and 12 months. Their findings indicate that lower levels of current inventory are associated with larger levels of negative future basis, implying that the convenience yield is an increasing function of inventory and that increasing inventory levels are negatively correlated with commodity price volatility. More specifically, they find that the largest inventory and basis correlation is associated with energy commodities, such as crude oil and natural gas, due to the high storage and transportation costs. Agriculture and soft commodities also exhibit high correlations due to the seasonality of production and the higher cost of storage relative to the commodities' value, relative to other commodities types such as precious metals. Also, they find that a negative inventory basis, or lower current inventory levels, has a stronger negative correlation to price volatility as opposed to instances of a positive inventory basis.

Johnson (1960) addresses the dichotomy of commodity market participants, namely hedgers and speculators. *Hedgers* are those desiring to reduce the risk of price fluctuations by going either long to secure a future need of acquiring commodities for production or short by selling commodities to generate revenue. On the other side of the transaction are speculators who, for an assumed risk premium provided by the hedgers, are willing to go long or short in the market and assume the price risk. The speculator, who may not desire to ever possess the underlying physical commodity, has the option of forgoing physical delivery or sale through the cancellation of the original contract, such as by closing a long futures contract with the purchase of an equivalent short futures contract. As a result, in many instances futures contracts end without the exchange of the physical commodity as contracts are either closed or rolled forward on an ongoing basis.

Before the advent of electronic trading, commodity exchanges such as the Chicago Board of Trade operated an auction market referred to as an *open outcry*. At the exchange locations, individuals who had seats on the exchange met on the trading floor, commonly referred to as the *pit*, openly negotiated futures contracts on either their behalf or for other clients and institutions, and often resorted to using hands signs as a method of communication during the chaotic trading hours (Debrouillard Group 2016; Encyclopedia Britannica 2016). This form of exchange was the dominant method of trading commodities until the turn of the twentieth century, at which point electronic trading began to shape the market. Open outcry has not fully disappeared because the Chicago Mercantile Exchange Group still allows open outcry trading for S&P 500 futures contracts and options, following a decision to close most other pits in 2015 (CME Group 2015).

By providing a gathering place for market participants, commodity exchanges provide numerous benefits, such as reducing associated transactions costs of buying or selling commodities, combined with the added functions of more accurate price discovery and transparency (UNCTAD 2009). Over time, as exchanges shifted toward a greater volume of futures trading as opposed to spot price transactions, the importance of the additional risk hedging component became the main focus of entities participating within the exchange. Starting in the twentieth century, the commodity derivatives markets saw a huge increase in volume. For example, between 2000 and 2009, actively traded futures and options contracts increased sixfold, a boom facilitated by a trend toward using electronic trading (Gensler 2009). During this time, commodity trading activity of large-scale investors such as money managers and index traders increased markedly. These market participants view commodities as an efficient diversification tool and a hedge against both inflation and U.S. dollar (USD) fluctuations, because most commodity futures are USD-denominated contracts (Mayer 2009).

For example, Gorton and Rouwenhorst (2006) study the weighted monthly index returns between 1959 and 2004. They find that commodity futures offered similar risk premiums to other investments but are negatively correlated with equity and bond returns, emphasizing the potential benefits in portfolio diversification. Substantial involvement of noncommercial and money managers by providing additional speculators to act as counterparties to hedgers can influence the commodities markets and cause futures prices to deviate from a foundation on fundamental factors in the market. These deviations could then affect other aspects of the market, such as current spot prices and elements of the cost of carry.

Carrying Costs

Brennan (1958) posits that, in theory, the difference between spot prices and futures prices for a commodity is equal to the marginal carry cost expense, less the marginal convenience yield, which is a decreasing function of supply. These costs are contingent on, but are not exclusive to, factors such as necessary transportation, storage and lease expense, inflation and interest rate in the market, and insurance costs needed to protect assets. Unless a firm enters into a futures contract that incorporates compensation for the positive carrying costs, the firm faces the assorted costs of all these factors and thus must optimize its commodity inventory levels to balance the marginal yield and marginal costs of current inventory levels.

Financial assets can have slight price discrepancies if the same security, such as a share of common stock, trades on two different exchanges in two different countries. However, these discrepancies are quite small, if they exist at all. In a study of the price discrepancies of IBM shares trading on the NYSE and the Paris stock market in 1995, Roehner (2000) reports a relative price differential between the two markets of about 0.7 percent with a 0.98 correlation. These differences can be explained by the various, and mostly fixed, transaction costs for international stock trading, such as brokerage charges, taxes, and currency conversion rates. In commodity markets, Roehner also studies the cash price differences for wheat trading in Omaha, Nebraska, and Portland, Oregon, and finds that the price differentials between 1980 and 1981 are 18 times greater than the 0.7 percent intermarket differential for IBM stock. Physical commodity markets differ from financial markets.

TRANSPORTATION COSTS

In contrast to financial assets, physical commodities are subject to an array of costs that can result in greater intermarket price discrepancies, largely due to the carrying costs that are contingent on the distance between the buyer, seller, and product market. Roehner (2000) posits that since nearly half of wheat produced in the United States is exported, Omaha's regional proximity to a coast is far greater than Portland's, since it lies in the middle of the United States, and this factor drives the commodity price discrepancy. When studying the price differential between Portland and Houston, Texas, another (near) coastal location, he finds the difference to be only 2.5 percent and concludes that these differences are not due to quality distinctions because grain specifications are very strict. In a separate study, Roehner (1996) reports the price differentials between different wheat classes on the order of only 2 to 5 percent, far less than the price differentials due to location.

Benirschka and Binkely (1995) posit that producer's price of commodities decreases as the distance to the relevant market increases, similar to Roehner's (2000) findings, as supported by a study of the spatial distribution of grain in the

Corn Belt states in 1978. Higher transportation costs lead to a lower product price, which in turns lowers the opportunity cost, or interest forgone, for holding the product. Therefore, product storage costs increase as distance increases due to the lower opportunity costs, which is a claim supported by the grain distribution in the Corn Belt states.

Transportation costs can be separated into three different components: terminal, line haul, and capital costs (Notteboom and Rodrigue 2016). Terminal costs include the cost from loading and unloading commodities, as well as transshipment costs, or similar handling costs to occur during the entire trip. Line haul costs are a function of the distance traveled and include costs such as labor and fuel that increase with the distance traveled. Capital costs include those relating to infrastructure, terminals, and vehicles, all of which depreciate over time and require future capital expenditures for maintenance and repairs.

Transportation costs, which can easily comprise 10 percent of the production costs for commodities, vary depending on the transportation method and time period. Competitive pressures in response to market levels of supply and demand set many transportation rates. On land, road and rail provide transportation for most commodity types, with transportation by pipeline available for energy products. Transportation by road is generally reserved for quick, flexible movement of small quantities, whereas rail is reserved for longer distances and larger quantities. The marginal cost of additional shipments is the same for transportation by road because incremental delivery requires additional trucks. However, the marginal cost decreases for rail because additional train cars can be added to the same trip. The most cost effective method of transportation is by maritime, due to the buoyancy and limited friction of water, allowing for an efficient method of moving large quantities at a lower cost per mile than other methods (Comtois, Rodrigue, and Slack 2016).

STORAGE COSTS

Firms looking to store commodities have several options ranging from creating and establishing their own storage facility to renting or leasing storage in a larger facility. Alexander and Kenkel (2012) highlight potential storage options for firms producing agricultural commodities, which involves on-farm storage, storage at condominium facilities, and storage at a commercial storage facility. On-farm storage offers benefits such as lower transportation costs, lower variable costs, and greater control over both the storage and marketing of sale because the farm owner is not subject to the limitations imposed by a specific commercial facility. The drawbacks, however, include high initial costs to establish the storage facility—a sunk cost that cannot be recovered if the farmer's needs change—as well as additional monitoring and quality control requirements. Condominium storage entails a farmer purchasing or entering into a long-term lease with a commercial facility, buying a fixed volume of storage, and capitalizing on the economies of scale of the large-scale facility while absorbing the drawbacks of less control via marketing flexibility. The farmer can potentially sell the right to storage at the facility at a later date but must pay a service fee based on the volume for the length of ownership. Commercial storage necessitates rent for various periods, contingent on the volume of storage required and subject to an array of variable costs, such as utility, handling, and monitoring costs as well as losses due to shrinkage and quality deterioration and forgone opportunities costs of interest if the commodities had been sold and proceeds invested. According to Lee and Elsayed (2005), manufacturers are becoming more reliant on outsourcing storage, as opposed to storage in their own warehouses, to help them focus not only on core value chain activities and low costs but also on expanding the breath of storage to better suit their needs. As a result, methods such as condominium and commercial storage facilities will likely become more popular, allowing firms to capitalize on economies of scale of storage created by other firms.

According to Roehner (1996), accounting for all factors in pricing commodities is nearly impossible. Commodities are sensitive to factors at the production level (weather conditions, and cost of production), international trade level (tariffs, quotas, transport, and storage), and consumption level (business fluctuations and changing consumer preferences), with transportation and storage needs playing a role at each level. The material impact of these factors can create greater volatility for firms relying on the spot market to buy or sell commodities given that spot rates are more susceptible to supply or demand shocks. A manufacturer may see its expenses grow exponentially if it lacks the proper procurement strategies and relies on the spot market for resources Moreover, a farmer could face bankruptcy if agricultural commodity prices were to collapse as the result of a supply glut. However, the aforementioned entities can reduce price risk through participation in the derivatives markets and use futures contracts coupled with physical trades to hedge their degree of exposure as desired.

Lease Rates and Interest Rates

Interest rates and potential returns on investment possibilities within a given market have a direct effect on commodity prices by changing the supply and demand factors as the opportunities costs change. The resulting effect of changing rates influences inventory levels of commodities because those storing commodities constantly must assess the marginal cost to marginal yield of inventory levels.

Schnabel (2010) models the effects of changing interest rates on spot prices and futures prices as shown in Equation 7.1:

$$\frac{d\left[\left(\frac{F}{P}\right)-1\right]}{dP} \tag{7.1}$$

where F is the one-year futures price and P is the current spot price. If the result is positive, this evidence implies that the spot price and futures price are positively related, and that spot prices will increase and market participants will increase inventory as interest rates increase and the opposite if interest rates decrease. If negative, the spot price and futures price are inversely related, so that spot prices will decrease and market participants will seek to decrease inventory as interest rates increase and the opposite if interest rates decrease. If zero, then the spot price and futures price are unrelated and no changes contingent on interest rates will occur within the market.

Marr-Johnson (2009) analyzes the effects of *lease rates* (i.e., the current rates for borrowing or lending commodities), supply and demand, and spot prices on precious metal markets. For the gold market in the late twentieth century, he finds that high interest rates for the USD and expected returns on the equity markets drove those in the market to sell gold, thus putting downward pressure on spot prices, to reinvest funds elsewhere or to possibly forgo other investment opportunities. As a result, the declining sentiment on gold led to more hedgers wanting to borrow gold, thus applying upward pressure on the lease rates on gold reserves, and in those who capitalized on the interest rate differentials by selling gold short in the futures market and borrowing gold in the spot market. This trend soon changed after 2000 when the conditions in the market reversed, leading to downward pressure on lease rates and upward pressure on spot prices.

Frankel (2006) posits that increases in real short-term U.S. interest rates lead to decreasing commodity prices. As support, she proposes three main channels that lead to the lower prices: increased incentive to extract resources today, decreased desire to carry inventory, and increased incentive for investors to invest in U.S. Treasuries as opposed to participating as speculators within the commodities markets. Most of these channels lead to increased commodity inventory for sale today, in which case the additional supply relative to the same levels of demand results in lower prices. In general, prices would fall until the commodities become undervalued to the extent of offering prospective appreciation, such as through the convenience yield, in relation to the increased interest rates and carrying costs. Once traders can achieve a desirable marginal yield, they will begin to buy the commodity again and establish a new equilibrium.

Trading Physical Commodities

The physical handling of commodities provides several ways to generate profit and sustain different business models by focusing on revenue generation and potential risks. Through producing or extracting commodities, producers seek to maximize revenue from selling raw resources to be used by other firms in value-added activities, and thus are likely to participate in the derivative markets to secure future sales. Manufacturers who use raw resources as inputs to operations focus on keeping input costs low and sales prices high, and thus will participate in the derivative markets to secure purchases and maintain inventory levels at a satisfactory price. Thus, manufacturers are keen to develop procurement strategies to optimize the levels of current inventory and associated marginal carrying costs to the ability to acquire more via the spot market or futures market and forgo the need for storage.

Aside from firms looking to profit solely from participating in the value chain of activities, commodity trading firms (CTFs) seek to profit from trading commodities and capitalizing on commodity mispricing within the commodity markets. Pirrong (2014) outlines the fundamentals of commodity trading firms, private or public firms that may either specialize in trading specific commodity types or trade within a large span of commodity sectors. Pirrong (p. 8) describes CTFs as "the visible manifestation of the invisible hand, directing resources to their highest value" due to their ability to undertake one or more of the commodity transformation types mentioned previously to generate profit, as opposed to purely speculating on general commodity price increases or decreases. CTFs typically seek to complete these transformations on a large scale given that volume size and margin of a transaction are positively correlated. Thus, larger volumes lead to larger returns.

Three of the largest CTFs are Vitol (mostly energy commodities), Glencore (agricultural, metals, and energy commotions), and Cargill (diverse portfolio of commodities). All these firms, like many other CTFs, operate facilities at the upstream, midstream, or downstream segments of their respective markets. This situation allows the CTFs to capitalize on the possible profits from transforming commodities through value chain processes and create refined products to meet the changing supply and demand factors of the commodity markets. The numerous segments also provide diversification benefits, as changing market conditions that adversely affect the margins of one segment are potentially offset by improving margins in another. The capital structure of CTFs can vary widely, from highly leveraged to virtually no debt, though often these firms try to match short- or long-term liabilities with investments of similar expected maturity. CTFs act to a certain extent as financial intermediaries in the commodity markets as well, extending lines of credit and other structured financing to customers. Typically, CTFs conduct extensive, ongoing research on current and future trends, thus lowering the credit risk by a reduction of the asymmetry of information.

Some large financial firms also trade physical commodities. However, as established per the Bank Holding Company Act of 1956, bank holding companies (BHCs) that owned or controlled major U.S. banks faced restrictions with respect to activities outside banking to prevent excessive power from accumulating within the financial sector (Omarova 2013). The integration of financial institutions and commodity commerce could lead to new risks not only associated with the financial institutions within the United States, but also with the overall systemic risk as large financial institutions expand operations. BHCs often had excessive power over the commercial markets, such as the ability to make lending and investment decisions that were advantageous to their affiliated commercial companies at the expense of competitors within the same market, thus obstructing macro productivity and growth trends.

Furthermore, the Glass-Steagall Act of 1933 restricted many BHCs to mostly spread-driven lending operations in the twentieth century, as opposed to capital market operations by investment banks. Yet, these restrictions largely disappeared in 1999 after the enactment of the Gramm-Leach-Bliley Act, which allowed for the creation of financial holding companies (FHCs) with increased access to non-financial activities. Following Gramm-Leach-Bliley, these non-financial activities were permissible if the FHC was to make a direct equity investment, up to 100 percent, in a commercial company through merchant banking or proving that its operations were complementary to other financial activities or continuing operations of a commercial company if it were merged into a FHC (Omarova 2013). A prime example of a FHC that capitalized on the shifting regulations to access the commercial commodities business was the Royal Bank of Scotland (RBS) in 2008. RBS established majority control of RBS Sempra Commodities, a joint venture with the U.S. utility group Sempra Energy focused on physical commodity trading, due to the complementary operations with RBS's derivatives operations at the time. Through the joint venture, RBS traded numerous physical commodities relating to the energy market, as well as hired third-party companies to process its commodities for future sale, setting a precedent of large opportunities in trading physical commodities for FHCs (Omarova 2013).

Following these regulatory changes early in the twenty-first century, three other financial institutions rose to dominance in the activities pertaining to investing in physical commodities: JP Morgan Chase & Company, Goldman Sachs Group, Inc., and Morgan Stanley. At the end of 2012, these three companies reported physical commodity inventory of $16.2 billion, $7.3 billion, and $11.7 billion, respectively (Omarova 2013). These FHCs could compete in the physical commodities markets with additional advantages over other competitors in the respective markets. Some advantages include lower borrowing costs and capital requirements where, in 2012, the Federal Reserve Commodities Team found that corporations with operations relevant to the oil and gas industries has an average capital ratio of 42 percent to cover losses, whereas subsidies of BHCs had an average of only 8 to 10 percent (Levin and McCain 2014).

Though profitable in the operations themselves, FHCs' inclusion in trading physical assets allowed them to capitalize on other advantages. FHCs would have a continuous flow of information about transportation and storage conditions in the market that would prove beneficial for trading derivatives of commodities markets. The ramification of financing institutions involved in the physical commodities market had spillover effects for other market participants, such as manufacturers reliant on the market for raw materials for production. For example, the Coca-Cola Company filed a complaint against the London Metals Exchange in 2011 based on Goldman Sachs Group, Inc.'s trend of accumulating massive amounts of aluminum in storage in Detroit and Chicago. Coca-Cola claimed that Goldman Sachs's actions disrupted global supply chains and led to increasing aluminum prices. Given that aluminum was an integral component of the cans created by Coca-Cola, the resulting disruption and increasing prices led to increased operating expenses (Omarova 2013).

CTFs are likely to persist as long as the physical commodities markets offer opportunities for well-informed firms to capitalize on instances of a mispricing. However, the future for financial institutions is not as positive. The U.S. Federal Reserve Bank is contemplating the application of increased capital charges on large banks participating in the commodity markets, which could be as steep as 1,250 percent for firms such as Goldman Sachs and Morgan Stanley (Borak and Hoffman 2016). These and similar firms will likely remain in the market if they can make profits, but exit if they face additional capital requirements resulting in lower margins and increased complexity.

Summary and Conclusions

Managing physical commodities can be a troublesome venture for participants in the commodity markets without the means of handling the large commitment.

Each commodity type possesses a unique set of characteristics, affecting both the carrying costs in holding the commodity over time and potential ways to profit, such as through resale, value-added activities, or processing to create other products. The integration of the spot and futures markets provides market participants with the means of smoothing inventory needs overtime and hedging risks. Price differentials between these markets reflect changing supply and demand factors that cause price fluctuations, but arbitrageurs seek to align the two intertemporal markets. The large-scale volume in physical commodities precludes investment by most retail investors and smaller institutions but leaves room for larger-scale CTFs and other institutions such as FHCs to capture large profits through capitalizing on price discrepancies.

Discussion Questions

1. Discuss the effects of pairing transactions in commodity spot and futures markets.
2. Discuss the short-term effects of commodity super cycles on the commodity markets.
3. Explain how the need for transportation and storage affects physical commodities.
4. Discuss the interconnection between market interest and lease rates with the commodity markets.
5. Identify the largest participants within the physical commodity markets.

References

Alexander, Corinne, and Phil Kenkel. 2012. "Economics of Commodity Storage." In W. David Hagstrum, Thomas W. Phillips, and Gerrit Cuperus (eds.), *Stored Product Protection*, 305-315. Manhattan: Kansas State University.

Benirschka, Martin, and James K. Binkley. 1995. "Optimal Storage and Marketing over Space and Time." *American Journal of Agricultural Economics* 77:3, 512-524.

Borak, Donna, and Liz Hoffman. 2016. "Fed Targets Big Bank Commodity Lines." September. Available at http://www.wsj.com/articles/fed-proposes-limits-on- bank-commodity-trading-1474646400.

Brennan, Michael J. 1958. "The Supply of Storage." *American Economic Review* 48:1, 50-72.

Brooks, Chris, Emese Lazar, Lazaros Symeonidis, and Marcel Prokopczuk. 2012. "Futures Basis, Inventory and Commodity Price Volatility: An Empirical Analysis." *Economic Modelling* 29:6, 2651-2663.

CME Group. 2015. "CME Group to Close Most Open Outcry Futures Trading in Chicago and New York by July; Most Options Markets to Remain Open." February. Available at http://www.prnewswire.com/news-releases/cme-group-to-close-most-open-outcry-futures-trading-in-chicago-and-new-york-by-july-most-options-markets-to-remain-open-300031191.html.

Comtois, Claude, Jean-Paul Rodrigue, and Brian Slack. 2016. "Transportation Modes, Modal Competition and Modal Shift." *The Geography of Transport Systems*. New York, NY: Routledge.

Cuddington, John T., and Daniel Jerrett. 2008. "Super Cycles in Real Metals Prices?" *IMF Staff Papers* 55:4, 541-565.

Debrouillard Group. 2016. "History." Available at https://tradingpithistory.com/history/.

Encyclopedia Britannica. 2016. "Chicago Board of Trade (CBOT)." September. Available at https://www.britannica.com/topic/Chicago-Board-of-Trade.

Erten, Bilge, and Jose A. Ocampo. 2012. "Super-cycles of Commodity Prices since the Mid-Nineteenth Century." Working Paper, United Nations Department of Economic and Social Affairs.

Frankel, Jeffrey A. 2006. "The Effect of Monetary Policy on Real Commodity Prices." Working Paper, National Bureau of Economic Research. Available at http://www.nber.org/papers/w12713.pdf.

Gensler, Gary. 2009. "Testimony before the United States Senate Subcommittee on Financial Services and General Government Committee on Appropriations." Available at http://www.cftc.gov/PressRoom/SpeechesTestimony/opagensler-2.

Gorton, Gary B., and Geert K. Rouwenhorst. 2006. "Facts and Fantasies about Commodity Futures." *Financial Analysts Journal* 62:2, 47-68.

Harvey, David I., Neil M. Kellard, Jakob B. Madsen, and Mark E. Wohar. 2010. "The Prebisch-Singer Hypothesis: Four Centuries of Evidence." *Review of Economics and Statistics* 92:2, 367-377.

Heap, Alan. 2005. "China—the Engine of a Commodities Super Cycle." March. Available at http://www.fallstreet.com/Commodities_China_Engine0331.pdf.

Johnson, Leland L. 1960. "The Theory of Hedging and Speculation in Commodity Futures." *Review of Economic Studies* 27:3, 139-151.

Lee, M. K., and E. A. Elsayed. 2005. "Optimization of Warehouse Storage Capacity under a Dedicated Storage Policy." *International Journal of Production Research* 43:9, 1785-1805.

Levin, Carl, and John McCain. 2014. "Wall Street Bank Involvement with Physical Commodities." *United States Senate Permanent Subcommittee on Investigations: Committee on Homeland Security and Governmental Affairs*. November. Available at https://www.hsgac.senate.gov/download/report-wall-street-involvement-with-physical-commodities.

Marr-Johnson, Merlin. 2009. "The Effect of Lease Rates on Precious Metals Markets." *Alchemist* 29, 20-22.

Mayer, Jörg. 2009. "The Growing Interdependence between Financial and Commodity Markets." October. Available at http://unctad.org/en/Docs/osgdp20093_en.pdf.

NASDAQ. 2012. "Commodity Family." OMX Group, Inc. Available at http://www.nasdaqtrader.com/content/ProductsServices/dataproducts/RealTimeIndexes/NASDAQCommodityFactSheet.pdf.

Notteboom, Theo, and Jean-Paul Rodrigue. 2016. "Transport Costs." *The Geography of Transportation Systems*. New York, NY: Routledge.

Omarova, Saule T. 2013. "The Merchants of Wall Street: Banking, Commerce, and Commodities." *Minnesota Law Review* 98, 265-355.

Pindyck, Robert S. 2001. "The Dynamics of Commodity Spot and Futures Markets: A Primer." *Energy Journal* 22:3, 1-28.

Pirrong, Craig. 2014 "The Economics of Commodity Trading Firms." March. Available at http://www.trafigura.com/media/1364/economics-commodity-trading-firms.pdf.

Roehner, Bertrand M. 1996. "The Role of Transportation Costs in the Economics of Commodity Markets." *American Journal of Agricultural Economics* 78:2, 339-353.

Roehner, Bertrand M. 2000. "The Correlation Length of Commodity Markets 1. Empirical Analysis." *European Physical Journal B: Condensed Matter and Complex Systems* 13:1, 175-187.

Schnepf, Randy. 2006. *Price Determination in Agricultural Commodity Markets: A Primer*. Library of Congress. Congressional Research Service.

Schnabel, Jacques A. 2010. "Interest Rates, Commodity Prices, and the Cost-of-Carry Model." *Journal of Risk Finance* 11:2, 221-223.

Trafigura. 2016. "Commodities Demystified: A Guide to Trading and the Global Supply Chain." Available at http://www.commoditiesdemystified.info/pdf/Commodities Demystified-summary-en.pdf.

United Nations Conference on Trade and Development (UNCTAD). 2009. "Overview of the World's Overview of the World's Commodity Exchanges—2007." Available at http://unctad.org/en/Docs/ditccom20084_en.pdf.

Weymar, Helmut F. 1966. "The Supply of Storage Revisited." *American Economic Review* 56:5, 1226-1234.

Working, Holbrook. 1948. "Theory of the Inverse Carrying Charge in Futures Market." *Journal of Farm Economics* 30:1, 1-28.

8

Agricultural

NICOLE MORAN
Senior Manager, Cornerstone Research

KELSEY SYVRUD
Associate, Cornerstone Research

Introduction

Agricultural commodities are products derived from agricultural activities, such as farming and growing crops. Some agricultural commodities, such as corn, wheat, and soybeans, are a direct product of agricultural activities, while others, such as soybean meal and soybean oil, are byproducts, derived from an underlying raw agricultural commodity. According to the World Bank, in 2014 agriculture contributed approximately \$2.894 trillion to worldwide wealth in terms of constant 2010 U.S. dollars (World Bank Group 2016a, 2016b). Many developing and emerging nations rely heavily on the revenue earned from exporting agricultural commodities as a major source of national income. For developed economies, the United States is the largest producer of agricultural goods, measured by gross domestic product (GDP), out of the G-10 countries with more than \$179 trillion of GDP (World Bank Group 2016a, 2016b).

Table 8.1 displays the 10 countries most reliant on agriculture in Panel A, the G-10 countries in Panel B, and the world in Panel C, ranked according to agriculture as a percentage of a country's GDP in 2014. This table reveals several key points. First, agriculture makes up, on average, more than 40 percent of the GDP for the 10 countries with the heaviest reliance on agriculture as an economic driver—frontier markets which are the least developed countries in the world. Second, agriculture makes up a small portion of GDP for many developed nations. For instance, agriculture contributed only 1.3 percent of the U.S. GDP in 2014, although this amount translates to more than \$179 billion (World Bank Group 2016a, 2016b). As Figure 8.1 shows, the United States trades billions of dollars in agricultural goods each month and agriculture is consistently a sector that creates a GDP surplus, not a deficit. For instance, in December 2015, the United States exported more than \$11 billion and imported more than \$9 billion in agricultural goods (ERS 2016).

This chapter focuses on agricultural commodities. Some main differences between agricultural commodities and non-agricultural commodities include seasonal production, the necessity of storage and gradual consumption until the next harvest, and

Table 8.1 **Selected Countries Ranked on Agriculture Value Added**

	U.S. Dollars (Billions)		*Percent of GDP*	
Country	*1997*	*2014*	*1997*	*2014*
Panel A. The 10 countries with the heaviest reliance on agriculture (as percent of GDP)				
Sierra Leone	770	1,567	58.65	54.06
Chad	—	5,955	39.94	52.62
Central African Republic	568	580	54.78	47.77
Guinea-Bissau	—	428	54.60	43.92
Togo	1,012	1,301	42.19	42.04
Ethiopia	6,907	16,026	57.72	41.92
Mali	1,315	5,483	39.35	40.33
Burundi	878	861	47.73	39.26
Niger	—	2,829	38.87	36.53
Comoros	149	242	40.89	35.58
Panel B. G-10 countries				
Italy	37,127	36,996	3.15	2.16
Netherlands	12,429	14,645	3.25	1.83
France	37,441	44,817	2.63	1.73
Sweden	5,914	7,200	2.42	1.38
United States	109,956	179,602	1.38	1.33
Japan	76,375	65,873	1.63	1.17
Switzerland	4,036	4,249	1.34	0.75
Belgium	2,997	3,315	1.48	0.70
United Kingdom	14,713	18,763	1.18	0.69
Germany	22,447	23,553	1.08	0.68
Canada	—	24,031	—	—
Panel C. World				
World	1,812,590	2,894,379	6.08	3.88

Note: This table lists agriculture value added as a dollar value and a percentage of each country's GDP in 1997 and 2014, ranked according to agriculture as a percentage of GDP in 2014. Panel A displays the 10 countries with the heaviest reliance on agriculture as a source of GDP. Panel B displays the G-10 countries. Panel C displays figures for the world. All dollar values are reported in terms of constant 2010 U.S. dollars. Values of "—" indicates no reported data for that country/year. The World Bank defines agriculture as corresponding to the International Standard Industrial Classification (ISIC) divisions 1 to 5 and includes forestry, hunting, and fishing, as well as cultivation of crops and livestock production.

Source: World Bank Group (2016a).

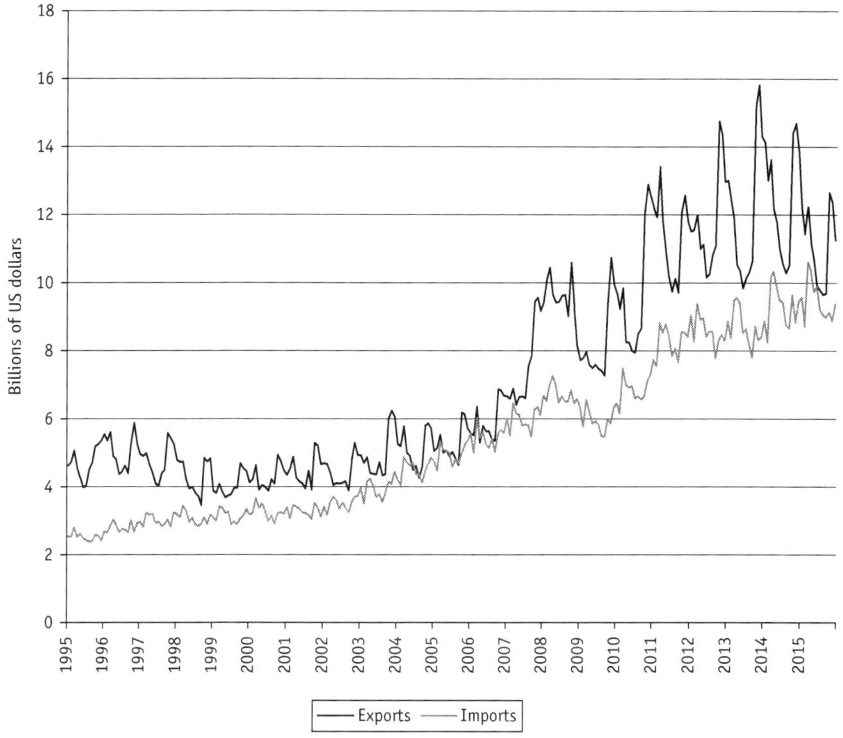

Figure 8.1 U.S. Agricultural Trade
This figure depicts the monthly exports and imports for agricultural trade in the United States. These figures are in billions of U.S. dollars for the time period of 1995 to 2015. Source: ERS (2016).

perishability. The chapter is organized as follows. The next section provides a background in investing in agricultural commodities, followed by a description of major price determinants. The subsequent section includes an in-depth description of 12 agricultural products traded on futures exchanges. The following section discusses where to find market information on agricultural commodities. The chapter closes with a short summary.

Investing in Agricultural Products

Investment and hedging markets have developed as a result of the importance of agriculture to the United States and global economies. Investments in agriculture are available in many forms, including physical products, over-the-counter (OTC) products, and exchange-traded futures and options. Investors may also use securities markets by investing in exchange-traded funds (ETFs) and stocks related to companies in the business of agricultural commodities (e.g., Cargill, ADM, and Bunge).

Physical products represent the actual ownership of the commodity itself, such as owning corn or soybeans in the physical form. OTC contracts are made bilaterally or through a dealer network rather than though a centralized exchange and can be physically or cash settled. For example, a flour mill might generate a forward contract with a wheat farmer. A forward contract is a legally binding contract to buy or sell specific assets at a specific price on a given date in the future. For example, the mill would agree to buy wheat from the farmer in three months at a set fixed price. This arrangement represents an example of a physically settled OTC contract, as the mill will physically obtain ownership of the wheat from the farmer at the end of three months based on the agreed price in the forward contract.

Commodity contract prices can also be determined via the *basis*, defined as the difference or spread between a futures price and specified cash price. For a given commodity with a fixed end date, *t*, the basis calculated as a formula can be written as Equation 8.1:

$$\text{Basis}_t = \text{Cash price}_t - \text{Futures price}_t \tag{8.1}$$

For example, the two parties may define their basis contract as the difference between the CME Group (CME) soft red winter wheat futures contract price and the prevailing Toledo wheat cash price published by the Agricultural Marketing Service (AMS). In this case, at the agreed end date of the contract, the two counterparties would exchange the physical commodity or cash payment based on the difference between the two prices.

Agricultural commodities can also be traded via the exchange-traded futures and options markets. The most cited and frequently consulted location for agricultural commodity prices is futures exchanges, with the two most prominent being the CME and the Intercontinental Exchange (ICE). Between 2007 and 2015, the average daily volume of agricultural commodity contracts traded on the CME has increased almost 74 percent (CME 2016).

The ICE is the other major exchange that trades agricultural commodities, specifically many soft commodities. A *soft commodity*, or softs, is a commodity such as cocoa, coffee, corn, fruits, livestock, soybeans, sugar, and wheat. Softs typically refers to commodities that are grown, rather than mined such as copper, gold, and oil, which are called *hard commodities*. The ICE became a publicly traded company in 2005 and quickly expanded, acquiring the New York Board of Trade in 2007, a major venue for trading futures and options on soft commodities (ICE 2007). Many of the CME's soft commodity futures contracts are tied to the pricing of the same commodity listed on ICE. Additionally, combinations of agricultural futures contracts may be traded on these exchanges to create additional products, such as calendar spreads, that may be of interest to investors.

Exchange-traded futures must have a close relation with the underlying cash agricultural commodity in which the futures contract is pricing. At expiration, the futures contract must converge to the price of the underlying commodity. Before expiration, the futures contract and underlying spot prices may differ due to storage costs and opportunity costs of foregone interest based on the time to expiration. If the futures price differs from the price of storage and opportunity costs, arbitrage can occur.

A lack of convergence between the futures and spot prices at expiration is symptomatic of problems with contract performance or contract design. In recent years, convergence problems have occurred in wheat and corn contracts traded on the CME. In response, the CME made contract design changes to improve the functioning and convergence of the contracts.

One of the changes included adding additional delivery points for the underlying physical commodity to be delivered on the futures contract to ensure the delivery points were in the flow of commerce for that agricultural product. The CME also changed the delivery mechanism of these contracts from a warehouse receipt to a shipping certificate. Although warehouse receipts required possessing the commodity at the warehouse in order to issue a certificate, the shipping certificate does not require possession of the commodity at the time of certificate issuance. The CME made the switch to provide more flexibility to companies making delivery of the commodity on futures contracts, as more delivery encourages convergence.

Another contract change was the storage rate charged by companies that delivered the shipping certificates to the buying party taking delivery. The buyer is not obligated to immediately take delivery of the physical commodity if the buyer pays the seller a futures contract specified storage charge. During the review of the futures contract specs, some individuals maintained that the exchange set storage rates were too low compared to actual market storage, which, when coupled with a "full carry" market, resulted in non-convergence. *Full carry* is defined when the difference between a nearer to expiration futures contract and a more deferred futures contract is roughly equivalent to the cost of storage and interest cost from holding the commodity from one maturity to another. The contract and market conditions incentivize the buyer to hold the shipping certificates, pay the storage rate, and then deliver the shipping certificates on positions in subsequent futures contracts. The strategy is called *cash and carry* and can be profitable in a low interest rate and full carry market.

On May 1, 1991, S&P launched the S&P GSCI (Goldman Sachs Commodity Index) Agriculture Index, an index based on the performance of agricultural commodities, and a sub-index of the S&P GSCI that includes non-agricultural and agricultural commodities (S&P 2016). Between 2005 and 2011, annual S&P GSCI Agriculture index returns ranged from a low of −28.8 percent in 2008 to a high of 34.2 percent in 2010. This index is volatile, with a 10-year standard deviation of 25.4 percent (Bloomberg 2016). According to Huchet-Bourdon (2011), between 2006 and 2008, rice prices increased by 130 percent, butter prices by 110 percent, soybean oil by 105 percent, corn by 83 percent, and whole milk powder by 79 percent. A sharp drop in commodity prices followed this run-up in prices.

Figure 8.2 shows the "boom" and "bust" in commodities prices for the GSCI Commodity and GSCI Agricultural indices relative to the S&P 500 index from May 20, 2006, to September 29, 2011. During the global financial crisis of 2007–2008, equity markets declined while commodity prices increased, attracting investors to the commodity indexes. Further, the increase in the production of biofuels drove demand for agricultural commodities, such as corn and soybeans, contributing to higher market prices for these products. Additionally, increased demand from emerging nations including China also supported increasing prices.

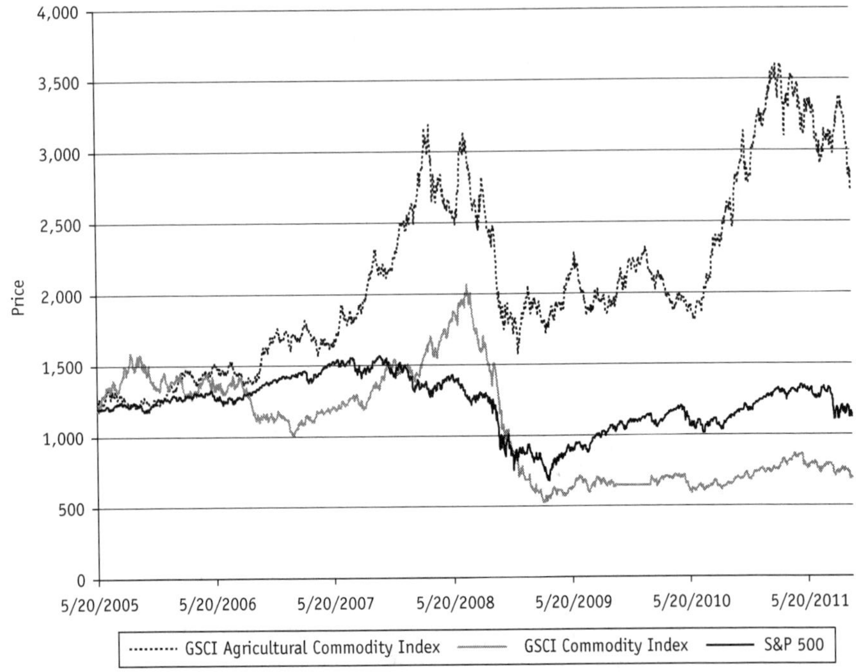

Figure 8.2 Price of S&P Indices: May 20, 2005 to September 29, 2011
This figure lists the daily closing price of the S&P GSCI Index, the S&P GSCI Agricultural Index, and the S&P 500 index from May 20, 2005 to September 29, 2011. These series have been pegged to a value of 1,191.08, the value of the S&P 500 on May 19, 2005. For days where price data are missing, the return for the day is set to zero. The process of pegging uses the daily returns of each of these indices in order to show how the price series have evolved compared to one another. Source: Bloomberg (2016).

Commodity indexes, such as the GSCI Agricultural index, were created to allow investors, such as hedge funds, pension funds, and other large institutional investors, the ability to invest in commodities without having to purchase the underlying physical commodities. Investment in commodities indexes increased substantially between 2003 and 2008. According to the 2009 report published by the U.S. Senate Permanent Subcommittee on Investigations (PSI 2009), the total value of investments in commodity indexes rose from $15 billion in 2003, to about $200 billion in mid-2008. This report created a debate between fundamental drivers of price and speculative investment impacts on price. In 2009, the U.S. Senate produced a report voicing concerns over index investment and investor speculation, specifically in the wheat market.

Figure 8.2 highlights the rise in agricultural commodity prices from 2006 into 2008. During this time, commodity index traders held roughly 35 to 50 percent of outstanding wheat contracts on the CME and about 20 to 30 percent of the outstanding contracts on the Kansas City Board of Trade (PSI 2009). Although the investment in agricultural commodities increased, fundamental economic factors also influenced higher agricultural products prices, including "slower growth in production and more rapid growth in demand that have contributed to a tightening of world balances of grains and oilseeds" (Trostle 2008, p. 1; Trostle, Marti, Rosen, and Westcott 2011).

Price Determinants of Agricultural Commodities

Although each commodity is subject to unique price determinants, some broad factors that impact many of the agricultural commodities include, but are not limited to, weather changes, storability and seasonality of each product, stocks-to-use ratios, and government regulation. Weather, including natural disasters, can drastically affect the prices of agricultural products. Early frosts or local droughts can have large price impacts, not only on domestic prices but also in the international markets. Many agricultural products have a finite supply each year, and as such, weather changes impact the available supply, and therefore prices of these products.

Many agricultural products, with the exception of dairy products, cannot be produced throughout the year and are subject to specific planting and harvesting seasons. Although demand for products such as corn may remain steady throughout the year, the production and therefore supply of corn is not constant. Each year, as corn is harvested, the large increase in the available supply typically lowers prices. Market prices serve as indicators to determine if the corn should be sold immediately or stored. In order for a seller to store corn, the seller must be compensated for the cost of storage and opportunity cost in future prices. Agricultural products, such as corn, can be stored for six months to a year, allowing the market to ration supply to match demand throughout the year (Glogoza and Nicolai 2014).

A common ratio monitored in the agricultural industry is the stocks-to-use ratio used to measure the supply and demand for commodities (Agricultural Market Information System 2015; Good and Irwin 2015). Specifically, the ratio measures the level of existing and carryover stock of a given product as a percentage of the commodity's total use. Stock that is carried over and stored from a previous production year can act as a buffer against unexpected supply and demand shocks in the current production year. The numerator of the ratio, or the stock level, is an indicator of the global supply available in the marketplace. The denominator of the ratio, or total use, is an indicator of the global demand for a commodity in a particular period. In general, low stocks relative to use indicate higher market volatility and prices and vice versa.

Government policies that attempt to stabilize product prices, produce a steady supply, and ensure quality of the produced products also affect prices. Policymakers use several tools, including subsidies, trade restrictions, and price controls. For instance, the U.S. government subsidizes crop insurance to protect farmers from catastrophic loss to help ensure a stable food supply. Related to international trade, governments may establish trade quotas or tariffs in efforts to limit the imports of foreign goods, or to raise the cost of imported goods for consumers, making domestically produced goods cheaper in comparison. Lastly, governments may also use price controls to stabilize market prices. Price ceilings may lead to lower production and price floors may lead to excessive production.

Major Agricultural Products

As Table 8.2 shows, the key agricultural commodities can be loosely classified into the following categories: (1) grains and oilseeds, (2) dairy, (3) softs, and (4) livestock (Bloomberg 2016; CME 2016). The following discussion focuses on the 12 largest agricultural commodities in international trade and those available on futures exchanges. Chapter 10 discusses livestock.

Table 8.3 displays generic production, consumption, import, and export data for each of the 12 discussed products within the United States and for the rest of the world (in table identified as "World Excluding the United States").

GRAINS AND OILSEEDS

The first category of agricultural commodities highlights grain and oilseed products. According to the Agricultural Marketing Resource Center (AMRC 2016), *grains* are those products identified as cereals suitable as food for humans, and oilseeds are grains also used for their oil content. The majority of these products are used for livestock feed, human consumption, and more recently to produce alternative fuels. This section provides overviews of corn, soybeans, wheat, and rice, which are four of the major grain and oilseed commodities.

Corn

In the United States, corn is the primary grain produced and used for livestock feed. According to the U.S. Department of Agriculture (USDA 2016a), corn accounts for more than 95 percent of the total U.S. feed grain production, and more than 90 million acres are devoted to the planting of corn each year. Before 2006, more than

Table 8.2 **Agricultural Commodity Classifications**

	Category			
	Grains and Oilseeds	***Dairy***	***Softs***	***Livestock***
Products	Corn	Milk	Cocoa	Live cattle
	Soybean	Dry milk	Coffee	Lean hog
	Soybean oil	Dry whey	Sugar	Feeder cattle
	Wheat	Butter	Cotton	
	Soybean meal	Cheese		
	Rough rice			

Note: This table classifies the major agricultural commodity products.

Source: CME Group (2016) and Bloomberg (2016).

Table 8.3 **Agricultural Commodity Supply and Demand Information**

	United States				*World Excluding the United States*			
	Produced	*Imports*	*Exports*	*Consumption*	*Produced*	*Imports*	*Exports*	*Consumption*
Panel A. Grains								
Corn	345,486	1,650	49,500	298,887	613,539	137,320	89,470	659,200
Soybean	106,934	680	52,798	54,955	206,038	130,183	78,065	261,345
Soybean oil	10,015	125	1,089	9,071	41,974	11,525	11,060	42,380
Soybean meal	40,769	363	10,705	30,391	177,089	63,827	56,070	185,243
Wheat	55,840	3,056	21,856	31,589	678,957	168,930	150,130	700,911
Rough rice	6,107	765	3,450	3,529	465,586	40,488	37,803	469,857
Panel B. Dairy								
Cows' milk	94,620	—	—	26,789	399,069	—	—	153,350
Whole milk powder	49	9	16	48	4,773	1,005	2,087	3,841
Nonfat dry milk	1,029	2	560	487	3,683	1,178	1,499	3,291
Dry whey	—	—	—	—	—	—	—	—
Butter	843	39	23	836	9,037	243	885	8,344
Cheese	5,370	157	317	5,152	13,562	1,493	962	13,033
Panel C. Softs								
Cocoa	—	445	17	—	—	2,498	2,708	—
Coffee	50	24,950	0	24,767	153,242	96,097	132,495	124,323
Sugar	8,104	2,931	0	10,887	156,819	51,506	54,871	160,912
Cotton	12,888	33	9,153	3,450	83,551	34,718	25,671	106,630

Note: This table lists production, trade, and consumption statistics for the major agricultural commodities during the 2015–2016 trade year. Unless otherwise stated, all values are in thousands of metric tons. Coffee is displayed in terms of thousand 60-kilogram bags, and cotton is displayed in terms of 1,000 hectare (HA) and 1,000 480-pound bales. Rough rice is proxied by milled rice. Due to availability, cocoa data are provided for the 2013 trade year. Values of "—" indicate no reported data for that commodity/trade year.

Source: USDA (2016), FAS (2016), and FAO (2016).

50 percent of U.S. corn production was used for livestock feed. More recently, a portion of demand for corn has shifted away from livestock feed and into the creation of biofuels. Figure 8.3 shows that in 1980, only 5 percent of corn went to the creation of biofuels but this amount increased to 80 percent by 2015. Between 1995 and 2013, the corn demand for food, seed, and industrial products increased 293 percent, while the demand related to the feed industry only rose 13 percent. Corn is also processed into various other products, including starch, corn oil, alcohol, and fuel ethanol, with fuel ethanol primarily driving the demand for corn in the last decade.

The United States is the largest producer of corn in the world. According to Panel A of Table 8.3, the United States produced 345,486 thousand metric tons of corn during the 2015–2016 trade year. The rest of the world produced 613,539 thousand metric tons, with China and Brazil as the second and third largest producers, respectively. The United States is also a major player in the corn trade. For example, in the 2015–2016 trade year, the United States comprised about 36 percent of all corn exported, which equates to roughly 14.3 percent of the total domestic production that year. Although the United States is a major corn exporter, much of the corn produced within the United States is consumed domestically. In 2015–2016, the United States consumed 298,887 thousand metric tons of corn, roughly 87 percent of total U.S. corn production.

Within the United States, the majority of corn is produced in the Heartland region with Illinois and Iowa as the two top corn-producing states, typically yielding about 33 percent of total domestic production (USDA 2016a). Within the United States, corn generally has a one-month planting cycle that starts between March and June of each year, with the majority of the planting occurring in March and April. Typically, corn is harvested between August and December, with the primary harvesting season happening in October and November (USDA 2010). The acreage devoted to corn in the United States has increased drastically from only 60.2 million acres in 1983 to 90 million acres by 2015. This increase is caused in part by the Federal Agricultural Improvement and Reform Act of 1996, which allowed farms to decide which crops to plant (USDA 2016a). Corn is storable from one crop year to the next, and storage life is dependent on the moisture content of the kernels and grain temperature (Glogoza and Nicolai 2014).

The price of corn has been highly volatile since the mid-2000s. The average price per bushel of corn in 2005 was $2.00, which then spiked to $6.89 in 2012, and decreased to $3.61 in 2015 (USDA 2006; Thiesse 2016a, 2016b). The use of corn for biofuels, mostly ethanol, has drastically influenced corn prices. In 2015, biofuels constituted more than 40 percent of U.S. corn consumption (USDA 2016a). Figure 8.4 depicts a positive correlation between the use of corn for biofuels and the price of corn between 2001 and 2015.

Corn is also one of the most actively traded agricultural futures. The primary exchange involved in the trading of corn is the CME. Corn futures are heavily traded, and therefore very liquid. One CME corn futures contract is for the delivery of 5,000 bushels. Mini-Corn futures contracts are also available for the delivery of only 1,000 bushels, as well as options on the corn futures (CME 2016). The settlement of these contracts, as with the other grain products, is *physical delivery,* which means if

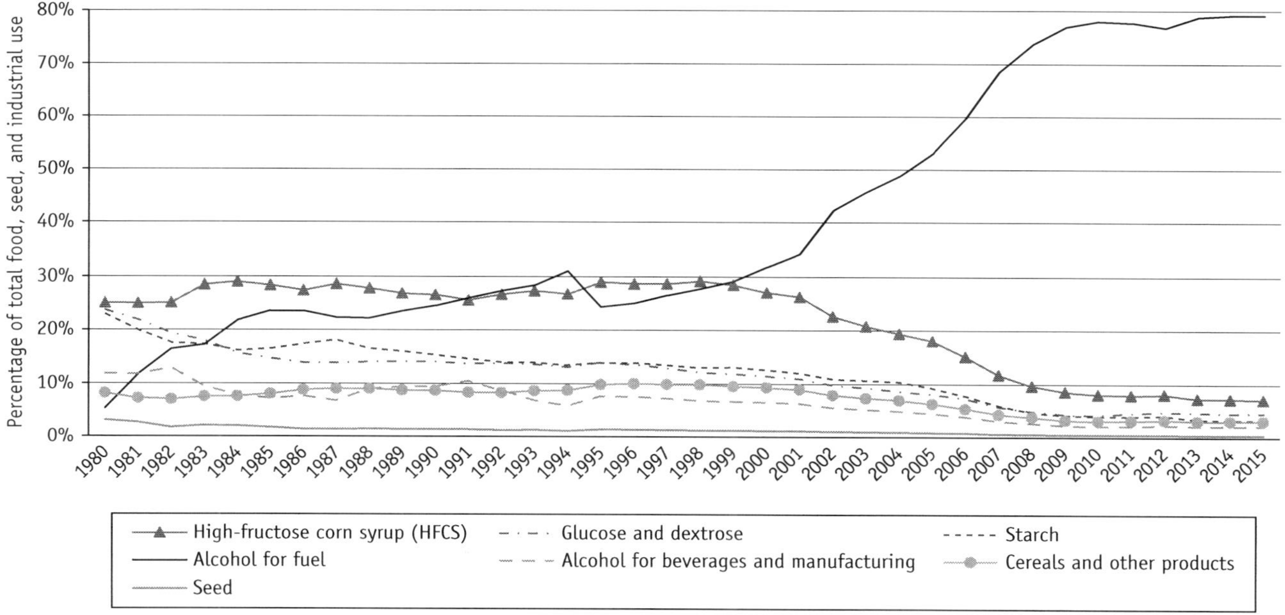

Figure 8.3 Usage of Corn Byproducts between 1980 and 2015
This figure lists the percentages of the total food, seed, and industrial use per byproduct between 1980 and 2015. Source: ERS (2016).

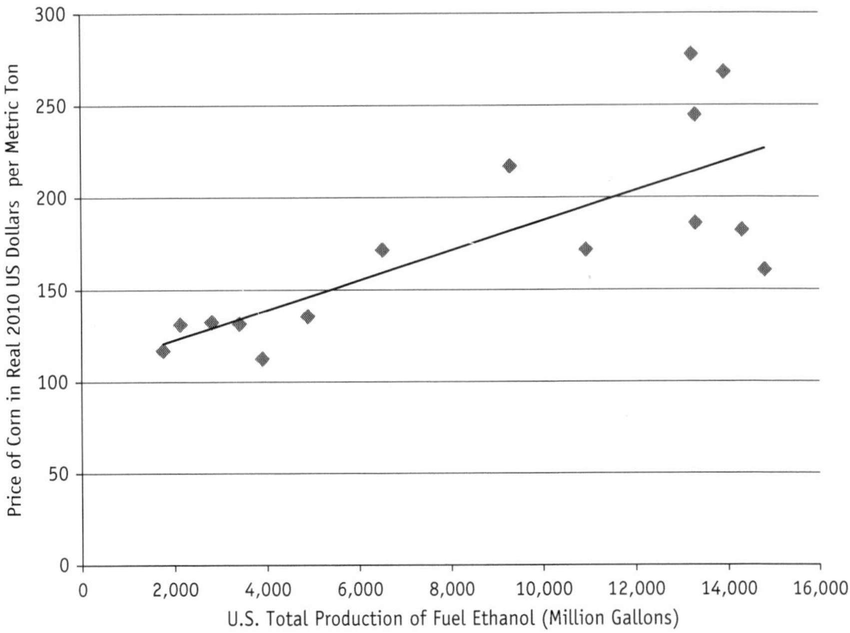

Figure 8.4 Corn Price versus Ethanol Usage between 2001 and 2015
This scatterplot charts the percentage of corn used in alcohol for fuel (ethanol) against the price of corn per metric ton between 2001 and 2015. All dollar values are reported in terms of real 2010 U.S. dollars. A linear line of best fit has been placed over the chart to highlight the relation between the price of corn and the total production of ethanol in the United States. Sources: EIA (2016b); World Bank Commodity Price Data (2016).

a futures contract is held to expiration, a shipping certificate is received that provides ownership of the corn that can be physically delivered by the seller of the contract.

Soybeans and Soybean Byproducts

In the United States, soybeans are the second most planted crop and account for approximately 90 percent of all oilseeds produced (USDA 2016d). Soybeans are rarely used in their raw state and are typically crushed to obtain the meal and oil. Although soybeans are an oilseed, only 20 percent of soybeans are used for oil, and in recent years, soybeans have primarily been used as meal due to their high protein content. Generally, soybean meal is used as livestock feed, but soybean meal is occasionally used for human food. Soybean oil is used as cooking oil, as well as in industrial products including paint, lubricants, and plastics. Over the last few years, soybeans have been used for biodiesel, accounting for about 30 percent of soybean consumption in the United States (Martin 2014). Figure 8.5 depicts the relation between soybean prices and biodiesel production within the United States from 2001 to 2015, and shows a strong positive correlation.

As with corn, the United States is the largest producer and exporter of soybeans in the world. According to the USDA (2016d), more than 80 million acres were planted

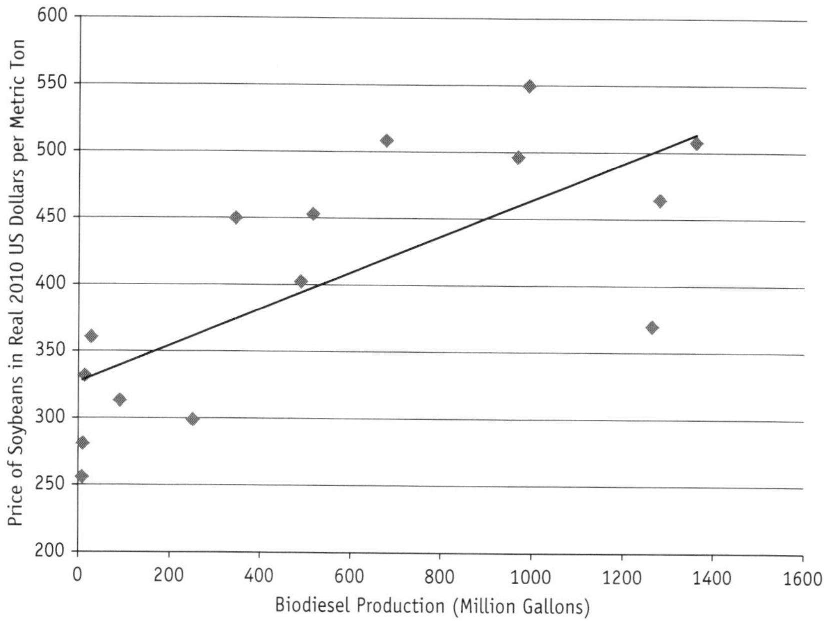

Figure 8.5 Soybean Price versus Biodiesel Production between 2001 and 2015
This scatterplot charts the production of biodiesel in million gallons against the price of soybeans per metric ton between 2001 and 2015. All dollar values are reported in terms of real 2010 U.S. dollars. A linear line of best fit has been placed over the chart to show the relation between the price of soybeans and production of biodiesel. Source: World Bank Commodity Price Data; EIA (2016a).

with soybeans in 2015. As Panel A of Table 8.3 shows, the United States produced 106,934 thousand metric tons of soybeans in the 2015–2016 trade year. The rest of the world produced 206,038 thousand metric tons, with Brazil and Argentina as the second and third largest producers. Although the United States is the top exporter of raw soybeans, Argentina is the top exporter of soybean byproducts: soybean oil and soybean meal. Argentina alone exports roughly half of all soybean byproducts worldwide. In the 2015–2016 trade year, the United States comprised about 41 percent of all soybeans exported, roughly 9 percent of all soybean oil exports, and 16 percent of exported soybean meal. In 2015–2016 the United States consumed 54,955 thousand metric tons of soybeans, about half of its total soybean production.

Within the United States, the majority of soybeans are planted in the upper Midwestern states, and as with corn, Illinois and Iowa are the two largest soybean producers. The planting cycle for soybeans begins in April and May and lasts until June and July of each year. The harvesting period generally starts in September and October and finishes in November and December (USDA 2010). Typically, soybeans are grown in a crop rotation with corn to maximize soil nutrients. Lauer, Porter, and Oplinger (1997) find that while this rotation optimizes corn yields, it does not maximize soybean yields. In a 2013 *Corn+Soybean Digest* article, soybean agronomist Shawn Conley states that a corn-soybean rotation is “a good risk-management strategy for both crops" (Morrison 2013, p. 3). This article highlights that crop rotation reduces nitrogen expenses, the use of insecticides, and the population of corn rootworms. As with corn, soybeans can be stored from one harvest to the next, and the length of time depends on the moisture content and grain temperature (Glogoza and Nicolai 2014).

The prices of soybeans have generally increased over the last decade. During the 2005 trade year the average price per bushel of soybeans was $5.66, spiked to $14.40 in 2012, and was $10.10 in 2014 (USDA 2016d). The use of soybeans in biodiesel, reaching 30 percent of U.S. soybean oil in 2013, has influenced soybean prices (CommodityBasis 2016). Additionally, high protein content makes soybeans an excellent food source for livestock and the demand will also influence soybean prices (Willis 2003).

The primary exchange trading soybean futures is the CME, which lists separate futures contracts for raw soybeans, crushed soybeans, soybean meal, and soybean oil. One CME soybean futures contract is for the delivery of 5,000 bushels. Mini-Soybean futures contracts are also available, as well as options on soybean futures. The settlement of these contracts, as with corn, is physical delivery.

Wheat

Wheat is the third most planted crop in the United States, although total acres of harvested wheat have declined by roughly 33 percent since peaking in 1981 (USDA 2016f). The decline is partially due to legislation granting farmers more choice in the production of crops and because of the reduced profitability of wheat relative to other crops. Wheat is the primary food grain produced within the United States, with human consumption being the principal use. Wheat is used to produce such items as bread, baked goods, noodles, crackers, and cereals. Wheat byproducts, such as bran, shorts, and middlings, are used as livestock feed, which is roughly 9 percent of wheat use (Zulauf 2016). Unlike corn and soybeans, renewable fuels are not a major use of wheat.

Wheat is the second largest crop produced worldwide by volume (USDA 2016f). The European Union (EU), China, and India are the three largest wheat-producing areas. The United States ranked fifth in wheat production. As Panel A of Table 8.3 shows, the United States produced 55,840 thousand metric tons of wheat in the 2015–2016 trade year, and the rest of the world produced 678,957 thousand metric tons. Much of the wheat produced within the United States is exported. In the 2015–2016 trade year, the United States comprised about 13 percent of all exported wheat, although it only accounts for roughly 8 percent of total wheat production. In 2015–2016 the United States consumed 31,589 thousand metric tons of wheat, about half of the total U.S. wheat production.

Within the United States, the majority of wheat is produced in Kansas and North Dakota. The two primary varieties of wheat grown within the United States are winter wheat and spring wheat. Winter wheat comprises more than two-thirds of U.S. wheat production. Five classifications are within the winter and spring wheat categories: (1) hard red winter (HRW), (2) hard red spring (HRS), (3) soft red winter (SRW), (4) white, and (5) durum. The various classifications have different uses, are produced in different regions of the United States, and have different planting and harvesting schedules. Winter wheat is generally planted in the fall and is then harvested in the spring. Spring wheat and Great Plains Durum wheat are planted in late spring and are harvested in late summer. Desert Durum wheat is generally planted in the winter months between December and February and harvested in the early summer (USDA 2010). As with the other grain products, wheat can be stored from one harvest to the next harvest (Glogoza and Nicolai 2014). Hard wheat has a higher protein and gluten content than the spring varieties and is generally priced higher than soft wheat (USDA 2016f). Generally, hard wheat is used to produce hard baked goods such as bread, and soft wheat is often used in soft baked goods (CommodityBasis 2016).

Wheat futures are one of the more actively traded contracts for agricultural commodities (CME 2015). The most liquid futures contract on the CME is tied to SRW wheat, and acts as the primary indicator of wheat prices overall, as many wheat grades are priced at a spread against the SRW wheat contract. The other two main wheat contracts are for Kansas HRW and Minneapolis HRS wheat contracts. The CME Group purchased the Kansas City exchange and the HRW contract in December 2012, and the Minneapolis exchange with the HRS contract continues to exist (CommodityBasis 2016). Each wheat futures contract is for the delivery of 5,000 bushels. Mini-Wheat futures and options on wheat futures are also available. Additionally, the CME recently started offering EU Wheat futures. The settlement of these contracts, as with the other grain products, is physical delivery (CME 2016).

Rough Rice

Rice is one of the principal commodities used for human consumption worldwide. While Asia accounts for roughly 90 percent of global rice production, the vast majority is domestically consumed. In the 2015–2016 trade year, China and India produced 145,770 and 104,300 thousand metric tons of milled rice, respectively. For the same time period, the top three exporting countries were India, Thailand, and Vietnam, each only exporting between 6,000 and 10,000 thousand metric tons of milled rice, and the United States is the fifth largest exporter of rice (FAS 2016b). Rice is primarily used as food; however a small portion is also distilled for use in alcoholic beverages like beer, sake, and soju (USDA 2016c).

Rough rice is raw rice, and the milling process removes the bran and husk, creating a variety of rice products. Five different rice byproducts can be produced from raw rice: hulls, bran, brown rice, whole-kernel rice, and broken milled rice. According to the USDA, 100 pounds of rough rice roughly translates to 60 pounds of whole-kernel milled rice, 10 pounds of broken milled rice, 9 pounds of bran, and 20 pounds of hull (USDA 2016c). The USDA reports production, consumption, and trade numbers for milled rice, not rough rice. According to Table 8.3, Panel A, the United States produced 6,107 thousand metric tons of rice in the 2015–2016 trade year. The rest of the world produced 465,586 thousand metric tons. More than half of the rice produced within the United States is exported. In the 2015–2016 trade year exports from the United States comprised around 8 percent of all exported rice, although the United States only accounts for roughly 1.3 percent of total rice production.

The three primary rice types grown within the United States are long-grain, medium-grain, and short-grain. More than two-thirds of U.S. rice production is long-grain rice, followed by medium-grain, while only 2 percent of production is short-grain. The four regions that produce the majority of U.S. rice are the Arkansas Grand Prairie, the Mississippi Delta, the Gulf Coast, and the Sacramento Valley of California (USDA

2016c). Each region specializes in producing the various rice categories. Long-grain rice is primarily grown in the southern states, with medium-grain grown in southern states as well as California. The short-grain rice is grown almost entirely in California. Generally, the planting cycle for rice lasts between April and June, and it is harvested between August and October of each year (USDA 2010). As with the other grain products, the ability to store rice is highly dependent on the temperature and moisture content (University of Arkansas 2016).

About half of rice produced in the United States is exported, compared with roughly 14 percent of corn and 39 percent of wheat (USDA 2016c). As a result, U.S. rice farmers are more exposed to changes in global markets; changes in demand by major rice importers, such as China and India, have large impacts on rice prices. Because different varieties of rice are very climate and region specific, climate changes or weather events can drastically affect the price of various types of rice. Rice, in general, is a high-cost commodity to cultivate. Fuel and fertilizer prices influence growing costs, which in turn affect the price farmers charge for the produced rice.

Investors can trade rough rice futures contracts at the CME. However, the futures market for rice is not as developed or liquid as the corn, wheat, and soybean markets. One rough rice futures contract is for the delivery of 2,000 hundredweights of rough rice and is physically delivered (CME 2016).

DAIRY

The second category of agricultural commodities highlighted in this chapter is dairy products. According to the Agricultural Marketing Resource Center (AMRC 2016), dairy consists of those products identified as accessory production from livestock that are used for human consumption, specifically products that contain or are made from milk. This section reviews four of the major dairy commodities: milk, dry whey, butter, and cheese.

Milk, Fluid and Dry

In the United States, milk is a household staple. The past few decades have seen a decreasing number of U.S. dairy farms, coinciding with an increase in the number of cows per farm. Of the 131,509 licensed dairy farms in 1992, more than 80,028 farms exited the business in the following years. By 2012 only 51,481 U.S. licensed dairy farms remained. Over that same period, however, the average herd size increased about 142 percent (Hoard's Dairyman 2012). The United States is the world's second largest producer of milk, second only to the European Union.

According to the USDA (2016d), milk produced in the United States contains about 87.3 percent water, 3.8 percent milk fat, and 8.9 percent skim solids. Fluid milk is highly perishable, with a short shelf life. Dry milk, or powdered milk, is manufactured by evaporating and drying the produced cow milk. Dry milk does not need to be refrigerated and has a much longer shelf life than traditional fluid milk. Although various powdered milk products are available, this section focuses on nonfat dry milk (NDM) and whole powdered milk (WPM), which are commonly used in baked goods and in infant formula. Dried milk products are also found in food aid supplies for developing nations due to their nonperishable nature.

According to Panel B of Table 8.3, the United States produced 94,620 thousand metric tons of cows' milk, 1,029 thousand metric tons of NDM, and 49 thousand metric tons of WPM during 2015. The United States is also the third largest consumer of milk worldwide. In 2015, U.S. consumption of 26,789 thousand metric tons of cows' milk was behind India's 59,750 and the European Union's 34,000 thousand metric tons. The United States is also third, behind India and the European Union, in consumption of NDM. For WMP China is by far the largest consumer, consuming roughly 40 percent of the global production. Due to the highly perishable nature of fluid milk, much of the U.S. trade is limited to dry and powdered forms of milk. The United States is the second largest exporter of NDM, exporting roughly 27 percent of all exported NDM in 2015. New Zealand exports about 66 percent and China imports roughly 34 percent of worldwide WPM.

In the United States, federal and state dairy programs set a minimum milk price based on the value of the byproducts made from the milk. These byproducts are classified into four "classes" of milk: Class I includes fluid milk used in beverage products; Class II refers to milk used in "soft" products such as ice cream and yogurt; Class III includes milk used to make hard cheeses; and Class IV is used to make butter and dry products such as NDM and WPM. Each class of milk is priced based on the average weekly wholesale market price of various products monitored by the USDA.

The annual average minimum farm milk prices have been hitting record highs since 2012. Prices were increasing in 2012 and 2013 and hit record-high levels in 2014, exceeding \$24 per 100 pounds, before plummeting in 2015 to levels around \$15 per 100 pounds (Hoard's Dairyman 2012). Andrew Novakovic, a professor of agricultural economics at Cornell University, suggests that this trend is part of the typical three-year price cycle for milk. The strengthening of the dollar against milk-importing nations currencies further exacerbated the record high prices in 2014 (Associated Press 2015). Domestically, high milk prices encourage increased milk production, which leads to an oversupply of milk. However, dairy products do not have the same storability as grain products.

Investors can trade fluid milk and NDM futures contracts at the CME. Currently, the CME does not have futures contracts related to WPM. The Class III and Class IV milk futures contracts are each tied to 200,000 pounds of the corresponding milk class. One NDM futures contract is tied to 44,000 pounds of nonfat dry milk. Although options are available to trade on the underlying milk product futures contracts, no Mini contracts are available. The settlement of these various milk contracts, unlike the grain and oilseeds commodities, is not physical delivery, but instead a cash settlement based on the USDA price information.

Dry Whey

According to the American Dairy Products Institute (ADPI) whey is specifically the liquid obtained from separating the coagulum from fluid milk during the cheesemaking process. The most common form of whey, dry whey, is often used in food additives, given its high levels of minerals, protein, and lactose. In fact, dry whey often contains up to 75 percent lactose, which provides a sweet taste that can be used to replace sugar (Canadian Dairy Commission 2011). Whey protein supplements and whey protein isolates have become popular in the health industry as a good source of protein.

Whey protein is one of the largest sources of food protein. In 2013, worldwide product of dry whey was about 180 million metric tons. According to the *Dairy Processing Handbook*, whey protein is the most nutritionally valuable protein available (Tetra Pak 2016). In 2013, the total whey production contained about 1.5 million metric tons of protein. Whey is used for various sports and infant nutrition products as well as in manufactured products such as bakery and confectionary items. Whey is produced throughout the year, and the shelf life for dry whey is a maximum of about 12 months.

Investors can trade dry whey futures contracts at the CME. The dry whey futures contracts are each tied to 44,000 pounds of dry whey. The settlement of the dry whey contracts, similar to other milk byproduct futures, is not physical delivery, but instead a cash settlement. The cash settlement of the contract is based on the USDA monthly weighted average price for dry whey. Although options are available to trade on these futures contracts, no Mini contracts are currently available.

Butter

Butter is produced by churning cream or milk to separate butterfat from buttermilk, primarily from cows' milk. As Table B of Table 8.3 shows, worldwide production reached about 9,880 thousand metric tons of butter in 2015. The United States is the world's third largest producer of butter, behind India and the European Union. India alone accounts for more than half of the total global production of butter. In 2015 India produced 5,035 thousand metric tons of butter, whereas during the same year the United States produced 843 thousand metric tons. Much of the butter produced within each country is consumed domestically. For instance, India's 2015 butter consumption reached 5,026 thousand metric tons, roughly 99 percent of its total domestic production. Likewise, the United States consumed 836 thousand metric tons of butter during 2015. Given that the majority of butter production is consumed domestically, this leads to relatively low trade numbers. Looking at the United States, total butter exports were only 23 thousand metric tons, and total imports were roughly 39 thousand metric tons for 2015.

Investors can trade cash-settled butter futures contracts at the CME. The butter futures contracts are each tied to 20,000 pounds of butter.

Cheese

Cheese is formed via the coagulation of casein, a milk protein. As with butter, cheese can be produced from different mammals' milk, but this section focuses on cheese produced from cows' milk. As Panel B of Table 8.3 shows, worldwide production of cheese was about 18,932 thousand metric tons on 2015. The United States is the world's second largest producer of cheese, behind the European Union, which accounts for more than half of the total global production of cheese. In 2015 the European Union produced 9,690 thousand metric tons, whereas during the same year, the United States produced 5,370 thousand metric tons, or roughly half the production of the European Union. The European Union and the United States are also the two largest consumers of cheese. In 2015, the United States exported 317 thousand metric tons of cheese, or roughly 5.9 percent of domestic production. During the same year, the United States imported 157 thousand metric tons.

The International Dairy Federation recognizes more than 500 different types of cheese. Although no universal standard is available to classify cheese, the most commonly used system categorizes cheese based on moisture content, and then further breaks down the categories based on fat content, curing, and ripening methods. The USDA applies standards and grades to various cheese products. For example, Bulk American cheese refers to American cheeses that are packaged in "bulk form," weighing at least 100 pounds.

Investors can trade cash-settled cheese futures contracts at the CME, each of which is tied to 20,000 pounds of cheese.

SOFTS

Soft commodities are those products that are primarily grown in tropical climates. These products are used for human consumption and in the manufacturing of goods. This section reviews four major soft commodities: cocoa, coffee, sugar, and cotton.

Cocoa

The cultivation of cocoa, a product of the cocoa tree, is highly dependent on a tropical environment. As such, these trees are generally located in countries close to the equator in Africa, Asia, and Latin America and are a key export of these countries. Cocoa beans are predominantly grown in Africa, producing more than 70 percent of the global supply. In fact, Côte d'Ivoire alone produces roughly one-third of the global cocoa supply (ICCO 2016). Although the United States does not play a major role in growing cocoa trees, cocoa is mostly processed in the United States and the Netherlands. Cocoa is used in various products, including animal feed and cocoa butter, and more commonly in manufactured goods like chocolate, beverages, and other confectionary goods.

According to the International Cocoa Organization (ICCO), the global production of cocoa reached about 4 million metric tons during the 2015–2016 trade year. During 2014, the Americas produced about 18 percent while Asian and Oceanic countries produced roughly 10 percent (ICCO 2016). According to Panel C of Table 8.3, U.S. imports amounted to 445 thousand metric tons of cocoa in 2013, making up about 15 percent of global cocoa bean imports, as the rest of the world imported roughly 2,498 thousand metric tons during the same period. In the 2013 trade year global cocoa exports reached 2,725 thousand metric tons, with the United States exporting 17 thousand metric tons, or slightly less than 1 percent of global exports.

Once planted, each cocoa tree takes about three to five years before it becomes productive (ICCO 1998). The actual harvesting of cocoa varies by country and variety and is spread over several months, once or twice a year. In Côte d'Ivoire, for example, the main crop is harvested between October and March with a secondary harvest season lasting from May to August (ICCO 2014). Generally, during each harvest, a cocoa tree produces about 20 pods, yielding roughly four pounds of cocoa. These yields are sensitive to environmental changes such as pests, diseases, droughts, floods, as well as climate changes (DraKoln 2016; WorldStandards 2016). Cocoa can be stored for 12 months or longer (GCCA 2008; GDV 2017).

Investors can trade cocoa futures contracts at the CME and the ICE. One futures contract is tied to 10 metric tons of cocoa. ICE contracts involve physical delivery, while the CME futures are financially settled (CME 2016; ICE 2016).

Coffee

According to the International Coffee Organization (ICO), coffee is the most widely traded tropical agricultural commodity (ICO 2016). More than 70 countries produce coffee. Coffee plants, like cocoa, grow best in tropical environments, and are primarily grown in the equatorial regions of Asia, India, Africa, and the Americas. During the 2015–2016 trade year, the top four exporting countries were Brazil, Vietnam, Colombia, and Indonesia, exporting 86,250 thousand 60-kilogram bags of coffee. During the same period, total global consumption of coffee reached 151.3 million 60-kilogram bags, with the European Union, United States, and Brazil consuming roughly 60 percent of this total. The United States is the second largest importer of coffee, behind the European Union. In 2016, more than 50 percent of Americans above the age of 18 drank coffee, and the average American coffee drinker consumed about 3.1 cups a day (National Coffee Association 2010).

As Panel C of Table 8.3 shows, global coffee production reached roughly 153 million 60-kilogram bags during the 2015–2016 trade year. More than one-third of all coffee is produced in South America, with Brazil producing around 32 percent, and Colombia producing almost 9 percent of global production in 2015–2016. Asia and Oceania are the second highest producing continents, with Vietnam producing almost 19.1 percent, and Indonesia producing roughly 7.6 percent during the 2015–2016 trade year. The United States does not produce coffee, except for a marginal amount in Hawaii. According to Panel C of Table 8.3, the United States imported almost 25 million 60-kilogram bags of coffee in the 2015–2016 trade year. This makes up nearly 21 percent of global coffee bean imports, as the rest of the world imported roughly 121 million bags during the same time period. During the same year, global coffee exports exceeded 132 million bags.

Globally, the two primary types of coffee beans are arabica and robusta. Arabica beans are generally more flavorful than robusta, and therefore generate a higher price in the market. Arabica beans generally grow in Central and South America. Brazil is both the largest producer of arabica beans and the leading coffee exporter. During the 2015–2016 trade year, Brazil produced 36,100 thousand 60-kilogram bags of arabica, which comprised roughly 41 percent of all Arabica production for that year. Arabica is forecast to reach record levels of production in the coming years, and is expected to comprise 60 percent of total coffee production (FAS 2016a). Robusta, however, has nearly twice the level of caffeine as Arabica, making it valuable despite its bitter taste. Additionally, robusta is sturdier than arabica, making it less susceptible to diseases, requiring less care, and generating higher yields than Arabica beans. Although Brazil also produces robusta beans, Vietnam is the top producer worldwide. During the 2015–2016 trade year, global robusta production reached 67,009 thousand 60-kilogram bags, of which Vietnam produced around 42 percent of the total. Brazil came in second for robusta production, producing roughly 20 percent during the same period.

Coffee beans come from coffee plants that can take from three to five years to reach maturity. Many corporations prefer to purchase robusta due primarily to the cheaper price. As with cocoa, coffee is also susceptible to climate and environmental changes. Natural disasters can cause heavy tolls on bean production, leading to price increases. Lastly, there is a growing interest in fair trade coffee, or coffee that has been produced up to fair trade standards, which seek to reward sustainable environmental farming practices and punish child and forced labor.

Investors can trade arabica coffee futures contracts at the CME. Additionally, the ICE trades coffee futures contracts, tied to either the arabica or robusta bean. One arabica coffee futures contract is tied to 37,500 pounds of arabica coffee beans. The ICE contracts are for physical delivery, while CME futures are financially settled. Physically settled robusta futures are limited to ICE, and each contract is equivalent to 10 thousand metric tons.

Sugar

Sugar is an important component of the diets of people worldwide. A study produced by the Food and Agriculture Organization (FAO) found that, in a global setting, about 53 pounds of sugar were consumed per person on an annual basis in 1999 (FAO 2002). This number is enhanced when focusing solely on the United States, as roughly 130 pounds of sugars and sweeteners are consumed per person within the United States each year (Walton 2012). The United States is the sixth largest producer of sugar behind Brazil, India, the European Union, Thailand, and China. Together, these six countries produce more than 60 percent of the annual sugar supply. Many of the top producing countries are also the largest consumers of sugar. India, the European Union, China, Brazil, and the United States are the top five largest consumers of sugar worldwide and represent roughly half of the total global sugar consumption. Today, sugar is used for many purposes including baking and cooking, as a preservative for perishable items, and as an additive to sweeten processed foods and drinks. Additionally, sugar byproducts are used to make ethanol for fuel.

According to Panel C of Table 8.3, the global production of sugar reached about 164,923 thousand metric tons during the 2015–2016 trade year. U.S. production of 8,104 thousand metric tons amounted to roughly 5 percent of global production. During the 2015–2016 trade year, the United States consumed 10,887 thousand metric tons of sugar. Over the past several decades the United States has increased sugar production, adopting new technologies, new equipment, and improved crops and devoting increased acreage. Besides being one of the world's largest producers and consumers of sugar, the United States is also one of the largest importers of sugar. U.S. imports amounted to 2,931 thousand metric tons of sugar during the 2015–2016 trade year. The majority of sugar produced in each country is consumed domestically. Such consumption has shaped the global sugar marketplace, resulting in many subsidies and tariffs associated with the sugar industry. For instance, the U.S. sugar program is a federal program designed to protect the domestic sugar industry, setting minimum prices, domestic marketing allotments, and tariff-rate quotas to help support domestic sugar production.

Generally, the two well-developed sources for sugar are sugar cane and sugar beets. Sugar cane is the primary source for sugar, on a global scale, comprising around 80 percent of the market (SUCDEN 2016). Sugar cane grows in tropical and semitropical climates, and typically takes one to two years to reach maturity. In the continental United States, sugar cane is primarily planted from late summer to early fall and is then harvested the following year. In tropical countries, sugar cane can be planted year round, so that the active growth season is shorter in the United States. Generally, this leads to tropical climates having higher yields than the continental United States. After sugar cane is harvested, the cane must be transported to a sugar mill within 16 hours of being cut to reduce the amount of sugar cane juice that evaporates.

In the United States, the sugar beet industry is the primary source of sugar, producing around 55 percent of all domestic sugar. Sugar beets are much sturdier than sugar cane, and can therefore be grown in different climates. Sugar beets have a four- to six-month growing season, and need a minimum of 100 days to produce a usable crop. Generally, in the Midwest, sugar beets are planted in the spring and harvested in the fall. Sugar beets can be stored for about six months after harvest, however a substantial loss of sugar can occur during storage. Once the sugar cane or sugar beet is processed into commercial sugars, sugar tends to have an indefinite shelf life due to its resistance to microbial growth.

The two primary sugar prices in the market are for raw cane sugar and refined beet sugar. The U.S. futures price for raw sugar cane, commonly called the Sugar Number 16 contract, is based off the price of sugar delivered to New York. Between 2010 and 2015, the USDA found that average annual price of U.S. raw cane sugar varied from 55.81 to 28.84 cents a pound (USDA 2016e). U.S. prices for raw cane sugar have been higher than the world raw sugar cane price since the early 1980s. The world raw cane sugar price, commonly called the Sugar Number 11 contract in the futures market, is based on the bulk spot price for sugar stored in Caribbean ports. The world raw sugar cane price has ranged from 13.42 to 28.42 cents per pound from 2010 to 2015 (USDA 2016e). Likewise, the refined U.S. beet sugar price tends to be higher than the world price, reflecting heavy government production subsidies and tariffs on imported sugar.

Investors can trade the CME's Sugar Number 11 futures contract. Additionally, the ICE trades Sugar Number 11 futures, Sugar Number 16 futures, white sugar futures, and others. Both the Sugar Number 11 and Sugar Number 16 futures are tied to raw sugar cane prices. One Sugar Number 11 futures contract is tied to 112,000 pounds of sugar. These contracts settle physically on ICE and financially on the CME. Currently, a futures market does not exist for U.S. refined sugar from sugar beets. However, a world refined sugar price is reflected in the Sugar Number 5 futures contract listed on the London International Financial Futures and Options Exchange.

Cotton

Cotton is a crucial component to the fiber industry and accounts for roughly 30 percent of total fiber use worldwide (USDA 2016b). According to the National Cotton Council of America (NCCA), the majority of cotton, around 64 percent, is used in apparel, while 31 percent is used in home furnishings, and 5 percent is used in industrial products (NCCA 2016). More than 75 countries produce cotton, with the cotton plant native to tropical and subtropical climates mainly in the Americas, Africa, and India (USDA 2016b). Combined, the United States, India, and China produce roughly 67 percent of the total global cotton production (FAS 2016b). Although the United States currently ranks third, behind India and China, in terms of global production, it is one of the largest exporters of cotton, exporting roughly 71 percent of total domestic production in 2015 (FAS 2016b). China is the world's largest consumer of cotton, accounting for 43 percent of the total world's use of cotton in 2007 (FAS 2016b). China produces many manufactured goods from cotton, which are then exported. The United States is one of the main importers of these goods. Although the United States is one of the top three cotton producers, roughly 97 percent of manufactured cotton goods came from imports in 2007, and of these goods, around 27 percent of the imports contained U.S.-produced cotton (ICAC 2008).

According to the USDA, global cotton production reached around 96,439 thousand metric tons during the 2015–2016 trade year. Panel C of Table 8.3 highlights that the United States produced 12,888 thousand metric tons, or roughly 13.4 percent of global production. The United States ranked sixth in terms of consumption of raw cotton, with China, India, and Pakistan accounting for roughly two-thirds of worldwide consumption (FAS 2016b). Trade is an incredibly important component of the cotton industry, as approximately 30 percent of all raw cotton is traded across borders before it is processed (USDA 2016b). According to the USDA, the percentage of unprocessed cotton that crosses international borders is larger than any of the four grain commodity products. During the 2015–2016 trade year, the United States exported 9,153 thousand metric tons and imported 33 thousand metric tons of cotton (FAS 2016b).

The USDA claims that the U.S. cotton industry generates about 200,000 jobs from farms to textile mills, accounting for more than $25 billion in products and services annually. The acreage devoted to cotton increased from the mid-1980s to the mid-2000s, from about 10 million to 15 million acres (USDA 2016b). However, starting in 2006, a large decrease in cotton acreage occurred as farmers switched to alternative crops such as corn and soybeans.

Globally, the four commercially grown varieties of cotton are upland cotton, extra-long staple cotton, tree cotton, and Levant cotton. Upland cotton makes up roughly 90 percent of the world production and is the primary variety of cotton grown in the United States (USDA 2016b; Calcot 2009; AMRC 2012). The USDA states that upland cotton production accounts for roughly 97 percent of the total U.S. cotton crop (USDA 2016b). The extra-long staple cotton is grown mostly in California, where the environment is ideal for cultivation. Generally, planting cotton in the United States starts in March and ends in June. The cotton is then harvested from September through December, except in Texas, where the harvest extends through January.

Another important component of the cotton crop, outside of the fiber, is the production of cottonseed. According to the NCCA, the annual production of cottonseed averages 5 million tons (NCCA 2016). More than 6 billion pounds of whole cottonseed and cottonseed meal are used as livestock feed, and another cotton byproduct, cottonseed oil, is used within the food industry (NCCA 2016). Besides cottonseed prices affecting overall cotton prices, grain prices and available subsidies also drive the price of cotton.

Since the 1930s, the United States has offered cotton subsidies to farmers. In 2005, these subsidies equated to $3.3 billion paid to U.S. cotton farmers, more than five times the subsidies offered to grain farmers (Environmental Working Group 2016). These subsidies led the United States to trade cotton below the cost of production, which some countries claimed was an unfair advantage, hurting developing economies that rely on cotton as a source of national income. In the early 2000s, Brazil filed a complaint with the World Trade Organization (WTO), which eventually sided with Brazil's claiming that U.S. subsidies were illegal. As a result of these trade disputes, the cotton industry has undergone change in local subsidy programs.

Investors can trade cotton futures contracts at the CME and the ICE, with one cotton futures contract tied to 50,000 pounds of cotton. ICE contracts settle with physical delivery, and the CME futures are financially settled (CME 2016; ICE 2016).

Market Information

Many sources of market and price information are available for agricultural commodity products. The organized exchanges for futures and options, including the CME and the ICE, provide readily available price, volume, and open interest data, including both end of day and intraday data. The USDA is a government agency that provides freely available information on agricultural commodities, including market reports, production and consumption data, as well as trade statistics both within the United States and worldwide. The AMS, an agency within the USDA, collects and publishes market information for many different types of commodities across many different geographic locations.

Other sources of information are available that provide international statistics as well. The Foreign Agricultural Service (FAS), the foreign affairs branch of the USDA, provides statistics and market information related to international trade, production, and consumption numbers for various agricultural products. The World Agricultural Supply and Demand Estimates (WASDE) is a monthly report published by the USDA that provides forecasts of supply and demand globally and within the United States for the major agricultural products. Farmers, governments, and market participants use the WASDE report, which is often considered to be the benchmark to which all other public and private agricultural forecasts are compared. The World Bank maintains the World Development Indicators (WDI) databank containing time-series data related to agricultural variables for countries all over the world. Besides the wealth of government-provided information, private publishers also offer data, such as DTN, which is a subscription service that delivers real-time weather, agricultural, and commodity market information. One of DTN's publications is *The Progressive Farmer*, which is produced 12 times a year (DTN 2010).

Summary and Conclusions

Agricultural commodities are a broad category consisting of many diverse products that are produced and traded worldwide. These products can be traded on multiple platforms with futures contracts as the prevailing financial instrument for investing in agricultural commodities. The three major categories of agricultural products include grains, dairy, and softs. Agricultural commodities are subject to factors such as perishability and seasonality, which distinguish them from other commodities such as metals and financials.

Discussion Questions

1. Discuss the various ways to settle futures contracts.
2. Discuss the use of subsidies in the agriculture industry.
3. Explain some common ways to invest in agricultural commodities.
4. Define basis and its importance in agricultural commodities.

References

Agricultural Market Information System (AMIS). 2015. "Stocks and Utilization." Available at http://www.amis-outlook.org/indicators/stocks/en/#.WEHl_9UrInR.

Agricultural Marketing Resource Center (AMRC). 2012. "Cotton." Available at http://www.agmrc.org/commodities-products/fiber/cotton/.

Agricultural Marketing Resource Center (AMRC). 2016. "Grains and Oilseeds." Available at http://www.agmrc.org/commodities-products/grains-oilseeds/.

Associated Press. 2015. "Plunge in Milk Prices Stresses Dairy Farmers." Available at http://www.agweb.com/article/plunge-in-milk-prices-stresses-dairy-farmers--naa-associated-press/.

Bloomberg. 2016. "Bloomberg Database."

Calcot Cotton Marketing Services (Calcot). 2009. "Cotton Production Information." Available at http://www.calcot.com/ourcotton.asp?flag=ourcotton.

Canadian Dairy Commission. 2011. "Whey Powder." October 17. Available at http://www.milkingredients.ca/index-eng.php?id=194.

CME Group (CME). 2015. "CBOT Black Sea Wheat Futures." Available at http://www.cmegroup.com/trading/agricultural/files/PM264_Fact_Card_Black_Sea_Wheat.pdf.

CME Group (CME). 2016. "CME Group Database."

CommodityBasis. 2016. "CommodityBasis Database."

DraKoln, Noble. 2016. "Commodities: Cocoa." *Investopedia*. Available at http://www.investopedia.com/university/commodities/commodities1.asp.

DTN. 2010. "DTN/The Progressive Farmer Technology Overview." Available at http://cdn2.hubspot.net/hub/116265/file-17528806-pdf/docs/dtn_technology_tour.pdf.

Environmental Working Group. "Farm Subsidy Primer." Available at https://farm.ewg.org/subsidyprimer.php

Food and Agriculture Organization of the United Nations (FAO). 2016. "FAOSTAT Database."

Food and Agriculture Organization of the United Nations (FAO). 2002. "World Agriculture: Towards 2015/2030." Available at http://www.fao.org/docrep/004/y3557e/y3557e00.htm#TopOfPage.

Gesamtverband der Deutschen Versicherungswirtschaft e.V. (GDV). 2017. "Cocoa/Cocoa beans." Transport Information Services, GDV. Available at http://www.tis-gdv.de/tis_e/ware/genuss/kakao/kakao.htm#verpackung.

Global Cold Chain Alliance (GCCA). 2008. "WFLO Commodity Storage Manual: Cocoa and Cocoa Beans." Available at http://www.gcca.org/wp-content/uploads/2012/09/CocoaCocoaBeans.pdf.

Glogoza, Phil, and Dave Nicolai. 2014. "Managing Stored Grain to Minimize Storage Losses." Working paper, University of Minnesota. Available at http://www.extension.umn.edu/agriculture/corn/harvest/managing-stored-grain/.

Good, Darrel, and Scott Irwin. 2015. "The Relationship between Stocks-to-Use and Corn Prices Revisited." *Farmdoc daily* 5:65, Department of Agricultural and Consumer Economics, University of Illinois at Urbana–Champaign. Available at http://farmdocdaily.illinois.edu/2015/04/relationship-stock-to-use-and-corn-prices.html.

Hoard's Dairyman. 2012. "U.S. Dairy Farm Numbers Drop by 1,621—Now Total 51,481." Hoards.com, February 27. Available at http://hoards.com/blog-4464-us-dairy-farm-numbers-drop-by-1621-%E2%80%94-now-total-51481.html.

Huchet-Bourdon, Marilyne. 2011. "Agricultural Commodity Price Volatility: An Overview." *OECD Food Agriculture and Fisheries Papers*, Paris.

Intercontinental Exchange (ICE). 2007. "Intercontinental Exchange and New Board of Trade Complete Merger." January 12. Available at http://ir.theice.com/press/press-releases/all-categories/2007/01-12-2007.

Intercontinental Exchange (ICE). 2016. Available at http://www.theice.com/products/254.

International Cocoa Organization (ICCO). 1998. "How Much Time Does It Take for a Cocoa Tree to Become Productive?" July 21. Available at https://www.icco.org/faq/57-cocoa-production/129-how-much-time-does-it-take-for-a-cocoa-tree-to-become-productive.html.

International Cocoa Organization (ICCO). 2014. "What Time of Year Is Cocoa Harvested?" July 23. Available at https://www.icco.org/faq/58-cocoa-harvesting/131-what-time-of-year-is-cocoa-harvested.html.

International Cocoa Organization (ICCO). 2016. "Production—Latest Figures from the Quarterly Bulletin of Cocoa Statistics." August 31. Available at https://www.icco.org/about-us/international-cocoa-agreements/cat_view/30-related-documents/46-statistics-production.html.

International Coffee Organization (ICO). 2016. "Mission." Available at http://www.ico.org/mission07_e.asp?section=About_Us.

International Cotton Advisory Committee (ICAC). 2008. "International Cotton Prices Forecast Higher in 2008/09." June 2. Available at https://www.icac.org/cotton_info/publications/press/2008/pr_june_08.pdf.

Lauer, Joel, Paul Porter, and Ed Oplinger. 1997. "The Corn and Soybean Rotation Effect." *Field Crops* 27:426. Available at http://corn.agronomy.wisc.edu/AA/1997/A014.html.

Martin, Jeremy. 2014. "Biodiesel Update: Now with More Soy." Union of Concerned Scientists. January 2. Available at http://blog.ucsusa.org/jeremy-martin/biodiesel-update-now-with-more-soy-360.

Morrison, Liz. 2013. "Including Soybeans in Crop Rotation Provides Advantages." *Corn + Soybean Digest*. September 25. Available at http://cornandsoybeandigest.com/soybeans/including-soybeans-crop-rotation-provides-advantages.

National Coffee Association (NCA). 2010. "2010 National Coffee Drinking Trends Study." Available at http://www.ncausa.org/i4a/pages/index.cfm?pageID=684.

National Cotton Council Association (NCCA). 2016. "World of Cotton." Available at http://www.cotton.org/econ/world/index.cfm.

S&P Dow Jones Indices (S&P). 2016. "S&P GSCI Agriculture." Available at http://us.spindices.com/indices/commodities/sp-gsci-agriculture.

SUCDEN. 2016. "World Sugar Production." Available at http://www.sucden.com/statistics/1_world-sugar-production.

Tetra Pak. 2016. *Dairy Processing Handbook*. Available at http://www.dairyprocessinghandbook.com/.

Thiesse, Kent. 2016a. "USDA Crop Predictions Sends Corn and Soybeans Prices Lower from July Estimates." *Corn + Soybean Digest*. August 15. Available at http://www.cornandsoybeandigest.com/blog/usda-crop-predictions-sends-corn-and-soybean-prices-lower-july-estimates.

Thiesse, Kent. 2016b. "USDA Projects Record Corn and Soybean Crop in 2016." *Corn + Soybean Digest*. November 14. Available at http://www.cornandsoybeandigest.com/blog/usda-projects-record-corn-and-soybean-crop-2016.

Trostle, Ronald. 2008. "Global Agriculture Supply and Demand: Factors Contributing to the Recent Increase in Food Commodity Prices." A Report from the Economic Research Service, United States Department of Agriculture. Available at https://www.ers.usda.gov/webdocs/publications/wrs0801/12274_wrs0801_1_.pdf?v=41057.

Trostle, Ronald, Daniel Marti, Stacey Rosen, and Paul Westcott. 2011. "Why Have Food Commodity Prices Risen Again?" A Report from the Economic Research Service, U.S. Department of Agriculture. Available at https://www.ers.usda.gov/webdocs/publications/wrs1103/7392_wrs1103.pdf.

University of Arkansas. 2016. "On-Farm Rice Drying and Storage." Division of Agriculture, University of Arkansas. Available at http://www.uaex.edu/farm-ranch/crops-commercial-horticulture/Grain_drying_and_storage/rice_drying_and_storage.aspx.

U.S. Department of Agriculture, Economic Research Service (ERS). 2016. "USDA Economic Research Service Database." Available at https://www.ers.usda.gov/data-products/.

U.S. Department of Agriculture, Foreign Agriculture Service (FAS). 2016a. "Coffee: World Markets and Trade—2016/17 Forecast Overview." Foreign Agriculture Service. Available at https://apps.fas.usda.gov/psdonline/circulars/coffee.pdf.

U.S. Department of Agriculture, Foreign Agriculture Service (FAS). 2016b. "USDA Foreign Agriculture Service Database."

U.S. Department of Agriculture (USDA). 2006. "USDA Issues Final 2006 Direct Payments and Final 2005-Crop Corn Counter-Cyclical Payments." October 12. Available at http://www.usda.gov/wps/portal/usda/usdamediafb?contentid=2006/10/0407.xml&printable=true&contentidonly=true.

U.S. Department of Agriculture (USDA). 2010. "Field Crops: Usual Planting and Harvesting Dates." Available at http://usda.mannlib.cornell.edu/usda/nass/planting//2010s/2010/planting-10-29-2010.pdf.

U.S. Department of Agriculture (USDA). 2016a. "Corn Background." Available at https://www.ers.usda.gov/topics/crops/corn/background/.

U.S. Department of Agriculture (USDA). 2016b. "Cotton & Wool Overview." Available at https://www.ers.usda.gov/topics/crops/cotton-wool/.

U.S. Department of Agriculture (USDA). 2016c. "Rice Background." Available at https://www.ers.usda.gov/topics/crops/rice/background/.

U.S. Department of Agriculture (USDA). 2016d. "Soybeans & Oil Crop Background." Available at https://www.ers.usda.gov/topics/crops/soybeans-oil-crops/background.aspx.

U.S. Department of Agriculture (USDA). 2016e. "Sugar & Sweeteners Background." Available at https://www.ers.usda.gov/topics/crops/sugar-sweeteners/background.aspx.

U.S. Department of Agriculture (USDA). 2016f. "Wheat Background." Available at https://www.ers.usda.gov/topics/crops/wheat/background/.

U.S. Energy Information Administration (EIA). 2016a. "EIA Monthly Energy Review Database."

U.S. Energy Information Administration (EIA). 2016b. "Renewable and Alternative Fuels Database."

U.S. Senate Permanent Subcommittee on Investigations (PSI). 2009. "Excessive Speculation in the Wheat Market: Majority and Minority Staff Report." June 24. Available at http://www.hsgac.senate.gov//imo/media/doc/REPORTExcessiveSpecullationintheWheatMarketwoexhibitschartsJune2409.pdf?attempt=2.

Walton, Alice. 2012. "How Much Sugar Are Americans Eating?" *Forbes*. August 30. Available at http://www.forbes.com/sites/alicegwalton/2012/08/30/how-much-sugar-are-americans-eating-infographic/#42de965a1f71.

Willis, Sara. 2003. "The use of Soybean Meal and Full Fat Soybean Meal by the Animal Feed Industry." 12th Australian Soybean Conference. Available at http://www.

australianoilseeds.com/__data/assets/file/0019/1198/Sarah_Willis-The_Use_of_Soybean_Meal_and_Full_Fat_Soybean_Meal_by_the_Animal_Feed_Industry.pdf.
World Bank Group. 2016a. "World Development Indicators Database."
World Bank Group. 2016b. "World Bank Commodity Price Database."
WorldStandards. 2016. "The Cacao Tree and Its Fruit." Available at http://www.worldstandards.eu/chocolate%20-%20cacao.html.
Zulauf, Carl. 2016. "U.S. Feeding of Wheat to Livestock." *Drovers* August 9. Available at http://www.cattlenetwork.com/news/industry/us-feeding-wheat-livestock.

9

Energy

MICHAEL A. PENICK
Senior Economist, U.S. Commodity Futures Trading Commission

LYNN RIGGS
Financial Economist, U.S. Commodity Futures Trading Commission

Introduction

Energy markets are vitally important to the world economy and fluctuations in energy prices can substantially affect consumers, manufacturers, airlines, and other energy users. Energy markets cover a broad range of different products from those in raw form (e.g., crude oil, natural gas, and coal) to those that have been transformed for a more specific purpose (e.g., gasoline, jet fuel, and ethanol). Given this diversity of products, energy products are usually categorized as follows: crude oil, refined crude oil products, natural gas, natural gas liquids, coal, electricity, petrochemicals, and biofuels. As with most commodities, energy commodities trade in both the spot and derivatives markets. Although modern futures trading began with agricultural futures contracts in the nineteenth century and expanded with the introduction of financial futures and precious metals futures in the 1970s, energy was the last major asset class to develop deep and liquid futures markets. For example, even though futures contracts on petroleum existed as far back as the nineteenth century and again in the 1930s, energy futures contracts became successful on a long-term basis only in the 1980s (Penick 2010). This was largely because price fluctuations historically presented relatively little risk to market participants due to regulation (particularly in natural gas markets) or market power held by certain oil producers.

This chapter discusses energy markets generally and then focuses on a subset of specific energy products for a more in-depth discussion of energy market structure and regulatory issues. The in-depth focuses on the benchmark, exchange-traded, energy futures markets—crude oil, gasoline, heating oil, and natural gas—as well as the cash and derivatives markets related to these futures contracts. Although numerous exchange-traded futures contracts and OTC derivatives are available in electricity, electricity markets are extremely complex and lack a liquid, benchmark futures contract. Markets for other energy commodities are relatively undeveloped. Hence, this chapter does not cover these markets in detail.

Market Fundamentals

Despite the wide array of energy products, Kaminski (2012) notes that energy markets in general share several common features. One of the most well-known shared features is that energy markets generally are characterized by inelastic short- and medium-term demand curves in which demand decreases rather slowly as prices increase. For example, a sharp increase in natural gas prices may cause consumers heating their homes with natural gas to lower their thermostats in winter or to raise them in summer given that natural gas prices affect electricity prices, but homeowners are unlikely to give up heating or air conditioning entirely because of high prices. On the supply side, short- and medium-term supply curves are relatively flat until storage and production capacity constraints start to bind at which point supply curves steepen or become vertical.

In the long run, both supply and demand curves are more elastic. For example, prolonged high energy prices may encourage technological innovation that in the long run increases supply or reduces demand, which can result in sharp price declines. Hence, consumers and producers can be more price sensitive in the long run even though they may be constrained in the short run. One example of such a technological innovation is hydraulic fracturing (fracking). After an extended period of high prices in the 2000s, the advent of fracking greatly expanded the production capacity and, hence, supply of natural gas in the United States, which contributed to the much lower prices in the 2010s. Similarly, crude oil experienced an extended period of high prices, which persisted longer than high natural gas prices, and market participants began to expect high prices to persist permanently (Dicker 2011). This market dynamic allowed for the development of technological innovations that enhanced producers' ability to obtain both crude oil from shale formations and additional crude oil from conventional oil fields that may previously have been considered too difficult or expensive to extract. These innovations led to a 73 percent increase in U.S. crude oil production between 2008 and 2014 (Aguilera and Radetzki 2016) and contributed to sharp declines in crude oil prices in the mid-2010s from above $100 per barrel to around $60 or below.

On the demand side, long periods of high prices can reduce demand by encouraging or making economically feasible the use of more energy-efficient goods—including a complete switch to alternative energy sources such as solar or wind power. As crude oil and gasoline prices rise, consumers switch to more fuel-efficient cars, as happened after Hurricanes Katrina and Rita damaged refineries and sharply drove up gasoline prices (Freeman 2005). From 2002 to 2010 (a period of high energy prices), total energy consumption by U.S. manufacturers decreased by 17 percent even though manufacturing gross output decreased only by 3 percent (U.S. Energy Information Administration 2013a). In 2014, several U.S. manufacturers reported renovation projects that would permanently convert residual fuel oil equipment to natural gas in response to relatively lower natural gas prices (U.S. Energy Information Administration 2016). Further, Google announced that in 2017 all the energy it consumes will be generated by wind and solar power and cited low price volatility as one reason for the shift to renewables (Hardy 2016). All of these long-run changes demonstrate the long-run elasticity of the demand curve.

Energy markets also tend to display periods of peak and off-peak demand. These periods can be intraday as with electricity or seasonal as with natural gas or petroleum products. For example, demand for natural gas varies by season with the highest demand in the winter for heating homes and businesses, while production rates are relatively steady. Since natural gas is a commonly used fuel for generating electricity, an increase in demand also occurs during the summer for air conditioning. During the spring and fall "shoulder" seasons, demand is relatively low. Hence, natural gas prices are typically highly seasonal and are more prone to higher levels of volatility due to weather events than other energy prices. In order to equate supply and demand over the course of the year, natural gas is stored, commonly in salt caverns, with storage levels increasing during the warm season (typically April to November) and decreasing during the cold season. The largest storage injections occur during the spring and fall, while storage increases more slowly during the summer in light of air conditioning demand.

Prices for crude oil and its refined products also exhibit seasonal changes, but seasonal patterns, particularly for crude oil, are less straightforward than with natural gas. Gasoline prices tend to rise during the summer due to both higher demand as consumers drive to vacation destinations and stricter emissions requirements in the United States. However, demand for heating oil is higher in the winter since consumers use heating oil for heating homes, especially in the northeastern United States.

Given the impact of production capacity and storage levels on energy prices, the Energy Information Administration (EIA) publishes calculations of related estimates on a weekly basis. For natural gas, the EIA typically releases estimates of storage levels on Thursdays at 10:30 a.m. Eastern time. For crude oil and its refined products, EIA releases an extensive set of data typically on Wednesdays at 10:30 a.m. Eastern time. For crude oil, EIA publishes estimates of production, inventories, and imports. For refined products, EIA publishes spot market prices as well as stocks of gasoline, heating oil, jet fuel, and other petroleum products. Figure 9.1 shows a graph of natural gas storage levels during 2015 and 2016 as provided by EIA, along with five-year ranges. Note that storage levels began the 2016 heating season at historically high levels, but declined sharply in December 2016 due to some very cold weather in December 2016. Likewise, the petroleum release can move the markets when the numbers differ from expectations. Figure 9.2 shows EIA's estimates of crude oil stocks in 2015 and 2016, along with five-year ranges. It also shows a lack of clear seasonality in crude oil stocks as compared to natural gas stocks.

Before EIA's regular release of these estimates, trading firms attempt to forecast the EIA figures, and these releases can result in substantial and sudden changes in prices if the EIA calculation differs markedly from the consensus estimates. Hence, prices can be volatile following these releases.

In energy markets, short-term spot markets are rather illiquid. Therefore, price discovery commonly occurs in the futures markets in which actively traded futures markets exist or in forward markets. Although energy commodity prices, like agricultural commodity prices, can vary widely within a particular commodity based on factors such as grade, variety, and location, energy futures contracts are typically structured differently than agricultural futures contracts. Agricultural futures contracts such as wheat and corn arose in the nineteenth century and currently provide for delivery of

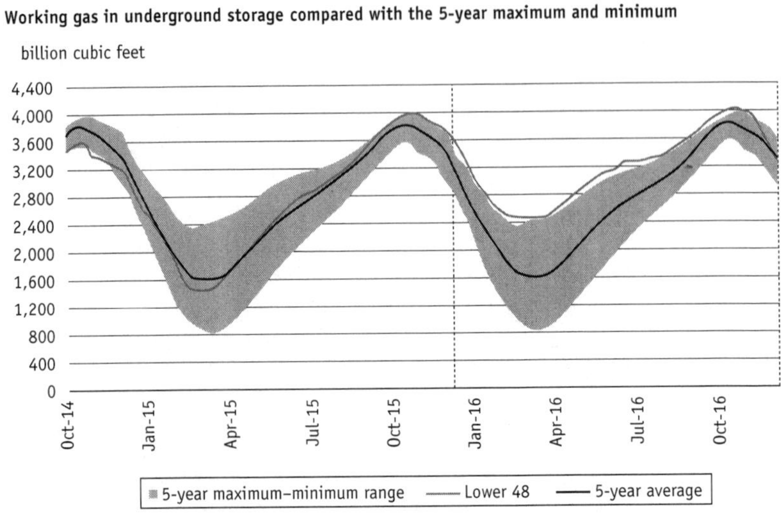

Figure 9.1 Natural Gas Storage Levels
This graph shows natural gas storage levels during 2015 and 2016 as provided by EIA, along with five-year ranges. Storage levels began the 2016 heating season at historically high levels, but declined sharply in December 2016 due to some very cold weather. The shaded area indicates the range between the historical minimum and maximum values for the weekly series from 2011 through 2015. The dashed vertical lines indicate current and year-ago weekly periods. The current chart is available at http://ir.eia.gov/ngs/ngs.html. Source: U.S. Energy Information Administration.

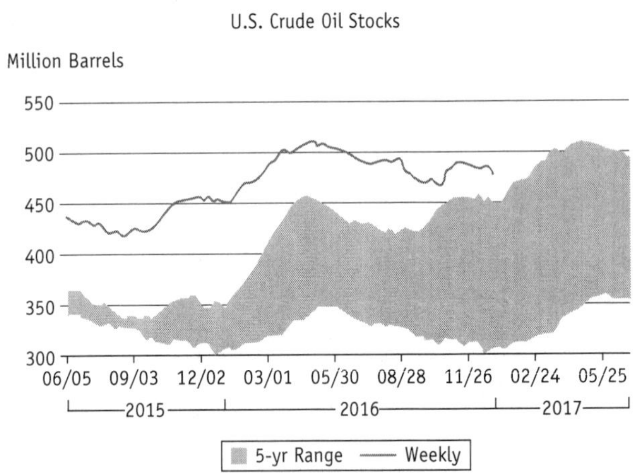

Figure 9.2 Crude Oil Stocks
This graph shows EIA's estimates of crude oil stocks in 2015 and 2016, along with five-year ranges. A lack of clear seasonality exists in crude oil stocks as compared to natural gas stocks. The current chart is available at http://www.eia.gov/petroleum/supply/weekly/pdf/figure1.pdf. Source: U.S. Energy Information Administration (2017).

a wide variety of grades and locations, typically under a system of fixed differentials. The result of this contract structure is that while more users can conveniently deliver against the futures contract, futures prices typically reflect the "cheapest-to-deliver" grade and location, which may vary over time. In contrast, energy futures contracts are structured to reflect the price of a single location, grade, and variety, and thus futures prices can consistently reflect a widely used benchmark in the industry. This contract structure also means that energy market participants widely use different derivative products in conjunction with benchmark energy futures contracts to provide more precise hedges for end-users.

Another common feature of energy markets is the use of long-term contracts in which prices of future deliveries are based on published benchmarks. These benchmarks can be futures prices or indexes of spot, near-term, or forward market prices as reported to price reporting agencies (PRAs) such as Platts or Argus.

Creating robust energy price indexes can be a difficult task since these spot markets can be thin and illiquid. Firms may have an incentive to report false prices or false transactions to PRAs in order to benefit their position in long-term contracts; and in thin or illiquid markets, these false reports can affect the index value. Between 2002 and 2004, the Commodity Futures Trading Commission (CFTC) brought numerous cases of false reporting of prices and volume as well as multiple cases of attempted manipulation of these benchmarks. Almost all of these cases involved settlement rather than litigation and often resulted in fines of $20 million or more. In response to these cases, numerous reforms have occurred at both the firm and the PRA level, including ensuring that staff members other than the traders themselves report the firm's transactions. Some firms also reduced the extent to which they report their transactions to the PRAs, which led to concerns among market participants about the quality and reliability of the benchmarks.

Following the financial crisis of 2007–2008, international regulators also took an interest in price reporting, particularly in the oil market. In 2012, the International Organization of Securities Commissions (IOSCO) recommended 12 principles for reforms of PRA operations, which were generally adopted by the PRAs in subsequent years (International Organization of Securities Commissions 2012). These principles related to various matters, including transparency of the methodology for calculating the benchmarks, favoring the use of actual transactions where possible along with completeness of reporting, audit trails, and procedures to address conflicts of interest. In 2016, ICE entered into an agreement with Platts to use anonymized versions of ICE's trade data as well as reports from firms in order to create more robust benchmarks in the natural gas market starting in 2017. This arrangement and potential similar deals in other energy markets could improve market confidence in the benchmarks.

Crude Oil and Refined Products Derivatives

The first modern attempt at an energy futures contract was a crude oil contract launched in 1974, shortly after the 1973 Arab oil embargo and subsequent increase in oil prices, by the New York Cotton Exchange (a predecessor to ICE Futures US).

This contract initially traded at a modest volume but was gone within two years. The New York Mercantile Exchange (NYMEX, now part of CME Group) was more successful with heating oil in 1978 and leaded gasoline in 1981. Both contracts continue to trade actively, but with some modifications to the contract specification from time to time as regulatory standards change. For example, leaded gasoline was banned in the United States for use by road vehicles in 1996 and is no longer traded. Instead, the current NYMEX gasoline futures contract provides for delivery of reformulated gasoline blendstock (RBOB). The NYMEX heating oil contract changed from requiring delivery of products with sulfur content up to 2,000 parts per million (0.2 percent) to delivery of ultra-low sulfur diesel (ULSD) that contains less than 15 parts per million of sulfur. This change took effect starting with the May 2013 contract as many states in the Northeast were requiring the switch to fuels with lower sulfur levels by 2018 (U.S. Energy Information Administration 2013b).

For both gasoline and heating oil (now ULSD), one contract delivers 42,000 gallons to New York Harbor, and trading terminates on the last day of the calendar month before the delivery month. In most energy futures contracts (unlike agricultural and metal futures contracts), trading terminates before the end of the delivery period. After trading terminates, contracts can continue to be offset via Exchange of Futures for Physical (EFP) transactions pursuant to exchange rules, usually only for the business day following the last trading day.

During the early 1980s, both the Chicago Board of Trade (CBOT, also now part of the CME Group) and NYMEX worked to design a futures contract on crude oil that would be more successful than previous crude oil futures contracts. At that time, futures exchanges needed prior approval from the CFTC before listing new futures contracts. Both crude oil contracts received CFTC approval on the same day, March 28, 1983, and were launched the following day. The NYMEX contract succeeded in generating substantial trading volume. Such volume may be because NYMEX already had successful contracts on gasoline and heating oil, which facilitated trading *crack spreads* (i.e., the differential between the price of gasoline and/or heating oil and the price of crude oil) on a single exchange. Another possibility is that the marketplace preferred NYMEX's West Texas Intermediate (WTI) light sweet crude oil contract over the CBOT's Louisiana-based contract for Louisiana light sweet crude oil (LLS).

As the Organization of Petroleum Exporting Countries (OPEC) became less successful during the mid-1980s at controlling oil prices, the need for risk-management tools increased, and the NYMEX WTI crude oil contract soon became one of the largest futures contracts on a physical commodity. The WTI contract provides for physical delivery of 1,000 barrels (42,000 gallons, the same size as the heating oil and gasoline futures contracts) of light sweet crude oil at Cushing, Oklahoma, during the delivery month. A fact worth noting is that "light" crude oil has lower viscosity and lower density than "heavy" crude oil and light crude oil flows easily at room temperature. "Sweet" crude oil has a lower sulfur content compared to high-sulfur "sour" crude oil. Light and/or sweet crude oil is generally easier and cheaper to refine than heavy and/or sour crude oil. Accordingly, lighter and sweeter grades typically command higher prices in the cash market than heavier, sourer grades. Moreover, refineries cannot easily substitute one grade of crude for another.

As is the case with most benchmark energy futures contracts, the NYMEX WTI crude oil futures contracts are listed for each calendar month with June and December generally being the most actively traded. Trading on the exchange typically terminates on the third business day before the twenty-fifth calendar day of the month proceeding the delivery month.

As NYMEX was developing its energy contracts, the International Petroleum Exchange (IPE, now ICE Futures Europe) in London was developing its own energy contracts. IPE was founded in 1980 with a gas oil (heating oil) futures contract and several other petroleum-based contracts. The IPE's most successful futures contract—Brent (North Sea) crude oil (also light and sweet)—began trading in 1988. ICE Futures Europe Brent futures contract is cash settled based on an index provided by the exchange (ICE Brent Index), but with a physical delivery option via EFP. The EFP process can also be used to deliver non-contract grades and locations at price differentials as agreed by the counterparties. Today, both the WTI and Brent contracts are considered major benchmarks, with Brent contract volume in recent years close behind the volume of WTI. In 2016, total volume in the NYMEX WTI futures contract was 277 million contracts as compared to 211 million contracts in ICE Brent futures contract. Figure 9.3 shows volume growth from 2006 to 2016 in both contracts (NYMEX CL and ICE B).

Futures exchanges also offer products allowing market participants to directly trade the crack spread (named after the "cracking" process by which crude oil is turned into its products such as gasoline and heating oil) in a single transaction: either the 3-2-1 crack spread (since a barrel of crude oil typically is refined into about two parts gasoline and one part heating oil) or a simple spread between crude oil and one product (gasoline or heating oil) alone. Various over-the-counter (OTC) derivatives debuted to facilitate more precise risk management and, as discussed in the next section, many of these products are now listed on futures exchanges and are traded as futures rather than swaps. For example, a common derivative, known as "contracts for differences," is cash settled to the difference in price between the price of a specified variety and location of crude oil and the spot price of Brent or WTI, generally based on published indexes from a PRA such as Platts or Argus. NYMEX and ICE also have listed options on their benchmark energy futures contracts.

Other futures contracts trade around the world for crude oil and its refined products. In Moscow and in India, for example, crude oil futures contracts actively trade. In Moscow, these crude oil futures have high volumes but small contract sizes.

Natural Gas Derivatives

The last major exchange-traded energy futures contract developed in the United States was in natural gas, launched by NYMEX in 1990. The contract provides for physical delivery of 10,000 mmbtu (million British thermal units) of natural gas at the Henry Hub in Louisiana, which is also the primary cash market benchmark. As with other energy futures contracts, contracts are listed monthly with trading terminating three business days before the delivery month. Volume in the NYMEX natural gas futures contract (NYMEX NG) was 97 million contracts in 2016. Figure 9.4

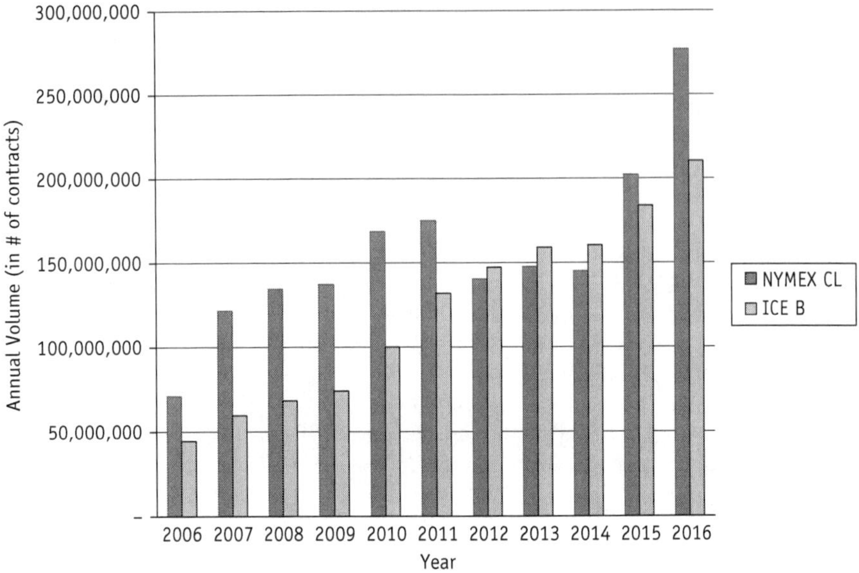

Figure 9.3 Total Annual Volume for Benchmark Crude Oil Futures—NYMEX CL and ICE B
Today, the NYMEX WTI Light, Sweet Crude Oil (NYMEX CL), and ICE Brent Crude (ICE B) contracts are considered major benchmarks, with Brent contract volume in recent years close behind the volume of WTI. In 2016, total volume in the NYMEX WTI futures contract was 277 million contracts as compared to 211 million contracts in ICE Brent futures contract. This graph shows volume growth from 2006 to 2016 in both contracts (NYMEX CL and ICE B). Source: FIA December Volume Report (2006–2011); NYMEX/COMEX Exchange Volume Report—Monthly (2012–2016); ICE Futures Europe Historical Monthly Volumes Report (2006-2011).

shows changes in total annual volume from 2006 to 2016. Substantial volume also occurs in "look-alike" contracts that are cash settled to the NYMEX settlement price on the last day of trading. The majority of volume in these cash-settled contracts is on ICE, but NYMEX also lists such contracts, known as Henry Hub swap futures.

The natural gas cash market developed in the 1980s and early 1990s after enactment of the Natural Gas Policy Act of 1978. Before this Act, natural gas prices had been subject to price controls following a Supreme Court decision known as the Phillips decision. The Act also created the Federal Energy Regulatory Commission (FERC). In subsequent years, FERC issued a series of orders and rulemakings, which eventually resulted in full deregulation of natural gas prices by 1992 (Sturm 1997).

For most commodities, a limited number of different contract types are traded. However, in natural gas, an enormous variety of derivatives contracts have become popular. Initially many of these traded OTC, but now many are regularly traded on futures exchanges. Although natural gas itself is generally uniform in terms of grades and varieties (as compared to crude oil), prices vary widely by location and the needs

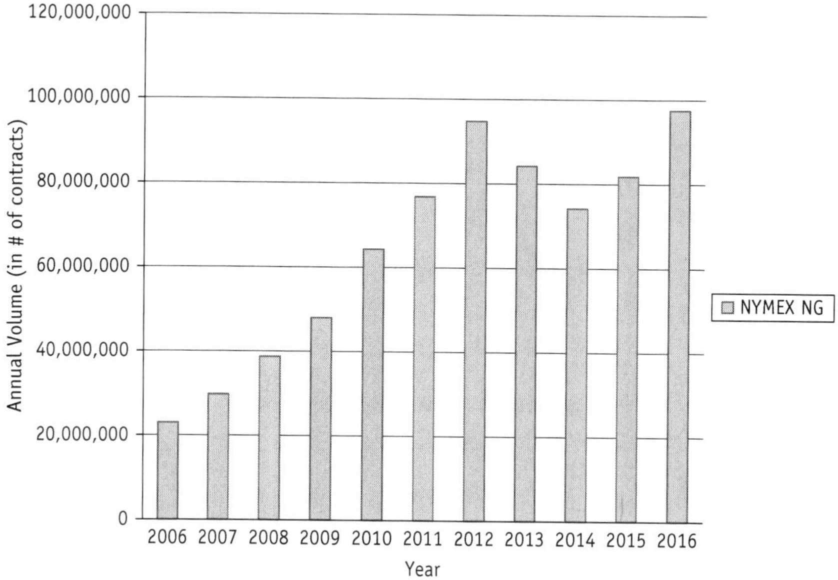

Figure 9.4 Total Annual Volume for Benchmark Natural Gas Futures—NYMEX NG
This figure shows that volume in the NYMEX natural gas futures contract (NYMEX NG) was at an all-time high of 97 million contracts in 2016. This volume is up from slightly more than 20 million contracts in 2006. This figure also shows changes in total annual volume from 2006 to 2016. Source: FIA December Volume Report (2006-2011); NYMEX/COMEX Exchange Volume Report—Monthly (2012-2016).

of end users can vary day-to-day based on localized weather conditions. Many of these OTC derivatives are designed to trade in conjunction with the main NYMEX Henry Hub natural gas futures contract to reflect these different needs. For example, while the NYMEX contract provides for delivery only at the Henry Hub, natural gas prices at other U.S. locations often vary widely from prices at the Henry Hub. In light of this situation, basis swap contracts were developed that are cash settled on the difference between the NYMEX futures price on the last trading day and the spot price at a specified location such as Chicago or New York, generally based on a published index from a PRA such as Platts. As discussed in the next section, basis contracts today are commonly listed by exchanges as futures contracts or options rather than swaps. A trader who needs to hedge the Chicago natural gas price can take a long position in both the NYMEX natural gas futures contract and a Chicago basis contract. The Chicago basis contract would generally provide a long position for Chicago natural gas and a short position in the NYMEX natural gas contract. Since the long and short NYMEX natural gas positions offset, this combination creates a synthetic futures contract on Chicago natural gas.

Another common type of derivative is the swing contract, which was originally structured as a swap but can also be a futures contract or option. According to Sturm (1997), a swing contract is based on daily prices as published by Platts in *Gas Daily* for a particular location. Although futures contracts in combination with basis contracts are typically used to hedge monthly price changes, a swing contract can be added to a position to further refine the hedge to reflect daily price changes. For example, a trader could add a Chicago swing contract to the NYMEX futures / Chicago basis contract position to create a synthetic futures contract that reflects daily changes in the Chicago natural gas price.

Origins of OTC Trading of Energy Derivatives

In 1999, the energy trading company Enron created an electronic trading platform called EnronOnline, which listed an enormous variety of energy derivatives as well as some non-energy products, such as lumber and even broadband. The EnronOnline platform made trading easy (as compared to previous OTC market structures) and contributed to a substantial expansion of the energy derivatives market. Enron rival Dynegy created a similar platform called DynegyDirect, but it was not as successful. EnronOnline was a one-to-many platform whereby Enron was the counterparty to every participant rather than a traditional exchange. EnronOnline briefly dominated the energy derivatives market until Enron declared bankruptcy in late 2001. Swiss bank UBS bought the EnronOnline platform but was unable to relaunch it successfully. DynegyDirect was shut down in 2002. In general, the OTC energy market seemed to be going into a tailspin in 2002. The creditworthiness of one's counterparty is important in the OTC markets because OTC derivatives, unlike exchange-traded derivatives, traditionally are not cleared. Following the Enron bankruptcy, the market called into question the creditworthiness of all OTC energy market participants and market volume declined sharply. Two big beneficiaries to this event were a new exchange called the Intercontinental Exchange (ICE) and the NYMEX.

ICE was founded in May 2000 by a consortium of energy trading firms and large banks. It began as a many-to-many electronic trading platform for OTC energy derivatives, typically the same products as were offered on EnronOnline. In 2001, ICE bought London's IPE and subsequently renamed that petroleum futures exchange ICE Futures Europe. Since then, ICE has made many additional acquisitions, including the New York Board of Trade, now ICE Futures US, and the New York Stock Exchange. When Enron declared bankruptcy, much of EnronOnline's business migrated to ICE. ICE benefited further as banks and investment banks entered the energy business and the OTC energy market recovered from the 2002 collapse.

NYMEX also benefited from the 2002 collapse in the OTC energy market, in part because some energy derivatives trading migrated from the OTC market to the exchange. As noted, futures contracts are cleared through a clearinghouse associated with an exchange, thus eliminating counterparty credit risk. The credit risk concerns in the OTC energy markets contributed to the volume increase at NYMEX. Moreover, in 2002, NYMEX established the ClearPort Internet-based platform on which market participants could either trade a wide variety of energy derivatives, or present privately negotiated energy derivatives transactions to ClearPort for clearing through the NYMEX clearinghouse (now the CME clearinghouse). Before submission, these OTC swaps would be converted to futures through an exchange for related position

(EFRP) process. ClearPort proved successful although its market share in trading generally was smaller than that of ICE trading platform. ClearPort was the first major platform in the United States for clearing OTC derivatives. As discussed later, most natural gas swaps have now been "futurized" and are traded directly as futures on NYMEX and ICE.

Regulatory Issues

The CFTC regulates energy futures, option, and swap markets and also has anti-manipulation authority over energy cash markets in interstate commerce. As noted, FERC regulates interstate natural gas markets, including anti-manipulation authority in those markets, but the CFTC has exclusive jurisdiction over natural gas futures markets. The remainder of this chapter discusses recent regulatory issues, including speculation in energy futures, potential position limits in energy markets, and the "futurization" of energy swaps to avoid various new regulations related to swap markets.

Speculation in Energy Commodities

Speculation in commodities markets has always been somewhat controversial; however, speculation appears to be an integral component of hedging markets (Working 1960). Markets for energy derivatives are no exception. Working (pp. 186–187) defines speculation in commodities as "the holding of a net long or a net short position, for gain, and not as a normal incident to operating for a producing, merchandising, or processing business." In the period studied by Working, speculators were fairly active in and well informed about the markets in which they invested. However, in the 1960s, a new form of speculation developed that took a more passive approach to trading, and is known as managed futures. Managed futures allow investors to diversify their portfolios and enhance returns by investing in commodities, or more to the point, in commodity derivatives. Even though managed futures began in the 1960s, investment in this new vehicle really did not take off until the 1980s when new research began to show the benefits of such investment. In 1980, less than $1 billion were under management through managed futures, but by 1994, this number was approximately $20 billion (Schneeweis and Spurgin 1997). Lintner (1997) appears to have been a catalyst for this area of research. He found that the return/risk ratio for a substantial portion of managed futures were higher than the ratios for diversified stock portfolios and, more importantly, that portfolios of stocks, bonds, or both combined with managed futures were substantially less risky for every expected return level than those portfolios without managed futures. Couple these results with other evidence that commodity prices are uncorrelated with the stock market, and suddenly investing in commodities became very popular. Chapter 12 contains further discussion of managed futures.

Since the introduction of managed futures, two other key financial product innovations—commodity index swaps and exchange-traded commodity funds—have allowed investors similar exposure to commodities in general and energy markets specifically. Both of these innovations created alternatives to managed futures in energy derivatives markets. The introduction of these new, largely passive investment vehicles—managed futures, commodity index swaps, and exchange-traded commodity funds—attracted a new pool of investors to commodity markets. In the literature, this trend is typically known as the "financialization" of commodities.

Between managed futures, commodity index swaps, and exchange-traded commodity funds, speculative activity in energy derivatives grew dramatically from the 1980s to 2008. As mentioned previously, assets under management (AUM) in managed futures went from less than $1 billion to about $20 billion in 1994. This number stayed under $50 billion until 2002, when it slightly exceeded $50 billion (Abrams, Ranjan, and Flores 2014). However, from 2002 to 2008, this market experienced substantial growth. According to Abrams et al., by 2004, these assets totaled slightly less than $150 billion and, by 2008, were just over $200 billion.

OTC commodity derivatives volume shows similar growth patterns to that of managed futures. For instance, OTC volume grew from less than $2 trillion in 2004 to more than $8 trillion in 2007 (Bunge and Burne 2012), and gross notional amounts outstanding grew from $1.4 trillion at the end of 2004 to peak at $13.2 trillion in the middle of 2008. To put this growth of OTC derivatives into context, Figure 9.5 shows the notional amounts outstanding and the gross market value for the global OTC commodity derivatives market starting in 1998. Growth in notional amounts outstanding for OTC commodity contracts was relatively stable from the middle of 1998 through the end of 2004 (with an annual growth rate of about 35 percent) compared to growth from the end of 2004 to the middle of 2008 (with an annual growth rate of 233 percent). In Figure 9.5, these trends appear to be more muted for the gross market value of these OTC derivatives contracts. However, the rates of growth are in fact more extreme. From the middle of 1998 through the end of 2004, the average annual growth rate in gross market value was 53 percent; whereas from the end of 2004 to the middle of 2008, the annual growth rate was 343 percent. After an extraordinary drop from the middle of 2008 to the end of 2008, both the notional amounts outstanding and the gross market value for OTC commodity derivatives have been in decline and, as of the end of 2016, are now close to where they were at the end of 2004. Although the BIS data covers all commodity derivatives with only a breakout for precious metals, the vast majority of the derivatives in Figure 9.5 are believed to be in energy. Mixon, Onur, and Riggs (2016) show that swaps for natural gas and light, sweet crude oil dominate the commodity swaps markets (see Figure 9.6).

The extraordinary growth in this relatively new pool of largely passive, speculative investment fueled concerns about its impact on rising commodity prices, and in particular, on rising fuel prices. According to a 2006 Senate staff report (U.S. Senate 2006), speculators had expended tens of billions of dollars in U.S. energy commodity markets in the previous few years and that speculation had contributed to rising U.S. energy prices. Shortly thereafter, the Senate published a second staff report about excessive speculation in the natural gas market (U.S. Senate 2007). In this report, the Senate staff finds that a single, speculative hedge fund was able to dominate the U.S. natural gas market in 2006 and that existing restraints on speculative trading

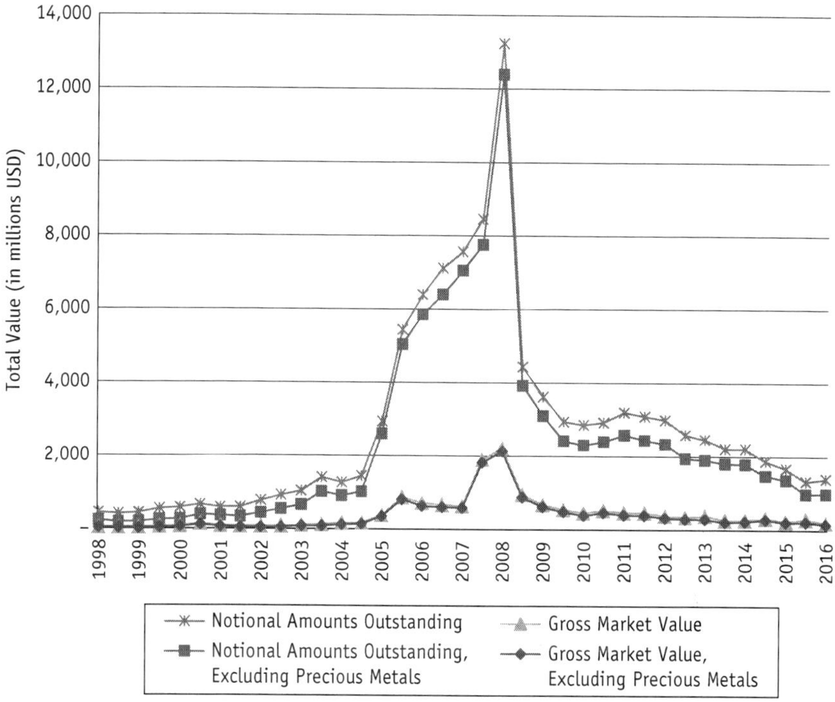

Figure 9.5 Global OTC Derivatives Market Commodity Contracts, All Instruments
This figure shows the notional amounts outstanding and the gross market value for the global OTC commodity derivatives market using data from the BIS Semiannual OTC Derivatives Statistics for the period June 30, 1998 to June 30, 2016. Growth in notional amounts outstanding for OTC commodity contracts was relatively stable from the middle of 1998 through the end of 2004 (with an annual growth rate of approximately 35 percent) compared to growth from the end of 2004 to the middle of 2008 (with an annual growth rate of 233 percent). These trends appear to be more muted for the gross market value of these OTC derivatives contracts. However, the rates of growth are in fact more extreme. From the middle of 1998 through the end of 2004, the average annual growth rate was 53 percent, whereas, from the end of 2004 to the middle of 2008, the annual growth rate was 343 percent. After an extraordinary drop from the middle of 2008 to the end of 2008, both the notional amounts outstanding and the gross market value for OTC commodity derivatives have been in decline and, as of the end of 2016, are now close to where they were at the end of 2004. Moreover, precious metals swaps are a relatively significant component of commodity swaps in terms of notionals. Source: Bank for International Settlements 2017.

to prevent price distortions were inadequate. Although debate still exists about the impact of financialization on commodity prices, these findings spurred various regulatory changes that provided greater oversight to these markets.

The CFTC has traditionally imposed position limits for certain agricultural futures contracts, but the exchange has administered position limits at its discretion on other futures and option contracts but not typically on swaps. The CME Group's

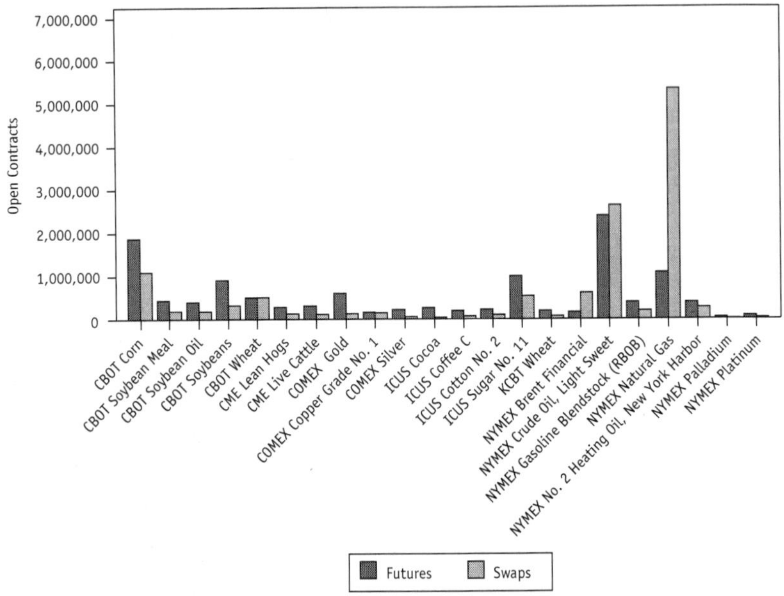

Figure 9.6 Average Daily Open Swaps versus Month-End Open Interest for Futures and Options Reported for June 2015
This figure shows the month-end open interest for select futures contracts relative to the average daily open swaps to which they are paired. Daily open swaps are averaged across the month of June 2015, and open interest values are month-end (June 30, 2015).

NYMEX exchange currently imposes spot-month position limits on its energy futures contracts. The intent of these spot-month limits is not only to deter excess speculation, but also (and arguably more importantly) to deter manipulation, particularly corners where one person (or a group of persons acting in concert) stands for delivery of a position that is very large relative to the economically deliverable supply. Exchanges also impose "position accountability" rules to non-spot month and all-months combined positions (for futures and options combined) under which an exchange can ask an entity with a position exceeding the position accountability level about the purpose of the position. In certain instances, an exchange can also ask the person not to increase the size of the position further.

The Dodd-Frank Wall Street Reform and Consumer Protection Act of 2010 (Dodd-Frank) amended the Commodity Exchange Act (CEA) to authorize the CFTC to establish position limits not just for futures and option contracts, but also for swaps that are economically equivalent to covered futures and options contracts. In late 2017, federal position limits for futures and swaps combined have not yet been imposed, but the CFTC has proposed regulations to set position limits for 24 commodities (Position Limits for Derivatives 2016). For energy markets, this proposal included limits for derivatives linked to the four main NYMEX energy contracts: Light Sweet Crude Oil (CL), NY Harbor ULSD (HO), RBOB Gasoline (RB), and Henry Hub Natural Gas (NG).

The Senate staff report on excessive speculation in the natural gas market (U.S. Senate 2007) was one of the first publications to report on both futures and swaps. However, this report only shows the use of futures and swaps for one entity in a very specific situation and, therefore, was not necessarily representative of the use of swaps and futures by market participants in general or even by speculators in particular. The lack of research on the use of swaps and futures was largely due to the opacity of the swaps markets. Research about swaps markets alone is relatively sparse, with much of that research on credit default swaps (CDSs) or interest rate swaps (IRSs). Research about commodity swaps markets is practically nonexistent with rare exceptions such as Peterson (2014). Hence, common ideas about swaps are generally based on what is known about CDSs and IRSs and little is known about energy swaps or even about commodity swaps in general. For example, market participants tend to view swaps as having long tenors (i.e., terms to maturity), and for CDSs and IRSs, this appears to be true. In CDSs, the typical tenor of an index swap is five years (Chen, Fleming, Jackson, Li, and Sarkar 2011). In IRSs, about 70 percent of gross notional are comprised of swaps with tenors greater than one year, and 35 to 40 percent are greater than five years (U.S. Commodity Futures Trading Commission 2016). According to Mixon et al. (2016), however, energy or other commodity swaps may not have such long tenors. They show that the tenor of exposure for WTI-linked swaps is relatively short-dated compared to IRSs or CDSs and is, in fact, very similar to the tenor of exposure for WTI futures and options open interest. For example, 71 percent of WTI open swaps and 78 percent of WTI futures and options open interest had a tenor of exposure less than one year. Moreover, about 2 percent of WTI open swaps and 2 percent of futures open interest had a tenor of exposure more than three years.

Mixon et al. (2016) examine both commodity swaps markets and futures markets. They conduct an in-depth analysis of swaps linked to WTI light sweet crude oil and the corresponding physical-delivery futures market for three groups of users: swap dealers, commercial end-users, and financial end-users (e.g., managed money, pension funds, and sovereign wealth funds). Although some activity in WTI derivatives by commercial end-users may fit Working's (1960) definition of speculative activity, all activity in WTI derivatives by financial end-users is likely to be speculative in nature. With that in mind, results from Mixon et al. for WTI futures and swaps largely resemble Working's (1960) results for futures—net long positions of financial end-users largely offset exposures of net short commercial end-users.

Mixon et al. (2016) add to Working (1960) by providing a view into the intermediation role played by swap dealers in this market across products and tenors of exposure in swaps. Basically, swap dealers sit in-between these two end-user groups. For example, financial end-users are the dominant users of index swaps for WTI exposure, and as a group, their net long WTI swap position is primarily composed of index swaps (about 80 percent). Furthermore, the vast majority of their net long WTI swap positions have a relatively short tenor (one year or less). In contrast, commercial end-users as a group hold a net short WTI swaps position comprised only of direct WTI swaps (i.e., swaps that are not index, basis, or inter-commodity spreads) and of slightly longer tenor but still primarily less than two years. Decomposing swap dealers' net positions in similar fashion shows their role as intermediaries in this market. For example, as a group, swap dealers hold a net long swap position composed entirely of direct WTI swaps similar in magnitude to the net short swap position for commercial end-users and a net short WTI position composed primarily of index swaps similar in magnitude to the net long swap position for financial end-users. Moreover, swap dealers in energy markets clearly use swaps and futures in combination to manage their overall net position. For example, swap dealers as a group held net long position in swaps that is similar in magnitude to their net short position in futures throughout 2014 (Mixon et al. 2016).

Effects of Regulation

As OTC derivatives, in particular swaps, became more actively traded in the 1990s, some debate existed as to whether these instruments were subject to the Commodity Exchange Act. The Commodity Futures Modernization Act of 2000 (CFMA) was hailed as providing legal certainty for the OTC derivatives markets (U.S. Commodity Futures Trading Commission 2000). Moreover, the CFMA allowed for electronic trading of these OTC derivatives. As previously noted, ICE started as a platform for electronic trading of OTC energy derivatives in 2000 and first began clearing OTC contracts in 2002. In 2002, NYMEX established the ClearPort platform for clearing energy derivatives.

The fact that clearing of OTC contracts began on ICE and NYMEX around the same time is no coincidence. A common belief is that clearing of OTC energy derivatives became popular after the collapse of Enron in December 2001 (Brunet and Shafe 2007) given that Enron's holdings were extensive. In 2000, Enron's financial reports indicated that their derivatives-related assets hit $12 billion, up from $2.2 billion, with most of the growth from its Internet trading system, EnronOnline (Schroeder 2002). At the end of September 2001, one estimate of Enron's gross derivatives trading liabilities, not accounting for collateral, was $18.7 billion (Henriques 2001).

With Enron's collapse, many traders realized the potential for counterparty risk and began clearing these OTC energy derivatives. ICE and NYMEX (NYMEX merged with CME in 2008), became the two main clearinghouses for these types of derivatives. "Over-the-counter energy clearing generated about $400 million or 30 percent of ICE's revenue last year [2011], and about $300 million, or 9 percent of the CME's" (Reuters 2012a).

OTC clearing of energy swaps stopped abruptly when, at the close of trading on October 12, 2012, ICE converted all of its OTC swaps contracts including existing positions to economically identical futures contracts and transferred trading from their OTC platform to their futures exchange, ICE Futures US. In a letter submitted to the CFTC on August 15, 2012 (Submission No. 12-45), ICE Futures US notified the CFTC of its plans to convert 435 swap and option contracts traded on ICE US OTC Commodity Markets LLC and cleared by ICE Clear Europe to futures contracts to be traded on ICE Futures US electronic central limit order book. In total, ICE apparently converted more than 800 OTC energy swaps to futures contracts (Acworth 2013).

At the same time, although not as abruptly, traders on NYMEX stopped converting OTC energy swaps to futures and began to trade the futures contracts directly

(Reuters 2012b). To maintain the bilateral nature of these trades, these new futures contracts are typically executed via privately negotiated "block trades" that are reported to the exchange and cleared through the clearing house (Reuters 2012b; Acworth 2013; Dunsky 2014). Although block trades traditionally have been limited to large transactions that were perceived as likely to have undue price impact if executed on the exchange's centralized market, NYMEX and ICE implemented very low block trading minimums for these products, often as little as one contract. The shift to blocks was dramatic. Before October 15, 2012, OTC swaps were 90 percent of all ClearPort activity, but on October 19, 2012, block-traded futures contracts accounted for 70 percent of volume (Reuters 2012b). In total, more than half of the notional daily trading of energy swaps (then estimated at $18 trillion) moved to futures (Leising 2013).

Many in the press dubbed this conversion of OTC swaps trading to futures trading as "futurization" and directly attributed the conversion to new regulations passed by the CFTC as a result of the 2010 enactment of Dodd-Frank. Before Dodd-Frank, OTC swap transactions were generally unregulated although certain natural gas and electricity swaps, known as significant price discovery contracts, were brought under limited CFTC oversight in 2008. Dodd-Frank brought these OTC energy derivatives fully under CFTC regulation. Moreover, October 12, 2012, was not a randomly selected date for the conversion but was specifically chosen because it marked the day when the swap definition went into effect and triggered the implementation of swap-related regulations. As Acworth (2013, p. 33) notes, "The main driving force in energy, according to exchange officials, was a desire by market participants to avoid certain Dodd-Frank rules, notably swap dealer registration, swap reporting requirements, and the extra-territorial impact of U.S. regulation." As of early 2017, very little clearing is done for commodity swaps. For the CME Group, the only cleared commodity swaps that appear to actively trade are four fertilizer swaps, one commodity index swap, and one grain and oilseed swap. The latter has the largest open interest and volume with 23,250 and 1,400 contracts respectively for January 9, 2017 (Chicago Mercantile Exchange 2017). ICE Swap Trade also appears to only have a handful of contracts that actively trade but has greater volume than CME (Intercontinental Exchange Swap Trade 2017).

By trading futures rather than swaps, market participants avoid triggering swap dealer or major swap participant (MSP) registration and all the additional requirements imposed on these entities as well as swap reporting requirements. Many participants apparently were worried about triggering the registration requirements for swap dealers or for MSPs mandated by Dodd-Frank and codified by CFTC regulations. These registration requirements are based on the amount of swap activity or exposure undertaken by firms such that firms exceeding some minimum threshold for either swap dealers or for MSPs must register as such. For swap dealers, the threshold is set as of 2018 at $8 billion in swap dealing per year, which is the same level as in 2012. For MSPs, a more complex test is available for determining the threshold as provided in CFTC regulation 1.3 for the legal definitions of swap dealer and MSP. More importantly than simply requiring registering as such, each designation has its own additional regulatory requirements as found in part 23 of the CFTC's regulations for the regulatory requirements associated with being a swap dealer or MSP. By early 2017, several large energy firms have registered as swap dealers but no currently registered MSPs exist.

The Dodd-Frank Act required, among other things, that more liquid swaps be subject to mandatory clearing and that swaps subject to the clearing mandate would also be required to be executed on a futures exchange or a new type of trading platform called a swap execution facility (SEF) if they are "made available to trade" on an exchange or SEF. To date, while the CFTC has subjected various interest-rate swaps and credit default swaps to the clearing mandate and the trading mandate, neither of these mandates has been implemented in the energy markets although, as noted, energy swaps were frequently cleared. Moreover, although the OTC cleared energy swaps traded on ICE and NYMEX would have been likely candidates for SEF trading, little information was available in late 2017 to ascertain the suitability of currently uncleared energy swaps for clearing or the trading mandate.

Summary and Conclusions

This chapter has described the structure of energy markets and discussed how market participants can use benchmark energy contracts, in conjunction with other derivatives, to create precise hedges of specific energy price risks to meet end-users' needs. The chapter continues with a discussion of speculation and position limits, and concludes with a discussion of the effects of new regulations, including "futurization" of swaps, whereby products that began as bilateral OTC swaps are now cleared and listed as futures contracts by futures exchanges.

Discussion Questions

1. Briefly explain why energy markets are important.
2. Describe some common features of energy markets.
3. Explain why supply and demand in energy markets are more elastic in the long run than in the short to medium term.
4. Explain how energy futures markets typically differ from other commodity futures markets such as agricultural markets.
5. Explain how and why the structure of energy derivative markets has changed over the last 30 years.
6. Describe two major legislative changes since 2000 that affected energy derivatives markets.

Disclaimer

Michael Penick and Lynn Riggs conducted and wrote the research presented for this chapter in their personal capacity and not in their official capacity as employees of the Commodity Futures Trading Commission (CFTC). The analyses and conclusions expressed in this chapter are those of the authors and do not reflect the views of other employees of the CFTC Office of the Chief Economist, other CFTC staff, the CFTC itself, or the United States Government.

References

Abrams, Ryan, Bhaduri Ranjan, and Elizabeth Flores. 2014. “Lintner Revisited: A Quantitative Analysis of Managed Futures Strategies.” White Paper, CME Group. Available at https://www.sigmanalysis.com/pdf/Lintner_Revisited_Quantitative_Analysis.pdf.

Acworth, Will. 2013. “Futurization: Dodd Frank Drives Swaps-to-Futures Migration.” *Futures Industry*, January, 33–36.

Aguilera, Roberto F., and Marian Radetzki. 2016. *The Price of Oil*. Cambridge: Cambridge University Press.

Bank for International Settlements. 2017. “Semiannual OTC Derivatives Statistics.” 1998-2016.

Brunet, Alexia, and Meredith Shafe. 2007. “Beyond Enron: Regulation in Energy Derivatives Trading.” *Northwestern Journal of International Law & Business* 27:3, 665–706.

Bunge, Jacob, and Katy Burne. 2012. “ICE Melts to Futures: Exchange to Overhaul Trading in Some Energy Contracts.” *Wall Street Journal*, July 30.

Chen, Kathryn, Michael Fleming, John Jackson, Ada Li, and Asani Sarkar. 2011. “An Analysis of CDS Transactions: Implications for Public Reporting.” Federal Reserve Bank of New York Staff Reports, no. 517.

Chicago Mercantile Exchange. 2017. CME Group Product Slate.

Dicker, Dan. 2011. *Oil's Endless Bid*. Hoboken, NJ: John Wiley & Sons, Inc.

Dunsky, Lisa. 2014. “EFRPs and Block Trades: Where Did They Come from and Where Are They Going?” *Futures & Derivatives Law Report* 34:1, 1–15.

Freeman, Sholnn. 2005. “Truck and SUV Sales Plunge as Gas Prices Rise.” *Washington Post*, October 4. Available at http://www.washingtonpost.com/wp-dyn/content/article/2005/10/03/AR2005100301657.html.

Hardy, Quentin. 2016. “Google Says It Will Run Entirely on Renewable Energy in 2017.” *New York Times*, December 6. Available at https://www.nytimes.com/2016/12/06/technology/google-says-it-will-run-entirely-on-renewable-energy-in-2017.html?_r=0.

Henriques, Diana B. 2001. “Enron's Collapse: The Derivatives Market That Deals in Risks Faces a Novel One.” *New York Times*, November 29. Available at http://www.nytimes.com/2001/11/29/business/enron-s-collapse-the-derivatives-market-that-deals-in-risks-faces-a-novel-one.html.

Intercontinental Exchange Swap Trade. 2017. “ICE Swap Trade Commodities End of Day Report.” Available at https://www.theice.com/marketdata/reports/158.

International Organization of Securities Commissions. 2012. *Principles for Oil Price Reporting Agencies: Final Report*. Madrid: International Organization of Securities Commissions. Available at http://www.iosco.org/library/pubdocs/pdf/IOSCOPD391.pdf.

Kaminski, Vincent. 2012. *Energy Markets*. London: Risk Books.

Leising, Matthew. 2013. “Energy Swaps Migrating to Futures on Dodd-Frank Rules.” *Bloomberg*, January 25. Available at https://www.bloomberg.com/news/articles/2013-01-25/energy-swaps-migrating-to-futures-as-dodd-frank-rules-take-hold.

Lintner, John. 1997. “The Potential Role of Managed Commodity-Financial Futures Accounts (and/or Funds) in Portfolios of Stocks and Bonds.” In Carl Peters and Ben Warwick (eds.), *The Handbook of Managed Futures: Performance, Evaluation, & Analysis*, rev. ed., 99–137. Chicago, IL: Irwin Professional Publishing, McGraw-Hill Companies Inc.

Mixon, Scott, Esen Onur, and Lynn Riggs. 2016. “Exploring Commodity Trading Activity: An Integrated Analysis of Swaps and Futures.” *Proceedings of the NCCC-134 Conference on*

Applied Commodity Price Analysis, Forecasting, and Market Risk Management. St. Louis, Missouri.

Penick, Michael A. 2010. "The Development and Current State of Derivatives Markets." In Robert W. Kolb and James Overdahl (eds.), *Financial Derivatives: Pricing and Risk Management*, 233–248. Hoboken, NJ: John Wiley & Sons, Inc.

Peterson, Paul E. 2014. "How Large Is the Agricultural Swaps Market?" *Proceedings of the NCCC-134 Conference on Applied Commodity Price Analysis, Forecasting, and Market Risk Management*. Available at http://www.farmdoc.illinois.edu/nccc134.

Position Limits for Derivatives. 2016. 81 Fed. Reg. 96704-96990 (to be codified at CFR 1, 15, 17, 19, 37, 38, 140, 150 and 151).

Reuters. 2012a. "CFTC Grants Last-Minute Relief on CME Commodity Swaps." October 12. Available at http://www.reuters.com/article/us-cme-swaps-idUSBRE89B15X20121012.

Reuters. 2012b. "CME Energy Swap Traders Swing Decisively to Futures-Data." October 23. Available at http://www.reuters.com/article/cme-swaps-idUSL1E8LNCU020121023.

Schneeweis, Thomas, and Richard Spurgin. 1997. "The Benefits of Managed Futures." In Carl Peters and Ben Warwick (eds.), *The Handbook of Managed Futures: Performance, Evaluation, & Analysis*, rev. ed., 17–48, Chicago, IL: Irwin Professional Publishing, McGraw-Hill Companies Inc.

Schroeder, Michael. 2002. "Enron's Dealing in Derivatives Helps Shift Spotlight to a Gap in Oversight." *Wall Street Journal*, January 28. Available at http://www.wsj.com/articles/SB1012168575563404120.

Sturm, Fletcher J. 1997. *Trading Natural Gas: Cash, Futures, Options and Swaps*. Tulsa, OK: PennWell Books.

U.S. Commodity Futures Trading Commission. 2000. Press Release #4479-00. December 15. Available at http://www.cftc.gov/opa/press00/opa4479-00.htm.

U.S. Commodity Futures Trading Commission. 2016. "Weekly Swaps Report."

U.S. Energy Information Administration. 2013a. "Manufacturing Energy Consumption Data Show Large Reductions in Both Manufacturing Energy Use and the Energy Intensity of Manufacturing Activity between 2002 and 2010." March 19. Available at https://www.eia.gov/consumption/manufacturing/reports/2010/decrease_use.php?src=<%20Consumption%20%20%20%20%20Manufacturing%20Energy%20Consumption%20Survey%20(MECS)-f3.

U.S. Energy Information Administration. 2013b. "Heating Oil Futures Contract Now Uses Ultra-Low Sulfur Diesel Fuel." *Today in Energy*. May 10. Available at http://www.eia.gov/todayinenergy/detail.php?id=11211.

U.S. Energy Information Administration. 2016. "Preliminary Estimates Show That U.S. Manufacturing Energy Consumption Increased between 2010 and 2014 MECS 2010 and 2014." October 13. Available at https://www.eia.gov/consumption/manufacturing/reports/2014/pre_estimates/?src=< Consumption Manufacturing Energy Consumption Survey (MECS)-f1.

U.S. Energy Information Administration. 2017. Monthly crude oil stocks available at https://www.eia.gov/petroleum/supply/monthly/.

U.S. Senate, Committee on Homeland Security and Governmental Affairs. 2006. *The Role of Market Speculation in Rising Oil and Gas Prices: A Need to Put the Cop Back on the Beat*. Washington, DC: Government Printing Office.

U.S. Senate, Committee on Homeland Security and Governmental Affairs. 2007. *Excessive Speculation in the Natural Gas Market*. Available at U.S. Senate Committee on Homeland Security & Governmental Affairs, Text from: *Committee Reports*. https://www.hsgac.senate.gov/subcommittees/investigations/issues/commodity-market-oversight.

Working, Holbrook. 1960. "Speculation on Hedging Markets." *Food Research Institute Studies* 2:May, 185–220.

10

Livestock

XIAOHU DENG
Assistant Professor of Finance, Tasmanian School of Business and Economics, University of Tasmania

ANDREW C. SPIELER
Professor of Finance, Frank G. Zarb School of Business, Hofstra University

DESMOND TSANG
Associate Professor of Accounting, Desautels Faculty of Management, McGill University

Introduction

Billions of people consume meat and other livestock products every day. The exponential growth rate in the world's population has facilitated an expansion in the livestock industry as producers attempt to meet increasing demand. Advances in technology and breeding practices have led to an evolution within the industry as production transitions from small family-run operations to large corporate production facilities. This commercialization of livestock production has created a layer of complexity that was once extraneous to the industry. The need for livestock producers to actively manage risks is vital to the profitability of their operations whether they are small ranchers or large corporate producers. Livestock futures contracts and options have become a staple in the price risk management strategies of all producers as well as a fertile ground for speculators who seek to capture profits by betting on the underlying's price movements. To effectively manage the risks associated with raising various types of livestock, understanding all aspects of the livestock industry from the process of raising animals to the external economic factors that affect the prices for livestock and livestock products has become critical.

Production

Understanding the production process of livestock provides a solid foundation that is essential to predicting future industry trends. Although similarities may exist in the methods used to raise different breeds of animals, gaining an awareness of the idiosyncrasies unique to raising specific types of livestock is important. From a financial perspective, the two most notable types of livestock are cattle (beef) and hogs (pork).

The following sections discuss the production cycles of cattle and hogs and some of the key characteristics unique to their respective production processes.

THE BEEF INDUSTRY

The production of cattle in the livestock industry begins with cow-calf producers or ranchers who breed herds of cattle. Ranchers use both natural and artificial breeding practices that emphasize the preservation of favorable genetics to be carried on between generations. The average size of a herd of cattle averages about 45 cows, each normally capable of giving birth to one calf per pregnancy with a nine-month gestation period (CME 2015a). Ranchers strategically breed their herds in the late summer months to avoid the risk of harsh winter conditions that could be fatal to young calves. In recent years, the cattle industry has shifted from small ranches to large cattle production operations. Calf producing operations with herds larger than 100 cows make up 9 percent of all calf producing operations and 51 percent of cattle inventory. Ranchers who use natural breeding methods rather than artificial insemination practices, typically employ one mature bull for every 20 to 25 cows (CME 2015a). Cows that miss annual pregnancies are often culled from the herd, sent off for slaughter, regardless of maturity. Calves are nursed by their mothers until they reach an age of six months when they are weaned from their mothers. At this age calves weigh an average of 500 to 600 pounds.

When weaned calves reach appropriate weights, ranchers will either contract with a stocker operation or sell the calves directly to a stocker operation that will place the weaned calves on land yielding a variety of harvest roughage such as summer grass or winter wheat. Stocker operators raise the weaned calves until they grow to a weight of 600 to 800 pounds. In this weight range, the calves are classified as feeder cattle and ready to be transferred to feedlots where they will continue to be fattened.

Feedlots in the United States are concentrated in the states of Colorado, Nebraska, Kansas, Oklahoma, and Texas with 2,000 operations producing 85 percent of fed cattle (CME 2015a). Feeder cattle owners have three options for transferring cattle to feedlots: (1) carry out feeding in their home operations, (2) transfer the cattle to a commercial feedlot while retaining ownership of the cattle, or (3) sell the feeder cattle outright to the feedlot. At this stage in the cattle production process, the feeder cattle receive high-energy feed consisting of grain, protein, supplements, and roughage that promote rapid weight gain. The majority of feeder cattle are comprised of steers (castrated males) and heifers (females that have not calved). Depending upon the type of feed, steers on feedlots gain an average of three pounds per day and consume an average of 24 pounds of feed per day, while heifers generally gain less weight per day and per pound of feed consumed. Feeder cattle typically remain in this stage of production for 90 to 300 days, ultimately reaching a weight of 1,000 to 1,300 pounds.

Weather conditions, feed prices, and the efficiency of the feedlot operation affect the length of time feeder cattle remain on feedlots. Extreme heat conditions can suppress the appetites of herds and lower daily weight gains, while extreme cold conditions can cause herds to use more energy to maintain body heat. Feedlot operators are more inclined to feed cattle when feed prices are lower, and are less inclined when feed prices are high. Vertical integration in the cattle production industry has led feedlots to shift toward very large and efficient operations, often employing in-house nutritionist and specialized equipment to monitor and maximize the amount of feed intake to weight gains. Larger operations allow feedlots to operate with greater economies of scale; however the complexity of larger operations increases the need to manage the price risk associated with inputs such as feeder cattle and the final output product—live cattle.

Once the cattle have reached weights of 1,000 to 1,300 pounds, they are classified as live cattle. At this point in production, live cattle are marketed to beef packers and processors through direct sales or auctions as either live animals or carcasses. In 2012, the average weight of live cattle for slaughter was about 1,305 pounds and the average carcass weight was 791 pounds (CME 2015a). Weights at which live cattle are marketed depend on current market conditions. Feedlots are inclined to keep cattle on feed when prices for live cattle are low. However, a limit exists to the amount of time cattle can remain on feedlots due to overly fattened cattle being subject to high pricing discounts.

PORK INDUSTRY

The consumption and demand for pork has increased substantially on a global scale and has effectuated many changes in the pork industry. To fully understand the market for pork and pork products requires developing knowledge of hog production and hog life cycles so that predictions can be made about changes or trends in the market. The life cycle of hog production can be divided up into three stages: (1) production of infant pigs, (2) fattening pigs to slaughter weights, and (3) slaughter and processing.

Hog production farms are comprised of four classifications: farrow-to-finish, finish-only, farrow-to-feeder, and farrow-to-wean. Farrow-to-finish farms handle the production of hogs from birth to the time they are ready for slaughter, while farrow-to-feeder and farrow-to-wean farms handle the production of hogs from birth until they reach a weight of 40 to 60 pounds and 10 to 15 pounds, respectively. Ultimately, all hogs from farrow-to-feeder and farrow-to-wean farms end up at finish-only farms. Finish-only farms raise hogs until they are of proper market weight and ready to be sold for slaughter. Changes in the hog industry have resulted in a movement to vertically coordinate the hog production process. Similar to the cattle industry, the majority of hog farms are finish-only and have shifted from small private operations to large corporate production facilities. In 2012, farms that produced more than 2,000 heads made up 87.5 percent of the hog inventory in the United States (CME 2015a). Most hog operations have become concentrated in the western Corn Belt and North Carolina.

The hog production life cycle begins with the breeding of baby piglets. Gilts (i.e., female pigs that have not given birth) and sows (i.e., female pigs that have given birth) are bred two times a year on a schedule that ensures a continuous flow of new hog inventory. Hog producers use three types of breeding methods: pen mating (a single boar with a group of sows and gilts), hand mating (a single boar and single sow or gilt), and artificial insemination. All three breeding methods emphasize preserving desirable genetic traits, such as health and leanness. After a four-month gestation period, sows and gilts give birth to a litter of nine to 10 piglets. Innovations in genetic engineering and breeding practices have led to substantial increases in the number of piglets per litter.

At an age of three to four months, baby pigs are weaned from their mothers and enter into the next stage of the hog production cycle. Male pigs will continue to be fattened to market slaughter weights, while most females are retained by farmers for two to three years to breed. After two to three years of breeding, female pigs are sold for slaughter. At an age of six months pigs will typically weigh an average of 270 pounds and are ready for slaughter. In 2012, the average weight of a live pig for slaughter was 275 pounds and the average carcass weight was 205 pounds (CME 2015a).

In the final stage of the hog production cycle, market-ready hogs are sold directly to packers and processors. The average hog carcass will yield 20 percent ham, 20 percent loin, 15 percent belly, 10 percent picnic, 5 percent spareribs, and 5 percent butt. A large portion of pork is processed and stored for substantial periods of time. Pork bellies, the meat processed into bacon, can be stored and frozen for up to a year before it is processed and packaged. Changes in the pork industry have also led to a handful of large corporate slaughterhouses controlling a large portion of market share. In 2012, the four largest hog slaughterhouses accounted for 64 percent of all hog slaughters (CME 2015a).

Financial Markets

Modern financial markets provide livestock producers and purchasers with multiple outlets to buy and sell their products, as well as a means to mitigate or transfer the risk associated with raising animals and producing livestock products. Understanding the financial markets and financial products available to livestock producers and purchasers is crucial for developing effective hedging and speculative strategies.

LIVESTOCK CASH MARKETS

Livestock cash markets facilitate the physical trading of livestock commodities, such as feeder cattle, live cattle, and lean hogs, between livestock producers and livestock purchasers. The production of different types of livestock has become concentrated to specific regions throughout the United States. Innovations in transportation and the expansion of infrastructure have led producers and purchasers of livestock to locate their facilities in the same geographical region so that delivery and the exchange process are economically efficient. The transaction process between producers and purchasers is carried out in local livestock auction markets at negotiated cash prices or through direct marketing methods where pricing methods can vary.

The price at which producers and purchasers transact in the cash market is referred to as the negotiated cash price or spot price. Spot price transactions take place in local auction barn sales, electronic auctions sales, and sales through dealers, brokers, and direct trades where livestock can be sold as live animals or as dressed carcasses. In theory, the spot price of any commodity is a function of current market supply and demand. However, the actual negotiated cash price in which producers and purchasers transact can be a function of the prevailing spot price, expected future spot prices, and premiums and discounts attributable to the quality of the livestock. Negotiated cash prices are required to be reported for price discovery and are tracked by the U.S. Department of Agriculture (USDA). Vertical integration of the livestock industry and the evolution of Alternative Marketing Arrangements (AMAs) have led to a decline of negotiated cash price transactions between livestock producers and purchasers.

AMAs have caused the majority of livestock transactions to shift from the cash market to more popular direct marketing methods. AMAs can include forward contracts, marketing agreements, production contracts, or packer ownership. Pricing methods in direct marketing transactions can vary and are directly negotiated between livestock buyers and sellers. Common price determination methods in direct marketing transactions include formula pricing, grid pricing, or frequent negotiations. Formula pricing involves the application of a mathematical formula that factors in other prices such as spot prices, future prices, and/or average purchase prices. Grid pricing establishes a base price that is adjusted by premiums and discounts for specific quality characteristics such as yield and grade. The base price used in grid pricing can be derived from formula pricing or any mutually agreeable pricing source such as spot prices, futures prices, or average prices of prior week purchases. Use of specific price determination methods in direct marketing transactions varies across different livestock industries. However, a commonality among all livestock industries is the shift from cash market transactions to direct marketing transactions.

LIVESTOCK FUTURES CONTRACTS

A *livestock futures contract* is a standardized, legally binding agreement between a buyer and a seller to accept delivery and make delivery of the underlying commodity at a predetermined delivery point, quantity, quality, and time period. A futures contract is not a written document; however, both the buyer and seller are legally bound to the implications inherent to the contract. All elements of the contract, such as the delivery point, quantity, quality, and time period, are standardized by the exchange facilitating the issuance and trading of the contract. The only element that is negotiable between the buyer and seller is the price of the contract. Price negotiation does not occur directly between buyers and sellers, but is innate in the bid-ask structure of exchanges (i.e., the interaction of demand from buyers and supply from sellers).

Although livestock futures contracts can either require physical delivery or cash settlement at expiration, the primary purpose of entering into a futures contract is price risk management, not to purchase the underlying commodity. Price risk management entails hedging the price at which a buyer can purchase or a seller can sell a commodity in the cash market, also referred to as the *spot price*. Using livestock futures contracts as a vehicle for price risk management requires entering into either a long futures position (obligation to buy) or a short futures position (obligation to sell). The decision to enter into a long or short futures position is determined by one's position in the cash market. Using livestock futures contracts to hedge price risk requires having opposing positions in the cash market and futures market. The effectiveness and optimization of price risk management is derived from the hedger's ability to record and predict changes in their basis. Basis is the relation between the cash market price and the future market price and will be discussed in more detail later in this chapter. Spot and future prices must be related because spot prices are derived from current supply and demand conditions in the market, whereas future prices are derived from expected supply and demand conditions at a later point in time. Implicitly, future prices predict the future spot price, and at the futures contract's expiration, spot and future prices should be interchangeable and any difference between the two should be a result of liquidity or other short-term market conditions.

LIVESTOCK OPTIONS

Although futures contracts can be very effective financial instruments for hedging or speculating changes in the price of livestock, the implications of a futures contract limit the ability to capitalize on favorable movements in prices. Livestock options offer the same protection from unfavorable movements in price as futures contracts without forgoing the opportunity to profit when prices move favorably. This situation is possible because options convey the right, but not the obligation, to buy (call) or sell (put) at a fixed price on or before a fixed expiration. Unlike long and short futures contracts, call and put options are not offsetting positions, but are two distinct financial instruments each with a buyer (holder), and seller (grantor or writer). The underlying of any livestock options contract is equivalent to a single futures contract in the respective month. For example, the underlying contract for a March Feeder Cattle option, call or put, is a March Feeder Cattle futures contract. Options that expire concurrent with the underlying futures expiration month are referred to as "standard" options. Additionally, other types of options are available with shorter life cycles than standard options such as serial options, which have a typical lifespan of 45 to 60 days, and weekly options that do not expire in the same month as the underlying futures contract. The underlying futures contract of a serial option is the futures contract expiring in the closest month after the option expires. Weekly options expire every Friday that is not an expiration date for standard or serial options. Weekly options are only listed on live cattle futures and are generally used to hedge event-driven risk such as upcoming government reports or regulations. Similar to a serial option, the underlying of a weekly option is the live cattle futures contract expiring in the closest month after the option expires.

The intrinsic value of the option is relative to the relation between the strike price and the underlying futures price. Hedgers and speculators are both concerned with the option's intrinsic value because the option's *premium*, the amount the holder of the option is required to pay for the rights, is the sum of the option's intrinsic value and a time premium. Livestock options are still one of the very few financial instruments traded on an open outcry platform.

PHYSICAL DELIVERY VERSUS CASH SETTLEMENT

Farmers, ranchers, feedlot operators, and food processors commonly use livestock futures contracts as a risk transfer mechanism, allowing risk reduction/transfer associated with weather conditions, interest rates, and market dynamics that impact commodity pricing. Speculators will also commonly buy (long) or sell (short) futures contracts to profit on expected movements in the price of the underlying asset. Often, the hedger or speculator who is long the contract (purchaser of the underlying commodity) does not have the ability or even the intention to take physical delivery of the underlying commodity. Given that neither counterparty expects to physically deliver or accept delivery of the asset, futures contracts are often closed out or offset by the losing party buying or selling an offsetting contract with the same underlying commodity and expiration date. Some contracts by nature are automatically closed out this way, such as lean hogs and feeder cattle, while other contracts, such as live cattle, will be subject to delivery if the party who is on the losing side of the contract does not enter into an offsetting position. The following example illustrates the concept of physical delivery versus cash settlement. Suppose a feedlot operator is bearish on live cattle prices and determines that hedging the price at which he can sell his live cattle on the cash market is necessary. To hedge the risk of falling prices, the feedlot operator enters into a short futures position, guaranteeing him a predetermined price at which he will be able to sell his live cattle at the contract's expiration. On the opposite side of the contract, a meatpacker is anticipating a bullish movement in the price of live cattle and enters into a long futures position in order to hedge the price at which it can buy live cattle. If the feedlot operator is correct and prices of live cattle are below the contract's predetermined price at the expiration date, the meatpacker that was long the futures contract is obligated to accept delivery at the contract's predetermined price. The meatpacker can forgo this obligation by selling back its long futures position in the market, thus entering an offsetting short futures position.

The majority of the time the contract will be closed out by the losing party electing to take a position in an offsetting contract. Physical delivery on live cattle futures occurs on less than 1 percent of traded contracts (CME 2015b). However, because live cattle futures contracts are inherently deliverable and require delivery for any contract that is not offset by the last trading day, if the meatpacker did not close out his long position he would have been required to accept delivery of 40,000 pounds of live cattle at a higher price than he could have purchased live cattle in the cash market. Although delivery of live cattle is uncommon, the fear and anticipation of delivery is a major feature of the futures market and it is important to note that the losing party must voluntarily elect to close out the contract in order to avoid making or accepting delivery. As mentioned previously, if the futures contract's underlying had been feeder cattle or lean hogs however, the losing position would have been automatically closed out by the exchange as physical delivery is not required and is never anticipated by either party.

OPEN OUTCRY VERSUS ELECTRONIC EXCHANGES

The stereotypical notion of traders shouting bids and offers on a crowded exchange floor is rapidly disappearing. However, this open outcry system continues to thrive in a small number of trading platforms. The Chicago Mercantile Exchange (CME), which facilitates trading of the largest volume of livestock futures contracts and options, operates both an open outcry platform and an automated electronic exchange called Globex. On the CME's open outcry platform only options can be traded, while Globex allows the trading of both futures contracts and options. Understanding the differences between open outcry and electronic exchanges is important because of the differences in the fundamental mechanics that underlie the two types of exchanges and how the trading process differs between the two systems.

In an open outcry, trades are executed in a ring-shaped trading pit. The process in which a trade order is delivered to the trading pit begins with a buyer or seller placing an order with a member firm. The party placing a trade may also inform the member firm of any trade restrictions or specific execution instructions such as a limit order or market order. A *limit order* instructs the trader to execute only at or better than the specified price, which in the case of a buy order is the ceiling price and a sell order is the floor price. A *market order* instructs the trader to execute the trade at the National Best Bid and Offer, commonly referred to as the NBBO. Once the member firm receives the order, it passes it on to its clerks located directly on the exchange floor. The clerk time stamps the order and hands it off to a runner who delivers the order to the member firm's broker in the trading pit. The broker now in possession of the trade instructions shouts out the order into the pit in search of another broker who can fill the order. As many brokers shout out orders at the same time, accurately conveying an order among the chaos can often be difficult. In order to augment the communication between brokers, brokers use a system of hand signals that indicate desires to buy or sell, the quantity of the contract, and the price. If a broker is required to fill a large order, he may do so by entering into trades with multiple brokers. The efficiency of the system of hand signals that brokers have developed in the trading pit enables brokers to transact with each other regardless of their proximity in the pit. Just from the use of hand signals brokers can execute trades with other brokers who are located on the opposite side of the trading pit. Once the order has been filled, the broker writes the details including price, quantity, and time as well as the buyer's or seller's identification number on a trade ticket and the information is sent off to the clearing agency. The execution price of the trade is entered into a computerized price reporting system for price discovery purposes. The final step of the trade entails the runner returning the filled order to the member firm's communications desk, which again time stamps the ticket and relays to the client that the trade has been executed. Trading pit brokers can typically execute about 60 trades per hour.

Rapid innovations in technology and the push for more efficient markets have caused trading platforms to shift from the traditional open outcry system to more modern electronic exchanges. Globex Exchange Trading System or more commonly Globex is an international automated order entry and matching system that is operated by Reuters Holdings PLC and the CME (Parikh and Lohse 1995). Globex operates continuously, unrestricted by borders and time zones, and facilitates the trades of various derivatives, although some types of derivative contracts have specified trading hours. The exchange operates using a broad array of order types including market and limit, and employs algorithms to facilitate order entry and the matching of bids and offers. Automatic exchanges such as Globex remove the human element that defines open outcry trading platforms and replaces it with a complex computerized exchange.

Major differences exist in the trading process on Globex compared to the trading process that takes place in the trading pit. Traders enter trades on Globex via a computer interface that allows them to view real-time data such as recent trades and a limited number of bids and offers in the order book. The *order book*, also referred to as the *limit order book*, is a record of unexecuted bids and offers that is maintained by computers on an electronic exchange and by a specialist in an open outcry exchange. Traders who want to place a buy or sell order can do so by navigating through an array of menus and options. Once a trader inputs an order into Globex, the order-entry algorithm facilitates the execution of the trade. The algorithm uses a standing price/time priority structure, arranging the best bids from highest to lowest price and the best offers from lowest to highest price. Trades are executed when bids and offers cross each other and orders with equal prices are executed based on time priority in the limit order book.

Once a trader enters an order and it is recorded in the limit order book, the trader can modify the order at any time before it is executed. However, if the trader does so, the order will lose its time priority in the limit order book, which can be detrimental to the execution of a trade in an illiquid market. This characteristic is a major disadvantage to trading on Globex compared to trading in an open outcry format. If a broker on the trading floor observes the market beginning to move away from him, he can easily alter his hand signals and shouting to account for the bullish or bearish movements. When a trader on Globex observes the market moving out of his favor, he cannot as easily modify his order without losing his priority in the order book.

LIVESTOCK FUTURES CONTRACT HIGHLIGHTS

Although livestock futures contracts with differing underlying commodities have many similarities that are standardized, the quantity, quality, and method of settlement may differ depending on the type of livestock the contract represents. The scope of this section is to discuss the different types of livestock futures contracts and the specific characteristics inherent to each type of contract. As with any contract, understanding what the contract represents and what obligations are required of the parties who enter into futures contracts is important. Table 10.1 summarizes the relevant futures contract details.

Feeder cattle are weaned calves that are typically less than one year of age and weigh between 600 and 800 pounds. Feedlot operators seeking to hedge the price at which they can purchase feeder cattle in the cash market and by farmers and ranchers seeking to hedge the price at which they can sell feeder cattle in the cash market often use feeder cattle futures. Feeder cattle futures contracts can only be traded on Globex, denoted by ticker symbol "GF," and are not traded in open outcry. Contracts are traded in sizes of 50,000 pounds or 500 hundredweight (cwt). The standardized quantity is denoted in pounds and not a specific number of feeder cattle due to the obvious fact that cattle differ in weight and size. Feeder cattle futures contracts are priced in cents per pound or dollars and cents per cwt. The minimum tick (minimum price change) of a contract is $0.00025 per pound or $0.025 per cwt, which equates to a minimum change of $12.50 per contract (500 cwt × $0.025 = $12.50). To prevent panic buying or selling in the market all feeder

Table 10.1 **CME Livestock Futures Contract Details**

	CME Live Cattle	*CME Feeder Cattle*	*CME Lean Hogs*
Contract size	40,000 pounds (lbs.) = 400 hundredweight (cwt)	50,000 pounds (lbs.) = 500 hundredweight (cwt)	40,000 pounds (lbs.) = 400 hundredweight (cwt)
Price unit	Cents per pound or dollars and cents per cwt	Cents per pound or dollars and cents per cwt	Cents per pound or dollars and Cents per cwt
Minimum tick	\$0.00025 per pound or \$0.025 per cwt = \$10/ contract	\$0.00025 per pound or \$0.025 per cwt = \$10/contract	\$0.00025 per pound or \$0.025 per cwt = \$10/contract
Daily price limits	\$0.03/pound above/ below the previous settlement price	\$0.045/pound above/ below the previous settlement price	\$0.03/pound above/ below the previous settlement price
Delivery type	Physical deliver	Cash settlement	Cash settlement
Contract months	Feb(G), Apr(J), Jun(M), Aug(Q), Oct(V), Dec(Z)	Jan(F), Mar(H), Apr(J), May(K), Aug(Q), Sep(U), Oct(V), Nov(X)	Feb(G), Apr(J), May(K), Jun(M), Jul(N), Aug(Q), Oct(V), Dec(Z)
Ticker symbol	LE	GF	HE

Note: This table summarizes the details of livestock futures contracts that trade on the Chicago Mercantile exchange.

Source: CME (2016).

cattle futures contracts are subject to daily price limits of \$0.045 per pound above or below the previous day's settlement price. If one or both of the first two listed contract months settle at the limit, the next business day the daily price limit will be expanded to \$0.0675 per pound. If on the next business day neither of the first two listed contract months settles at the limit, the daily price limit reverts to \$0.045 per pound on the following business day. Feeder cattle futures contracts are listed for expiration in the months of January, March, April, May, August, September, October, and November, and are all cash-settled. As previously discussed, the exchange automatically closes out a cash-settled futures contract such that physical delivery is never anticipated for feeder cattle futures contracts.

Following the cattle production process, feeder cattle become live cattle when they reach a weight of 1,000 to 1,300 pounds. Live cattle futures contracts have many similarities to feeder cattle futures contracts as well as some important differences. Like feeder cattle futures contracts, live cattle futures contracts are only traded on Globex, denoted by the ticker symbol "LE," and are unavailable to be traded in open outcry. Live cattle futures contracts also have a minimum tick of $0.00025 per pound or $0.025 per cwt. However, a live cattle futures contract represents 40,000 pounds or 400 cwt of live cattle, thus resulting in a minimum price change of $10 per contract (400 cwt × $0.025 = $10). The daily price limit for live cattle futures contracts is $0.03 per pound above or below the previous settlement price. If one or both of the first two listed contract months settle at the limit, the next business day the daily price limits will be expanded to $0.045 per pound above or below the previous day's settlement price. Assuming one or both of the first two listed contract months do not settle at the limit again, the daily price limit reverts to $0.03 per pound on the following business day. Live cattle futures contracts are listed for expiration in the months of February, April, June, August, October, and December, and are subject to physical delivery. The settlement method of live cattle futures contracts is the most noteworthy difference from feeder cattle futures contracts. If the hedger or speculator fails to take the necessary steps to close out positions in a contract before expiration, the hedge or speculator will be legally bound to accept or deliver 40,000 pounds of live cattle. Physical delivery rarely occurs because transportation and storage costs make it uneconomical and the primary purpose of the futures market is to hedge price risk and not purchase commodities. Yet, instances occur where physical delivery would have an economic advantage. At the time of the contract's maturity, if the basis is wider than anticipated and greater than the cost of delivery, making physical delivery on the contract would be advantageous rather than to close the contract (Wellman 1992).

Lean hog futures contracts trade similarly to live cattle futures contracts in that a single contract represent 40,000 pounds or 400 cwt of lean hog and is priced in cents per pound or dollars and cents per cwt. Lean hog futures contracts, like live cattle and feeder cattle, are only traded on Globex, denoted by the ticker symbol "HE," and are unavailable to be traded in open outcry. Similar to both live cattle and feeder cattle futures contracts, lean hog futures contracts have a minimum price tick of $0.00025 per pound or $0.025 per cwt, which equates to a minimum price change of $10 per contract (400 cwt × $0.025 = $10). Lean hog futures contracts also have daily price limits of $0.03 per pound above the previous day's settlement price and are subject to the same limit expansion guidelines as live cattle futures contracts. Lean hog futures contracts expire in the months of February, April, May, June, July, August, October, and December, and are cash-settled contracts. Lean hog futures contracts are used to hedge price risk at all levels of production in the pork industry because lean hogs are the only type of futures contracts in the pork market since the 2011 delisting of pork belly futures contracts.

In 1961, the Chicago Mercantile Exchange began listing pork belly futures contracts for meatpackers and food companies to hedge seasonal price risk and for traders to speculate on price direction. In the early decades of pork belly futures, demand was the highest in the summer months when many of its complementary products such as hamburgers were also in high demand. Slaughtering pigs and hogs, however, occurred year-round, often creating the need to freeze meat at different points throughout the year, primarily in the winter months, until demand called for it to be processed into bacon.

Over time, demand increased and consumers began eating more bacon year-round, causing a shift in the landscape of the pork belly market as the need for freezer storage of pork bellies began to diminish. With a steadying demand for pork bellies throughout all four seasons, the need to hedge seasonal price risk became irrelevant to many meat processors and food companies. Inevitably, open interest in pork belly futures contracts dwindled to almost nothing and volatility was excessively high. In July 2011, the CME announced to the public and regulatory authorities that it would be delisting all pork belly futures contracts. For decades, pork bellies were one of the most heavily traded CME contracts, but the change in market dynamics eliminated the need to hedge the price risk of bacon.

LIVESTOCK OPTION HIGHLIGHTS

Although hedgers and speculators heavily use livestock futures contracts for price risk management and speculation, livestock options can be just as effective at managing price risk and much less risky for speculative purposes. Each livestock option represents the right to either buy or sell one livestock futures contract with the same underlying. The premiums for all livestock options are priced in cents per pound and have minimum premium fluctuations of $0.00025 per pound for a full tick and $0.000125 per pound for a half tick. Strike prices for all puts and calls on all livestock options are listed in intervals of $0.02 per pound for all months and $0.01 per pound for the first two upcoming months. Unlike livestock futures contracts, livestock options are traded both on Globex and in the trading pit. Livestock options allow hedgers and speculators to avoid the commitment associated with live cattle futures contracts, because options do not legally bind the option holder to exercise their right to buy or sell. Table 10.2 summarizes the relevant option contract details.

CALCULATING BASIS

Although many traders use livestock futures contracts for speculative purposes, the fundamental application of livestock futures contracts is to provide market participants with exposure to commodities a means to hedge price-associated risk. The most critical concept that represents the effectiveness of a hedging strategy is "basis." *Basis* reflects the unique relation between cash market prices and futures contract prices. Understanding basis is critical because it allows livestock producers and processors to determine if they should use futures or alternative hedging instruments to manage price risks, if they need to make modifications to their risk management strategy, when they should close out their positions, and where they should ultimately buy or sell their livestock in the cash market.

Hedgers can have more than one basis to monitor if they sell livestock in multiple cash markets. This situation occurs because spot prices may differ between cash markets and the basis reflecting prices in one cash market may be different than the basis reflecting prices in another cash market. Hedgers only need to be concerned with spot prices that are relevant to the cash markets in which they commonly transact. Basis is also informative in determining which cash market offers better prices for buying or selling.

Current basis and deferred basis are determined using different futures prices. When calculating a current basis, which is the most common, the hedger should use

Table 10.2 **CME Livestock Option Details**

	Live Cattle Options	*Feeder Cattle Options*	*Lean Hogs Options*
Underlying contract	40,000 pounds (lbs.) CME Live Cattle Futures	50,000 pounds (lbs.) CME Feeder Cattle Futures	40,000 pounds (lbs.) CME Lean Hog Futures
Premium price unit	Cents per pound	Cents per pound	Cents per pound
Minimum premium fluctuation	$0.02/pound for all months $0.01/pound for front two months	$0.02/pound for all months $0.01/pound for front two months	$0.02/pound for all months $0.01/pound for front two months
Strike price intervals	$0.03/pound above/below the previous settlement price	$0.045/pound above/below the previous settlement price	$0.03/pound above/below the previous settlement price
Contract months	Standard: Feb, Apr, Jun, Aug, Oct, Dec Serial: Jan, Mar, May, Jul, Sep, Nov	Standard: Jan, Mar, Apr, May, Aug, Sep, Oct, Nov	Standard: Feb, Apr, May, Jun, Jul, Aug, Oct, Dec
Ticker symbol (Globex):	LE	GF	HE
Ticker symbol (Open Outcry):	Call: CK, Put: PK	Call: KF, Put: JF	Call: GH, Put: PH

Note: This table summarizes the details of livestock option contracts that trade on the Chicago Mercantile exchange.

Source: CME (2016).

the most current spot price minus the futures price in the nearest succeeding month. For example, if a rancher wants to calculate his basis in the month of October, he would take the current cash price from a specific cash market and then subtract the November futures price. To calculate a deferred basis, the hedger should use a forward cash market quote minus the futures contract price in the nearest month succeeding the month of the forward cash market quote. For example, if a rancher in the month of October is planning to sell some of his live cattle herd in the upcoming spring, the deferred basis would be the March cash quote minus the April futures price. Implicitly, a deferred basis reflects what the current basis should be at some point in the future. If the hedger believes that the forward cash market quote offers a better basis than what he expects at the time of physical delivery, the hedger should elect to use the cash contract. However, if the hedger expects a better basis than what the forward cash contract offers, he may instead want to use futures to manage the price risk.

The relation between local cash markets and futures prices may fluctuate over time, changing the basis. For a meaningful relation to exist between cash and futures markets, cash and futures market prices must move up and down with each other, thus exhibiting some level of correlation. However, this movement does not mean that prices must move with the same magnitude. When cash market prices and futures prices move with different magnitudes the basis will either strengthen (widen) or weaken (converge).

A basis can strengthen when prices in markets increase or decrease. When prices increase, the basis will strengthen if the cash market price increases more than the futures contract price. When prices decrease, the basis will strengthen if the cash market price declines less than the decline in the futures contract price. Analogously, the basis can also weaken in both declining and increasing price environments. When prices increase, the basis will weaken if the cash market price increases less than the futures contract price. When prices decrease, the basis will weaken if the cash market price decreases more than the futures contract price.

Hedgers can benefit from both a strengthening and weakening basis depending on whether they are short hedgers or long hedgers. Short hedgers or sellers of livestock will benefit from a strengthening basis where the cash market is stronger than the futures market. Long hedgers or purchasers of livestock will benefit from a weakening basis where the cash market is weaker than the futures market. In other words, sellers of livestock prefer for basis to become more positive (or less negative) and purchasers of livestock prefer for basis to become less positive (or more negative).

Calculating basis is a simple concept, but also very important to understand in order to effectively manage risk. The due diligence of recording and monitoring changes in a hedger's basis is essential to the performance of his hedging and should not be underestimated.

ECONOMICS OF LIVESTOCK SUPPLY AND DEMAND

Understanding the production cycles of hogs and cattle is essential to forecasting prices of livestock. However, to make accurate estimates hedgers and speculators need to understand the economic factors that influence and cause changes in the production cycles. Hedgers and speculators must distinguish between factors that change the quantity supplied and demanded, as opposed to factors that cause a change in supply and demand—two very different and critical economic concepts.

Using a pipeline approach to estimate slaughter and production of either hogs or cattle is an effective way to forecast changes in the prices of livestock. When using this type of estimation process, being cognizant of the economic factors that can cause changes in the quantity supplied or cause the supply curve to shift is crucial. A change in the quantity supplied or movement along the supply curve represents a short-term immediate effect resulting from a change in the price of livestock itself. Short-term changes in quantities of livestock supplied generally have minimal impact on long-term market trends and often result from unexpected circumstances such as harsh winters or disease outbreaks. Conversely, factors external to the production pipeline cause a shift in the supply curve and are more often realized in the long term or following production cycles. External factors that can result in a shift of the supply curve are changes in the price of inputs, substitute goods, joint products, technological advancements, and institutional factors.

In the livestock production process the most important inputs influencing supply are the prices of feed and feeder animals. Increases or decreases in the prices for these inputs will cause the supply curve to shift either left or right. For example, if the price for feed or feeder animals increases, ceteris paribus, the supply curve for fed animals will shift to the left, resulting in a lower quantity supplied at the same price. The increase in price of the inputs makes production less attractive based on the current supply curve. In other words, because an increase in the price of feed or feeder animals makes producing fed animals more expensive, producers will be less inclined to continue feeding animals or purchase feeder animals at current price levels. A decrease in the price of the same inputs, ceteris paribus, would make production of fed animals more attractive and result in a shift of the supply curve to the right, or a greater quantity supplied at the same price.

The shift in the supply curve, left or right, will normally not be realized immediately. In fact, in the short term the change in the price of feed or feeder animals may have a reverse impact on supply. For example, if the price of feed decreases, a resulting shift in the supply curve to the right would likely result in the long term. However, in the short term, the supply of fed animals may decrease because producers may be more inclined to keep animals on feed for a longer period and fatten them to greater weights.

Substitutes are competing goods that offer comparable levels of utility and are produced with similar resources and are interchangeable among consumers. Changes in the price of a good will affect the supply of the substitute good. For example, because meat products may be substitutes, a decrease in the price of cattle will shift the supply curve for hogs to outward. The decrease in the price of cattle leads livestock producers to shift resources toward greater hog production or other goods with relatively higher prices. The opposite occurs if the price of cattle increases.

Joint products are goods that are derived from a single commodity and are produced proportionally to the supply of the commodity. Pork bellies and hog carcasses are an example of joint products. Unlike substitutes, an increase in the price of a joint product causes the supply curve for the other joint product to shift rightward. Similarly, a decrease in the price of a joint product causes the supply curve for the other joint product to shift leftward.

Technological advancements shift the supply curve to the right because advancements in technology generally increase profit margins and productivity. Common technological advancements in the livestock industry pertain to improvements in genetics and feed, and the introduction of new breeds, all of which lead to higher yields of lean meat from hog and cattle carcasses.

Institutional factors have a large impact on supply in the livestock industry, such as interest rates, regulations, restrictions, and government programs with oversight over the livestock production standards and waste disposal. Institutional factors can cause supply curves to shift either left or right. For example, decreases in interest rates will shift supply curves outward because cheaper capital enables livestock producers to expand or make improvements to their existing operations. Stricter waste disposal regulations may result in a leftward shift in supply curves as costs associated with disposing waste increase.

Aside from supply concerns, many factors affect the demand for livestock and livestock products. A strong understanding of such factors is critical to demand forecasts and ultimately developing a price risk management strategy. Factors affecting demand include changes in consumer attitudes and their decisions to consume different products and services. Similar to supply, differentiating a change in quantity demanded from a change in demand is essential. A change in quantity demanded is a movement along the existing demand curve and is generally a short-term movement resulting from occurrences such as seasonality of livestock products and their complements. A change in demand results in a leftward or rightward shift of the existing demand curve and is caused by factors such as changes in demographics (e.g., population and age), income, the price of substitutes and complements, and consumer preferences.

Increases in population growth will result in a concomitant increase in demand. However, the population age distribution may also change. For example, an increase in newborns and children will have less impact on demand compared to their later teenage and adult years. Because temporal shifts in population growth and distribution occur over years if not decades, any change is only relevant to long-term analysis and generally has limited impact on short-term trends and analysis.

Changes in income also affect the demand curve. However, the relation is more complex than for population factors. For example, when incomes rise the demand curve for expensive cuts of beef may shift rightward (or perhaps even to the left if consumers substitute sushi for meat). However, the demand curve for less expensive meats such as ground beef may shift leftward. Furthermore, although an increase in income allows consumers to afford more expensive meat, an upper limit exists to the amount of meat people can consume regardless of income.

Substitutes have supply similar effect on demand. When the price of a substitute good increases, the demand curve for the opposing good shifts outward and vice versa. Complementary goods, goods whose demand is positively correlated to changes in price of another good, exhibit a positive cross elasticity of demand. For example, barbeque sauce is a complement to many meat products such as hamburgers or pork. Therefore, if the price for hamburgers or pork decreases, consumers will demand more hamburgers and pork as well as more barbeque sauce. The result is a rightward shift in the supply curve for both barbeque sauce and the underlying meat.

Changes in consumer preferences can result in changes in demand. However, predicting changes in consumer preferences can be very difficult. Many external factors influence consumer preferences, such as changes in income, social influences, corporate advertising, and available substitutes. Analyzing factors that affect consumer preferences particularly in the short term can be difficult because consumer preference generally changes over longer periods; an exception would be the 2003 outbreak of mad cow disease (Schlenker and Villas-Boas 2009).

International Livestock

Worldwide, growing populations and incomes have resulted in large increases in demand for meat and livestock products. The livestock industry has been a major catalyst and focused on the development in emerging markets and poor countries as a means to modernize their economies. Although the United States is a dominant participant in international livestock exports and imports, several key countries, including China, Japan, Indonesia, Ethiopia, Brazil, and Australia, have increasingly grown their respective market shares in the global livestock industry.

Australia is a large exporter of Brahman-cattle, a popular breed for meat processing that is also common in the United States, Brazil, and Argentina. In contrast to the United States, a net importer of cattle, Australia exports about two-thirds of its cattle production to countries such as Japan, South Korea, and the United States. Australian cattle production is concentrated on the coasts, where rain falls in monsoonal conditions during the summer months in the north and during the winter months in the south. Heavy rainfalls are optimal for the pasture system used by many cattle producers in Australia. Under a pasture system, cattle are placed on large pastures where they feed on grass rather than supplemental feeds such as wheat and corn. Pasture systems are more cost efficient than grain feeding and produce leaner meats with little to no marbling (i.e., fat content). As cattle producers locate further inland, annual rainfall amounts decline, limiting the amount of Australian cattle that can be sustained per hectare.

In Ethiopia, agriculture plays a major role in economic development, accounting for 42 percent of GDP, 77 percent of employment, and 84 percent of exports (Ethiopian ATA 2016). Unlike modern economies, the Ethiopian livestock sector is comprised of subsistence farmers who consume most of their production. Growth in the livestock sector has been stagnated by few incentives for subsistence farmers to expand production and limited access to financing. However, Ethiopia has one of the largest livestock populations in Africa with around 54 million cattle and 50 million goats and sheep (Leta and Mesele 2014). The government of Ethiopia has focused on incentivizing livestock producers as well as encouraging the employment of modern farming practices such as using fertilizers to grow feed and advanced breeding methods.

Brazil has made remarkable strides over the last few decades to modernize its economy. In 2015, Brazil was the second largest cattle producer at 9.4 million metric tons, only trailing the United States, which produced 10.8 million metric tons (US Department of Agriculture 2016). Cattle production is concentrated in the central tropical region of Brazil, where climate conditions are most appropriate for raising herds and growing feed. Brazilian cattle producers raise herds that yield a variety of beef including grain-fed, certified, lean, and marbled beef. The Brazilian government has negotiated foreign trade agreements with countries in Asia and the Middle East to facilitate its goal of growing its exports and market share in the livestock industry. Brazil has also developed its own financial exchange that facilitates the issuances and trading of livestock futures and options.

Overall, several factors incentivize the development of livestock industries in emerging markets. Countries such as Brazil have become leaders on par with the United States in global livestock production and are exponentially growing their market share. Over time, if this trend continues, major changes may result in global supply and demand conditions. Understanding and tracking developments in international livestock markets to forecast changes in supply and demand, as well as changes in exports and imports, are important.

Summary and Conclusions

In the livestock industry, both producers and consumers must have a sound knowledge of the factors that influence prices for livestock and livestock products and the risks associated with different levels of production. Animals have unique life cycles and production processes that may present risk specific to that type of livestock. Understanding of these factors helps predict future supply and demand. Both livestock producers and purchasers must actively engage in price risk management to maximize the profitability of their operations. A price risk management strategy can only be successful if hedgers understand the risks associated with their operations and allow for their strategy to take a dynamic approach when dealing with these risks.

Modern financial markets provide many financial products to facilitate the unique risk management strategies of operations of all sizes. Hedgers must be proactive in their risk management strategies by continuously monitoring supply and demand conditions, regulations, and other external economic factors. Hedgers using financial products in their risk management strategies must also continuously monitor their basis for each cash market they transact in and keep well-documented records. Speculators must also have a deep understanding of the livestock industry to develop successful trading strategies. The livestock industry remains a means to propel developing countries into modern economies. Governments of developing nations nurturing their livestock industries act as a catalyst for the globalization of livestock production. Ultimately, as livestock industries in developing countries adopt technological advancements and improved breeding practices, they will be able to compete on a global scale, facilitating globalization and adding an additional layer of complexity to the industry.

Discussion Questions

1. Jameson Meatpackers is a large buyer of live cattle. Jameson purchases its live cattle from various feedlots and engages in grid pricing using the current spot price for its base price and adjusting for premiums and discounts depending on the quality of the live cattle. Jameson is concerned that over the next few months, spot prices for live cattle are likely to increase. As a hedging measure, Jameson enters a short position on 100 live cattle futures contracts. Explain whether this strategy is appropriate for Jameson in order to hedge an increase in the spot prices of live cattle.

2. Jameson Meatpackers purchases hogs in two cash markets located in the western Corn Belt. John Jameson oversees basis calculations and record-keeping. He receives a lean hog futures quote for next month for $0.5025 per pound. He also knows that all week he can buy hogs in the two cash markets Jameson transacts in, in Market A for $0.50 per pound and in Market B for $0.505 per pound. Describe how many and what type of bases Jameson must calculate. Explain what Jameson can infer from these calculations. Explain what basis changes Jameson is expecting if he entered a long position on a lean hogs futures contract at $0.5025 per pound.
3. Describe the differences between live cattle and feeder cattle futures contracts.
4. Before the delisting of pork belly futures contracts, a trader wanted to speculate on pork belly pricings using options. Explain whether and why the trader would have been better off placing his trade on Globex or in an open outcry.
5. Explain how changes in the quantity supplied and demanded for livestock differ from changes in supply/demand.

References

Chicago Mercantile Exchange (CME). 2015a. "Livestock Futures and Options: Introduction to the Underlying Market Fundamentals." Available at https://www.cmegroup.com/trading/agricultural/files/livestock-fundamentals.pdf.

Chicago Mercantile Exchange (CME). 2015b. "Self-Study Guide to Hedging with Livestock Futures and Options." Available at http://www.cmegroup.com/trading/agricultural/files/AC-215_SelfStuy_GuideNYMEX.pdf.

Chicago Mercantile Exchange (CME). 2016. "Livestock Futures and Options." Available at http://www.cmegroup.com/trading/agricultural/livestock.html.

Ethiopian ATA. 2016. "Production and Productivity." Available at http://www.ata.gov.et/programs/production-productivity/.

Leta, Samson, and Mesele Frehiwot. 2014. "Spatial Analysis of Cattle and Shoat Population in Ethiopia: Growth Trend, Distribution and Market Access." March. Available at https://springerplus.springeropen.com/articles/10.1186/2193-1801-3-310.

Parikh, Satu S., and Gerald L. Lohse. 1995. "Electronic Futures Market versus Floor Trading: Implications for Interface Design." Working paper, Finance Department, Operations and Information Management Department, University of Pennsylvania.

Schlenker, Wolfram, and Sophia B. Villas-Boas. 2009. "Consumer and Market Responses to Mad Cow Disease." *American Journal of Agricultural Economics* 91:4, 1140-1152.

US. Department of Agriculture (USDA). 2016. "Livestock and Poultry: World Markets and Trade." October. Available at https://apps.fas.usda.gov/psdonline/circulars/livestock_poultry.PDF.

Wellman, Allen C. 1992. "G84-726 Delivering Slaughter Steers on a Live Cattle Futures Contract." April. Available at http://digitalcommons.unl.edu/cgi/viewcontent.cgi?article=1637&context=extensionhist.

11

Metals

GREG LEONARD
Senior Advisor, Cornerstone Research

CHANEL O'NEILL
Principal, Cornerstone Research

Introduction

Trading metals physical and derivatives is generally similar to trading in other commodities. Futures and options on standardized metal specifications, units, and delivery locations are traded for eventual cash or physical settlement on a number of exchanges. Over-the-counter (OTC) physical and derivatives trading is also common. As with most commodity trading, only a small percentage of derivatives trades is ultimately physically settled, and only a small percentage of physical trading is included in the setting of reference spot prices. As with most commodities, the academic literature finds that metals have relatively flat real prices over the long term but experience cyclical pricing. This chapter explores the sources and uses of various exchange-traded metals, highlights differences across exchanges, and then examines the individual metals, including recent changes in trading, products, and market structure. The individual metals sections follow the industry and trading convention of grouping metals into precious metals, non-ferrous base metals, and ferrous metals.

Metal Sourcing

Metal is primarily sourced from mines. The time from exploration to commercial production often exceeds 25 years, which can result in long periods when increasing demand is met with price increases until more supply can be brought online (Cuddington and Jerrett 2008). Due to the length of these price cycles, they are sometimes called super cycles. Metal trading strategies may be based on these super cycles.

Different metals are often joint outputs of individual mines. For example, lead, zinc, copper, gold, and silver are usually found together. In the case of silver, about one-third comes from silver mines, another third from lead-zinc mines, and the final third from gold and copper mines (O'Connell et al. 2016c). Thus, calculations of expected mine profitability often depend on the prices of several metals.

Mining of some metals is concentrated in a few countries, while other metals are more evenly dispersed. Platinum and palladium are the most geographically concentrated of the major metals, with approximately 75 percent of production from South Africa and Russia. When a metal is primarily sourced from just a few countries, events in one of those countries may affect market prices. For example, a 17 percent increase in the price of platinum accompanied a series of strikes at South African platinum mines in August through October 2012 (Saefong 2012). Table 11.1 summarizes the top mining sources of each metal, as well as scrap's contribution to production, when available.

Although metal is primarily sourced from mines, the underlying fundamentals of metals markets differ from energy and agricultural commodities in that scrap metal is a major source of supply for many metals. For example, about one-third of steel and aluminum production as well as about one-quarter of gold production is sourced from scrap. This secondary production has the potential to mitigate supply-demand imbalances that would otherwise be addressed through higher prices.

Several other nuances of metal production should be kept in mind when evaluating which news is likely to affect metal prices. The first nuance is that mined production and metal production often occur in different locations. For example, China is the source of about 20 percent of the ore used to produce aluminum but produces over half of the world's aluminum, relying on imports to fill the production gap (USGS 2016). A second nuance is that metal concentration varies substantially across ores. For example, high-grade iron ore from Australia or Brazil contains on the order of 60 percent iron, while iron ore mined in China averages only 20 to 30 percent iron (Lian et al. 2015). Thus, despite China being the largest producer of iron ore by ore weight, it is not the largest producer of iron ore as measured by refined metal produced from the ore, as shown in Table 11.1. Even seemingly small differences in ore concentration can have a large effect on transport and refining costs. For example, Yap (2014) reported that nickel ore from Indonesia has an average ore concentration of 1.8 percent nickel, while ore from the Philippines has an average concentration of 1.5 percent, which translates into 20 percent more ore transport and processing with Philippine than Indonesian ore for the same amount of refined metal.

A third nuance is that metal production costs are highly dependent on energy costs because metal production is energy intensive. For example, electricity typically accounts for about one-third of aluminum production costs (Burns 2015). Energy, or more specifically coking coal and coke, typically accounts for 20 percent of steel production costs (Obayashi 2016). Steel is often produced from a blast furnace using coke as an energy source, which in turn is produced from metallurgical, or coking, coal. The *Steel Index*, a Platts publication, reports coking coal and coke prices as well as iron ore and steel prices, reflecting the large impact of energy cost on steel.

Metal Demand

Most metal is used in industry, and multiple metals are often used in the same product, such as cars, electronics, industrial machinery, or household appliances. More broadly, metals are often used together in the same industry, such as construction

Table 11.1 **Precious Metal Sourcing in 2014**

	First-Ranked Producing Country		*Second-Ranked Producing Country*					
Metal	***Country***	***Share of Mined Production (%)***	***Country***	***Share of Mined Production (%)***	***Mined Production***	***Secondary Production (Scrap)***	***Primary and Secondary Production***	***Share of Production from Scrap (%)***
Panel A. Precious Metals								
Gold	China	15	Australia	9	3,010.0	1,125.0	4,135.0	27
Silver	Mexico	19	China	15	26,800.0	5,240.0	32,040.0	16
Platinum	South Africa	64	Russia	16	146.0	39.7	185.7	21
Palladium	Russia	43	South Africa	30	193.0	76.2	269.2	28
Panel B. Base Metals								
Bauxite (Aluminum Ore)	Australia	32	China	22	245.0			
Aluminum					54.0	24.2	78.2	31
Copper	Chile	31	China	10	18.5	3.9	22.2	18
Lead	China	49	Australia	15	4.9	5.8	10.6	55
Nickel	Indonesia	31	Philippines	12	2.7	N/A	N/A	N/A
Tin	China	38	Indonesia	15	0.3	0.0	0.4	N/A
Zinc	China	37	Australia	12	13.3	N/A	13.3	N/A
Iron Ore-A[a]	China	45	Australia	22	3,373.6			
Iron Ore-B[b]	Australia	36	Brazil	19	2,054.1			
Steel					1,085.0[c]	585.0[c]	1,670.0	35

Note: This table shows sources of precious metals (metric tonnes) and base metals (millions of metric tonnes), by country.

[a] Measured in raw tonnage.

[b] Measured by converting Chinese ore to world average Fe content.

[c] Estimated based on 2014 scrap estimate

Source: O'Connell et al. (2016a, 2016b, 2016c) USGS (2016); International Aluminium Institute (2016); Willeke et al. (2016); World Steel Association Economics Committee (2016). All USGS data are compiled from USGS Mineral Yearbook (2014), except nickel data, which are from the USGS Mineral Yearbook (2013)

and transportation, and are also often used in sectors that have highly correlated economic growth. For example, the six London Metals Exchange (LME) base metals—aluminum, copper, lead, nickel, tin, and zinc—are all critical inputs in construction, transportation, and heavy industry manufacturing. The precious metals platinum and palladium are also used primarily in the transportation sector as inputs to catalytic converters.

Although metal prices tend to move together over the long term, daily price movements and forward curves of different metals do not consistently move together. Based on extensive academic research, monthly base and precious metal price movements are positively correlated over the long term, between and even more strongly within groups (Rossen 2014). Correlations based on daily data show strong and persistent positive correlations between returns on gold and returns on both silver and platinum, but weaker correlations between other metals pairs. Forward curves show substantial differences across metals, with some metals in contango and others in backwardation.

Metal Trading on Exchange

The most important exchanges for metal derivatives trading are the LME; COMEX, one of the CME Group exchanges (CME); and the Shanghai Futures Exchange (SHFE). For precious metals, the CME is the most important followed by the SHFE. Both exchanges have large trading volumes on gold and silver futures, and the CME also offers platinum and palladium futures. The LME and the SHFE have the largest volumes on the six non-ferrous base metals. The SHFE also has the largest trading volume in steel futures.

Beyond differences in metals traded, the three exchanges and the contracts they offer differ in various ways. The LME, as the oldest of the three exchanges, has conventions not seen on other exchanges. For example, it offers spot and futures trading, with daily contracts out to three months, weekly contracts out to six months, and monthly contracts beyond that. In contrast, the CME and SHFE offer monthly contracts. The similarities in specifications between the CME and the SHFE contracts (e.g., monthly rather than daily contracts) facilitate trading strategies and hedging using contracts on both of these exchanges.

The exchanges differ in which contract maturity is quoted as the reference price for each metal. This can complicate price comparisons and the ability to arbitrage across the exchanges. On the LME, the two reference prices are the three-month contract and spot, and other contracts are often quoted at a spread to these contracts. LME trading volume concentrates in the three-month contract. The CME reference contract, known as the active month, varies by metal and is defined in its contract specifications. The SHFE has not developed a reference month convention, although trading volume tends to concentrate in the contract three months out for base metals, following LME convention, and in the June and December contracts for gold and silver. Jointly trading SHFE contracts along with contracts on the LME and the CME is also complicated by evolving Chinese currency controls and differences in quotation currency. The LME and the CME both quote in USD, while the SHFE quotes in RMB.

Another difference across exchanges is in the offering of options, an important part of hedging and speculating. The SHFE, the newest exchange, offers only futures, while the other two exchanges have substantial trading in options.

A final important difference across exchanges is the locations of delivery warehouses. The LME has by far the greatest geographic spread in its warehousing network with facilities in 14 countries (set in areas of net consumption). The other two exchanges offer only regional delivery, but the SHFE offers delivery in China, the world's largest metal producer and consumer, where the LME has no warehouses. Although the LME remains the dominant base metal exchange, it has been losing volume to the SHFE. The differing value of a metric ton (MT) of each metal affects the importance of delivery location. At 2016 prices, gold may was worth $40 million or more per MT, silver was valued on the order of $500,000 per MT, non-ferrous base metals were valued on the order of $1,000 to $20,000 per MT, and steel was on the order of $500 per MT. Although putting gold on a plane from New York to London to settle a contract might be profitable, the delivery expense for base metals makes local delivery more essential. Even for gold, however, delivery location can be critical due to import/export controls and tax rules.

Other exchanges are important for one or two metals, including the Shanghai Gold Exchange (SGE) and the Dalian Commodity Exchange (DCE) for iron ore. Table 11.2 lists the top 15 metal futures contracts.

Precious Metals

The precious metals grouping of gold, silver, platinum, and palladium owes as much to history as common features. There exist metals both rarer and more expensive. Gold, silver, and, to a lesser extent, platinum were traditionally used in jewelry, coins, or other stores of value given their rarity and resistance to corrosion. Palladium was a late addition to the precious metal group, while other rare and expensive metals were not labeled precious metals.

TYPES OF PRECIOUS METALS

Gold and silver are more malleable and have lower melting points than platinum and palladium, facilitating their early use in coins and jewelry. Figure 11.1 provides more details on current end uses of gold and silver. Platinum and palladium are primarily consumed by industrial applications.

Gold

Gold has the largest trading volume by value of the four precious metals and is more frequently traded as a type of currency, or store of value, than as an industrial input. Mine output affects gold prices, but mine output by country and company is not sufficiently concentrated for individual production country or company events to cause supply shocks. Another reason that one producer is unlikely to cause a supply shock is

Table 11.2 **Top 15 Metal Futures Contracts in 2015**

Commodity	*Exchange*	*Contract Size*	*Number of Contracts Traded in 2015* **(million)**	*Total Volume Traded in 2015* **(million MT)**	*Options Available*
Precious Metal					
Gold (GC)	CME	100 troy ounce	41.8	130,160	Yes
Gold	SHFE	1 kg	25.3	25,317	No
Silver	SHFE	15 kg	144.8	2,171,797	No
Silver (SI)	CME	5,000 troy ounce	13.5	2,092,397	Yes
Base Metal (Non-Ferrous)					
Aluminum	LME	25 MT	59.9	1,497	Yes
Aluminum	SHFE	5 MT	22.9	115	No
Copper Grade A	LME	25 MT	38.6	964	Yes
Copper	SHFE	5 MT	88.3	442	No
Copper (HG)	CME	25,000 lb	17.0	193	Yes
Nickel—Primary	LME	6 MT	20.0	120	No
Nickel	SHFE	1 MT	63.6	64	No
Zinc—Special High Grade	LME	25 MT	28.8	719	Yes
Zinc	SHFE	5 MT	45.2	226	No
Ferrous Metal					
Iron Ore	DCE	100 MT	259.6	25,957	No
Steel Rebar	SHFE	10 MT	541.0	5,410	No

Note: This table provides details about the top 15 metal futures contracts in 2015., which are based on the number of contracts traded and/or cleared in 2015 at 78 exchanges worldwide compiled by FIA. The table excludes ETFs and Micro contracts, which were included in the original ranking.

Source: Acworth (2016), CME Group (2016a), DCE (2016), LME (2016a), and SHFE (2016).

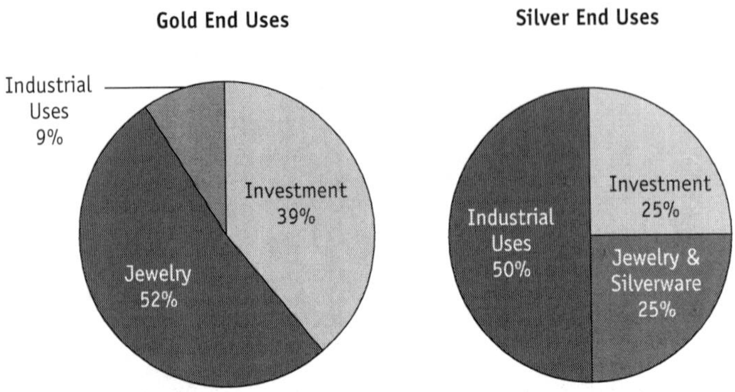

Figure 11.1 Gold and Silver End Uses in 2014
This figure shows the primary end uses of newly-produced gold and silver. Source: O'Connell et al. (2016a, 2016b).

that gold stores are large relative to annual production. Bar and coin holdings amount to about 70,000 MT, compared to annual gold production of 4,000 MT (O'Connell et al. 2016a). Central banks hold about 30,000 MT of this 70,000 MT, making central banks major players in this market in a way not usually found in other metals. The combination of large stores of gold relative to production, the use of gold as currency, and large central bank holdings and trading make the dynamics of the gold market different from other metals.

Because gold is held in large amounts as a store of value, having gold in backwardation is historically unusual. That is, if the future price of gold were lower than the current price, one would expect sales from current stores of gold until the current price were no higher than the future price. However, gold has spent considerable time in backwardation since 2013. One explanation for this backwardation is that the price of gold is quoted in a currency (USD) with a negative real interest rate or with expected deflation.

Although gold supply is relatively dispersed, gold demand is concentrated in India and China, the world's largest gold consumers, with each accounting for about 25 percent of non-bar gold consumed each year (O'Connell et al. 2016a). Economic conditions in these countries can noticeably affect gold demand. For example, according to O'Connell et al. (2016a), Indian households dependent on agricultural income account for an estimated one-third of India's gold demand, and that demand is highly sensitive to monsoon conditions. In years with unfavorable conditions, Indian households may be net sellers rather than net buyers of gold.

Silver

Silver is the little sibling of gold, in that an estimated 25 percent of demand is as a store of value—less than for gold but more than for any other metal. Silver is most commonly used for industrial applications, such as electronics and photovoltaic cells. Silver mined production is relatively dispersed, with Mexico, China, and Peru as the world's largest producers, accounting for nearly 50 percent of world mine production (O'Connell et al. 2016c).

Platinum Group Metals

The six platinum group metals—platinum and palladium plus rhodium, osmium, ruthenium, and iridium—have similar physical and chemical properties and tend to occur together in the same mineral deposits, primarily in South Africa. Of the six, only platinum and palladium are exchange traded, although rhodium exchange-traded funds (ETFs) are available. About half of platinum and palladium production goes into vehicle catalytic converters, according to the USGS (2016). South Africa and Russia are responsible for about 75 percent of global mined production. This concentration in production causes the prices of platinum and palladium to respond to events in these countries, such as mining strikes and trade embargoes.

TRADING AND PRICING

Gold, silver, platinum, and palladium are the only metals with international standard currency codes for interbank clearing (ISO 4217). Despite the currency designation, platinum and palladium have never gained popularity as coinage, although commemorative coins are available.

Physical Spot Trading

The London Bullion Market Association (LBMA) and Shanghai Gold Exchange (SGE) are the organizations with the largest reported trading volumes of spot gold and silver. The LBMA is not an exchange but rather a trading association that facilitates OTC trading of bullion with delivery in London ("loco" delivery) through provision of vaulting services, designated market makers, and promulgation of product standards and trading practices. The SGE offers trading in gold, silver, and platinum spot products, as well as facilitating OTC trading like the LBMA (SGE 2016a). In China, VAT is imposed on gold bar trading except when trading is reported to an exchange, which strongly encourages trading to be reported to the SGE. The SGEI is the International Board subsidiary of the SGE, allowing foreign entities to participate in gold trading on the SGEI as well as in some SGE contracts with vaulting in a free trade zone. The SGEI offers only gold spot contracts.

The LBMA remains the dominant clearinghouse. Monthly LBMA cleared trading volume in gold averaged 12,500 MT in 2016 (LBMA 2017), while the SGE reports monthly average trading volume in gold of about 600 MT in exchange spot, 2,000 in exchange deferred delivery, and 1,500 MT in OTC spot, forwards, and swaps that are exchange cleared (SGE 2017). Comparing SGE and LBMA trading volumes is complicated by a lack of reporting of LBMA trading. Unlike China, the United Kingdom does not have VAT incentives to encourage OTC reporting. Murray (2011) found that LBMA Clearing Statistics contained approximately 10 percent of member trading.

Platinum and palladium have much lower trading volumes than gold and silver. In London, spot traders in these metals are served by the London Platinum and Palladium Market (LPPM), which is organized similarly to the LBMA.

Precious Metal Auctions

Round-the-clock spot prices are available to traders from various sources, including online OTC dealer quotes; SGE reported prices of the latest trades in its exchange-traded spot gold, silver, and platinum products; and theoretical spot prices derived from futures prices. However, traders have traditionally relied on the results of a once- or twice-daily auction as the reference price for precious metals. In the last several years, the administration of all of these auctions has been changed to increase transparency.

The auctions generally work as follows. The organization offers a starting price, and members and the clients of members submit buy and sell orders at that price. If the difference between the buy and sell orders is fairly small, defined as being within the auction-defined imbalance threshold amount, the auction closes, and orders are settled at that price, with the imbalance divided among the member orders. If the difference between the buy and sell orders exceeds the imbalance threshold, the organization begins a second round by proposing a new price, and members and their clients again submit orders. The rounds continue until the difference between buys and sells is within the imbalance threshold. Although the auctions are generally similar, they differ in various ways, some of which are described in Table 11.3.

China is following several strategies to increase its role in setting spot gold prices. Chinese banks have increased their role in spot gold price setting by becoming members of the LBMA Gold Price auction. Also, the SGE now operates its own Shanghai Gold Benchmark Price auction, with rules similar to the LMBA Gold Price (SGE (2016a)). In 2016, monthly trading volume in the SGE Gold Benchmark Price averaged approximately 65 MT (SGE 2017), as compared to 225 MT for the LBMA Gold Price (ICE 2017).

Many other countries offer precious metal spot trading, OTC or on exchange, but none of these countries produces a well-recognized spot reference price. Large amounts of gold are traded in Switzerland, Hong Kong, and the Middle East, but none of these regions are price setters. As discussed below, several of the exchanges in other countries offer precious metal reference prices based on futures contracts.

Derivatives Trading

The largest gold and silver derivative exchanges are the CME, SGE, SHFE, Multi Commodity Exchange of India (MCX), and Tokyo Commodity Exchange (TOCOM). For futures trading, the CME and the SHFE offer the highest trading volumes. As Table 11.2 shows, the CME has the largest gold trading volume of these exchanges. For silver, the SHFE is the largest market by number of futures contracts traded, but the CME is the largest market by value traded owing to the larger CME contract size. The SHFE contracts are for 1 kg of gold or 15 kg of silver, substantially smaller than the CME contracts of 100 troy oz. of gold (about 3 kg) or 5,000 troy oz. of silver (about 155 kg) (CME 2016a; SHFE 2016).

The SHFE offers gold and silver futures contracts with expiry up to one year. The CME offers a larger set of contracts than does the SHFE, offering both futures and

Table 11.3 **Precious Metals Auctions**

Fix Name	*LBMA Gold Price*	*Shanghai Gold Fix*	*LBMA Silver Price*	*LBMA Platinum and Palladium Prices*
Administered by	ICE	SGE	CME and Thomson Reuters	LME
Date of Initiation or New Administration	3/20/2015	4/19/2016	8/5/2014	12/1/2014
Times per Day	Twice	Twice	Once	Twice
Round Length	30 seconds	First round: 1 minute + 10-second supplementary session. Subsequent rounds: 30 seconds + 10-second supplementary session.	30 seconds	Not fixed
Imbalance Threshold	10,000 oz.	400 kg	3 lakh (300,000 oz.)	4,000 oz.
Clearing	By participants; Central proposed to start in 2017	Central	By participants	By participants
Method to Maintain Privacy of Member Client Orders	Clients of members may place orders directly	Clients of members may place orders directly	Members have two traders, one for house orders and one for client orders	Members may segregate house and client orders. Direct access may be granted to clients of members.

Note: This table describes precious metals auctions around the world.

Source: CME Group (2016b), ICE (2016), LME (2016b), and SGE (2016b).

options in all four precious metals, contracts with different sizes, and contracts with expiry up to six years for gold, up to five years for silver, and up to 15 months for platinum and palladium.

The SHFE does not have official "active" or reference months, but volume tends to concentrate in the June and December contracts. The CME reference price contract is the "active" contract. The active month is the nearest "base" contract month that is not the current delivery month. Table 11.4 shows the active contract for each precious metal for each month.

MCX offers a range of gold and silver futures with high trading volume by number of contracts, but this volume can be misleading as the most traded contracts have smaller contract sizes than the most traded contracts elsewhere. For example, MCX offers a 1 kg gold contract but its most traded contract is its mini, 100 g contract. For silver, MCX's most frequently traded contract is also the mini, with a contract size of 5 kg (MCX 2016).

The TOCOM offers even-month futures in the four precious metals for up to one year out, plus gold options and a gold rolling spot contract. The reference price contract is for expiry closest to one year out. In 2015, the TOCOM started offering gold rolling spot futures, which have no maturity date but rather have positions rolled from one trading day to the next. The gold rolling spot future has several times the trading volume

Table 11.4 **CME Precious Metal Reference Price Contract**

	Active Month Contract			
Current Month	*Gold*	*Silver*	*Platinum*	*Palladium*
Jan	Feb	Mar	Apr	Mar
Feb	Apr	Mar	Apr	Mar
Mar	Apr	May	Apr	Jun
Apr	Jun	May	Jul	Jun
May	Jun	Jul	Jul	Jun
Jun	Aug	Jul	Jul	Sep
Jul	Aug	Sep	Oct	Sep
Aug	Dec	Sep	Oct	Sep
Sep	Dec	Dec	Oct	Dec
Oct	Dec	Dec	Jan	Dec
Nov	Dec	Dec	Jan	Dec
Dec	Feb	Mar	Jan	Mar

Note: This table maps current month to the active month contract for CME precious metals futures contracts.

Source: CME (2016a).

of the standard expiry gold futures, although the contract size is smaller. The theoretical spot price is calculated every five minutes based on the one-month and six-month future prices. The contract is cash settled (TOCOM 2016).

The SGE offers both "price matching" products—exchange traded products—and "price asking" products—arranged OTC but reported to and cleared with the SGE. The price matching products are spot and deferred delivery spot. The SGE's largest trading volumes are in deferred delivery spot ("T+D"), which have similarities with the TOCOM rolling gold spot future. Once daily, all the longs/shorts can submit their intentions to take/make delivery. If more intentions to take delivery are available than those to make delivery, all the shorts of gold (T+D) must pay the longs' deferred compensation fee to long positions. If more intentions to make delivery are available than those to take delivery, those holding long positions in gold (T+D) must pay the deferred compensation fee to short positions. The SGE also offers T+N deferred delivery contracts, which require deferred interest to be paid annually.

Investors can take positions in precious metals in ways beyond those mentioned above, with gold having the largest set of well-developed alternatives. These alternatives include OTC forwards and swaps, ETN/Fs investing in either futures or physical metal held in vaults, lending or borrowing gold or silver, and stock in mining companies. Because mining companies vary in how much of their production they hedge or lock into fixed price contracts, any attempt to gain metal exposure through mining companies requires research into the metal mix of their ore and their strategies with respect to contracting and hedging.

In summary, many markets and products are available for trading gold risk, with a smaller number available for other precious metals. Trading of gold, and markets and products for trading gold, in China have expanded significantly in recent years, but other precious metals have not received the same attention.

Non-ferrous Base Metals

Non-ferrous base metals have traditionally been grouped together both in trading venue (e.g., the LME), and in academic analysis (e.g., super cycle literature). Industrial metal indices tend to contain four or five metals: aluminum, copper, nickel, zinc, and sometimes lead, although the LME offers its own index (LMEX) of all six metals, including tin.

Although the country of origin varies across the base metals, China is both the largest refined base metal producer and largest consumer of base metals, followed by the United States. Table 11.1 shows world production of the six base metals and the largest mined sources. Table 11.5 shows top-end uses as well as China's share of consumption.

TYPES OF NON-FERROUS BASE METALS

Non-ferrous base metals are more common and less expensive than the precious metals, but less common and more expensive than iron. Unlike precious metals, base metals oxidize easily.

Table 11.5 **Base Metal Consumption in 2014**

Metal	*Global Consumption (million MT)*	*First-Ranked Consuming Country*	*First-Ranked Consuming Country's Market Share (%)*	*Second-Ranked Consuming Country*	*Second-Ranked Consuming Country's Market Share (%)*	*First-Ranked Consuming Industry*
Aluminum	78.2	China	50	N/A	N/A	Building and Construction
Copper	22.9	China	48	U.S.	8	Equipment
Lead	10.9	China	43	U.S.	15	Batteries
Nickel	1.9	China	50	N/A	N/A	Stainless Steel
Tin	0.4	China	45	N/A	N/A	Solder
Zinc	13.7	China	48	U.S.	N/A	Galvanizing Industry
Steel	1,543.0	China	48	U.S.	7	Building and Infrastructure

Note: This table shows that China is the first-ranked consuming country on various base metals.

Source: International Aluminium Institute (2016). International Copper Study Group (2016), International Nickel Study Group (2015), International Trade Administration (2016). ITRI (2016), RUSAL (2016). Sanderson (2016), and USGS (2016).

Aluminum

Aluminum's use exceeds that of any other metal except iron and is important in virtually all segments of the world economy, including transportation (e.g., automobiles, airplanes, trucks, railcars, and marine vessels), packaging (e.g., cans and foil), construction (e.g., windows, doors, and siding), consumer durables (e.g., appliances and cooking utensils), electrical transmission lines, and machinery.

Bauxite (aluminum ore) is refined into alumina (Al_2O_3), which is then smelted using electrolysis to create aluminum. Aluminum production is particularly energy intensive, with energy typically accounting for about one-third of production costs (Burns 2015). Pure aluminum is a very soft metal and is generally used as an alloy with other metals. Semi fabricators create alloys and process them into semi-fabricated products, such as sheet, plate, foil, extrusions, drawing stock, wire, pigments and powder, forgings, and impacts.

Both aluminum and aluminum alloy contracts are traded on exchange. In the second half of 2016, the CME began offering cash-settled contracts on alumina, the precursor product to aluminum.

Copper

Many sectors consume copper, primarily for electrical uses. China consumes about half of world copper production. Beyond Chinese industry, China's Strategic Reserve Bureau (SRB) also plays an important role in Chinese markets. The SRB maintains reserves in various metals, including copper, and its activities have sometimes had a marked effect on copper prices. For example, in 2005, authorities discovered that a trader for the SRB manipulated the LME copper price (Economist 2005). More recently, in 2008 in response to the financial crisis, the SRB purchased about 2 percent of world annual demand for copper and aluminum largely to prop up the prices of Chinese metal producers (USGS 2008).

Copper ore is often initially processed at the mine into copper concentrate, which is about 30 percent copper. Benchmark costs to process copper concentrate into copper are commonly referred to as treatment and refining charges (TC/RCs), contributing on the order of 5 to 20 percent to the price of copper. TC/RCs are publicly available price indices. Copper concentrate contracts sometimes specify a purchase price based on the current LME price less the current TC/RC. Although TC/RCs are the basis for setting prices in contracts for other metals, benchmark rates are not well-publicized.

Chile is the world's largest source of mined copper, with about one-third of worldwide production. This large role suggests that developments in the mining sector in Chile have the potential to impact copper prices globally.

Nickel

Nickel's primary use is in stainless steel (65 percent) (Nickel Institute 2016). Major changes have occurred in the nickel market in the last decade, taking advantage of nickel and iron often occurring together in ore and nickel and iron often being used together to make stainless steel. A decade ago Chinese producers largely switched from importing high-purity, high-cost nickel to importing low-purity, low-cost nickel-iron ore and refining it into nickel pig iron, consisting of about 10 percent nickel and 90 percent iron, as an intermediate product for stainless steel production in China.

Before 2014, China sourced much of the nickel-iron ore from Indonesia, with Indonesia and the Philippines being the world's largest producers of nickel ore with 31 and 12 percent of the market share, respectively, in 2013 (USGS 2013). In early 2014, however, an Indonesian ban on metal ore exports came into effect. This ban was enacted in 2009 and implemented with a delay in an attempt to create local Indonesian jobs by encouraging firms to build smelters in Indonesia and to shift exports from raw materials to higher-value finished metals. As a result, the Philippines became the world's top nickel ore exporter and now accounts for around one-quarter of the world's mined nickel, most of which is shipped to China. In January 2017, the Indonesian government eased the export ban on nickel and other ores.

Other Base Metals

The other major non-ferrous base metals traded on the LME are lead, zinc, and tin. Mine sources of lead and zinc are generally found together. China's mines produce nearly 40 percent of the world's lead and zinc. Lead's primary use is in batteries (80 percent), for cars, backup electrical systems, forklifts, and others (International Lead and Zinc Study Group 2016). Zinc's primary use is in galvanized steel (50 percent) and other alloys (34 percent) (International Lead and Zinc Study Group 2016). Tin is primarily used as a protective coating or as an alloy with other metals. China and Indonesia are the leading producers of tin, sourcing more than half of worldwide mine production, Indonesia's 2014 ban on metal ore exports has reduced its overall production, and Myanmar has taken on supplying China with additional ore.

TRADING AND PRICING

The LME and the SHFE have the largest reported futures trading volumes in base metals and offer trading with physical settlement in the same six non-ferrous base metals: aluminum, copper, nickel, lead, tin, and zinc. The SHFE added nickel and tin futures in 2015. The LME also offers trading in spot and options. Table 11.2 provided the trading volumes in the top metals. The LME offers delivery at LME-approved warehouses worldwide, but not in China, while the SHFE offers delivery at approved warehouses in China.

Of the non-ferrous base metals, aluminum and copper have the largest turnover and are the only ones for which the CME offers actively traded contracts. In 2015, the CME announced the launch of zinc and lead futures contracts, but these are not listed as traded contracts on the CME website as of the end of 2016. The CME-approved warehouses are concentrated in the United States, with some approved warehouses in Europe. The CME aluminum regional contracts rely on Platts or Metal Bulletin prices and are cash settled.

Beyond the six metals actively traded on the LME, other non-ferrous base metals do not have much trading activity on major exchanges. The LME offers trading in cobalt and molybdenum. Fanya minor metals exchange in China was founded in

2011 with trading in 14 minor metals, but it collapsed in 2015. Argus, CRU, Platts, and Metal Bulletin offer daily, weekly, or monthly prices in different minor metals.

In summary, the LME remains the dominant trading venue for non-ferrous base metals but has not yet placed warehouses in China, while the SHFE has been gaining substantial market share in base metal derivatives trading with its network of China warehouses. The CME has a meaningful presence in copper and aluminum regional premia.

DELIVERY, EXCHANGE WAREHOUSES, AND REGIONAL PRICE DIFFERENTIAL CONTRACTS

When a physically-settled futures contract is held to delivery, the seller may settle the contract with a warrant from any of the exchange's warehouses. A warrant is proof of ownership of exchange-approved metal meeting the contract specifications in a particular exchange-approved warehouse. The buyer has no control over delivery location, which has resulted in some problems for the LME in recent years and ultimately the rise of regional premium contracts.

As with other exchanges, the LME monitors but does not own the facilities that take delivery of physical metal, issue warrants in exchange, and deliver metal against canceled warrants. LME warehouses are not required to deliver metal on a canceled warrant within a fixed period but rather to deliver a minimum amount per day. This process has led to wait times of more than two years for delivery from some warehouses, peaking between 2011 and 2014. Rent is owed until delivery occurs. The load-out waits did not necessarily discourage new metal holders from storing their metal at a given facility because they could exit their holdings by delivering the warrant to a buyer. As previously mentioned, buyers must accept a warrant to metal in any LME warehouse as payment. If the new warrant owner wants to continue to store the metal in the warehouse, the warehouse will charge rent. If the warrant owner wants metal delivery from that warehouse, the warrant is then canceled and delivery is requested.

These long wait times had several effects. For example, several government agencies initiated investigations and private lawsuits were filed. The LME initiated its own investigation and policy review, first in 2010 and then again in 2013. The 2013 policy review has resulted in several new rules to reduce load-out wait times. As of December 2016, wait times were no more than 20 days for all metals and warehouses except one aluminum warehouse in Vlissingen in the Netherlands, with a wait time of 8 months (LME 2017).

One of the effects of long load-out times was to depress LME prices relative to "all-in" prices for metal delivery at a particular location, driving up regional price premia over the LME price. Although regional aluminum premia had traditionally been under $200 per MT, they consistently exceeded $200 between 2011 and 2013. In response, the LME and the CME introduced regional premium contracts on aluminum. The CME contracts are cash settled based on Platts regional price indices, while the LME contracts are physically settled, whereby the buyer provides an LME warrant and the cash premium and receives from the seller a warrant to metal in a LME premium warehouse in the region defined by the contract.

As already discussed, aluminum has the highest trading volume of the non-ferrous base metals. To date, exchange-traded regional premium contracts are available on no other metals. While no other metal had wait times as long as aluminum, copper, lead, and zinc had wait times of up to six months between 2011 and 2014.

As an alternative to using the LME in combination with regional premium contracts, traders who seek delivery in a particular region can trade on exchanges with more geographically concentrated warehouses, such as the CME in the United States or the SHFE in China. The CME's warehouse capacity is much more geographically concentrated than the LME's, with warehouses in 13 U.S. cities and in three European cities since 2015. The CME has been steadily building its storage network partly as a result of controversy surrounding the dominant LME warehouse system.

In summary, the LME and SHFE are the major exchanges in non-ferrous base metals trading, with price discovery occurring on both exchanges. The CME continues to play a role with a small number of traditional products and a number of new products.

Ferrous Base Metals

Ferrous metals refer to iron and steel. Steel is generally defined as iron alloys with up to approximately 2 percent carbon content. More steel is produced every year than all other metals combined. In fact, steel makes up more than 90 percent of metal produced.

TYPES OF FERROUS BASE METALS

Steel production is the primary use of iron, with nearly 98 percent of the world's iron ore used to produce it. China is the world's largest producer of iron ore, but the ore tends to have low iron content. Controlling for iron content, Australia and Brazil are the two largest iron ore producers.

Besides iron ore, other products upstream of steel production include coking coal and pig iron. Coking coal is used to make coke, which is then used in blast furnaces to make steel. Steel produced from iron ore, as opposed to steel scrap, requires about 8 kg of coking coal per 10 kg of steel (World Steel Association 2016). Around 15 percent of world coal production goes into steel production (World Steel Association 2016). For these reasons both coke and coking coal are sometimes analyzed as steel inputs.

Pig iron, iron ingot with about 5 percent carbon content, is a potential intermediate product between iron ore and steel, if the iron is not immediately processed into steel via a continuous process. In recent years, nickel pig iron has been produced from nickel-iron ore and used as an input in stainless steel. Steel pricing services also offer price quotes on pig iron.

TRADING AND PRICING

Steel and iron have not traditionally had substantial trading as derivatives. As China has become a major steel producer in the last decade, world pricing methods for both iron ore and steel have shifted considerably.

Iron Ore

BHP Billiton and Rio Tinto in Australia and Vale in Brazil are known as the Big Three iron ore producers. For more than 30 years through 2008, the price of iron ore was set through annual negotiations between the Big Three and large steelmakers in Asia, but this system broke down in 2009.

In 2008, Platts, the Metal Bulletin, and Steel Business Briefing (commonly known by its index name, The Steel Index, TSI) each launched iron ore price indices for delivery into China. OTC spot, forward, and swap trading based on these indices quickly followed. In 2009, the Singapore Exchange (SGX) launched clearing of standardized iron ore swaps based on the TSI index, with a contract size of 500 MT (SGX 2016). By 2010, most iron ore purchasing had shifted to spot purchases or short-term contracts based off of these price indices.

In 2013, China's state-owned Dalian Commodity Exchange (DCE) launched a physically-settled iron ore futures contract, with a contract size of 100 MT. Since 2013, DCE iron ore contract trading volume has surpassed SGX's. Goldman Sachs estimates that individuals account for 70 percent of Dalian volumes (Ng 2016). As Table 11.1 shows, the DCE iron ore contract was the second most traded metal future (measured by number of contracts) in the world in 2015. The DCE also offers coking coal and coke futures, which were actively traded in 2016.

Steel

Like iron ore, steel has not traditionally traded on an exchange. Today, contracts are available on scrap as well as on steel formed into coil, plate, rod, billet, and rebar. In the 1990s, three different exchanges in China were set up to trade steel price risk, but by 1994 all of them were closed due to lack of business. The LME and the CME both launched steel futures contracts in 2008. The LME's contract is physically settled, while the CME's contract is cash settled based on price indices provided by CRU. The CME has launched additional steel contracts since 2008, including, in 2012, a steel-scrap future settled against American Metal Market's newly-created scrap index. The LME has also launched additional steel contracts since 2008.

Although the SHFE did not launch physically-settled steel futures contracts until a year after the LME and the CME launched their steel contracts, it has attracted by far the largest trading volumes. The SHFE steel rebar contract had the largest trading volume (measured by number of contracts) of any metal futures contract in the world in both 2014 and 2015. Steel contracts offer delivery at LME warehouses worldwide and at SHFE warehouses in China, in contrast to iron ore contracts, which are all priced for delivery into China.

In summary, in the last decade iron ore and steel derivatives have gone from not existing to having the largest trading volumes of all the metal contracts, and the contracts with substantial volumes are all for delivery in China.

Summary and Conclusions

In summary, the rise of China's industry in recent years has led to a shift in global metal exchange trading to China. Although the LME and the CME remain the reference price sources and dominant venues in derivatives trading of base and precious metals respectively by volume for now, that status may soon be shared with Chinese exchanges. In ferrous metals, Chinese exchanges are already the dominant venues.

Discussion Questions

1. Discuss how metals are related to each other in sourcing and use.
2. Explain how gold fundamentals differ from other metals.
3. Explain how the process for setting precious metal spot prices has changed.
4. Explain how price discovery around iron ore and steel has changed.
5. Discuss the market changes that resulted from long LME load-out wait times.

Disclaimer

The views expressed in this article are solely those of the authors, who are responsible for the content, and do not necessarily represent the views of Cornerstone Research.

Acknowledgments

The authors thank Alice Dai, Daisy Ding, and Prachi Sharma for their research and editing contributions to this chapter.

References

Acworth, Will. 2016. "Asia Takes the Lead: 2015 Annual Survey, Global Derivatives Volume." *MarketVoice Magazine,* March. Available at http://marketvoicemag.org/sites/default/files/pdf/March2016_TopStoryupd.pdf.

Burns, Stuart. 2015. "Power Costs in the Production of Primary Aluminum." *Metal Miner.*

CME Group. 2016a. "Contract Specs." Available at http://www.cmegroup.com/trading/metals/.

CME Group. 2016b. "The LBMA Silver Price." Available at http://www.cmegroup.com/international/emea/lbma-silver-price.html.

Cuddington, John T., and Daniel Jerrett. 2008. "Super Cycles in Real Metal Prices?" *IMF Staff Papers* 55:4, 541–565.

Dalian Commodity Exchange (DCE). 2016. "Iron Ore Futures." Available at http://www.dce.com.cn/DCE/Products/Industrial/Iron%20Ore/491886/index.html.

Economist. 2005. "China's Copper Crisis." Available at http://www.economist.com/node/5164898.

Industrial Technology Research Institute (ITRI). 2016. "Annual Report 2015." Available at https://www.itri.co.uk/images/ITRI_Annual_Report_2015-WEB.pdf.

Intercontinental Exchange (ICE). 2016. "ICE Benchmark Administration (IBA): LBMA Gold Price." Available at https://www.theice.com/iba/lbma-gold-price.

Intercontinental Exchange (ICE). 2017. "LBMA Gold Price Quarterly Volume Report." Q1–Q4 2016. Available at https://www.theice.com/iba/historical-data.

International Aluminium Institute. 2016. "Global Mass Flow 2014 [2015 draft]." Available at http://www.world-aluminium.org/publications/.

International Copper Study Group. 2016. "The World Copper Factbook 2016." Available at http://www.icsg.org/index.php/component/jdownloads/viewdownload/170/2202.

International Lead and Zinc Study Group. 2016. "End Uses of Lead" and "End Uses of Zinc." Available at http://www.ilzsg.org/static/enduses.aspx.

International Nickel Study Group. 2015. "Statistics." Available at http://www.insg.org/stats.aspx.

International Trade Administration. 2016. "Global Steel Report." U.S. Department of Commerce.

Lian, Ruby, David Stanway, et al. 2015. "More Chinese Iron Ore Mines Seen Shutting in 2015—Executive." Reuters.

London Bullion Market Association (LBMA). 2017. "London Bullion Market Clearing Statistics." Available at http://www.lbma.org.uk/clearing-statistics.

London Metals Exchange (LME). 2016a. "Contract Specifications." Available at https://www.lme.com/en-gb/metals/non-ferrous/.

London Metals Exchange (LME). 2016b. "LBMA Platinum Price and LBMA Palladium Price Discovery Process." Available at https://www.lme.com/~/media/Files/Metals/Precious%20Metals/LBMA%20Platinum%20and%20Palladium%20Prices%20%20Price%20Discovery%20Process%20Schedule%201.pdf.

London Metals Exchange (LME). 2017. "Warehouse Company Stocks and Queue Data." Available at https://www.lme.com/en-gb/metals/reports/stocks/queue/

Multi Commodity Exchange of India (MCX). 2016. "Contract Specifications." Available at https://www.mcxindia.com/products.

Murray, Stewart. 2011. "Loco London Liquidity Survey." *Alchemist* 63, 9–10.

Ng, Jasime. 2016. "Goldman Says 'Size Doesn't Matter' as SGX's Iron Holds Sway." Bloomberg.

Nickel Institute. 2016 "About Nickel." Available at http://www.nickelinstitute.org/NickelUseInSociety/AboutNickel/NickelMetaltheFacts.aspx.

Obayashi, Yuka. 2016. "Nippon Steel Says High Coking Coal Prices Likely to Stay Awhile." Reuters.

O'Connell, Rhona, William Tankard, et al. 2016a. "GFMS Gold Survey 2016." Thomson Reuters.

O'Connell, Rhona, William Tankard, et al. 2016b. "GFMS Platinum Group Metals Survey 2016." Thomson Reuters.

O'Connell, Rhona, William Tankard, et al. 2016c. "The Silver Institute, World Silver Survey 2016." Thomson Reuters.

Rossen, Anja. 2014. "What Are Metal Prices Like? Co-movement, Price Cycles and Long-Run Trends." *Resources Policy* 45, 255–276.

RUSAL. 2016. "Aluminium Consumption by Regions in 2013 and 2015." Available at http://www.rusal.ru/en/aluminium/consumers/.

Saefong, Myra P. 2012. "What Strikes in South Africa Really Mean to Metals." *MarketWatch*.

Sanderson, Henry. 2016. "Commodities demand and China: an explainer." *Financial Times*.

Shanghai Futures Exchange (SHFE). 2016. "Contract Text." Available at http://www.shfe.com.cn/en/.

Shanghai Gold Exchange (SGE). 2016a. "Contracts Introduce." Available at http://www.en.sge.com.cn/.

Shanghai Gold Exchange (SGE). 2016b. "Shanghai Gold Benchmark Price: White Paper." Available at www.en.sge.com.cn/upload/resources/file/2016/04/21/32499.pdf.

Shanghai Gold Exchange (SGE). 2017. "Monthly Report of Data Highlights (December, 2016)." Available at http://www.en.sge.com.cn/datas/data-hilights---monthly-report/.

Singapore Exchange (SGX). 2016. "Iron Ore." Available at http://www.sgx.com/wps/portal/sgxweb/home/products/derivatives/commodities/ironore_steel/iron/contracts.

Tokyo Commodities Exchange (TOCOM). 2016. "New Way to Tap into Gold Investment." Available at https://www.tocom.or.jp/goldrolling/index.html.

U.S. Geological Survey (USGS). 2008. "USGS Minerals Yearbook." Available at http://minerals.usgs.gov/minerals/pubs/commodity.

U.S. Geological Survey (USGS). 2013. "USGS Minerals Yearbook." Available at http://minerals.usgs.gov/minerals/pubs/commodity.

U.S. Geological Survey (USGS). 2014. "USGS Minerals Yearbook." Available at http://minerals.usgs.gov/minerals/pubs/commodity.

U.S. Geological Survey (USGS). 2016. "USGS Minerals Yearbook." Available at http://minerals.usgs.gov/minerals/pubs/commodity.

Willeke, Rolf, et al. 2016. "World Steel Recycling in Figures 2011–2015." Bureau of International Recycling.

World Steel Association. 2016. "Fact Sheet: Steel and Raw Materials." Available at http://www.worldsteel.org/publications/fact-sheets.html.

World Steel Association Economics Committee. 2016. "Steel Statistical Yearbook 2016." Available at https://www.worldsteel.org/en/dam/jcr:37ad1117-fefc-4df3-b84f-6295478ae460/Steel+Statistical+Yearbook+2016.pdf.

Yap, Cecilia. 2014. "Philippines Sees Nickel Boon on Indonesia's Ban: Southeast Asia." Bloomberg.

Part Three

METHODS TO INVEST IN COMMODITIES

12

Commodity Trading Advisors and Managed Futures

KORAY D. SIMSEK
Associate Professor of Finance, Rollins College, Crummer Graduate School of Business

HALIL KIYMAZ
Bank of America Professor of Finance, Rollins College, Crummer Graduate School of Business

Introduction

The term *managed futures* encompasses active trading strategies that use global derivative markets. Initially, this investment category exclusively focused on commodity futures. Today, even though commodities still constitute a sizable chunk of the managed futures industry, non-commodity futures have been instrumental in the growth of this investment class.

Investors gain access to managed futures through three main channels. Historically, the oldest managed futures investment vehicles were public commodity (futures) funds, which began trading in 1948 (Kat 2004). Despite the introduction of currency futures and other new contracts in the 1970s, helping the growth of these funds, they have not been able to establish a strong base. In 2007, managed futures mutual funds entered the scene, partly due to the positive performance of managed futures strategies during the Great Recession of 2008–2009. Their numbers have increased remarkably since 2010. As of January 19, 2017, the Morningstar (2017) database lists 50 mutual funds, three exchange-traded funds (ETFs), and one exchange-traded note in the alternative managed futures category.

The remaining two managed futures investment vehicles are private: commodity trading advisors (CTAs) and commodity pool operators (CPOs). According to the National Futures Association (NFA), the self-regulatory organization for the U.S. derivatives industry, and the Commodity Futures Trading Commission (CFTC), the federal agency that regulates the U.S. futures markets, a CTA is an entity that, for compensation or profit, advises others as to the value of or the advisability of buying or selling futures contracts, options on futures, retail off-exchange forex contracts, or swaps. Therefore, if investors choose to directly invest with a CTA, they would have a separate managed futures account. This route is open to qualified investors as CTAs charge hedge-fund-level management and incentive fees. By contrast, a CPO's structure is similar to a fund of hedge funds. It pools the funds investors place with the CPO and hires one or more CTAs to manage the funds in the pool. Although these regulatory terms are true to their origins, CTAs and CPOs no longer trade commodities exclusively. Many CTAs have diversified investment strategies and some are completely invested in financial futures.

The remainder of the chapter is organized as follows. The next section provides a discussion of the characteristics of managed futures strategies and CTAs and offers current market information. The third section offers an overview of the available indices and the databases used in the managed futures industry. The fourth section provides a review of the academic literature on performance and persistence of managed futures. The fifth section contains a survey of studies focusing on the diversification benefits of managed futures. The final section offers a summary and conclusions.

Characteristics of the Managed Futures Industry

The managed futures industry has grown remarkably since 2000. Figure 12.1 shows the growth of assets under management (AUM) for the CTAs reporting to the Barclay Hedge (2017) database. The pattern is remarkably similar to that of the growth of the derivative markets. Figure 12.1 also displays the market share of CTAs in the alternative investments universe defined by adding the hedge funds reporting to the same database. The recent performance of alternative investment classes appears to dictate the fund flows. Managed futures outperformed hedge funds during the Great

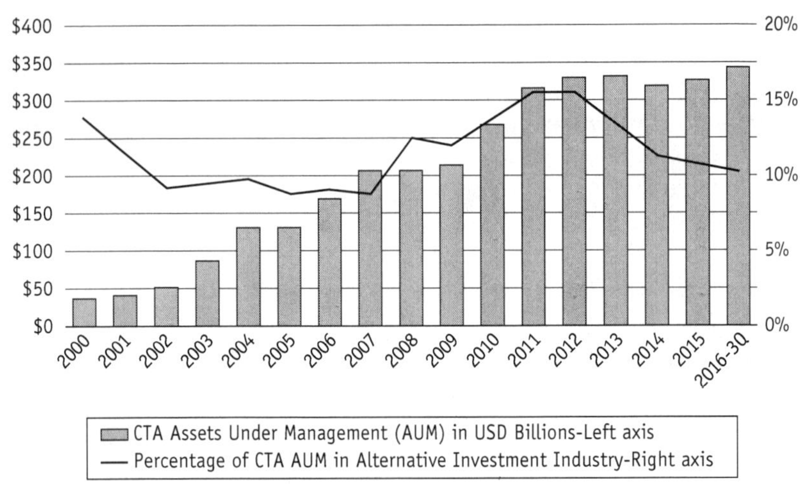

Figure 12.1 Growth of CTAs
This figure shows in columns (left axis) the growth of the assets managed by the CTAs reporting to the Barclay Hedge database since 2000. The black line (right axis) displays the ratio of this amount to the total AUM in the alternative investment industry defined as the group of CTAs and hedge funds reporting to the same database. Source: The authors' calculations using data from Barclay Hedge (2017).

Recession, which may have increased their relative popularity shortly thereafter. Yet, during the equity bull market after the Great Recession, CTAs experienced negative performance, which likely contributed to a slowdown of fund inflows.

Managed futures mutual funds have also displayed remarkable growth since first trading in 2007. As of January 19, 2017, 54 mutual funds and ETFs listed under this category in the Morningstar (2017) database are managing $29 billion even though many are just a few years old.

CTAs are typically classified across two dimensions: their trading strategies and the markets in which they trade. CTAs use two major trading strategies: discretionary and systematic. Discretionary CTAs trade based on their fundamental analysis of economic data such as macroeconomic news and global supply/demand imbalances. They adopt a fully active management style. By contrast, systematic CTAs trade on rules and algorithms based on quantitative models. They do not exert sentiment or judgment. Some CTAs employ both fundamental and systematic trading strategies in an effort to diversify against failure of an algorithmic trading rule even when they are not diversified with respect to the markets in which they trade.

Most systematic CTAs are trend-following in nature. They base their trading decisions on quantitative measures of trends, such as moving average and exponential smoothing, and try to exploit momentum in futures prices. When the prices rise, they increase exposure and vice versa. By exiting the market during decreases, they avoid overexposure. CTAs may differ with respect to the time horizon of the trend pattern they measure. They typically use stop-loss and take-profit rules as well as filters such as trading volume and volatility. In most cases, CTAs trade long and short positions diversified across multiple futures contracts.

Some systematic CTAs trade based on price reversals, a common phenomenon in commodity and interest rate markets. These counter-trend-followers employ quantitative mean-reversion models and technical analysis indicators to detect shifts in trends.

With respect to the futures markets in which they trade, CTAs are either fully diversified or focused on a specific set of markets. Fully diversified CTAs trade numerous contracts and could systematically weight them equally or based on measures such as volatility. Specialized CTAs could trade in a single market such as currencies, agricultural commodities, metals, energy, and equities. They could also operate in larger sets such as financials that encompass currencies and equities or physicals that cover all commodities.

Although the popularity of these different CTA strategies differs over time, Table 12.1 presents a recent breakdown of CTA AUM within each group previously mentioned. The individual CTA amounts may not necessarily add up to the total CTA AUM as some managers self-report belonging to more than one category or no category and are excluded.

How successful are managed futures strategies and CTAs? Researchers have extensively studied this question since the industry gained visibility in the early 1980s. The following sections present a review of these studies, including recent findings using larger data sets. Figure 12.2 presents a long-term historical performance of CTAs against other asset classes. Each line in this figure represents the growth of $100 invested in the respective asset class at the beginning of 1980. Using one of

Table 12.1 **Assets under Management for Various CTA Classes: 2016**

Assets under Management (USD billions)	*Q3 2016*	*Q2 2016*	*Q1 2016*
All CTAs	$342.3	$333.7	$333.9
Agricultural CTAs	$1.8	$1.8	$1.6
Currency CTAs	$19.5	$19.0	$19.6
Diversified CTAs	$203.6	$207.2	$198.0
Financial/Metal CTAs	$93.1	$87.6	$88.0
Discretionary CTAs	$26.0	$28.2	$28.3
Systematic CTAs	$290.4	$288.7	$275.6

Note: This table shows the value of assets managed by the CTAs reporting to the Barclay Hedge database in the first three quarters of 2016. Some CTAs may not fall into the strict definition of these classes and are considered as "Others." As a result, the sum of the values in either the bottom or middle panel does not add up to the total AUM given in the first row of the table.

Source: The authors' calculations using data from Barclay Hedge (2017).

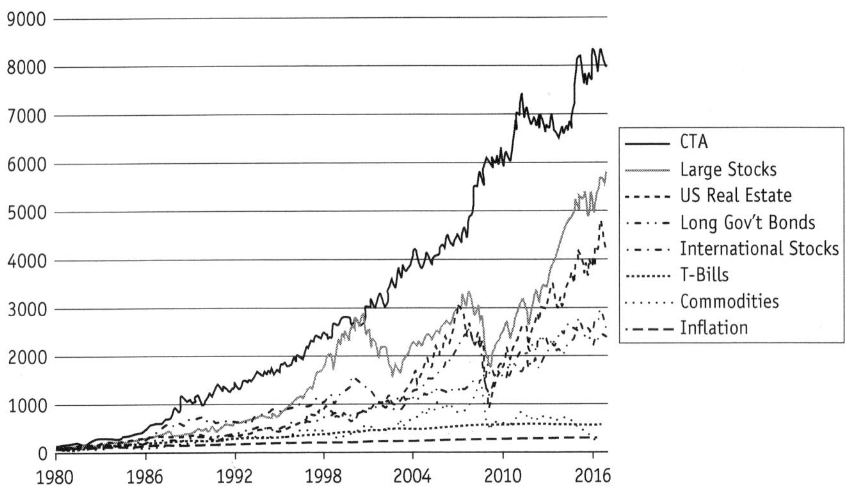

Figure 12.2 Performance of CTAs and Various Asset Classes
This figure displays the growth of $100 invested in each asset class at the beginning of 1980. The equal-weighted CISDM CTA index is the clear winner overall and is not exposed to a substantial drawdown except between 2011 and 2014. The remaining asset classes are represented by the following indices: Large Stocks: S&P 500, International Stocks: MSCI EAFE, U.S. Real Estate: FTSE NAREIT (U.S. Composite), Commodities: S&P GSCI, T-Bills: BofA Merrill Lynch U.S. T-Bill (3M), Long Government Bonds: Bloomberg Barclays U.S. Treasury—Long, Inflation: U.S. CPI-U. All monthly returns are computed using the total return indices. Source: Authors' calculations using data from CISDM (2017) and FactSet.

the oldest indices in the industry, CISDM (2017) CTA Equal-Weighted, reveals a smooth and rewarding ride for CTAs. The most striking aspect about this figure is that the performance is not attributable to commodity investing by itself. The worst-performing index is the long-only commodity index S&P GSCI, which barely beats inflation. The almost perfect compatibility of managed futures strategies and commodities make this happen.

This time-series chart provides two stylized facts that enable this superior result: low correlation with other asset classes and positive performance during equity market downturns. Table 12.2 provides evidence with respect to the low-correlation argument. The first column clearly shows that CTAs enjoy very desirable (close to zero and negative) correlation characteristics with major asset classes. Once again, the almost zero correlation with the long-only commodity index underscores the long-short trend-following nature of the CTAs.

To demonstrate how CTAs perform during down equity markets, the worst 15 months in the history of the S&P 500 index are selected and compared against the return on the CISDM CTA EW index for the same months. Table 12.3 shows these months sorted by S&P 500 returns. Usual suspects, such as months that include Black Monday in 1987, the ruble crisis of 1998, and the Lehman bankruptcy in 2008, are all on the list. The CTA index outperforms the S&P 500 index by a minimum of about seven percentage points and mostly provides positive returns.

These simple illustrations rely on the premise that the indices represent the returns generated by the CTAs. The next section focuses on understanding various indices used in the managed futures industry and provides an overview of the databases from which they are computed.

Benchmarking the Managed Futures Industry: Indices and Databases

Benchmarks in the traditional investment universe have been well established, especially with respect to equities. Investors can readily assess the performance of mutual funds, given their holdings- or returns-based style analysis, using various indices as commonly accepted benchmarks involving market cap or value/growth attributes. In the fixed income domain, several well-defined government or corporate bond indices exist and serve as benchmarks. One advantage of these indices or benchmarks is that their constituents are publicly traded and data are less susceptible to any quality issues.

By contrast, the managed futures industry is largely private. Public commodity funds and, more recently, managed futures mutual funds constitute exceptions that present a small fraction of these markets. This leaves index providers with two choices: obtain data by enlisting managers operating in the industry or use futures contracts to create strategies similar to those of the CTAs. Schneeweis, Gupta, and Remillard (2008) provide a detailed overview that encompasses indices of both types. Rollinger and Hoffman (2015) present a comparative analysis of several manager-based CTA indices.

Table 12.2 **Correlations between Monthly Returns of Various Asset Classes**

	CTAs	*Large Stocks*	*International Stocks*	*U.S. Real Estate*	*Commodities*	*T-Bills*	*Long Government Bonds*
Large Stocks	−0.072						
International Stocks	−0.065	0.663					
U.S. Real Estate	−0.037	0.572	0.476				
Commodities	0.006	0.176	0.266	0.129			
T-Bills	0.227	0.039	0.033	0.031	−0.001		
Long Government Bonds	0.139	0.045	0.001	0.108	−0.135	0.115	
Inflation	0.109	−0.023	−0.026	−0.013	0.215	0.291	−0.205

Note: This table shows the correlation matrix calculated using the monthly returns of various asset classes between 1980 and 2016, including CTAs that are represented by the CISDM (2017) CTA EW index. The remaining asset classes are represented by the following indices. Large stocks: S&P 500, International stocks: MSCI EAFE, U.S. Real Estate: Financial Times Stock Index National Association of Real Estate Investment Trusts (FTSE NAREIT) (US Composite), Commodities: S&P GSCI, T-Bills: BofA Merrill Lynch U.S. T-Bill (3M), Long Government Bonds: Bloomberg Barclays U.S. Treasury—Long, Inflation: U.S. Consumer Price Index for All Urban Consumers (CPI-U). All monthly returns are computed using the total return indices.

Source: The authors' calculations using data from CISDM (2017) and FactSet.

Table 12.3 **CTA Performance during the Worst 15 Months of the Equity Market between January 1980 and November 2016**

Month	*CISDM CTA EW (%)*	*S&P 500 (%)*
October 1987	14.88	−21.58
October 2008	5.79	−16.70
August 1998	7.21	−14.31
September 2002	2.54	−10.90
February 2009	−0.08	−10.36
March 1980	13.61	−9.75
February 2001	−0.13	−9.10
August 1990	6.67	−9.08
September 2008	0.28	−8.55
September 1986	−1.63	−8.32
June 2008	3.29	−8.28
January 2009	−0.15	−8.26
November 1987	8.33	−8.19
September 2001	2.39	−8.04
May 2010	−1.14	−8.01
Average	**4.12**	**−10.63**

Note: This table shows the worst 15 months of the S&P 500 Total Return index between January 1980 and November 2016. In each of these 15 months, the CISDM (2017) CTA EW index outperformed the equity market by a sizable margin.

Source: Authors' calculations using data from CISDM (2017) and FactSet.

Although no universal consensus exists on the common characteristics of a "good" index, Schneeweis et al. (2008) contend that five important attributes should be considered in CTA index construction. *Unambiguity* concerns the transparency of the index with respect to full disclosure of the constituents and their weights as well as clear guidelines for inclusion/exclusion. *Measurability* refers to providing data to investors for possible replication and verification. *Appropriateness* implies that constituents, weighting schemes, and rebalancing frequencies are suitable for a typical investor. *Accountability* refers to the presence of a committee that makes the changes based on established, well-defined procedures. Finally, *investability* means that, while the index itself may not be directly investible, its returns are achievable with low cost and minimum tracking error.

CTA database providers construct manager-based indices using the data reported by the managers in their respective databases. Reporting is a choice made by the managers. As such, some managers may choose to report to one or more database providers whereas others may prefer not to report performance data. This situation implies that no database and therefore no manager-based index can fully represent the CTA industry. Database providers use several selection criteria to determine which CTA to include in a particular index. Some providers have indices consisting of a fixed number of CTAs, whereas others have both narrowly-defined and broad-based CTA indices.

Besides general manager-based CTA indices, style-specific indices are also available. For example, Barclay Hedge (2017) maintains a broad-based managed futures industry index called Barclay CTA Index with 532 programs included in 2016. Within these managers, those who report their approach to be at least 95 percent as systematic are included in the Barclay Systematic Traders Index. If managers self-declare their style as at least 65 percent discretionary, they are included in the Barclay Discretionary Traders Index. Naturally, some managers may not fall into either category and are only part of the broad-based index. Societe Generale (2017) has an even more narrowly-defined style benchmark, SG Trend Index, which is comprised of the 10 largest trend-following CTAs in their database.

Finally, some databases provide market-specific CTA indices. If the manager trades across a wide range of futures markets, the CTA becomes a constituent of the Diversified index, which is typically the largest group. If the manager self-reports as trading primarily in a certain futures market segment, the CTA becomes assigned to an index named after the sector, such as agricultural, currency, financial, metals, or equities.

Certain technical differences exist in index construction methodology. Some indices use an equal-weighting method of aggregating CTA returns whereas others use AUM as weights. The asset-weighted method seems to represent the industry better while the equal-weighting method provides information on the average CTA's performance. Rebalancing these weights back to the original equal weights or the prevailing asset weights is done at a constant frequency. If CTAs report their returns more frequently than the rebalancing period, this may create a discrepancy between the targeted weights and the actual weights. The selection criteria are also applied to reform the constituents at a predetermined frequency.

Most manager-based CTA indices are not directly investible. According to Rollinger and Hoffman (2015), the iSTOXX® Efficient Capital® Managed Futures 20 Index is the only directly investible index in their analysis.

Investors could understandably be concerned over the differences in the definition and the construction of these indices. However, Rollinger and Hoffman (2015) show an average correlation of monthly returns among 11 manager-based indices between 2003 and 2014 period of 0.94 with a minimum monthly correlation of 0.89. Regardless of their characteristics, CTA indices are similar to one another.

Although manager-based indices have become popular for understanding industry performance, passive CTA indices that use rule-based futures trading strategies have also attracted interest because they have the potential to replicate the performance of diversified trend-following CTAs in a simple way. One of the oldest indices in this group is the MLM Index™, launched by Mount Lucas Management LP in 1988. Other examples include the Credit Suisse Managed Futures Liquid Index, Morningstar Diversified Futures Index, and S&P Systematic Global Macro Index. They are all based on long-short positions in a wide range of futures contracts with equal- or value-weighting. Whether the positions are long or short depends on momentum-type of trading rules and other details such as rolling contracts, and rebalancing frequency is explicitly determined in the rulebooks of the indices. Some of these indices also have sub-indices with respect to the futures market segments such as commodities, equities, or currencies.

Given the nature of subjectivity in index design, several issues should be addressed before statistical analysis. According to Schneeweis et al. (2008), four types of biases should be of concern: selection, backfill, new manager, and survivorship biases.

Selection bias arises due to the index construction methodologies used by the database provider and is almost inevitable. Although the high correlation previously reported is somewhat comforting, one should be careful in selecting indices based on their objective.

Under normal circumstances, CTAs voluntarily report their results to index providers. Those who do not report create a misleading representation of the industry or the strategy. This self-selection creates an issue as they may choose to start reporting their performance only after their results become positive. This situation is the root cause of *backfill bias*. Most of the major CTA indices are relatively safe in this respect as many have been around since the early 1990s.

To alleviate new manager bias, which may distort especially the equal-weighted indices due to their lower AUM and less diversified portfolios, index providers ignore the first one or two years of reported returns or apply a filter for AUM. If one uses only the surviving members of a database to create an index and calculates its historical returns using the same database, the inevitable result is survivorship bias. This approach results in overestimating performance statistics because dead funds whose returns would be much lower than surviving firm returns would be ignored in computing index returns. The next section provides details on the magnitude of this bias in historical data and how the academic literature deals with this issue. On the upside, major CTA indices are now in a more mature stage of their life cycle and, therefore, the impact of survivorship bias on empirical studies is limited.

Performance Evaluation of Managed Futures

Lintner (1983) is the first empirical study to analyze the benefits of managed futures strategies. He investigates the stand-alone risk-return profiles of 15 CTAs and eight public commodity funds between July 1979 and December 1982 as well as the diversification benefits via low correlation with stocks and bonds. Lintner represents the CTAs with a composite index using the trading profits, net of fees, resulting from all their accounts, including public commodity funds, and shows that this index outperforms a well-diversified stock-bond portfolio based on return-risk ratio. He notes that this composite index is superior to the average CTA due to the low correlation among the individual CTAs. With respect to the public commodity funds, Elton, Gruber, and Rentzler (1987, 1989, 1990) and Irwin, Krukemyer, and Zulauf (1993) challenge Lintner's finding that these funds cannot beat the risk-free rate.

Edwards and Liew (1999) revisit this horse-racing approach for the extended sample between 1982 and 1996 using a data set that has CTAs, CPOs, and public commodity funds. For each of these three categories, they create three investment styles: random selection of a fund within each category, an equal-weighted market portfolio, and a value-weighted market portfolio. Using the Sharpe ratio as the comparison metric, only one of these nine stylized investments managed to outperform the large capitalization stocks in all time periods, including big bull markets of 1980s and 1990s. Abrams, Bhaduri, and Flores (2014) provide overwhelming evidence to uphold the arguments laid out in Lintner (1983) with respect to including managed futures in an institutional portfolio through CTAs.

Among many biases that exist in the CTA databases, survivorship bias has attracted the most attention. Schneeweis, Spurgin, and McCarthy (1996) use a limited database of 56 CTAs to document evidence for survivorship bias in risk and return estimates despite the annual dissolution rate being around 10 percent. They point out that the impact of this bias is limited in a portfolio setting. Fung and Hsieh (1997) analyze the 1989–1995 period and find an average annual attrition rate of about 20 percent, implying that on average one out of five CTAs would cease to operate each year. They also measure the magnitude of the survivorship bias at 3.4 percent annually by comparing the average returns of surviving funds against those of all funds in the database. Brown, Goetzmann, and Park (2001) extend the data set through 1998 and find a lower survival rate as they measure the half-life of CTAs as two years, compared to 30 months for hedge funds.

Gregoriou, Hübner, Papageorgiou, and Rouah (2005) attribute the high mortality rates in these early studies to the absence of extreme market events during the selected time periods. They implement the most comprehensive CTA mortality analysis to that date and extend the sample period to 1990–2003, which includes the equity market collapse of 2001 among other major bearish moves. They implement a rich set of statistical methods and show that the median survival time for CTAs is about 4.5 years, much longer than Brown et al. (2001) find. As expected, they find that CTAs with higher management fees fail faster whereas those with above-average monthly returns and less liquidity constraints survive longer. Their results also demonstrate that currency, diversified, and financials/metals CTAs are more likely to survive.

Understanding the drivers of CTA returns has been a prime target in the literature as traditional factor models fail to capture the dynamics of managed futures. McCarthy, Schneeweis, and Spurgin (1997) document some evidence of performance persistence in CTAs. However, as in Schneeweis et al. (1996), their data set of CTAs is limited to 56 managers, making their conclusions weak. Fung and Hsieh (2001) follow Fung and Hsieh (1997) and define option-based factors to explain the trend-following CTA returns. This fresh parametric approach is based on ground intuitive reasoning as well as empirical support, which helped others such as Kazemi and Li (2009) pursue this direction for modeling returns of alternative investments.

Fung and Hsieh maintain that the most basic form of trend-following strategy, which they call the "primitive trend-following strategy" (PTFS), can be modeled after an option trading strategy called "lookback straddle." A *lookback straddle* consists of owning a lookback call and a lookback put option in a one-to-one ratio. The lookback call option gives its owner the right to buy the underlying futures contract at its minimum price during the life of the option, whereas the lookback put option gives the right to sell at the highest price. In combination, the owner perceives the maximum payout possible, which is the difference between the highest and the lowest prices during the lifetime of the strategy.

Fung and Hsieh (2001) generate the returns to PTFS using observable, exchange-traded option prices in five different markets, and empirically demonstrate that lookback straddle returns resemble the returns of trend-following CTAs. They find that these five PTFS factors explain almost 48 percent of the variation in CTA returns, whereas the next best model utilizing traditional factors can explain only 7.5 percent. They attribute this remarkable success to common characteristics of PTFS and CTA returns. One characteristic is the strong positive skewness that both strategies display through positive returns in extreme up and down markets. Furthermore, this similarity is more pronounced in currencies, commodities, and interest rates. Finally, both strategies deliver positive performance when market volatility increases. These findings have been extremely important, as the presence of systematic risk in CTAs is documented for the first time in the literature. Yet, at the individual fund level, the results are inconsistent, which implies that these factors may not serve well as benchmarking individual CTAs.

Kazemi and Li (2009) study the period between 1994 and 2004 using the CISDM database. Besides performing a risk-adjusted return assessment of CTAs, they also investigate their market timing abilities, which they define as the skill of managers to anticipate changes in market trends and to adjust their risk exposures accordingly. First, following Fung and Hsieh (2001), Kazemi and Li define new risk factors based on the returns of the most heavily traded futures contracts and present within multifactor models that explain CTA returns better than other parametric models. Using these multifactor models, they can identify market timing skills (beta) as well as selection abilities (alpha) of different types of CTAs. They show that discretionary CTAs have higher alphas but lower betas as compared with systematic CTAs. Focusing on individual CTA performance, Kazemi and Li note that most of the CTA returns originate from successful market timing and document the negative relation between market timing and selection, which is also observed in the hedge fund universe.

Gregoriou, Hübner, and Kooli (2010) use the Barclay CTA database for the 1995–2008 period. After removing backfill and survivorship biases, they run parametric models to explain CTA returns. More specifically, they assess the alphas for different classifications of CTAs based on the standard capital asset pricing model (CAPM), Fama and French (1993) three-factor model, Carhart (1997) four-factor model, and a custom multifactor model that has option-based factors. They find that alphas begin to disappear when the option-based factors are considered. More specifically, their results indicate that only four out of 12 CTA categories appear to significantly outperform the market and that diversified CTAs generate the highest alpha. Not surprisingly, in support of the findings of Fung and Hsieh (1997), option-based factors are the strongest drivers of CTA returns in almost all cases.

Gregoriou et al. (2010) also investigate the performance persistence of CTAs across different time periods by using median alpha performance as the cutoff. They document that diversified, financial/metal, and systematic CTAs consistently outperform the other categories whereas arbitrage CTAs always rank at the bottom. Furthermore, they find that CTAs displaying persistence over at least three months are more likely to be persistent over a longer period. However, all these persistence results disappear, except for agricultural CTAs, when they perform a quartile-based persistence analysis.

As Hurst, Ooi, and Pedersen (2013) show, CTA returns can be explained by time-series momentum strategies, which exhibit large correlations with managed futures indices and individual CTA returns. Even for the largest and most successful managers, alphas disappear after controlling for time-series momentum strategies.

Despite the abundance of positive findings favoring CTAs in the literature, some studies are critical of the performance of CTAs. Bhardwaj, Gorton, and Rouwenhorst (2014) use the Lipper-TASS database between 1994 and 2012 and various filters to remove backfill and survivorship biases. They find that CTAs do not provide significant alphas net of fees, even though the gross performance is significantly positive. Despite these poor results, they acknowledge the persistence of CTAs as an asset class and attribute this persistence to the lack of market discipline and regulation. The findings of Bhardwaj et al. have also attracted much interest in the industry. Zweig (2017) discusses the presence of fees in the case of managed futures mutual funds and contends that, despite a general move toward lower fees, the lack of transparency in disclosing these fees appears to be a common concern.

Bianchi, Drew, and Fan (2016) present a behavioral perspective for explaining the superior returns of momentum-based commodity strategies typically used by CTAs. Besides providing evidence for the investors' anchoring around the 52-week high and low commodity futures prices, they also document the decline in the profitability of such strategies, which cannot be attributed to either behavioral theories or the efficient market hypothesis. They contend that behavioral biases of traders might have changed over time, especially since the introduction of the Commodities Futures Modernization Act in 2001 and the expansion of CTAs, managed futures, and other commodity investment methods.

Do, Faff, Lajbcygier, Veeraraghavan, and Tupitsyn (2016) investigate factors contributing to the growth of the CTA industry in terms of both numbers and fund flows. They find that positive performance of the industry has negative effects on the fund flows to new CTAs in the short run due to fierce competition. This effect becomes positive in the long run as investor sentiment toward CTAs improves markedly. They also show that investors are unsuccessful in choosing high-performing CTAs, mostly because the flows follow past performance, which does not persist in CTAs.

Tee (2013) presents a detailed review of the managed futures academic literature through 2010 without providing a direct commodity focus. Miffre (2016) provides an extensive literature review of long-short commodity investing, which is an approach commonly adopted by CTAs and managed futures mutual funds. She concludes that most of the recent academic studies provide evidence for the superiority of this strategy over long-only portfolios that often track indices such as the S&P GSCI.

Diversification Benefits of Managed Futures

As previously noted, Lintner (1983) is the first to provide empirical evidence on the potential of managed futures for portfolio diversification by reporting their low correlation with stocks and stock-bond portfolios. Apart from being one of the first studies to document the survivorship bias in CTAs, Fung and Hsieh (1997) also provide insights about how to explain CTA returns with respect to market conditions. They note that survivorship bias does not affect the performance of the trend-following CTAs as the other types are affected. Next, they observe an option-like return diagram for these managers. In other words, when equity markets crash, CTAs provide positive and typically large returns, hinting at the presence of diversification benefits.

Edwards and Liew (1999) find that CTAs and CPOs significantly increase portfolio Sharpe ratios when they are added to a diversified stock and bond portfolio by receiving allocations of 25 to 50 percent, depending on the portfolio constraints. They also show that passive commodity indices such as MLM or CRB (Commodity Research Bureau) cannot substitute these funds in the diversified portfolio even though MLM has an average correlation of 0.4 with them.

Kat (2004) goes one step further and recognizes the comparability of managed futures with hedge funds as diversifiers of traditional stock-bond portfolios. He finds that managed futures, represented by the Stark 300 index between 1994 and 2001, have better diversification benefits than hedge funds but lower expected returns. He demonstrates that adding both to a traditional portfolio significantly reduces risk, while maintaining the returns, and has no negative effects on skewness and kurtosis as long as managed futures constitute half of the alternative investments.

Edwards and Caglayan (2001) compare the diversification benefits of CTAs with hedge funds by recognizing how they behave differently in bear and bull markets. As in Kat (2004), hedge funds outperform CTAs. However, during equity bear markets, CTAs have higher returns than hedge funds and display negative correlations with equities. A few subcategories of hedge funds overturn these results and the authors acknowledge that their sample period of 1990–1998 may not be robust to general conclusions.

Liang (2004) compares CTAs with two other popular alternative investment classes—hedge funds and funds-of-funds—both on a stand-alone and portfolio basis. Focusing on the 1994–2001 period, he finds that CTAs are the worst-performing category and survivorship bias cannot explain this result. However, Liang provides evidence that CTAs are also the best diversifying investment class, protecting against downside risk and improving the risk-return trade-off in a portfolio setting.

Many recognize the MLM Index™, launched by Mount Lucas Management LP in 1988, as the first price-based benchmark for evaluating managed futures performance. One of its sub-indices, the MLM Commodity Index™, is a monthly-rebalanced equal-weighted portfolio of 11 commodity futures contracts that carry a long or short exposure based on a simple trend-following algorithm. Mulvey,

Kaul, and Simsek (2004) present a detailed empirical analysis of the MLM Index™ and its components. Their back-tests demonstrate the diversification benefits of managed futures in a portfolio setting and attribute a substantial part of these benefits to rebalancing gains at the index and portfolio level. These findings confirm the results of Jensen, Johnson, and Mercer (2002) showing that the level of risk-reduction is superior to that of an unmanaged long-only futures index, the GSCI. The composition of the index has slightly changed since the publication of these studies.

Schneeweis, Spurgin, and Szado (2013) conduct a comprehensive empirical analysis of three commonly used indices that track the performance of CTAs between 1994 and 2009. They find that the composition of the indices and the time period of the analysis are key issues affecting the results of such studies.

Summary and Conclusions

This chapter presents an overview of the managed futures strategies and CTAs that implement these strategies for investors. Since the early 1980s, managed futures have become popular strategies among CTAs. More recently, managed futures mutual funds also began trading. Various benchmarks and databases are available to track the performance of managed futures. These strategies have excellent diversification benefits due to their low correlation with other assets. They also display positive performance when all other asset classes crash, as demonstrated during the Great Recession. The majority of the literature confirms these stylized characteristics despite disagreement about how to explain managed futures returns. Notwithstanding these findings, recent studies also pose important questions about relatively high fees and performance persistence in managed futures products. As CTAs often follow long-short strategies in futures markets, where shorting is easy, a trend toward low-cost passive investing in the CTA industry may emerge.

Discussion Questions

1. Discuss the differences between managed futures and commodity trading advisors (CTAs).
2. Identify various types of managed futures strategies and summarize their important characteristics.
3. Discuss the stylized facts about managed futures returns.
4. Discuss the research findings about the stand-alone performance of CTAs.

References

Abrams, Ryan, Ranjan Bhaduri, and Elizabeth Flores. 2014. "Lintner Revisited: A Quantitative Analysis of Managed Futures Strategies." CME Group Report. June. Available at http://www.cmegroup.com/education/files/lintner-revisited-quantitative-analysis.pdf.

Barclay Hedge. 2017. "CTA Industry—Assets under Management." January. Available at http://www.barclayhedge.com/research/indices/cta/Money_Under_Management.html.

Bhardwaj, Geetesh, Gary B. Gorton, and K. Geert Rouwenhorst. 2014. "Fooling Some of the People All of the Time: The Inefficient Performance and Persistence of Commodity Trading Advisors." *Review of Financial Studies* 27:11, 3099–3132.

Bianchi, Robert J., Michael E. Drew, and John Hua Fan. 2016. "Commodities Momentum: A Behavioral Perspective." *Journal of Banking and Finance* 72:C, 133–150.

Brown, Stephen J., William N. Goetzmann, and James Park. 2001. "Careers and Survival: Competition and Risk in the Hedge Fund and CTA Industry." *Journal of Finance* 56:5, 1869–1886.

Carhart, Mark M. 1997. "On Persistence in Mutual Fund Performance." *Journal of Finance* 52:1, 57–82.

Center for International Securities and Derivatives Markets (CISDM). 2017. "Center for International Securities and Derivatives Markets CISDM Indices." January. Available at https://www.isenberg.umass.edu/centers/center-for-international-securities-and-derivatives-markets/cisdm-indices.

Do, Viet, Robert Faff, Paul Lajbcygier, Madhu Veeraraghavan, and Mikhail Tupitsyn. 2016. "Factors Affecting the Birth and Fund Flows of CTAs." *Australian Journal of Management* 41:2, 324–352.

Edwards, Franklin R., and Mustafa O. Caglayan. 2001. "Hedge Fund and Commodity Fund Investments in Bull and Bear Markets." *Journal of Portfolio Management* 24:7, 97–108.

Edwards, Franklin R., and Jimmy Liew. 1999. "Managed Commodity Funds." *Journal of Futures Markets* 19:4, 377–411.

Elton, Edwin J., Martin J. Gruber, and Joel C. Rentzler. 1987. "Professionally Managed Publicly Traded Commodity Funds." *Journal of Business* 60:2, 175–199.

Elton, Edwin J., Martin J. Gruber, and Joel C. Rentzler. 1989. "New Public Offerings, Information, and Investor Rationality: The Case of Publicly Offered Commodity Funds." *Journal of Business* 62:1, 1–15.

Elton, Edwin J., Martin J. Gruber, and Joel C. Rentzler. 1990. "The Performance of Publicly Offered Commodity Funds." *Financial Analysts Journal* 46:4, 23–30.

Fama, Eugene F., and Kenneth R. French. 1993. "Common Risk Factors in the Returns on Bonds and Stocks." *Journal of Financial Economics* 33:1, 3–56.

Fung, William, and David A. Hsieh. 1997. "Survivorship Bias and Investment Style in the Returns of CTAs." *Journal of Portfolio Management* 24:1, 30–41.

Fung, William, and David A. Hsieh. 2001. "The Risk in Hedge Fund Strategies: Theory and Evidence from Trend Followers." *Review of Financial Studies* 14:2, 313–341.

Gregoriou, Greg N., Georges Hübner, and Maher Kooli. 2010. "Performance and Persistence of Commodity Trading Advisors: Further Evidence." *Journal of Futures Markets* 30:8, 725–752.

Gregoriou, Greg N., Georges Hübner, Nicolas Papageorgiou, and Fabrice Rouah. 2005. "Survival of Commodity Trading Advisors: 1990–2003." *Journal of Futures Markets* 25:8, 795–815.

Hurst, Brian, Yao Hua Ooi, and Lasse Heje Pedersen. 2013. "Demystifying Managed Futures." *Journal of Investment Management* 11:3, 42–58.

Irwin, Scott H., Terry R. Krukemyer, and Carl R. Zulauf. 1993. "Investment Performance of Public Commodity Pools: 1979–1990." *Journal of Futures Markets* 13:7, 799–820.

Jensen, Gerald R., Robert R. Johnson, and Jeffrey M. Mercer. 2002. "Tactical Asset Allocation and Commodity Futures." *Journal of Portfolio Management* 28:4, 100–111.

Kat, Harry M. 2004. "Managed Futures and Hedge Funds: A Match Made in Heaven." In Greg N. Gregoriou, Vassilios N. Karavas, François-Serge Lhabitant, and Fabrice Rouah (eds.), *Commodity Trading Advisors: Risk, Performance Analysis, and Selection*, 5–17. Hoboken, NJ: John Wiley & Sons, Inc.

Kazemi, Hossein, and Ying Li. 2009. "Market Timing of CTAs: An Examination of Systematic CTAs vs. Discretionary CTAs." *Journal of Futures Markets* 29:11, 1067–1099.

Liang, Bing. 2004. "Alternative Investments: CTAs, Hedge Funds, and Funds-of-Funds." *Journal of Investment Management* 2:4, 76–93.

Lintner, John V. 1983. "The Potential Role of Managed Futures Accounts (and/or Funds) in Portfolios of Stocks and Bonds." Presentation to the Annual Conference of the Financial Analysts Federation in Managed Futures, Toronto, Canada.

McCarthy, David, Thomas Schneeweis, and Richard Spurgin. 1997. "Informational Content in Historical CTA Performance." *Journal of Futures Markets* 17:3, 317–339.

Miffre, Joëlle. 2016. "Long-Short Commodity Investing: A Review of the Literature." *Journal of Commodity Markets* 1:1, 3–13.

Morningstar. 2017. "Premium Fund Screener." January. Available at http://screen.morningstar.com/AdvFunds/Selector.html.

Mulvey, John M., Shiv Siddhant N. Kaul, and Koray D. Simsek. 2004. "Evaluating a Trend-Following Commodity Index for Multi-period Asset Allocation." *Journal of Alternative Investments* 7:1, 54–69.

Rollinger, Thomas N., and Scott T. Hoffman. 2015. "A Comparison of CTA Indexes." White Paper, Red Rock Capital, February. Available at http://www.redrockcapital.com/A_Comparison_of_CTA_Indexes__Feb_2015_.pdf.

Schneeweis, Thomas, Raj Gupta, and Jason Remillard. 2008. "CTA/Managed Futures Strategy Benchmarks: Performance and Review." In Frank J. Fabozzi, Roland Füss, and Dieter G. Kaiser (eds.), *The Handbook of Commodity Investing*, 266–310. Hoboken, NJ: John Wiley & Sons, Inc.

Schneeweis, Thomas, Richard Spurgin, and David McCarthy. 1996. "Survivor Bias in Commodity Trading Performance." *Journal of Futures Markets* 16:7, 757–772.

Schneeweis, Thomas, Richard Spurgin, and Edward Szado. 2013. "Managed Futures Research: A Composite CTA Performance Review." *Journal of Alternative Investments* 15:3, 32–61.

Societe Generale. 2017. "SG Prime Services Indices." January. Available at https://cib.societegenerale.com/en/prime-services-indices/.

Tee, Kai-Hong. 2013. "An Overview of Managed Futures' Performance: 1983 to Post-2008 Credit Crisis." In H. Kent Baker and Greg Filbeck (eds.), *Alternative Investments: Instruments, Performance, Benchmarks, and Strategies*, 437–452. Hoboken, NJ: John Wiley & Sons, Inc.

Zweig, Jason. 2017. "The Hidden Fees Inside Managed Future Funds." *Wall Street Journal*, January 27, B1. Available at http://blogs.wsj.com/moneybeat/2017/01/27/thehiddenfeesinsidemanagedfuturefunds/.

13

Commodity Exchange-Traded Funds

CHRISTOPHER MILLIKEN
Vice President, Hennion & Walsh, Inc.

EHSAN NIKBAKHT
Professor of Finance, Frank G. Zarb School of Business, Hofstra University

ANDREW C. SPIELER
Professor of Finance, Frank G. Zarb School of Business, Hofstra University

Introduction

An increasingly popular way to access the commodity market has been through exchange-traded funds (ETFs). An ETF is a security that trades on a national stock exchange and represents a basket of underlying holdings, most often with the objective of replicating the performance of a specified index. To a lesser extent, a small segment of the ETF market consists of actively managed funds, whose aim is to provide shareholders with total return. In either case, the price at which ETFs trade is determined primarily in the secondary market and rarely drifts far from the fund's net asset value (NAV), which is the sum of the value of the fund's underlying holdings. State Street Corporation introduced ETFs in the United States in 1993. ETFs now represent a large portion of pooled investment vehicles with more than $2 trillion in assets invested across nearly 2,000 products (Cantor Fitzgerald 2016). Most ETFs are structured as open-end investment vehicles registered under the Investment Company Act of 1940 with the aim of tracking an equity index. Yet, a growing number of ETFs are designed to track the performance of a specified commodity or a basket of commodities and use an alternative path of registration (Huntington, Treff, and Tzouganatos 2013).

The SPDRs (pronounced "Spiders") are issued by State Street's ETF division, the first ETF provider to issue a fund that tracks the performance of a commodity. SPDR is short for S&P Depository Receipt and pays homage to the first U.S.-listed ETF, launched by State Street in 1993. Launched in November 2004, the SPDR Gold Shares ETF *GLD* tracks the spot price of gold (SPDR 2015). About two months after GLD launched, in January 2005, iShares, the largest provider of ETFs both in number of funds offered and by assets under management (AUM), launched the iShares Gold Trust ETF (*IAU*). IAU's objective is also to track the spot price of gold (iShares 2016).

Unlike the majority of ETFs which are open-end funds, the SPDR Gold Shares and the iShares Gold Trust are grantor trusts and maintain a physical investment in gold in order to track the commodity. Although these first two commodity ETFs, subsequently referred to as ETCs, are grantor trusts, the vast majority of products in today's market are exchanged-traded notes (ETNs). An *ETN* is technically a senior, unsecured debt security issued by a financial institution with the stated objective of tracking an underlying index (Financial Industry Regulatory Authority 2012). ETNs are publicly traded in the secondary market on national stock exchanges just like traditional ETFs. Given the prevalence of this structure, this chapter discusses issues specific to ETNs. A less common, but still popular, form of registration is the commodity pool structure, or partnership ETF. Commodity pools are set up as partnerships and are registered with the Commodity Futures Trading Commission (CFTC) rather than with the Securities Exchange Commission (SEC) (Antoniewicz and Heinrichs 2014). They achieve their objective by investing in the futures contracts of the underlying commodity and can freely invest in derivatives without having to worry about violating the parameters for a Registered Investment Company (RIC), which all open-end funds must oblige. Last, ETCs can be legally structured as traditional open-end funds. This chapter discusses each structure, the associated regulatory bodies covering each structure, and their advantages and disadvantages.

The 10 years after the launch of GLD witnessed the launching of more than 140 ETFs whose objective is to track individual commodities, groups of commodities, or a broad-based commodity basket. A few examples of individual commodities that investors can now access through an ETF include oil, silver, copper, livestock, and wheat. By purchasing an ETC, investors can track the performance of an index whose underlying components are a narrow group of commodities with similar characteristics. An energy ETC, for example, can be built to track a blended index of Brent crude oil, heating oil, light crude oil, natural gas, and gasoline. More broadly speaking, providers have created ETFs designed to track indexes representing a basket of commodities.

To better illustrate an ETC that tracks a commodity basket, consider the largest such fund with more than $2.2 billion in assets, the PowerShares DB Commodity Index Tracking Fund (DBC) launched in 2006. Its objective is to provide investment results similar to the Deutsche Bank Index Quant Group Optimum Yield Diversified Commodity Index Excess Return. Figure 13.1 displays the 14 components of the DBC with approximate weights on July 31, 2016.

Another variety of ETCs include managed futures accounts (MTAs) run by commodity trading advisors (CTAs). These investments, like the commodity pool trusts previously discussed, register with the CFTC through the National Futures Association (NFA). MTAs typically go long or short in futures contracts to seek a total return objective that will produce a return path that is uncorrelated with other asset classes such as stocks and bonds (BarclayHedge 2016). The end goal of the MTA is to produce a positive, non-correlated total return.

Some ETCs have the objective of providing the leveraged and/or inverse return of a specific commodity or group of commodities. These ETFs provide investors with

Commodity	Base Weight (%)
Aluminum	4
Brent crude	12
Copper-Grade A	4
Corn	6
Gold	8
Heating oil	12
Light crude	12
Natural gas	6
RBOB gasoline	12
Silver	2
Soybeans	6
Sugar #11	6
Wheat	6
Zinc	4

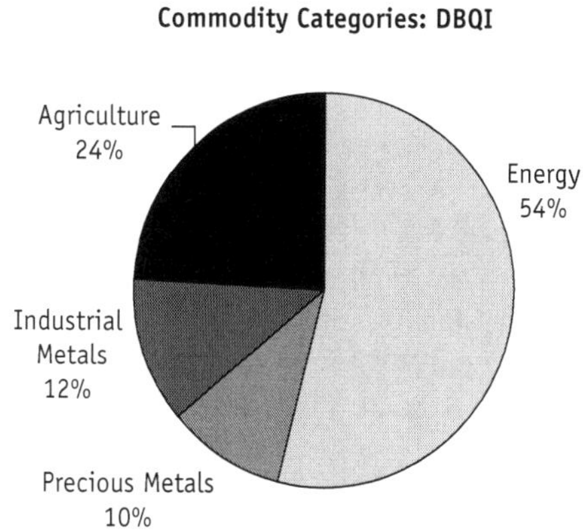

Figure 13.1 Overview of a Diversified ETC
This table and pie chart show the allocations to the underlying commodities in the ETC DBIQ. Source: PowerShares (2016a).

a multiple or inverse daily return of the reference commodity without the need to borrow funds on margin or enter into a short sale. A major downside to leveraged and/or inverse ETFs is the tracking error caused by the daily resetting factor. Due to compounding, in a volatile trading environment that is mean reverting, the fund will underperform the index, but in a trending market, the fund is likely to outperform. Convenience is certainly a benefit, but these products are often misunderstood. Thus, investors should proceed only after thoroughly understanding the risks (Securities and Exchange Commission 2009).

This chapter focuses on ETCs tracking the performance of an underlying commodity and not funds that enter into indirect commodity investments, which consist of purchasing the common stock of companies engaged in the commodity business. An indirect investment in commodities could include buying the Materials Selection Sector SPDR Fund (XLB), which invests in a portfolio of stocks that includes Freeport-McMoran, the world's largest copper miner. Although some of the products discussed also invest in common stocks, the underlying objective remains to provide investors with a return structure that tracks the spot or futures price of the underlying commodity or basket of commodities.

This chapter provides an overview of various ways investors can access the commodity market through the ETF wrapper. The chapter also discusses the growth of these relatively new products and their future from both a regulatory and product development viewpoint. Additionally, this comprehensive overview identifies the users of these products and the strategies employed. Because the regulatory landscape is an essential component of this discussion, the chapter also reviews various funds listed on U.S. exchanges and the regulatory bodies that oversee them.

Growth of ETCs

ETCs debuted in 2004 and 2005 with two products that provided exposure to gold. Over the next 11 years, these markets grew substantially. By 2016, more than 140 individual funds had almost $80 billion in AUM (Bloomberg 2016). While ETFs as investment vehicles have enjoyed many consecutive years of growth in both fund issuance and AUM, the growth of ETCs has tempered. Two reasons are likely to explain this slowdown. First, the market has been become saturated with enough products to fulfill investor appetites, and providers do not believe bringing competing ETFs to market would be profitable. In support of this argument is the current "war on fees" that the ETF industry is experiencing (ETF Trends 2016). Bringing a new product to market in an area where a fund already exists forces the new provider to compete by offering a lower fee and operate with tighter margins, an unattractive and potentially unprofitable endeavor.

The other reason issuance has slowed is that the vast majority of ETCs (63 percent) are structured as ETNs, or senior, unsecured debt securities issued by financial institutions. Of the 89 ETNs in the marketplace in late 2016, 64 originated between 2006 and 2008, a period coinciding with the lead-up to and beginning of the financial crisis of 2007-2008. Considering that ETNs, unlike ETFs, carry the risk of default by the issuer, securities that depend on the going concern of financial firms such as Merrill Lynch, Barclays, and Deutsche Bank were understandably less attractive to investors after the collapse of Lehman Brothers and near collapse of the entire financial system. Jorgensen and Washer (2011) show that demand for ETNs fell in the aftermath of the collapse of Lehman Brothers and continued to fall through the end of 2008. Their study reports that as credit spreads widen, ETN demand falls. According to Jorgensen and Washer (p. 56), "Demand for DJP was negatively related to investor credit risk aversion . . . the demand for ETN is negatively correlated to credit spreads." Figure 13.2 provides a visual display of yearly issuance by product type.

Evidence of lower demand following the financial crisis is the release of only one ETN in 2009, the UBS-ETRACS Bloomberg Commodity Index Total Return ETN (DJCI), and none in 2010.

With respect to the remaining 37 percent of the ETC marketplace not structured as ETNs, growth in fund issuance appears to have tempered as well, albeit not to the dramatic extent witnessed in the years after 2008. Although commodity pool issuance peaked in 2008 with the release of 10 funds, six came to market in 2011. The release of the last commodity pool developed before 2017 occurred in 2013 by iShares and since then no providers have chosen this structure. The two less common structures for ETCs are grantor trusts and open-end funds, with eight products each. The last grantor trusts issued came to market in 2014, and like each of the other trusts in the market today, tracked the price of a precious metal by physically holding the underlying asset in a vault. ETCs registered as open-end investment companies are becoming a more popular choice for providers because they do not issue the unattractive K-1 tax form that commodity pools must issue (Justice 2010). First Trust issued the first ETC structured as an open-end fund in 2013. By the end of 2016, seven additional funds emerged in the same manner (Bloomberg 2016). Specific techniques

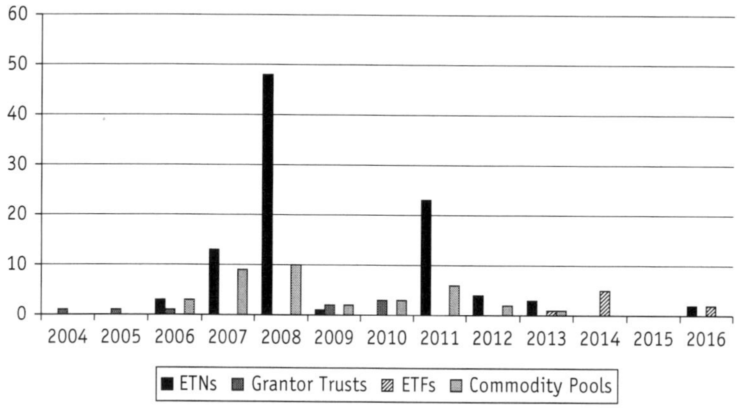

Figure 13.2 Issuance by Product Type
This graph shows the number of ETCs issued each year organized by regulatory structure. Source: Author calculations using data from a Bloomberg terminal on September 30, 2016.

used to maintain RIC status, which is required for open-end funds, afford the ability to use derivative contracts in these funds.

The number of ETC fund sponsors has grown from two in 2005 to 19 by July 2016. This growth stems from traditional providers of ETFs such as iShares and PowerShares as well as some of the largest financial companies such as Barclays, Deutsche Bank, and UBS. ETNs make up a large share of the ETC universe. Because ETNs depend on the creditworthiness of their provider and their provider's ability to hedge their exposure, large banks are among the few institutions capable of and willing to create these securities. Of the 19 ETC providers, about 40 percent are investment banks or financial holding companies. The remaining 60 percent have more narrowly focused business lines that center on creating and distributing ETFs (Bloomberg 2016).

Uses and Users of ETCs

ETCs grant individual and institutional market participants the ability to invest in commodities such as oil, gold, or grain as easily as they could in the stock of a publicly traded company. Before 2004, investors seeking exposure to a given commodity likely had only two choices. The first choice was to buy stock in a company whose earnings and share price were tied to the commodity. For example, someone looking to gain exposure to oil might buy shares of Exxon Mobil. This approach is an indirect investment because the gains and losses on the stock investment are not perfectly correlated with the performance of the commodity. Deviations can occur for different reasons including the positive changes in the prospect of future cash flows such as a technological development or negative changes such as an accounting scandal.

Gorton and Rouwenhorst (2006) explore this issue by comparing a basket of commodities futures contracts with a relevant basket of commodity-based equities from

July 1959 through December 2004. They find that the equities (an indirect commodity investment) exhibit a closer correlation to the S&P 500 Index than they do with the commodity futures index and thus offer less diversification benefit.

The second option for investors to gain exposure to commodities was to use the futures markets. A *futures contract* is an agreement between two parties for the delivery of a specified amount of a specified good at an agreed upon price. Futures require capital to be posted (margin), do not perfectly track the spot price of the commodity, and can be intimidating for investors because they have been called "potentially [the] riskiest financial products available in the United States" (Financial Industry Regulatory Authority 2016). For these reasons, very few individual investors use the futures market to gain exposure to commodities, and the institutional investors who do have to hire a specialist with experience in this area, raising costs.

Today, an investor with as little as a few hundred dollars can gain access to a broad basket of commodities that do the work of investing in futures contracts. Given that ETCs trade on public stock exchanges, investing is simple and costs are low with few restrictions in most types of accounts. Institutional investors also can take advantage of these benefits, reduce internal costs, and potentially increase liquidity.

A common use of futures contracts is by commercial traders who engage in the futures market to hedge their exposure to given commodity. For example, consider a wheat farmer who through the normal course of production grows 1,000 bushels of wheat intended for sale, but not yet sold. Between the time of harvesting the wheat and collecting cash, the farmer has exposure to price risk, which could work out to his benefit if wheat prices rise or to his detriment if prices fall. Rather than assume this risk, the farmer could hedge the long wheat position by selling a futures contract on wheat, locking in the sale price.

Conversely, consider the producer of flour who knows that in two months, it will need to buy 1,000 bushels of wheat. In this example, the price risk is the opposite of the farmer's and the flour producer benefits from a drop in the value of wheat and, conversely, loses out if prices rise. To hedge this exposure, the flour producer could purchase a futures contract on wheat, locking in the price so gains in the contract's value offset any increase in costs.

An important distinction exists between using futures to hedge exposure to a given commodity and attempting to do the same thing through the purchase or short sale of an ETC that tracks the underlying commodity. Because the design of an ETC is to offer perpetual exposure, the provider will often buy the front month futures contract, or the contract that comes due the following month, and roll that contract into the next month before expiration (Iachini 2013a). As soon discussed in more detail, this strategy exposes the ETC to roll yield on a monthly basis. *Roll yield* is the cost or gain associated with buying the next month's futures contract whose price differs from the price of the current month's contract. Ultimately, roll yield either increases or decreases the return to the futures investor and creates a divergence between the return of the spot price of the commodity and the return the commodities futures holder realizes. Thus, the outright purchase of a futures contract with a given expiration exposes the buyer to a onetime effect of roll yield, avoiding the compound effects associated with a series of monthly rolls inherent with the ETC structure.

For investors who have no exposure to price risk in the product market, an allocation to commodities serves as a diversification and risk-reduction tool. Many investors build portfolios containing a mix of stocks and bonds, with the more conservative investors allocating a greater portion of their wealth to bonds and those more comfortable taking risk allocating a greater portion to stocks. Taking a portion of the portfolio, however, and investing in an asset class such as commodities, which have historically lower correlations with stocks or bonds, can potentially lower the amount of risk taken by the investor without sacrificing return potential. Georgiev (2001) shows that combining a portfolio of U.S. stocks and bonds with the Goldman Sachs Commodity Index (GSCI) lowers the standard deviation of the portfolio's annual returns by 0.9 percent and does not cause a change to the portfolio's Sharpe ratio. In an international context, a global portfolio of stocks and bonds when combined with the GSCI reduces the portfolio standard deviation by 0.5 percent while increasing the Sharpe ratio. Although this example considers a basket of commodities, investors often use gold as a stand-alone holding as a hedge against inflation and currency depreciation as well as a place to store wealth during geopolitical or financial distress (SPDR Gold Shares 2015).

Besides using commodities to reduce portfolio risk or hedge against price changes of the underlying, speculators, or noncommercial investors, trade commodity futures as a means of generating returns. For example, if speculators believe that the price of oil is set to rise, they could buy oil futures contracts, wait until the expected appreciation occurs, and then sell the contracts for a gain or hold until cash settlement at expiration. ETCs enable a larger set of investors to invest in commodities and eliminate the need to directly invest in futures.

In this same example, an investor can speculate on price gains in oil using an ETC. This speculative transaction can now take place in almost any type of account as simply as buying a common stock. Of course, this simple scenario can be applied to any individual commodity or group of commodities that an investor believes will appreciate. Conversely, investors believing that the price of a commodity or group of commodities is set to decline could sell the ETC short rather than selling futures contracts.

The design of some ETCs is to deliver a multiple of two to three times the return of the underlying and grant investors the ability to take a leveraged bet on the future price direction. The intention of these products is to replicate the stated multiple of price performance over the course of a single trading day. Due to the effects of compounding, investors cannot rely on ETCs to replicate the price performance of the underlying over longer periods of time (Financial Industry Regulatory Authority 2012). Of course, downward movements in price will generate larger losses from the leveraged position relative to the change in the actual commodity price. Due to the increased risk associated with leveraged ETCs and the fact they track the performance of the underlying only over a single day, these products are popular among active traders with high risk tolerances and short time frames.

Speculators use inverse ETCs, not unlike the leveraged funds previously discussed, as a substitute for short selling traditional funds. However, because of the limited choices of products available and typically higher transaction costs, those looking for inverse exposure to the future price direction of a commodity are likely to sell the ETC short rather than buy an inverse product.

Regulatory Environment and Legal Structure

Perhaps more so than in any other category or asset class of ETFs, those ETFs tracking commodities are the most complicated from a regulatory standpoint. More than 95 percent of ETFs that trade on U.S. exchanges are structured as open-end investment companies under the Investment Company Act of 1940 ("1940 Act"). Issuers must register these products with the SEC under the Securities Act of 1933, the Securities Exchange Act of 1934, and the Investment Advisors Act of 1940. ETFs registered in this format are required to abide by strict rules in terms of the concentration of underlying holdings, types of securities held, and amount of income received ultimately passed through to the shareholders (Antoniewicz and Heinrichs 2014). However, due to these restrictions, very few ETCs choose this structure, instead forming as ETNs.

An ETN is technically a senior, unsecured debt security issued by a financial institution (Financial Industry Regulatory Authority 2012). This is a critical point of differentiation from ETFs because ETN shareholders do not own a portfolio of underlying assets but represent a general claim against the issuer's assets in the case of bankruptcy, and thus introducing a degree of credit risk (Jorgensen and Washer 2011). In contrast to the fixed coupons of a traditional fixed income security, the ETN's value is adjusted based on changes in the underlying index. For example, consider the largest, non-leveraged, commodity ETN by AUM, the iPath Bloomberg Commodity Index Total Return Fund (DJP), whose intent is to track the performance of a basket of commodities. During the course of a trading day, if the value of the underlying, as measured by the designated index, increased by 5 percent, then the ETN provider promises to redeem shares at a value of 5 percent more than the prior day. Conversely, if the value of the basket of commodities and designated index fell by 5 percent, then the fund provider would redeem shares of the ETN at a price 5 percent lower than the previous day.

The benefits of the ETN structure are limited tracking error and favorable tax treatment. *Tracking error* is the standard deviation of the difference in the return of an ETF versus the return of the underlying index. A provider of an ETN backs the product with a basket of securities and builds tracking error into the fee charged rather than forcing the shareholders to bear the burden of transaction costs, cash drag, and imperfect replication. Compared to other ETF structures, the ETN is the most tax efficient since taxes are only assessed on capital gains when the fund is sold. Traditional ETFs can pass through capital gains and dividends to shareholders while they hold the fund regardless of whether the investor sold shares and/or received dividends throughout the course of the year (Justice 2010).

On the downside, since an ETN is a senior, unsecured debt security, the shareholders of an ETN are subject not only to the risk of loss of principal due to the underlying security falling in value but also to the risk of default on behalf of the provider. Therefore, having Wall Street's biggest banks such as Barclays, Deutsche Bank, and

UBS issue the majority of ETNs is not surprising. Although default by these large institutions was once unthinkable, the financial crisis of 2007–2008 brought these banks to the brink of collapse and made default risk an important consideration in the ETN market. Empirical evidence supports a fall in demand associated with heightened credit risk during this period (Jorgensen and Washer 2011). In the immediate aftermath of the financial crisis, the inherent default risk of ETNs has reduced the popularity of this structure. Providers have instead focused on a traditional open-end, grantor trust, or commodity pool structures.

Grantor trusts currently represent the majority of commodity ETFs as measured by AUM, thanks to a behemoth in the group, the SPDR Gold Shares ETF (GLD), which has $41.5 billion in assets. GLD is the largest ETC by a factor of more than four times and is the eighth largest ETF overall. The second largest ETC by AUM is also a grantor trust. The iShares Gold Trust (IAU) has nearly $10 billion in assets. Despite having aggregated a large share of assets, only eight ETCs are grantor trusts at the end of 2016 (Bloomberg 2016).

According to Vanguard (2016), grantor trusts are required to hold a fixed portfolio of securities, which makes them ideal for holding physical commodities, specifically non-perishable precious metals. This means a physical amount of the precious metal held in a vault and not in futures contracts backs every dollar invested in a grantor trust. Specifically, for the SPDR Gold Shares Fund, the gold is in the form of London Good Delivery bars, or 400-oz. bars, and held in the London vaults of HSBC Bank plc. The issuer passes through the cost of storage to investors in the form of the expense ratio (SPDR 2015). Unlike an open-end fund, a grantor trust is not required to register under the 1940 Act, but is regulated by the Securities Act of 1933 and Securities Exchange Act of 1934 (Antoniewicz and Heinrichs 2014). From a tax standpoint, the assumption is that the shareholder in the grantor trust owns a proportionate share of the underlying commodity and no realized capital gains are generated or investment income passed through while the trust is held. Upon the sale of shares, the investor is subject to taxes at the ordinary income rate (Justice 2010).

Because having a direct investment in most commodities is impractical due to storage costs and spoilage, many ETCs choose to track the price of the underlying by investing in futures contracts. Due to restrictions on investing in derivatives for funds registered under the 1940 Act, ETCs that engage in trading futures contracts often use a commodity pool or partnership structure. Partnership ETFs are regulated by the CFTC and National Futures Association (NFA) as well as the Securities Act of 1933 and Securities Exchange Act of 1940 (BarclayHedge 2016).

With more than $11 billion in AUM across 36 funds, the commodity pool or partnership ETF is the second largest fund structure used by ETCs. A *commodity pool* is an unincorporated business entity that chooses to be taxed in the same manner as a limited partnership. With partnerships, commodity pools pass through realized gains and losses as well as income to the shareholders who receive a K-1 tax document at the end of each calendar year (Justice 2010). Traditionally, the Internal Revenue Service (IRS) would deem a publicly traded limited partnership taxable even when held inside of a retirement account. This tax treatment falls under an IRS clause known as Unrelated Business Taxable Income (UBTI), but because an ETC generates income passively through futures contracts, it does not apply (Iachini 2013b).

To be classified as and remain a RIC, an ETF must generate 90 percent of its income from passive securities such as stocks and bonds. A futures contract does not meet the definition of passive security and so ETFs wanting to use futures contracts as the primary underlying security cannot register as an open-end fund. More recently, however, providers have been able to navigate around this restriction using two different techniques. The first approach is to blend passive securities with futures contracts and construct or manage the portfolio in a way that ensures 90 percent of the income comes from the passive investments. The second method is to create an offshore subsidiary through the19b-4 filing that effectively manages a portfolio of securities using the same mandate as the ETF. The subsidiary has no restrictions on investing in derivatives and the fund in turn can invest up to 25 percent of its assets in the offshore entity. The ETF invests the remaining fund assets in cash equivalents to be held as collateral and other securities considered passive.

One common thread in the registration of each variety of funds is the requirement to register with the SEC under both the Securities Act of 1933 and the Securities Exchange Act of 1934. The governments created both acts in the wake of the Great Depression to address two separate issues. The Securities Act of 1933 primarily deals with transparency in financial statements and established laws against misrepresentation. The biggest impact on commodity ETFs is the requirement for readily available information concerning the description, management, and financial statements of the security being offered (i.e. prospectus). The Securities Exchange Act of 1934 deals primarily with the listing of shares on a public stock exchange. ETFs, regardless of their structure, are required to seek exemption of some provisions of this law including extending credit to customers, confirmations, and delivering notice of certain specified actions. In general, the Securities Exchange Act of 1934 sets forth requirements to establish fairness and investor confidence, which affects every ETF trading in the United States (Huntington et al. 2013).

Physically Backed ETCs

As previously mentioned, some ETCs achieve their stated objective by investing in futures contracts or other derivatives tracking the price of the underlying commodity or basket of commodities. Grantor trusts, however, achieve their objective by investing in the physical good and storing the good in a vault. Hence, an ETC structured as a grantor trust can track the pure value of the underlying without the influence of supply and demand for futures contracts. The following section provides a discussion of this condition.

Most of the ETCs in the market aim to track the price of goods that are perishable. Grains, coffee, sugar, and oil incur substantial storage costs but do not maintain their physical structure indefinitely. For this reason, each of the eight grantor trust ETFs tracks the price of precious metals, which theoretically can last forever in storage and require minimal maintenance. Investors have the choice of purchasing shares in ETCs that track the price of gold, silver, platinum, palladium, or a basket of precious metals and in doing so technically own a stake in the physical metal. Because ETFs offer in-kind redemptions, sufficiently large shareholders can potentially redeem a stake in the ETC for physical delivery of the underlying, a feature unavailable to investors in ETCs with other structures (SPDR 2015).

The price performance of grantor trust funds has predictably tracked the spot price of the underlying commodity. Plamondon and Luft (2012) study how closely physically backed funds track the spot price of their underlying commodity. Using regressing analysis, they find that beta is statistically indistinguishable from 1.0 with a high R^2. The authors analyze the returns from each of the grantor trust ETFs that track gold with at least five years of available data, the SPDR Gold Trust, iShares Gold Trust, and ETFS Physical Swiss Gold Share. The results confirm pair-wise correlations with the spot price of gold of more than 0.99 when measured on a weekly basis. The expense ratio explains the only significant divergence in price between the ETCs and the spot price of gold. However, investors in these products have to consider the commission charge when making a purchase or sale. The expense ratios range from 0.25 to 0.60 percent and cover the storage and administrative costs of the provider (Bloomberg 2016).

To highlight the efficiency of grantor trusts in tracking the price of the underlying, Figure 13.3 shows the cumulative return of the spot price of gold, the iShares Gold Trust, IAU (a grantor trust), the PowerShares DB Gold Fund, DGL (a commodity pool) from the inception of the PowerShares DB Gold Fund on January 5, 2007.

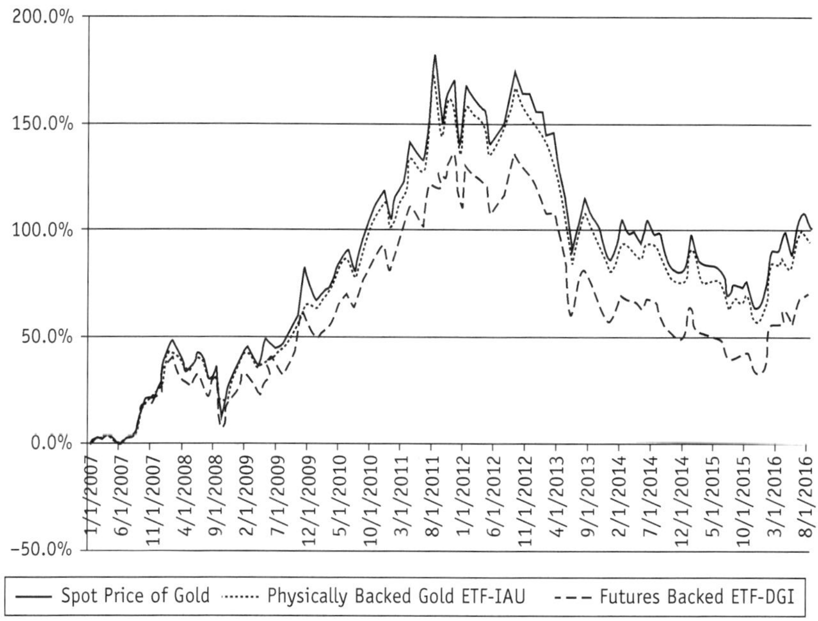

Figure 13.3 Price Return of Gold and Gold ETCs
This graph shows the total return of the spot price of gold and two popular ETCs, IAU and DGI, from January 2007 to August 2016. Source: Author calculations using data from a Bloomberg terminal on September 9, 2016.

Figure 13.3 highlights the performance of these funds between February 2007 and August 2016, when the spot price of gold increased 102 percent. An investor holding the iShares Gold Trust would have experienced a gain of 94 percent, while an investor holding the PowerShares DB Gold Fund (DGL) would have experienced a gain of 63 percent. Besides illustrating the difference in return between a futures-backed and a physically backed fund, the return pattern of these three products exhibits the compounding effect of the expense ratio. Despite closely tracking the spot price of gold, IAU cumulative returns lagged by 8 percent due to the low but impactful annual expense ratio of 0.25 percent paid on a daily basis. Further, this analysis excludes commission charges and taxes, which would have further reduced the total return for the investor in IAU and DGL.

The PowerShares DB Gold Fund lagged the spot return of gold by 39 percent since February 2007 and, as noted, invests in futures contracts rather than holding the physical good. Besides the expense ratio of 0.78 percent that DGL charges, the costs of entering a futures contract at a price higher than the spot price of gold induces contango, which also reduces returns when the investor rolls forward futures contracts. The next section discusses contango in more detail.

Investment strategy and return differential aside, IAU and DGL exhibit very similar correlation with the spot price of gold and nearly identical volatility. IAU's and DGL's correlation with gold, as measured by monthly returns over the same period considered previously, was more than 0.99. The volatility each fund experienced, as measured by the standard deviation of monthly returns, was 5.6 percent, in line with the spot price of gold, which also registered 5.6 percent (Bloomberg 2016).

Futures-Backed Funds

Commodity pools, or partnership ETFs, do not register as open-end investment companies under the Investment Company Act of 1940 but register instead with the CFTC (Antoniewicz and Heinrichs 2014). This affords fund providers the freedom to invest in futures contracts and other derivatives to achieve their stated objective. The vast majority of ETFs seek to track an underlying equity index by purchasing shares of the underlying companies in proportion to their weight in the associated index. For an ETF tracking a commodity, however, replicating the performance of the underlying is not as straightforward. Buying a physical commodity and storing it for future sale require ongoing management and incur costs that are simply too prohibitive. As discussed previously, this strategy is sensible when the underlying is a precious metal that does not spoil and investors can easily buy and sell with relatively low transaction costs. Funds can also attempt to replicate the performance of a particular commodity by investing in the common stock of companies that engage in mining or producing the underlying because their cash flows and stock price are positively correlated with the commodity. Unfortunately, this strategy is an unreliable method to track the commodity performance because many factors go into the pricing of a company's stock that are independent of the pricing structure of the underlying commodity. According to Plamondon and Luft (2012, p. 3), "Purchasing shares of commodity producing firms had considerable tracking error, [and] rising commodity prices may not translate to superior share performance for producers." Due to these factors, using stocks to access the commodity markets is not widely popular.

Fund providers have determined that the most accurate and feasible way to replicate the performance of a commodity is by purchasing futures contracts. The CFTC regulates futures contracts, which are standardized to make trading easier and more efficient. To guard against the risk of default on behalf of the counterparty, the exchange on which it trades guarantees each contract. The structure of a typical contract enables settling each month at a range of prices for cash delivery, meaning instead of delivering the physical good, investors exchange the cash difference between purchase price and settlement price (CME Group 2013).

When engaging in a futures-based strategy, the ETC often buys contracts that come due the following month (i.e., front month contracts). Before the contracts come due, the ETC manager sells them and uses the proceeds to buy the next month's contracts. This process continues in perpetuity with the notional value of the holdings equating to the market value of the ETC. This process is known as rolling futures contracts. Often times, however, the price of a futures contract is either higher or lower than the spot price of the underlying commodity. This causes the holder of the contracts to experience a gain or loss that is unrelated to price changes in the underlying, a return known as a *roll yield* (Kosev and Williams 2011). Interest rates, carry costs, and supply and demand dynamics all affect roll yield.

When the futures price is trading above the spot price, the contract is in *contango*. During contango, the owner of the futures contract experiences a negative roll yield. Conversely, when the futures price is trading below the spot price, the contract is in *backwardation*, which benefits the holder of the futures contract from the positive roll yield. The roll yield from contango and backwardation can substantially affect ETC returns. Consider Figure 13.4, which shows the total return of the United States Oil Fund, USO, compared to the spot price of oil measured between September 30, 2015, and September 30, 2016.

Clearly, the spot price of oil has substantially outperformed the United States Oil Fund, which achieves its exposure by investing in the front month oil futures and rolling over the contracts each month. Speculators pouring into the long side of futures contracts drive the price upward due to supply and demand dynamics and erode gains in the spot price. The spot price of WTI Crude Oil increased 7.1 percent over this one-year period, while an investor in USO lost 25.5 percent. According to the *Wall Street Journal* (2009), the predictable nature of USO's rolling allows speculative, predatory traders to benefit at the expense of shareholders and amplify the negative roll yield.

Some ETCs attempt to mitigate the effects of contango and maximize the potential positive roll yield associated with backwardation by actively managing the futures contracts that they buy. For example, the PowerShares DB Oil Fund (DBO) invests in futures contracts associated with West Texas Intermediate (WTI) crude oil with the intent of identifying the most advantageous contracts available. Although this strategy can potentially outperform the spot price of oil when a market is in backwardation, it cannot eliminate negative roll yield entirely for markets in contango (PowerShares 2016b). As with any ETF, investors must also consider the commissions, expense ratio, and trading costs.

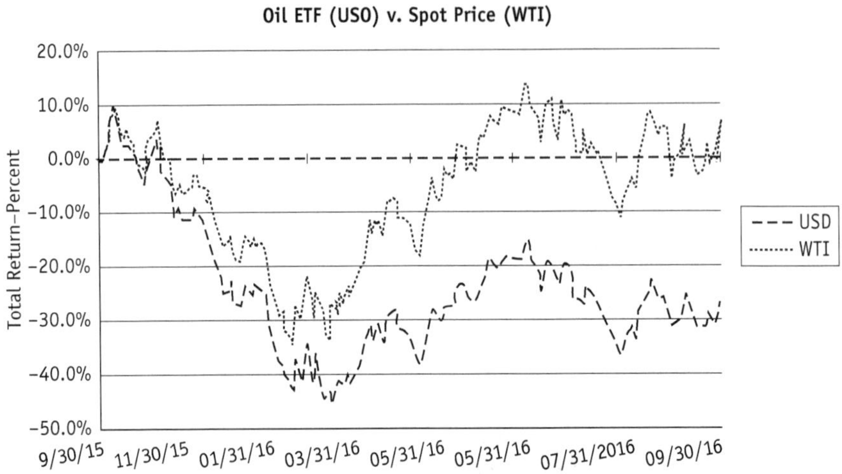

Figure 13.4 Spot Price of Crude Oil and Crude Oil ETF
This graph shows the total return of the spot price of WTI oil compared to the ETC USO. Source: Author calculations using data from a Bloomberg terminal on September 30, 2016.

Effects on the Underlying Market

Before 2004, limitations exist in how the majority of investors could invest in the commodities market, but ETCs changed this situation. Easy access to these markets allowed additional capital to enter that investors previously invested elsewhere. Although the first ETCs invested in physical commodities, the majority of ETCs bought futures contracts or tracked an index of futures contracts, thus requiring the issuer to hedge with offsetting purchases or sales of futures contracts. The additional inflow of capital has caused many to question what underlying effect ETCs have had on the volatility and liquidity of the commodities futures market. Besides questions about the effect on the underlying market, special attention should be paid to the regularity with which an ETC is rebalanced and the potential for predatory traders to take advantage of this regularity.

The additional inflow of capital has both positive and negative effects on financial markets. All else equal, the more capital invested, the more liquid a market becomes, which tightens bid-ask spreads and improves price discovery. Conversely, the increased volume of trading paired with the daily tradability of ETFs could heighten volatility in the underlying market and cross asset volatility. As with most innovations in financial markets, actual trading experience helps to identify product flaws and to promote effective regulation. Academics, governmental bodies, and industry participants are increasingly focusing on ETC research.

Market participants often interpret an increase in volatility as an increase in risk and therefore view it as a negative side effect. Corbet and Twomey (2014) show that ETCs with an investment in a futures market below \$2.15B decrease the associated volatility within that market. However, ETCs with larger investments in markets have the opposite effect, increasing the volatility of the underlying market. The resulting higher volatility is reflective of the daily trading afforded to investors who use the ETF wrapper and the associated buying and selling of futures contracts by fund providers in these markets. Smaller ETCs actually lower the volatility of the futures markets they aim to track. Corbet and Twomey find that the increased liquidity due to more market participants (i.e., the ETF providers) results in lower overall volatility and thus benefits existing market participants.

As discussed, certain ETCs invest in a basket of commodities offering investors diversified exposure. When creating or redeeming shares of a diversified ETC, the provider must make the subsequent purchases or sales of futures contracts to ensure that the notional value of these contracts matches the market value of the fund. Thus, market participants in futures contracts for energy, agricultural, and precious metal commodities, for example, either buy or sell simultaneously. Corbet and Twomey (2014) find that this trading activity leads the cross-asset correlations of futures contracts to rise across various commodities. They report that the correlation of soybeans with WTI crude oil was essentially zero between 1986 and 2004. However, since 2004, the correlation has increased to 0.6. The authors report a similar increase between oil and cotton (0.5), live cattle (0.4), and copper (0.6).

Most ETFs provide great transparency in the rebalancing schedules and with respect to the types of contracts purchased in accordance with their underlying strategy. This predictable trading behavior can be gamed to the detriment of shareholders. Consider the example where a speculative futures trader is aware that a large ETC is about to sell the current month's futures contract and buy the following month's contract. The speculator can front run this trade by placing sell orders in advance of the ETC and use the proceeds generated from the short sale to buy the next month's contract. When the ETC actually places its sale orders, supply will inundate the market, prices will drop, and the short sale will prove profitable. Conversely, when the ETC places buy orders, demand will spike, prices will rise, and the speculator's long bet will win. Bijerga, Loder, and Robinson (2010) suggest that professional traders can exploit the roll process of ETFs at the "little guy's" expense. Cui and Meyer (2009) single out the United States Oil Fund (USO) and report that due to the fund's size, rolling futures contracts is impossible with moving the market and creates opportunities for predatory traders.

Bessembinder, Carrion, Tuttle, and Venkataraman (2012) study whether predatory trading is economically viable or if a trader would rather benefit from creating liquidity and capturing the bid-ask spread. By reviewing the trading associated with eight crude oil ETCs, the study finds that ETCs pay about 30 basis points to complete roll trades, which is in line with the trading costs in large-cap equities. They find no evidence that predatory trading is the cause for this cost and instead believe that "sunshine trading," trading related to a preannouncement that attracts liquidity suppliers, is more likely.

Summary and Conclusions

ETFs enable individual and institutional investors to invest in a liquid, transparent basket of securities that is both cost and tax efficient. Although mutual funds have to abide strictly by the rules of the Investment Company Act of 1940, ETFs can seek relief under this Act, which allows for trading on an exchange or, alternatively, can structure themselves under a different format entirely. By choosing an alternative path to registration, ETF and ETN managers can use investment strategies not offered through the mutual fund wrapper and, before 2004, largely unavailable for the vast majority of investors. Due to these developments, the commodity market and the concomitant diversification benefits are readily available to retail investors.

ETCs garnered investor attention after their debut but appear to have saturated the market as new issuance has declined. Overall, AUM in ETCs have continued to grow marginally and innovative new strategies have the potential to attract additional capital and/or improve the investor risk-return trade-off. As is the case with any investment product, investors need to understand the underlying holdings of these products and appreciate that each individual strategy carries with it inherent drawbacks and costs that will affect the investor's return.

Although the benefits of ETCs are clear, the easier flow of capital to a market that previously had been difficult to access also has the potential for unintended consequences. Due to the increased accessibility of futures contracts, lasting changes have taken place that have both enhanced the integrity of futures markets and introduced a new form of capital. To date, the benefits appear to exceed the costs. Regulators and market participants alike, however, need to continue to monitor futures market behavior during times of stress to ensure that the unintended consequences cause no harm to ETC shareholders and the commercial traders depending on futures to keep their business and their share of the U.S. economy running smoothly.

Discussion Questions

1. Differentiate between an exchange-traded note (ETN) and an exchange-traded fund (ETF).
2. Describe the benefits of including an ETC in a diversified portfolio of stocks and bonds.
3. Explain the types of commodities investors can access through ETCs.
4. Aside from the ETN, identify what types of regulatory structures under which an ETC might file.
5. Describe two effects that the growth in ETCs might have on the futures markets.

References

Antoniewicz, Rochelle, and Jane Heinrichs. 2014. "Understanding Exchange Traded Funds: How ETFs Work." *ICI Research Perspective* 20:5, 11–13. Available at www.ici.org/pdf/per20-05.pdf.

BarclayHedge. 2016. "Managed Futures Overview." Available at http://www.barclayhedge.com/research/educational-articles/managed-futures-articles/managed-futures-overview.html.

Bessembinder, Hendrik, Allen Carrion, Laura Tuttle, and Kumar Venkataraman. 2012. "Predatory or Sunshine Trading? Evidence from Crude Oil ETF Rolls." Working paper, Southern Methodist University.

Bijerga, Alan, Asjylyn Loder, and Peter Robinson. 2010. "ETFs Imperil Investors as Contango, Pre-roll Conspire." Bloomberg Newsroom. July 22, 2010.

Bloomberg Terminal. 2016. "Selected Data." New York: Bloomberg L.P.

Cantor Fitzgerald. 2016. "ETF Spotlight: US." 2016.

CME Group. 2013. "A Trader's Guide to Futures." August 2016. Available at https://www.cmegroup.com/education/files/a-traders-guide-to-futures.pdf.

Corbet, Shaen, and Cian Twomey. 2014. "Have Exchange Traded Funds Influenced Commodity Market Volatility?" *International Journal of Economics and Financial Issues* 4:2, 323-335.

Cui, Carolyn, and Gregory Meyer. 2009. "U.S. Oil Funds Finds Itself at the Mercy of Traders." *Wall Street Journal*, March 6. Available at https://www.wsj.com/articles/SB123629874701846317.

ETF Trends. 2016. "ETF Fee Cuts." Available at https://www.etftrends.com/tag/etf-fee-cuts/.

Financial Industry Regulatory Authority (FINRA). 2012. "Exchange-Traded Notes—Avoid Unpleasant Surprises." Available at http://www.finra.org/investors/alerts/exchange-traded-notes-avoid-surprises.

Financial Industry Regulatory Authority (FINRA). 2016. "Security Futures—Know Your Risks, or Risk Your Future." August. Available at http://www.finra.org/investors/security-futures-know-your-risks-or-risk-your-future.

Georgiev, Georgi. 2001. "Benefits of Commodity Investment." *Journal of Alternative Investments* 4:1, 40-48.

Gorton, Gary, and Geert K. Rouwenhorst. 2006. "Facts and Fantasies about Commodity Futures." *Financial Analysts Journal* 62:2, 47-68.

Huntington, Jack P., Bruce Treff, and Ioannia Tzouganatos. 2013. "ETF Regulatory and Operational Considerations." *Citi Transaction Services*. Available at https://www.citibank.com/mss/docs/com_reg_article_jan13.pdf.

Iachini, Michael. 2013a. "Commodity ETFs: Spot and Futures Prices." Available at http://www.schwab.com/public/schwab/nn/articles/Commodity-ETFs-Spot-and-Futures-Prices.

Iachini, Michael. 2013b. "ETFs and Taxes: What You Need to Know." Available at http://www.schwab.com/public/schwab/nn/articles/ETFs-and-Taxes-What-You-Need-to-Know.

iShares Gold Trust. 2016. "Prospectus." August. Available at https://www.ishares.com/us/literature/prospectus/p-ishares-gold-trust-prospectus-12-31.pdf.

Jorgensen, Randy, and Kenneth Washer. 2011. "Exchange Traded Notes and the Lehman Bankruptcy." *Academy of Accounting and Financial Studies Journal* 15:1, 47-58. Available at http://www.alliedacademies.org/articles/aafsjvol15si12011.pdf#page=55.

Justice, Paul. 2010. "A Basic Tax Guide for Holders of Commodity ETFs, ETNs and Trusts." *Morningstar and Seeking Alpha*. Available at http://www.nasdaq.com/article/a-basic-tax-guide-for-holders-of-commodity-etfs-etns-and-trusts-cm17739.

Kosev, Mitch, and Thomas Williams. 2011. "Exchange-Traded Funds." Reserve Bank of Australia. Available at http://www.rba.gov.au/publications/bulletin/2011/mar/8.html.

Plamondon, John P., and Carl F. Luft. 2012. "Commodity Exchange Traded Funds: Observations on Risk Exposure and Performance." Working paper, DePaul University, Department of Finance.

PowerShares. 2016a. "PowerShares DB Commodity Index Tracking Fund." October. Available at https://www.invesco.com/portal/site/us/financial-professional/etfs/product-detail?productId=DBC.

PowerShares. 2016b. "PowerShares DB Oil Fund Fact Card." October. Available at https://www.invesco.com/static/us/financialprofessional/contentdetail?contentId=3619e01e98630410VgnVCM10000046f1bf0aRCRD&dnsName=us.

Securities and Exchange Commission. 2009. "Leveraged and Inverse ETFs: Specialized Products with Extra Risks for Buy-and-Hold Investors." August. Available at https://www.sec.gov/investor/pubs/leveragedetfs-alert.htm.

SPDR Gold Shares. 2015. "FAQs." August. Available at http://www.spdrgoldshares.com/usa/faqs/.

Vanguard. 2016. "What Are the Five ETF Structures." Available at https://advisors.vanguard.com/VGApp/iip/site/advisor/etfcenter/article/ETF_FiveStructures.

14

Commodity Mutual Funds

GUSTAVO CAMILO
Associate, Cornerstone Research

JANKO CIZEL
Associate, Cornerstone Research

PAUL ZUREK
Principal, Cornerstone Research

Introduction

Commodity mutual funds (CMFs) are a category of mutual funds (MFs) that are one of the most common publicly offered regulated investment vehicles. Other such vehicles include exchange-traded funds (ETFs) and certain managed futures funds. As detailed in this chapter, CMFs are distinct entities from ETFs, managed futures funds, and hedge funds even if they all invest in commodity-related assets. As with all investments, some of the key issues regarding CMFs relate to their unique institutional details, the degree to which they provide exposures to the relevant markets, and assets, fees, risks, and performance.

This chapter is organized as follows. First, the chapter describes institutional features and risks of CMFs, preceded by a discussion of the database of fund performance used in the chapter. Next, trends in fund flows and correlations are discussed, followed by a discussion of CMF fees and performance during the 1996–2016 sample period.

Institutional Features and Risks

MFs, in general, are organized as investment companies and have assets and liabilities on their balance sheets but can perhaps be more intuitively thought of simply as pools of assets on which fund investors hold claims. They are frequently actively managed (i.e., seek to generate returns above some benchmark by employing professional managers who pick securities in which to invest) and invest in assets such as stocks, bonds, and other securities. CMFs invest in assets whose values are broadly related to the values of commodities, such as shares of companies involved in the extraction of oil, gas, or precious metals and the production of petroleum-based products. Some

CMFs have as their objective to track the performance of the overall commodities markets, while others are more specialized with a focus on energy or precious metals.

Throughout the chapter, information from a database of mutual funds and their returns (Center for Research in Security Prices at the University of Chicago Bias-Free U.S. Mutual Fund Database [CRSP MF database]) is used to shed light on the performance and characteristics of CMFs. The CRSP MF database is described in more detail in the following section. Table 14.1 shows the 20 largest CMFs in the database by assets under management (AUM) as of June 2016. AUM is the total value of assets held by the fund even if the assets are subject to claims by lenders or other claimants, and, therefore, AUM is generally not all available for distribution to investors. As shown in Table 14.1, Vanguard Specialized—Energy Fund was the largest CMF with more than $10 billion in AUM. The 20 largest funds include funds that focus on the overall commodities markets (e.g., Credit Suisse Commodity Return Strategy Fund) or specific sectors such as energy and precious metals (e.g., the aforementioned Vanguard Specialized—Energy Fund and the Vanguard Specialized—Gold & Precious Metals Fund).

MFs, including CMFs, sell shares to the public. Each share is typically a fractional claim on the fund's assets net of any liabilities. The *net asset value* (NAV), defined as the value of the fund's assets available for distribution to investors, determines the prices of MF shares at which investors can buy and sell. In other words, the prices are not generally determined by supply and demand for shares on an exchange. The calculation of NAV is performed by the fund on a regular—but not real-time—basis, typically once per business day when the market closes. NAV reflects the value of the assets (AUM) minus the value of non-equity claims such as any borrowing by the fund. Restrictions generally exist on MFs borrowing and using leverage. Most MFs are "open-end" companies, which means that no predetermined maximum number of shares exists and that shares are issued and retired based on investor demand.

The fact that investors buy and sell shares directly from the fund at its end-of-day NAV distinguishes MFs from ETFs, which trade on exchanges and whose prices vary on an intraday basis as investors' demand to buy and supply to sell shares changes through time. Because supply and demand determines ETF prices, ETFs disclose holdings more frequently than MFs so that investors can assess the intraday value of the underlying assets when making buy and sell decisions. Nevertheless, MFs are generally much more liquid and transparent than hedge funds, which typically do not provide NAV calculations to investors as frequently as MFs do and tend to be secretive about their investment holdings and strategies.

Like CMFs, managed futures funds are another type of commodity-focused investments. Managed futures funds are also actively managed pools of assets. However, unlike most CMFs that invest in stocks and bonds, managed futures funds invest in futures contracts and other derivatives through strategies such as taking both long and short positions in the underlying assets. The Securities and Exchange Commission (SEC) regulates publicly sold managed futures funds because they are organized as investment companies. However, some managed futures funds are not offered to the public and resemble hedge funds. Both types of managed futures funds are subject to regulation by the Commodity Futures Trading Commission (CFTC), which is a regulator of futures and options trading in the United States.

Table 14.1 **Top CMFs by Assets under Management**

Rank	*Fund Name*	*AUM as of June 2016 ($ millions)*
1	Vanguard Specialized—Energy	10,084
2	PIMCO Funds: Pacific Investment Management Series: Commodity Real Return Strategy Fund	6,573
3	T Rowe Price Real Assets Fund, Inc.	4,092
4	Credit Suisse Commodity Return Strategy Fund	4,064
5	SteelPath MLP Funds Trust: SteelPath MLP Alpha Fund	3,544
6	SteelPath MLP Funds Trust: SteelPath MLP Income Fund	3,472
7	Price (T. Rowe) New Era Fund	3,311
8	Fidelity Fixed Income Trust: Fidelity Series Commodity Strategy Fund	2,979
9	SteelPath MLP Funds Trust: SteelPath MLP Select 40 Fund	2,898
10	Vanguard Specialized—Gold & Prec. Metals	2,694
11	Scudder Institutional Funds: Scudder Commodity Securities Fund	2,583
12	Fidelity Select—Energy	2,481
13	Van Eck Funds: Global Hard Assets Fund	2,473
14	Investment Managers Series Trust: Center Coast MLP Focus Fund	2,440
15	PIMCO Funds: CommoditiesPLUS Strategy Fund	2,351
16	Goldman Sachs Trust: Goldman Sachs MLP Energy Infrastructure Fund	2,294
17	FlexShares Trust: FlexShares Morningstar Global Upstream Natural Resources Index Fund	2,186
18	Prudential Global Natural Resources Fund	2,079
19	Robertson Stephens Inv Tr:Glbl Natrl Res	2,048
20	Fidelity Select—American Gold	1,689

Note: This table shows the largest CMFs in the CRSP Mutual Fund database as of June 2016.

Source: CRSP Survivorship-Bias-Free Mutual Fund Database.

The goal of the SEC in regulating MFs is to protect investors. The SEC establishes standards for liquidity and leverage, among other metrics, and mandates the ability of investors to redeem or sell shares back to the fund upon demand. Investment advisers manage MFs and are also regulated by the SEC. Investment advisers employ investment professionals who make investment decisions. These advisers receive compensation for their services and to cover expenses incurred in managing the fund in the form of fees paid by investors (e.g., fees when buying or selling shares and ongoing management fees). Investors may also pay commissions (called loads) to brokers who facilitate the buying and selling of shares. Unlike hedge funds, many but not all MFs do not charge performance-based fees such as carried interest. Instead, management fees are based on the amount of AUM and are paid regardless of fund performance. Of course, investors may choose to redeem shares in poorly performing funds, thereby reducing AUM and the amount of fees received by the adviser.

Many MFs are actively managed. *Actively managed investments* are investments chosen by a portfolio manager to maximize return (or most commonly, risk-adjusted return or return above a certain benchmark) by identifying and buying assets that are relatively underpriced and by selling assets that are relatively overpriced. However, MFs, unlike investment vehicles such as hedge funds, are typically prohibited from short selling, which limits their ability to profit from selling overpriced assets that they do not already own in their portfolios. Passive management is another investment strategy that, unlike active management, minimizes discretionary investment decisions in favor of selecting investments that yield returns similar to the returns of a pre-specified benchmark. Some MFs and many ETFs are passively managed.

MF returns are composed of unrealized capital gains or losses and distributions. These unrealized capital gains or losses arise due to changes in the value of the investments that are held in the portfolio. Distributions from MFs include dividends as well as cash flows from asset sales. Such distributions may be reinvested in the fund, frequently at a lower up-front cost than new shares acquired outright. CMFs, like other MFs, must generally pass through to investors any realized gains that are not offset by realized losses.

Investors select CMFs for at least two reasons. First, investing in CMFs provides exposure to various commodities markets and may provide diversification against other investments. Second, because CMFs are actively managed, they provide the potential of superior returns if fund managers have the skill to select underpriced securities. Empirical evidence on how well CMFs track commodity price index returns and how they have performed historically is addressed in the remainder of the chapter.

What are potential disadvantages and risks to investors who invest in CMFs? A key risk is underperformance, either through outright capital losses or through returns that do not adequately compensate investors for the risks being borne, especially after taking into account fees. Liquidity risk is also a consideration. When faced with large redemption requests, CMFs may be unable to orderly liquidate their holdings, especially when redemption requests occur during times of market distress. This risk can result in loss to all fund investors, not only those redeeming shares, because the costs of liquidating positions are generally borne by all investors equally. Lastly, investors in CMFs may be subject to unfavorable tax treatment. As noted, MFs must pass through any realized gains that are not offset by realized losses to investors. Although such distributed net gains also lower NAV (acting as an unrealized loss), they may result in accelerated tax liabilities.

CRSP MF Database

As mentioned in the previous section, the analysis in this chapter uses data from the June 2016 vintage of the CRSP MF database, which provides information on U.S. mutual fund returns, net asset values, fund fees, and other information. One of the benefits of the database is that it is not subject to survivorship bias, because it continues to report data for funds that exit the sample.

Survivorship bias in a fund database occurs when only funds that are presently reporting are included in the database while funds that have ceased reporting are not. Funds exit the database due to either idiosyncratic reasons or poor performance. The latter can be problematic because a database that systematically excludes poor performance may result in incorrect inferences about average fund performance.

Even though the CRSP MF database is free of survivorship bias, Elton, Gruber, and Blake (2001) find that the database may suffer from omission bias for funds with NAVs below $15 million (i.e., it systematically omits funds below that size). Thus, the analysis in this chapter only focuses on funds with NAVs above this threshold. The CRSP MF database coverage starts in 1964, but the analysis is limited to the years between 1996 and 2016 because fund style information, which is used to identify CMFs in the database, becomes available only in the second half of the 1990s. Additionally, other data items, such as fund expenses, also become available only in the 1990s.

CMFs are identified as those funds that satisfy one of the following two criteria: (1) the Lipper or CRSP classification code assigned to the fund is in one of the commodity categories; or (2) the fund name contains the word "commodity" or the name of a specific commodity (e.g., "gold"). The resulting list of funds is then filtered by excluding commodity ETFs and managed futures funds and by only keeping funds with available return data at some point between 1996 and 2016. CMFs in the sample are further categorized according to the type of commodity on which they focus. In particular, gold CMFs are identified as CMFs whose name contains the word "gold," and energy CMFs are identified as the funds whose name contains the words "oil" or "energy." Applying these criteria results in a set of 207 CMFs. Table 14.2 shows the number of funds available over the sample period.

Trends in CMF Fund Flows and Performance

Historically, CMF AUM has been a relatively small fraction of all MF AUM. In June 2016, CMF AUM totaled about $120 billion, which represents 0.61 percent of all MF AUM in the CRSP MF database ($19.7 trillion). CMFs were also small relative to the size of the commodities markets. For example, the World Gold Council (2011) estimates that the size of the world gold market was about $2.4 trillion in 2010, while

Table 14.2 **Commodity Mutual Funds in the CRSP Mutual Fund Database**

	All CMFs			*Energy CMFs*			*Gold CMFs*		
Year	*# Funds*	*# Entries*	*# Exits*	*# Funds*	*# Entries*	*# Exits*	*# Funds*	*# Entries*	*# Exits*
1996	56	0	0	9	0	0	26	0	0
1997	60	7	1	9	1	0	26	0	1
1998	64	4	3	11	2	0	26	1	0
1999	63	1	2	12	0	0	25	0	2
2000	60	1	4	13	1	0	21	0	3
2001	58	2	3	13	0	0	20	0	2
2002	58	1	1	13	0	0	19	0	0
2003	58	1	1	13	0	0	19	0	0
2004	61	5	0	14	2	0	19	0	0
2005	67	8	2	15	0	0	19	0	0
2006	72	4	0	18	4	0	19	0	0
2007	81	11	0	19	1	0	21	2	0
2008	92	28	1	21	5	0	21	0	0
2009	115	11	2	26	3	1	21	0	0
2010	127	15	1	29	5	0	21	0	0
2011	141	14	2	35	4	0	20	0	1
2012	153	18	7	40	6	0	20	2	0
2013	166	15	2	45	4	0	23	2	0
2014	175	11	4	51	7	1	25	1	0
2015	174	3	11	55	3	1	24	0	2
2016	169	0	1	54	0	0	23	0	0

Note: This table shows the number of CMFs in the CRSP Mutual Fund database.

Source: CRSP Survivorship-Bias-Free Mutual Fund Database.

the AUM of gold CMFs in the same year was only about $38 billion in the database, or 1.6 percent of the total figure. In 2016, gold CMFs accounted for approximately 38 percent of all CMF funds in the database by AUM, whereas energy CMFs accounted for around 14 percent.

Nevertheless, as Figure 14.1 shows, CMF AUM experienced substantial growth between 2003 and 2011, increasing from $10.3 billion to $154.1 billion. This partially coincides with the so-called commodity boom that occurred from 2004 to 2008, a

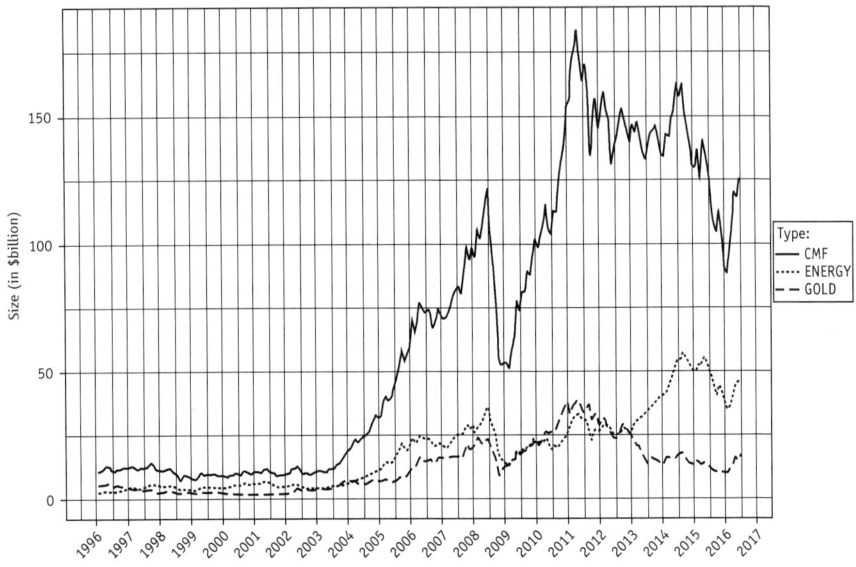

Figure 14.1 Assets under Management of CMFs over Time
This figure shows the level of CMF AUM between 1996 and 2016. Source: CRSP Survivorship-Bias-Free Mutual Fund Database.

period associated with an increase in prices of a broad basket of commodities, in particular, energy, metal, and agricultural commodities.

Despite a pause in growth and in fact a decline during the financial crisis of 2007–2008, CMF AUM continued to grow well into the first half of 2011. After 2011, CMF AUM declined to reach its June 2016 level of about $120 billion. The trends of gold and energy CMF AUM more or less tracked overall CMF trends until 2011, after which energy CMF AUM grew substantially until the decline in oil prices in the second half of 2014.

Both prices of the underlying commodity investments and net investment flows into CMFs drive the dynamics of CMF AUM because net investments create new shares and increase AUM. Figure 14.2 disaggregates flows from capital gains and plots cumulative flows for CMFs. CMFs experienced substantial investment inflows from 2003 to 2006 and from 2009 to 2011. Additionally, energy CMFs had positive net flows between 2013 and 2016 despite the adverse price movements in energy commodities after 2014.

Some contend that the financialization of commodity markets, characterized by the increased participation of institutional investors in commodities, has been one of the key drivers of commodity price dynamics during the 2000s. Although little empirical evidence is available on the effects of CMF flows on commodity prices, a strong causal relationship with CMF flows is relatively unlikely for two reasons. First, CMFs represent only a small fraction of the overall commodity market and are unlikely to generate investment flows that are sufficiently large to systematically affect commodity prices. Second, CMFs tend to invest only indirectly in commodities.

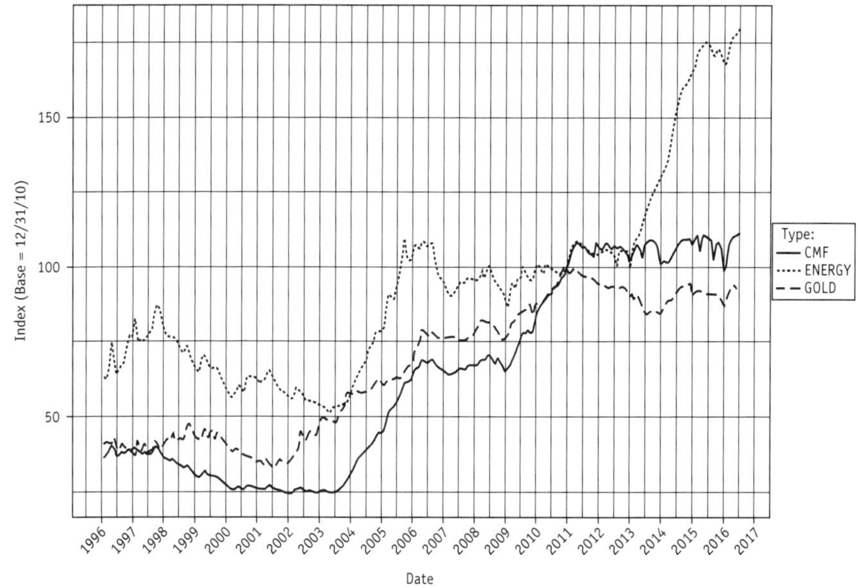

Figure 14.2 Investment Flows into CMFs
This figure shows cumulative net investment flows into CMFs between 1996 and 2016. Source: CRSP Survivorship-Bias-Free Mutual Fund Database.

Relation between CMF and Benchmark Returns

This section presents correlations between CMF returns and various benchmarks such as commodity price indexes. Analyzing correlations is informative for at least two reasons. First, investors may decide to buy CMFs to gain exposure to the underlying commodity. Second, correlations with other investment alternatives are important from the perspective of portfolio optimization.

One consideration when performing a correlation analysis is to determine the relevant benchmark against which correlations are measured. The difference between an MF's return and a benchmark return is commonly called *tracking error*. Many reasons help to explain why an MF does not perfectly track a given benchmark. For example, when CMF returns are compared to commodity price indices as benchmarks, differences in performance may arise given that many CMFs invest in equity and other securities of companies involved in commodities markets as opposed to investing directly in physical commodities. For the funds in the CRSP MF database, for instance, the average level of equity holdings is 81.4 percent.

Beyond correlations between CMF returns and returns of commodity indices, correlations with other benchmarks such as market returns and changes in inflation can shed light on whether CMFs provide a hedge against broad equity market returns and/or changes in price levels. In general, different investors may use different benchmarks to evaluate performance depending on the circumstances.

After choosing a benchmark, another issue that needs to be addressed involves the appropriate time horizon for calculating correlations. In some contexts, daily or even intraday return correlations may be appropriate. However, given that mutual funds are not typically considered to be short-term investments, the analysis here focuses on monthly and longer horizons. By the nature of how they are traded, MFs are not ideal for investors who have a short investment horizon and desire to trade frequently because all of a given day's purchases of MF shares occur at one single price determined by the NAV that is computed at the end of the business day. Moreover, various MFs actively discourage frequent trading by imposing exit fees and by otherwise placing restrictions on frequent trading.

Table 14.3 presents results of the correlation analysis comparing CMF returns to a commodities price index, a gold price index, equity market returns, and inflation. Correlations are measured monthly and computed over the entire sample starting in 1996.

Over this period, CMF returns were positively correlated with a broad index of commodity prices as well as with overall equity market returns given that CMFs invest in the equity of companies involved in the commodities markets. The correlation with equity market returns was in fact stronger than the correlation with commodity prices. CMFs also exhibited a positive—although relatively small—correlation with inflation, consistent with CMFs providing some degree of an inflation hedge. Interestingly, commodity prices were more highly correlated with inflation over this period than CMF returns, suggesting that a direct investment in commodities would have provided a superior hedge against inflation.

Table 14.3 also shows correlations for gold CMFs. Somewhat surprisingly, average gold CMF returns were highly correlated with overall CMF returns (0.79) but relatively less correlated with changes in an index of gold prices (0.35). This may reflect the fact that gold CMFs invest largely in equity of companies involved in the gold market and not directly in gold. This result may also be driven by the divergence in the performance of gold CMFs from gold prices starting in late 2011 and early 2012. Gold CMF returns also had a small but insignificant positive correlation with inflation.

Figure 14.3 plots the monthly correlations between CMF returns and changes in a commodity price index, and gold CMF returns and changes in a gold price index on a rolling basis using a three-year window. Correlations varied over time. For example, correlations between returns of energy CMFs and changes in an energy price index fell substantially in early 2000s and did not recover until the financial crisis.

Lastly, besides measures of monthly return correlations, the performance of an investment in CMFs relative to the performance of a hypothetical investment in a commodities price index is also examined. Figure 14.4 shows the performance of a $100 investment made in 1996 into gold CMFs, a gold price index, and gold ETFs. Gold CMFs exhibit relatively larger deviations from the gold price index than do ETFs. A large divergence in performance between an investment in gold CMFs and a hypothetical investment in gold occurred sometime in late 2011 or early 2012 and led to gold CMFs substantially underperforming relative to gold ETFs and the gold price index.

Table 14.3 **Correlations between CMF Returns and Other Commodity Series**

	CMF Returns	*Broad Commodity Price Index*	*Gold CMFs Return*	*Gold Commodity Price Index*	*Market Excess Return*	*CPI Inflation*	*Lagged CPI Inflation*
CMF returns	1						
Broad commodity price index	0.393***	1					
Gold CMFs return	0.790***	0.251***	1				
Gold commodity price index	0.177***	0.262***	0.348***	1			
Market excess return	0.630***	0.162**	0.299***	−0.108*	1		
CPI inflation	0.169***	0.625***	0.041	0.199***	0.033	1	
Lagged CPI inflation	−0.003	0.188***	−0.144**	−0.067	0.025	0.485***	1

Note: This table shows the correlations between CMF returns and the following series: Broad Commodity Price Index returns, Gold CMF returns, Gold Commodity Price Index, Market Excess Return, CPI Inflation, and CPI Inflation Lagged by One Month. ***, **, and * denote statistical significance at 0.01, 0.05, and 0.10 level, respectively.

Source: CRSP Survivorship-Bias-Free Mutual Fund Database, IMF Primary Commodity Prices.

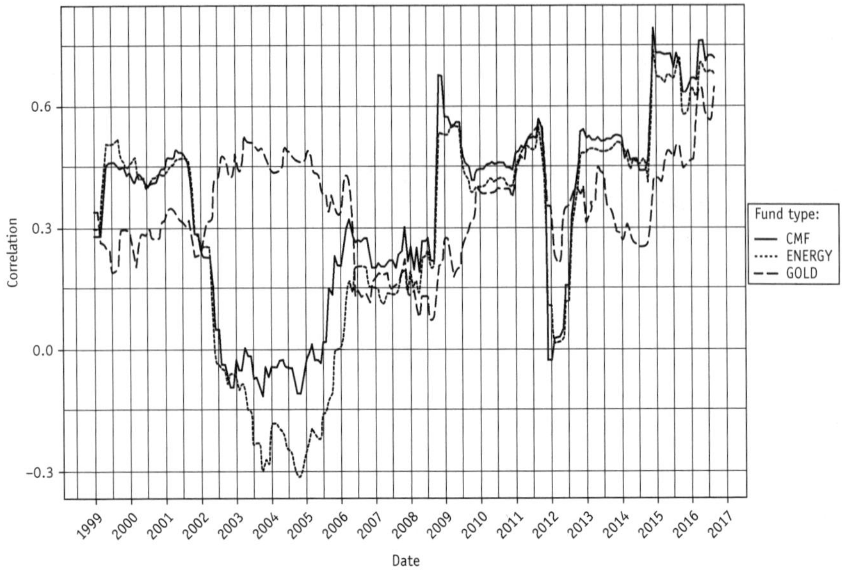

Figure 14.3 Three-Year Rolling Correlations between Commodity Indices and CMF Returns

This figure shows 36-month rolling correlations between CMF returns and the corresponding commodity price index returns. Source: CRSP Survivorship-Bias-Free Mutual Fund Database, IMF Primary Commodity Prices.

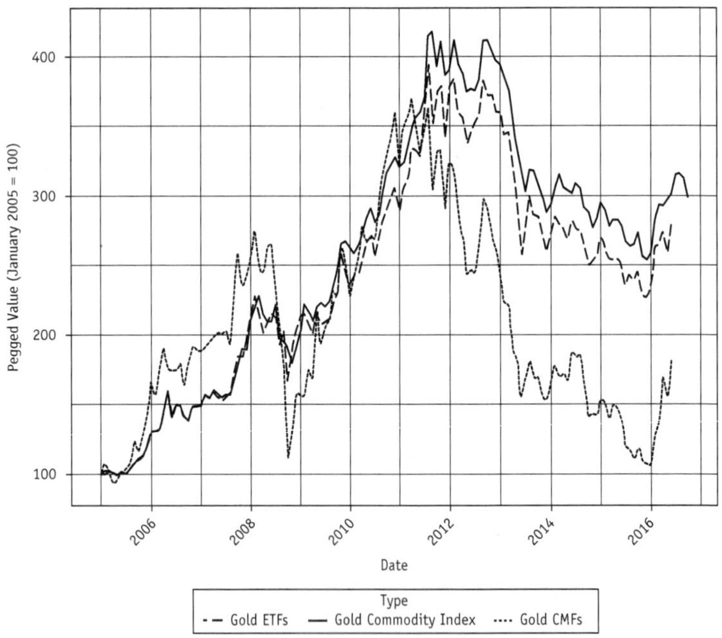

Figure 14.4 Return Indices for Gold CMFs, Gold ETFs, and Gold Prices

This figure displays average cumulative returns for gold ETFs, gold CMFs, and a gold commodity price index, all pegged to 100 in January 2005. Source: CRSP Survivorship-Bias-Free Mutual Fund Database, IMF Primary Commodity Prices.

Costs of Investing in CMFs

As previously explained, MFs are actively managed investments involving various fees to investors. MF fees are generally higher than fees associated with passively managed ETFs. The level of fees is a relevant consideration because, on average, risk-adjusted CMF performance is negative net of fees. CMF performance net of fees will be discussed in more detail in the following section.

Many MFs do not charge asymmetric fees like hedge funds and private equity funds, for which manager compensation depends in part on fund performance. Instead, investors pay MF fees regardless of performance, which means that even in years of poor performance, investors are responsible for paying fees. SEC regulations require that funds disclose fees in a prospectus.

Funds have several types of fees. Fees associated with buying and selling shares are the sales loads and other fund-imposed purchase fees, redemption fees, and exchange fees. Ongoing fees include management fees, 12b-1 fees, and other expenses. Some mutual funds offer multiple types of shares that represent claims to the same net assets but differ in their fee structures. For example, some classes may be subject to front-end loads and lower ongoing expenses, while other classes forgo front-end loads in exchange for higher ongoing expenses.

Sales loads are commissions that investors pay to brokers who facilitate the selling of mutual fund shares. Investors pay up-front loads at the time of purchase. These fees can be as high as a few percentage points of the amount being invested. For example, a $1,000 investment into a mutual fund with a 5 percent up-front load would result in only $950 being invested and $50 is paid to the broker. Some funds have back-end loads that investors pay when selling shares. Back-end loads typically decline with the length of time an investor has held the shares. Investors may also pay purchase fees to the fund (as opposed to the broker) at the time they buy shares. Certain funds also impose redemption fees when shares are sold; these redemption fees work to discourage short-term in-and-out trading of fund shares. Lastly, funds may assess exchange fees when transferring shares into another fund in the same fund family.

Unlike fees associated with the buying and selling of shares, ongoing fees compensate the fund manager for managing the fund's portfolio, including the manager's asset-picking ability, as well as covering the fund's ongoing operating expenses. A *12b-1 fee* is another ongoing fee that is intended to compensate for marketing the fund to new investors.

A fund's reported *annual expense ratio* is defined as the sum of ongoing fund expenses divided by a measure of the fund's average net assets over the year. Figure 14.5 plots reported annual expense ratios for CMFs in the CRSP MF database over the sample period, with average expense ratios being shown on an equally weighted and value-weighted basis for CMFs as a group and for gold and energy CMFs separately. Expense ratios have declined over time and presently average around 1 percent on a value-weighted basis. Additionally, equally weighted expense ratios are higher, presently about 25 basis points above value-weighted ratios, which is consistent with smaller funds having higher expense ratios. Third, gold CMFs exhibited consistently higher average expense ratios than the overall CMF category, while energy CMFs

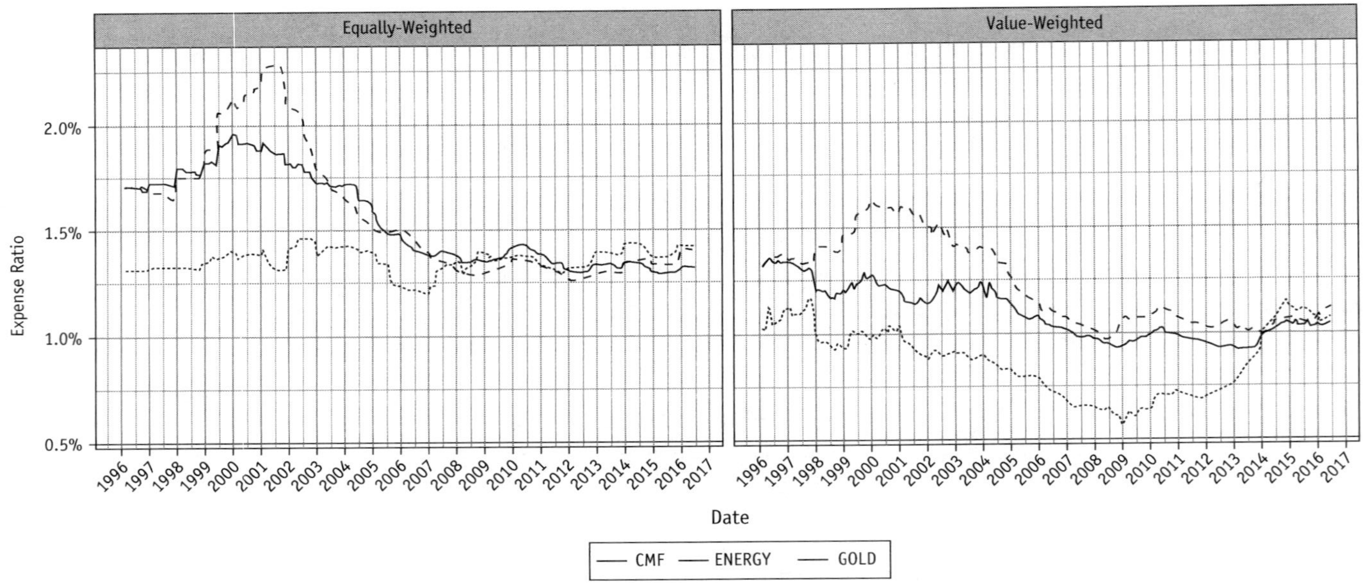

Figure 14.5 CMF Expense Ratios over Time
This figure displays the average expense ratios of CMFs during the sample period. Source: CRSP Survivorship-Bias-Free Mutual Fund Database.

had lower expense ratios until recently, when expense ratios for all three categories have largely converged.

Historical CMF Performance

This section examines the historical performance of CMFs between 1996 and 2016. The analysis focuses on 207 CMFs, which are further categorized into gold CMFs, energy CMFs, and other CMFs. Fund performance is examined along four dimensions. First, historical fund returns and Sharpe ratios are analyzed. Second, the Carhart (1997) four-factor model (Fama-French three factors and momentum) is used to adjust CMF returns for various sources of systematic risk to measure risk-adjusted performance (alpha). Third, explanatory regressions of risk-adjusted performance are used to determine drivers of excess returns during the sample period. Lastly, persistence of CMF fund returns is analyzed to answer the question of whether high (low) performing funds in the sample continued to generate high (low) returns in subsequent years.

Table 14.4 displays historical returns and Sharpe ratios for all CMFs and for groupings of CMFs based on their investment strategy (i.e., gold CMFs, energy CMFs, and other CMFs). Because performance may have varied over time, Table 14.4 reports fund performance over several sub-periods: the commodity boom of 2004 to 2008, the financial crisis of 2008 to 2010, and the post-crisis period of 2011 to 2016 associated with declining commodity prices.

The first grouping of columns displays average annualized monthly historical returns after fees. As Panel A of Table 14.4 shows, over the entire sample period, average annualized performance was 11.6 percent for all CMFs, while gold and energy CMFs had higher average returns of 12.7 and 17.0 percent, respectively. Given that the CRSP MF database also includes MFs that exited during the sample period, funds with short lifespans are relatively underweighted in the equally weighted average calculation. To determine whether the exiting funds had different performance, the second column assigns weights to observations based on the inverse of the number of observations in the sample. This yields an average return for all CMFs of 5.3 percent. This finding is consistent with funds that have relatively few observations in the data set having lower returns. The third column displays returns weighted by average AUM in the relevant period, which gives more weight to larger funds. This calculation yields an average return of 8.2 percent, implying that the largest funds had lower returns without adjusting for risks over the sample period.

The second set of columns displays the excess return over the risk-free rate, which is proxied by the one-month Treasury-bill rate. The third grouping of columns shows the annualized monthly Sharpe ratio (Sharpe 1966), which is a metric used to evaluate investment performance, and is defined as the excess return divided by the standard deviation. The Sharpe ratio can be interpreted as excess return per unit of standard deviation risk. Higher values of the ratio indicate better performance. Alternative methods might use another benchmark return instead of the risk-free rate in the excess return calculation.

Table 14.4 **Historical Performance of CMFs**

	Actual Return[1]			*Excess Return*[2]			*Sharpe Ratio*[3]		
	Un-Weighted Mean[4]	*Freq-Weighted Mean*[5]	*Value-Weighted Mean*[6]	*Un-Weighted Mean*[4]	*Freq-Weighted Mean*[5]	*Value-Weighted Mean*[6]	*Un-Weighted Mean*[4]	*Freq-Weighted Mean*[5]	*Value-Weighted Mean*[6]
Panel A. Entire Sample Period (1996–2016)									
All CMFs	0.116*** (0.035)	0.053* (0.033)	0.082*** (0.031)	0.062** (0.025)	0.027 (0.023)	0.058** (0.027)	0.193** (0.096)	0.049 (0.100)	0.189 (0.116)
Gold CMFs	0.127*** (0.042)	0.092** (0.043)	0.103** (0.051)	0.082* (0.046)	0.054 (0.046)	0.084* (0.048)	0.176 (0.137)	0.067 (0.145)	0.177 (0.149)
Energy CMFs	0.170** (0.072)	0.061 (0.061)	0.135*** (0.039)	0.085*** (0.023)	0.063** (0.025)	0.092*** (0.023)	0.363*** (0.092)	0.322*** (0.113)	0.415*** (0.095)
Other CMFs	0.086*** (0.028)	0.042* (0.025)	0.047* (0.026)	0.044* (0.023)	0.011 (0.023)	0.031 (0.024)	0.135 (0.107)	−0.042 (0.119)	0.080 (0.130)
Panel B. Commodity Boom Period (2004–2008)									
All CMFs	0.261*** (0.024)	0.233*** (0.032)	0.254*** (0.032)	0.231*** (0.023)	0.210*** (0.026)	0.220*** (0.034)	0.868*** (0.104)	0.816*** (0.122)	0.922*** (0.151)
Gold CMFs	0.333*** (0.028)	0.323*** (0.033)	0.325*** (0.016)	0.302*** (0.029)	0.297*** (0.030)	0.286*** (0.019)	0.851*** (0.055)	0.845*** (0.061)	0.889*** (0.074)
Energy CMFs	0.287*** (0.044)	0.315*** (0.045)	0.280*** (0.040)	0.230*** (0.044)	0.237*** (0.044)	0.242*** (0.041)	0.948*** (0.176)	0.951*** (0.170)	1.056*** (0.194)
Other CMFs	0.208*** (0.033)	0.179*** (0.040)	0.205*** (0.033)	0.181*** (0.031)	0.164*** (0.032)	0.172*** (0.035)	0.841*** (0.151)	0.754*** (0.163)	0.836*** (0.164)
Panel C. Global Financial Crisis (2008–2010)									
All CMFs	0.083* (0.050)	0.061 (0.041)	0.095** (0.048)	0.065 (0.044)	0.040 (0.042)	0.064 (0.043)	0.195 (0.182)	0.124 (0.171)	0.214 (0.188)
Gold CMFs	0.199*** (0.046)	0.166*** (0.049)	0.209*** (0.042)	0.182*** (0.037)	0.173*** (0.033)	0.182*** (0.036)	0.450*** (0.141)	0.424*** (0.133)	0.455*** (0.135)
Energy CMFs	0.053 (0.081)	0.060 (0.086)	0.075 (0.058)	0.024 (0.053)	0.016 (0.051)	0.046 (0.050)	0.101 (0.199)	0.082 (0.188)	0.187 (0.203)
Other CMFs	0.043 (0.037)	0.039 (0.029)	0.060 (0.044)	0.021 (0.043)	0.010 (0.040)	0.025 (0.041)	0.102 (0.190)	0.052 (0.172)	0.129 (0.188)

Panel D. Post-Crisis Period (2011–2016)									
All CMFs	0.025 (0.033)	−0.002 (0.033)	0.023 (0.033)	0.025 (0.033)	0.006 (0.028)	0.021 (0.032)	0.044 (0.121)	−0.046 (0.124)	0.023 (0.136)
Gold CMFs	−0.012 (0.073)	−0.025 (0.064)	0.006 (0.077)	−0.013 (0.072)	−0.024 (0.063)	0.004 (0.077)	−0.124 (0.215)	−0.205 (0.206)	−0.085 (0.229)
Energy CMFs	0.045 (0.036)	−0.004 (0.058)	0.059** (0.024)	0.055** (0.027)	0.045 (0.030)	0.060** (0.024)	0.272** (0.118)	0.279* (0.152)	0.299*** (0.107)
Other CMFs	0.026 (0.031)	0.002 (0.026)	0.013 (0.031)	0.025 (0.034)	−0.002 (0.029)	0.010 (0.031)	0.003 (0.143)	−0.138 (0.148)	−0.055 (0.162)

Note: This table reports three measures of historical CMF performance: (1) the average actual return, (2) the average excess return, and (3) the average Sharpe ratio.

[1] The column reports annualized returns, averaged across funds and time periods, which are computed for each year by averaging the funds return, raising one plus the average monthly return to the power of 12, and then subtracting one. Standard errors, reported in parentheses, are double clustered by fund and year as in Petersen (2009).

[2] The column reports annualized excess returns averaged across funds and time periods. The risk-free rate is the one-month U.S. Treasury bill, taken from Ken French's website. Standard errors, reported in parentheses, are double clustered by fund and year.

[3] The column reports Sharpe ratios, averaged across funds and time periods, which is the ratio of the average return of the fund, divided by the monthly standard deviation, and then annualized by multiplying by the square root of 12. Standard errors, reported in parentheses, are double clustered by fund and year.

[4] This average is the simple arithmetic mean with no weighting.

[5] This average is computed by weighting the individual fund variables by the inverse of the number of months that the fund was present in the sample. This weighting scheme adjusts for the fact that funds which exit the sample early are underweighted in the equally weighted estimate.

[6] This average is computed by weighting the individual fund variables by the fund's AUM.

[7] ***, **, and * denote statistical significance at 0.01, 0.05, and 0.10 level, respectively.

Source: CRSP Survivorship-Bias-Free Mutual Fund Database.

The equally weighted average Sharpe ratio for CMFs during the sample period was 0.19, with energy CMFs outperforming other CMFs. Sharpe ratios for CMFs varied over different periods, but generally trailed the performance of the broad market, as the average Sharpe ratio for the S&P 500 index over the same period was 0.53.

Risk-adjusted fund performance (alpha) is measured by comparing CMF returns to the returns that an investor could have earned by investing in a portfolio of traded securities with a similar risk profile. The empirical asset pricing literature frequently assumes that returns of any fund or security can be described as a linear combination of tradable asset pricing factors. Fund performance is considered as "abnormal" or excess to the extent that it cannot be explained by these factors. Equation 14.1 models returns as being described by the Carhart four-factor model, which includes the three Fama-French factors and a momentum factor:

$$R_{it} - R_t^f = \alpha_i + \beta_i^{Mkt} F_t^{Mkt} + \beta_i^{HML} F_t^{HML} + \beta_i^{SMB} F_t^{SMB} + \beta_i^{Mom} F_t^{Mom} + \varepsilon_{it}, \qquad (14.1)$$

where R_{it} is the return of CMF i in period t; R_t^f is the risk-free rate in period t; F_t^{Mkt} is the excess market return in period t; F_t^{HML} is the "high minus low" book-to-market portfolio return in period t; F_t^{SMB} is the "small minus big" factor portfolio return in period t; F_t^{Mom} is the "momentum factor" return in period t; and ε_{it} is the residual. The data on the risk-free rate and the factor returns were obtained from Kenneth French's website (http://mba.tuck.dartmouth.edu/pages/faculty/ken.french/Data_Library).

The model is estimated for each CMF individually using 36-month rolling windows. Table 14.5 shows the average estimated coefficients. CMFs tended to have large factor loadings on the market factor throughout the sample period and in particular during the financial crisis, which indicates that CMFs were exposed to significant market risk. Loadings on the momentum factor varied in sign during the sample period and were highest and positive during the middle of the period during the commodity boom and during the financial crisis.

A statistically significant negative estimated alpha coefficient means that the fund underperformed the four-factor benchmark. Conversely, a statistically significantly positive coefficient indicates superior fund performance relative to the benchmark. As discussed in the previous section, fund returns are reported net of management fees and other ongoing expenses, and as a consequence, the alpha is measured after fees.

As Table 14.6 shows, CMF alphas over the entire sample period were on average negative but often not statistically significant. This is true across all categories of funds. This result is even stronger on a frequency-weighted basis, suggesting that funds that exit the sample after a short period of time exhibit more negative performance on average. Conversely, on a value-weighted basis, average alphas are generally positive and are statistically significant for gold and energy CMFs. This result is consistent with stronger risk-adjusted relative performance of the larger funds in the sample. This finding is unlike the prior result that large funds had lower performance without adjusting for risk. Interestingly, average alphas were positive across all categories during the commodity boom and financial crisis periods and generally negative in the post-crisis period. In general, the academic literature

Table 14.5 **Factor Loadings of CMFs**

	Market Factor	*SMB*	*HML*	*Momentum*
Panel A. Entire Sample Period (1996–2016)				
All CMFs	0.760	0.052	−0.112	−0.019
Gold CMFs	0.534	0.387	−0.279	−0.041
Energy CMFs	0.909	−0.106	0.018	0.024
Other CMFs	0.799	−0.033	−0.096	−0.022
Panel B. Commodity Boom Period (2004–2008)				
All CMFs	0.802	0.402	0.271	0.665
Gold CMFs	0.730	0.788	−0.034	0.880
Energy CMFs	0.905	0.179	0.576	0.654
Other CMFs	0.798	0.263	0.315	0.530
Panel C. Global Financial Crisis (2008–2010)				
All CMFs	1.024	−0.111	−0.366	0.216
Gold CMFs	0.702	0.309	−0.582	0.058
Energy CMFs	1.226	−0.231	−0.281	0.381
Other CMFs	1.085	−0.251	−0.304	0.217
Panel D. Post-Crisis Period (2011–2016)				
All CMFs	0.734	0.029	−0.191	−0.176
Gold CMFs	0.346	0.590	−0.436	−0.478
Energy CMFs	0.909	−0.151	−0.052	−0.093
Other CMFs	0.768	−0.052	−0.189	−0.126

Note: This table shows the estimated factor loadings, averaged across CMFs. Loadings are estimated from fund-by-fund time-series Fama-French + Momentum factor rolling regressions. For each fund, the estimation is conducted over 36-month estimation windows, with the window moved in one-month incremental steps.

Source: CRSP Survivorship-Bias-Free Mutual Fund Database.

finds that few funds can generate positive alphas after considering costs (Fama and French 2010).

Table 14.7 presents a multiple regression analysis of the determinants of alpha. In this analysis, the average alpha for each fund is regressed on the fund's expense ratio and turnover ratio, which is a measure of how frequently a fund trades, and on the natural logarithm of AUM as a measure of fund size. Overall, fund expense ratios are

Table 14.6 **Risk-Adjusted Performance of CMFs**

	Alpha[1] (annualized)									
	Un-Weighted Mean[2]	*Frequency-Weighted Mean[3]*	*Value-Weighted Mean[4]*	*Minimum*	*1st Percentile*	*25th Percentile*	*Median*	*75th Percentile*	*99th Percentile*	*Max*
Panel A. Entire Sample Period (1996–2016)										
All CMFs	−0.013 (0.008)	−0.051*** (0.008)	0.017* (0.010)	−0.562	−0.349	−0.114	−0.012	0.075	0.341	0.701
Gold CMFs	0.019 (0.017)	−0.050* (0.027)	0.096*** (0.016)	−0.562	−0.429	−0.144	0.043	0.171	0.417	0.553
Energy CMFs	−0.008 (0.010)	−0.030*** (0.011)	0.019*** (0.007)	−0.410	−0.275	−0.099	−0.002	0.072	0.278	0.701
Other CMFs	−0.029*** (0.008)	−0.058*** (0.008)	−0.010 (0.012)	−0.438	−0.254	−0.118	−0.031	0.049	0.241	0.441
Panel B. Commodity Boom Period (2004–2008)										
All CMFs	0.083*** (0.009)	0.076*** (0.009)	0.112*** (0.009)	−0.257	−0.123	0.021	0.077	0.133	0.346	0.445
Gold CMFs	0.127*** (0.015)	0.126*** (0.015)	0.137*** (0.013)	−0.153	−0.080	0.047	0.112	0.206	0.392	0.445
Energy CMFs	0.074*** (0.013)	0.073*** (0.012)	0.105*** (0.014)	−0.218	−0.117	0.030	0.081	0.122	0.250	0.304
Other CMFs	0.058*** (0.011)	0.053*** (0.011)	0.107*** (0.010)	−0.257	−0.133	0.001	0.060	0.110	0.292	0.441

Panel C. Global Financial Crisis (2008–2010)										
All CMFs	0.089*** (0.010)	0.070*** (0.010)	0.113*** (0.015)	−0.298	−0.134	0.032	0.081	0.133	0.374	0.522
Gold CMFs	0.180*** (0.016)	0.175*** (0.017)	0.218*** (0.017)	−0.042	−0.001	0.101	0.176	0.250	0.400	0.438
Energy CMFs	0.050*** (0.013)	0.039** (0.016)	0.085*** (0.010)	−0.219	−0.175	0.016	0.063	0.095	0.183	0.207
Other CMFs	0.060*** (0.009)	0.045*** (0.011)	0.077*** (0.012)	−0.298	−0.131	0.013	0.066	0.105	0.245	0.330
Panel D. Post–Crisis Period (2011–2016)										
All CMFs	−0.069*** (0.008)	−0.073*** (0.007)	−0.046*** (0.010)	−0.410	−0.286	−0.145	−0.082	−0.003	0.247	0.384
Gold CMFs	−0.045** (0.021)	−0.069*** (0.023)	0.025 (0.026)	−0.356	−0.321	−0.184	−0.067	0.072	0.306	0.384
Energy CMFs	−0.069*** (0.010)	−0.056*** (0.012)	−0.039*** (0.013)	−0.410	−0.320	−0.130	−0.079	0.003	0.127	0.291
Other CMFs	−0.076*** (0.008)	−0.082*** (0.008)	−0.066*** (0.009)	−0.336	−0.253	−0.145	−0.085	−0.015	0.156	0.298

Note: The table shows risk-adjusted performance for CMFs, measured by fund alpha.

[1] Alphas are estimated from fund-by-fund time-series Fama-French + Momentum factor rolling regressions. For each fund, the estimation is conducted over 36-month estimation windows, with the window moved in one-month incremental steps.

[2] The column reports CMF alpha, averaged across funds and time periods. Standard errors, reported in parentheses, are double clustered by fund and year-month as in Petersen (2009).

[3] The column reports CMF alpha, averaged across funds and time periods, where the average is computed by weighting individual fund alphas by the inverse of the number of months that the fund was present in the sample. This weighting scheme adjusts for the fact that funds which exit the sample early are underweighted in the equally weighted estimate. Standard errors, reported in parentheses, are double clustered by fund and year-month.

[4] The column reports CMF alpha, averaged across funds and time periods, where the average is computed by weighting individual fund alphas by the fund's AUM. Standard errors, reported in parentheses, are double clustered by fund and year-month.

[5] ***, **, and * denote statistical significance at 0.01, 0.05, and 0.10 level, respectively.

Source: CRSP Survivorship-Bias-Free Mutual Fund Database.

Table 14.7 **Explaining the Risk-Adjusted Performance of CMFs**

	Dependent Variable Is the Annualized Alpha[1]			
	All CMF	*Energy CMF*	*Gold CMF*	*Other CMF*
Panel A. Entire Sample Period (1996–2016)				
Expense ratio	–2.601	6.456	–3.325***	0.887
	(1.860)	(5.462)	(0.689)	(2.117)
Turnover ratio	–0.003***	–0.004***	0.001	–0.003**
	(0.001)	(0.001)	(0.004)	(0.001)
Log of AUM	0.031***	0.009	0.003	0.026***
	(0.007)	(0.008)	(0.009)	(0.006)
N	11135	2767	2931	5437
Adjusted R^2	0.629	0.706	0.927	0.661
Panel B. Commodity Boom Period (2004–2008)				
Expense ratio	–0.859	4.585	8.685**	1.588
	(3.139)	(4.665)	(3.898)	(2.944)
Turnover ratio	–0.002	–0.005***	–0.003	–0.002**
	(0.001)	(0.001)	(0.009)	(0.001)
Log of AUM	0.053***	0.044**	0.074***	0.030**
	(0.016)	(0.021)	(0.017)	(0.015)
N	2661	598	818	1245
Adjusted R^2	0.599	0.711	0.926	0.597
Panel C. Global Financial Crisis (2008–2010)				
Expense ratio	–2.889	4.912	–11.383**	–2.999
	(2.170)	(3.559)	(4.473)	(2.718)
Turnover ratio	–0.007	0.002	0.025	–0.009**
	(0.005)	(0.003)	(0.019)	(0.004)
Log of AUM	0.060***	0.067***	0.078***	0.032***
	(0.014)	(0.017)	(0.028)	(0.010)
N	1815	420	484	911
Adjusted R^2	0.802	0.844	0.902	0.797

Table 14.7 **Continued**

	Dependent Variable Is the Annualized Alpha[1]			
	All CMF	*Energy CMF*	*Gold CMF*	*Other CMF*
Panel D. Post–Crisis Period (2011–2016)				
Expense ratio	0.817	−0.609	2.869	0.460
	(4.280)	(15.401)	(2.224)	(5.538)
Turnover ratio	0.000	0.001	0.015**	−0.001
	(0.002)	(0.004)	(0.007)	(0.002)
Log of AUM	0.053***	0.014	0.122***	0.026***
	(0.010)	(0.011)	(0.036)	(0.008)
N	4965	1406	950	2609
Adjusted R^2	0.623	0.663	0.942	0.763

Note: The table shows estimation results from panel regression in which fund alpha is regressed on the fund's expense ratio, turnover ratio, and the logarithm of AUM.

[1] The table shows estimation results from the regression of fund-specific alphas on the fund's expense ratio, turnover ratio, and the logarithm of assets under management. The specification includes time and fund-fixed effects. Standard errors (in parentheses) are double clustered by fund and year-month as in Petersen (2009).

[2] Alphas are estimated from fund-by-fund time-series Fama-French + Momentum factor rolling regressions. For each fund, the estimation is conducted over 36-month estimation windows, with the window moved in one-month incremental steps.

[3] ***, **, and * denote statistical significance at 0.01, 0.05, and 0.10 level, respectively.

Source: CRSP Survivorship-Bias-Free Mutual Fund Database.

not a significant determinant of a fund's alpha, except for gold CMFs, for which the effect was inconsistent across periods. Yet, their turnover ratios are negatively correlated with alpha, indicating that funds trading often performed worse on average than less active funds after adjusting for risk. CMF AUM is also positively correlated with alpha, indicating that larger funds tended to have better performance on average—this finding generally held true across fund types and sub-periods.

Finally, Figure 14.6 shows an analysis of persistence of CMF returns similar to the one in Carhart (1997). First, in each period, CMFs are sorted into 10 portfolios according to their returns over the past 12 months (worst performers in decile 1 and best performers in decile 10), and then their performance is tracked over the following five years. Figure 14.5 displays the average monthly excess return across time, following portfolio formation. A large degree of regression to the mean appears such that the top and bottom decile portfolios perform very similarly one year after being assigned to their respective deciles. On average, nearly 90 percent turnover in the funds composing the top and bottom deciles occurs over the full sample period, with

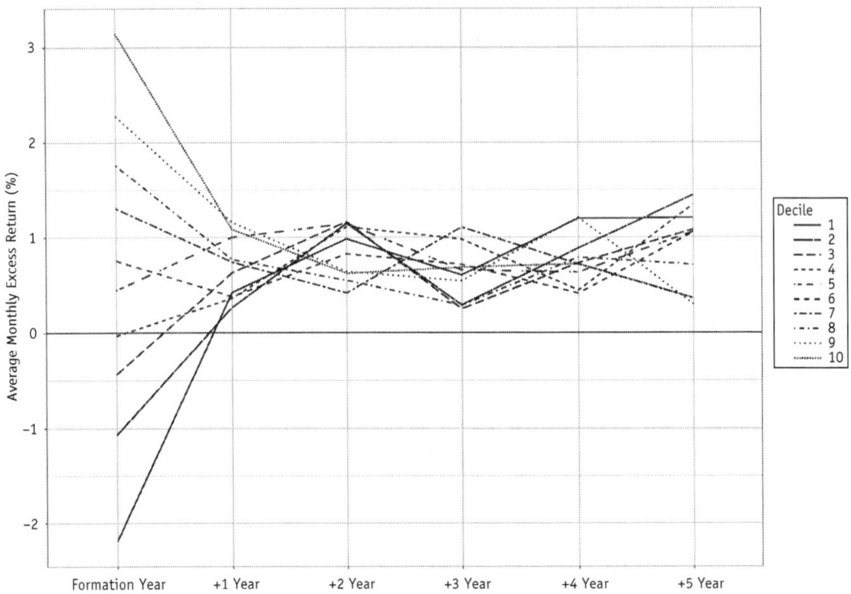

Figure 14.6 Persistence of CMF Returns
This figure shows the average monthly excess returns for 10 portfolios formed by sorting funds into deciles by performance during the formation year. Source: CRSP Survivorship-Bias-Free Mutual Fund Database.

complete turnover in these deciles during some of the years. Therefore, based on this metric, funds with high (low) returns in a given period are generally unlikely to stay high (low) performers in future periods.

Summary and Conclusions

The chapter described the main institutional features of CMFs, such as active management, the assets in which the funds invest, the process through which shares are bought and sold, fees borne by investors, and risks associated with investing in the funds. Unlike certain other investment alternatives in the commodity space such as ETFs, CMFs are predominantly actively managed. CMFs also tend to invest heavily in the equity of companies engaged in commodity markets but do not necessarily invest directly in the commodities themselves. CMFs also do not trade on exchanges, and investors make investments directly with the funds or through brokers. CMFs, like other MFs, have a fee structure that includes not only ongoing management fees and expenses but also sales loads and fees payable when shares are sold. Key risks of investing in CMFs include the risk of capital loss, liquidity risk, and the risk of adverse tax treatment of capital gains.

CMF AUM generally increased between 1996 and 2016, driven by both capital gains and investment flows. Evidence shows that correlations between CMFs and commodity price changes are positive but lower than those of commodity ETFs that invest directly in underlying commodities. Finally, using data on fund fees and performance between 1996 and 2016, the chapter documents a decline in fund expense ratios over time, negative average risk-adjusted performance, except for large funds, and a general lack of persistence in fund returns over the sample period.

Discussion Questions

1. Discuss whether commodity mutual funds (CMFs) are feasible instruments to take advantage of short-term swings in commodity prices.
2. State whether a commodity price index would be expected to have a higher correlation with a CMF or with a commodity ETF and explain why.
3. Discuss the long-run trends in CMF expense ratios.
4. Discuss whether CMF managers have generated alpha, on average, relative to the Fama-French factors and momentum between 1996 and 2016.

Disclaimer

The views expressed in this chapter are solely those of the authors, who are responsible for the content, and do not necessarily represent the views of Cornerstone Research.

References

Carhart, Mark M. 1997. "On Persistence in Mutual Fund Performance." *Journal of Finance* 52:1, 57–82.

Elton, E. J., Martin J. Gruber, and Christopher R. Blake. 2001. "A First Look at the Accuracy of CRSP Mutual Fund Database and a Comparison of the CRSP and Morningstar Mutual Fund Databases." *Journal of Finance* 56:6, 2415–2430.

Fama, Eugene F., and Kenneth R. French. 2010. "Luck versus Skill in the Cross-Section of Mutual Fund Returns." *Journal of Finance* 65:5, 1915–1947.

Petersen, Michael A. 2009. "Estimating Standard Errors in Finance Panel Data Sets: Comparing Approaches." *Review of Financial Studies* 22:1, 435–480.

Sharpe, William F. 1966. "Mutual Fund Performance." *Journal of Business* 39:1, 119–138.

World Gold Council. 2011. "Liquidity in the Global Gold Market." Report available at https://www.gold.org/research/liquidity-global-gold-market.

Part Four

PERFORMANCE OF COMMODITIES

15

Pricing of Futures Contracts

TIMOTHY A. KRAUSE
Assistant Professor of Finance, Penn State Behrend
Faculty Advisor, Intrieri Family Student Managed Fund

Introduction

The literature on the pricing of futures contracts is well-established. Black (1976, p. 167) provides one of the first analyses of futures pricing relations, noting that the "value of a futures contract is zero at the start of each day." This comment provides the basis for the "no arbitrage" arguments that define futures pricing. Futures contracts are inextricably related to the value of the asset underlying the contract, and are thus governed by no arbitrage pricing restrictions that define the mathematical relation. The price of a crude oil future is inextricably linked to the price of delivering 1,000 barrels (bbls) of West Texas Intermediate (WTI) crude oil to a delivery point in Cushing, Oklahoma. The price of a natural gas future is inextricably linked to the price of delivering 1 million (MM) BTU's worth of natural gas to the Henry Hub delivery point in Erath, Louisiana. Similar arguments can be made for all traded futures products, including those based on financial assets (e.g., stocks, bonds, and interest rates), agricultural products, energy commodities, and precious metals. Hull (2017) provides an extensive analysis of these issues.

The finance literature extensively examines the pricing of futures contracts. The purpose of this chapter is to synthesize much of the academic and practitioner-oriented exposition on the topic in a comprehensive, yet accessible format. The first part of the chapter explains the basic theoretical pricing models for various underlying asset classes that rely on the concept of "no arbitrage" arguments. That section includes two brief empirical analyses to highlight the accuracy and effectiveness of these models in explaining the theoretical modeling of the relation between futures and spot prices. The section concludes with a discussion of two economic theories that seek to explain these relations. The second section describes several different intermarket spreads among various closely-related commodities to demonstrate their usefulness in providing price information to commodity producers and consumers. The chapter then includes a discussion of the process to empirically model energy futures prices using a generalized autoregressive conditional heteroskedastic (GARCH) process. The GARCH model closely follows actual out-of-sample, daily futures prices, but concluding that this information could provide profitable trading rules to capitalize on this information is questionable. A summary and conclusions section follows.

Basic Futures Pricing

Given that futures contracts are agreements to exchange some commodity, cash, or other asset in the future (the "underling asset"), futures prices must inevitably converge to the underlying asset spot (cash) price at the expiration of the contract. Before expiration, however, the relation between the futures contract may vary. This relation, the difference between futures and spot prices, is known as the *basis*. When a futures price exceeds the price of the underlying asset, this situation is known as "contango." When the spot price exceeds the futures price, the situation is called "normal backwardation." Technically, futures markets are in "normal backwardation" when the "expected" spot price of the underlying asset exceeds the futures price, but the best estimate of the future value of the underlying asset is its current price, assuming prices follow a random walk. A similar argument can be made for futures market "contango."

Figure 15.1 displays the simulated price paths for a three-month crude oil futures contract and the underlying spot price for West Texas Intermediate (WTI), the underlying asset for crude oil futures traded on the NYMEX, which is now part of the CME Group. As the graph shows, the initial basis is about \$2 (\$43 minus \$41) and gradually converges to zero at contract expiration. For most of the contract's life, the market was in a state of normal backwardation (i.e., the futures price is below the spot price), but the basis varies substantially during the contract's life. This section of the chapter discusses the determination of futures prices by the evolution of the basis.

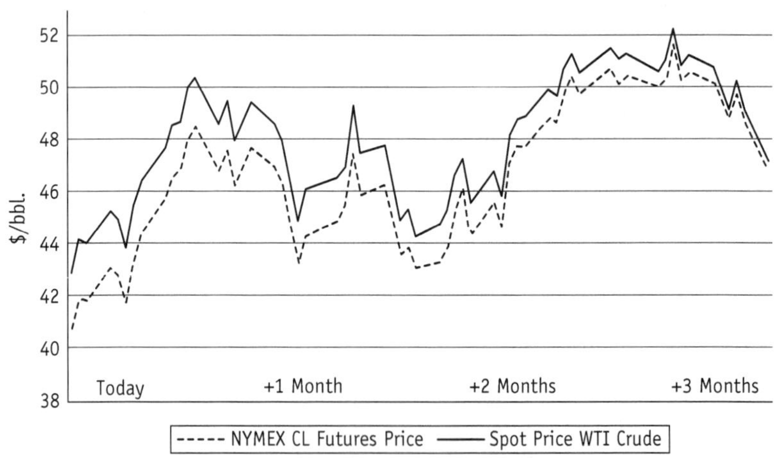

Figure 15.1 Convergence of Futures and Spot Prices in the Crude Oil Market
This figure shows the process of futures prices converging to the spot price of crude oil at contract expiration.

FUTURES PRICING WITH SHORT SALES

The use of "no arbitrage" arguments characterizes futures pricing. That is, a certain relation must exist between a futures price and its underlying asset or else arbitrageurs will have the opportunity to make a risk-free profit with no initial investment. This condition is one that efficient markets will not tolerate. Several assumptions apply to the initial "no arbitrage" paradigm. First, no transactions costs exist and taxes are applied in a uniform fashion to trading profits. Second, all market participants can borrow and lend money at the risk-free rate and markets are deep enough in terms of market participants and capital to exploit arbitrage opportunities in a timely fashion. Although these assumptions are not particularly realistic, making adjustments to deal with these over-restrictive terms is not difficult. As an introduction, suppose that gold is currently trading at \$1,500/ounce (oz) in the spot market. Interest rates for borrowing and lending for one year are 1 percent and storage/leasing costs are zero. An arbitrageur observes that a one-year futures contract for an ounce of gold is trading at \$1,520. To capitalize on this situation, the arbitrageur borrows \$1,500 for one year at 1 percent and simultaneously sells a one-year futures contract at \$1,520. At the end of the year, the trader delivers the gold in exchange for \$1,520 and repays the loan of \$1,500 plus accrued interest (in the continuously compounded environment that is assumed in derivatives pricing) of $1{,}500e^{rt} = 1{,}500e^{0.01*1}$ = \$1,515.08. The net profit, which required no initial investment, is thus \$1,520.00 – \$1,515.08 = \$4.92/oz. A similar argument can be made if the futures price is below its theoretical "fair value," in which case the arbitrageur would buy futures and short the underlying spot asset. Equation 15.1 describes this situation as follows:

$$F_t = S_0 e^{rt} \quad (15.1)$$

where F_t represents the fair value of a futures contract with expiration at time *t*; S_0 is the current spot price of the asset; *e* is the exponential function for continuous compounding; *r* represents the risk-free rate of interest; and *t* represent time in terms of years. Any deviation of the futures price from this fundamental relation will be arbitraged away in the marketplace. This fundamental relation for gold applies because a facility, similar to that for stocks and bonds, exists to borrow and short physical gold, albeit with a fee. Similar to a stock brokerage account, companies such as the global metals trading firm Kitco Metals, Inc. (www.kitcometals.com) enable investors to borrow physical gold from other firm customers and sell it in the marketplace, albeit at a cost. The investor is betting that the price of gold will decline and that she can buy it back at a lower price at a later date. Kitco reports that the rate for leasing and shorting gold approximated slightly less than 0.5 percent since 2006. However, a temporary spike existed up to about 3.0 percent during the global financial crisis of 2007–2008 (Kitco Metals Inc. 2016). A simple adjustment to the fundamental futures pricing Equation 15.1 can be made in this situation. Equation 15.2 shows the pricing relation for commodities that require a fee for leasing assets to sell them short.

$$F_t = S_0 e^{(r-u)t} \quad (15.2)$$

where u is the annualized leasing cost (in percent) for the commodity. Observant market participants will "arbitrage away" any deviations from this fundamental relation.

INVESTMENT ASSETS WITH KNOWN INCOME AND/OR YIELD

In contrast to physical assets with storage and/or leasing costs, futures on financial assets have different pricing considerations. Because stock indices pay a generally known or estimable dividend yield, futures prices must be adjusted to account for the income foregone by buying a futures contract instead of the basket of stocks to replicate the index. The futures pricing models for individual stocks must account for the estimated discrete dividends that the company will pay over the course of the life of the futures contract. Finally, the pricing of futures contracts on foreign currencies must account for the differential in risk-free interest rates between domestic and foreign markets.

Stock Index Futures

Because of the particularly liquid nature of stock index arbitrage, the example of stock index futures provides an enlightening illustration of the relation between spot and futures prices. Although the New York Stock Exchange (NYSE) stopped reporting the volume of program trading and index arbitrage trades in May 2016, these trades have averaged a substantial percentage of total trading volume at the NYSE. For example, the final NYSE program trading report (Barron's 2016) indicates that program trading represented 20.5 percent of all NYSE volume for the week ending April 29, 2016. A stock index provides an index dividend yield and most S&P 500 index stocks are easily "shortable." Thus, because most S&P 500 index stocks are quite liquid, the calculation of futures prices is simple. For stock indices that provide a reasonably accurate estimate of their yield (e.g., the S&P 500 index), currently about 2 percent, Equation 15.3 shows the basic futures pricing equation for equity index contracts:

$$F_t = S_0 e^{(r-dy)t} \tag{15.3}$$

where dy equals the dividend yield on the S&P 500 index. Thus, the dividend yield on the index partially offsets the benefit from owning futures relative to the risk-free rate. In recent years, the dividend yield more than offsets the effect of the risk-free rate. As of late November 2016, with 21 days until December futures expiration), the S&P futures closed at 2211.30, with the underlying index settling at 2213.35. Assuming a risk-free rate of 0.34 percent (current one-month U.S. Treasury bills), a dividend yield of 2.08 percent, and 21 days to expiration, Equation 15.3 results in a "fair value" of 2,211.14, which is within 0.16 of the actual futures closing price. Due to the large volume of index arbitrage that occurs in U.S. equity markets, the fundamental futures pricing equation for S&P 500 index futures contracts should seemingly keep the spot/futures relation "in line" with the fundamental futures pricing equation.

In order to see if the theorized futures/spot relation holds up over time, this chapter explores closing spot prices and the March 2016 S&P 500 futures contract from December 15, 2015 (about when this contract became the "front month" active contract) until its expiration on March 16, 2016. Futures and spot closing prices are obtained from Bloomberg Professional®, while the dividend yield and the 30-day Treasury-bill rate is provided by the OptionMetrics® database. Using these data, the daily futures contract closing "fair value" is calculated using closing spot prices and 30-day treasuries as the risk-free rate since most futures markets participants finance their activities on a short-term basis and the number of days to expiration. Table 15.1 shows summary statistics for this brief analysis.

As Table 15.1 shows, the mean deviation from fair value is less than $1, or two "ticks" in these futures contracts given the minimum price fluctuation is $0.50. Additionally, the percent deviation is 4.8 basis points or 0.048 percent of the futures contract value, which is reasonable given transaction costs in the futures and equity markets program trading paradigm. That is, a "window" exists around the fair value price in which trading due to transaction costs in unprofitable. Trading institutions will only intervene if the deviation from fair value exceeds the transaction costs of the trade. The median values of the deviations are slightly higher, but still well within a "reasonable" range, especially given large outliers in the data as indicated by the minimum and maximum values. These outliers are probably the result of news that occurred close to the markets' closing times that sharply affected futures prices but were unable to be "arbitraged away" before the respective equity and futures markets closed on these days. Thus, the basic futures pricing equation for stock index futures generally seems to hold.

Single Stock Futures

Single stock futures began trading in the United States in 2002 on the OneChicago exchange, a joint venture of the CBOE, CBOT, and the CME Group. Futures on

Table 15.1 **Summary Statistics for S&P 500 March 2016 Futures Contract Deviation from "Fair Value" between December 15, 2015 and March 16, 2016**

Statistic	*n*	*$ Deviation from "Fair Value"*	*% Deviation from "Fair Value"*
Mean	62	−0.944	−0.048
Median	62	−1.663	−0.085
Standard deviation	62	5.096	0.262
Minimum	62	−8.433	−0.433
Maximum	62	30.897	1.586

Note: This table presents summary statistics from a representative S&P 500 Index futures contract showing deviations from fair value that indicate potential mispricing, but which are not economically significant.

single stocks can be priced using dividend yields as well, but subtracting the present value of the expected dividend payments that will occur during the life of the futures contract is more precise. Thus, Equation 15.4 shows the pricing for these contracts by modifying the basic futures pricing equation:

$$F_t = (S_0 - I)e^{rt} \tag{15.4}$$

where *I* equals the present value of the expected dividend payments, discounted at the risk-free rate of interest. Single stock futures have been widely traded in Europe for some time because they substitute for stock holdings in securities that are subject of many European countries' "stamp taxes" (effectively a tax on stock trading). As noted previously, such instruments have been available in the United States since 2002, but trading volumes are still fairly limited.

Foreign Currency Futures

Many individual investors are now familiar with spot currency trading given the proliferation of global trading services in spot markets for small retail investors. However, an extremely active and large market exists in currency futures, mainly involving large banks, financial institutions, and multinational corporations. These futures are priced in similar fashion to stock index futures, except that the dividend yield in Equation 15.3 is replaced with the risk-free rate in the foreign currency (*rf*). This substitution is because the "income" received from owning a foreign currency is assumed to be equal to that country's risk-free rate. Thus, Equation 15.3 is modified to form the pricing equation for foreign exchange futures in Equation 15.5:

$$F_t = S_0 e^{(r\text{-}rf)} \tag{15.5}$$

A MODEL FOR CONSUMPTION COMMODITIES WITHOUT SHORT SALES

This section considers futures contracts on commodities in which short sales are impossible, such as futures prices of consumption assets, including energy products that are generally only stored for the purposes of future use. However, for an asset to be an investment asset, it need not be held solely for investment purposes. What is required is that some individuals hold it for investment purposes and that these individuals are prepared to sell their holdings and go long forward contracts, if the latter look more attractive. This explains why silver, although it has industrial uses, is generally regarded as an investment asset. The most basic futures pricing relation relies on the concept of "no arbitrage," as mentioned previously. This concept states that, among other things, risk-free profits with no initial investment are impossible in reasonably efficient markets. The availability of arbitrage profits will be "traded away" such that futures must be efficiently priced to preclude such opportunities. Several key assumptions apply to the basic futures pricing model, although adjustments to these basic futures pricing equations can be made to account for "real world" violations of these assumptions.

This chapter previously described the particular details of gold futures pricing given that this commodity can be borrowed and sold short. Yet, the more frequently observed phenomenon in commodity markets is that the consumption commodity is unavailable to short. These consumption commodities, such energy products as crude oil, natural gas, and heating oil, are not readily available to short because these commodities are needed for consumption in the physical economy. These constraints are also applicable to a wide variety of perishable commodities such as wheat, corn, soybeans, coffee, sugar, live cattle, lean hogs, milk, and other agricultural commodities that cannot be stored indefinitely.

Because the facility to short the physical commodity is normally unavailable, only an upper bound on futures prices for these communities can be established, as shown in Equation 15.6:

$$F_t \leq S_0 e^{(r+u)t} \tag{15.6}$$

The inability to describe an exact futures pricing equation for such commodities stems from the fact that "no arbitrage" arguments can only be used for one side of the trade. The reason for this limitation is because arbitrageurs can buy the physical asset and sell futures against it (enforcing the "upper bound" for futures prices), but arbitrageurs cannot enforce a lower bound because they cannot short the commodity and buy futures. However, an argument can be made that if this relation reaches extreme levels, producers of commodity products will sell these products in the open market instead of maintaining them in inventory. This process will naturally force the relative prices of futures and spot markets back into line with our futures pricing equations.

For commodities products that are not normally available to short, such as consumption commodities like crude oil and natural gas, a "convenience yield" emerges that quantifies the benefit that comes from having the commodity immediately available for sale. Equation 15.7 shows the modified pricing relation:

$$F_t = S_0 e^{(r+u-y)(t)} \tag{15.7}$$

where y quantifies denotes the imputable, although not directly observable, convenience yield. The *convenience yield* is the *ex ante,* unknowable value to having a commodity on hand to sell in the event of a favorable move in commodity prices.

In similar fashion to the earlier analysis of the futures/spot relation of S&P 500 index futures, in order to examine the potential accuracy of Equation 15.7, commodity price information for the "front month" continuous crude oil futures contract between January 4, 2015 and November 30, 2016 is extracted from Bloomberg Professional®. From the same source, WTI spot crude oil prices, the 30-day Treasury-bill rate, and one-month storage costs for one barrel of oil are obtained. Storage costs are estimated by the Louisiana Offshore Oil Port (LOOP) one-month crude oil storage futures that started trading on March 16, 2015. For data points between January

4, 2015 and March 16, 2015, the closing price from March 16 is used. Compared to the previous analysis of the S&P 500 index, the longer time frame examined here is necessary because crude oil futures do not seem to be as "efficient" as S&P 500 index futures in that the basis experienced substantial deviations from "fair value" in 2015 due to a severe price correction and imbalances in the supply/demand equilibrium. Specifically, the basis rose substantially during 2015 because of a large jump in storage costs (u) that occurred due to a substantial oversupply of crude oil that led to a subsequent decline in crude oil prices from a closing high price of $64.99/bbl on May 12, 2015 to $34.99/bbl on January 20, 2016, a decline of 46.16 percent.

Figure 15.2 details the divergent relation between spot and futures prices during this period. The left axis and the solid line indicate the price of crude oil futures and the right axis and the dashed line denote deviations from fair value as calculated by Equation 15.6. Deviations from this value provide information regarding the convenience yield (y).

As previously mentioned, financial theory posits that the crude oil basis may be negative because of the presence of a convenience yield (y) that exists due the ability to sell the commodity immediately because it is currently on hand. However, during the period from January 2015 to April 2016 that saw a sharp sell-off in the price of oil, futures were consistently priced above their theoretical "fair value" (above zero on the right axis) and thus the convenience yield was not large enough to offset interest and storage costs. The crude oil futures basis reaches extremely high levels, indicating a shortage of storage capacity and skyrocketing costs, at one point approaching $10/bbl. These two events are related because as the price of oil was falling during

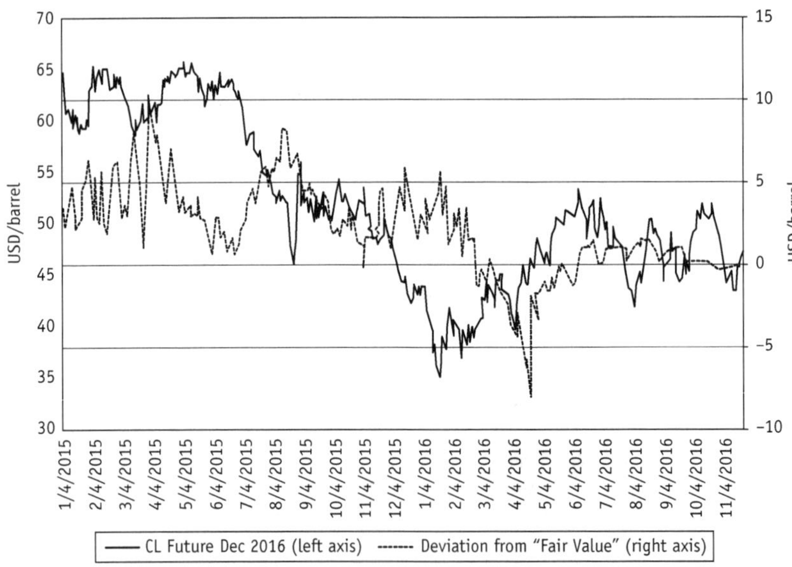

Figure 15.2 Crude Oil Futures Prices and Deviations from Fair Value between January 4, 2015 and November 21, 2016

This chart describes crude oil futures and their deviations from the fair value equation 15.7 for consumption commodities.

Table 15.2 **Summary Statistics for Crude Oil Futures Deviation from "Fair Value" between January 4, 2015 and November 22, 2016**

Statistic	*N*	*$ Deviation from "Fair Value"*	*% Deviation from "Fair Value"*
Mean	477	2.04	3.72
Median	477	0.87	3.50
Standard deviation	477	2.71	5.26
Minimum	477	−8.19	−17.62
Maximum	477	10.26	17.18

Note: This table presents summary statistics from a "front month" continuous crude oil futures contract showing deviations from fair value that indicate potential mispricing, which are economically significant and relate to imbalances in the supply/demand equilibrium for crude oil.

this time frame, storage costs were high as producers sought to delay sales of oil in hopes of obtaining higher prices. At certain times during this period, some oil companies even chose to store oil in tanker ships at a higher cost than land storage rather than sell it near the average $36 per barrel cost of production in the United States (Kristopher 2016).

From the point of extreme oversupply in 2015, crude oil prices start to decline to a nadir in early March 2016, when the supply/demand imbalance seems to have been reconciled and futures prices are in line with fair values. Eventually, both the basis and deviations from fair value become negative in anticipation of price increases, which do not occur until June 2016 when the supply/demand balance once again reaches equilibrium, and deviations around fair value are attenuated and generally are indistinguishable from zero. Table 15.2 provides summary statistics for the data described in Figure 15.2. Deviations from fair value are much greater and more volatile for crude oil futures than observed earlier for S&P 500 index futures.

GENERALIZING THE COST OF CARRY

To this point, the chapter has discussed the specific institutional details of futures pricing for investment and consumption assets, but these relations can more generally be defined in terms of the "cost of carry." In the previous example, the cost of carry (*c*) describes the net cost of carrying a futures position that offsets the equivalent cost of carrying a spot position in the underlying asset. For assets that are easily available to short, the cost of carry is simply the risk-free interest rate, but for consumption commodities and some investment assets such as gold, the cost of carry must be adjusted for additional storage and/or leasing costs. Equation 15.8 describes this relation:

$$F_t \leq S_0 e^{ct} \tag{15.8}$$

Table 15.3 **Cost of Carry and Futures Prices**

Futures Contract	*Pricing Equation*	*Cost of Carry*
No income or storage costs	$F_t = S_0 e^{rt}$	$c = r$
With storage and/or leasing costs (% a year)	$F_t = S_0 e^{(r+u)t}$	$c = (r + u)$
Known percentage yield (e.g., stock index)	$F_t = S_0 e^{(r-dy)t}$	$c = (r - dy)$
Known dollar income (e.g., dividends)	$F_t = (S_0 - I)e^{rt}$	$c = r$ *(less present value of discrete dividends)*
Currencies	$F_t = S_0 e^{(r-rf)t}$	$c = (r - r_f)$
Cost of carry, leasing costs, and convenience yield	$F_t = S_0 e^{(c+u-y)t}$	$c = (c + u - y)$

This table summarizes various futures pricing equations with different underlying assets.

where $c = (r + u - y)$ for consumption commodities and $c = (r + u)$ for investment assets that incur only storage and/or leasing costs. Alternatively, the term c can be defined in other terms for assets that provide known incomes and or investment yields, and a summary of the relevant pricing equations is presented in Table 15.3.

INTEREST RATE/FIXED INCOME FUTURES

Because of some unique institutional aspects of fixed income futures, this section of the chapter provides a more detailed discussion of these instruments. U.S. Treasury instruments are generally viewed as being free of credit risk, which may be a questionable assumption given S&P's downgrade of the country's credit rating in 2011, but that topic is beyond the scope of this chapter. Interest rates as set by the Federal Reserve Bank solely determine U.S. government interest rate futures prices. Equation 15.9 shows how Treasury bill futures prices in the United States are determined:

$$P = \frac{360}{n}(100 - Y) \tag{15.9}$$

where Y is the cash price per \$100 of bond value; P is the quoted price; and n is the number of days until expiration. Treasury bond futures are quoted in terms of their *cash* or *clean price*, which is the sum of the quoted price plus accrued interest since the last coupon payment ("dirty" price). Treasury bond futures prices are determined in a slightly different manner because coupon payments are involved. Equation 15.10 shows the basic futures pricing relation for Treasury bond futures:

$$\text{Cash price received by party with short position} = \\ \text{Most Recent Settlement Price} \times \text{Conversion factor} + \text{Accrued interest} \tag{15.10}$$

The U.S. government provides the conversion factor to translate any particular bond issue to be equivalent to a 6 percent coupon bond with a matching maturity. This settlement procedure leads to the "wild card" play where any of a range of eligible bonds can be delivered in futures settlement procedures. The Treasury futures settlement price is set at 2:00 p.m. in Chicago, but cash Treasury bonds trade until 4:00 p.m. This timing difference creates a window of opportunity (or "optionality") for the party that is short a futures contract to buy a particular bond at an advantageous price (i.e., cash bond prices fall in the 2:00 to 4:00 p.m. window) and notify the broker of the investor's intent to deliver the bond at the converted settlement price.

RATIONAL EXPECTATIONS VERSUS RISK AVERSION HYPOTHESES IN FUTURES PRICING

Although the cost of carry model is widely accepted in practice and in the academic literature, alternative theories about variations in the basis are available. Goss (1992) provides a discussion of the *rational expectations* model in futures markets. The hypothesis of this model posits that current futures prices reflect the collective market opinion about expected future spot prices. If futures prices diverge too far from expectations, traders step in to take advantage of the "arbitrage" opportunity. The price-correcting activity of these traders drives prices back in line with expectations.

Keynes (1930) and Hicks (1939) provide another alternative. Their theory, sometimes called "contango / normal backwardation," states that, in certain markets, commodity-producing hedgers are net sellers of futures contracts and speculators are net buyers. Because speculators require compensation for their risk in order to trade in futures markets, futures prices are generally below expected future spot prices (normal backwardation) in those markets. Conversely, when commodity consumers make the majority of hedging trades, futures prices must be above future expected spot prices in order to compensate speculators for their risk.

Figlewski, Kose, and Merrick (1986) subscribe to the cost of carry model and state that both of the other theories do not account for the activities of true arbitrageurs, as opposed to the "implicit" arbitrage of the rational expectations theory. The authors do not dispute the fact that expectations of future spot prices may have a role in shaping the evolution of futures prices, but they think that the current spot price includes these expectations. Their theory is therefore more consistent with the efficient markets hypothesis. Chow, McAleer, and Sequeira (2000, p. 249) provide an extensive survey and examination of the issues as well as an empirical study, finding "substantial evidence in favor of the cost of carry hypothesis," noting the importance of the convenience yield. Gorton, Hayashi, and Rouwenhorst (2012) conduct a thorough examination of the convenience yield and conclude that it is related to commodity inventories, rejecting the Keynesian hypothesis.

Futures Spread Relations and Relative Pricing

Thus far, this chapter has examined futures contracts as "stand-alone" entities, but important relations exist among commodity futures contracts that can be used to assess the value of a particular contract relative to other contracts. This class of futures spreads is known as "intermarket spreads."

Spread trading is a technique that takes advantage of the relative price movement between futures contracts and can be used to assess differing relations among raw commodities ("basic materials") and finished products ("complex goods"). *Intermarket spreads* involve the simultaneous purchase and sale of different, but related, commodities whose prices have historically moved in a parallel fashion. In energy markets, three particular spreads exist that are popular with traders and hedgers.

First, the "crack" spread involves trading crude oil futures (symbol CL) against RBOB gasoline (reformulated gasoline blendstock for oxygen blending—symbol RB) and heating oil (HO) futures. Because three barrels of CL can be "cracked" (refined, actually) into roughly two barrels of RB and one barrel of HO, this combination is sometimes known as the 3:2:1 spread. For example, in January 2017, March 2017 CL futures were trading at $53.200 per barrel (1000 bbls per contract). RBOB gasoline futures were trading for $1.522 per gallon with 42,000 gallons in each contract. Thus, each barrel of crude oil will be converted into $1.522(42,000)/1000 bbls/contract(2/3) = $42.637 worth of gasoline. Heating oil futures, also for 42,000 gallons, were trading for $1.620/gallon. Thus, each barrel of crude oil will be converted into $1.620(42,000/1,000 bbls/contract) (1/3) = $22.65 worth of heating oil. Adding the proceeds from the sale of RB and HO futures results in revenue of $42.637 + $22.650 = $65.288 per barrel of oil. Thus, the "crack spread can be locked in by an oil refiner by selling the appropriate number (20 and 10) of gasoline and heating oil futures at $1.522 and $1.620, respectively, while simultaneously buying 30 crude oil futures at $53.20 per barrel. This locks in a gross profit of $65.288 – $53.20 = $12.088. As long as the company's refining and overhead costs are less than this amount per barrel, the company can also lock in a net profit. Table 15.4 shows the calculations described in this section, assuming a refining cost of $8.00 per barrel and a calculated net profit of $4.09 per barrel given prevailing futures market prices at the time. Although space limitations prohibit an extended discussion of the institutional details (more information on the specifics is available at www.cmegroup.com), similar relations apply to the other commodities such as the crude oil to diesel fuel (ULSD) spread and the crude oil to jet fuel (JF) spread, which are constructed similarly to the crack spread. In addition to the usefulness of this spread trade to oil refiners, speculators may exploit extreme variations in this spread and find profitable trading opportunities.

Another spread trading opportunity reflects the relation between the main raw commodity used in electricity (natural gas) and the price of electricity. This relation is known as the "spark spread." This spread reflects the opportunity to profit from the relation between natural gas prices and the price of electricity, both of which are observable in CME Group futures prices. The *dark spread* describes the similar relation between the price of coal and the price of electricity, both of which are also directly observable from CME prices. Both of these relations are characterized by the *heat rate* (i.e., efficiency of power plants), which translates the price of electricity produced by each of these commodities.

Table 15.4 **"Crack Spread" Calculation Example**

Refinery Hedge Calculation

Month	*CL$*	*Contracts*	*RBOB$*	*Contracts*	*HO$*	*Contracts*	*CL$*
Mar-17	53.20	30	1.522	20	1.620	10	53.20

1	**2**	**3**	**4**	**5**
RB$/Bbl	**2/3 RB**	**HO$/ Bbl**	**1/3 HO**	**Revenue from RB & HO**
63.924	42.637	68.019	22.650	65.288

		6		**7**
Revenue minus CL		**Spread/ Bbl**	**Refining Cost**	**Net Profit**
53.200	=	12.088	$8.00	$4.09

Steps	Using 3:2:1 ratio (3 Bbl CL = 2 Bbl RB & 1 Bbl HO)
1	Calculate RB price per Bbl (per gal price x 42).
2	Calculate RB revenue per Bbl (RB price x 2/3).
3	Calculate HO price per Bbl (per gal price x 42).
4	Calculate HO revenue per Bbl (HO price x 1/3).
5	Calculate RB & HO revenue per Bbl.
6	Calculate crack spread (RB & HO revenue less CL).
7	Subtract cost to refine to obtain net profit.

Note: This table describes the calculation of the "crack spread" involving crude oil and its two main distillates, gasoline and heating oil.

Similarly, the *frac spread* reflects the relation among the price of natural gas and natural gas liquids (NGLs). Refiners break down unrefined (raw) natural gas into usable heating fuel and natural gas liquids such as propane and ethylene. Mack (2014) provides a more in-depth analysis of these energy market spreads and their relation to physical energy production. Production/consumption futures pricing relations also exist in agricultural markets. These relations are known as *crush spreads* because the first evolution of this type of spread involves "crushing" soybeans into soybean meal and soybean oil. All three products are available for trading in futures markets. Another crush spread involves the relation between corn and ethanol futures because corn is the primary input in the production of ethanol. Finally, the spread known as the *cattle crush* replicates the operations of a typical beef feedlot because the inputs to the spread involve feeder cattle and corn, while the final output of this process is live cattle. Barrett and Kolb (1995) provide a thorough analysis of these agricultural market spreads.

Futures spreads among different classes of equity indexes now exist such as the S&P 500 index versus the S&P 400 mid-cap index. Although this chapter only discusses the most popular inter-commodity spreads in this section, literally hundreds of these types of spreads exist and are listed on the CME Group website, including many that include contracts from other U.S. and international derivatives exchanges. First, intermarket sector spreads, such as the spread between treasury yields and Eurodollar interest rates (the TED spread), provide one example. Another such spread is the AAA bond yield over treasuries. Conversely, intra-market spreads compare the yields of two similar bond yields with the same maturity, such as the bonds of Coca-Cola (KO) and Pepsico (PEP). A particularly popular spread of late is the WTI (i.e., West Texas Intermediate crude oil, the underlying asset of U.S. crude oil futures) versus Brent crude that is produced in the North Sea (Segal 2013). Locational spreads refer to the fact that prices for certain exchange traded contracts require delivery at a specific location (e.g., Cushing, Oklahoma, for crude oil), while producers and/or consumers require delivery at other geographic locations, such as New York, New York. Transportation spreads examine the cost/benefit analysis, for example, of transporting crude oil from the Alaskan pipeline to Cushing or New York. Energy companies are constantly monitoring the economic benefits of delivering their products to potential sales outlets given production, transportation, and marketing costs.

Modeling and Forecasting Futures Prices Using a GARCH Process

To examine some empirical examples of commodity futures pricing behavior, this section analyzes actual energy market price data using NYMEX daily futures and spot prices for crude oil and natural gas obtained from the Energy Information Administration between 2010 and 2016. For each of these commodity futures products, univariate EGARCH-*t* models are used between January 4, 2010 and October 31, 2016 to predict out-of-sample futures prices for the next month between November 1 and November 30, 2016.

The model provides reasonably good estimates of future commodity futures prices and it is robust to heteroskedasticity, autocorrelation, and asymmetric volatility, which are three generally important features of financial market data. Both the augmented the Dickey-Fuller test (Dickey and Fuller 1979) and the Phillips-Peron test (Phillips and Perron 1988) indicate that the levels of these two commodities are characterized by non-stationarity (i.e., clear trends are present in the data). Thus, first differences are used in this forecasting example to remove spurious correlation caused by these trends. The first differences of these series (today's price minus yesterday's

Table 15.5 **Summary Statistics for Energy Futures Returns between January 4, 2010 and November 30, 2016**

	n	*Mean*	*Median*	*Max*	*Min*	*Standard Deviation*	*Skewness*	*Kurtosis*
△ CL	1,736	−0.018	−0.015	7.370	−9.440	1.446	−0.211	5.618
△ NG	1,736	−0.001	−0.002	0.600	−0.690	0.099	0.239	7.683

Note: This table provides summary statistics for crude oil and natural gas futures in the sample under study.

price), however, are stationary at the 0.01 significance level for both of these tests, and the Phillips-Peron test (1988) is robust to heteroskedasticity or changing volatility and autocorrelation consistent (HAC) standard errors. Table 15.5 provides summary statistics for the price difference data.

Evidence exists that certain economic data can be modeled using simple autoregressive (AR) processes (e.g., Engle 1982), and AR models may be fine for data series such as inflation that are not particularly volatile. However, in recent years, energy prices have been extremely volatile, price volatility has varied widely over time (heteroskedasticity), and it has exhibited serial (auto-) correlation. Thus, the GARCH model (Engle 1982; Bollerslev 1987) is a more robust methodology to model and forecast energy prices. Specifically, this chapter uses Nelson's (1991) EGARCH-*t* model to predict energy futures prices. This model is robust to HAC errors even when using the Newey-West adjustment procedure (Newey and West 1987), and it accommodates the effects of asymmetric volatility in financial markets (i.e., prices are more volatile in down markets than in up markets). This analytical technique is an advanced form of the AR model and the term "conditional" means that future values are based on prior price changes and prior volatility. *Heteroskedasticity* refers to the fact that volatility is not constant, an artifact that exists in much of financial market data. In a more extensive analysis of energy commodity prices than the one presented here, Yaziz, Ahmad, Nian, and Muhammad (2011) examine the merits and drawbacks of modeling energy prices using several econometric techniques, finding statistically significant results for GARCH models. However similar to the results in this chapter, whether these forecasting models can generate profitable trading signals is uncertain. The EGARCH model is described by Equations 15.11 and 15.12, which are maximized via log likelihood following the Broyden-Fletcher-Goldfarb-Shanno (BFGS) procedure and Nelson (1991):

$$y_t = c_1 + b_1 y_{t-1} + \varepsilon_t \tag{15.11}$$

$$\log_t^2 = c_2 + d_1\left[\frac{|\varepsilon_{t-1}|}{\sigma_{t-1}} - E\left\{\frac{|\varepsilon_{t-1}|}{\sigma_{t-1}}\right\}\right] + f_1\left(\frac{\varepsilon_{t-1}}{\sigma_{t-1}}\right) + g_1 \log_{t-1}^2 \tag{15.12}$$

where $E\left\{\frac{|\varepsilon_{t-1}|}{\sigma_{t-1}}\right\} = E\{|z_{z-1}|\} = \sqrt{\frac{\nu-2}{\pi}}\left(\frac{\frac{\Gamma(\nu-1)}{2}}{\Gamma\left(\frac{\nu}{2}\right)}\right)$ and ν represents the degrees of freedom in the equation system. Because most financial market data are non-normal, the standard errors of the equation system are adjusted using the procedure of Newey and West (1987).

The terms in the AR(1) model as shown in Equation 15.11 are self-explanatory, while the terms in Equation 15.12 for the conditional variance are derived as follows. First, the coefficient d_1 describes the price series' sensitivity to asymmetric volatility, the empirically observed phenomenon that prices are more volatile following negative price changes. In the equity markets literature, this is sometimes referred to as the *leverage effect*. The coefficient on the f_1 terms is known as the ARCH effect because it describes the effect of previous standardized innovation on future changes in the conditional variance. The coefficient for g_1 measures the GARCH effect of prior changes in price variance on future volatility innovations. Finally the value of ν indicates the level of non-normality in the data as measured by degrees of freedom. Any value of ν greater than two indicates that the data are not properly characterized by the normal bell curve.

Table 15.6 contains the results of estimating these equations. In Panel A regarding crude oil futures, the results of the mean equation are statistically insignificant, although the negative coefficient for $\boldsymbol{b}_1$ indicates possible evidence of mean-reverting behavior. However, the conditional variance model results are much more robust. The coefficient for $\boldsymbol{d}_1$ (asymmetric volatility) is positive and significant at the 1 percent level. Thus, the futures returns are more volatile following negative prior day returns. The coefficient $\boldsymbol{f}_1$ is negative and significant, indicating some small mean reversion in the conditional variance. However, the coefficient $\boldsymbol{g}_1$ is large and statistically significant, an indication of volatility persistence, which is a common finding in financial market data. Finally, the statistically significant value of ν indicates that the data are not characterized by the normal distribution; thus the Newey-West correction is appropriate.

Panel B of Table 15.6 documents similar results for the natural gas futures. In this case the negative autocorrelation coefficient in the mean model is significant at the 0.10 level, confirming the prior marginally significant evidence of mean-reverting behavior in crude oil futures prices. Similar results are obtained for the other coefficients in the equation system except the coefficient for f_1, which is positive for natural gas futures and was negative for the crude oil futures. This finding indicates that volatility innovations for natural gas futures may contain more of a trending effect than for those of crude oil futures, which may be related to a higher seasonality component of natural gas futures given their importance for heating homes in the winter months given that the out-of-sample results are conducted in November as demand is rising in advance of the winter months.

Although analyzing the marginal effects of the GARCH model coefficients is worthwhile, the model's real utility lies in its ability to provide forward looking

Table 15.6 **AR(1) EGARCH-t (1,1) Model for Crude Oil and Natural Gas Futures Prices between January 5, 2010 and October 31, 2016**

Coefficient	*Value*	*Standard Error*	*z-Statistic*	*p-Value*
Panel A Crude Oil Futures				
Mean Model—AR(1)				
c_1	−0.018	0.031	−0.584	0.559
b_1	−0.029	0.023	−1.258	0.209
Volatility Model—EGARCH-*t*(1,1)				
c_2	−0.061	0.016	−3.936	0.000
d_1	0.093	0.022	4.244	0.000
f_1	−0.040	0.013	−3.171	0.002
g_1	0.983	0.007	131.573	0.000
v	9.721	1.603	6.063	0.000
Observations			1,716	
Log Likelihood			−2,975.68	
Panel B Natural Gas Futures				
Mean Model—AR(1)				
c_1	−0.001	0.002	−0.636	0.525
b_1	−0.047	0.025	−1.866	0.062
Volatility Model—EGARCH-*t*(1,1)				
c_2	−0.215	0.049	−4.382	0.000
d_1	0.128	0.025	5.148	0.000
f_1	0.048	0.014	3.337	0.001
g_1	0.976	0.008	124.752	0.000
v	8.157	1.253	6.511	0.000
Observations			1,716	
Log Likelihood			1,715.08	

Note: This table provides point estimates for the measures of statistical inference for AR(1) EGARCH-t (1,1) models for crude oil and natural gas futures prices in the sample period.

forecasts. Using the equation coefficient estimates from the prior estimations generates a series of one-day ahead forecasts for the month of November 2016, which follows the sample period of the original analysis. Figures 15.3 and 15.4 provide graphs of the forecasts and actual prices for crude oil and natural gas futures prices, respectively. As is evident, the models provide fairly accurate estimates of the futures prices on a one-day ahead basis. However, most of the forecasting "power" stems from the fact that the one-day forecasts are updated each day with daily price changes in November. The actual forecast changes are much smaller (i.e., median average absolute daily change of 0.201) than the median of actual median absolute price changes (0.610). Additionally, 19 out-of-sample observations exist and the model predicts the correct direction of the next day price change only nine times. Whether these results can be used to profitably trade on this information is beyond the scope of this chapter and seems unlikely without further refinement. Any such effort would likely be improved by accounting for the seasonality that is commonly observed in energy futures prices. The analysis here does not account for this seasonality, but a clear uptrend in natural gas futures occurs from mid- to late November as the winter months approached. Academic studies such as Yaziz et al. (2011) that show statistically significant forecasting ability should be evaluated with an eye toward whether the forecasts can be used in an economically significant manner.

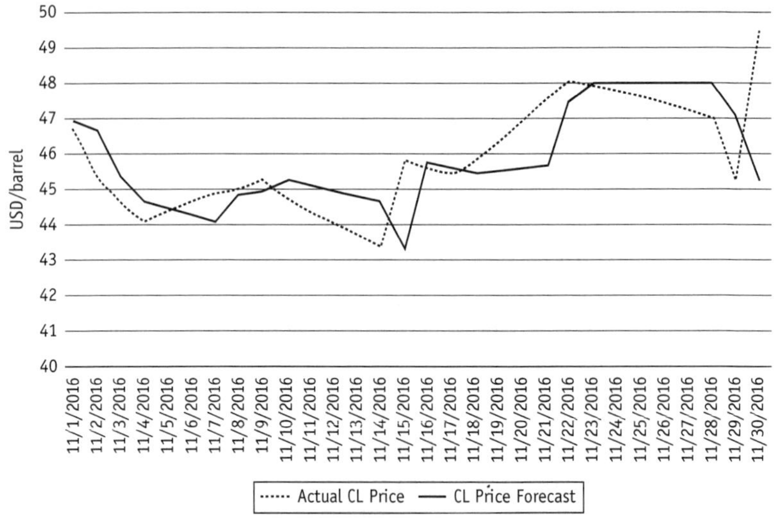

Figure 15.3 Out-of-Sample Forecast of Crude Oil Futures Prices Using an AR(1) EGARCH-t(1,1) Model
Figures 15.3 and 15.4 provide graphical representations of the AR(1) EGARCH-t (1,1) forecast model for crude oil and natural gas futures prices, respectively.

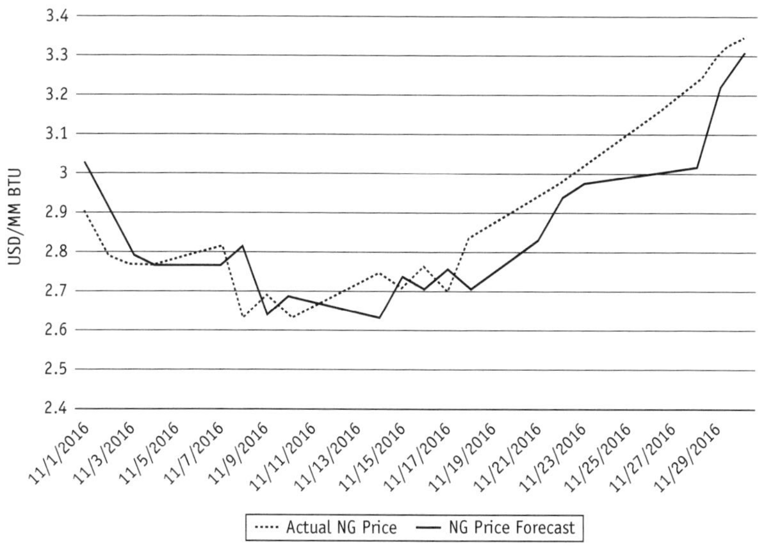

Figure 15.4 Out-of-Sample Forecast of Natural Gas Futures Prices Using an AR(1) EGARCH-t(1,1) Model
Figures 15.3 and 15.4 provide graphical representations of the AR(1) EGARCH-t (1,1) forecast model for crude oil and natural gas futures prices, respectively.

Summary and Conclusions

This chapter discusses the fundamental futures pricing equations according to "no arbitrage" arguments to determine exact relations between spot and futures prices. These equations can be modified to account for differing costs of carry and violations of initial model assumptions, and the models are generally accepted to be empirically correct. The chapter discusses futures pricing for single stocks, stock indices, foreign currencies, commodities, and fixed income products. Although the evidence in this chapter demonstrates that these models work very well for stock index futures, the results vary for crude oil futures due to their dependence on the supply/demand situation in the spot (cash) oil market. In this case, academic theories cannot be universally applied.

This chapter discusses futures spread pricing relative to a wide range of energy and agricultural commodities and shows that relative pricing provides useful information to commodity producers and consumers. The chapter presents two economic theories about futures pricing, although the cost of carry model is generally accepted by academics and certainly by practitioners. Relative commodity pricing among related commodity complexes provides indications to producers and consumers about industry inputs and outputs. Lastly, the chapter provides a limited empirical study indicating that the GARCH family of econometric models may be useful in forecasting crude oil and natural gas futures, but the models are most likely not economically useful for implementing trading strategies.

Discussion Questions

1. A stock index currently stands at 2,170. The risk-free interest rate is 1 percent a year (with continuous compounding) and the dividend yield on the index is 2 percent a year. Calculate the futures price for a six-month contract.
2. If the stock index futures price in the market in question 1 were 2,150, explain what an arbitrageur would do to make a risk-free profit from the situation, and the amount that the arbitrageur would theoretically make per contract. Assume the "unit" or "tick" value of the futures contract in this example is $50.
3. Explain the cost of carry for (a) non-dividend-paying stock, (b) dividend-paying stock, (c) stock index, (d) a commodity with storage costs, and (e) a foreign currency.
4. Assume that silver is currently trading for $20 per ounce in the spot market, interest rates are 2 percent a year for a one-year maturity, and there is a cost of 3 percent a year to store a large quantity of silver bullion. Calculate the futures price of silver for delivery in one year.

References

Barrett, W. Brian, and Robert W. Kolb. 1995. "Analysis of Spreads in Agricultural Futures." *Journal of Futures Markets* 15:1, 69–86.

Barron's. 2016. "NYSE Program Trading." May. Available at http://www.barrons.com/public/page/9_0210-nysepgtd.html.

Black, Fischer. 1976. "The Pricing of Commodity Contracts." *Journal of Financial Economics* 3:1–2, 167–179.

Bollerslev, Tim. 1987. "A Conditionally Heteroskedastic Time Series Model for Speculative Prices and Rates of Return." *Review of Economics and Statistics* 69:3, 542–547.

Chow, Ying-Foon, Michael McAleer, and John Sequeira. 2000. "Pricing of Forward and Futures Contracts." *Journal of Economic Surveys* 14:2, 215–253.

Dickey, David A., and Wayne A. Fuller. 1979. "Distribution of the Estimators for Autoregressive Time Series with a Unit Root." *Journal of the American Statistical Association* 74:366, 427–431.

Engle, Robert F. 1982. "Autoregressive Conditional Heteroscedasticity with Estimates of the Variance of United Kingdom Inflation." *Econometrica* 50:5, 987–1007.

Figlewski, Stephen, John Kose, and John Merrick. 1986. *Hedging with Financial Futures for Institutional Investors: From Theory to Practice.* Cambridge, MA: Ballinger.

Gorton, Gary B., Fumio Hayashi, and K. Geert Rouwenhorst. 2012. "The Fundamentals of Commodity Futures Returns." *Review of Finance* 17:1, 35–105.

Goss, Barry. 1992. *Rational Expectations and Efficiency in Futures Markets.* London: Routledge.

Hicks, John. R. 1939. *Value and Capital.* Oxford: Clarendon Press.

Hull, John. 2017. *Options, Futures, and Other Derivatives,* 10th edition. Boston, MA: Pearson.

Keynes, John. M. 1930. *A Treatise on Money.* London: Macmillan.

Kitco Metals Inc. 2016. "Gold Lease Rate Chart." November 15. Available at http://www.kitco.com/lease.chart.html.

Kristopher, Gordon. 2016. "Crude Oil's Total Cost of Production Impacts Major Oil Producers." January 13. Available at http://marketrealist.com/2016/01/crude-oils-total-cost-production-impacts-major-oil-producers/.

Mack, Iris. 2014. *Energy Trading and Risk Management: A Practical Approach to Hedging, Trading and Portfolio Diversification*. Singapore: Wiley Finance.

Nelson, Daniel B. 1991. "Conditional Heteroskedasticity in Asset Returns: A New Approach." *Econometrica* 59:2, 347–370.

Newey, Whitney K., and Kenneth D. West. 1987. "Hypothesis Testing with Efficient Method of Moments Estimation." *International Economic Review* 28:3, 777–787.

Phillips, Peter C. B., and Pierre Perron. 1988. "Testing for a Unit Root in Time Series Regression." *Biometrika* 75:2, 335–346.

Segal, Gerald. 2013. "CME Group Reports Record Crude Spread Trading Volumes." October 25. Available at http://www.leaprate.com/2013/10/cme-group-reports-record-crude-spread-trading-volumes/.

Yaziz, Siti R., Maizah H. Ahmad, Lee C. Nian, and Noryanti Muhammad. 2011. "A Comparative Study on Box-Jenkins and GARCH Models in Forecasting Crude Oil Prices." *Journal of Applied Sciences* 11:7, 1129–1135.

16

Return Characteristics of Commodities

DIANNA PREECE
Professor of Finance, University of Louisville

Introduction

Commodities are raw materials or agricultural products that can be bought or sold. The four main commodity sectors are agriculture, meat and livestock, metals, and energy, the largest category. Examples of commodities include corn, crude oil, and gold. Commodities are interchangeable, meaning that the raw material is uniform and thus the source of the commodity does not matter. For example, an investor does not care whether gold is mined in South Africa or the United States because the gold is interchangeable. Crude oil, corn, wheat, and copper are likewise interchangeable commodities. Commodity values affect the lives of everyone regardless of whether they hold commodity exposure as a part of an investment portfolio. Commodity prices are relevant to policymakers who are concerned about rising food prices and food shortages. They are also concerned about the role commodity prices play in terms of inflation pressures.

Commodities are classified as alternative investments that are held largely by institutional investors. Like other alternative assets, regulation is limited. Commodity investors benefit from the alternative asset class in several ways. Before the financial crisis of 2007–2008, a passive investment strategy in commodities generally meant high, equity-like average returns, a hedge or at least a partial hedge against inflation, and negative return correlations with traditional asset classes such as stocks and bonds (Stockton 2007). These characteristics make commodities desirable in a diversified portfolio.

Trading in commodities dates back thousands of years. Commodities ranging from livestock to spices were traded in ancient civilizations. Evidence shows that trading in commodities futures dates back 6,000 years to the trading of rice futures (called "rice tickets") in China (Babcock 2016). Futures trading in commodities provides a natural solution to the problem of maintaining year-around supplies of agricultural products, although the market has expanded well beyond commodities to financial instruments over the centuries. In the United States, futures trading began in the mid-1800s in grain markets. Both hedgers and speculators participated, and continue to participate, in the market.

Both the size and diversity of commodity markets have expanded. After the post-2000 boom in commodity prices, firms invested more in exploration, production, and commodity investment activities. As commodity prices fell from peak levels after the financial crisis to a bottom in 2011, firms cut back on investments (World Bank Group 2016). Since then, many institutional investors have increased their allocation to commodities. The ever-growing presence of financial investors in commodity markets raises concerns about the role speculators play in commodity prices and commodity price volatility. A famous example is that of the Hunt brothers cornering the global market for silver in 1980 (Christopher 2016). The Hunt brothers contended that they were simply trying to hedge against the extremely high, late-1970s inflation. However, in 1980 they and other family members owned about two-thirds of all privately held silver. The silver bet ultimately backfired and wiped out a large amount of the Hunt fortune. However, the case illustrates the difficulty of distinguishing between manipulation of markets, which affects investor returns, and normal trading for legitimate purposes.

Commodity investments represent claims on raw materials. Financial investments typically represent claims on underlying assets or cash flow streams. The unique characteristics of commodity investments mean that popular investment strategies are generally unsuitable. Although traditional and alternative investments often use similar investment strategies, the investment characteristics of commodities necessitate that investors use different approaches to valuation and investment strategies.

Investors can gain exposure to commodities through several outlets. For example, they can buy the physical commodity directly, but direct ownership requires transporting the commodity and storing it to maintain its value. As such, the allocation to direct investment in commodities has been historically small (Greer 2000). Alternatively, investors can gain exposure to commodities through derivatives such as futures, forwards, swaps, or options. For many reasons, not the least of which is convenience, most direct commodity investments are made through derivatives. Indirect ownership of commodities is most common. Investors can buy the stock or bonds of companies that produce, market, or transport commodities. Alternatively, investors can gain exposure through vehicles such as mutual funds or limited partnerships that make direct commodity investments. These funds may invest in commodity firms or firms that finance commodity production.

The number of available passive investable commodity indexes and commodity-linked alternatives that provide direct access to commodities continues to increase. Examples include exchanged-traded indexes such as the Goldman Sachs Commodity Index (GSCI) and the Bridge/Commodity Research Bureau (CRB) Index. The Chase Physical Commodity Index, Dow-Jones-AIG Commodity Index, and J. P. Morgan Commodity Index are commodity-linked investments. Physical commodities must be transported and stored, which is not something many investors are willing or able to do. Because futures contracts expire, long-term investments in commodities through futures contracts must be repeatedly rolled over, posing a challenge for some investors.

The returns on commodity investments vary over time. Commodities generally perform well during periods of inflation. In the late 1970s, interest rates were almost 18 percent and commodities reached record highs. In the 2000s, commodities saw a boom until they, like most asset classes, bottomed out in 2008. For example, gold reached \$850 per ounce in 1980, reached a low of \$250 per ounce in 1999 and exceeded $1,900 per ounce in August, 2011. Although commodities took considerable time to recover after the financial crisis of 2007–2008, beginning in late 2015 investors started paying attention again, with some believing that the time was right for commodities to turn around (Treadgold 2015), primarily because they thought prices had finally reached the post-crisis bottom. Also, key commodities trade in dollars and an expectation of a fallback of the dollar and an expected increase in interest rates in late 2015 moving into 2016 were good signs for commodities.

In simple terms, two opportune times exist to buy commodities. First, investors may choose to buy commodities when they are cheap. In this case, investors are making a "value" play. Alternatively, they may purchase commodity investments when commodities are expensive (e.g., when hitting multi-year highs), and investors want to catch the trend (i.e., momentum investing).

The advent of commodity exchange-traded funds (ETFs) has made buying commodities easier for a long-term investment. Commodity ETFs either invest in the physical commodities, often focusing on a single commodity, holding them in physical storage, or focus on investments in commodity futures contracts. Some ETFs attempt to track the performance of commodity indexes through direct investments and positions in derivatives (e.g., commodity futures contracts). Traditional ETFs consist of a portfolio of public equities linked by an investment style or strategy (e.g., emerging market stocks, financial services stocks, and utility stocks). By contrast, commodity ETFs use direct commodity investments and futures contracts to track the performance of a commodity or group of commodities. For example, the SPDR Gold Shares ETF, which tracks the performance of gold, is one of the largest gold ETFs.

In terms of the characteristics of commodity returns, the extensive literature dates to seminal work by Greer (1978) and Bodie and Rosansky (1980). The primary themes that run through academic studies of commodities as an investment vehicle are the roles of commodities as diversifiers, inflation hedges, and return providers. However, sorting through the literature based on these three topics is difficult because most work since the mid-1980s involves all three issues. As such, the following discussion examines relevant literature relating to the characteristics of commodity returns in chronological order.

The chapter proceeds as follows. The second section offers a description of the association between commodity spot prices and futures prices to help provide understanding of the decisions investors make between holding the underlying commodity and taking long positions in commodity futures contracts to gain exposure to the asset class. The next section provides a description of the various types of returns that commodity investors earn, followed by a review of return characteristics contained in the academic literature. Finally, the chapter provides a summary and conclusions.

Spot Prices and Futures Prices

Understanding the drivers of commodity futures returns is necessary to form expectations about them. First, commodity investors must understand the relation between spot and futures prices. How are commodity futures priced in equilibrium? Equation 16.1 shows this equilibrium pricing relation:

$$F_0 = SP_0(1+r+s-c) \tag{16.1}$$

where F_0 is the current futures price; SP_0 is the current spot price; r is the risk-free rate; s is the annual cost to store the physical commodity; and c is the convenience yield that results from holding the physical commodity.

Examining the characteristics of commodity returns requires considering both the returns of holding the physical commodity and the returns from taking long positions in commodity futures contracts. To gain exposure to the commodity, investors can either borrow the money to buy the commodity and store it until time T, or take a long position in the futures contract and settle it at time T (Gray 2016).

CONVENIENCE YIELD

The *convenience yield* is the non-monetary benefit (i.e., the implied return) received from physically holding a commodity. The convenience yield is inversely related to the level of inventory of the commodity (i.e., it is a risk premium). According to Fama and French (1988), the theory of storage, which explains the convenience yield, helps to clarify the seasonal behavior of spot and futures prices of agricultural commodities. It evolved over time, beginning with Keynes's theory of normal backwardation, and then successively by Kaldor (1939), Working (1948), Brennan (1958), and Telser (1958). In general, before harvests, when inventories are low, futures prices tend to be below spot prices because market participants assume the commodity will be more available in the future. In contrast, when inventories are high, market participants do not see value in holding the commodity because current scarcity is low. The *cost of carry* includes financing, storage, and potential spoilage costs. The convenience yield is an adjustment to the cost of carry.

Based on Equation 16.1, the futures price is equal to the spot price adjusted for the cost of carry (i.e., for the cost of borrowing, storage, and the convenience yield). If financing and storing a commodity cost investors more than they can gain in convenience, the futures price will be higher than the spot price and the futures market will be in *contango*. If storage and financing the commodity cost investors less relative to the benefit of holding the commodity (i.e., the convenience yield), the futures price will be lower than the spot price and the market will be in *backwardation*. The next section describes contango and backwardation in greater detail. According to Gray (2016), a futures contract is basically owning an asset in the future secured by a loan. The costs and benefits, such as the convenience of having a commodity on hand, and the cost of storing that commodity, are endured by another party.

Sources of Commodity Returns

Commodity futures generate three sources of returns: (1) changes in the spot price, (2) the roll yield, and (3) the collateral yield. This section provides a discussion of each source of return.

COLLATERAL RETURN

The *collateral return,* also called the Treasury-bill (T-bill) return, the cash return, or the collateral yield, is the return generated from collateral. Because commodity futures are leveraged by nature, an investor may have a large amount of uninvested cash. *Collateralized commodity futures,* which are unlevered positions in commodity futures contracts, require collateralization of the risk exposure of the contract. Cash is used to collateralize the unlevered position. In other words, the futures contract requires the investor to pay a price for the asset at some time in the future. Because the investor does not pay for the commodity at the contract's inception, the funds needed to pay in the future can be invested in other assets, usually risk-free assets, such as T-bills, for the life of the contract. Returns are generated from the collateral investments. These returns are the interest earned on T-bills or other risk-free assets that are purchased to collateralize the face amount of the commodity futures held for investment. The collateral yield is comprised of the expected rate of inflation plus a real rate of return (i.e., the nominal risk-free rate of interest). The collateral return is important because it is the actual inflation hedge, not the underlying commodities. This hedge occurs because the T-bill yield adjusts as the rate of inflation changes (Greer 2000).

SPOT RETURN

The spot price of a commodity is the current price. The *spot price* is the price quoted for immediate or short-term delivery of the commodity. The *spot return* reflects change in the underlying commodity (i.e., spot) price. As the supply and demand for a commodity changes, so does the commodity's price. Many factors lead to changes in the supply or demand of a commodity, including changes in weather patterns, seasonal factors, and real demand increases (e.g., the increasing demand for meat as citizens in countries such as China become wealthier and shift from plant-based toward meat-based diets). Increasing (decreasing) commodity prices result in positive (negative) spot returns for commodity index investors. Spot prices are driven by the supply and demand characteristics of the particular commodity market and are volatile. Spot returns are a primary driver of unhedged futures returns.

Spot returns are typically below cash returns and are much more volatile. The spot return implies a direct investment in the physical commodity, one which most investors do not make because of transportation and storage costs. As a result, the roll return, a source of return that results from investing in commodity futures to gain exposure to commodities, is relevant to investors who choose not to hold physical commodities. Over long periods, the historical spot return average is approximately the rate of inflation.

ROLL RETURN

The roll return or roll yield results when a commodities investor wants to hold a long position in futures over a long period of time. The investor must sell or "close out" positions in futures contracts that are expiring and reinvest in longer-term contracts.

The *roll return* is the gain (or loss) associated with rolling a futures contract forward. Contracts are sold as they approach maturity and are replaced with new contracts to maintain the risk exposure in the portfolio. A large contributor to differences in commodity futures returns is the return derived from rolling futures contracts before they expire. Whether the market is in *contango* or *backwardation* will determine whether the roll yield is positive or negative.

CONTANGO AND BACKWARDATION

An investor must decide on the maturity of the new contract that will replace the expiring contract. However, the prices of nearer term contracts do not generally match the prices of longer-term contracts. The *term structure of futures prices,* which is the shape of the futures curve, affects the investor's return. An investor must consider whether the market is in *contango* or *backwardation*. When the price of a commodity for future delivery is higher than the spot price, the futures market is in contango. When the market is in backwardation, the futures curve is downward sloping. That is, longer-out futures contracts have lower prices than contracts that mature sooner and the futures price is less than the spot price. However, as a contract expires, the futures price converges to the spot price. In the case of a backwardation, cheaper contracts converge from below to the spot price, resulting in a positive roll yield. In other words, in a *backwardated futures market,* the price rolls up to the spot price. This relation means roll returns are positive in backwardated markets and negative in contangoed markets. Stated differently, in a backwardated market, the futures curve is downward sloping. As the investor replaces expiring contracts with longer maturity contracts, they are less expensive (i.e., the downward sloping curve) so the investor "saves money" and earns a positive return.

Roll yields are typically small, but stable. The roll return is important as it makes commodity returns competitive with that of equity investments. A 2007 Vanguard report presented evidence that the roll return was shrinking, and perhaps disappearing altogether (Stockton 2007). The report uses the energy futures market as an example. If the roll yield is indeed disappearing, investors should be wary of using past commodity returns as expectations for future returns. Investors must be forward-looking when including commodities in a portfolio. The *income return,* or the sum of the roll yield and the collateral yield, makes up the greatest portion of a commodity futures portfolio's return. Figure 16.1 illustrates the concepts of contango and backwardation.

BROAD COMMODITY INDEXES AND RETURNS

Many, if not most, investors gain exposure to commodities via futures contracts, indexes, and ETFs. Many broad commodity indexes are available that track several commodity sectors. For example, in March 2016, gold was up 16 percent year-to-date and natural gas was down 21 percent (Roy 2016). Many in the popular press were heralding the fact that commodities had turned the corner and that investors should again return to commodities. As Roy notes, however, if investors who were on the

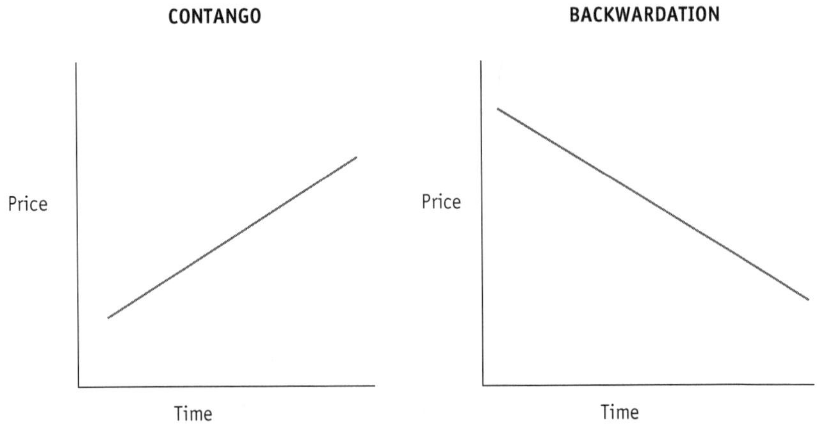

Figure 16.1 An Illustration of Contango and Backwardation in Futures Markets
This figure illustrates that the upward sloping (contango) futures curve and the "normal" downward sloping (backwardated) futures curve.

wrong side, such as being long natural gas rather than gold in 2016, returns would not have reflected the "turnaround." Additionally, because the indexes are broad, gains in one commodity sector may be washed out by losses in another. Although research suggests investing in a broad basket for diversification and inflation hedging properties, diversification can lead to lower returns as some commodities perform well while others falter. However, this may be said about diversifying across any asset class. For example, losses in some stocks will offset gains in others in a diversified equity portfolio.

Noting the possible resurgence of inflation coupled with greater volatility in stock and bond markets in the late 1990s, Greer (2000) indicates that institutional investors were increasingly interested in long-only passive unleveraged commodity indexes to access sources of commodity returns and to hedge against inflation. An unleveraged commodity index represents the return that an investor would earn holding passive long positions in commodity futures. Greer contends that although Halpern and Warsager (1998) examine commodity returns in periods of low and high inflation, periods of unexpected inflation are actually a cause for concern for institutional investors. Unlike many alternative assets requiring investors to select and monitor active managers (e.g., private equity investments), fully investable, passive commodity indexes exist.

Greer (2000) explores four questions in his study of unleveraged commodity index investments. First, do these investments offer an inherent return? Second, are the returns negatively correlated (or uncorrelated) with stock and bond returns? Third, are the returns positively correlated with the rate of inflation or with changes in the rate of inflation? Fourth, is the return sufficient (i.e., higher than the return on cash) to justify an allocation to commodity indexes? According to Greer, the basis of commodity returns is threefold: (1) the T-bill rate, which includes expected inflation plus a real rate of return; (2) insurance, which is the price of uncertainty; and

(3) rebalancing. Although not necessarily a source of returns, expectational variance also affects the pattern of commodity returns. Using data from 1970 to 1999, Greer finds that total returns from unleveraged commodity indexes are positive and "equity-like," commodity returns are negatively correlated with stock and bond returns, and commodity index returns are positively correlated with inflation and more positively correlated with changes in inflation.

The next section provides a discussion of the academic literature on the characteristics of commodity returns. As noted, most studies examine many of the same issues, using different data sets, time horizons, and methodologies. Given the difficulty of categorizing the studies by topic because so much crossover exists among them, the literature review is presented largely in chronological order.

Commodity Return Literature Review

Greer (1978) is one of the first to propose commodities as a conservative investment to hedge against inflation. Examining inflation and commodities in a period of high inflation in the United States, he maintains that commodities, considered highly speculative by most market participants at the time, have a legitimate place in the portfolios of conservative institutional investors. Greer notes that investors cannot achieve a hedge against inflation in a portfolio of stocks or of stocks and bonds. He finds that between 1960 and 1974, an index of collateralized commodity futures outperforms equities. Additionally, the commodity futures had a lower maximum drawdown. Greer is also one of the first to find that an allocation to commodities improves the risk-return trade-off of a traditional stock portfolio. Additionally, he indicates that the approach of investing in collateralized commodity futures does not require a prediction about the rate of inflation.

Following Greer (1978), Bodie and Rosansky (1980) take a comprehensive look at nearly all commodities and their returns between 1950 and 1976. In 1950, 10 commodities were actively traded, increasing to 23 by 1976. The authors calculate a quarterly series of returns for 23 commodity futures using two separate definitions of return. First, they define return simply as the percentage change in the price of the futures contract over a three-month holding period. In their second measure of return, the authors include the return the investor could have earned on the collateral (i.e., the collateral yield). They examine an equally-weighted portfolio of collateralized commodity futures. Bodie and Rosansky find that over the sample period the commodity futures earned equity-like returns, much higher than the nominal risk-free rate of interest. The mean and variance of returns were similar to that of the S&P 500 index. However, they find that the commodity futures had more positively skewed returns than stock returns. Over the study period, commodities had both a higher maximum return and a higher minimum return than equities. They find that stocks and commodities had nominal losses in seven of the study years, but the average annual loss for the benchmark commodity futures contract was only 2.87 percent compared to an 11.46 percent average loss for equities. The authors contend that these results imply greater upside and less downside potential for commodities relative to investments in equities. They also find that commodities outperform government bonds. Additionally, Bodie and Rosansky confirm Greer's results and find that the commodity futures portfolio was a good inflation hedge. The commodity futures portfolio performed best during periods of high inflation (e.g., the early 1950s, late 1960s, and early 1970s) while equities provided a poor inflation hedge over the same period.

Fama and French (1988) continue the work, exploring the nature of commodities and commodity returns, examining the relation between commodities, specifically industrial metals, and the business cycle. The authors test the dominant model of commodity futures prices, the *theory of storage* (Working 1949; Brennan 1958; Telser 1958). The theory suggests that as commodity inventories rise, the marginal convenience yield on inventory falls. The convenience yield, previously described, is the implied return on holding inventories. Fama and French suggest that as inventories rise, the marginal convenience yield falls at a decreasing rate. The authors hypothesize that, when inventories are low, commodity futures prices are less volatile than spot prices. They test the hypothesis using industrial metals (e.g., copper, tin, lead, aluminum, and zinc) and precious metals (e.g., silver, gold, and platinum) between 1972 and 1983. They use daily observations from the London Metals Exchange (LME). Fama and French also examine the price behavior of silver during the period, copper and gold futures prices from the New York Commodity Exchange (COMEX), and platinum prices from the New York Mercantile Exchange (NYM).

Fama and French (1988) find that unlike agricultural commodities, industrial metals are unaffected by seasonality. However, the business cycle affects industrial metals. The authors contribute to the existing literature showing that metal prices follow the patterns predicted by the theory of storage, but due to business activities, not harvests and seasonal differences in inventories. According to their study, metal manufacturers do not respond quickly to demand shocks that occur at the peak of the business cycle, resulting in inventory shortages. As inventories fall, futures prices are below spot prices. Fama and French also find that spot prices are more variable than futures prices around peaks in the business cycle (i.e., when inventories are low). Yet, when inventories are high, the changes in forward and spot prices are nearly perfectly positively correlated. The authors find weaker results for precious metals. Storage costs are lower for precious metals. This relation means that inventories are generally high enough to keep convenience yields near zero. As such, the nearly perfect positive correlation between spot and forward prices holds in precious metal markets. The general conclusion is that for industrial metals, the business cycle is an important and significant variable affecting the variability of spot and forward prices.

Keynes (1930) first posits the theory of normal backwardation in *A Treatise on Money*. He suggests that the ease or difficulty of storing a commodity is critical to the benefit of allocating a portion of a portfolio to the asset class. The theory is that the futures price is less than the future spot price and converges up to the future spot price over time. To test the hypothesis of normal backwardation suggested by Keynes, Kolb (1992) examines 980,800 daily futures prices for 29 commodities between 1957 and 1988. He finds that most commodities do not follow contango or normal backwardation. However, feeder cattle, live beef, live hogs, and orange juice follow normal backwardation. He also finds these commodities have positive returns. In a later paper, Kolb (1996) finds that only the contracts on commodities that are difficult to store, such as live beef, live hogs, oil, and copper, generate positive returns. Till and Eagleeye (2003, 2005) examine and confirm the notion that futures contracts of difficult to store commodities such as live cattle, gasoline, and copper are strongly and routinely backwardated and, as a result, generate historically positive returns because they have positive roll returns.

Furthering the early research on commodities as an inflation hedge, Bjornson and Carter (1997) examine the association between commodity futures returns and the business cycle. The authors suggest that risk premia change with changes in the business cycle and monetary conditions. In periods of inflation, commodity prices tend to increase while stock and bond values suffer. Long positions in commodity futures benefit from increases in the prices of underlying commodities. Thus, Bjornson and Carter, along with Bodie (1983), Jensen, Johnson, and Mercer (2000), and Gorton and Rouwenhorst (2006a) confirm the usefulness of commodities futures as a hedge against inflation. Extending the work, Jensen et al. consider how commodities perform under expansive versus restrictive monetary policy regimes. They find that both on a stand-alone basis and in a broader portfolio context, commodity futures perform well during periods of restrictive monetary policy and poorly during expansionary periods. The authors contend that investors should use monetary policy stringency to guide asset allocation decisions to alternative assets, such as commodities, that are considered inflationary hedges.

Satyanarayan and Varangis (1994) examine the benefits of adding commodity futures to a portfolio of domestic and international stocks and bonds. They also consider the benefits of adding emerging market assets to an investment portfolio. The authors add an allocation of the Goldman Sachs Commodity Index (GSCI), now called the S&P GSCI, to represent commodities in a traditional, but internationally diversified stock and bond portfolio. The S&P GSCI is a tradable index that is available to market participants on the Chicago Mercantile Exchange (CME). They find that the allocation does indeed lower the risk of the traditional, internationally diversified portfolio. The standard deviation of the portfolio is reduced while returns are maintained.

When considering research that involves an exposure to the S&P GSCI, an important fact to note is that energy heavily influences the index. The S&P GSCI has a much higher exposure to energy (e.g., around 70 percent in much of the 2000s) than to any other commodity. The index is currently comprised of 24 commodity sectors (24 commodities' nearby futures contracts), including energy, industrial, and precious metals, as well as agricultural and livestock products. According to Goldman Sachs, the return from the S&P GSCI Total Return is substantially different from buying the underlying physical commodities (S&P GSCI Components and Weights 2017).

Froot (1995) considers several real asset categories in terms of their abilities to reduce portfolio volatility. He finds that for a traditional portfolio to benefit from (i.e., see a reduction in risk) an allocation to commodities, the allocation must be primarily weighted toward oil, either directly or via a product such as the S&P GSCI, which, as noted, is heavily weighted toward the energy sector. The author finds that gold, real estate, the equities of real estate, and energy firms do not reduce the volatility of a traditional asset portfolio. Froot asserts that if investors intend to add an allocation to real assets, they must do so based on the return prospects alone. They cannot rely on the traditional view that these assets, owing to low or negative correlation with traditional asset classes, will reduce the volatility of portfolio returns.

Anson (1998) examines the component parts of commodity returns: the spot, collateral, and roll returns. He suggests that commodity futures indexes have beneficial aspects relative to financial futures and options. First, commodity futures indexes are long-only strategies, unlike hedge funds or managed futures, which may hold long and short positions. Second, the indexes invest in non-financial commodity futures. This distinction is important for diversification. The same factors that influence stock and bond prices also affect financial futures. Stock and bond prices are inversely related to inflation, while commodities are generally positively correlated with inflation. This difference suggests that commodities are likely to be good diversifiers. Examining the total returns of commodity futures between 1985 and 1997, Anson finds that roll returns and collateral returns predominantly drive total returns. Anson concludes that spot returns primarily provide diversification benefits. Spot commodity prices often do well in periods of financial stress, which is the same time stocks and bonds generally perform poorly.

Idzorek (2006) studies the role of commodities in a portfolio context. He considers the strategic asset allocation decision combining commodities with portfolios of stocks and bonds. He uses three approaches to show that including commodities in portfolios of traditional assets improves the risk-return trade-off. Specifically, Idzorek shows that including commodity futures contracts in a diversified portfolio improves diversification and the efficient frontier. The efficient frontier shifts up and to the left. He develops a technique to estimate the market capitalization of commodities and then uses the capital asset pricing model (CAPM), not usually applicable to commodities due to the lack of market capitalization, to demonstrate the advantage of adding commodities to a traditional, diversified portfolio.

Erb and Harvey (2006) examine an assertion that many researchers before them have made, namely, that investors can earn equity-like returns taking long-only positions in commodity futures. Using data between December 1969 and May 2004, the authors first examine the returns of individual commodity futures as a stand-alone investment. They find that during the period the S&P GSCI had a 12.24 percent return with a standard deviation of 18.35 percent compared to an 11.20 percent S&P 500 index return with a standard deviation of 15.64 percent. A 50 percent S&P GSCI and 50 percent S&P 500 index portfolio had a return of 12.54 percent with a standard deviation of 11.86 percent during the period, an increase in return and a decrease in standard deviation relative to the S&P 500 index portfolio. However, Erb and Harvey find that on an historical excess return basis, commodity returns are roughly zero, indicating that the often touted "equity-like returns" to commodities is incorrect. The *diversification return* is an incremental return that results from rebalancing a portfolio. The authors find that commodities may provide equity-like returns if investors can earn a high enough diversification return or if the portfolio is skewed toward individual commodities that are expected to have considerably positive roll or spot returns in the future. Even when the volatility of assets is high, if the correlations between them are low enough, investors can earn a substantial diversification return derived from rebalancing the portfolio. Willenbrock (2011) contends that the diversification returns result not from a reduction in variance, as most studies suggest, but from rebalancing.

Gorton and Rouwenhorst (2006a) use an equally-weighted index of commodity futures monthly returns between July 1959 and March 2004 to examine whether commodity futures act as a hedge against inflation. The authors discover that commodity futures are positively correlated with inflation. They find that commodity futures are negatively correlated with stocks and bonds. The conclusion, consistent with much of the earlier research on the characteristics of commodity returns including the Erb and Harvey (2006) study, is that commodity futures benefit traditional portfolios, providing desirable risk-return benefits.

Gorton and Rouwenhorst (2006b) assert that the diversification return is a mathematical property of the geometric average. The geometric average of the returns of the underlying assets in a portfolio will be, unless the assets are perfectly positively correlated, less than the geometric average of the portfolio returns as a whole. The authors show that the diversification return results from this mathematical property, and not, as Erb and Harvey claim, from rebalancing.

Willenbrock (2011) enters this debate about the diversification return. The author finds that the diversification return is indeed a function of rebalancing. He shows that rebalancing forces investors to sell appreciated assets and buy assets that have depreciated in order to bring the portfolio back to its prescribed weights. This strategy is contrarian in nature according to Willenbrock because the investor increases (decreases) the allocation to assets that have decreased (increased) in value. This "buying low, selling high" strategy results in a positive return, one that is often ascribed to lower variance (Erb and Harvey 2006) or to the mathematical property of geometric returns (Gorton and Rouwenhorst 2006b). According to Willenbrock, reduced variance is necessary, but not sufficient, to earn a diversification return. The author also shows the return on a buy-and-hold strategy results from the weights on assets that have performed well increase. However, unlike the risk profile of a rebalanced portfolio that is constant, a buy-and-hold strategy changes the portfolio's risk profile. Willenbrock solves the return puzzle, showing that the Gorton and Rouwenhorst (2006a) commodities portfolio earns a positive diversification return if rebalanced, and a buy-and-hold return, as described, if not. He maintains that no contradiction exists and that the Gorton and Rouwenhorst portfolio earns excess returns under both conditions but for different reasons.

Following this line of research about rebalancing to earn a diversification return, Sanders and Irwin (2012) contend that roll yields are irrelevant to long-only futures returns. The authors demonstrate that two assets with a zero percent geometric return over 10 periods can be combined into an equally-weighted portfolio that earns a diversification return of 4 percent, if rebalanced each period.

In relation to the findings of the Satyanarayan and Varangis (1994), Smimou (2010) notes that early research such as that conducted by Bodie and Rosansky (1980), Satyanarayan and Varangis (1994), Anson (1998), and Gorton and Rouwenhorst (2006a) relies on published commodity indexes such as the S&P GSCI or on equally-weighted benchmark portfolios, and largely ignores the effects of individual commodity futures. He contends that studies on the benefits of holding commodities and on the benefits of international diversification should consider diversifying with international agricultural commodity futures. Siminou examines the period January 1985 to February 2007 to avoid discontinuities in commodity futures and computes the returns based on a buy-and-hold strategy. The author finds substantial benefits are available to U.S. investors from holding international agricultural commodity futures contracts. The benefits stem from the size of the negative correlation coefficients. He asserts that U.S. investors can improve portfolio performance by adding an allocation to foreign agricultural commodity futures.

Gorton, Hayashi, and Rouwenhorst (2012) examine commodity risk premiums in commodity futures contracts. The authors use a large data set of 31 commodity futures and commodity inventories (i.e., physical inventories) between 1971 and 2010. They find that commodity risk premiums are largely dependent on storage levels. Risk premiums vary across the type of commodity and across time. According to the study, investors can use spot returns, the volatilities of spot returns, historical futures returns, and the futures basis to discover commodity futures risk premiums. These data incorporate inventory levels that impact returns and risk premiums.

More than three decades after Greer's seminal work on the role of commodities as an inflation hedge, Fulli-Lemaire (2013), contributes to this body of work by reexamining the issue. He contends that two basic, but compelling, reasons explain why people invest in commodities. First, commodities have earned sound nominal returns and have enhanced risk-adjusted returns because of low or negative correlation with traditional assets. Second, he posits, like many before him, that commodities offer the possibility of an inflation hedge. He points out, however, that commodities are cyclical and may suffer sharp declines, as they did following the financial crisis of 2007–2008. As such, Fulli-Lemaire maintains that the decision to include commodities in a portfolio is not trivial and must be broached with caution. He also maintains that commodity price shocks no longer pass through to the core inflation rate. Because of these fundamental macro changes, he contends that investors should use forecasted core inflation data to determine an ex ante strategic allocation to commodities. Because core inflation risk is now small according to the author, it should be left unhedged. Fulli-Lemaire also builds an indicator that is a function of the spread between core and headline inflation and uses it to define a dynamic commodity allocation rule.

Erb and Harvey (2016) revisit their earlier work on commodities to see if the results still hold. They analyze commodity futures return data between December 2004 and June 2015. They find a -4.6 percent return per year during the period, lower than the S&P 500 index return of 7.4 percent and the Barclays US Aggregate Bond Index return of 4.5 percent. The authors blame the poor returns on low income returns, the roll yield plus collateral returns, which they liken to the dividend yield or bond yield on a traditional asset. These periods of low income returns can last for long periods, such as 10 years or more. Erb and Harvey contend that investors searching for a "safe" return from investing in commodity futures may not realize the expected return.

In contrast to Erb and Harvey (2016), Bhardwaj, Gorton, and Rouwenhorst (2015), reviewing their 2006 results, find that their positive findings on commodity returns from 2006 still largely hold. They extend the original July 1959 to December

2004 period to December 2014 in the more recent study. The authors note that while short, the additional 10-year period is rich with economic diversity, including a U.S. housing boom followed by the largest financial crisis since the Great Depression, and a global economic expansion led by China. The authors find a 3.7 percent average annual risk premium to commodity futures over the new period, comparable to the long-term average (5.23 percent between 1959 and 2004). Lower collateral returns resulting from a period of low interest rates contributed markedly to the decline. Bhardwaj et al. find that correlation with traditional assets increases during periods of financial distress, as in the financial crisis of 2007-2008.

Gray (2016) suggests that the differences between the conclusions of the studies by Bhardwaj et al. (2015) and Erb and Harvey (2016) regarding commodity futures returns lie in the methodologies. Erb and Harvey examine indexes weighted by trading volume or macroeconomic factors, which results in evidence skewed by the experience of energy futures, particularly oil futures. Bhardwaj et al. minimize the influence of a single sector by examining equally-weighted commodity futures indexes. Using equally-weighted versus volume-weighted indexes leads to very different results, as evidenced by the two studies.

Main, Irwin, Sanders, and Smith (2016) try to explain the poor performance of commodities since the heyday of the mid-2000s. They suggest that conclusions in many influential academic studies about commodity futures returns (Erb and Harvey 2006; Gorton and Rouwenhorst 2006a) contributed to the increase in the allocation to commodities in mainstream investment portfolios. Since the mid-2000s, however, commodities have generally performed poorly. The authors suggest that roll yields, as described in the literature, are a fallacy because of an "apples to oranges" comparison problem. The spot price–futures price comparison is not an apple-to-apple comparison because futures investors neither hold the physical commodity nor bear the storage cost. Main et al. find that generally idiosyncratic shifts in the supply and demand of commodities primarily drive returns. They suggest that investors can earn returns taking long positions in low-storage-cost commodities and short positions in high-storage-cost commodities.

Finally, in an extremely long-term look at commodity futures, Levine, Ooi, and Richardson (2016) examine commodity futures returns dating back to 1877. They find that on average commodity returns have been positive. During the long history, commodity returns varied significantly based on inflation, business cycles, and periods of contango versus backwardation. The authors also find that returns are tied to the underlying physical commodities in that spot returns largely drive futures returns over time. Levine et al. also find, in support of much of the earlier research, that returns have low correlation with stock and bond returns and perform well during periods of higher inflation.

Summary and Conclusions

Much interest exists in allocating a portion of a diversified portfolio to commodities. Commodities, like other alternative assets, increased proportionally in the portfolios of institutional investors in recent years. Since record prices in the 2000s and a spate of influential research touting their advantages in the mid-2000s such as Erb and Harvey (2006) and Gorton and Rouwenhorst (2006a), commodities have become commonplace, especially in the portfolios of institutional investors but also to some degree in the portfolios of retail investors. According to Kat (2006), institutions invested more than $75 billion in commodities in the mid-2000s. A Barclay's survey also suggests that institutions intended to substantially increase their exposures to commodities in the latter half of the 2000s. Kat notes an explosion in growth in China as support on the demand side, underinvestment by commodity producers resulting in shortages on the supply side, and research, such as Gorton and Rouwenhorst's (2006a), as fodder for the increased interest and investment. Commodity-linked funds, ETFs, trackers, and other structured products expanded to meet investor demands.

Proponents have praised commodities for their role in portfolios for primarily three reasons. First, studies such as Gorton and Rouwenhorst (2006a) find that commodities have earned equity-like returns with volatility comparable to equities. Second, studies, including that by Gorton and Rouwenhorst, find that commodity returns are negatively correlated with stock and bond returns. Finally, empirical evidence shows that commodity futures are positively correlated with inflation. All of these characteristics make commodities an ideal diversifier in a traditional portfolio of stocks and bonds.

Debate in the literature still exists about the true source of commodity returns. The collateral yield, roll yield, and spot return are all, to varying degrees, given credit for the performance of commodity futures in various studies. However, since the financial crisis of 2007-2008, commodities have generally performed poorly, inciting another round of academic studies aimed at determining if commodities are indeed useful in terms of returns and properties that make them good diversifiers in portfolios of traditional assets. By late 2015 and into 2016, many in the popular press and writing for investment blogs were arguing that investors should again consider commodities, that they had reached their low point and could only go up (Treadgold 2015). But recent academic research by Erb and Harvey (2016) concludes that commodities earned a negative return since 2004. In contrast, Bhardwaj et al. (2015) reexamine commodity returns, including additional data from year-end 2004 through December 2014, updating their initial study, and find their original results largely hold true. Investors who examine research on the return characteristics and performance of commodities can find support for either allocating to commodities or forgoing commodities in diversified portfolios. Given no clear-cut case for or against them, the answer to whether investors should add commodities to a portfolio is "it depends."

Discussion Questions

1. Explain the primary disadvantage of owning physical commodities.
2. Explain the concept of a convenience yield.
3. Describe three sources of commodity futures returns.
4. Describe three advantages of adding commodities to a diversified portfolio.

References

Anson, Mark J. P. 1998. “Spot Returns, Roll Yield, and Diversification with Commodity Futures.” *Journal of Alternative Investments* 1:3, 16–32.

Babcock, Bruce. 2016. “Commodity Futures Trading for Beginners.” Reality Based Trading Company. Available at http://www.rb-trading.com/begin4.html.

Bhardwaj, Geetesh, Gary B. Gorton, and K. Geert Rouwenhorst. 2015. “Facts and Fantasies about Commodity Futures Ten Years Later.” Available at http://faculty.som.yale.edu/garygorton/documents/FactsandFantasiesaboutCommodity.pdf.

Bjornson, Bruce, and Colin A. Carter. 1997. “New Evidence on Agricultural Commodity Return Performance under Time Varying Risk.” *Journal of Agricultural Economics* 79:3, 918–930.

Bodie, Zvi. 1983. “Commodity Futures as a Hedge against Inflation.” *Journal of Portfolio Management* 9:3, 12–17.

Bodie, Zvi, and Victor I. Rosansky. 1980. “Risk and Return in Commodity Futures.” *Financial Analysts Journal* 36:3, 27–39.

Brennan, Michael J. 1958. “The Supply of Storage.” *American Economic Review* 48:1, 50–72.

Christopher, Ben. 2016. “How the Hunt Brothers Cornered the Silver Market Then Lost It All.” *Priceonomics*. Available at https://priceonomics.com/how-the-hunt-brothers-cornered-the-silver-market/.

Erb, Claude B., and Campbell R. Harvey. 2006. “The Strategic and Tactical Value of Commodity Futures.” *Financial Analysts Journal* 62:2, 69–97.

Erb, Claude B., and Campbell R. Harvey. 2016. “Conquering Misperceptions about Commodity Futures Investing.” *Financial Analysts Journal* 72:4, 26–35.

Fama, Eugene F., and Kenneth R. French. 1988. “Business Cycles and the Behavior of Metals Prices.” *Journal of Finance* 43:5, 1075–1093.

Froot, Kenneth A. 1995. “Hedging Portfolios with Real Assets: Which Real Assets Can Help Protect Financial Portfolios?” *Journal of Portfolio Management* 21:4, 60–77.

Fulli-Lemaire, Nicolas. 2013. “An Inflation Hedging Strategy with Commodities: A Core Driven Global Macro.” *Journal of Investment Strategies* 2:3, 23–50.

Gorton, Gary B., and K. Geert Rouwenhorst. 2006a. “Facts and Fantasies about Commodities Futures.” *Financial Analysts Journal* 62:2, 47–68.

Gorton, Gary B., and K. Geert Rouwenhorst. 2006b. “A Note on Erb and Harvey.” Yale ICF Working Paper No. 06-02. Available at http://papers.ssrn.com/sol3/papers.cfm?abstract id=869064.

Gorton, Gary B., Fumio Hayashi, and K. Geert Rouwenhorst. 2012. “The Fundamentals of Commodity Futures Returns.” *Review of Finance* 17:1, 35–105.

Gray, Wesley R. 2016. “Commodity Futures Investing: Complex and Unique.” Alpha Architect. Available at http://blog.alphaarchitect.com/2016/12/21/commodity-investing-is-complex-and-volatile-but-unique/#gs.7w7GCHI.

Greer, Robert J. 1978. “Conservative Commodities: A Key Inflation Hedge.” *Journal of Portfolio Management* 4:4, 26–29.

Greer, Robert J. 2000. “The Nature of Commodity Index Returns.” *Journal of Alternative Investments* 3:1, 45–53.

Halpern, Philip, and Randy Warsager. 1998. “The Performance of Energy and Non-energy Based Commodity Investment Vehicles in Periods of Inflation.” *Journal of Alternative Investments* 1:1, 75–81.

Idzorek, Thomas M. 2006. “Strategic Asset Allocation and Commodities.” Chicago, IL. Ibbotson Associates, commissioned by PIMCO, March 27.

Jensen, Gerald R., Robert R. Johnson, and Jeffrey M. Mercer. 2000. “Efficient Use of Commodity Futures in Diversified Portfolios.” *Journal of Futures Markets* 20:5, 489–506.

Kaldor, Nicholas. 1939. “Speculation and Economic Stability.” *Review of Economic Studies* 7:1, 1–27.

Kat, Harry M. 2006. "Is the Case for Investing in Commodities Really That Obvious?" Eurekahedge. Available at http://www.eurekahedge.com/NewsAndEvents/News/883/Is_the_Case_for_Investing_in_Commodities_Really_that_Obvious.

Keynes, John M. 1930. *A Treatise on Money*. London: Macmillan.

Kolb, Robert W. 1992. "Is Normal Backwardation Normal?" *Journal of Futures Markets* 12:1, 75–90.

Kolb, Robert W. 1996. "The Systematic Risk of Futures Markets." *Journal of Futures Markets* 16:6, 631–634.

Levine, Ari, Yao Hua Ooi, and Matthew P. Richardson. 2016. "Commodities for the Long Run." Available at https://papers.ssrn.com/sol3/papers.cfm?abstract_id=2856435.

Main, Scott, Scott H. Irwin, Dwight R. Sanders, and Aaron D. Smith. 2016. "How Could We Have Been So Wrong? The Puzzle of Disappointing Returns to Commodity Investments." Available at http://www.farmdoc.illinois.edu/irwin/research/Main_Irwin_Sanders_Smith_JOCM.pdf.

Roy, Sumit. 2016. "Choosing the Right Commodity ETF." Available at http://www.etf.com/sections/fund-flows/choosing-right-commodity-etf?qt-etf_related_articles=0.

S&P GSCI Components and Weights. 2017. Available at http://www.goldmansachs.com/what-we-do/securities/products-and-business-groups/products/gsci/components-weights-index-levels.html.

Sanders, Dwight R., and Scott H. Irwin. 2012. "A Reappraisal of Investing in Commodity Futures Markets." *Applied Economic Perspectives* 34:3, 515-530.

Satyanarayan, Sudhakar, and Panos Varangis. 1994. "An Efficient Frontier for International Portfolios with Commodity Assets." Policy Research Working Paper 1266, World Bank, International Economics Department, International Trade Division. Available at https://ideas.repec.org/p/wbk/wbrwps/1266.html.

Smimou, Kamal, 2010. "Stock Market and Agricultural Futures Diversification: An International Perspective." *Journal of Alternative Investments* 12:4, 36–57.

Stockton, Kimberly A. 2007. "Understanding Alternative Investments: The Role of Commodities in a Portfolio." Available at http://www.vanguard.com/pdf/s552.pdf?221002207.

Telser, Lester G. 1958. "Futures Trading and the Storage of Cotton and Wheat." *Journal of Political Economy* 66:3, 233–255.

Till, Hillary, and Joseph Eagleeye. 2003. "The Risks of Commodity Investing." In Lars Jaeger (ed.), *The New Generation of Risk Management for Hedge Fund and Private Equity Investment*. London: Euromoney Books. Available at http://www.premiacap.com/publications/EB_091004.pdf.

Till, Hilary, and Joseph Eagleeye. 2005. "Understanding Managed Futures." Available at http://dx.doi.org/10.2139/ssrn.2628543.

Treadgold, Tim. 2015. "After the Crash, the First Signs of a Commodity-Market Recovery Are Emerging." *Forbes*. Available at https://www.forbes.com/sites/timtreadgold/2015/12/23/after-the-crash-the-first-signs-of-a-commodity-market-recovery-are-emerging/#18b3462318b3.

Willenbrock, Scott. 2011. "Diversification Return, Portfolio Rebalancing, and the Commodity Return Puzzle." *Financial Analysts Journal* 67:4, 42–49.

Working, Holbrook. 1948. "Theory of the Inverse Carrying Charge in Futures Markets." *Journal of Farm Economics* 30:1, 1–27.

Working, Holbrook. 1949. "The Theory of the Price of Storage." *American Economic Review* 39:6, 1254-1262.

World Bank Group. 2016. "Commodity Markets Outlook, April." Washington, DC: World Bank. Available at http://pubdocs.worldbank.org/en/677121461693540498/CMO-April-2016-Full-Report.pdf.

17

Issues in Benchmarking Commodity Performance

AARON FILBECK, CFA, CAIA
Investment Analyst, The Joseph Group Capital Management

Introduction

As investors look for diversification opportunities while maintaining return expectations, many have turned to alternative asset classes such as commodity investments. Commodity investments have historically held a strong relation with economic activity, with supply and demand driving price movements. Commodity sectors have also exhibited lower correlations to one another. This relation is a stark contrast to relations between traditional asset classes such as equities or fixed income, which tend to exhibit high cross-sectional correlations. These factors have allowed commodities to provide diversification benefits relative to other traditional asset classes (Whitton, Thuerbach, and Botting 2015).

Historically, commodity prices have exhibited a positive correlation with inflation. As inflation increases, commodity spot prices have typically moved upward as prices reflect the changes in the consumer price index (CPI). As Stockton (2007) notes, sources of commodity returns in futures markets come from collateral, spot, and roll returns. *Collateral returns* are the returns on the collateral investors post on margin in order to purchase futures contracts. Collateral typically includes U.S. Treasuries or investment grade bonds. *Spot returns* are the change in the current price of commodities. Over the long term, commodity spot returns have not deviated substantially from inflation, so any excess return comes from roll returns. *Roll returns* are the returns that result from closing out futures contracts and initiating others. They provide the active manager or commodity index with a positive or negative excess return to the spot and collateral returns of a futures contract.

Although investors can physically buy and sell commodities, trading commodity investments typically occurs via futures contracts listed on exchanges. Futures markets allow market participants to buy ("go long") and sell ("short") contracts on future commodity prices, or "lock in" a pre-specified price by which they agree to buy or sell the underlying commodity at the expiration of the contract. Typically, these contracts do not result in physical delivery of an asset, but instead a cash exchange takes place. Futures market participants comprise two broad categories: hedgers and speculators. *Hedgers* are those participating in futures markets such as farmers, companies, or product producers to lock in future commodity prices in order to solidify costs or revenues depending on the trade. Speculators represent everyone else. Speculators take large risks, especially with respect to anticipating future price movements hoping to make quick, large gains. They do not intend to take physical possession of the underlying commodity. Thus, speculators are market participants who take the other side of a hedger's trade and speculate on commodity prices, or simply try to gain exposure to the asset class as a whole.

Many ways exist to gain exposure to commodity investments. The original form of "active management" within this asset class came from commercial trading. Participants actively managing in the commodity markets benefited from physically possessing commodities or wanted to hedge the price of a future sale. From 2003 to 2008, passive commodity investments, or index funds, grew by a magnitude of about 300 percent, as institutional investors discovered the benefits of gaining exposure to the asset class (Masters 2008). A large inflow into commodity futures markets from institutional investors, such as pension funds and endowments, brought forth some of the issues that may exist with commodity index funds and benchmark construction. In fact, Masters contends that these institutional investors are a root cause of the commodity bubble and subsequent crash in the mid-2000s.

The purpose of this chapter is to introduce existing commodity indexes and to discuss some of the issues associated with index construction and performance benchmarking. Many investors may not fully grasp the complexity of the asset class, commodity futures contracts, or the underlying construction of commodity benchmarks.

The remainder of this chapter addresses key topics and problems associated with commodity investments and the implications these problems pose for traditional commodity indexes. The chapter also provides a conceptual review of the differences between the three generations of commodity indexes and offers specific examples and detailed comparisons between them. Although every index operates differently, the way in which each index approaches exposure with futures markets term structure sets the generations apart. The chapter then offers a discussion of the issues that surround benchmarking commodity performance on a relative or absolute basis. The chapter addresses contradictions with modern portfolio theory (MPT) as well as commodity financialization, co-integration with public equity markets, and questions the true "passiveness" of commodity indexes. Each section provides a literature review, taking into account some of common views within each topic. The final section offers a summary and conclusions.

Generations of Commodity Benchmarks

Gaining investment exposure to commodities as an asset class can be as simple as tracking an index. However, three different classifications, or generations, of commodity indexes currently exist for reporting performance. The nature of their construction (passive or active) based on term structures in contango or backwardation distinguish the indexes within these categories. A term structure in *contango* means that the futures curve is upward sloping, resulting in the futures price being above the current spot price. The *futures curve* is a graphic representation that plots current (spot) and expected future (futures) prices of commodity investments. A term structure is in *backwardation* when the term structure of the futures curve is downward sloping and the futures price is lower than the current spot price.

DEFINING THE THREE GENERATIONS

The construction of each generation of commodity indexes differs to account for markets in contango or backwardation, with each progressive generation becoming more active in its approach. The first generation of indexes is long only and does not account for the fundamentals of backwardation or contango. The second generation is also long only, but takes a more active approach by attempting to smooth the negative effects of contango and take advantage of backwardation. The third generation considers both long and short positions to take advantage of positive price appreciation during backwardation and negative price appreciation during contango markets, respectively.

Changes in commodity prices occur due to changes in supply or demand levels. Supply represents "what is available to everyone" or what producers provide for consumption. Demand is "what is needed by everyone," or what consumers require from production to satisfy needs. Commodity prices are in equilibrium when suppliers and consumers agree on a quantity and price goods that satisfies both parties. When either supply or demand changes drastically, price changes occur.

For example, if a frost occurs in the Midwestern part of the United States and kills corn crops in multiple cornfields, supply levels decrease accordingly. If consumer demand for corn remains constant, consumers may have difficulty buying corn and, if so, will drive corn prices higher to satisfy their demand. A farmer who owns a cornfield unaffected by the frost now holds a product that has become more valuable due to a price increase. Consumers with an unchanged demand for corn should theoretically be willing to pay a higher price to satisfy their demand, and producers now hold a more valuable commodity.

The supply and demand relation to commodity markets is what futures markets attempt to replicate, and what generations of commodity indexes attempt to exploit. The rest of the section provides examples of indexes distinctly categorized within these three generations.

FIRST GENERATION

First-generation commodity indexes have a natural long bias within their construction, and only invest in individual commodity futures contracts that are nearing expiration, otherwise known as *front-month contracts*. A *long bias* in the index means that the index follows the price of the commodity and never benefits from falling commodity prices. Miffre (2014) maintains that first-generation indexes only exist to provide investors with broad exposure to commodity markets. Two commonly used and widely recognized first-generation indexes are the Standard & Poor's Goldman Sachs Commodity Index (S&P-GSCI) and the Dow Jones-UBS Commodity Index.

The S&P-GSCI, or GSCI for short, originated in 1991 and is a global-production weighted index based on the average of the last five years of world production values and represents an unlevered, long-only basket of 24 commodities futures contracts, including six energy, eight agricultural, five industrial metals, three livestock, and two precious metals contracts (Goldman Sachs 2005). As of the annual rebalancing meeting for 2017, held by the S&P GSCI Advisory Panel on October 6, 2016, the expectation is that energy commodities will continue to make up 56 percent of the index, with WTI crude oil holding the largest weight. Additionally, seven of the 24 representative commodities hold weights of less than 1 percent each within the index allocation (Goldman Sachs 2016).

For each commodity, the index holds a front-month futures contract. A *front-month contract* is the contract that is nearest to expiration. Futures contacts require cash or physical delivery of the underlying commodity at the contract's expiration. Therefore, for an investor or index to maintain exposure required closing the existing contract and reinitiating a new one before expiration to maintain exposure, a process called "rolling." For example, if a contract's expiration is August 5, and the investor holds a long position in the contract, the investor must take an offsetting short position in the same contract and initiate a new long position in a later-date contract. This process repeats until the investor no longer wants to have exposure to the commodity. According to Feldman and Till (2006), the portfolio's rolling procedure requires each contract to be rolled to the next front-month contract one month before expiration, and the GSCI transactions take place in between the fifth and ninth business day of each month.

The other popular first-generation commodity index is the Bloomberg Commodity Index (BCOM). The index originated in 1998 and was renamed the Dow Jones-UBS Commodity Index (DJ-UBSCI) in 2009 when UBS acquired the index from AIG (Reuters 2009). Bloomberg (2014) discusses the rebranding of the index to its current name after a strategic partnership between UBS and Bloomberg, LP. The index is quantity-based, meaning it uses a fixed number of contracts for each commodity within the index allocation. Individual commodities are limited to 15 percent, and sectors to 33 percent of the index allocation. The index allocates across individual commodities and consists of seven agricultural, five energy, four industrial metals, two precious metals, and two livestock contracts. Liquidity and production weights determine commodity weights in the index. Therefore, the index tends to underweight long-term storage commodities such as precious metals.

Similar to the GSCI, investors roll BCOM contracts one month before maturity. However, the BCOM weights energy commodities less than the GSCI due to its construction. The index has historically performed best when agriculture and metals outperform or have greater backwardation than energy contracts.

SECOND GENERATION

Second-generation indexes are also long-only indexes. However, they take a slightly more active approach to mitigating the effects of rolling futures contracts in contangoed markets than first-generation indexes. Many second-generation indexes exist but differ slightly due to their construction. The UBS Bloomberg Constant Maturity

Commodity Index (CMCI) originated in 2007 with the intent to provide enhanced exposure to commodity investments, primarily by using a daily rolling mechanism and allocating commodities across various maturities on the futures curve (Business Wire 2012). According the UBS (2015), this "tenor-diversification" process serves two additional purposes in addition to commodity exposure. First, by continuously rolling small portions of the underlying futures contracts daily, the index mitigates potential roll return impact surrounding the predetermined roll schedule that is prevalent in first-generation commodity indexes. As noted in the previous section, most first-generation indexes roll their contracts within the first two weeks of each month to the next front-month contract.

Second, tenor-diversification mitigates concentration at the short end of the futures curve, and limits negative roll returns when the futures curve is in market contango. Term structures often change over time, so holding contracts across different maturities provides diversification to mitigate any drastic changes or the slope of the curve. In other words, a first-generation commodity index will always have to roll its contracts every month, meaning the index is more sensitive to term structure movements. If a commodity's term structure is in steep contango, rolling short-term contracts more often results in more consistent negative roll returns.

The Merrill Lynch Commodity Index eXtra (MLCX), released as trackable benchmark in 2006, was designed to provide investors with a highly liquid and cost-effective index for commodity investments (Business Wire 2006). Rather than hold front-month or current month contracts, the MLCX opts to hold futures contracts that expire two months out, and rolls the two-month contracts to the third month during the first 15 business days of every current month. Morrison (2006) claims the construction of the index allows for mitigation of large negative impacts from contangoed markets when first-generation indexes are buying new contracts. The construction of the index also results in having an average contract maturity that is close to one month to six weeks longer than first-generation indexes (Hougan 2006).

Another index, the Deutsche Bank Liquid Commodity Index—Optimum Yield, uses a quantitative methodology to determine the attractiveness of various commodity futures contracts. The underlying methodology analyzes each contract's rising or falling prices, and selects the contracts to initiate long positions based on various factors. One of the most important factors upon which investors base this decision is selecting contracts with minimal negative returns in contangoed markets or maximization of returns in backwardated markets. Analyzing this methodology, Skapa (2013) finds that back-tested returns, in conjunction with live returns, provide evidence that this type of index has historically produced higher returns than first-generation indexes, while maintaining a similar risk level.

THIRD GENERATION

Third-generation commodity indexes are the most recent development of index construction methodologies, taking a hybrid approach of systematic passive exposure to commodity futures contracts and active management overlays. Third-generation indexes build upon the previous generation by taking long positions in backwardated commodity markets and short positions in commodities in contangoed markets.

By design, this construction methodology provides both the risk management capabilities of second-generation indexes and additional levels of return enhancement. Return enhancements come from providing investors with the opportunity to benefit from commodities that decline in price, as well as mitigate the negative effects of passively rolling contracts in contango, which might deteriorate returns (Miffre 2014).

The UBS Bloomberg CMCI Active Index (CMCI Active) builds upon the construction methodology of its second-generation predecessor—the CMCI Index. As previously described, the CMCI uses a continuous rolling pattern and maturity, or tenor, diversification methodology. These two factors remain in place, but now with additional enhancements. The CMCI Active introduces an active management overlay to its construction. According to UBS (2011), the CMCI Index uses a research team of analysts who are involved in making a combination of strategic and tactical decisions at allocation, component, tenor, and sector levels. The bases of these decisions stem from the fundamental research of the team members that allow the index to blend a mix of passive and active management.

The SummerHaven Dynamic Commodity Index (SDCI) debuted in 2010. The index is rebalanced monthly, selecting 14 commodities contracts from a universe of 27 contracts using a three-step process. The first step is to select the seven commodities with the greatest backwardation, or smallest contango. Of the remaining 20 contracts, the other seven contracts represent those contracts with the greatest price momentum during the previous 12 months. The final step of the process is contract selection. For the 14 commodities represented, the index selects the individual contract with the largest backwardation or smallest contango. Each contract does not have a limit on the length of the contract, as long as the contract does not expire in the subsequent month before rebalancing.

According to the SDCI (2016), the index methodology requires that the index represent each of the six commodity sectors. If a commodity sector lacks representation, a substitution occurs for the commodity with the highest price momentum within the omitted sector. The substituted commodity has the lowest price momentum among the seven momentum commodities.

Issues Surrounding Commodity Benchmarking

Distinct differences exist among the three generations of commodity indexes. The differences in weighting methodology, long and short exposure, and rolling procedures can introduce inefficiencies and biases into passive investment vehicles such as index mutual funds and exchange-traded funds (ETFs), as well as return benchmarking. This section discusses common issues associated with major commodity indexes, such as using them to benchmark performance for the asset class as a whole.

MODERN PORTFOLIO THEORY AND VALUATION

Markowitz (1952) introduces the concept of modern portfolio theory (MPT), which has served as a foundation for modern-day portfolio management. The theory uses a mean-variance optimization approach that attempts to maximize portfolio returns for each possible level of portfolio risk, measured by variance. Investors typically plot the mean-variance combinations along a graph that represents the "efficient frontier." Markowitz relies on the idea that risk and return are positively related, and investors who want to achieve greater expected returns must take on more risk. Investors achieve mean-variance optimization by combining assets or asset classes with less than perfect correlations to one another, which might lead to risk or volatility levels not mattering as much as correlations leading to decreases in total portfolio risk (Dubois 2013).

Distinguishing between financial and real assets becomes important when performing valuation methodologies to determine asset values. According to Skapa (2013), financial assets represent a residual claim to a company's assets, whereas real assets can be consumed or transformed. This distinction becomes important because the approach in valuing both types of assets differs.

One of the most universally known and accepted ways of valuing equity securities is the capital asset pricing model (CAPM). Under this model, a stock's source of return comes from the risk-free rate and a risk premium. The risk premium is the product of the excess return of the market above the risk-free rate, otherwise known as the *market risk premium*, and the company's beta, as a measure of systematic risk (Sharpe 1964). The CAPM generally does not apply to real assets or commodity investments. Most commodity investments do not raise capital or distribute cash flows. Additionally, commodities are consumed or transformed and do not act as a residual claim toward a particular asset. As a result, commodities are heavily dependent on supply and demand characteristics. Empirical research reports that an equally weighted, non-rebalanced portfolio basket of commodities results in an excess return over the risk-free rate of zero (Erb and Harvey 2006). This finding indicates that a traditional valuation methodology holds little explanatory power and is inappropriate for commodity investments.

An individual or a company may hold physical commodities as an asset, either because it provides value in its current state or as an input to produce something that holds value to that entity. Using a simple example, oil as a physical commodity has many uses, such as producing gasoline, which holds value to consumers. Depending on the person or company, holding a barrel of oil has two sources of value: the value of owning and potentially selling it or transforming it into gasoline. These multiple sources of value imply that the value of a barrel of oil can be determined by finding the price at which the seller is willing to part with it and the buyer is willing to pay for it. If either the buyer or the seller demands a price that is outside of equilibrium, the transaction should theoretically not take place if the participants are rational.

ELECTRONIC TRADING AND "FINANCIALIZATION"

Due to the presence of commodity index funds and other passive investment vehicles, Irwin and Sanders (2012) observed that correlations between commodity and capital markets increased in the latter half of the 2000s. The observation could suggest that commodity prices do not have the same fundamental drivers as they once did. Monetary flows in and out of commodity futures markets could also drive commodity prices. If this supposition were true, the diversification benefits and fundamental hedges provided by commodities would no longer be as strong or certain as previously.

According to Masters (2008), the dollar amount of assets allocated to passive commodity index funds was approximately $13 billion in 2003. By the end of 2008, that number rose to about $200 billion in long positions on commodity indexes (Chilton 2011). The financial crisis of 2007–2008 produced a large sell-off in commodities, prompting questions about whether this sell-off was due to fundamental shifts, or the possibility of an asset bubble due to investor speculation. Supporting the idea that investors have increasingly become responsible for these asset price bubbles, Masters, testifying before the US. Senate Committee on Homeland Security and Governmental Affairs, states that he believed institutional investor speculation was a driver of commodity price inflation.

Chilton (2011) also references to institutional investors as "index speculators," which differentiated them from typical speculators. *Index speculation* involves buying index funds of popular commodity indexes, effectively allocating dollars to every single commodity type in the index. This strategy differed from that of typical speculators, who buy and sell as counterparties on individual contracts for hedgers and producers. All else equal, by purchasing the entire index, all commodity prices should theoretically increase, despite underlying fundamental drivers. By 2008, institutional investors had become the largest speculators in the commodity futures markets (Masters 2008). In his testimony, Masters describes this shift as a demand shock, stating that supply characteristics remained constant from 2003 to 2008, yet commodity prices had increased in multiples without much change in consumer demand. Masters notes that by allocating capital to commodity markets as a strategic piece of their asset allocation, index speculators can effectively ignore commodity prices and supply and demand characteristics in favor of having exposure to the asset class. Although allocating to index funds may be more widely accepted in public equity markets, commodity prices tend to have an immediate effect on the economy. For example, rising gas prices may have an adverse effect on consumer spending, even if no fundamental reason exists for the price increase.

Irwin and Sanders (2012) test what they deem "Masters' hypothesis." Brunnermeier (2008) defines the occurrence of an *asset bubble* as when asset prices rise above their fundamental value due to the irrational behavior of investors and their belief that they can buy the asset now and sell it later for a higher price. Many academic researchers empirically question Masters's (2008) claims. This section later examines some of these arguments.

Irwin and Sanders (2012) examine the relation among futures contracts, index funds, and commodity markets. They study Masters's arguments, attempting to confirm or refute his assertions and to determine if a bubble occurred in the commodity markets during the financial crisis of 2007–2008. Irwin and Sanders find no evidence of a linkage between commodity index performance and bubble-like characteristics. Throughout, they emphasize that the methodology Masters uses for making such claims has too many errors and omissions for it to be reliable, despite assertions that commodity markets were not fully integrated with financial markets until investors began using passive investment vehicles, such as index funds. Therefore, Irwin and Sanders claim that commodity index funds may reflect economic shocks more efficiently than before, potentially due to lesser constraints on liquidity. Movements from peak to trough could be more indicative of a normal commodity cycle and are not necessarily indicative of irrational investor behavior.

Hamilton (2008) examines Masters's argument as well, and comes to the same conclusion that a relationship does not exist between bubble-like characteristics and commodity prices. Hamilton argues that the price elasticity for commodities creates a limit on how much commodity prices can increase in the long term. This limit occurs because many commodities have physical producers and consumers, which indicates the presence of a supply and demand relation. He uses crude oil as an example: if crude oil prices increase, less benefit exists for consumption and a higher benefit to produce. Overproduction will occur, which will force prices back down to an equilibrium price. While short-term fluctuations can cause futures prices to suddenly increase, he argues it is unsustainable over the long-term.

Another structural change in commodity markets has been the increase in electronic trading over the past decade. Electronic trading in commodity markets once accounted for less than 10 percent of volume in traditional commodity markets in the early 2000s, in favor of the "open outcry" system. The "open outcry" system is a 150-year-old trading mechanism that involves financial professionals trading stocks, bonds, and futures contracts. Traders placed trades by shouting or using hand signals in "the pit" of an exchange to determine buy and sell order pricing. The purpose of this system was to allow for "price discovery" of the price that the market participants were willing to pay to own an asset. Given technological advancements since the early 2000s, this system of trading dwindled in favor of electronic access trading and more efficient price discovery (Irwin and Sanders 2012).

According to Irwin and Sanders (2012), the surge in electronic trading leads to increased market efficiency due to lower transaction costs and access to information. Conversely, Zaremba (2016) contends that electronic trading has invited noncommercial traders and market speculators to participate in commodity markets due to lower barriers to entry, thereby stimulating a structural change in market participant demographics. This specific change, called *financialization,* describes a growing presence and reliance on financial professionals in a market. The proportion of noncommercial traders, or speculators, holding commodity futures contracts increased from 23 percent in 1986 to 45 percent in 2013 (Zaremba 2016).

The increased participation of speculators presents a dilemma: Do commodity markets in their current electronic form truly reflect a fundamental environment or investor speculation? Zaremba (2016) tests this theory by observing cross-sectional data of 26 commodities between 1987 and 2013, constructing back-tested hypothetical commodity strategies, to determine the effect of financialization during this period. He constructed the back-tested strategies to replicate long and short portfolios that followed term-structure and momentum-based commodity strategies over periods in which different levels of financialization might exist. In short, the test analyzes performance during a period where financialization is high, and then removes the effect of noncommercial traders' presence in the market to see the effect on returns.

Zaremba (2016) concludes that highly financialized markets produce lower excess returns, lower standard deviations, and more negative skewness than the same strategies implemented in non-financialized markets. In other words, the presence of noncommercial traders in these observations led to lowered volatility at the expense of lower excess returns and negative drawdown events. The result was similar to the term structure spread or momentum strategies, but only statistically significant in the nearest to second nearest term structure rolling strategy. Although the results told a similar story, momentum strategies lacked statistical significance.

Irwin and Sanders (2012) and Zaremba (2016) provide thorough evidentiary support for their claims on reasons for or against changes in commodity markets. However, the important part about these multiple arguments is not that commodity benchmarks and futures markets may or may not truly represent performance. Instead, additional factors and alternative underlying characteristics, such as institutional investor behavior and continued ease of trading, could affect performance.

The increased use of electronic trading, which lowered barriers to entry into these markets, led to more speculators gaining access to these commodity markets. The argument becomes whether increased presence has led to greater market efficiency or irrational investor behavior. On one side of the argument, ease of access and more sophisticated, electronic trading platforms can lead to better price discovery and lower trading costs can lead quicker reaction to new information (Irwin and Sanders 2012). Conversely, ease of access could lead to an increase in less sophisticated investors and speculators alike, which could lead to an increase in irrational decision-making (Zaremba 2016). When using commodity indexes as a way to benchmark performance, investors should understand these arguments and their effect on asset prices.

CO-INTEGRATION WITH EQUITY MARKETS

With any increase in noncommercial trading and speculation, questions surround co-integration and increased correlations between traditional asset classes, such as publicly traded equity markets and commodity markets. *Co-integration* is the statistical relation between asset price movements over time. The key differentiator between co-integration and correlation is the type of relation between the two asset prices. The prices of two correlated assets move in similar patterns over time. For example, if Stock A's price declines over a specific period and Stock B's price has a high correlation with Stock A's price, then Stock B's price will also decline during the same period. Co-integration involves the association between two assets. Even if two assets have low correlations to one another, they may move similarly or be driven by similar fundamental factors over a specific period.

Büyükşahin, Haigh, and Robe (2010) analyze weekly correlations between the Dow Jones Industrial Average Index (DJIA), the Standard & Poor's 500 Index (S&P 500), S&P-GSCI, and DJ-UBSCI between 1991 and 2008. They discover both commodity indexes' mean returns exhibited low to negative correlations to both equity indexes over multiple periods leading up to late 2008. The authors divide their co-movement analysis into three periods to see if any co-movement divergence occurred in times of extreme market movements. The cross-sectional correlations remained relative stable over various market cycles. They compared co-movements occurring between both June 2003 and May 2008 and June 2003 and November 2008, where June 2003 marked the starting period where the authors claimed many noncommercial and institutional investors began allocating to commodity investments as a strategic piece of their portfolio.

The co-movement results leading up to May 2008 showed that the presence of these investors did not change the statistical relation between equity and commodity markets. However, when they extended the sample period to include the months leading up to November 2008, the total relation increased noticeably. In the fall of 2008, correlations between the two commodity and equity indexes rose dramatically as the financial crisis of 2007–2008 began and equity markets fell. This rise suggests that electronically traded commodity markets cannot provide proper diversification benefits when investors need these benefits the most. Thus, index performance may deviate from true fundamentals in favor of investor behavior during times of extreme market events. Therefore, analysts must consider using statistical techniques such as co-integration or conditional correlation.

From 2009 onward, the linkage and correlation between commodity prices and equity markets have increased, beyond that discovered by Büyükşahin et al. (2010). Kawamoto, Morishita, and Higashi (2011) decompose multiple cross-sectional drivers of commodity price levels between 2006 and 2010, studying investor flows, stock prices, industrial production, and monetary policy as potential drivers of commodity price levels. Their results show that these factors rotate as contributors to commodity prices but primary drivers rotate depending on the environment. They conclude that the empirical evidence confirms the rotational nature of the association between these factors and commodity prices. In particular, the data support that a completely different dominant factor drove commodity price booms between both January 2007 and June 2008 and January 2009 and January 2011. Investor flows from securitized assets into commodity prices, termed as a "flight to simplicity," primarily drove the commodity boom of 2007-2008. The rise in commodity prices between 2009 and 2011 resulted from a combination of current and continued anticipated accommodative monetary policy, and a change in production levels led by emerging countries.

Between 2006 and 2011, institutional investors continued to increase commodity allocations within portfolios. The shift in investors viewing commodities as an asset class rather than a consumable good led to decreased impacts of fundamental supply and demand shocks on commodity prices over this same period. By 2011, commodity price movements tracked traditional asset classes closer than the price movements of commodities as consumption goods (Kawamoto et al. 2011).

PASSIVE INDEXES OR ACTIVE STRATEGIES?

As noted in previous sections, commodity indexes differ by generation and within generations. To use a commodity index as a performance benchmark, investors must be aware of whether the index represents the commodity constituents or the allocation of the underlying futures contracts. As an example, the GSCI and DJ-UBSCI are both popular first-generation commodity indexes but with different index weighting rules. The GSCI has historically had a much higher allocation to energy commodities such as oil, while the DJ-UBSCI has a maximum limit of 33 percent to any sector. Although both have exposure to similar commodity baskets, energy prices should primarily dictate GSCI performance. Additionally, roll schedule differences affect performance. A publicly traded equity index undergoes rebalancing, but the underlying securities do not undergo expiration the same way futures contracts do.

Because of the major differences between publicly traded equity indexes and commodity indexes, as well as the differences in how commodity indexes are constructed, tangible implications exist for commodity performance benchmarking. Regarding commodity performance, Erb and Harvey (2006) find that the mean return of the average commodity futures contract was not statistically significant from zero, but a rebalanced and equally weighted portfolio produced a return that was statistically greater than zero. They conclude that the geometric return of a rebalanced portfolio exceeded the weighted average return of its constituents, if the constituents had low correlations to one another and high average standard deviations.

When observing the historical return streams of the GSCI, DJ-UBSCI, and the Reuters-CRB Futures Price Trade Index (CRB) between 1994 and 2001, all three indexes produced different mean returns and standard deviations due to the weighting and constituents within each index. The mean return of the GSCI was the highest, accompanied by the highest volatility over the period, while the CRB produced the lowest return with the lowest volatility. This dispersion or returns over the observed time period was due to being overweight commodities that performed well and underweight those that did not. As noted previously, GSCI has a much higher allocation to energy commodities, whereas the DJ-UBSCI and CRB offer a more balanced representation of commodity investments. Because rolling patterns are similar among the three first-generation indexes, the differences in return and standard deviation resulted from differences in allocation weightings. This finding means the effect of the individual commodity contracts becomes more prevalent in overall index performance, and index performance could have an implicit bias toward one commodity group over another.

Erb and Harvey (2006) take this idea a step further and assert that no true index exists in commodity investments. They describe current benchmarks as strategies rather than true passive benchmarks. Theoretically, this classification is because investors take offsetting long and short positions against one another in commodity markets, effectively taking the overall market exposure or "capitalization" to zero. Unlike a publicly traded equity or bond index, which may weight index constituents by market capitalization, commodities do not actually have a market capitalization due to the netting principles of futures markets. Instead, the basis of commodity indexes is alternative weighting methodologies such as worldwide production or liquidity. The GSCI weights its constituents by worldwide production, which skews the performance of the index toward energy commodities, which happened to outperform during the period observed.

Similarly, Atwill and Liebel (2016, p. 2) expand upon the argument against first-generation commodity indexes acting as true passive representations of broader commodity markets, claiming:

> Index providers, who needed to have some consistent weighting mechanism to apply, have developed a variety of supposed proxies to play a similar role in their indexes . . . . There is no clear argument that any one of these is better than another, and some critics maintain that these proxies suffer from overzealous back testing, to generate impressive historical performance. Even more apparent, these indexes are not attempting to provide a "slice of the market," as most mainstream equity indexes do, but instead are simply very explicit commodity trading strategies based on different arbitrary metrics for measuring the importance of a given commodity contract.

An equity index may follow a simple rules-based approach to give an investor exposure to a specific size, sector, or industry. Market capitalization is the most popular form of an equity index using company's equity measure to determine its weight relative to others in the index. Investors can easily replicate market capitalization indexes across with investment vehicles such as mutual funds or ETFs due to both their transparency in methodology, and the fact that every share of equity in a company is homogenous, or no different from one another.

Conversely, a commodity index must use much more subjective or qualitative metrics, such as "world production" or "economic significance," that are then translated into quantitative weights. Commodity indexes technically do not have market capitalization weights due to the nature of futures markets and their clearinghouses. A clearinghouse in a futures market balances the supply and demand of each commodity contract, meaning that when one party buys a contract, another party sells a contract. The gains of one investor offsets the losses of another, resulting in futures markets being a "zero-sum game" and no technical market capitalization is present (Atwill and Liebel 2016).

Again, the drastic differences in mean return and volatility, as measured by standard deviation, confirm that popular commodity indexes do not often mirror one another. Just by using a small sample, and observing the differences between first-generation commodity indexes, whether it is the differences in weighting components, what is included, or the qualifications for inclusion, all support the assertions of Erb and Harvey (2006) and Atwill and Liebel (2016).

Summary and Conclusions

Commodity indexes and investment strategies are as diverse as those in public equity and fixed income markets. However, different issues surround commodity indexes, including the misrepresentations of the asset class or simple existing inefficiencies that analysts have not frequently addressed. This chapter explored some of the issues that exist within the asset class, including the differences in commodity index generations and how each protects against or exploits the negative effects of market contango.

First-generation indexes completely ignore the negative effects of contango, but each progressive generation has addressed these effects differently. Second-generation indexes are long only, and holistically and systematically buy the futures contracts with the smallest level of contango, minimizing roll return and volatility. Third-generation indexes have the ability to take both long and short positions in futures markets, opting to short contangoed markets and go long backwardated ones. When trying to benchmark the performance of these strategies, selecting the appropriate benchmark becomes crucial. Understanding both the generational differences between commodity benchmarks and indexes, as well as the cross-sectional diversity within the generations, is important.

Historically, different fundamental factors, such as supply and demand and inflation expectations, drive commodity markets. However, as noncommercial traders and speculators, such as pension funds endowments, have entered into commodity futures markets, correlations between commodity prices and other traditional asset classes have increased. Rising correlations and returns driven by investor behavior can have a negative impact on the diversification that commodities once offered. In fact, Büyükşahin et al. (2010) find that during times of fear, correlations between commodity markets and traditional asset classes spiked, a time when commodities lacked proper diversification benefits when investors needed it most.

Finally, one of the biggest issues with commodity indexes and passive investments is the idea that commodity indexes do not truly represent the asset class as a whole. Although traditional asset classes, such as global equities and fixed income, take a more tangible rules-based approach to their index construction (e.g., market capitalization-weighted indexes), some contend that commodity indexes are different variations of strategies rather than standard benchmarks.

Understanding all of these issues becomes important when performing attribution analysis for an active manager, attributing asset class performance based on commodity index performance, or even including commodities as part of a globally diversified portfolio. Index weightings and philosophy, as well as trading strategies, all become important components to analyzing past returns and implementing a forward-looking framework to extrapolate future returns.

Discussion Questions

1. Define a futures curve and what it means for such a curve to be in "contango" or "backwardation."
2. Discuss the major differences between the three generations of commodity indexes and how each generation generally addresses the issues of contango on a futures curve.
3. Discuss the concept of "financialization," including the arguments Masters (2008) and Irwin and Sanders (2012) make about its effect on commodity futures markets.
4. Define "co-integration" and discuss its applicability to the association between commodity futures markets and public equity markets.
5. Discuss the claim that commodity indexes are not truly passive indexes.

References

Atwill, Tim, and Greg Liebel. 2016. "Commodity Investing: Indexes Are Not Your Friend." Parametric Portfolio Associates. Available at https://www.parametricportfolio.com/insights-research/paper/commodity-investing-indexes-are-not-your-friends.

Bloomberg. 2014. "Bloomberg Indexes to Oversee Leading Global Commodity Indexes." April 10. Available at https://www.bloomberg.com/company/announcements/bloomberg-indexes-oversee-leading-global-commodity-indexes/.

Brunnermeier, Markus K. 2008. "Bubbles." In Steven N. Durlauf and L. E. Blume (eds.), *The New Palgrave Dictionary of Economics*, 2nd edition, 578–582. New York, NY: Palgrave Macmillan.

Business Wire. 2006. "Headline Maker: Merrill Lynch Announces 2007 Composition and Weights for the Merrill Lynch Commodity Index." December 6. Available at http://www.businesswire.com/news/home/20061207005428/en/Merrill-Lynch-Announces-2007-Composition-Weights-Merrill.

Business Wire. 2012. "UBS Launches ETRACS Exchange Traded Note Providing Exposure across Commodities and across Their Respective Futures Maturities." Available at http://www.businesswire.com/news/home/20120426006159/en/UBS-Launches-ETRACS-Exchange-Traded-Note-Providing.

Büyükşahin, Bahattin, Michael S. Haigh, and Michel A. Robe. 2010. "Commodities and Equities: Ever a 'Market of One'?" *Journal of Alternative Investments* 12:3, 76–95.

Chilton, Bartt. 2011. "Speculators and Commodity Prices." U.S. Commodity Futures and Trading Commission. March 16. Available at http://www.cftc.gov/PressRoom/SpeechesTestimony/opachilton-41.

Dubois, Robert. 2013. "Asset Price Trend Theory: Reframing Portfolio Theory from the Ground Up." *Journal of Wealth Management* 16:3, 11–30.

Erb, Claude B., and Campbell R. Harvey. 2006. "The Strategic and Tactical Value of Commodity Futures." *Financial Analysts Journal* 62:2, 69–97.

Feldman, Barry, and Hilary Till. 2006. "Backwardation and Commodity Futures Performance: Evidence from Evolving Agricultural Markets." *Journal of Alternative Investments* 9:3, 24–39.

Goldman Sachs. 2005. *The GSCI Manual: A Guide to the Goldman Sachs Commodity Index*. New York, NY: Goldman Sachs & Co. Available at http://www2.goldmansachs.com/gsci/docs/GSCI_Manual_2005_FINAL.pdf.

Goldman Sachs. 2016. "Review of 2017 S&P GSCI Index Rebalancing." Available at http://us.spindices.com/documents/index-news-and-announcements/20161006-sp-gsci-rebalance-advisory-panel.pdf?force_download=true.

Hamilton, James D. 2008. "Understanding Crude Oil Prices." National Bureau of Economic Research. November. Available at http://www.nber.org/papers/w14492.

Hougan, Matt. 2006. "Merrill Lynch Launches Commodity Index." ETF.com, June. Available at http://www.etf.com/sections/features/729.html?nopaging=1.

Irwin, Scott H., and Dwight R. Sanders. 2012. "Financialization and Structural Change in Commodity Futures Markets." *Journal of Agricultural and Applied Economics* 44:3, 371–396.

Kawamoto, Takuji, Takeshe Kimura, Kentaro Morishita, and Masato Higashi. 2011. "What Has Caused the Surge in Global Commodity Prices and Strengthened Cross-Market Linkage?" St. Louis, MO: Federal Reserve Bank of St Louis.

Markowitz, Harry. 1952. "Portfolio Selection." *Journal of Finance* 7:1, 77–91.

Masters, Michael. 2008. "Testimony of Michael W. Masters." May 28. Available at http://www.hsgac.senate.gov//imo/media/doc/052008Masters.pdf?attempt=2.

Miffre, Joëlle. 2014. "Comparing First, Second, and Third Generation Commodity Indices." *Alternative Investment Analyst Review* 3:2, 22–33.

Morrison, Kevin. 2006. "Crusaders against 'Contango.'" *Financial Times*, September. Available at http://www.ft.com/cms/s/0/4ae7b15c-41fb-11db-b4ab-0000779e2340.html?ft_site=falcon&desktop=true#axzz4LvxIlIuk.

Reuters. 2009. "DJ-AIG Commodities Index Becomes DJ-UBS in Acquisition." May 7. Available at http://uk.reuters.com/article/commodities-ubs-idUKN0731630220090507.

Sharpe, William F. 1964. "Capital Asset Prices: A Theory of Market Equilibrium under Conditions of Risk." *Journal of Finance* 19:3, 425–442.

Skapa, Stanislav. 2013. "Commodities as a Tool of Risk Diversification." *Equilibrium* 8:2, 65–77.

Stockton, Kimberly. 2007. "Understanding Alternative Investments: The Role of Commodities in a Portfolio." Available at http://www.vanguard.com/pdf/s552.pdf?221002207.

SummerHaven Dynamic Commodity Index (SDCI). 2016. "SDCI Index Methodology." SummerHaven Index Management. Available at https://www.summerhavenindex.com/guest/sdci_methodology.html.

UBS. 2011. "CMCI Active Presentation." UBS Index Presentation. Available at https://www.ubs.com/global/en/investment-bank/bloomberg-cmci/universe/strategy-indices/active/_jcr_content/par/linklist/link_0.1053590426.file/bGluay9wYXRoPS9jb250ZW50L2RhbS91YnMvZ2xvYmFsL2ludmVzdG1lbnRfYmFuay9ibG9vbWJlcmctY21jaS9DTUNJX0FjdGl2ZS1QcmVzZW50YXRpb24ucGRm/CMCI_Active-Presentation.pdf.

UBS. 2015. *Fact Sheet—UBS Bloomberg CMCI.* Available at https://www.bbhub.io/indices/sites/2/2015/12/CMCI-Commodity-Composite-Index-Fact-Sheet.pdf.

Whitton, Bransby, Klaus Thuerbach, and Kate Botting. 2015. "Commodities Remain a Valuable Portfolio Allocation." PIMCO. Available at https://www.pimco.com/insights/investment-strategies/featured-solutions/commodities-remain-a-valuable-portfolio-allocation.

Zaremba, Adam. 2016. "Strategies Based on Momentum and Term Structure in Financialized Commodity Markets." *Business and Economics Research Journal* 7:1, 31–46.

18

Volatility Transmission across Commodity Futures Markets

FRANKIE HO-CHI CHAU
Associate Professor, Durham University Business School, Durham University, United Kingdom

RATAPORN DEESOMSAK
Assistant Professor, Durham University Business School, Durham University, United Kingdom

Introduction

In the wake of the financial crisis of 2007–2008, also called the global financial crisis (GFC), interest in the commodity markets soared as many turned to so-called "alternative investments" to hedge against heightened uncertainty and adverse economic conditions. Institutional investors started to expand their investable asset universe beyond the traditional asset classes of stocks, bonds, and cash. Commodities have gained greater prominence in recent years. According to the World Bank (2012), investment fund activity in commodities was about $330 billion as of the first quarter of 2012, which was nine times higher than in the early 2000s, when this activity started becoming a popular investment vehicle within the financial community.

Despite this growing popularity, the recent increased volatility in crude oil prices and the spillover effects on other commodity markets have brought about a renewed concern about excessive fluctuations and volatility spillovers among the global commodity markets. Some claim that the large inflow of investment capital to commodity futures markets in the past decade, a phenomenon often called *financialization*, has distorted commodity prices and caused excessive volatility (Nazlioglu, Erdem, and Soytas 2013; Cheng and Xiong 2014). According to many economists, however, little evidence supports the view that large investment inflows in commodity markets are cause for concern (Stoll and Whaley 2010; Irwin and Sanders 2011). Figure 18.1 plots commodity futures prices for oil, metals, and agricultural product between 2005 and 2016. As the figure shows, commodity futures prices experienced a boom-bust cycle between 2005 and 2016. Most commodity prices began to increase in early 2005, leading to the longest commodity price boom since the World War II. Oil prices briefly approached $150 a barrel in July 2008 but as global demand collapsed, oil prices halved during the GFC. In searching for explanations for this pronounced cycle in commodity prices, researchers believe that the main drivers may include

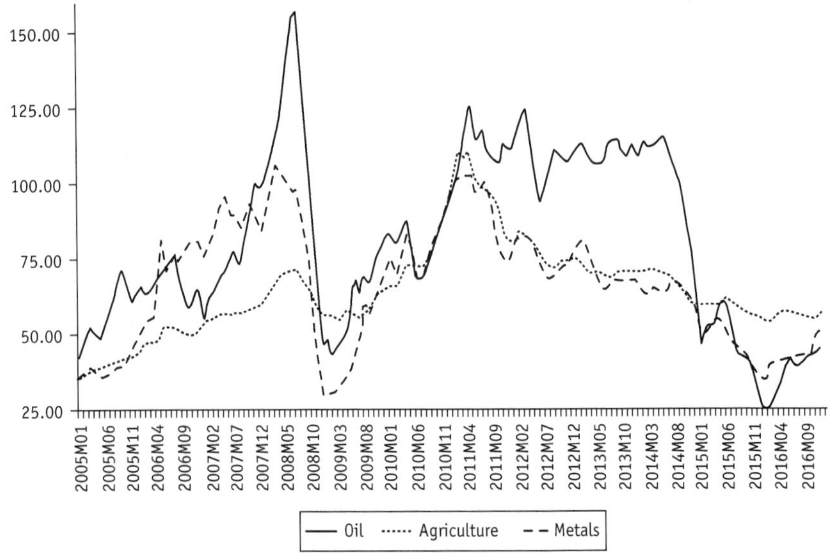

Figure 18.1 Commodity Price Movements between 2005 and 2016
The figure shows commodity futures prices for crude oil, metals, and agricultural materials between 2005 and 2016 (US$, January 2011 = 100). Source: World Bank Group (2016).

(1) the growing demand from emerging economies, especially China, (2) low interest rates and effective dollar depreciation, and (3) improved liquidity attributable to the growing interest of institutional investors, including hedge funds and exchange-traded funds (ETFs).

Notwithstanding the causes of this boom-bust cycle, a sudden increase in volatility in commodity prices spurred a heated debate in the literature. This chapter investigates this controversial issue by examining the level and direction of volatility transmission across three major classes of commodities: agricultural products (corn, coffee, and soybeans), energy (crude oil and gas), and metals (copper, gold, and silver). Intuitively, a better understanding of the fundamental process through which volatility transmits across the commodity markets is particularly important for investors and regulators whose strategic asset allocation decisions and policy formulation, respectively, are often influenced by the uncertainty in these markets (Chng 2009; Kang, McIver, and Yoon 2017). Moreover, to the extent that volatility is caused by trading in response to the arrival of new information to the markets (Ross 1989), a thorough assessment of volatility spillovers among commodity markets has important implications about information flows and price discovery in these markets.

The investigation of volatility linkage between commodity markets has been an expanding area for both academic and regulatory research, particularly after the GFC (Nazlioglu et al. 2013; Olson, Vivian, and Wohar 2014; Antonakakis and Kizys, 2015; Bouri 2015). For instance, using the causality-in-variance approach of Hafner and Herwartz (2006), Olson et al. (2014) investigate the relation between the energy and equity markets and show that low S&P 500 index returns cause substantial increases in the volatility of the Goldman Sachs energy index. However, only a weak response exists from the S&P 500 volatility index to energy price shocks. Antonakakis and Kizys (2015) employ the spillover index of Diebold and Yilmaz (2012) to examine the dynamic link between returns and volatilities of commodity and currency markets. Based on weekly data between January 6, 1987 and July 22, 2014, they find that the observed transmission process is both time and event dependent. In particular, the dynamic spillover effects originating in gold and silver reach an unprecedented level during the GFC. After the GFC, however, the role of gold and silver as net transmitters of shocks weakened. Similarly, applying the newly developed causality-in-variance test and impulse response functions, Nazlioglu et al. (2013) show that the dynamics of volatility transmission between energy and agricultural markets changes significantly following the food price crisis. Their results show that while no risk transmission exists between oil and agricultural commodity markets in the pre-crisis period, oil market volatility spills on the agricultural markets in the post-crisis period. More recently, Yaya, Tumala, and Udomboso (2016) investigate volatility persistence and returns spillovers between oil and gold markets using the Constant Conditional Correlation generalized autoregressive conditional heteroscedasticity (CCC-GARCH) modeling framework and find that oil-gold volatility spillovers exist between 1986 and 2015. However, return spillover effects switch from bidirectional before the crisis period to unidirectional (i.e., from gold to oil market) after the crisis.

However, despite the widespread attention given to this research area, the majority of studies focus on the energy-equity return relations (Arouri, Jouini, and Nguyen 2011; Olson et al. 2014; Bouri 2015), the cross-market linkages between energy and metals markets (Reboredo 2013; Yaya et al. 2016), and the volatility spillovers between energy and agricultural markets (Nazlioglu et al. 2013). Little research investigates the interrelations among the price and volatility of the three major commodity classes—agricultural products, energy, and metals. This observation is somewhat surprising given the growing concern that "financial stress is more systemic and thus more dangerous for the economy as a whole if financial instability spreads more widely across the whole system" (Holló, Kremer, and Duca 2012, p. 1). One noticeable exception is Kang et al. (2017), who examine return and volatility spillover effects among six commodity futures markets—gold, silver, West Texas Intermediate (WTI) crude oil, corn, wheat, and rice—by employing the multivariate GARCH model and the spillover index. Although Kang et al. attempt to measure the intensity and direction of volatility transmissions across the major commodity markets, they only examine six commodities between 2002 and 2016 and thus do not fully consider the changing nature of volatility spillovers during the early 1990s global recession.

To address these important issues, this chapter builds on the work of Chau and Deesomsak (2014) and proposes an indicator of volatility transmission across commodity futures markets labeled the Commodity Volatility Spillover Index (CVSI) to assess interdependence in the major commodity futures markets and to identify periods of excessive spillover that may lead to global commodity price instability. Specifically, using the spillover index approach of Diebold and Yilmaz (2012), this study tracks estimates of both total and directional volatility spillovers across the energy, precious metals, and agriculture commodity markets. In contrast to other studies, this chapter directly accounts for important linkages among the major commodity futures markets in an interconnected world by considering the average and time-varying interconnectedness of each market's volatility shocks.

This chapter adds to the existing literature in several ways. First, the development of a new index of volatility spillover incorporates the important interaction and transmission of risk across the three major classes of commodities, providing investors and regulators with an early warning indicator for emergent crises. Second, the directional CVSI helps to identify the origin of systemic stress and to detect systemically important commodity markets. Finally, the conditional version of our CVSI tracks the time-varying movements and trends of both total and directional volatility spillovers. Overall, the findings of this study are important in understanding the level and transmission mechanism of risk across commodity futures markets and are relevant to regulators in formulating effective policies to tackle excessive volatility, particularly during the turbulence periods. They should also provide new insights into channels of information transmission, which may improve investment decisions and inform portfolio investors' trading strategies.

The remainder of this chapter is organized as follows. The next section describes the data and econometric modeling framework used to measure the intensity and direction of volatility transmission across different categories of commodity futures markets. Next, the main empirical findings of this chapter are presented and analyzed. The final section summarizes and concludes the chapter.

Data and Methodology

This section describes the data and modeling framework of the study. It begins with a brief description of the data followed by an overview of Diebold and Yilmaz's (2012) spillover index, which identifies dynamic volatility spillover effects across commodity futures markets.

DATA DESCRIPTION

The data used in this chapter include the weekly observations for three categories of commodity futures markets, including the agricultural (CBOT corn and soybeans and ICE coffee), energy (NYMEX Brent crude oil, WTI, and natural gas), and precious metals (COMEX copper, gold, and silver). Using weekly time-series data alleviates the concerns over non-synchronicities and bid-ask effects in daily data (Antonakakis and Kizys 2015; Batten, Ciner, and Lucey 2015). In particular, Wednesday closing prices of these nine globally important commodity futures markets are obtained from Thomson Reuters Datastream. The sample period is between April 4, 1990 and December 28, 2016. Unlike Kang et al. (2017), this study examines the period covering the early 1990s global recession, the more recent GFC, as well as periods of economic growth. To construct a continuous series of futures prices, successive settlement rates are collected from a contract closest to expiration until the last day before the delivery month, and then switching to the next nearest contract from the first day of the delivery month. Following Lien and Shrestha (2005), the crossover returns are deleted from the data set to avoid the rollover risk when the nearby futures contract switches months.

The continuously compounded returns are calculated as logarithmic relatives $R_t = 100 \times ln(P_t / P_{t-1})$, where P_t is the Wednesday closing futures price. Figure 18.2 displays a time-series plot of price (Panel A) and return (Panel B) movements of the nine chosen commodity futures during the sample period. Several facts emerge: (1) although the return series appear to be stationary as expected, they fluctuate substantially over time with peaks in the periods corresponding to crisis events; (2) energy prices are generally more volatile than other commodities, as indicated by the magnitude of their price movements; (3) WTI and Brent crude oil future prices increased dramatically during the GFC, and only revert to somewhat lower levels in 2009 and 2010; and (4) the prices of precious metals such as gold and silver were relatively stable before 2004 but experienced substantial growth thereafter. The growing demand for precious metals may be because investors perceive these assets as "safe heaven" investments, especially in the periods of financial turmoil (i.e., the so-called "flight-to-quality" phenomenon). Antonakakis and Kizys (2015) and Kang et al. (2017) document similar findings.

Table 18.1 presents the descriptive statistics of the weekly commodity futures markets returns. The statistics reported are the mean, standard deviation, measures of skewness and kurtosis, Jarque-Bera (JB) statistic, and the Ljung-Box statistic (LB) for 12 lags. Consistent with the extant literature, the futures returns series clearly depart from normality, as indicated by significant JB statistics. In particular, almost all commodity futures returns are negatively skewed and slightly leptokurtic. The LB statistics provide evidence of significant temporal dependencies in the first moment of these return distributions, with the exception of soybean and silver futures. Given that the variables in the vector autoregression (VAR) must be stationary, the study tests for the presence of a unit root in these return series. In addition to the augmented Dicker-Fuller (ADF) and Phillips-Perron (PP) tests, this chapter also presents the Dickey-Fuller Generalized Least Squares (DF-GLS) unit root test proposed by Ng and Perron (2001), which has better properties than many conventional unit root tests (Elliott, Rothenberg, and Stock 1996). The test results reported in Panel B of Table 18.1 are consistent with those of Kang et al. (2017) and indicate that commodity futures returns are first-order nonstationary processes.

As an initial gauge of the dynamic interactions between commodity futures markets returns, this study estimates correlation coefficients during the sample period. The results reported in Panel C of Table 18.1 show positive and statistically significant correlations exist among these nine commodity futures markets with corn-soybeans, gold-silver, and Brent crude oil–WTI pairs sharing the highest correlations of 0.61, 0.74, and 0.89 respectively. Nonetheless, the interaction of commodity futures may give rise to correlation patterns that are more complex than a simple correlation coefficient can capture. Thus, investigating the extent to which risk and volatility originating in one commodity market affect the others and identifying the channels through which a market's financial stress spills over across different commodity futures markets are both interesting and informative.

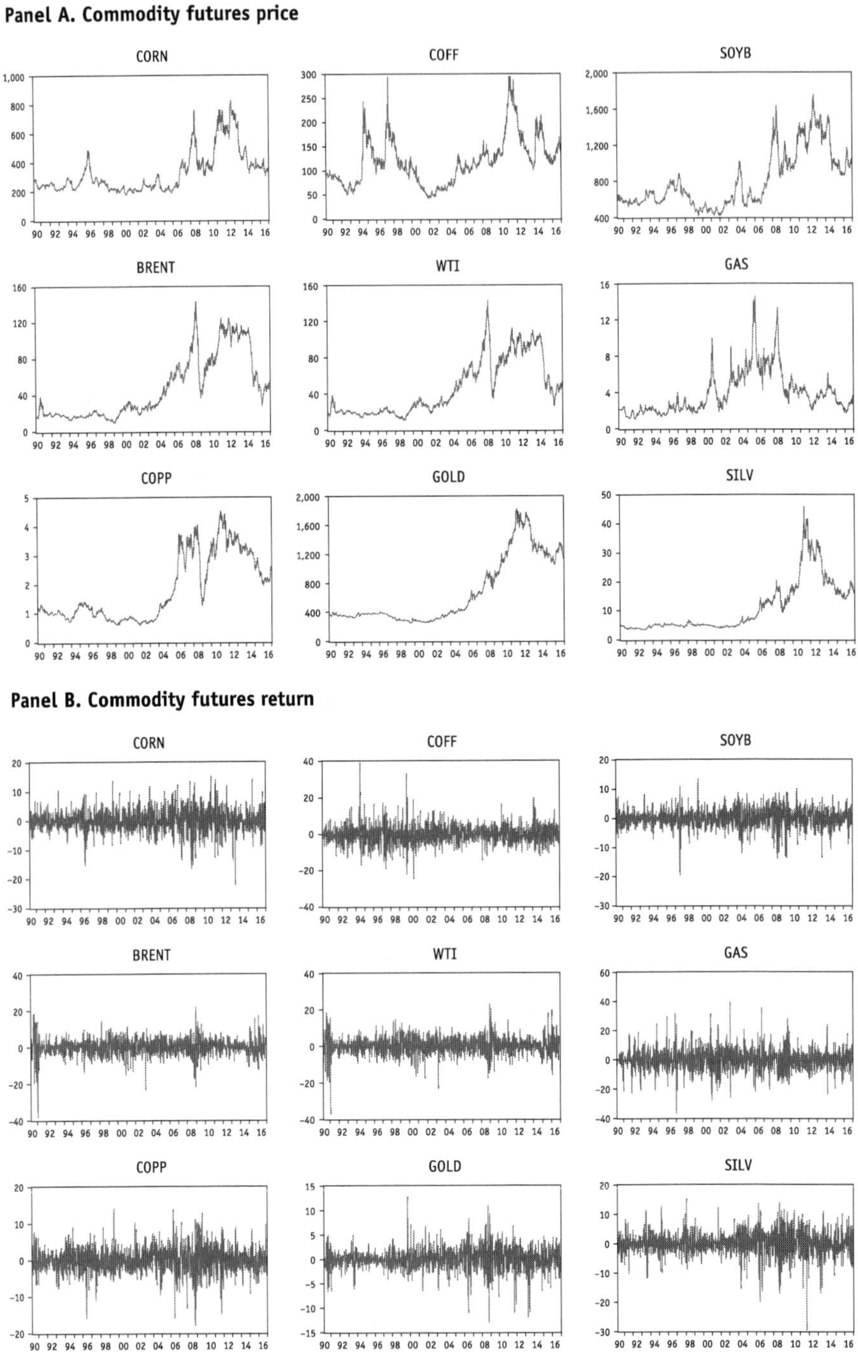

Figure 18.2 Time-Series Plot of Commodity Futures Markets Movements
The figure shows a time-series plot of the price (Panel A) and return (Panel B) movements of nine commodity futures markets during the sample period between April 4, 1990 and December 28, 2016.

Table 18.1 **Descriptive Statistics of Commodity Futures Returns**

	Corn	*Coffee*	*Soybeans*	*Brent Oil*	*WTI*	*Natural Gas*	*Copper*	*Gold*	*Silver*
Panel A. Summary statistics									
Mean	0.019	0.024	0.038	0.081	0.072	0.041	0.052	0.079	0.081
Standard deviation	3.781	5.291	3.252	4.730	4.951	7.485	3.466	2.255	3.977
Skewness	−0.146	0.531	−0.497	−0.568	−0.341	0.172	−0.274	−0.312	−0.604
Kurtosis	5.523	7.615	5.550	8.060	7.029	5.416	5.475	7.468	7.283
JB	374.857***	1303.640***	435.596***	1563.524***	970.464***	346.095***	373.490***	1182.888***	1151.190***
LB(12)	20.836*	41.152***	16.097	22.33**	40.246***	34.492***	35.368***	28.506***	16.732
Panel B. Unit root tests									
ADF	−38.823***	−40.225***	−24.571***	−38.922***	−20.546***	−40.531***	−24.501***	−37.238***	−37.951***
PP	−38.793***	−40.245***	−37.665***	−39.031***	−38.954***	−40.527***	−38.507***	−37.589***	−38.209***
DF-GLS	−8.339***	−40.217***	−24.376***	−2.616***	−2.709***	−6.849***	−6.152***	−5.728***	−36.285***

(*continued*)

Table 18.1 **Continued**

	Corn	*Coffee*	*Soybeans*	*Brent Oil*	*WTI*	*Natural Gas*	*Copper*	*Gold*	*Silver*
Panel C. Correlation coefficients									
Corn	1								
Coffee	0.1576***	1							
Soybeans	0.6074***	0.1645***	1						
Brent oil	0.1515***	0.0897***	0.1903***	1					
WTI	0.1300***	0.0953***	0.1729***	0.8867***	1				
Natural gas	0.0920***	0.0342	0.1017***	0.2045***	0.2200***				
Copper	0.1669***	0.1320***	0.2071***	0.2461***	0.2526***	0.0501*	1		
Gold	0.1710***	0.1381***	0.1690***	0.2485***	0.2342***	0.0579**	0.2909***	1	
Silver	0.2000 ***	0.1919***	0.2114***	0.2516***	0.2417***	0.0879***	0.3529***	0.7441***	1

Note: This table reports the sample mean, standard deviation, skewness, and kurtosis for the commodity futures returns. JB is the Jarque-Bera test for normality and LB(12) is the Ljung-Box Q test of serial correlation. The unit root tests include a constant term, with lag length determined by the Schwartz Information Criteria. Critical values for ADF, PP, and DF-GLS tests are from Mackinnon (1996). *, **, and *** denote significance at 10%, 5%, and 1% levels, respectively.

MODELING FRAMEWORK

With the rapid development of financial econometrics in the past few decades, researchers have advanced various modeling approaches to investigate the co-movements and spillovers of key financial market variables (e.g., asset return and volatility). For instance, a growing body of literature uses multivariate GARCH models to investigate return and volatility spillovers between oil market and the equity market (Arouri et al. 2011). Although multivariate GARCH models offer substantial insights in the dynamic interactions between commodity markets, the analysis in this chapter distinguishes between idiosyncratic shocks to each commodity futures market and the spillover of shocks across markets, and more importantly, identifies how shocks to each market affect other markets. In other words, the chapter uses a more advanced approach to capture how quickly volatility builds and spreads across commodity markets over time. To achieve this goal, this study follows the methodology set forth in Diebold and Yilmaz (2009, 2012) hereafter DY, generating what they term a spillover index. The spillover index is built upon the familiar notion of variance decomposition associated with an N-variable vector autoregression (VAR). The remainder of this section provides a brief overview of the DY's spillover index methodology.

Consider a covariance stationary of N-variable VAR of pth-order, $x_t = \sum_{i=1}^{p} \Phi_i x_{t-i} + \varepsilon_t$, where $\varepsilon_t \sim (0, \Sigma)$. In the context of current chapter, $x_t = (x_{1t}, x_{2t} \ldots x_{nt})$ represents a vector of conditional volatility estimated by a standard GARCH (1,1) model; Φ is a $N \times N$ parameter matrix and ε is the vector of independently and identically distributed error terms with zero mean and variance of covariance matrix Σ. The moving average (MA) representation is $x_t = \sum_{i=0}^{\infty} A_i x_{t-i}$ where A_i is an $N \times N$ coefficient matrices following the recursion $A_i = \Phi_1 A_{t-1} + \Phi_2 A_{t-2} + \ldots + \Phi_p A_{t-p}$ with A_0 as an $N \times N$ identify matrix and $A_i = 0$ for $i < 0$. Variance decomposition allows decomposing the fraction of H-step-ahead forecast error variance into own variance shares and cross variance shares, or spillovers. The *own variance shares* refer to the part of the forecast error variance in forecasting x_i due to shocks to x_i itself for $i = 1,2,\ldots,N$, whereas the *cross variance shares* represent the part that is attributable to shocks from another variable x_j for $j = 1,2,\ldots,N$ (and $i \neq j$). Diebold and Yilmaz (2009) propose using the Cholesky-decomposition to decompose the variance. However, the Cholesky-decomposition depends on the ordering of the variables. Diebold and Yilmaz (2012) resolve this ordering problem by exploiting the generalized VAR framework of Koop, Pesaran, and Potter (1996) and Pesaran and Shin (1998) (collectively called KPPS hereafter), producing the variance decomposition invariant to ordering.

More specifically, the KPPS H-step-ahead error forecast variance decomposition is given by Equation 18.1:

$$\theta_{ij}^{g}(H) = \frac{\sigma_{ii}^{-1} \sum_{h=0}^{H-1} \left(e_i' A_h \sum e_j \right)^2}{\sum_{h=0}^{H-1} \left(e_i' A_h \sum A_h' e_i \right)} \tag{18.1}$$

where Σ represents the variance matrix for error vector ε; σ_{ii} is the standard deviation of the error term for i^{th} equation; and e_i is the selection vector with one for the *i*th element and zero otherwise. Unlike Cholesky factor orthogonalization, the KPPS H-step-ahead error forecast variance decomposition does not try to orthogonalize the shock but instead allows for correlated shocks and accounts for them appropriately using the historical distribution of the errors. However, as Diebold and Yilmaz (2012, p. 58) state, "As the shocks to each variable are not orthogonalized, the sum of contributions to the variance of forecast error (that is, the row sum of the elements of the variance decomposition table) is not necessarily equal to one." Thus, each entry of the variance decomposition matrix in Equation 18.1 must be normalized to use the information from the variance decomposition matrix.

Equation 18.2 shows the normalization of the entry for the variance decomposition matrix by the row sum:

$$\tilde{\theta}_{ij}^{g}(H) = \frac{\theta_{ij}^{g}(H)}{\sum_{j=1}^{N} \theta_{ij}^{g}(H)} \tag{18.2}$$

where $\sum_{j=1}^{N} \tilde{\theta}_{ij}^{g}(H) = 1$ and $\sum_{i,j=1}^{N} \tilde{\theta}_{ij}^{g}(H) = N$.

Using the normalized entry for the generalized variance decomposition matrix in Equation 18.2, Diebold and Yilmaz construct the total spillover index as Equation 18.3:

$$S^{g}(H) = \frac{\sum_{\substack{i,j=1 \\ i \neq j}}^{N} \tilde{\theta}_{ij}^{g}(H)}{\sum_{i,j=1}^{N} \tilde{\theta}_{ij}^{g}(H)} \times 100 = \frac{\sum_{\substack{i,j=1 \\ i \neq j}}^{N} \tilde{\theta}_{ij}^{g}(H)}{N} \times 100 \tag{18.3}$$

Besides the total spillover index, information from KPPS variance decomposition also enables measuring the directional spillovers across the markets in order to understand how shocks to the commodity markets are carried across and transferred among the major commodity assets. In particular, Equation 18.4 shows how the directional spillover received by market *i* *from* all other markets *j* can be calculated:

$$S_{i\bullet}^{g}(H) = \frac{\sum_{j=1, i \neq j}^{N} \tilde{\theta}_{ij}^{g}(H)}{\sum_{j=1}^{N} \tilde{\theta}_{ij}^{g}(H)} \times 100 \tag{18.4}$$

Similarly, the directional spillover transmitted by market *i* to all other markets *j* can be measured as shown in Equation 18.5:

$$S_{\bullet i}^{g}(H) = \frac{\sum_{j=1, i \neq j}^{N} \tilde{\theta}_{ji}^{g}(H)}{\sum_{j=1}^{N} \tilde{\theta}_{ji}^{g}(H)} \times 100 \tag{18.5}$$

Finally, obtaining the net directional spillover from market *i* to all other markets *j* involves calculating the difference between Equations 18.4 and 18.5 and as shown in Equation 18.6:

$$S_i^g(H) = S_{\bullet i}^g(H) - S_{i \bullet}^g(H) \tag{18.6}$$

This net directional spillover provides critical information about how much (in net terms) each of the commodity futures market contributes to volatility transmission within the overall system.

International financial markets have become increasingly interconnected because of the advances in technology and increasing globalization. Financial events in any part of the world now influence every part of the world. Although this interconnectedness has created opportunities for improving efficiency, it also has the potential to amplify financial shocks and spark contagion across marketplaces globally. The GFC highlights this risk as the collapse of one financial institution rippled through markets worldwide, affecting thousands of financial firms and ultimately threatening global financial stability (Diebold and Yilmaz 2012). The generality of the DY spillover measures (both total and directional) is often useful allowing for identification of the main transmitters and recipients of shocks in such a globalized financial world. The next section uses these spillover results to derive some intuitive measures of volatility spillovers, called the Commodity Volatility Spillover Index (CVSI). The chapter then uses the CVSI to study the levels and trends of volatility interdependence in the major commodity futures markets—including energy, precious metals, and agriculture commodity assets. Antonakakis and Kizys (2015) and Kang et al. (2017) provide further discussion about the empirical advantages of DY's method.

Empirical Findings

To investigate the level and direction of volatility transmission across the major classes of commodities, this study uses the generalized VAR framework of Diebold and Yilmaz (2012) to construct total and directional net spillovers. This section presents the estimation results of a nine-variate VAR incorporating the GARCH(1,1) volatility estimates of nine commodity futures (i.e., corn, coffee, soybean, Brent oil, WTI, natural gas, copper, gold, and silver). Then, in an attempt to check the sensitivity of estimation results, it reports several robustness tests results.

VOLATILITY LINKAGE AND TRANSMISSION MECHANISM

The previous section illustrates how the Diebold and Yilmaz (2012) spillover index framework can be used to construct an indicator of volatility transmission to monitor the levels of stress spillovers across major commodity markets. This section presents both total and directional spillover indices and examines their time-series dynamics over the sample period. Two associated tools of DY's methodology are spillover tables and spillover plots. However, as DY emphasize, while a spillover table provides a useful summary of the total (i.e., average) spillover behavior over the whole sample, this point estimate is a static measure that, by definition, cannot capture the secular and cyclical movements in spillovers. In fact, changes in spillovers are particularly important when examining turbulence in the commodity markets and how dynamics in commodity markets evolve. Thus, besides reporting the unconditional full-sample spillover table, this chapter also presents the time-varying conditional spillover plots to assess the nature and direction of volatility spillover variation over time.

Unconditional Full-Sample Volatility Spillover

Following Diebold and Yilmaz (2012), this study applies a second-order VAR with 10-step-ahead forecasts to do the generalized variance decomposition of conditional volatility of nine major commodity futures markets, including agricultural (corn, coffee, and soybeans), energy (Brent crude oil, WTI, and natural gas), and precious metals (copper, gold, and silver). As a robustness check, the chapter also calculates the total spillover indices for a fourth-order VAR with five-step forecast horizons. As reported in the robustness tests section, the results show that the levels of spillover are similar, irrespective of the choices of order of VAR or the forecast horizon. Table 18.2 provides the average levels of both total and directional spillovers over the full-sample period. The off-diagonal column sums, which are labeled "Contribution to others," and row sums, which are labeled "From others," are the "TO" and "FROM" directional spillovers, and "TO-FROM" differences are the net directional spillovers. The lower-right corner of the table reports the total spillover index.

As Table 18.2 shows, the total financial stress spillover is not sizable (the total spillover index is 24.8 percent), indicating that, on average, over the sample period between April 11, 1990 and December 28, 2016, the cross-market volatility spillovers explain less than a quarter of the variations in these major commodity futures markets, while idiosyncratic shocks to individual commodity market volatility levels explain the remaining 75.2 percent variations. These results are directly comparable to those of Antonakakis and Kizys (2015) and Kang et al. (2017). In terms of the directional spillovers transmitted TO others, global oil price volatility as measured by the two major categories of crude oil (i.e., Brent oil [45.7 percent] and WTI [43.3 percent]) appears to be the largest average contributor to volatility spillovers in other commodity futures markets, followed by silver (35.8 percent) and gold (33.4 percent). Interestingly, judging by the directional spillovers received FROM others, these energy and metal markets are also the largest recipients of volatility spillovers from others, with Brent oil, WTI, silver, and gold receiving 45.0 percent, 45.4 percent, 31.3 percent, and 30.0 percent, respectively. In contrast, coffee barely transmits any financial volatility to other commodity markets and coffee does not receive any volatility spillovers from other markets. The net directional spillovers (TO—FROM) confirm that agricultural markets (corn, coffee, and soybeans) are generally the net recipient of commodity volatility spillover. Silver (4.5 percent) and gold (3.4 percent), conversely, are the net transmitters of volatility. The results also indicate that natural gas is the most exogenous market because 97.8 percent of natural gas market variations are due to volatility shocks generated in its market.

Table 18.2 **Volatility Spillover Table, Commodity Futures Markets: Full Sample**

	Corn	*Coffee*	*Soybeans*	*Brent Oil*	*WTI*	*Natural Gas*	*Copper*	*Gold*	*Silver*	*From Others*
Corn	76.44	0.16	15.06	0.02	0.14	0.84	4.21	1.09	2.03	23.60
Coffee	0.09	94.59	0.39	0.84	0.16	1.22	0.93	0.61	1.17	5.40
Soybeans	18.71	0.26	76.37	0.04	0.32	0.88	2.01	0.29	1.12	23.60
Brent oil	0.11	0.07	0.48	55.02	38.33	0.96	1.22	2.14	1.69	45.00
WTI	0.18	0.02	0.24	39.85	54.57	0.38	0.83	2.59	1.35	45.40
Natural gas	0.40	0.12	0.10	0.14	0.16	97.79	0.83	0.13	0.33	2.20
Copper	0.87	0.24	0.38	2.58	2.56	0.10	83.52	3.21	6.56	16.50
Gold	1.05	0.61	1.40	1.19	1.16	0.10	3.02	69.96	21.52	30.00
Silver	1.17	0.31	1.79	1.03	0.47	0.06	3.08	23.39	68.71	31.30
Contribution to others	22.60	1.80	19.80	45.70	43.30	4.50	16.10	33.40	35.80	223.00
Contribution incl. own	99.00	96.40	96.20	100.70	97.90	102.30	99.60	103.40	104.50	Spillover
Net spillovers (TO—FROM)	−1.00	−3.60	−3.80	0.70	−2.10	2.30	−0.40	3.40	4.50	Index = 24.8%

Note: This table reports the full sample (i.e. average) total and directional volatility spillovers. The second-order VARs with 10-step-ahead forecasts are used to do the generalized variance decomposition for nine major commodity futures markets. The off-diagonal column sums (labeled "Contribution to others") and row sums (labeled "From others" are the "TO" and "FROM" directional spillovers, and "TO-FROM" differences are the net directional spillovers. The total spillover index is given in the lower-right corner of the table.

These findings are consistent with the results of previous studies showing that precious metals (e.g., silver and gold) play an important role in the development of risk and uncertainty in the financial system (Antonakakis and Kizys 2015; Batten et al. 2015). According to a survey conducted by O'Connor, Lucey, Batten, and Baur (2015), silver and gold are closely associated throughout history and can be treated as "safe havens" or hedges against stocks and bonds in times of panic and extreme market stress. Thus, the market often interprets the unanticipated increases in the price of these precious metals as a signal of future adverse conditions and uncertainty producing sharp movements in the global commodity prices. Despite these concerns, the results raise an important question on whether the "scapegoating" of one particular asset (e.g., gold or silver) can help policymakers reach reliable policy conclusions. On the contrary, this chapter contends that focusing on one particular market might serve to distract regulatory attention from the central problems inherent in the operations and interconnectedness of the global commodity market as a whole. The call for further regulation on trading of these commodity futures markets, such as higher margins, narrower fluctuation limits, and restrictions on the issue of contracts may not be fully justified.

Despite this advised caution, regulators have historically reacted to market volatility with these precise measures. For instance, on August 11, 2011, the world's largest gold futures market, Chicago Mercantile Exchange (CME), raised the margins on its gold futures by 22 percent, effectively reducing the demand for gold and associated volatility. This change was not an isolated event, as Shanghai Gold Exchange (SGE) also raised its margin requirements on gold to 11 percent in the same month.

Conditional Time-Varying Volatility Spillover

In this section, this study calculates the conditional spillover indices by re-estimating the second-order VAR weekly, using a 200-week rolling estimation window, which is roughly four years of weekly data, to assess the time-varying nature of both total and directional volatility spillovers. This study also checks the sensitivity of the findings to the 200-week estimation window by replicating results with a 100-week rolling estimation window.

Figure 18.3 presents the conditional total volatility spillover plot. Several important observations can be drawn from this figure. First, as expected, the spillover index varies considerably over time. Starting at a value of around 38 percent in the first window, the spillover index fluctuates mostly between 30 and 40 percent. However, during the onsets of the GFC and Eurozone debt crisis, the cross-market volatility spillovers show very sharp jumps and exceed the 50 percent mark during 2010 and 2011. Second, although the index fluctuates over time, Figure 18.3 allows differentiation between several cycles, typically corresponding to the GFC and the food crisis. Lastly, the spillover index also tends to increase rapidly during the beginning periods marked as recessions. Examination of how the intensity of commodity volatility spillovers affects the overall economic activity and the evolution of financial crises is worthy of further study, but is beyond the scope of this chapter.

Besides the conditional total spillover plot, this chapter also presents the time-varying directional spillover plots in order to allow policymakers to derive an

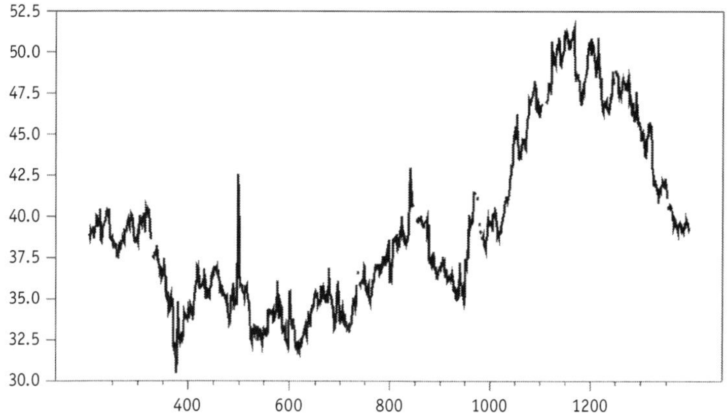

Figure 18.3 Time-Varying Volatility Spillover across Commodity Futures Markets
This figure shows the total volatility spillover across nine major commodity futures markets. The values are calculated by re-estimating the second-order VAR, using a 200-week rolling estimation window with a 10-week forecast horizon. Generalized variance decomposition method is used. The sample period is between April 11, 1990 and December 28, 2016.

early-warning system for identifying the "origin" of stress. These basic measures should assist policymakers in taking appropriate regulatory actions as necessary. This study focuses on the net directional spillover plots presented in Figure 18.4 to demonstrate the time-varying differences between directional TO and directional FROM spillovers (i.e., TO—FROM) for each commodity futures market. Consistent with the unconditional findings reported in Table 18.2, these time-series plots are quite revealing about the net spillovers of energy and metal markets to others. The high net spillovers from crude oil to other markets are most evident after the 2000s, around the European debt crises, and the intensification of the GFC. The gold market was also an important source of commodity volatility spillovers with its net spillovers reaching almost 40 percent around the burst of dot-com bubble. However, since late 2003, its role was reversed and gold received almost 20 percent of volatility from other markets in 2006. The agricultural futures markets, conversely, were the net recipient of commodity volatility spillovers over most of the sample period.

Taken together, the evidence thus far suggests that important volatility episodes and fluctuations exist across major commodity markets; the total cross-market spillovers were limited until the onsets of the GFC. As the crisis intensified, so too did the commodity volatility spillovers with much stress carrying over from the energy and metal markets to others. These findings are important in understanding the level and transmission mechanism of financial stress across the major commodity markets and are relevant to the market regulators in formulating effective policies to tackle financial stress transmission, particularly during turbulent periods.

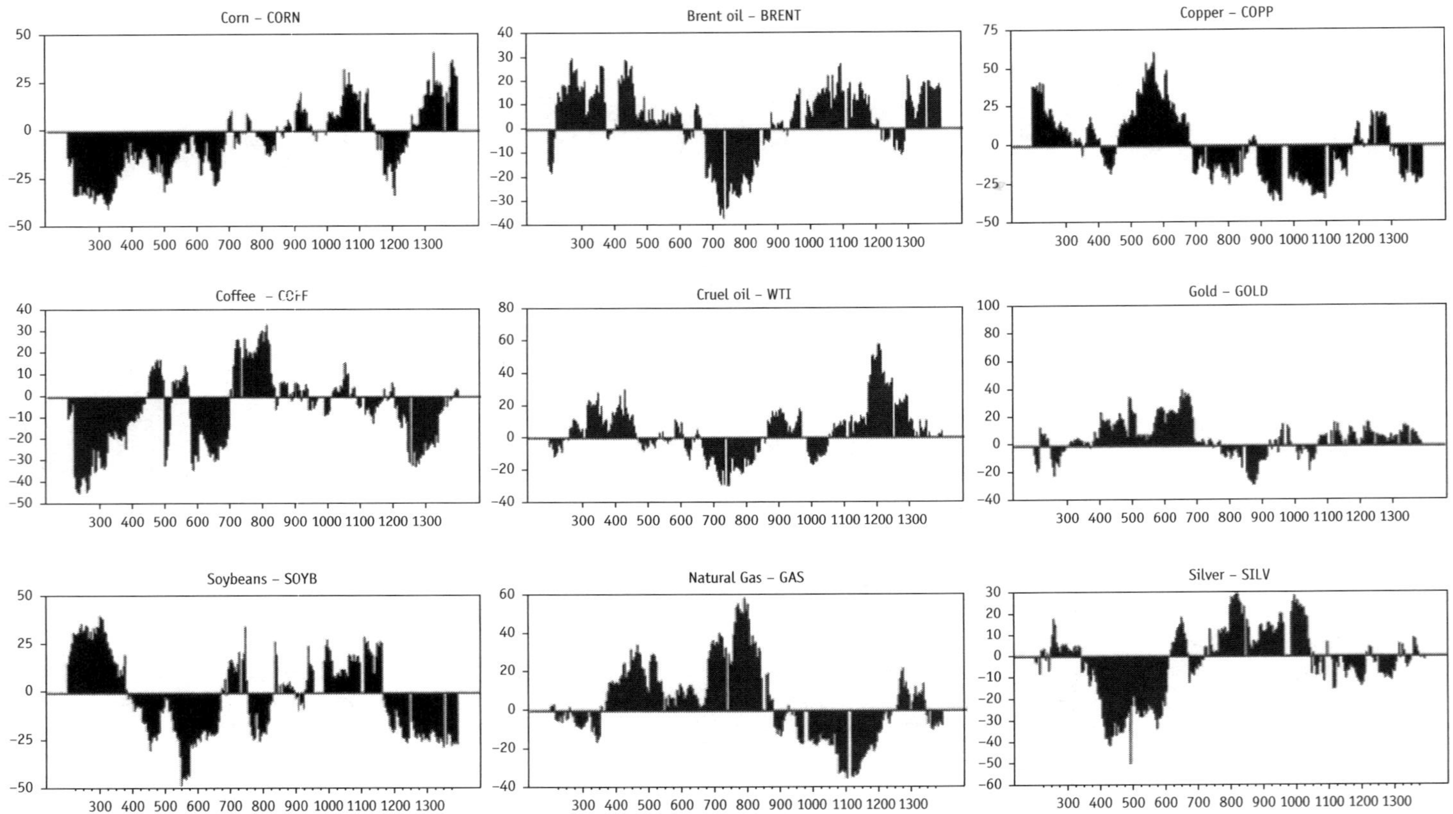

Figure 18.4 Net Volatility Spillovers across Commodity Futures Markets

This figure shows the net volatility spillover across nine major commodity futures markets. The values are calculated by subtracting directional "TO" from directional "FROM" spillovers. Positive (negative) values of the net spillover suggest that the market is a net transmitter (receiver) of volatility spillovers. The second-order VAR is employed using a 200-week rolling estimation window with 10-week forecast horizon. The sample period is between April 11, 1990 and December 28, 2016.

ROBUSTNESS TESTS

To check the sensitivity of these base results, this study re-estimates and plots the total volatility spillover indices based on (1) a five-week forecast horizon, (2) a fourth-order VAR model, and (3) a 100-week rolling window. The figures presented in Figure 18.5 show that the total spillover plot is insensitive to the choices of forecast horizon, order of VAR model, or the estimation window size. The spillover indices appear to

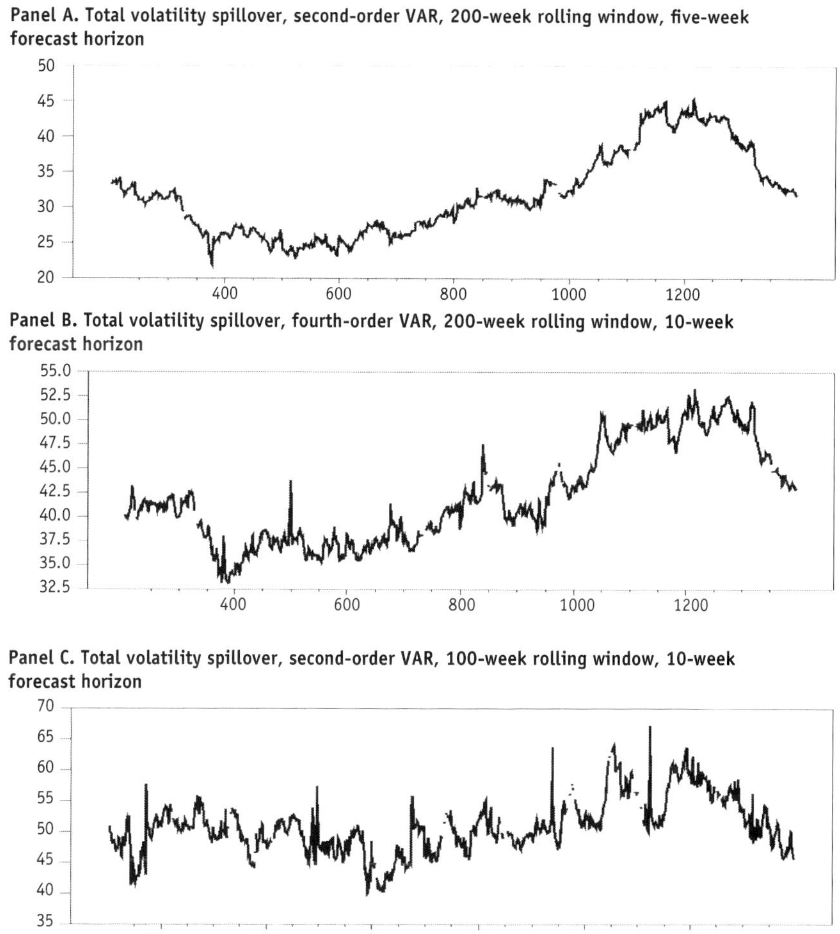

Figure 18.5 Robustness Tests

These figures show the total volatility spillover indices calculated by re-estimating using (1) the second-order VAR, using a 200-week rolling estimation window with five-week forecast horizon (Panel A), (2) the fourth-order VAR, using a 200-week rolling estimation window with 10-week forecast horizon (Panel B), and (3) the second-order VAR, using a 100-week rolling estimation window with 10-week forecast horizon (Panel C).

follow similar patterns. Several previous studies carry out similar robustness checks (Antonakakis and Kizys 2015; Kang et al. 2017).

Summary and Conclusions

Commodity futures markets have witnessed staggering growth since the early 2000s. Commodity futures have become a popular asset class for institutional investors, just like stocks and bonds. This phenomenon is sometimes called the financialization of commodity markets. In fact, the observed steep rises in the commodity prices and volatility has spurred a heated debate in both public and policy circles as to whether financialization of commodity markets destabilised commodity futures markets. Moreover, the debate among policymakers has culminated in questions about the need for more government regulation in these markets.

This chapter examines this controversial topic, investigating the intensity and direction of volatility transmission across three major classes of commodities, including agricultural products (corn, coffee, and soybeans), energy (crude oil and gas), and metals (copper, gold, and silver). To this end, this chapter develops an indicator of volatility transmission across commodity futures markets, the Commodity Volatility Spillover Index (CVSI), to better understand the current state of market instability and to provide regulators with an early warning system for emergent crises. Building on the work of Diebold and Yilmaz (2012) and Chau and Deesomsak (2014), this study derives several conditional and unconditional measures capturing both level and transmission mechanism of volatility across the nine major commodity futures markets.

The evidence points to important stress episodes and fluctuations in volatility spillovers across markets over time; the total cross-market stress spillovers are limited until the onsets of various global crises. As crises intensify, so too do the financial stress spillovers, with considerable stress generally carrying over from energy and metal markets to other commodity futures markets. These results also reveal that coffee and natural gas are exogenous markets that barely transmit any volatility to, or receive volatility spillovers from, other commodity futures markets.

Overall, these findings provide clear evidence on the importance of crude oil and gold in ensuring global commodity market stability. In this light, crude oil and gold are of great importance to the regulatory authorities and policymakers who have a responsibility of safeguarding market stability and promoting economic growth. However, the evidence shows that interconnectedness in the modern world has substantially increased the complexity and fragility of the commodities network. Although crude oil and gold markets provide important signals of economic instability, scapegoating one particular sector (e.g., oil or gold) for the collapse of commodity prices might not be optimal in reaching reliable policy conclusions. On the contrary, focusing on crude oil and gold market regulation may distract regulatory attention from other central problems inherent in the operations and interconnectedness of the global commodity market as a whole. In this light, the claim for further regulation on these specific commodity futures markets, such as higher margins and narrower fluctuation limits, may not be justified.

Several important directions for future research exist, both substantive and methodological. Substantive research should include an examination of how the intensity of commodity volatility spillovers affects the overall economic activity and the evolution of financial crises. Further research could also examine the volatility spillovers within a certain commodity class (e.g., precious metals) as well as other asset classes and multiple asset classes in order to provide additional insights into the linkages and interconnectedness among the global financial markets. On the methodological front, the modeling framework adopted in this chapter can be extended by providing a comparative assessment of our volatility spillover indicator (CVSI) against those generated by other methods such as the multivariate-GARCH model and the causality-in-variance approach of Hafner and Herwartz (2006). Besides, structural breaks may exist in the dynamic volatility spillovers over a long time period and extending the Diebold and Yilmaz's (2012) spillover index approach to a Markov-switching framework would be an interesting area for future research.

Discussion Questions

1. Identify the three major classes of commodities.
2. Explain the term "financialization of commodity markets."
3. Identify three main reasons for the boom and bust in commodity prices.
4. Identify which commodity futures markets are the largest contributors (recipients) of volatility spillovers to (from) others between 1990 and 2016.

References

Antonakakis, Nikolas, and Renatas Kizys. 2015. "Dynamic Spillovers between Commodity and Currency Markets." *International Review of Financial Analysis* 41:October, 303–319.

Arouri, Mohamed E. H., Jamel Jouini, and Duc K. Nguyen. 2011. "Volatility Spillovers between Oil Prices and Stock Sector Returns: Implications for Portfolio Management." *Journal of International Money and Finance* 30:7, 1387–1405.

Batten, Jonathan A., Cetin Ciner, and Brian M. Lucey. 2015. "Which Precious Metals Spill Over on Which, When and Why? Some Evidence." *Applied Economics Letters* 22:6, 466–473.

Bouri, Elie. 2015. "A Broadened Causality in Variance Approach to Assess the Risk Dynamics between Crude Oil Prices and the Jordanian Stock Market." *Energy Policy* 85:October, 271–279.

Chau, Frankie, and Rataporn Deesomsak. 2014. "Does Linkage Fuel the Fire? The Transmission of Financial Stress across the Markets." *International Review of Financial Analysis* 36:December, 57–70.

Cheng, Ing-Haw., and Wei Xiong. 2014. "Financialization of Commodity Markets." *Annual Review of Financial Economics* 6, 419–441.

Chng, Michael T. 2009. "Economic Linkages across Commodity Futures: Hedging and Trading Implications." *Journal of Banking and Finance* 33:5, 958–970.

Diebold, Francis X., and Kamil Yilmaz. 2009. "Measuring Financial Asset Return and Volatility Spillovers, with Application to Global Equity Markets." *Economic Journal* 119:534, 158–171.

Diebold, Francis X., and Kamil Yilmaz. 2012. "Better to Give Than to Receive: Predictive Directional Measurement of Volatility Spillovers." *International Journal of Forecasting* 28:1, 57–66.

Elliott, Graham, Thomas J. Rothenberg, and James H. Stock. 1996. "Efficient Tests for an Autoregressive Unit Root." *Econometrica* 64:4, 813–836.

Hafner, Christian M., and Helmut Herwartz. 2006. "Volatility Impulse Response for Multivariate GARCH Models: An Exchange Rate Illustration." *Journal of International Money and Finance* 25:5, 719–740.

Holló, Daniel, Manfred Kremer, and Macro L. Duca. 2012. "CISS—a Composite Indicator of Systemic Stress in the Financial System." Working paper, Macroprudential Research Network (MaRs), European Central Bank.

Irwin, Scott H., and Dwight R. Sanders. 2011. "Index Funds, Financialization, and Commodity Futures Markets." *Applied Economic Perspectives and Policy* 33:1, 1–31.

Kang, Sang H., Ron McIver, and Seong-Min Yoon. 2017. "Dynamic Spillovers Effects among Crude Oil, Precious Metals, and Agricultural Commodity Futures Markets." *Energy Economics* 62, 19–32.

Koop, Gary, Hashem M. Pesaran, and Simon M. Potter. 1996. "Impulse Response Analysis in Nonlinear Multivariate Models." *Journal of Econometrics* 74:1, 119–147.

Lien, Donald, and Keshab Shrestha. 2015. "Estimating the Optimal Hedge Ratio with Focus Information Criterion." *Journal of Futures Markets* 25:10, 1011–1024.

MacKinnon, James G. 1996. "Numerical Distribution Functions for Unit Root and Cointegration Tests." *Journal of Applied Econometrics* 11:6, 601–618.

Nazlioglu, Saban., Cumhur Erdem, and Ugur Soytas. 2013. "Volatility Spillover between Oil and Agricultural Commodity Markets." *Energy Economics* 36:March, 658–665.

Ng, Serena, and Pierre Perron. 2001. "Lag Length Selection and the Construction of Unit Root Tests with Good Size and Power." *Econometrica* 69:6, 1519–1554.

O'Connor, Fergal A., Brian M. Lucey, Jonathan A. Batten, and Dirk G. Baur. 2015. "The Financial Economics of Gold—a Survey." *International Review of Financial* Analysis 41:October, 186–205.

Olson, Eric, Andrew J. Vivian, and Mark E. Wohar. 2014. "The Relationship between Energy and Equity Markets: Evidence from Volatility Impulse Response Functions." *Energy Economics* 43:May, 297–305.

Pesaran, Hashem M., and Yongcheol Shin. 1998. "Generalized Impulse Response Analysis in Linear Multivariate Models." *Economics Letters* 58:1, 17–29.

Reboredo, Juan C. 2013. "Is Gold a Safe Haven or a Hedge for the US Dollar? Implications for Risk Management." *Journal of Banking and Finance* 37:8, 2665–2676.

Ross, Stephen A. 1989. "Information and Volatility: The No-Arbitrage Martingale Approach to Timing and Resolution Irrelevancy." *Journal of Finance* 44:1, 1–17.

Stoll, Hans R., and Robert E. Whaley. 2010. "Commodity Index Investing and Commodity Futures Prices." *Journal of Applied Finance* 20:1, 7–46.

World Bank. 2012. "Prospect for Commodity Markets." *Global Economic Prospect* 4, 1–165.

World Bank Group. 2016. "Commodity Markets Outlook, October 2016: OPEC in Historical Context." Quarterly Report, October, 1–72. Washington, DC: World Bank. Available at https://openknowledge.worldbank.org/handle/10986/25240.

Yaya, OlaOluwa S., Mohammed M. Tumala, and Christopher G. Udomboso. 2016. "Volatility Persistence and Returns Spillovers between Oil and Gold Prices: Analysis before and after the Global Financial Crisis." *Resources Policy* 49:September, 273–281.

Part Five

STRATEGIES AND PORTFOLIO MANAGEMENT

19

Commodities in International and Emerging Markets

KAMAL SMIMOU
Associate Professor of Finance, University of Ontario Institute of Technology

Introduction

According to Stoll and Whaley (2010), trading costs have declined in all markets, thereby promoting market liquidity and depth and the advent of alternative investments. Gorton and Rouwenhorst (2006) and Erb and Harvey (2006) present strong evidence in support of adding commodity futures contracts to a diversified stock portfolio to lower the risk of the overall rate of return. Erb and Harvey point out that commodity futures are not correlated with one another, proposing to consider them unrelated assets rather than as a homogenous market of similar assets (Capie, Mills, and Wood 2005; Smimou 2010; Joy 2011; Beckmann, Belke, and Czudaj 2014). Ex post studies have examined the gains of international diversification in equity and bond markets, including emerging markets. For instance, Errunza and Rosenberg (1982) stress the importance of including corporate securities of less developed countries in international portfolios (Errunza 1983; Gilmore and McManus 2002), highlighting the need to fully understand the linkage between the fundamentals of emerging markets and global commodity futures. Furthermore, many hedge funds managers build various investment strategies (e.g., commodity-based strategies, global macro, managed futures, or multiple strategies that include emerging-market investing) and seek to profit from changes in global economies (Sarafrazi, Hammoudeh, and Santos 2014).

This chapter attempts to examine financial issues within international and emerging markets to gain insights that would be impossible by amalgamating all the assets and ignoring country-specific factors (Acharya, Lochstoer, and Ramadorai 2013; Hu and Xiong 2017). It examines two research questions. What is the impact of U.S.-listed global commodity futures on the business cycle and financial fundamentals (equity and bond) of emerging markets? What is the additional contribution and impact of changes within that dynamic relation when taking into consideration the movement of U.S. dollar index futures?

Literature Review and Related Studies

Using an adapted definition from Luo and Tung (2007), Jormanainen and Koveshnikov (2012) define emerging markets as those having undergone major transformation in the recent past with rapidly growing national economies in which industries have undergone and continue to undergo dramatic structural changes and hold promise despite a volatile and weak legal system (Smimou and Karabegovic 2010; Kearney 2012). Surveys on emerging markets by Bekaert and Harvey (2003), Phylaktis (2006), and Lien and Zhang (2008) all promote future research on emerging markets, notably on some essential topics including asset management, market integration and contagion, and derivative markets, along with behavioral and cultural perspectives (Bekaert, Harvey, and Ng 2005). As examples of the latter, Lucey and Zhang (2010) examine cultural effects on equity market correlations, and Aggarwal, Kearney, and Lucey (2012) study such effects on foreign portfolio investment.

Highlighting the inter-market relations between emerging markets and the rest of the world, Garcia-Herrero, Woolridge, and Yang (2009) show that Asian foreign investment is concentrated in financial markets outside the region. Berger, Pukthuanthong, and Yang (2011) emphasize the frontier market's low levels of integration with the world market, which may offer benefits to regional investors. Chen, Rogoffand, and Rossi (2010) indicate that commodity prices may help forecast an individual country's stock market indices. Because their study did not fully explore this area of research, this chapter adds information and insight with its focus on some newly defined relations between global commodity futures markets and selected emerging markets.

COMMODITIES AND ECONOMIC GROWTH

Given the renaissance of emerging market economies such as India and China, these countries are in the commodity-intensive stage of development. They have taken advantage of a sizable surge in demand for global commodities to further enhance the expansionary mode of their industries and infrastructure. The price increases of some commodities reflect broad fundamentals corroborated by strong demand from some emerging markets and supply constraints, while the decline of commodity prices during the global financial crisis of 2007–2008 was associated with a sharp fall in global growth. Thus, seeing links between the movement of some commodity prices and the economic growth of various emerging nations is unsurprising.

A stream of research attempts to investigate the potential influence of macroeconomic announcements on certain commodities. Cai, Cheung, and Wong (2001) find that employment reports and gross domestic product (GDP), consumer price index (CPI), and personal income announcements have the greatest impact in the United States. In their examination of the effect of macroeconomic news on metal futures, Elder, Miao, and Ramchander (2012) note the importance of commodity futures, under the assumptions that metal futures act as a hedge against inflation, in offering valuable diversification opportunities, and play the role of a monetary intermediary in time of crisis or uncertainty. While examining the link between economies of emerging markets and the global market, Brei and Buzaushina (2015) find that enduring downturns in the economy and domestic lending followed sharp increases in a country's risk. Thus, the authors suggest the existence of a financial accelerator structure that supports the weakening of financial conditions augmented by currency depreciation and adverse balance sheet effects.

COMMODITIES AND EQUITY MARKETS

Another stream of research attempts to discuss the link between commodities and equity markets. Batten, Szilagyi, and Wagner (2015) highlight the time-varying nature of the benefits of commodities both individually and in portfolios as a vehicle of diversification for emerging-market investors. Using spot market data, they show that Asian investors receive positive risk-adjusted returns in gold and rice markets but not in any of the other commodities when included with traditional stock and bond portfolios. Öztek and Öcal (2017) attempt to model time-varying correlations between commodity and stock markets (the S&P 500 index) to uncover the dynamic nature of correlations in the aftermath of the financial crisis of 2007–2008. They consider market conditions in trying to explain the properties and structure of these correlations. Öztek and Öcal find that the agricultural commodity market provides promising portfolio diversification opportunities during calm periods, yet those opportunities vanish during financial crises. Additionally, they find that market volatility during the financial crisis highly affected the relation between the precious metal sub-index and stock market index. This conclusion calls for further examination to uncover the relations between stock markets and other commodity markets.

Furthermore, studies also examine the advantage of derivative products in emerging markets. For instance, Atilgan, Demirtas, and Simsek (2016) present a comprehensive review of literature on derivative products in emerging markets. Chen, Firth, and Xin (2005) tackle the question of efficiency by examining the response of returns to information shocks in China's commodity futures markets. They find that less actively traded futures (e.g., copper and soybeans), are not as efficient in responding to shocks.

COMMODITIES AND BOND MARKETS

Recently, Bouri, Boyrie, and Pavlova (2017) investigate the volatility transmission from commodities to sovereign credit default swaps of emerging and frontier markets. Using daily data of seven emerging and six frontier countries, they find a noticeable spillover from commodity markets to sovereign credit default swap (CDS) spreads of emerging and frontier markets—commodity prices affect 10 out of 17 CDS spreads. In the same vein, Cifarelli and Paladino (2006) discuss the dynamic relations between sovereign bond spreads of 10 emerging market countries in Asia and Latin America, finding a conditional covariation increases in turbulent periods. Jaramillo and Weber (2013) consider the global spillovers into emerging market bond markets for 26 emerging economies, and show that the global risk appetite and liquidity conditions influence domestic bond yields. Weakness of emerging markets is not uniform but depends on country-specific factors.

The examination of the major global commodities traded in futures markets and their impact on the bond market of emerging markets has value. Juttner, Chung, and

Leung (2006) and Kennedy and Palerm (2014) analyze the influences of external/global versus domestic variables on emerging markets bond index (EMBI) spreads and suggest that external conditions explain many of the movements.

Commodity Market Dynamics and Cross-Asset Linkages

This section describes the data for this study and offers some descriptive statistics. It also highlights the nature of the correlation among selected commodities and the business cycle and movement of equity markets of selected emerging countries. Additionally, the section presents some preliminary analysis involving the gold evolution.

DATA AND EMPIRICAL ANALYSIS

To understand the behavior of U.S.-listed global commodity futures, this study relies on the most liquid commodity trades at the Intercontinental Exchange (ICE) and the Chicago Mercantile Exchange (CME). The empirical analysis uses both weekly and annual data for various types of testing to match the frequency of other available data (i.e., to align those variables with the appropriate control variables that are only available on an annual basis). The continuity of the data series is preserved by selecting only those contracts that satisfy the rolling criteria denoted in this chapter and are actively traded between January 2000 and December 2016, describing three basic commodity groups: (1) energy (WTI crude oil and natural gas), (2) metals (gold, silver, platinum, and copper), and (3) agricultural (grains and softs including corn, soybeans, rice, cotton, coffee, sugar, and cocoa).

Using global commodity futures to tap the impact of the commodity has many benefits given that their movements reflect news and changes in economic and financial conditions more quickly than do consumer and spot prices. Additionally, their trading hours cover an extended number of days and hours per week.

From a practical perspective, the monthly roll in the commodity futures is spread over the entire month preceding the first delivery day and sometimes longer. Following past studies such as de Ville de Goyet, Dhaene, and Sercu (2008), this study assumes that a roll occurs from the expiring month to the next nearest contract when its volume exceeds the volume of the expiring month. Furthermore, three portfolios (indices) are computed as the equally weighted average of all selected commodities in each of the three commodity groups, closely following Gorton and Rouwenhorst (2006), De Miguel, Garlappi, and Uppal (2009), and Batten et al. (2015). Creating equally weighted portfolios from the highly liquid to the less liquid commodities mitigates the effect of the on-index commodities versus off-index commodities.

As documented in past empirical studies, controlling for movements in the U.S. dollar index is essential. Thus, ICE U.S. Dollar Index (USDX) futures—a leading benchmark for the international value of the U.S. dollar and the world's most widely traded six currencies—is included, following the same roll procedure. Having all indices and commodities in a common currency avoids concerns of possible exchange-rate effects.

Following Auer (2016), this study selects a set of equity indices from MSCI to tap the movement of the selected emerging equity markets. The benefits of using MSCI indices include (1) the ability to use a longer time span than what could be achieved from nationally computed indices and (2) the ability to eliminate or reduce the impact of different index methodologies on empirical results because of the standardization on their constructions.

From Datastream, the study uses the main commodity futures as well as macroeconomic and market variables such as GDP, central bank policy rates, inflation rates, equity indices, and bond indices of all selected countries. The 22 countries represent four chosen emerging market groups designated according to economic cohesiveness and "subjective" similarity of their political institutions. The African (AF) group consists of South Africa, Kenya, and Nigeria, while the Latin American (LA) group consists of Brazil, Argentina, Venezuela, Bolivia, and Mexico. The Middle East and North Africa (MENA) group consists of Saudi Arabia, Kuwait, Qatar, Oman, Egypt, UAE, Iraq, Iran, Algeria, and Morocco. Lastly, the Special Emerging (SE) group represents Russia, India, China, and Turkey. All the data for GDP and equity and bond indices are valued in U.S. dollars.

DESCRIPTIVE STATISTICS

Table 19.1 provides the descriptive statistics of the relevant futures returns. Among the futures contracts, gold, followed by silver, sugar, and copper, had the highest average weekly returns (0.16, 0.13, 0.13, and 0.12 percent, respectively), while coffee and cotton had the lowest returns between January 2000 and December 2016.

Table 19.1 examines correlations among selected variables and between selected contracts vis-à-vis domestic business cycle (GDP growth) and equity market movements as shown in Table 19.2. Results in Table 19.1 show that the benefit of diversification stems from the positive and low returns among all commodities. Gold futures proved to be quite effective in reducing the risk through diversification when combined with rice or cotton or sugar (Daskalaki and Skiadopoulos 2011; O'Connor and Lucey 2012; Agyei-Ampomah, Gounopoulos, and Mazouz 2014).

Table 19.2 reveals that energies show higher correlation with GDP growth in a majority of the MENA countries, Russia, Brazil, Argentina, and Mexico, given their dependence on crude oil production. Yet, no statistically significant correlation exists between energies and economic growth in the African group. Broadly speaking, metals exhibit higher correlations with economic growth for the majority of selected countries—19 out of 22 countries have a positive correlation.

EVOLUTION OF GOLD RESERVES IN EMERGING COUNTRIES

As presented in the previous section, gold futures and metals have significant correlations with economic growth and equity markets of selected countries. Thus, examining gold reserves across selected countries is worthwhile because gold is among the most liquid and widely followed commodities. According to the World Gold Council (2016), central bank reserves follow the mandate of safety, liquidity, and return. If central banks

Table 19.1 **Summary Statistics and Correlation Coefficients among Selected Commodities**

Variables / *Statistics*	1. *Oil (WTI)*	2. *Natural Gas*	3. *Gold*	4. *Silver*	5. *Platinum*	6. *Copper*	7. *Corn*	8. *Soybeans*	9. *Rice*	10. *Cotton*	11. *Coffee*	12. *Sugar*	13. *Cocoa*
Mean %	0.09	0.05	0.16	0.13	0.09	0.12	0.06	0.09	0.04	0.03	0.00	0.13	0.10
Minimum	−0.21	−0.23	−0.11	−0.27	−0.19	−0.17	−0.20	−0.16	−0.16	−0.32	−0.18	−0.30	−0.24
Maximum	0.24	0.24	0.18	0.19	0.22	0.19	0.13	0.11	0.13	0.15	0.18	0.20	0.16
Standard Deviation	0.05	0.06	0.03	0.04	0.03	0.04	0.04	0.04	0.04	0.04	0.05	0.04	0.04
Skewness	−0.38	0.07	0.03	−0.85	−0.25	−0.27	−0.20	−0.54	−0.28	−0.46	0.08	−0.4	−0.26
Reward-to-risk (R-R ratio)	0.02	0.01	0.06	0.03	0.03	0.03	0.02	0.02	0.01	0.01	0.00	0.03	0.03
Kurtosis	2.25	0.77	4.07	4.43	6.08	2.34	1.65	1.79	1.54	4.37	1.17	4.69	1.38
Jarque-Bera	205.9***	22.3***	604.4***	822.3***	1355.2***	209.3***	104.8***	159.9***	98.1***	729.6***	50.82***	824.9***	79.4***
1.	1.0	0.28***	0.19***	0.26***	0.31***	0.35***	0.21***	0.25***	0.11***	0.19***	0.16***	0.13***	0.17***
2.		1.0	0.11***	0.14***	0.14***	0.10***	0.10***	0.12***	0.06*	0.03	0.12***	0.06*	0.07**
3.			1.0	0.77***	0.58***	0.35***	0.20***	0.17***	0.10***	0.11***	0.17***	0.15***	0.25***
4.				1.0	0.60***	0.45***	0.25***	0.25***	0.13***	0.15***	0.24***	0.16***	0.26***

5.	1.0	0.47***	0.24***	0.25***	0.16***	0.19***	0.19***	0.13***	0.21***
6.		1.0	0.20***	0.30***	0.18***	0.20***	0.2***	0.18***	0.18***
7.			1.0	0.54***	0.22***	0.21***	0.18***	0.10***	0.15***
8.				1.0	0.26***	0.25***	0.22***	0.13***	0.17***
9.					1.0	0.11***	0.1***	0.07**	0.12***
10.						1.0	0.18***	0.12***	0.16***
11.							1.0	0.18***	0.21***
12.								1.0	0.18***
13.									1.0

Note: This table presents the summary statistics for the weekly returns of major selected commodity futures between January 2000 and December 2016. (n = 866). ***, **, and * indicate statistical significance at the 1%, 5%, and 10% levels, respectively. Reward-to-risk was computed by dividing the mean return of each variable (e.g., the average amount of profit the trader expects to have made when the position is closed [i.e., the reward]) by the standard deviation (e.g., the amount she stands to lose if the price moves in the unexpected direction [i.e., the risk]). Weekly returns of selected futures are not expressed as annualized figures.

Table 19.2 **Correlation Coefficients between Constructed Commodity Indexes and GDP, and Selected Equity Markets**

Countries	*Variables*	*Energies*	*Metals*	*Agricultural (Grains and Softs)*		*Energies*	*Metals*	*Agricultural (Grains and Softs)*	*The Dollar Index*
South Africa	GDP Growth	0.33	0.56**	0.53**	Domestic Equity Market	0.27***	0.45***	0.33***	–0.34***
Kenya		0.31	0.29	0.46**		0.06*	0.08**	0.07**	–0.12***
Nigeria		0.37	0.71***	0.25		0.09**	0.03	0.04	0.00
Saudi Arabia		0.54**	0.79**	0.41*		0.07**	–0.04	0.06*	–0.00
Kuwait		0.50**	0.69***	0.33		0.09**	0.14***	0.03	–0.09***
Qatar		0.55**	0.74***	0.36		0.17***	0.10***	0.16***	–0.09**
Oman		0.56**	0.70***	0.34		0.18***	0.13***	0.10***	–0.07**
Egypt		0.084	0.13	0.16		0.15***	0.13***	0.09***	–0.08**
UAE		0.55**	0.76***	0.36		0.18***	0.09**	0.05	–0.06
Iraq		0.74***	0.77***	0.71**		n.a.	n.a.	**n.a**	**n.a**
Iran		0.28	0.71***	0.66***		n.a.	n.a.	**n.a**	**n.a**
Algeria		0.59***	0.79***	0.58***		n.a.	n.a.	**n.a**	**n.a**

Morocco	0.19	0.41*	0.67***	0.08***	0.22***	0.20***	–0.37***
Brazil	0.46**	0.68***	0.65***	0.23***	0.36***	0.27***	–0.23***
Argentina	0.55**	0.51**	0.63***	0.22***	0.25***	0.22***	–0.19***
Venezuela	0.37	0.23	0.13	0.00	0.04	0.00	–0.02
Bolivia	0.29	0.53**	0.66***	n.a.	n.a.	**n.a**	**n.a**
Mexico	0.51**	0.62***	0.09	0.20***	0.28***	0.20***	–0.18***
Russia	0.62***	0.74***	0.48**	0.22***	0.28***	0.20***	–0.14***
India	0.10	0.51**	0.38	0.15***	0.23***	0.17***	–0.17***
China	0.33	0.71***	0.72***	0.20***	0.27***	0.21***	–0.18***
Turkey	0.05	0.45*	0.42*	0.13***	0.20***	0.16***	–0.16***

Note: This table shows the correlation coefficients between the constructed equally commodity portfolios and GDP growth using yearly data and the correlation coefficients between the constructed commodity portfolios and the domestic equity market returns using weekly data between 1997 and 2015. ***, **, and * indicate statistical significance at the 1%, 5%, and 10% levels, respectively. Some countries, as indicated, do not have either a reliable investable equity index or do not have equity markets; in both cases, I denote not available (n.a.).

purchase or change their positions on gold as insurance for their country's reserves, then the possibility exists that emerging-market investors may expand their positions in the gold market to hedge their equity portfolios, which is the safe haven argument. Therefore, the change in gold reserves should help in understanding the movement of the demand side of gold commodity, and hence possibly capture any noticeable surge or decline of central bank reserves.

The clear message that emerges from Figure 19.1 is that Iraq, Mexico, and Turkey have the highest changes in gold reserves, between 20 and 52 percent; while Venezuela decreased its gold reserves by −11.5 percent over the same period. The proportion of gold commodity in the total reserves may be used as a proxy for the gold demand from the central bank such that a high demand indicates that more trades will occur in the future. Some emerging nations, such as South Africa (10.9 percent), Egypt (19.9 percent), Turkey (14.9 percent), and Venezuela (65.2 percent), show a proportion of holdings in gold reserve beyond the normal 10 percent threshold, which may be expected given the economic challenges and political turmoil these nations face. Thus in that context, any negative movement of the gold commodity may have sizable ramifications on their economic outlook and equity and/or bond markets.

For instance, the World Gold Council's gold demand and supply statistics for the first quarter of 2016 show that the consumption (as a percent of gold produced in the world) is about 37.36 percent in jewelry, 47.88 percent in investments, 6.27 percent

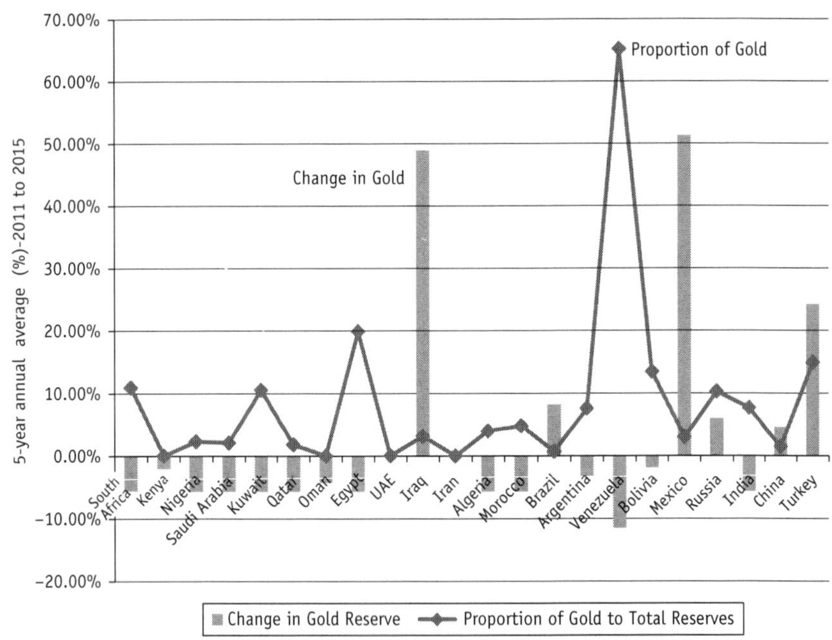

Figure 19.1 Evolution of Gold Reserve Holdings of Emerging Countries
This figure shows changes in gold reserves and the proportion of gold commodity to total reserves of selected countries over a five-year window using annual data. Source: Thomson Reuters Datastream and the author's computations.

in industry, and 8.49 percent in central banks and other institutions. Hu and Xiong (2017) show that stock prices across East Asian economies exhibit significant positive reactions to changes of futures prices of commodities traded in the United States—serving as barometers of the global economy (Killian 2009; Kilian and Murphy 2014; Singleton 2014).

Economics of Commodity and Emerging Markets

This section presents the nature of the relation between global commodities and business cycles of selected emerging countries, followed by the examination of the impact of commodities on domestic equity markets of those countries. Additionally, this section puts forth empirical evidence by looking more closely at the impacts of constructed commodity futures indexes on bond markets of a group of emerging countries.

GLOBAL COMMODITIES AND THE BUSINESS CYCLE OF EMERGING MARKETS

The first phase of this discussion is an examination of the relations between macroeconomic variables such as economic growth (proxy business cycle) and behavior of commodity futures, while controlling for the U.S. dollar index movement, policy interest rates, and inflation (e.g., Smimou 2014). Equation 19.1 shows the tested regression equation:

$$\begin{aligned} Y_{it} &= \alpha_0 + \varphi_1 \times COM_t + \varphi_2 \times COM_{t-1} + \\ &\quad \omega_1 \times Dol_t + \omega_{12} \times Dol_{t-1} + \pi \times Inf_t + \theta \times Int_t +_i \end{aligned} \qquad \textbf{(19.1)}$$

where Y_{it} denotes the economic growth over the year t for country i. The impact of COM futures is proxied by the three constructed equally-weighted portfolio-based energies (ENG), metals (MET), and agricultural (AGR) commodity futures. The model includes the change in the U.S dollar index futures contract (*Dol*) and two control independent variables: inflation (*Inf*) and central bank policy rate (*Int*) of each country. The model also includes the commodity effects on selected assets by assuming that real variables potentially respond to the movement in commodity markets contemporaneously or with a lag, and this impact may differ across various regions and countries.

In this subsection, the study employs panel estimation, which has several advantages compared to a study on the individual-country level. A panel framework increases the efficiency and power of the regressions relative to country-specific estimates, which might be prone to problems associated with low degrees of freedom. Using panel data may also help to uncover a common dynamic across countries that might be hidden by individual country-level analyses (Gavin and Theodorou 2005). Sensoy, Ozturk, Hacihasanoglu, and Tabak (2016) find that the increase in average correlations among the debt indexes of emerging markets after the financial crisis of 2007–2008 is more likely caused by clusters of countries that exhibit high within-cluster co-movement but not between-cluster co-movement. In this study, establishing four different emerging markets that are not homogenous groups of countries mitigates this issue. For instance, some emerging markets, such as Russia, Brazil, Venezuela, and Saudi Arabia, are commodity exporters, which have benefited from increasing export revenues associated with favorable commodity prices.

Table 19.3 reveals results for various specifications. Panel A shows the positive impact of energy portfolios for all emerging groups except the African group. The coefficient of energy futures price changes on the economic growth of selected emerging groups ranges between 0.12 and 0.18, indicating that between 12 and 18 percent of the economic growth of those emerging countries is attributed to the energy futures market.

Furthermore, Panel B shows that metals exhibit a higher contemporaneous impact on the economic growth of all selected emerging countries, highlighting the importance of gold across many nations. The coefficients on metals hover between 0.25 (AF) and 0.36 (MENA). Although this study finds strong evidence for the relations between commodities and GDP growth using annual data, instances exist (Panel C specifications 1 to 11) when global agricultural markets have some positive effect on GDP growth in most countries; the effect is more pronounced for the Latin America (LA) group. This fact highlights the importance of agriculture in these countries, particularly for Brazil and Argentina. An annual increase of 1 percent in the standard deviation of global agricultural commodities contributes a 0.41 percent increase in GDP for the LA group.

Again, in the emerging-market context, the contemporaneous change in the U.S. dollar has a significant impact on the business cycle, highlighting the dependence on and role of the U.S. dollar as global currency of trade across many regions. The results in Table 19.4 also highlight the dynamic relations between equity or bond and global commodity futures markets across various emerging economies.

RELATION BETWEEN EMERGING EQUITY MARKETS AND GLOBAL COMMODITIES

In this section, the study uses weekly data to examine the relations between energy futures markets and a set of emerging equity indices from selected countries. The interaction of the most liquid commodity futures markets with emerging economy financial markets can be considered an ideal testing ground for empirical appraisal. Doing that, this study indirectly examines if the predictive ability of commodity futures movement is contingent upon the appropriate match between economic fundamentals (e.g., growth opportunities, exchange rates, and interest rates) and factors specific to equity market and firm (e.g., institutional factors). For instance, Brazil and Saudi Arabia are commodity-based economies with both real economy and equity markets that are heavy influenced by commodities.

Each regression in Table 19.4 estimates if the energy futures market at $t-1$ has a positive or negative relation with the future performance emerging market equity markets. Panel A in Table 19.4 shows that contemporaneous energy commodity movements are statistically and economically related to equity markets in Russia, Brazil, Argentina, and South Africa, with estimated coefficients between 0.20 and 0.35. Turkey is an exception,

Table 19.3 **Movement of Global Commodities and Emerging Market Business Cycles**

Panel A. Energy Futures Portfolio, EW_{ENG} Variables⇓ Models ⇒	*(1)*	*(2)*	*(3)*	*(4)*	*(5)*	*(6)*	*(7)*	*(8)*	*(9)*	*(10)*	*(11)*	*(12)*
Groups→	*SP Emerging Group*			*MENA Group*			*LA Group*			*AF Group*		
Const.	0.097***	0.080**	0.110***	0.061***	0.029	0.026	0.050**	0.070	0.061	0.048	0.140***	0.200**
	[0.020]	[0.037]	[0.026]	[0.011]	[0.018]	[0.025]	[0.020]	[0.040]	[0.043]	[0.040]	[0.040]	[0.09]
EW_{ENG}	0.120*	0.110*	0.120**	0.150***	0.160***	0.18***	0.150***	0.14***	0.14***	0.075	0.083	0.100
	[0.060]	[0.060]	[0.050]	[0.033]	[0.034]	[0.037]	[0.050]	[0.04]	[0.044]	[0.056]	[0.050]	[0.070]
L. EW_{ENG} (One-Period Lag EW_{ENG})	0.080	0.080	0.090*	0.070**	0.073**	0.087***	–0.003	–0.013	–0.014	–0.03	–0.030	–0.006
	[0.050]	[0.050]	[0.050]	[0.030]	[0.030]	[0.030]	[0.060]	[0.06]	[0.06]	[0.07]	[0.060]	[0.070]
U.S. Dollar (Dol_t)	–0.680***	–0.690***	–0.820***	–0.770***	–0.770***	–0.75***	–0.50***	–0.51***	–0.54***	–0.620***	–0.650***	–0.770***
	[0.190]	[0.190]	[0.170]	[0.120]	[0.110]	[0.12]	[0.16]	[0.16]	[0.18]	[0.200]	[0.19]	[0.260]
L. U.S. Dollar (One-Period Lag Dol_{t-1})	0.010	0.001	0.120	–0.05	–0.021	0.034	–0.51**	–0.51**	–0.44**	0.045	–0.090	0.270
	[0.180]	[0.180]	[0.160]	[0.12]	[0.110]	[0.12]	[0.21]	[0.21]	[0.19]	[0.240]	[0.240]	[0.330]
Inflation rate	–0.130	–0.090	–0.510**	0.180	0.290*	0.27**	0.005	–0.300	–0.220	0.460	–0.020	0.100
	[0.150]	[0.170]	[0.190]	[0.120]	[0.150]	[0.13]	[0.220]	[0.530]	[0.400]	[0.530]	[0.460]	[0.660]
Central Bank Policy Rate (interest rate)			0.100			0.012			–0.840			–0.420
			[0.074]			[0.470]			[0.670]			[0.810]
Country Effect	No	Yes	Yes	No	Yes	Yes	No	Yes	Yes	No	Yes	Yes
Adjusted R^2	**0.21**	**0.19**	**0.37**	**0.38**	**0.40**	**0.42**	**0.26**	**0.25**	**0.36**	**0.17**	**0.19**	**0.25**

(continued)

Table 19.3 **Continued**

Panel B. Metals Futures Portfolio, EW_{META} Variables⇓ Models ⇒	*(1)*	*(2)*	*(3)*	*(4)*	*(5)*	*(6)*	*(7)*	*(8)*	*(9)*	*(10)*	*(11)*	*(12)*
Groups→	SP Emerging Countries Group				MENA Group			LA Group			AF Group	
Const.	0.079***	0.064*	0.085***	0.042***	0.010	0.017	0.035*	0.054	0.047	0.026	0.110**	0.170**
	[0.020]	[0.038]	[0.025]	[0.010]	[0.020]	[0.025]	[0.020]	[0.045]	[0.045]	[0.040]	[0.040]	[0.080]
EW_{META}	0.320***	0.330***	0.320***	0.360***	0.360***	0.360***	0.340***	0.330***	0.310***	0.310***	0.320***	0.250**
	[0.070]	[0.067]	[0.066]	[0.041]	[0.040]	[0.040]	[0.070]	[0.070]	[0.070]	[0.110]	[0.110]	[0.110]
L. EW_{META}	0.095	0.090	0.100*	0.190***	0.190***	0.200***	0.021	0.009	0.014	−0.090	−0.070	−0.090
(One-Period Lag EW_{META})	[0.060]	[0.060]	[0.056]	[0.038]	[0.035]	[0.036]	[0.070]	[0.078]	[0.080]	[0.110]	[0.110]	[0.100]
U.S. Dollar (Dol_t)	−0.290	−0.300	−0.44**	−0.370***	−0.380***	−0.370***	−0.240	−0.260	−0.310	−0.370	−0.390*	−0.600**
	[0.190]	[0.200]	[0.170]	[0.110]	[0.100]	[0.110]	[0.180]	[0.190]	[0.200]	[0.230]	[0.230]	[0.290]
L. U.S. Dollar	−0.033	−0.047	0.078	−0.020	−0.007	0.021	−0.590**	−0.590***	−0.510***	−0.054	−0.090	0.050
(One-Period Lag Dol_{t-1})	[0.140]	[0.150]	[0.140]	[0.110]	[0.090]	[0.090]	[0.220]	[0.210]	[0.180]	[0.200]	[0.180]	[0.220]
Inflation rate	−0.100	−0.060	−0.470***	0.098	0.140	0.140	−0.010	−0.310	−0.240	0.560	0.100	0.260
	[0.150]	[0.170]	[0.170]	[0.120]	[0.120]	[0.110]	[0.240]	[0.560]	[0.410]	[0.480]	[0.440]	[0.680]
Central Bank Policy			0.110*			0.110			-0.910			-0.420
Rate (interest rate)			[0.064]			[0.37]			[0.730]			[0.700]
Country Effect	No	Yes	Yes	No	Yes	Yes	No	Yes	Yes	No	Yes	Yes
Adjusted R^2	0.31	0.295	0.43	0.53	0.56	0.57	0.275	0.27	0.384	0.28	0.30	0.33

Panel C. Agricultural Futures Portfolio, EW_{Agr} Variables⇓ Models ⇒	*(1)*	*(2)*	*(3)*	*(4)*	*(5)*	*(6)*	*(7)*	*(8)*	*(9)*	*(10)*	*(11)*	*(12)*
Groups→	SP Emerging Countries Group			MENA Group			LA Group			AF Group		
Const.	0.100***	0.086**	0.110***	0.068***	0.038***	0.024	0.056***	0.077*	0.047	0.053	0.140***	0.190*
	[0.017]	[0.040]	[0.030]	[0.012]	[0.014]	[0.023]	[0.020]	[0.045]	[0.047]	[0.040]	[0.050]	[0.101]
EW_{Agr}	0.260**	0.270**	0.180*	0.270***	0.260***	0.330***	0.370***	0.380***	0.410***	0.170	0.210*	0.173
	[0.110]	[0.110]	[0.110]	[0.064]	[0.060]	[0.060]	[0.120]	[0.130]	[0.120]	[0.120]	[0.110]	[0.120]
L. EW_{Agr} (One-Period Lag EW_{Agr})	−0.043	−0.046	−0.06	−0.014	−0.015	−0.014	0.012	0.034	0.043	−0.120	−0.110	−0.087
	[0.080]	[0.080]	[0.090]	[0.070]	[0.060]	[0.060]	[0.080]	[0.080]	[0.090]	[0.090]	[0.090]	[0.130]
U.S. Dollar (Dol_t)	−0.530**	−0.540**	−0.730***	−0.650***	−0.660***	−0.620***	−0.380**	−0.380**	−0.400*	−0.670***	−0.670***	−0.840***
	[0.230]	[0.230]	[0.210]	[0.130]	[0.120]	[0.130]	[0.170]	[0.180]	[0.210]	[0.210]	[0.220]	[0.270]
L. U.S. Dollar (One-Period Lag Dol_{t-1})	−0.130	−0.150	−0.067	−0.180	−0.160	−0.150	−0.540***	−0.510***	−0.420**	−0.060	−0.110	0.150
	[0.160]	[0.170]	[0.170]	[0.120]	[0.110]	[0.110]	[0.200]	[0.180]	[0.160]	[0.240]	[0.220]	[0.300]
Inflation rate	−0.100	−0.060	−0.480***	0.160	0.230	0.170	−0.052	−0.450	−0.510	0.440	−0.074	0.075
	[0.140]	[0.160]	[0.170]	[0.150]	[0.160]	[0.150]	[0.240]	[0.550]	[0.440]	[0.510]	[0.440]	[0.690]
Central Bank Policy Rate (interest rate)			0.120*			0.360			−0.740			−0.390
			[0.070]			[0.500]			[0.640]			[0.870]
Country Effect	No	Yes	Yes	No	Yes	Yes	No	Yes	Yes	No	Yes	Yes
Adjusted R^2	0.21	0.19	0.29	0.32	0.34	0.36	0.24	0.24	0.37	0.17	0.19	0.23

Note: This table shows the regression analysis and in-sample predictability tests for constructed commodity portfolios (energy, metals, and agricultural) while conditioning for some macroeconomic variables (i.e., inflation, monetary policy interest rate, and the U.S. dollar index futures) using annual data. The dependent variable is economic growth (Domestic GDP growth). Twenty-two countries are grouped into four different classifications: (1) Special Emerging group consists of Russia, India, China, and Turkey; (2) Latin America (LA) group consists of Brazil, Argentina, Venezuela, Bolivia, plus Mexico; (3) Middle East and North African (MENA) group consists of Saudi Arabia, Kuwait, Qatar, Oman, Egypt, UAE, Iraq, Iran, Algeria, and Morocco; and (4) Africa (AF) group consists of South Africa, Kenya, and Nigeria. *, **, and *** indicate a significant difference from zero at the 10%, 5%, and 1% levels, respectively. Robust standard errors are provided in brackets below the estimated coefficients and are corrected for heteroskedasticity using White's (1980) heteroskedasticity-consistent covariance matrix of the parameter estimates, as in MacKinnon (1985). All Durbin-Watson test statistics, though not reported here, do not reject the hypothesis of random residuals of the regressions at the 5% level. L. stands for the Lag.

Table 19.4 **Movement of Global Commodities and Emerging Equity Markets**

Panel A. Energy Futures Portfolio, EW_{ENG} and Equity Markets

Variables ⇒ Equity Market of Countries⇓	*Const.*	*EW_{ENG}*	*L. EW_{ENG} (One-Period Lag EW_{ENG})*	*U.S. Dollar (Dol_t)*	*L. U.S. Dollar (One-Period Lag Dol_{t-1})*	*Adjusted R^2*
Russia	-0.001 [0.002]	0.357*** [0.072]	0.019 [0.064]	–0.660*** [0.220]	–0.440* [0.240]	**0.061**
India	0.0015 [0.001]	0.110*** [0.030]	0.001 [0.029]	–0.470*** [0.120]	–0.340*** [0.120]	**0.050**
China	–0.001 [0.001]	0.180*** [0.034]	0.023 [0.035]	–0.540*** [0.130]	–0.320** [0.130]	**0.065**
Turkey	0.001 [0.002]	0.150*** [0.056]	–0.110** [0.052]	–0.820*** [0.210]	–0.370* [0.200]	**0.038**
Brazil	0.001 [0.002]	0.236*** [0.041]	0.008 [0.041]	–0.860*** [0.150]	–0.120 [0.180]	**0.085**
Argentina	–0.001 [0.002]	0.247*** [0.041]	0.045 [0.0450]	–0.750*** [0.160]	–0.087 [0.180]	**0.068**
Venezuela	0.001 [0.003]	–0.002 [0.061]	–0.045 [0.061]	–0.180 [0.350]	0.070 [0.330]	**0.001**
Mexico	0.0014 [0.001]	0.160*** [0.034]	–0.023 [0.032]	–0.490*** [0.120]	–0.090 [0.140]	**0.057**
Saudi Arabia	0.001 [0.001]	0.024 [0.030]	0.110*** [0.030]	0.062 [0.120]	–0.220* [0.130]	**0.024**

Kuwait	0.0006	0.020	0.030	–0.120	–0.190*	**0.015**
	[0.001]	[0.023]	[0.023]	[0.080]	[0.110]	
Qatar	0.0012	0.077**	0.082***	–0.106	–0.330**	**0.040**
	[0.001]	[0.026]	[0.026]	[0.100]	[0.130]	
Oman	0.0007	0.073***	0.043*	–0.054	–0.110	**0.032**
	[0.001]	[0.021]	[0.020]	[0.070]	[0.150]	
Egypt	0.001	0.140***	0.047	–0.130	–0.320***	**0.036**
	[0.0012]	[0.035]	[0.031]	[0.130]	[0.120]	
UAE	0.001	0.110***	0.060*	0.090	–0.320	**0.030**
	[0.001]	[0.033]	[0.030]	[0.120]	[0.20]	
Morocco	0.001	–0.003	–0.037	–0.810***	–0.120*	**0.144**
	[0.001]	[0.020]	[0.022]	[0.068]	[0.070]	
South Africa	0.001	0.200***	–0.063**	–1.090***	–0.078	**0.162**
	[0.001]	[0.033]	[0.032]	[0.110]	[0.120]	
Kenya	0.002*	0.020	0.005	–0.290**	–0.270**	**0.020**
	[0.001]	[0.026]	[0.030]	[0.120]	[0.120]	
Nigeria	0.001	0.077**	0.048	0.105	–0.29**	**0.020**
	[0.001]	[0.032]	[0.035]	[0.120]	[0.130]	

(*continued*)

Table 19.4 **Continued**

Panel B. Metals' Futures Portfolio, EW_{META} and Equity Markets						
Variables ⇒ Equity Market of Countries⇓	*Const.*	*EW_{META}*	*L. EW_{META} (One-period Lag EW_{META})*	*U.S. Dollar (Dolt)*	*L. U.S. Dollar (One-period Lag Dolt-1)*	*Adjusted R^2*
Russia	–0.001 [0.002]	0.750*** [0.100]	0.170 [0.103]	–0.183 [0.240]	–0.270 [0.240]	**0.084**
India	0.001 [0.001]	0.27*** [0.051]	0.220*** [0.060]	–0.270** [0.120]	–0.110 [0.120]	**0.087**
China	–0.001 [0.001]	0.404*** [0.052]	0.105* [0.062]	–0.270** [0.135]	–0.220 [0.140]	**0.089**
Turkey	0.001 [0.002]	0.404*** [0.083]	0.075 [0.088]	–0.530** [0.210]	–0.184 [0.203]	**0.046**
Brazil	0.001 [0.002]	0.630*** [0.065]	0.051 [0.080]	–0.408** [0.165]	–0.072 [0.178]	**0.138**
Argentina	–0.001 [0.002]	0.435*** [0.067]	0.008 [0.075]	–0.510*** [0.166]	–0.110 [0.180]	**0.070**
Venezuela	0.001 [0.003]	0.179 [0.120]	–0.042 [0.076]	0.008 [0.270]	0.067 [0.360]	**0.002**
Mexico	0.001 [0.001]	0.376*** [0.056]	0.008 [0.070]	–0.240* [0.130]	0.054 [0.130]	**0.083**
Saudi Arabia	0.001 [0.001]	–0.087 [0.080]	0.150* [0.080]	–0.049 [0.120]	–0.150 [0.120]	**0.021**

Kuwait	0.001	0.118**	0.044	–0.025	–0.180	**0.026**
	[0.001]	[0.050]	[0.050]	[0.090]	[0.110]	
Qatar	0.001	0.110*	0.160***	–0.065	–0.240*	**0.040**
	[0.001]	[0.050]	[0.060]	[0.100]	[0.120]	
Oman	0.001	0.106***	0.107*	–0.010	–0.043	**0.303**
	[0.001]	[0.040]	[0.050]	[0.080]	[0.140]	
Egypt	–0.000	0.185***	0.170**	–0.063	–0.170	**0.0363**
	[0.0012]	[0.054]	[0.070]	[0.130]	[0.110]	
UAE	0.001	0.081	0.165*	0.080	–0.200	**0.022**
	[0.001]	[0.076]	[0.090]	[0.130]	[0.180]	
Morocco	0.001	0.073**	0.060	–0.730***	-0.031	**0.148**
	[0.001]	[0.033]	[0.040]	[0.060]	[0.078]	
South Africa	0.001	0.560***	0.015	–0.670***	0.002	**0.233**
	[0.001]	[0.054]	[0.060]	[0.120]	[0.110]	
Kenya	0.002	0.030	0.087	–.270**	–0.180*	**0.020**
	[0.001]	[0.050]	[0.060]	[0.110]	[0.110]	
Nigeria	0.001	0.012	0.064	0.050	–0.270**	**0.008**
	[0.001]	[0.060]	[0.070]	[0.120]	[0.130]	

(*continued*)

Table 19.4 **Continued**

Panel C. Agricultural (Grains and Softs) Futures Portfolio, EW_{AGR} and Equity Markets

Variables ⇒ Equity Market of Countries⇓	*Const.*	EW_{AGR}	*L.* EW_{AGR} *(One–period Lag* EW_{AGR}*)*	*U.S. Dollar (Dolt)*	*L. U.S. Dollar (One-period Lag Dolt-1)*	*Adjusted* R^2
Russia	–0.001 [0.002]	0.600*** [0.120]	0.057 [0.103]	–0.590** [0.230]	–0.430* [0.240]	**0.050**
India	0.0012 [0.001]	0.237*** [0.061]	–0.012 [0.065]	–0.410*** [0.120]	–0.370*** [0.110]	**0.052**
China	–0.001 [0.001]	0.338*** [0.066]	–0.004 [0.070]	–0.480*** [0.137]	–0.347** [0.141]	**0.062**
Turkey	0.001 [0.002]	0.380*** [0.096]	–0.004 [0.100]	–0.706*** [0.200]	–0.280 [0.204]	**0.038**
Brazil	0.001 [0.002]	0.530*** [0.077]	–0.030 [0.084]	–0.730*** [0.150]	–0.165 [0.170]	**0.095**
Argentina	–0.001 [0.002]	0.448*** [0.084]	–0.057 [0.080]	–0.678*** [0.162]	–0.170 [0.170]	**0.062**
Venezuela	0.001 [0.003]	–0.020 [0.110]	–0.043 [0.074]	–0.200 [0.350]	0.082 [0.350]	**0.001**
Mexico	0.002 [0.001]	0.290*** [0.064]	–0.070 [0.076]	–0.440*** [0.120]	–0.120 [0.130]	**0.054**
Saudi Arabia	0.001 [0.001]	0.086 [0.060]	0.170** [0.070]	0.090 [0.120]	–0.190 [0.120]	**0.020**

Kuwait	0.001	0.006	0.100**	–0.140	–0.140	**0.019**
	[0.001]	[0.040]	[0.040]	[0.090]	[0.100]	
Qatar	0.001	0.230***	0.220***	–0.028	–0.250**	**0.062**
	[0.001]	[0.062]	[0.066]	[0.100]	[0.120]	
Oman	0.0008	0.104**	0.107**	–0.053	–0.073	**0.025**
	[0.001]	[0.044]	[0.054]	[0.081]	[0.130]	
Egypt	0.001	0.140**	0.130*	–0.170	–0.280**	**0.023**
	[0.001]	[0.066]	[0.076]	[0.140]	[0.120]	
UAE	0.001	0.056	0.140*	0.028	–0.270	**0.016**
	[0.001]	[0.070]	[0.087]	[0.130]	[0.170]	
Morocco	0.001	0.095***	–0.015	–0.740***	–0.107	**0.146**
	[0.001]	[0.035]	[0.035]	[0.065]	[0.070]	
South Africa	0.001	0.430***	–0.084	–0.970***	–0.085	**0.171**
	[0.001]	[0.060]	[0.060]	[0.120]	[0.120]	
Kenya	0.002	0.050	0.080	–0.280**	–0.220**	**0.02**
	[0.001]	[0.063]	[0.060]	[0.110]	[0.110]	
Nigeria	0.001	0.080	0.021	0.090	–0.320**	**0.008**
	[0.001]	[0.060]	[0.070]	[0.120]	[0.130]	

Note: This table shows the regression analysis and in-sample predictability tests for constructed commodity portfolios (energy, metals, and agricultural) on the domestic equity markets of the selected countries while conditioning for the U.S. dollar index futures using *weekly* data. The dependent variable is domestic equity market (proxied by a relevant investable equity index associated with each country). For all those selected countries, the estimation covers the same time frame between January 1997 and December 2016 ($n = 1{,}044$) except for Nigeria, Kenya, Saudi Arabia, Kuwait, Qatar, Oman, and the UAE, the estimation covers from June 2002 to December 2016 ($n = 760$). Robust standard errors are provided in brackets below estimated coefficients. *, **, and *** indicate a significant difference from zero at the 10%, 5%, and 1% levels, respectively.

showing a negative lingering effect followed by a higher contemporaneous positive impact of the global energy futures market on the equity market. Qatar, Oman, and UAE exhibit double positive effects for both trailing and contemporaneous prices, so that increasing global energy futures prices lead to higher equity market prices. South Africa shows the double effects as well, but with negative relations. The economic fundamentals of the MENA and Africa regions easily explain this distinction by either lack of efficiency or liquidity—perhaps the equity markets in those countries do not fully respond quickly to the movement of global commodity markets. This relation may allow sophisticated but late investors to enjoy a higher reward to risk by positioning their trading strategies accordingly in both emerging equity and global commodity markets (Bekaert and Harvey 2002, 2003).

In Panel B, the results indicate that global metals have a larger effect than energy futures, in all emerging equity markets except Venezuela, Kenya, and Nigeria. Metals futures are positively related to some equity markets. Panel C indicates that agricultural futures prove to be reliable contributors to emerging equity markets as well.

RELATION BETWEEN EMERGING BOND MARKETS AND GLOBAL COMMODITIES

This subsection explores the dynamic relations between the bond market of emerging nations and global commodity markets. For instance, during periods with strong energy markets (oil and its refined fuels), energy-exporting countries and energy-dependent countries (energy companies also) do well in their debt obligations. During downturns in global energy products, however, these countries find themselves strapped by the need to raise further capital (external debt or domestic bonds).

The basis for this empirical examination is the premise that markets, notably energy and metals markets, are leading economic indicators and follow the business cycle in tandem, as shown in Table 19.2. Bonds tend to be sensitive to interest-rate movements, while commodities tend to boom when inflationary pressures start to develop, peaking when they become unsustainable. According to Murphy (2004), this finding may allow investors who are observing the relations among commodities, bond prices, and currencies to develop intelligent investment strategies.

Results in Table 19.5, Panel A, reveal that global energy markets do not have a consistent pattern across all emerging nations. In fact, an increase of the energy futures market is associated with and/or leads to increasing bond markets for a majority of selected countries but has no impact in Mexico, Egypt, Morocco, or Kenya. Seven out of 19 countries show a trailing positive effect of energy in the bond market, with the exception of South Africa, which shows the reverse (i.e., energy market advances are followed by higher bond market declines in the next period). This result lends support to the contention that a surge of energy commodity markets could cause some challenges to the affluence of emerging bond markets.

Qualitatively, the same observation is more pronounced when using the other commodity index in Panel B, with a higher explanatory power than in results from Panel A. Here 16 out of 19 countries show a positive contemporaneous or trailing effect of precious metals on the direction and performance of their domestic market. Furthermore,

Table 19.5 **Movement of Global Commodities and Emerging Bond Markets**

Panel A. Energy Futures Portfolio, EW_{ENG} and Bond Markets

Variables ⇒ Bond Market Proxy of Countries⇓	*Const.*	*EW_{ENG}*	*L. EW_{ENG} (One-Period Lag EW_{ENG})*	*U.S. Dollar (Dol_t)*	*L. U.S. Dollar (One-Period Lag Dol_{t-1})*	*Adjusted R^2*	*Sample Size*
Russia	0.000 [0.001]	0.072*** [0.019]	0.046** [0.020]	–0.090 [0.078]	–0.230*** [0.065]	**0.127**	**578**
India	0.000 [0.001]	0.022 [0.020]	0.025** [0.011]	–0.044 [0.055]	–0.175 [0.130]	**0.038**	**593**
China	0.000 [0.001]	–0.005 [0.009]	0.028*** [0.009]	–0.153*** [0.044]	–0.100** [0.047]	**0.086**	**593**
Turkey	–0.000 [0.001]	0.027* [0.015]	–0.014 [0.016]	–0.167** [0.065]	–0.161*** [0.050]	**0.030**	**975**
Brazil	0.001 [0.001]	0.036* [0.020]	0.009 [0.016]	–0.150** [0.073]	–0.080 [0.070]	**0.013**	**1044**
Argentina	–0.000 [0.001]	0.089*** [0.030]	0.053 [0.047]	–0.380** [0.150]	–0.250* [0.130]	**0.040**	**975**
Venezuela	–0.001 [0.001]	0.157*** [0.024]	0.080*** [0.030]	–0.270*** [0.098]	–0.300*** [0.001]	**0.095**	**975**
Bolivia	0.001 [0.001]	0.0076 [0.018]	0.055** [0.023]	–0.043 [0.076]	0.130 [0.081]	**0.025**	**196**

(continued)

Table 19.5 **Continued**

Panel A. Energy Futures Portfolio, EW_{ENG} and Bond Markets							
Variables ⇒ Bond Market Proxy of Countries⇓	*Const.*	*EW_{ENG}*	*L. EW_{ENG} (One-Period Lag EW_{ENG})*	*U.S. Dollar (Dol_t)*	*L. U.S. Dollar (One-Period Lag Dol_{t-1})*	*Adjusted R^2*	*Sample Size*
Mexico	–0.000 [0.000]	0.021 [0.017]	0.029 [0.020]	–0.210*** [0.064]	–0.056 [0.060]	**0.081**	**578**
Kuwait	–0.001 [0.000]	0.024 [0.015]	–0.004 [0.011]	–0.014 [0.061]	0.008 [0.038]	**0.007**	**196**
Qatar	–0.000 [0.000]	0.011 [0.015]	0.021* [0.011]	0.020 [0.054]	–0.015 [0.045]	**0.007**	**593**
Oman	0.001 [0.000]	0.014* [0.008]	0.003 [0.008]	–0.045 [0.035]	0.0088 [0.043]	**0.006**	**196**
Egypt	0.001* [0.001]	0.0134 [0.012]	–0.006 [0.013]	–0.120** [0.05]	–0.050 [0.047]	**0.011**	**593**
UAE	–0.000 [0.000]	0.014* [0.008]	–0.003 [0.008]	–0.031 [0.034]	–0.027 [0.034]	**0.012**	**196**
Morocco	0.000 [0.001]	0.020 [0.020]	–0.012 [0.023]	–0.140* [0.085]	–0.109 [0.100]	**0.006**	**196**
South Africa	–0.001 [0.001]	0.057** [0.024]	–0.074*** [0.024]	–0.920*** [0.086]	0.058 [0.089]	**0.134**	**1044**
Kenya	–0.002 [0.001]	–0.026 [0.025]	0.003 [0.030]	–0.201* [0.110]	0.120 [0.110]	**0.001**	**308**
Nigeria	0.000 [0.001]	0.043** [0.016]	0.016 [0.020]	–0.140** [0.068]	–0.170** [0.070]	**0.078**	**308**

Panel B. Metals' Futures Portfolio, EW_{META} and Bond Markets

Variables ⇒ Bond Market Proxy of Countries⇓	*Const.*	*EW_{META}*	*L. EW_{META} (One-Period Lag EW_{META})*	*U.S. Dollar (Dolt)*	*L. U.S. Dollar (One-Period Lag Dolt-1)*	*Adjusted R^2*	*Sample Size*
Russia	–0.000 [0.001]	0.070** [0.027]	0.066** [0.031]	–0.077 [0.070]	–0.180*** [0.060]	**0.109**	**578**
India	0.000 [0.001]	0.012 [0.023]	0.052* [0.028]	–0.054 [0.044]	–0.130 [0.091]	**0.041**	**593**
China	–0.000 [0.000]	0.020 [0.017]	0.055*** [0.019]	–0.120** [0.054]	–0.060 [0.050]	**0.107**	**593**
Turkey	–0.000 [0.001]	0.088*** [0.024]	0.030 [0.025]	–0.094 [0.068]	–0.110** [0.051]	**0.042**	**975**
Brazil	0.000 [0.001]	0.105*** [0.027]	0.036 [0.032]	–0.070 [0.077]	–0.049 [0.070]	**0.024**	**1044**
Argentina	–0.000 [0.001]	0.209*** [0.058]	0.166 [0.101]	–0.230* [0.120]	–0.103 [0.120]	**0.060**	**975**
Venezuela	–0.001 [0.001]	0.183*** [0.041]	0.098 [0.063]	–0.210** [0.094]	–0.250** [0.099]	**0.065**	**975**
Bolivia	0.001 [0.001]	0.053 [0.050]	0.016 [0.043]	–0.004 [0.062]	0.106 [0.108]	**0.003**	**196**
Mexico	–0.001 [0.000]	0.045* [0.026]	0.019 [0.029]	–0.170*** [0.060]	–0.060 [0.055]	**0.080**	**578**

(*continued*)

Table 19.5 **Continued**

Panel B. Metals' Futures Portfolio, EW_{META} and Bond Markets

Variables ⇒ Bond Market Proxy of Countries⇓	*Const.*	*EW_{ENG}*	*L. EW_{ENG} (One-Period Lag EW_{ENG})*	*U.S. Dollar (Dol_t)*	*L. U.S. Dollar (One-Period Lag Dol_{t-1})*	*Adjusted R^2*	*Sample Size*
Kuwait	–0.000 [0.000]	0.043** [0.018]	–0.020 [0.020]	0.008 [0.043]	–0.002 [0.044]	**0.020**	**196**
Qatar	–0.000 [0.000]	0.014 [0.017]	0.013 [0.016]	0.024 [0.057]	–0.200 [0.044]	**0.006**	**593**
Oman	0.001** [0.000]	0.056*** [0.020]	0.012 [0.023]	–0.001 [0.040]	0.027 [0.035]	**0.062**	**196**
Egypt	0.001* [0.001]	0.075*** [0.020]	0.034 [0.021]	–0.033 [0.047]	0.013 [0.052]	**0.040**	**593**
UAE	–0.000 [0.000]	0.044*** [0.015]	0.002 [0.015]	0.002 [0.032]	–0.016 [0.034]	**0.057**	**196**
Morocco	0.000 [0.001]	0.128*** [0.046]	0.0505 [0.051]	–0.028 [0.084]	–0.027 [0.097]	**0.066**	**196**
South Africa	–0.001 [0.001]	0.250*** [0.046]	–0.024 [0.038]	–0.704*** [0.097]	0.104 [0.088]	**0.158**	**1044**
Kenya	–0.002 [0.001]	–0.002 [0.045]	0.140* [0.080]	–0.170 [0.110]	0.290* [0.160]	**0.031**	**308**
Nigeria	0.001 [0.001]	0.099*** [0.038]	0.000 [0.023]	–0.067 [0.080]	–0.160** [0.060]	**0.110**	**308**

Note: This table shows regression analysis and in-sample predictability tests for constructed commodity portfolios (energy, metals, and agricultural) on the domestic bond markets of the selected countries while conditioning for the U.S. dollar index futures using weekly data. The dependent variable is *domestic* bond market (proxied by a relevant bond index associated with each country). Robust standard errors are provided in brackets below estimated coefficients. *, **, and *** indicate significant difference from zero at the 10%, 5%, and 1% levels, respectively. Results of Panel C showing the impact of agricultural commodity portfolios on domestic bond markets per country are not reported but are available from the author upon request.

in Panel C, coefficients for 10 out of 19 selected countries range from 0.039 (Egypt) to 0.17 (Argentina) to 0.19 percent (South Africa), reflecting Argentina's and South Africa's dependence on agriculture to fuel prosperity.

Overall, although a relation exists between global commodities and domestic markets, the contribution of some commodities to the variance of the domestic economic growth and/or domestic equity and bond markets for emerging countries may seem surprising, given that some of these countries import or export commodities. Also, perhaps other factors such as political risk, economic slowdown, currency regimes, changes in monetary policy, economic growth prospects, equity market volatility, and global economic factors could all be candidates that drive movements in selected emerging markets.

Summary and Conclusions

This chapter is motivated by the debate over the importance of the emerging markets in the development of various investment strategies, and by recent studies that examine the relevance of global commodity futures markets. It examines (1) the impact of actively-traded commodity futures on the business cycle of emerging markets and (2) how global commodity price changes affect emerging equity and bond markets. The chapter shows that U.S.-listed commodity price movements exhibit sizable contemporaneous effects on the business cycle of emerging market countries. In that regard, differences exist among the emerging markets and across selected commodities. Increased energy prices are associated with improving emerging market business cycles except for African countries. Additionally, increasing metals prices show an almost consistently positive effect on the GDP of emerging nations, and agricultural commodities have a more pronounced and stronger impact on the Latin American nations than on other countries.

The preponderance of the evidence indicates important trading opportunities between global commodity price changes and emerging equity and bond markets, notably for countries lacking liquidity and efficiency such as the MENA and African regions. This result has practical and policy implications because it spotlights the underlying factors that influence economic growth in emerging markets. From a global perspective, institutional investors can learn from the predictive ability of U.S.-listed global commodity futures when assessing potential investment instruments available in the global financial markets. A better understanding of emerging market business cycles and their main drivers will prove beneficial to many investors as they analyze the prospects for various global industries.

Discussion Questions

1. Discuss several conventional facts about global commodity markets and how they relate to the movement of both equity and bond returns.
2. Explain some benefits of international diversification in equity and bond markets, including the emerging markets.

3. Define an emerging market and discuss how the inclusion of global commodity futures could enhance investment strategies in emerging markets.
4. Discuss the importance and role of the open interest of commodity futures in guiding investment decisions of global investors, notably those considering the emerging markets.
5. Explain the nature of the relation between global commodity movement and business cycle of the emerging markets.
6. Identify and discuss a possible channel that links the state of global commodities and the overall outlook for emerging bond markets.

References

Acharya, V. V., L. A. Lochstoer, and T. Ramadorai. 2013. "Limits to Arbitrage and Hedging: Evidence from Commodity Markets." *Journal of Financial Economics* 109, 441–465.

Aggarwal, R., C. Kearney, and B. Lucey. 2012. "Gravity and Culture in Foreign Portfolio Investment." *Journal of Banking and Finance* 36:2, 525–538.

Agyei-Ampomah, S., D. Gounopoulos, and K. Mazouz. 2014, March. "Does Gold Offer a Better Protection against Losses in Sovereign Debt Bonds Than Other Metals?" *Journal of Banking and Finance* 40, 507–521.

Atilgan, Y., O. K. Demirtas, and K. D. Simsek. 2016. "Derivative Markets in Emerging Economies: A Survey." *International Review of Economics and Finance* 42, 88–102.

Auer, B. R. 2016. "On Time-Varying Predictability of Emerging Stock Market Returns." *Emerging Markets Review* 27, 1–13.

Batten, J. A., P. G. Szilagyi, and N. F. Wagner. 2015. "Should Emerging Market Investors Buy Commodities?" *Applied Economics* 47:39, 4228–4246.

Beckmann, J., A. Belke, and R. Czudaj. 2014. "Does Global Liquidity Drive Commodity Prices?" *Journal of Banking and Finance* 48, 224–234.

Bekaert, G., and C. R. Harvey. 2002. "Research in Emerging Markets Finance: Looking to the Future." *Emerging Markets Review* 3:4, 429–448.

Bekaert, G., and C. R. Harvey. 2003. "Emerging Markets Finance." *Journal of Empirical Finance* 10:1, 3–55.

Bekaert, G., C. R. Harvey, and A. Ng. 2005. "Market Integration and Contagion." *Journal of Business* 78, 39–69.

Berger, D., K. Pukthuanthong, and J. Yang. 2011. "International Diversification with Frontier Markets." *Journal of Financial Economics* 101, 227–242.

Bouri, E., M. E. de Boyrie, and I. Pavlova. 2017. "Volatility Transmission from Commodity Markets to Sovereign CDS Spreads in Emerging and Frontier Countries." *International Review of Financial Analysis* 49:January, 155–165.

Brei, M., and A. Buzaushina. 2015. "International Financial Shocks in Emerging Markets." *Journal of International Money and Finance* 58, 51–54.

Cai, J., Y.-L. Cheung, and M. C. Wong. 2001. "What Moves the Gold Market?" *Journal of Futures Markets* 21:3, 257–278.

Capie, F., T. C. Mills, and G. Wood. 2005. "Gold as a Hedge against the Dollar." *Journal of International Financial Markets, Institutions, and Money* 15, 343–352.

Chen, G., M. Firth, and Y. Xin. 2005. "The Response of Volume and Returns to the Information Shocks in China's Commodity Futures Markets." *Journal of Futures Markets* 25:9, 893–916.

Chen, Y., K. Rogoffand, and B. Rossi. 2010. "Can Exchange Rates Forecast Commodity Prices?" *Quarterly Journal of Economics* 125, 1145–1194.

Cifarelli, G., and G. Paladino. 2006. "Volatility Co-movements between Emerging Sovereign Bonds: Is There Segmentation between Geographical Areas?" *Global Finance Journal* 16, 245–263.

Daskalaki, C., and G. Skiadopoulos. 2011. "Should Investors Include Commodities in Their Portfolios After All? New Evidence." *Journal of Banking and Finance* 35:10, 2606–2626.

De Miguel, V., L. Garlappi, and R. Uppal. 2009. "Optimal versus Naive Diversification: How Inefficient Is the 1/N Portfolio Strategy?" *Review of Financial Studies* 22, 1915–1953.

de Ville de Goyet, C., G. Dhaene, and P. Sercu. 2008. "Testing the Martingale Hypothesis for Futures Prices: Implications for Hedgers." *Journal of Futures Markets* 28:11, 1040–1065.

Elder, J., Miao, H., and S. Ramchander. 2012. "Impact of Macroeconomic News on Metal Futures." *Journal of Banking and Finance* 36, 51–65.

Erb, C. B., and C. R. Harvey. 2006. "The Strategic and Tactical Value of Commodity Futures." *Financial Analysts Journal* 62:2, 69–97.

Errunza, V. 1983. "Emerging Markets: A New Opportunity for Improving Global Portfolio Performance." *Financial Analysts Journal* 39:5, 51–58.

Errunza, V., and B. Rosenberg. 1982. "Investment in Developed and Less Developed Countries." *Journal of Financial and Quantitative Analysis* 17:5, 741–763.

Garcia-Herrero, A., P. Wooldridge, and D. Yang. 2009. "Why Don't Asians Invest in Asia? The Determinants of Cross-Border Portfolio Holdings." *Asian Economic Papers* 8, 228–246.

Gavin, W., and A. Theodorou. 2005. "A Common Model Approach to Macroeconomics: Using Panel Data to Reduce Sampling Error." *Journal of Forecasting* 24, 203–219.

Gilmore, C., and G. McManus. 2002. "International Portfolio Diversification: US and Central European Equity Markets." *Emerging Markets Review* 3:1, 69–83.

Gorton, G., and G. K. Rouwenhorst. 2006. "Facts and Fantasies about Commodity Futures." *Financial Analysts Journal* 62:2, 47–67.

Hu, C., and W. Xiong. 2017. "Are Commodity Futures Prices a Barometer of the Global Economy?" In G. E. Weyl, E. L. Glaeser, and T. Santos (eds.), *Apres le deluge: Finance and the Common Good after the Crisis.* Chicago: University of Chicago Press.

Jaramillo, L., and A. Weber. 2013. "Bond Yields in Emerging Economies: It Matters What State You Are In." *Emerging Markets Review* 17, 169–185.

Jormanainen, I., and A. Koveshnikov. 2012. "International Activities of Emerging Market Firms." *Management International Review* 52:5, 691–725.

Joy, M. 2011. "Gold and the US Dollar: Hedge or Haven?" *Finance Research Letters* 8:3, 120–131.

Juttner, D., D. Chung, and W. Leung. 2006. "Emerging Market Bond Return: An Investor Perspective." *Journal of Multinational Financial Management* 16, 105–121.

Kearney, C. 2012. "Emerging Markets Research: Trends, Issues, and Future Directions." *Emerging Markets Review* 13, 159–183.

Kennedy, M., and A. Palerm. 2014. "Emerging Market Bond Spreads: The Role of Global and Domestic Factors from 2002–2011." *Journal of International Money and Finance* 43, 7–87.

Kilian, L. 2009. "Not All Oil Price Shocks Are Alike: Disentangling Demand and Supply Shocks in the Crude Oil Market." *American Economic Review* 99, 1053–1069.

Kilian, L., and D. Murphy. 2014. "The Role of Inventories and Speculative Trading in the Global Market for Crude Oil." *Journal of Applied Econometrics* 29:3, 454–478.

Lien, D., and M. Zhang. 2008. "A Survey of Emerging Derivatives Markets." *Emerging Markets Finance and Trade* 44:2, 39–69.

Lucey, B., and Q. Zhang. 2010. "Does Cultural Distance Matter in International Stock Market Comovement? Evidence from Emerging Economies around the World." *Emerging Markets Review* 11, 62–78.

Luo, Y., and R. L. Tung. 2007. "International Expansion of Emerging Market Enterprises: A Spring-Board Perspective." *Journal of International Business Studies* 38:4, 481–498.

MacKinnon, J. G. 1985. "Some Heteroskedasticity-Consistent Covariance Matrix Estimators with Improved Finite Sample Properties." *Journal of Econometrics* 29:3, 305.

Murphy, J. J. 2004. *Intermarket Analysis: Profiting from Global Market Relationships.* Hoboken, NJ: John Wiley & Sons, Inc.

O'Connor, F. A., and B. Lucey. 2012. "Gold's Negative Relationship to the US Dollar." *Alchemist* 66, 16.

Oztek, M. F., and N. Ocal. 2017. "Financial Crises and the Nature of Correlation between Commodity and Stock Markets." *International Review of Economics and Finance* 48, 56–68.

Phylaktis, K. 2006. "Emerging Markets Finance: Overview of the Special Issue." *Journal of International Money and Finance* 25:3, 349–357.

Sarafrazi, S., S. Hammoudeh, and P. Araujo Santos. 2014. "Downside Risk, Portfolio Diversification and the Financial Crisis in the Euro-zone." *Journal of International Financial Markets, Institutions and Money* 32:September, 368–396.

Sensoy, A., K. Ozturk, E. Hacihasanoglu, and B. M. Tabak. 2016. "Not All Emerging Markets Are the Same: A Classification Approach with Correlation Based-Networks." *Journal of Financial Stability*, In Press.

Singleton, K. 2014. "Investor Flows and the 2008 Boom/Bust in Oil Prices." *Management Science* 60, 300–318.

Smimou, K. 2010. "Stock Market and Agricultural Futures Diversification: An International Perspective." *Journal of Alternative Investments* 12:4, 36–57.

Smimou, K. 2014. "Consumer Attitudes, Stock Market Liquidity, and the Macro Economy: A Canadian Perspective." *International Review of Financial Analysis* 33:May, 186–209.

Smimou, K., and A. Karabegovic. 2010. "On the Relationship between Economic Freedom and Equity Returns in the Emerging Markets: Evidence from the Middle East and North Africa (MENA) Stock Markets." *Emerging Markets Review* 11:2, 119–151.

Stoll, H. R., and R. E. Whaley. 2010. "Commodity Index Investing and Commodity Futures Prices." *Journal of Applied Finance* 20:1, 7–46.

White, H. 1980. "A Heteroskedasticity-Consistent Covariance Matrix Estimator and a Direct Test for Heteroskedasticity." *Econometrica* 48, 817–838.

World Gold Council. 2016. "The Gold Market in 2016." http://www.gold.org/.

20

Commodity Trading Strategies, Common Mistakes, and Catastrophic Blowups

HILARY TILL
Principal, Premia Research LLC

JOSEPH EAGLEEYE
Principal, Quartile Risk, LLC

RICHARD HECKINGER
Member, Working Group on Financial Markets, Federal Reserve Bank of Chicago

Introduction

Gaining expertise in commodity derivatives markets occurs by working in niche commodity-processor companies, banks that specialize in hedging project risk for natural-resource companies, or fund companies that have strict rules on keeping their trade secrets proprietary. This chapter aims to help fill the knowledge gap about these markets by providing useful information highlighted in the following sections on futures strategies, common trading mistakes, and catastrophic derivatives blowups. A summary and conclusions section follows.

Commodity Trading Strategies

This section discusses the most common strategies employed by futures traders, namely: trend-following and calendar-spread trading.

COMMODITY TRADING ADVISORS

Although two basic types of commodity trading advisors (CTAs)—discretionary and trend-following—exist, the investment category is dominated by trend-followers. As Campbell and Company (2013, p. 7) note, "[M]ore than 70 percent of managed futures funds [are estimated to] rely on trend-following strategies." As discussed in Till and Eagleeye (2005), trend-followers are also known as *systematic traders*. The operative word here is systematic. Automated programs screen the markets using various technical factors to determine the beginning or end of a trend across different time frames. As

Lungarella (2002, p. 10) writes, "The trading is based on the systematic application of quantitative models that use moving averages, break-outs of price ranges, or other technical rules to generate the 'buy' and 'sell' signals for a set of markets."

In this investment process, automation is important and discretionary overrides of the investment process tend to be taboo. Discretionary traders occupy the other end of this bifurcated CTA spectrum. For discretionary traders, Lugarella (2002, p. 9) explains that "[p]ersonal experience and judgment are the basis of trading decisions. They tend to trade more concentrated portfolios and use fundamental data to assess the markets, and also technical analysis to improve the timing."

Description of Trend-Following

The basic idea underlying trend-following strategies is that all markets trend at one time or another. As put forward by Rulle (2003, p. 5), "A trend-following program may trade as many as 80 different markets globally on a 24-hour basis. Trend-followers try to capture long-term trends, typically between 1 and 6 months in duration when they occur."

Trend-followers will scan the markets with quantitative screens designed to detect a trend. Once the model signals a trend, a trade will be implemented. Successful trend-followers curb losses on losing trades and let the winners ride. That is, they quickly exit false trends and lever into real trends, which is the distinguishing feature among trend-following CTAs. In a sense, alpha may come from this dynamic leverage. As Fung and Hsieh (2003, p. 78) explain, "[T]rend-following alpha will reflect the skill in leveraging the right bets and deleveraging the bad ones as well as using superior entry/exit strategies. Negative alphas will be accorded to those managers that failed to lever the right bets and showed no ability in avoiding losing bets irrespective of the level of overall portfolio return—luck should not be rewarded."

Persistence of Momentum Strategies

Can such simply described strategies continue to be successful? A 2012 AQR Capital Management white paper shows how persistent momentum profits have been (at least in the past) across time, as summarized in Till (2016). Table 20.1 illustrates the persistence of momentum profits.

AQR constructed a simple momentum strategy as follows. It created "an equal-weighted combination of 1-month, 3-month, and 12-month momentum strategies for 59 markets across 4 major classes—24 commodities, 11 equity indices, 15 bond markets, and 9 currency pairs—from January 1903 to June 2012," explains Hurst, Ooi, and Pedersen (2012, p. 2).

Excerpting further from the AQR authors' white paper, Hurst et al. (2012, p. 2) state: "Since not all markets have return data going back to 1903, . . . [the researchers constructed] the strategies using the largest number of assets for which return data exist[ed] at each point in time." They used "futures returns when . . . available." And then "[p]rior to the availability of futures data," they used "cash index returns financed at local short rates for each country" as proxies for futures returns. Each position was sized to "target the same amount of volatility" and "positions across the three strategies . . . [were] aggregated each month, and scaled such that the combined portfolio . . . [had a] volatility target of 10 percent."

Table 20.1 **Hypothetical Performance of Time-Series Momentum**

Time Period	*Gross of Fee Returns (Annualized %)*	*Net of 2/20 Fee Returns (Annualized %)*	*Realized Volatility (Annualized %)*	*Sharpe Ratio, Net of Fees*	*Correlation to S&P 500 Returns*	*Correlation to U.S. 10-year Bond Returns*
Full Sample						
Jan 1903–Jun 2012	20.0	14.3	9.9	1.00	–0.05	–0.05
By Decade						
Jan 1903–Dec 1912	18.8	13.4	10.1	0.84	–0.30	–0.59
Jan 1913–Dec 1922	17.1	11.9	10.4	0.70	–0.12	–0.11
Jan 1923–Dec 1932	17.1	11.9	9.7	0.92	–0.07	0.10
Jan 1933–Dec 1942	9.7	6.0	9.2	0.66	0.00	0.55
Jan 1943–Dec 1952	19.4	13.7	11.7	1.08	0.21	0.22
Jan 1953–Dec 1962	24.8	18.4	10.0	1.51	0.21	–0.18
Jan 1963–Dec 1972	26.9	19.6	9.2	1.42	–0.14	–0.35
Jan 1973–Dec 1982	40.3	30.3	9.2	1.89	–0.19	–0.40
Jan 1983–Dec 1992	17.8	12.5	9.4	0.53	0.15	0.13
Jan 1993–Dec 2002	19.3	13.6	8.4	1.04	–0.21	0.32
Jan 2003–Jun 2012	11.4	7.5	9.7	0.61	–0.22	0.20

Note: This table shows the strategy performance after simulated transaction costs both gross and net of hypothetical 2-and-20 fees.

Source: Adapted from Exhibit 1 in Hurst et al. (2012).

In viewing Table 20.1, Hurst et al. (2012, p. 3) note that "[t]rends appear to be a pervasive characteristic of speculative financial markets over the long term" and theorize that "price trends exist in part due to long-standing behavioral biases exhibited by investors, such as anchoring and herding, as well as the trading activity of non-profit seeking participants, such as central banks and corporate hedging programs." Assuming these factors continue, the long-term profitability from momentum strategies might not just be a matter of history.

CALENDAR-SPREAD TRADING

In contrast to highly scalable CTA programs, proprietary futures traders often specialize in understanding the factors that impact the spread between two (or more) of a commodity futures contract's delivery months. This strategy is known as *calendar-spread trading*. By way of further explanation, in all commodity futures markets, a different price typically exists for each commodity, depending on when the commodity is to be delivered. For example, with natural gas, a futures contract whose delivery is in October will have a different price than a contract whose delivery is in December. Accordingly, a futures trader may trade the spread between the October versus December futures contracts.

Calendar spread opportunities arise when a seemingly predictable one-sided commercial or institutional interest exists in particular futures contract(s): a proprietary trader will thereby take the other side of this "flow." Examples of one-sided flow have occurred during seasonal inventory build-and-draw cycles and during the scheduled times when futures contracts are rolled in commodity indices, as discussed in the next section.

Trading Strategies Keyed to Seasonal Inventory Build-and-Draw Cycles

Figure 20.1 shows the futures curve for natural gas on June 28, 2016. The term structure of a commodity futures market is classified as a curve because each delivery-month contract is plotted on the x-axis with their respective prices on the y-axis, thus, tracing out a curve.

As Till (2006) explains, when the near-month futures contracts trade at a discount to further-delivery contracts, the futures curve is in *contango*. When the near-month futures contracts instead trade at a premium to further-delivery contracts, the futures curve is in *backwardation*. The yearly futures curves for natural gas in Figure 20.1 approximately mirror the average seasonal inventory build-and-draw pattern shown in Figure 20.2. The prices of summer and fall futures contracts typically trade at a discount to the winter contracts. The markets thus provide a return for storing natural gas. An owner of a storage facility can buy summer natural gas and simultaneously sell winter natural gas via the futures markets. This difference is the storage operator's return for storage. When the summer futures contract matures, the storage operator can take delivery of the physical natural gas, and inject this natural gas into storage. Later when the operator's winter futures contract matures, the operator can make delivery of the physical natural gas by drawing physical natural gas out of storage for this purpose. As long as the operator's financing and physical outlay costs

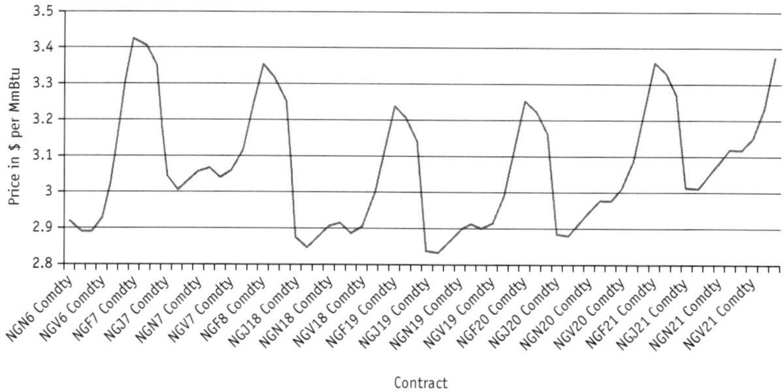

Figure 20.1 NYMEX Natural Gas Futures Curve as of June 28, 2016
This graph plots futures prices for natural gas contracts, maturing from July 2016 through October 2021 on June 28, 2016. Source of Data: Bloomberg.

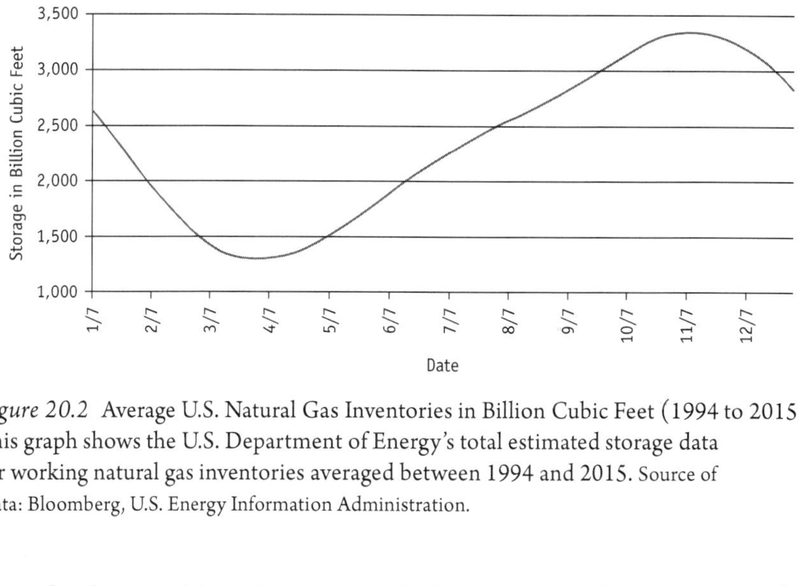

Figure 20.2 Average U.S. Natural Gas Inventories in Billion Cubic Feet (1994 to 2015)
This graph shows the U.S. Department of Energy's total estimated storage data for working natural gas inventories averaged between 1994 and 2015. Source of Data: Bloomberg, U.S. Energy Information Administration.

are under the spread locked in through the futures market, this operation will be profitable.

Now to the extent that the hedging activity by storage operators causes trends in calendar spreads, a speculator can potentially have a profitable edge in taking the other side of these trades. This chapter discusses the drawbacks from such a strategy in a later section: one needs to be quite careful about sizing and valuation.

Cootner (1967) described analogous price-pressure effects in the grain futures markets, which were keyed off the following factors: (1) peaks and troughs in visible grain supplies, (2) peaks and troughs in hedging positions from data provided by the Commodity Exchange Authority, a predecessor organization to the Commodity

Futures Trading Commission (CFTC), and (3) fixed calendar dates that line up on average with factors (1) and/or (2). In practice, these effects can potentially be monetized through calendar spreads.

Trading Strategies Keyed to Commodity Index Rolls

Another example of calendar-spread trading arises from commodity-index roll dates. Unlike an equity index, one unique aspect of a commodity futures index is that its precise rules need to specify on what dates each of its contracts has to be rolled before the maturity of each contract. These rules are known as *roll rules*. The rules specify when a particular index constituent should be sold and a further-maturity contract should be bought. In advance of such a procedure, speculators in futures contracts such as in the wheat market have historically sold the front-month while buying the next-month contract, establishing what is known as a *bear calendar spread*. They would then unwind this position during index roll dates, preferably profitably, but not always, as described in Collins (2007).

Common Mistakes

This section discusses the following three common mistakes in futures trading: (1) targeting absolute returns rather than risk; (2) establishing inappropriate sizing; and (3) treating trading as an "intellectual challenge" rather than as an exercise in "self-mastery and endurance."

REQUIRING RETURNS

According to Till (2008), many experienced traders note how ephemeral trading strategies are, or at least, how all strategies have life cycles. As Cashin (2008, p. 1) notes, the late Gerald Loeb, who was a highly successful financier and founding partner of E.F. Hutton, once declared, "Just when you think you found the key to the market, they change the locks."

As a matter of fact, Patel, Suri, and Weisman (2007) quantify one of the consequences of Loeb's observation. The expected drawdown for a strategy is positively related to how consistently profitable a strategy is, if a threshold of returns is constantly demanded. As Patel et al. (p. 21) note, the markets have "periodic market efficiency," which is another way of saying all strategies have a limited lifespan. Equation 20.1 shows the "tail loss" when a strategy finally and inevitably outlives its usefulness.

$$\text{Loss} = \left[\begin{array}{l}(\text{Demanded Returns})(\text{Probability of the Strategy Succeeding})/\\ \text{Probability of the Strategy Failing}\end{array}\right]. \qquad (20.1)$$

For strategies that target an absolute level of return, the natural consequences of this goal are that losses are proportional to gains and inversely proportional to their probability of occurrence.

Ethical issues do not arise when applying Patel et al.'s (2007) analysis to proprietary trading firms because in this case the partners' capital is at risk. The partners accept that drawdowns are endogenous to the trading strategy. As a result, they may not target absolute returns, knowing that trading strategies are fleeting. As Eagleeye (2007, p. 492) notes, "One can manage risk . . . [but] one can't demand a threshold return from the market." Enduring proprietary trading firms instead typically target risk.

Patel et al.'s (2007) analysis involves severe consequences for fund investors. Such investors historically have based their investment decisions on past track records, which may not be predictive of future results. They also pay traders based on short-term results, with no clawbacks of fees if the strategy suffers disastrous results. The previous natural gas spread trading example serves to illustrate the negative consequences to the "dangerous attraction" to absolute-return targeting, as discussed next.

Figure 20.3 illustrates how consistent a strategy of trading natural gas using bear calendar spreads was between spring 2004 and spring 2006. As discussed previously, a *bear calendar spread* consists of taking a short position in a nearer-month futures contract while simultaneously taking a long position in a later-delivery contract of the same futures market.

By early summer 2006, the profitability of this strategy had declined by about half of the performance of the previous two years. If commodity futures traders had responded by doubling up their position size to try to maintain an absolute-return target, then in July and August of 2006, they would have sustained losses about twice the size of the trader's year-to-date profits. The significance of such a loss is that when a trader's risk-and-return results differ dramatically from client and/or prime-broker expectations, this can set off a "critical liquidation cycle," as described by De Souza and Smirnov

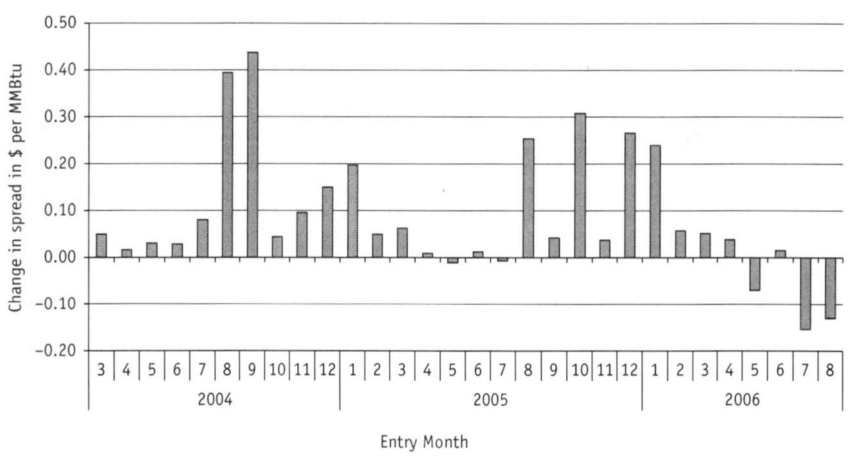

Figure 20.3 Natural Gas Bear-Calendar Spread P/L, One-Month Horizon, January 2004 through August 2006

This figure illustrates the consistency of a strategy of trading natural gas using bear calendar spreads between spring 2004 and spring 2006, after which performance degraded. Source of data: Bloomberg.

(2004). In a "critical liquidation cycle," client redemptions and/or additional demands for collateral from creditors cause a trader to liquidate positions in a distressed manner, which can then cause further losses that imperil a fund's survival, as both the fund's investors and creditors lose faith in the manager. Unfortunately, once a fund incurs a threshold level of losses, successive rounds of distressed liquidations will quickly cause a step-function decrease in the fund's net asset value.

SIZING

Interestingly, natural gas seems to be frequently at the center of many trading debacles. Natural gas derivatives trading offers traders and investors a potentially alluring combination of scalability and volatility, and also at times, pockets of predictability.

But even with the natural gas markets, a surprisingly common mistake has been adopting the appropriate sizing for trading this seemingly scalable market. This realization is a key lesson from the hedge fund natural gas trading disasters suffered by both MotherRock and Amaranth in 2006. Later in February 2008, the Houston-based energy hedge fund Saracen was reported to have also had difficulties with natural gas trading positions.

The commodity markets do not have natural two-sided flow. For experienced traders in the fixed income, equity, and currency markets, this point may not be obvious. The commodity markets have *nodal liquidity*. If a commercial market participant needs to initiate or lift hedges, large-scale transactions will take place, but not at a speculator's convenience. Before initiating a position, particularly one that is large compared to the size of the marketplace, a trader needs a clear understanding of what flow or catalyst will allow the trader out of a position.

A commodity-market observer can readily identify when a massively-sized distressed liquidation is occurring, particularly in a spread market. If no geopolitical, economic, or weather news exists about a market, and a spread relation changes by many standard deviations relative to recent history, this combination is a clear signal that a market participant is unwinding a position in a distressed fashion (Till 2006). In summary, a key risk-management objective in speculative commodity futures trading is to keep sizing within a relatively small fraction of daily trading volume and open interest. Apparently, this objective can be a difficult restriction for futures traders to live by when prior success brings an influx of capital that is beyond what a commodity trading program can nimbly manage.

PSYCHOLOGICAL DISCIPLINE AND RISK TOLERANCE

In discussing the crucial elements of an investment process, a common mistake is to leave out one vital aspect of trading, which is a manager's *risk tolerance* (Till and Eagleeye 2006). Vince (1992, p. xv) states that monetizing market inefficiencies

> requires more than an understanding of money management concepts. It requires discipline to tolerate and endure emotional pain to a level that 19 out of 20 people cannot bear . . .. Anyone who claims to be intrigued by the "intellectual challenge of the markets" is not a trader. The markets are as intellectually challenging as a fistfight . . .. Ultimately, trading is an exercise in self-mastery and endurance.

In futures trading, psychological discipline is just as crucial as finding structural sources of return and designing an appropriate risk management methodology around them. Taleb (2001) explains why following a disciplined investment process is challenging for a manager. He provides an example of a return-generating process that has annual returns in excess of Treasury bills of 15 percent with an annualized volatility of 10 percent. At first glance, carrying out a trading strategy with such superior risk and return characteristics might be considered trivial. But Taleb also notes that with such a return-generating process, only a 54 percent chance of making money exists on any given day. If the investor felt the pain of loss say 2.5 times more acutely than the joy of a gain, then carrying out this superior investment strategy could be potentially exhausting and perhaps almost impossible.

Catastrophic Blowups

Previous sections of this chapter describe the fundamental underpinnings of the natural gas spread trading strategy and how inappropriate sizing of this strategy can lead to disastrous results. This outcome exactly describes the Amaranth hedge fund debacle, which is covered in this section along with one other blowup, which occurred at MF Global. Although the lessons from the Amaranth blowup can best be understood in terms of market-risk principles, the lessons from the MF Global bankruptcy are best understood in terms of due diligence principles.

AMARANTH

Till (2008) serves as the basis of discussion for this section's case study on Amaranth. Amaranth Advisors, LLC was a multi-strategy hedge fund, founded in 2000 and headquartered in Greenwich, Connecticut. The founder's original expertise was in convertible bonds. The fund later became involved in merger arbitrage, long-short equity, leveraged loans, blank-check companies, and energy trading. As of June 30, 2006, energy trades accounted for about half of the fund's capital and generated about 75 percent of its profits.

Davis (2006) provides an excellent overview on Amaranth's energy trading. Davis (p. A1) reports that Amaranth's head energy trader sometimes held "open positions to buy or sell tens of billions of dollars of commodities." Amaranth's energy trading operation was based in Calgary, Alberta. "[Amaranth's head energy trader] saw that a surplus of [natural] gas . . . [in the] summer [in the United States] could lead to low prices, but he also made bets that would pay off if, say, a hurricane or cold winter sharply reduced supplies by the end of winter." Excerpting from key points in Davis's (p. A1) article:

- Amaranth's hedge energy trader "also was willing to buy gas in even further-away years, as part of complex strategies."
- "Buying what is known as 'winter' gas years into the future is a risky proposition because that market has many fewer traders than do contracts for months close at hand."
- "Unlike oil, [natural] gas can't readily be moved about the globe to fill local shortages or relieve local supplies."

- "[Natural gas] traders . . . make complex wagers on gas at multiple points in the future, betting, say, that it will be cheap in the summer if there is a lot of supply, but expensive by a certain point in the winter. [Amaranth's head trader would] closely watch how weather affects prices and whether conditions will lead to more, or less, gas in a finite number of underground storage caverns."

Amaranth's structural position-taking may have assisted energy companies in their need to hedge their far-forward production, including through 2010. Davis (2006, p. A1) writes: "[Amaranth's energy book] was up for the year roughly $2 billion by April [2006], scoring a return of 11 percent to 13 percent that month alone, say investors in the Amaranth fund. Then ... [the energy strategies] ... had a loss of nearly $1 billion in May [2006] when prices of gas for delivery far in the future suddenly collapsed, investors add. [The energy traders] won back the $1 billion over the summer."

As of August 31, 2006, the fund had about $9.2 billion in assets under management. On Monday, September 18, 2006, market participants became aware of Amaranth's distress. The founder had issued a letter to investors informing them that the fund had lost an estimated 50 percent of their assets since its end-August value. Additionally, Hamilton (2006) notes the fund had lost $560 million on Thursday, September 14, 2006 alone.

According to Davis, Zuckerman, and Sender (2007), the fund had scrambled to transfer its positions to third-party financial institutions during the weekend of September 16 and 17, 2006. Merrill Lynch had agreed to take on 25 percent of the fund's natural gas positions for a payment of about $250 million. The fund then lost $800 million more through Tuesday, September 19, 2006, due to the natural gas market moving severely against its positions. On Wednesday, September 20, 2006, the fund succeeded in transferring its remaining energy positions to Citadel Investment Group and to its clearing broker, J.P. Morgan Chase, at a $2.15 billion discount to their September 19, 2006 mark-to-market value. Apparently, the two firms equally shared the risk of Amaranth's positions. On Thursday, September 21, 2006, the natural gas curve stabilized. The hedge fund's losses ultimately totaled $6.6 billion.

On June 25, 2007, the U.S. Senate Permanent Subcommittee on Investigations released a report on the Amaranth debacle, entitled "Excessive Speculation in the Natural Gas Market." The 135-page report and its further 345 pages of appendices provided details on the Amaranth case. In carrying out its forensic analysis, the Senate subcommittee examined several million individual trades. The subcommittee obtained this information by subpoenaing records from the New York Mercantile Exchange (NYMEX), the Intercontinental Exchange (ICE), Amaranth, and other traders.

Amaranth's spread trading strategy involved taking long positions in winter contract deliveries and short positions in non-winter contract deliveries. These positions would have benefited from potential weather events such as hurricanes and cold-shocks from 2006 through 2010. Although one can justify the economic rationale for Amaranth's strategy, both trade sizing and value matter even more so. The U.S. Senate Permanent Subcommittee on Investigations Staff Report (2007, p. 52) found that in late July 2006, Amaranth's natural gas positions for delivery in January 2007 represented "a volume of natural gas that equaled the entire amount of natural gas eventually used in that month by U.S. residential consumers nationwide."

Drawing from the U.S. Senate's report, Table 20.2 summarizes the scale of Amaranth's natural gas trading activity. Figure 20.4 draws from the report's appendix to show the positioning of the fund through May 2009, as of the end of August 2006. The U.S. Senate report excludes similar charts for the fund's positions past the May 2009 maturity date and also its miscellaneous commodity investments.

Amaranth's position sizes were obviously too large for a financial entity that had no physical energy assets. If a financial firm cannot make or take physical delivery of a commodity, then that firm's exit strategy is very constrained. Also, the fund had entered into these vast positions at exceedingly wide levels for these spreads.

Using the Senate report's documented positions for Amaranth as of August 31, 2006, Till (2008) finds that two spreads were 93 percent correlated to Amaranth's natural gas book: (1) the November 2006 versus October 2006 (NGX-V6) spread and (2) the March 2007 versus April 2007 (NGH-J7) spread.

Examining the past spread values for the November-versus-October-2006 spread and the March-versus-April-2007 spread helps to understand the riskiness of Amaranth's

Table 20.2 **Scale of Amaranth's Natural Gas Trading: Excerpted from the U.S. Senate Report of June 25, 2007**

At times Amaranth controlled up to 40 percent of all the open interest on NYMEX for the winter months (October 2006 through March 2007).	pp. 51–52
In late July 2006, Amaranth held a total of more than 80,000 NYMEX and ICE contracts for January 2007, representing a volume of natural gas that equaled the entire amount of natural gas eventually used in that month by U.S. residential consumers nationwide.	p. 52
On July 31, 2006, Amaranth's trading in the March and April 2007 contracts represented almost 70 percent of the total NYMEX trading volume in each of these contracts on that date.	p. 52
Amaranth also held large positions in other winter and summer months spanning the five-year period from 2006 to 2010.	p. 52
For example, Amaranth held 60 percent of the outstanding contracts (open interest) in all NYMEX natural gas futures contracts in 2010.	p. 52
On July 24, 2006, Amaranth's futures position as a % of NYMEX futures open interest in the December 2007 contract was 81 percent.	p. 94
On August 28, 2006, Amaranth accounted for over 40 percent of the total volume on ICE, and over 25 percent of the entire volume of exchange-traded futures and swaps on NYMEX and on ICE on that date.	p. 101

Note: This table summarizes the scale of Amaranth's natural gas trading activity.

Source: Excerpted from U.S. Senate Permanent Subcommittee on Investigations Staff Report (2007). The right-hand column shows on what page of the Staff Report each point is derived from.

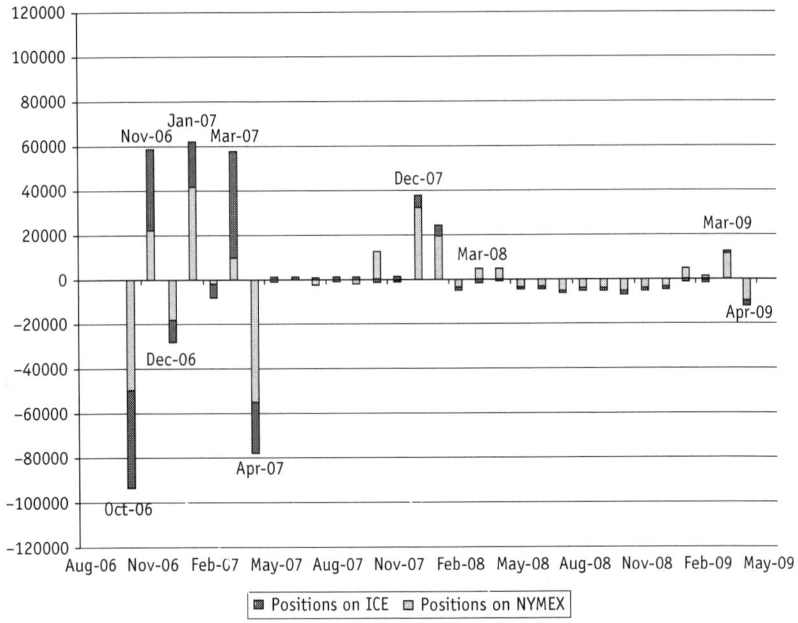

Figure 20.4 Amaranth's Forward Curve on August 31, 2006 Natural Gas Contracts on NYMEX and ICE
This chart illustrates the natural-gas contract positioning of the hedge fund Amaranth, which held contracts that matured from October 2006 through April 2009. Source: Adapted from U.S. Senate Permanent Subcommittee on Investigations Staff Report (2007), Appendix V, p. 38.

documented August 31, 2006 portfolio. If these two spreads had reverted to levels that had prevailed at the end-of-August during the previous six years, up to –36 percent could have been lost under normal conditions, as shown in Table 20.3.

This analysis is based on Amaranth's portfolio as of August 31, 2006, which was two weeks before the fund's implosion. One caveat with this analysis is that it is based solely on the positions documented in the U.S. Senate report's graphical appendix. In mid-September 2006, the fund had lost more than $2 billion month-to-date. At this point the critical-liquidation-cycle was initiated for the fund, a vicious circle in which distressed liquidations cause even greater losses, leading to even greater calls for margin from a fund's credit-providers, which then leads to even more distressed trading. In the case of Amaranth, no natural (financial) counterparty existed who could entirely take on the fund's positions during a very short period when the fund became distressed in mid-September 2006. The natural counterparties to Amaranth's trades were the physical-market participants who had either locked in the value of forward production or storage. The physical-market participants would likely have had physical assets against their derivatives positions so would have had little pressing economic need to unwind these trades at Amaranth's convenience. Michael Cosgrove, then president of Amerex Brokers, confirmed the identity of Amaranth's counterparties in Farrington

Table 20.3 **Scenario Analysis of Amaranth's Key Risk Positions: August 31, 2006**

	Natural Gas		
Number of Contracts	*Spread Symbol*	*Spread*	*8/31/06 Level*
(105,620)	NGV-X	October–November	2.18
59,543	NGH-J	March–April	2.14

Date	*NGV-X*	*NGH-J*	*Losses due to V-X*	*Losses due to H-J*	*Total Losses*	*Portfolio Loss (%)*
8/31/2000	–0.058	0.26	$(2,241,256,400)	$(1,119,408,400)	$(3,360,664,800)	–36.5
8/31/2001	–0.33	0.09	$(1,953,970,000)	$(1,220,631,500)	$(3,174,601,500)	–34.5
8/31/2002	–0.33	0.113	$(1,953,970,000)	$(1,206,936,610)	$(3,160,906,610)	–34.4
8/31/2003	–0.25	0.44	$(2,038,466,000)	$(1,012,231,000)	$(3,050,697,000)	–33.2
8/30/2004	–0.643	0.57	$(1,623,379,400)	$(934,825,100)	$(2,558,204,500)	–27.8
8/31/2005	–0.185	2.24	$(2,107,119,000)	$59,543,000	$(2,047,576,000)	–22.3

Note: This table is a scenario analysis of winter vs. non-winter spreads reverted to past spread relations.

(2006, p. 22). "There were storage managers, pipeline companies and retail marketers who had absorbed the other side of the Amaranth position as hedges against their physical businesses," according to Cosgrove.

The time needed to unwind the Amaranth positions can be inferred by seeing if any footprints existed in natural gas price patterns from September 20, 2006 onward. Figure 20.5 shows the evolution of natural gas spreads in which the long legs are the winter contracts, and the short legs are summer and spring contracts, which in turn are collectively correlated to Amaranth's actual positions. The graph in this figure is from September 1, 2006 through December 31, 2006. This graph shows the spreads recovered in late September during the immediate aftermath of the portfolio transfer, indicating a (temporary) absence of liquidation pressure. At the end of September 2006, Citadel assumed the entire Amaranth portfolio, taking on J.P. Morgan's half of Amaranth's positions, by paying J.P. Morgan $725 million. Citadel also received all the remaining concessionary payments from Amaranth. As Figure 20.5 shows, the natural gas spreads smoothly declined throughout October, and largely bottomed out by the end of October.

At the end of November 2006, widespread public reports existed about the contents of Citadel's bond prospectus, which provided some commentary on the timing of the unwinding of Amaranth's trades. The Citadel document said that the firm had reduced the risk of its Amaranth positions by two-thirds during the first two weeks of October. Given that the natural gas curve bottomed out at the end of October, an inference is that Citadel essentially finished unwinding the risk of the remaining positions during the last two weeks of October. Commercial-market hedgers could have been the natural other side to Citadel's orderly unwind of October 2006 because they could realize their substantial hedging windfall at this time.

As Figure 20.5 shows, further liquidation pressure does not appear on the natural gas curve in November and December 2006. Given how stable the curve was during this time, this period is when normal two-sided flow likely resumed. Given how orderly Citadel's unwind was during October 2006, the firm probably only sustained relatively small losses during this time. Therefore, Citadel was apparently able to realize substantial net profits, given the $1.425 billion payment that Citadel ultimately received for agreeing to take on Amaranth's distressed portfolio ($1.425-billion = $2.15 billion [concessionary payment received by Citadel and J.P. Morgan] minus the $725 million that Citadel paid J.P. Morgan so that Citadel could fully take on the entire Amaranth energy portfolio and all remaining concessionary payments).

Szala (2014) draws attention to a November 2006 statement by the then co-head of J.P. Morgan's investment bank about the bank's Amaranth stance. As excerpted by Szala (p. 11), the investment banker explained that "through its hedge fund relationships, such as trade clearing, 'we have the insight into what's going on in these funds' and can 'respond quickly to opportunities when they come up. Amaranth was one obvious example of that.' He added, 'I imagine there will be others . . . where our ability to be both on the inside, but not compromised, is extremely powerful [as a way] to generate profits.'"

Robert Greer, then of PIMCO, and now a Scholar-in-Residence at the University of Colorado Denver Business School's J.P. Morgan Center for Commodities, notes a key

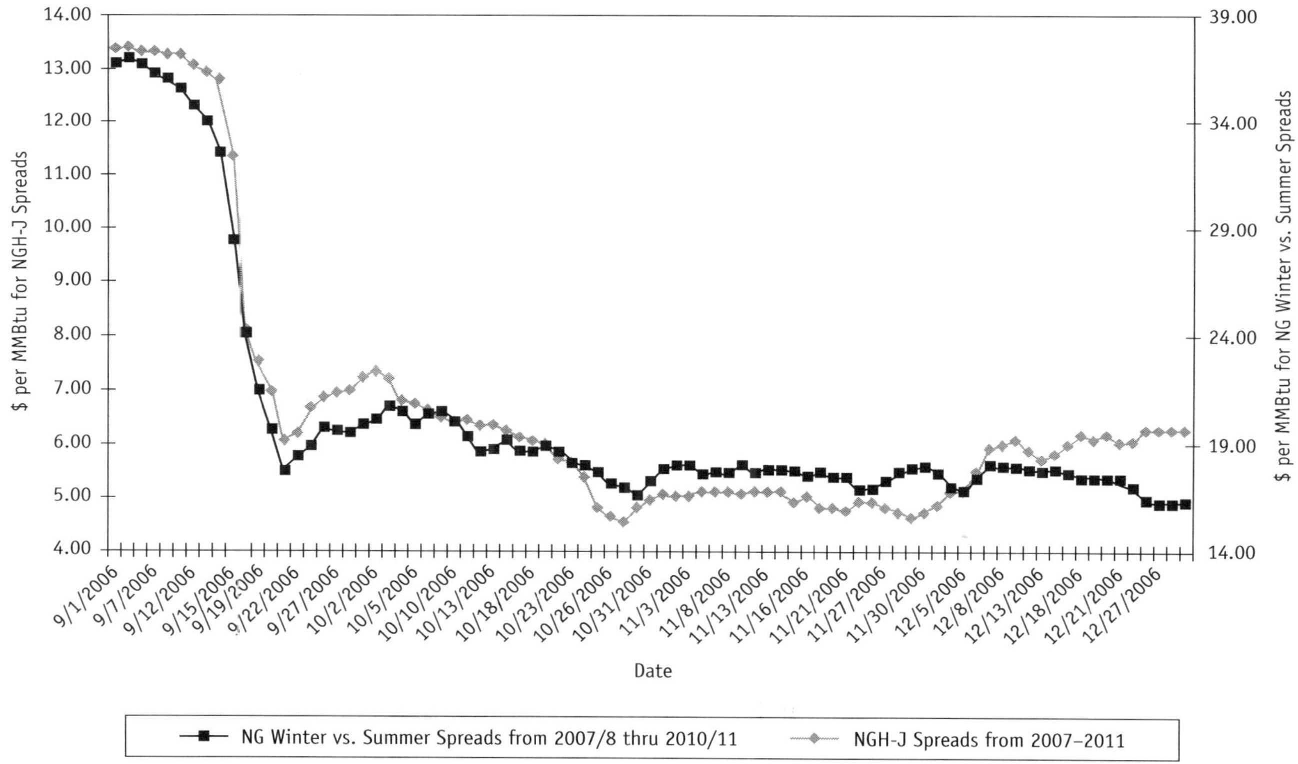

Figure 20.5 Natural Gas Spreads: September 1, 2006 through December 31, 2006

This graph shows the evolution of natural gas spreads in which the long legs are the winter contracts, and the short legs are summer and spring contracts, which in turn were collectively correlated to Amaranth's actual positions. Note: NG is an abbreviation for natural gas. H and J are symbols for the March and April futures contracts respectively. Source of data: Bloomberg.

lesson from the Amaranth debacle. Hougan (2008, p. 3) quotes Greer, who said, "[T]he market showed that someone can actually be so big that the market will punish them, rather than reward them for their size."

The Regulatory Response

Both the CFTC and the Federal Energy Regulatory Commission (FERC) pursued actions against the hedge fund, which were announced on July 25 and 26, 2007, respectively. Although the Senate report focused on whether Amaranth's position-taking pushed up the price of forward winter natural gas prices, the CFTC's and FERC's investigations were much more narrowly focused on Amaranth's trading activities on several days of 2006, leading to allegations against Amaranth and its head natural gas trader of attempted and actual manipulation, respectively.

Zajac (2013, p. 1) reports that "[i]n August 2009, . . . [Amaranth] agreed to pay $7.5 million to end U.S. cases brought by FERC and the CFTC over price manipulation. [Then] [o]n April 11 [2013], a federal judge in Manhattan gave final approval to a $77.1 million settlement by Amaranth to resolve a class action brought by traders."

The regulatory actions, in turn, against Amaranth's head natural gas trader became complicated by confusion about the FERC's authority over the U.S. energy futures markets. A federal court ruling finally resolved the matter on March 15, 2013. Zajac (2013, p. 1) states that the U.S. Court of Appeals in Washington, DC ruled that the "'FERC lacks jurisdiction to charge . . . [Amaranth's head trader] with manipulation of natural gas futures contracts.' The Commodity Exchange Act gives the CFTC 'exclusive jurisdiction.'"

Van Voris and Hurtado (2014, p. 1) report that a year-and-a-half later, on September 15, 2014, the former Amaranth trader "agreed to pay $750,000 to settle a Commodity Futures Trading Commission lawsuit claiming he tried to rig prices of natural gas contracts . . .. Under the agreement, which 'fully resolves' the commission's claims against him, . . . [the trader] also agreed to a partial ban on futures trading . . .. [The trader] neither admitted nor denied wrongdoing."

MF GLOBAL

Although large-scale trading losses at hedge funds such as at Amaranth have historically not been unusual, market participants were, nonetheless, shocked by the aftermath of the 2011 bankruptcy of the futures commission merchant (FCM) MF Global. Even during the 2005 collapse of the FCM Refco, and during the worst of the global financial crisis (GFC) of 2007–2008, the transfer of futures customer funds and positions to healthy FCMs occurred smoothly and almost flawlessly. Not so with the MF Global bankruptcy, three years after the GFC. This section of the chapter attempts to lift the shroud of mystery that seems to have descended upon this complicated bankruptcy. Heckinger (2016) serves as the basis of discussion for this section's case study on MF Global.

On October 31, 2011, the broker-dealer (B/D) and FCM firm of the MF Global Group (i.e., MFG, the group, and all its parts) collapsed, causing substantial financial distress to its customers, many of whom were small investors or hedgers such as farmers, ranchers, or commodity merchants such as grain elevator operators. About $1.6 billion of customers' funds were not immediately available for liquidation proceedings due to the apparent misallocation of customer funds, which were not segregated from firm accounts, and the use of the funds to fund proprietary trading, which resulted in the encumbrance of such funds.

By late 2015, recovery and distribution actions of the respective bankruptcy trustees and administrators appointed to liquidate the firm made all customers whole, depending on the jurisdiction and particular MFG business entity. Other creditors such as vendors or suppliers of services to MFG received around 95 percent of the value of their claims. In the five years following its collapse, trustee/administrator reports, legal proceedings, and journalists thoroughly documented this episode.

A run on its liabilities and a hasty sale of its assets at possibly concessionary prices known as a *fire sale* characterized MFG's collapse. As MFG suffered a *crisis of liquidity* (i.e., the inability to fund its proprietary positions), customers did not exit the firm en masse, at least not initially.

The eventual exit by customers amounted to $1.1 billion and accelerated when MFG was in the throes of credit downgrades. In particular, credit downgrades by Moody's Investors Service and Standard & Poor's between October 24 and 27, 2011 reduced MFG's rating to junk status. The $1.1 billion reduction in MFG's customer funds represented a drain on MFG's liquidity certainly, but likely it was of insufficient magnitude or happened rapidly enough to cause the firm to collapse at the start of MFG's liquidity crisis.

Simply put, some actual or potential providers of liquidity to MFG, such as commercial banks, reduced their liquidity provision at the same time that counterparties demanded additional collateral from MFG by increasing their margin requirements. MFG used multiple sources of liquidity, and, in some cases, the liquidity providers and the demanders were the same firms. Such arrangements are common in broad-based client relationships between, say, banks and their commercial customers.

In this context, MFG faced various entities with banks in particular as their customer (i.e., the bank as MFG's agent) and/or their counterparty (i.e., the bank as the other side of a dealt position). MFG's other key counterparties were the various central counterparties (CCPs or clearinghouses) that required collateral and liquidity for positions held by MFG with the opposite sides of the positions guaranteed by the CCPs.

The liquidity crisis was experienced with respect to MFG's proprietary trading of mainly European sovereign debt. The strategy, as diagrammed in Figure 20.6, was based on earning the yield to maturity of the securities, but the strategy had the risk of default by the issuers. As with most investment strategies, the other risks included the market (price/yield) risks of changes in interest rates overall and/or changes in the credit rating attached to the securities.

MFG's liquidity risk was based on the need to fund its positions through the full maturity of the securities, of which most positions were one year or less, thereby vacating the opportunity to sell the securities before maturity to take a profit or loss. The use of *repurchase agreements* (i.e., the sale of securities with an agreement to repurchase them at a later agreed upon date) exacerbated this "lock-in" aspect of MFG's strategy to affect the so-called repo to maturity (RTM) strategy. With an RTM, the maturity of repo funding matches the maturity of the security being financed.

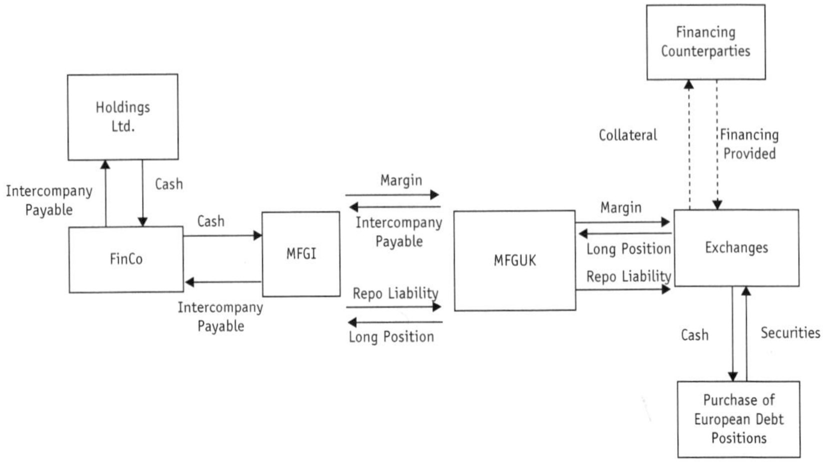

Figure 20.6 End-to-End Structure of MF Global's Euro RTM Transaction
This figure diagrams how MF Global carried out its leveraged European sovereign-debt trades, focusing on the various financing relationships in doing so. Note: "MFGI" is an abbreviation for MF Global Inc., "an indirect subsidiary of MF Global Holdings Ltd." MFG UK is an abbreviation for MF Global U.K. Limited, which "was the MF Global entity that was a member of the clearinghouses in Europe." The "Euro RTMs" were trades in European sovereign debt, which, in turn, were "financed through repurchase to maturity transactions." "On the dates MFGI entered into the various Euro RTMs, it recognized a gain in the amount of the difference or spread between (1) the effective interest rate received by MF Global on the debt securities and (2) the repurchase rate (or the financing rate) paid by MF Global to the counterparty. MFG UK recognized a gain in the amount of the markup for its role as counterparty to both MFGI and the clearinghouses. The trades were held by MFGI so that it, rather than MFG UK, bore the risk of default or restructuring of the sovereign debt. On July 1, 2010, MFGI and MFG UK entered into an investment management agreement related to the Euro RTM trades, which provided that MFG UK would identify market opportunities related to the sovereign debt of certain European governments. Pursuant to this agreement, MFG UK received 80 percent of the consolidated net revenue of such transactions, while MFGI received 20 percent of the revenue, held the trades, and took the risk that the sovereigns would default or restructure their debt." Source: MF Global Holdings Ltd. Trustee Report (2013), p. 33.

Two reasons motivated MFG to use the RTM strategy. First, the firm could use the cash generated by the repo (minus the *margin haircut*, which is the amount held back from the repo to cover the risk of the deal) to fund further positions, thereby creating leverage. Second, MFG realized profits on the RTM immediately because the accounting rules characterized the securities in the repo positions as "sold." The other leg of the repo transaction (i.e., the repurchase from the RTM counterparty at the maturity of the repo) was characterized as a forward purchase agreement (a derivatives transaction) that was marked-to-market with variations recognized as current profit or loss. Regardless, the consequence was that MFG was committed to using its capital to fund the strategy for the full duration. In effect, this strategy was akin to a highly levered portfolio of zero-coupon securities held until maturity.

However, as with market and credit risks, liquidity risks might change over time. MFG faced possible downgrades in the credit ratings of the sovereign issuers such as Italy and Ireland and the securities being financed could be subject to margin calls for additional collateral. Such downgrades occurred and required MFG to obtain additional funding and liquidity to meet the calls. Concomitantly, due to its re-leveraging of positions, MFG itself was put on alert/watch lists by regulators and rating agencies, and its eventual downgrades caused additional margin calls, reflecting MFG's increased counterparty credit (and liquidity) risk.

The main, relevant regulators were the U.S. Financial Industry Regulatory Authority (FINRA), a supervisor of U.S. B/Ds, and the Financial Services Authority (FSA), a supervisor of UK financial intermediaries (now the Financial Conduct Authority). Each questioned the adequacy of MFG's capital to support the RTM strategy, specifically imposing a default risk capital charge to cover the sovereign debt that was the collateral for the RTM.

Institutionally, MFG's back office systems were appropriate for FCM and B/D business, and were not well-suited to managing a book of leveraged proprietary positions. Further, its use of two settlement banks—J.P. Morgan Chase and Bank of New York Mellon—to settle its securities (fixed income) transactions, as well as for access to immediate liquidity versus pending settlements (so-called in-the-box securities) complicated its liquidity management. This situation resulted in cases where liquidity was available at one bank but needed at the other. Its settlement banks were also key liquidity providers/agents, and as previously noted demanders of liquidity as MFG's counterparties, among others. As the downgrades occurred, MFG's access to liquidity would have been stressed at only one bank, and the use of two banks increased its operational and coordination risks substantially.

The trustees and administrators note that MFG apparently used customer-segregated funds, held in respect of its FCM activities, to fund some of the margin calls. The exact extent of such use was in doubt due to the chaotic conditions at MFG during its last weeks, compounded by its inadequate management information and control systems. The consensus was that between $1 billion and $1.6 billion was possibly used inappropriately. Regardless of that possible violation, any amount of customer funds that may have been used was beyond MFG's capital and balance-sheet ratios, thereby allowing the firm to fund risks that it should not have been capable of taking.

In seeking liquidity, MFG sought to sell assets at essentially a fire sale. Due to the haste of and administrative chaos surrounding such attempted sales, and failures by counterparties to consummate the deals and the claiming of proceeds by settlement agents for monies owed, MFG was left with unsold securities, especially corporate bonds. The unsold securities required full funding, thereby locking up potential liquidity. Given MFG's market standing at the time, potential buyers of any of MFG's assets were unwilling to accept the settlement risk attached to trades with MFG. Even for securities that MFG was able to repo, the counterparties increased their haircuts; closed out their reverse repos, calling for their cash back by returning the securities, as might have been allowed in the terms of the repo, to MFG; or took both actions. In response, MFG attempted to extend its fire sale to securities it had lent out after paying back the collateral in cash to the borrower, a further drain on its liquidity. MFG continued attempts to sell, possibly by auction, whole portfolios of holdings and further attempted to unwind some of its RTM positions. This latter effort itself called for short-term liquidity, in that the return of the securities to allow their sale from its CCP counterparties would require MFG to return the cash provided from the original repo, net of the margin already paid. Further, it would require that MFG take a charge but not a cash transaction for the profit already realized from the RTM.

These efforts were inadequate to save the firm. Furthermore, due to questions about the status of customer funds and the extremely short time available (i.e., a week from the downgrades), such efforts did not allow for its sale to another firm. MFG in all its parts was liquidated and its customers were left with unhedged positions and/or their assets tied up in liquidation proceedings for about four years.

Lessons Learned and Reforms

Among the possible lessons learned is that the public face—the customer business of MFG, and the institutional face—the proprietary business of MFG, were very different. Customers relied on the rigorous and consistent regulations that existed on their behalf, with little knowledge of the risks the firm was taking overall and possibly by use of their monies without their consent. Customers that could exit from the firm did so but many may have not had much choice due to the suddenness of MFG's demise. Some customers may have had a false sense of security expecting that, in the event of a default, regulatory safeguards (e.g., funds segregation) would protect them. Such expectations were reasonable given the explicit segregation requirements, but further, their reasonable expectation that MFG was well managed and in compliance with applicable laws, regulations, and rules. The segregation of customer monies and positions is part of law in the United States (U.S. Commodity Exchange Act, Section 4d), for example, and is available to customers of intermediaries in other jurisdictions.

Customers believed they were dealing with a reliable agent, and generally they did not have full knowledge of the "other" MFG, namely the firm's proprietary trading activities. Customers' collective faith in the customer-facing business exposed the moral hazard implications of the protections.

These severe tests of customer protections raised new regulatory questions as to the adequacy of their scope and application. New, more specific, customer funds segregation structures were proposed and implemented. Among them are the legally separate operationally comingled (known as LSOC) accounts that, as the name implies, would provide more visibility to any one customer's funds versus the comingled account used for operational purposes such as clearing. Another innovation was individual segregated accounts so that funds would be totally segregated on behalf of the customer. On their own initiative, many customers withdrew any excess margin that might have formerly been left at an FCM.

Another lesson from the MF Global collapse is to pay more attention to the full scope of an FCM's business activities. In comparison to customers of MFG who assumed they were dealing with an agent, MFG's counterparties had access to more instantaneous data as counterparties or agents. Customers lacked a full picture of MFG's financial condition except for periodic corporate filings and disclosures.

Reacting to what information they had, the institutional counterparties had several remedies, such as demanding more collateral to protect their interests, which they did. Customers, many of whom were hedgers, had difficulty either extracting their funds or re-establishing their hedge positions in a timely manner. Consequently, they suffered real and opportunity costs from the lack of access to FCM services.

Other claimants, creditors of various classes, had little choice but to hope for sufficient recovery of assets to cover their claims against the estates of MFG. Civil and criminal judgments are still being resolved. For example, on January 4, 2017, Jon Corzine, the former MFG CEO, settled with the CFTC and paid $5 million out of his own pocket to settle claims from the case. The regulator also set a lifetime ban on him personally trading other people's money in the futures industry. As Robinson (2016, p. 1) notes, "The CFTC alleges Corzine didn't fix inadequate controls that led to $1 billion in missing customer funds, that he was aware of the New York-based firm's extreme shortage of cash and that he didn't ask questions about the origins of funds used to make transfers that he ordered."

Ultimately, MFG's counterparties of all kinds were satisfied in whole or in large part, but their collective trust in the regulation and management of financial intermediaries in general was tested. Key among the results of the demise of MFG are the provision of additional customer protections, and more rigorous investor due diligence in choosing agents and counterparties.

Summary and Conclusions

This chapter examined two categories of trading strategies—trend-following and calendar spreads—as well as common, but avoidable, trading mistakes, including demanding a threshold return from the market, inappropriate trade sizing, and having an insufficient appreciation for the psychological discipline required for trading. It also discussed the surprisingly catastrophic derivatives blowups at a hedge fund and a futures commission merchant.

Typically, the daily mark-to-market process in futures markets serves to limit catastrophic losses, but interestingly this was not helpful in the two case studies covered in this chapter. With Amaranth, the immense scale of the hedge fund's positions meant that a severe cost existed to quickly liquidate its positions. With MF Global, the FCM unlawfully used customer funds in large-scale proprietary trades that the firm ultimately could not fund.

Gaining expertise in the commodity markets usually occurs through trial-and-error experiences, some of which can be painful. The goal of this chapter has been to provide enough cautionary notes and lessons to help others avoid similar debacles in their own careers.

Acknowledgments

The authors gratefully acknowledge the research assistance from both Katherine Farren, CAIA, of Premia Risk Consultancy, Inc., and Hendrik Schwarz.

Discussion Questions

1. Discuss distinguishing features among trend-following CTAs.
2. Define a futures calendar spread.
3. Discuss three common mistakes that occur in commodity trading strategies.
4. Discuss key lessons learned from the Amaranth debacle.
5. Discuss key lessons learned for FCM clients from the MF Global bankruptcy.

References

Campbell & Company. 2013. "Prospects for CTAs in a Rising Interesting Rate Environment." Working Paper. January. Available at https://www.thehedgefundjournal.com/sites/default/files/Campbell%20CTAS.pdf.

Cashin, Art. 2008. "Market Commentary." UBS Financial Services. March 18.

Collins, Daniel. 2007. "Commodity Indexes Getting More Complex." *Futures Magazine*, July, 58–61.

Cootner, Paul. 1967. "Speculation and Hedging." *Food Research Institute Studies* Supplement 7, 64–105.

Davis, Ann. 2006. "How Giant Bets on Natural Gas Sank Brash Hedge Fund Trader." *Wall Street Journal Online*. September 19. Available at http://www.wsj.com/articles/SB115861715980366723.

Davis, Ann, Greg Zuckerman, and Henny Sender. 2007. "Hedge Fund Hardball: Amid Amaranth's Crisis, Other Players Profited." *Wall Street Journal Online*. January 30. Available at http://www.wsj.com/articles/SB117012628156391989.

De Souza, Clifford, and Mikhail Smirnov. 2004. "Dynamic Leverage." *Journal of Portfolio Management* 31:1, 25–39.

Eagleeye, Joseph. 2007. "Risk Management, Strategy Development, and Portfolio Construction in a Commodity Futures Programme." In Hilary Till and Joseph Eagleeye (eds.), *Intelligent Commodity Investing*, 491–497. London: Risk Books.

Farrington, Stella. 2006. "Lessons Learned." *Energy Risk*, December, 20–24.

Fung, William, and David Hsieh. 2003. "The Risk in Hedge Fund Strategies: Alternative Alphas and Alternative Betas." In Lars Jaeger (ed.), *The New Generation of Risk Management for Hedge Funds and Private Equity Investments*, 72–87. London: Euromoney Books.

Hamilton, Dane. 2006. "Amaranth Says Determined to Stay in Business." *Globe Investor*. September 22. Available at http://www.globeinvestor.com/servlet/WireFeedRedirect?cf=GlobeInvestor/config&vg=BigAdVariableGenerator&date=20060922&archive=roc&slug=2006-09-22T202458Z_01_N22203575_RTRIDST_0_BUSINESS-FUNDS-AMARANTH-COL.

Heckinger, Richard. 2016. "MF Global Five Years On." *Global Commodities Applied Research Digest* 1:1, 137–141.

Hougan, Matthew. 2008. "An Interview with Bob Greer." HardAssetsInvestor.com. March 25. Available at http://www.etf.com/sections/features-and-news/742-an-interview-with-bob-greer?nopaging=1.

Hurst, Brian, Yao Hua Ooi, and Lasse Pedersen. 2012. "A Century of Evidence of Trend-Following Investing." Working Paper: AQR Capital Management. Fall.

Lungarella, Guido. 2002. "Managed Futures: A Real Alternative." *swissHEDGE*. Fourth Quarter, 9–13.

MF Global Holdings Ltd. Trustee Report. 2013. Morrison & Foerster LLP, Attorneys for the Chapter 11 Trustee. "Report of Investigation of Louis J. Freeh, Chapter 11 Trustee of MF Global Holdings LTD., *et al.*" In re *MF Global Holdings LTD., et al.*, Debtors, United States Bankruptcy Court Southern District of New York, Case No. 11-15059 (MG), (Jointly Administered). April 4.

Patel, Sandeep, Anil Suri, and Andrew Weisman. 2007. "Chasing Your Tail." Working paper, Merrill Lynch. March 29.

Robinson, Matthew. 2016. "Corzine Set to Reach a $5 Million CFTC Deal on MF Global." *Bloomberg News*, October 6. Available at https://www.bloomberg.com/news/articles/2016-10-06/corzine-said-to-be-close-to-5-million-cftc-deal-over-mf-global.

Rulle, Michael. 2003. "Trend-Following: Performance, Risk and Correlation Characteristics." Working paper, Graham Capital Management.

Szala, Ginger. 2014. "Cover Story: In-House [Im]Prop[er] Trading." *InsideAdvantage* newsletter, Spring, 10–13.

Taleb, Nassim. 2001. *Fooled by Randomness*. New York: Texere.

Till, Hilary. 2006. "EDHEC Comments on the Amaranth Case: Early Lessons from the Debacle." October 2. Working paper, EDHEC-Risk Institute.

Till, Hilary. 2008. "Case Studies and Risk Management Lessons in Commodity Derivatives Trading." In Helyette Geman (ed.), *Risk Management in Commodity Markets: From Shipping to Agriculturals and Energy*, 255–291. Chichester, UK: John Wiley & Sons Ltd.

Till, Hilary. 2016. "What Are the Sources of Return for CTAs and Commodity Indexes? A Brief Survey of Relevant Research." *Journal of Wealth Management* 18:4, 108–123.

Till, Hilary, and Joseph Eagleeye. 2005. "A Hedge Fund Investor's Guide to Understanding Managed Futures." In Greg Gregoriou, Georges Hubner, Nicolas Papageorgiou, and Fabrice Rouah (eds.), *Hedge Funds: Insights in Performance Measurement, Risk Analysis*, 473–490. Hoboken, NJ: John Wiley & Sons, Inc.

Till, Hilary, and Joseph Eagleeye. 2006. "Commodities—Active Strategies for Enhanced Return." In Robert Greer (ed.), *The Handbook of Inflation Hedging Investments*, 127–157. New York: McGraw-Hill.

U.S. Senate Permanent Subcommittee on Investigations Staff Report. 2007. "Excessive Speculation in the Natural Gas Market." June 25. Available at https://www.hsgac.senate.gov/download/report-psi-staff-report-excessive-speculation-in-the-natural-gas-market-6/25/07.

Van Voris, Bob, and Patricia Hurtado. 2014. "Ex-Amaranth Trades Reaches $750,000 Settlement with CFTC." *Bloomberg News*, September 15. Available at https://www.bloomberg.com/news/articles/2014-09-15/ex-amaranth-trader-reaches-750-000-settlement-with-cftc.

Vince, Ralph. 1992. *The Mathematics of Money Management*. New York: John Wiley & Sons.

Zajac, Andrew. 2013. "FERC Lacks Power to Regulate Futures, Court Rules." *Bloomberg News*, March 15. Available at https://www.bloomberg.com/news/articles/2013-03-15/ferc-ruled-lacking-authority-to-regulate-futures-contracts-1-.

21

Asset Allocation Strategies and Commodities

CLAUDIO BOIDO
Professor, University of Siena

Introduction

At the beginning of the twenty-first century, after the equity market collapsed during the dot-com bubble, more asset managers started selecting commodities as an alternative asset class because commodity and stock returns often have low correlations. This change resulted in an inflow of billions of dollars into commodity markets from financial institutions and high net worth individuals. At that time the most popular choice was to invest in an index composed of commodities. The most commonly used indexes were the S&P Goldman Sachs Commodity Index (GSCI) and the Dow Jones-UBS Commodity Index (DJ-UBSCI), both characterized by larger weights of commodities in the energy sector. Investors in commodity index products purportedly had the ability to influence the movement of commodity prices because traditional speculators and commercial hedgers did not have the strength to modify trends in commodity prices. Reasons cited for the inclusion of commodity exposure in portfolios before the financial crisis of 2007–2008 included the following:

- commodity futures had historically offered a competitive return to U.S equity securities;
- commodity returns were negatively correlated with the returns of stocks and bonds; and
- commodity returns remained positively correlated with inflation.

Commodities help investors to make better decisions about asset allocation because they can improve the efficient frontier. Between 1959 and 2006, commodities were negatively correlated with equities and bonds and positively correlated with inflation, while maintaining a risk/return profile comparable with equities. The opportunity set for commodity markets has dramatically changed from a market of mines, refineries, and farms to a market of exchange-traded funds (ETFs), hedge funds, and financial futures. Some label this change as the financialization of commodity markets. Before the early 2000s, asset managers often did not consider commodity markets as part of financial markets. Beginning in 2001, billions of investments flowed into commodity markets from financial institutions and this flow stimulated the process of financialization among commodity markets. This shift has reduced the ability for commodities to enhance a portfolio's risk-adjusted returns. Indeed, the risk premium decreased from 5.23 percent between 1959 and 2004 to 3.67 percent between 2006 and 2015. The correlation between commodities and other assets and commodities and inflation increased markedly, especially between September and October 2008.

The strong growth of markets in Brazil, Russia, India, and China (i.e., the BRICs) contributed to the recent commodity price boom, especially in the energy and metals sectors. In these markets, the demand for commodities depends on the strength of the economic growth and is negatively related to the appreciation of the U.S. dollar. The correlation between the S&P GSCI and Morgan Stanley Capital International (MSCI) Emerging Markets Index was close to zero or negative until 2004, and then increased to 0.5 during 2009 (Bhardwaj, Gorton, and Rouwenhorst 2016). This trend is compatible with both the growth of demand for goods and the development of emerging markets. Researchers have identified different factors to explain the strong volatility in oil and non-energy commodities. These factors included the financial crisis of 2007–2008, which reduced the appeal for asset managers to include commodities in their portfolio, the global economic recession that followed, and the financialization process, which underlined the weakness of producers in controlling the effective supply and demand of commodities

This backdrop raises many questions as the world has emerged from the financial crisis. How have asset managers changed their way of thinking after the financial turmoil? What is the difference between passive and active managers in commodity investment? Is following the so-called "smart strategies" in commodity investment a winning solution? This chapter introduces the following topics in sequential order: asset management, commodity investment performance, and correlation. A summary and conclusions section wraps up the chapter.

Asset Management

Asset managers consist of two different types: active and passive. *Active managers* try to combine the right choices in their portfolio in pursuit of a superior combination of risk and return, often selecting alternative investments as part of their portfolios. Alternative investments offer the opportunity to earn an absolute return or an independent return from the performance in equity or debt markets. *Passive managers* try to replicate the risk and return of a predetermined target expressed in the form of a benchmark, so the performance of their funds is compared to the benchmark return. Active managers pursue strategies to maximize alpha, while passive managers focus on market capitalization strategies to gain market exposure.

Asset managers use alpha and beta to explain the source of their returns. *Beta* is the covariance of the asset's return with the return of the market portfolio divided by the variance of the returns of the market portfolio. The financial interpretation of beta is a measure of systematic or non-diversifiable risk. The capital asset pricing model (CAPM) is a single factor model in which the factor is the market. Multifactor asset pricing models such as those by Fama and French (1993) and Carhart (1997) include multiple betas. The expression "the strategy beats the beta" implies the asset manager is looking for an excess return or a higher expected return. When asset managers try to earn more, without taking additional systematic risk, they are searching for alpha. *Alpha* is an excess return after accounting for expectations based on the risk-free rate, systematic risk, and risk premiums. Alpha is associated with the asset manager's knowledge and skill. The original concept of alpha was from Jensen's (1968) work with the CAPM, linked to empirical application of the single factor model and later applied also to multifactor market models. Alpha and beta are generally unobservable but are often estimated based on historical data. An asset's true alpha and beta can change over time.

The asset management industry uses the concept of *return drivers,* which are the underlying factors that create a portfolio's risk and return. In this context, asset managers use the difference between a beta driver linked to the movement of the selected market and an alpha driver if the manager seeks extra returns. Beta drivers capture the market risk premium. Fundamentally, a passive asset manager follows a simple strategy of "buy and hold" to generate returns, which match the market's movement before netting fees. In contrast, alpha drivers seek excess returns with alternative assets such as commodities, which typically have low correlations with traditional assets. With active management high risk-adjusted returns would be the result of skilled (alpha) active asset managers.

The difficulty in capturing alpha has led many asset managers to search for new opportunities in commodity markets. As a result, the asset management industry has created new benchmarks for assessing returns named alternative beta and smart beta. *Alternative beta* is the exposure to systematic risk linked to special sectors of investment such as shipping, timber, and farmland rather than a simple stock market index. The term *smart beta* refers to the strategy that applies to a rule-based portfolio weighting scheme based on one or different features in the underlying asset such as volatility. Smart beta is highly successful if it generates a superior risk/return combination over those systematic risk exposures. The strategies of smart beta are commonly based on single or multiple characteristics such as small-cap stocks, value stocks, low volatility stocks, and price momentum. If investors believe that some characteristics will be more in favor, they could change the portfolio weight to favor these preferred characteristics.

Smart beta strategies are successful because they can be implemented according to the following scheme: (1) capitalizing on an attractive risk premium, (2) using fixed rules that are based on measurable security features, (3) using weights other than market capitalization weights, and (4) selecting large portfolios instead of concentrated ones.

Buffett (2016) observes that diversification helps those who do not know the financial markets, while it is less relevant for investors who know more about markets. In effect, diversification is a good rule for Markowitz (1952) portfolio selection if concentrated portfolios reflect higher risk that negatively affects risk-adjusted returns. Buffett suggests that the right balance between diversification and concentration also depends on the investor's skill to take and to diversify risk.

Active asset management describes the difference between the managed portfolio return and the benchmark portfolio return. *Active risk* is the standard deviation of the active return. *Active management* is the practice of skilled professional managers who try to outperform the market. These managers buy or sell securities in pursuit of searching for a superior combination of risk and return. Recently this pursuit has been less successful for active managers, with active funds more likely to underperform than outperform. In this context, many investors increasingly select index funds to take market risk, avoiding the elusive alpha because alpha is a zero-sum game.

Active managers select asset classes by applying active selection and by using market timing, sector, or country rotation. Indeed, their portfolios largely replicate the preferred benchmarks and only between 15 and 35 percent of the portfolio is truly actively managed. The objective is to follow the selected benchmarks over the short term but to allow their choices to achieve an optimal result in the longer run.

The *information ratio* (IR) is a ratio of portfolio returns above the returns of a benchmark to the volatility of those returns. The IR measures a portfolio manager's ability to generate excess returns relative to a benchmark. Grinold and Kahn (1999) offer a new perspective involving active management strategies. They state that a portfolio's IR is the product of both the manager's "skill" in selecting securities and the breadth of the strategy, or an opportunity to diversify across independent investment decisions, over the course of a year. In this context, skill, also called the *information coefficient,* is measured by the correlation between the manager's expected and achieved returns, and breadth is the square root of the number of independent positions in the portfolio. This research affirmed that active deviations are a function of two factors: skill (playing well) and breadth (playing often). In this way, investors can reach the same target IR, but the manager who trades infrequently needs a much higher success rate than the one who takes positions more often. The right trade-off between skill and breadth is one way to obtain high portfolio returns. An active manager imagines earning active returns through skill. However, this goal is difficult to achieve because keeping the same IR is easier by focusing on breadth. Active managers engage in many trades to achieve high returns and justify their expensive fees, without having outstanding skill, but simply by selling alpha as the "holy grail."

Clarke, Da Silva, and Thorley (2002) introduce the concept of a "transfer coefficient" to account for the constraints that active managers face when implementing a smart strategy. A *transfer coefficient* is the correlation between active weights and forecasted residual returns and it is equal to one in the absence of constraints in portfolio construction. These authors test the application of the "fundamental law of active management" to measure ex post performance attribution. Of course, the practical application of the fundamental law of active management remains difficult. In fact, two main problems inhibit tests of this law. First, the analyst must know the manager's expected returns, which are difficult to obtain, to compute the information coefficient. Second, this law is based on the assumption that managers follow the theoretical principles developed by researchers.

Commodity Investments

Alternative assets represent an opportunity for active managers to focus on commodities with major benchmarks being established after the 1990s. Asset managers include commodities in their portfolios for several reasons. First, commodity markets offer returns that may generate high alphas. Second, commodities are an asset class offering opportunities for growth. Third, including commodities offers better diversification than a traditional portfolio. Finally, commodities are an excellent protection against inflation risk.

Two factors dictate the choice of commodities by investors. One factor is the increasing supply of new financial products for gaining exposure to commodities. The other factor is the decreasing performance of equities and real estate after the tech bubble of 2000 and the financial crisis of 2007–2008, which drove investors to seek alternative asset classes. The following section describes the different instruments for gaining exposure to commodities: physical commodities, equity of commodity companies, derivative contracts, mutual funds, and ETFs.

PHYSICAL COMMODITIES

Direct investment in physical commodities represents the most obvious and easiest way to invest in commodities. The problem is low liquidity in these physical assets related to the costs associated with trading, insuring, and storing of the commodity. Investors more commonly directly invest in physical commodities during both financial crises and periods of great future uncertainty. In this context, conservative investors buy and hold precious metals such as gold in a pure physical form (gold bars) or as a currency (silver coins) to protect their portfolio against inflation, financial turbulence, and increased volatility in asset classes.

EQUITY OF COMMODITY COMPANIES

Investors can also take long or short positions in equities of companies whose core business is commodities to gain exposure to this asset class. Equity investments represent a good opportunity to gain commodity exposure with low costs compared to physical assets. Obviously, commodities-based equities are correlated to the stock index and investing in equities facilitates risk/return assessments similar to beta market strategies. This consideration underlines the issue of whether commodities offer consistent diversification benefits over time. As previously noted, the correlation between commodities and equities was positive between 2005 and 2014 but spiked between 2009 and 2011.

DERIVATIVE CONTRACTS

Using derivative contracts such as futures and options is a simple and efficient way to gain commodities exposure in a portfolio. In this way, asset managers obtain the benefits of selecting commodities in their portfolio while avoiding the management of the physical goods. Investors can use less cash due to minimal margin requirements but are responsible for requirements associated with "marking to market." Asset managers may allocate their liquidity in derivatives on one commodity or a basket of commodities. In the latter case, they assume passive strategies because their investment follows the variation of the commodity index.

Another alternative is to invest in a commodity swap to exchange cash flows having a value, which depends on the underlying commodity. Given that a commodity swap is a contract traded in the over-the-counter (OTC) market, a swap involves both counterparty and commodity risk.

Still another approach is to use commodity linked notes consisting of two parts: a security of a fixed income instrument plus an exposure in commodity in derivative contracts. Investors gain exposure in commodities but at maturity they receive the initial principal amount plus a return linked to the positive variation of underlying asset's commodity price.

MUTUAL FUNDS AND ETFS

Retail investors can also gain commodity exposure through mutual funds and ETFs. Mutual funds investing in commodities do so by investing in commodity indexes or in the equity of commodity firms. Mutual funds generally have higher fees compared to ETFs. In fact, ETFs offer a good opportunity to enter into a wide range of commodities and commodities indexes including energy, hydrocarbons, metals, industrial, and agriculture at relatively low fees. ETFs are traded on stock exchanges like equity, a feature appreciated by small investors. The most popular products are based on the performance of commodity indices such as the Commodity Research Bureau (CRB) Commodity Index, Goldman Sachs Commodity Index (GSCI), and Deutsche Bank Commodity Index (DBC). Other ETFs track the performances of individual commodities. In this way, retail investors can add an alternative asset class such as commodities to their portfolios.

Commodity ETFs can be constructed using two different underlying instruments. The first commodity-based ETFs use futures contracts as the underlying, while the second hold the actual physical commodities in storage. The futures-based approach is exposed to *rolling costs*, which are costs caused because the ETFs must roll the futures contracts that are to expire into future dated ones. According to Guedj, Li, and McCann (2011), commodity ETF returns failed to track the changes in commodity prices, so this tracking error reduces the ability of ETFs to effectively diversify and hedge. An investor can also choose ETFs created to track the price stocks of companies whose core business is linked to commodities.

Some have termed the inflows into these investment vehicles and the decrease of the trading in the physical market as the *financialization of commodity markets* (Domanski and Heath 2007). These changes reflect a diminished role for the typical operators of commodities relative to hedge funds and ETFs. Some fear that financialization has caused an irregular price trend that may not reflect the relation between the demand and supply of physical commodities but rather reflects speculative pressure. Above all, both hard and soft commodities have experienced a run-up and run-down in prices. For example, during the financial crisis of 2007–2008, oil moved from $65 per barrel in June 2007 to $145 in July 2008 before falling to $31 in December 2008. High volatility of prices also occurred for cotton, gold, copper, and coffee. Factors likely causing these irregular trends are different macroeconomic factors such as the weak demand from emerging markets, the crisis of the U.S. dollar, quantitative easing by the Federal

Reserve and the European Central Bank (ECB), inflation, and the presence of financial speculation linked to the supply and demand of physical commodities. According to some researchers, stigmatizing commodity index investing as speculation is wrong (Irwin, Sanders, and Merrin 2009; Stoll and Whaley 2010). Additionally, ETF or other fund flows do not cause changes of commodity futures prices. However, Tang and Xiong (2012) show that the benefits of diversification were stronger in 2000 and claim that the subsequent increase in commodity index investing led to commodity price changes unrelated to the balance between the physical asset's supply and demand.

Performance and Correlation

Asset managers tend to judge the performance of commodities relative to an index or assess their sources of return in commodity futures. These sources depend on three different components: the change in spot price, return on margin collateral, and roll return. Table 21.1 indicates how over the past 40 years a commodity investment has a better performance than the S&P 500 index and Europe/Australasia/Far East (EAFE) index, confirming that their long-term return performance is comparable to that of some equities.

As Table 21.1 shows, the GSCI performed best with a monthly return of 0.979 percent compared to the S&P 500 index and EAFE, but it had the highest standard deviation of 5.763 percent. The most speculative sub-sector is energy with a monthly return of 1.180 percent and a standard deviation of 9.315 percent. This result justifies the final return of the GSCI index in which the weight of the energy sector is strong.

Table 21.1 **Investment Performance of Commodities and Equities: Monthly Data between 1970 and 2009**

Index	*Monthly Return*	*Standard Deviation*	*Skewness*	*Kurtosis*
GSCI	0.979	5.763	0.082	2.858
Energy	1.180	9.315	0.043	1.873
Livestock	0.768	5.223	0.056	1.556
Agriculture	0.523	5.851	0.741	3.713
Metals	0.964	7.038	0.553	4.164
Precious Metals	0.816	6.692	1.218	7.732
S&P 500	0.669	4.497	−0.458	1.931
EAFE	0.934	4.947	−0.323	1.215

Note: This table presents the performance characteristics of several commodity futures sub-indexes relative to the U.S. equity market as reflected in the S&P 500 index and the developed non-U.S. equity market as reflected in the Europe/Australasia/Far East (EAFE).

Source: Jensen and Mercier (2011).

Precious metals have a relatively high standard deviation (6.692 percent) even if some view metals as a safe haven for many investors. In this case, behavioral finance suggests that investor confidence wavered during the financial crisis of 2007–2008 and the track record of precious metals, most notably gold, is irregular. Table 21.1 also shows *positive skewness*, which means that positive returns are more common than negative returns. A common view is that commodities with positive skewness have positive risk, consistent with their reaction during the financial crisis. The last row indicates kurtosis or peakedness. In this sample, the precious metals sector reflects high kurtosis, which means that extreme returns are more common for precious metals.

A primary reason asset managers select commodities in their portfolio is because these investments exhibit a low correlation with traditional asset classes. Table 21.2 examines the results between 1970 and 2009 (Jensen and Mercer 2011).

These results show that commodities comprise an alternative asset class with low or negative correlation with traditional assets. Historically the correlation coefficient between the GSCI and the S&P 500 index has been low (0.034). The GSCI and fixed income indexes (U.S. Treasury bonds and Treasury bills) actually exhibit negative and low correlations, respectively. Lastly, the correlation between the GSCI and inflation is positive (0.318). Therefore, during the longer time interval analyzed, the standard properties for selecting commodities in portfolio are confirmed, but in shorter time intervals (e.g., between 1990 and 2009), commodities exhibit lower returns and higher correlations.

Correlations increase in the presence of a financial crisis (Bhardwaj and Dunsby 2013). Bhardwaj, Gorton, and Rouwenhorst (2015) re-examine conclusions from Gorton and Rouwenhorst (2006) by extending the study to include 2005 to 2014, a period that includes the global economic expansion and industrialization of China, the U.S. housing boom and bust, the financial crisis of 2007–2008, and the extraordinary Federal Reserve and ECB monetary policy stimuli that drove interest rates toward zero. During this period the correlation between commodities and other asset classes increased. Table 21.3 highlights a positive commodity equity correlation (0.5) between

Table 21.2 **Correlation of Commodities with Traditional Assets and Inflation between 1979 and 2009**

	GSCI	*Energy*	*Livestock*	*Agriculture*	*Metals*	*Precious Metals*
S&P 500	0.034	0.112	0.216	−0.078	0.159	−0.065
EAFE	0.335	0.018	0.419	0.031	0.260	0.048
T-Bonds	−0.263	−0.024	−0.076	−0.211	−0.322	−0.220
T-Bills	0.021	0.161	0.169	0.064	−0.105	−0.030
Inflation	0.318	0.588	0.166	0.372	0.115	0.411

Note: This table reports correlation coefficient between the traditional asset classes, inflation, the GSCI, and each of the GSCI's component indexes.

Source: Jensen and Mercier (2011).

Table 21.3 **Correlations of Monthly Commodity Futures Return**

	July 1959–2004	*2005–2014*
Stocks	0.05	0.52
Bonds	–0.14	0.05
Inflation	0.02	0.25

Note: This table presents the increase in the correlation of commodity futures with equities, bonds, and inflation during 1959–2004 and 2005–2014.

Source: Bhardwaj et al. (2016).

2005 and 2014, as shown in Bhardwaj et al. (2016), compared to the negative relation during the period up to 2004.

Because the correlation between commodities and bonds is reasonably stable, the recent period does not differ from earlier periods. The correlation between equities and commodities spiked between 2009 and 2011, reaching magnitudes similar to the earlier spikes in the 1960s and 1980s. Daskalaki and Skiadopoulos (2011) and Tang and Xiong (2012) reach a similar conclusion: the correlation between commodities and equities has risen over recent years and the commodity hedge against inflation is valid for most periods. Additionally, a minor effect may exist for commodities hedging other types of inflation such as monetary inflation (Ang 2012). Commodity futures returns have also shown a positive skewness compared to the negative skewness in equity returns. During the last decade, the co-movements between various commodities have increased and the prices of non-energy futures are linked to oil prices.

A growing emerging economy demand explains the increasing return correlation between commodities and MSCI Emerging Markets. These co-movements were stable in China during the financial turmoil compared to the large increases in the United States. An analogous situation involving co-movements occurred in the 1970s and early 1980, which was a period marked by persistent oil supply shocks, stagflation, and high inflation.

Commodity Strategies

What proportion of a portfolio should be invested in commodities? The answer depends on the investor's perspective. According to Norrish (2015), the preferences of investors are the following: Bloomberg Global Equity 58 percent, Barclays Multiverse 45.8 percent, and commodities 0.24 percent. In this context, Facebook's market capitalization (0.29 percent) exceeds the total market value of commodity investment. Alternatively, Idzorek (2006) finds that optimal allocation to commodities is 9.1 percent for conservative portfolios, 21.9 percent for moderate portfolios, and 23.2 percent for aggressive portfolios.

At first glance, the traditional portfolio consisting of 60/40 equity and bonds may seem to be well diversified. However, because this traditional portfolio suffered during the financial crisis of 2007–2008, investors decided to turn their attention to alternative assets to enhance portfolio returns and to reduce correlations with traditional assets. In the context of commodity markets, investors define *commodity beta* as exposure to one of the original indexes (i.e., S&P Goldman Sachs Commodity Index or Bloomberg Commodity Index, formerly DJ-UBS Commodity Index). These indexes have different volatilities related to their composition. The S&P GSCI includes 24 commodities with volatility, measured as the standard deviation of returns, of 24 percent over the long term, while the BCOM consists of 22 commodities with volatility of 22 percent.

As previously described, asset managers could search for uncorrelated returns by pushing to earn alpha, perhaps by identifying assets with uncorrelated returns. The research concerning this objective addresses investment styles. Asness, Ilmanen, Israel, and Moskowitz (2015, p. 28) define an investment style as "a disciplined and systematic method of investing that produces unique long term positive average returns across markets and asset classes with low zero correlation with major log only asset classes." The difficulty in diversifying investment portfolios has led some investors to investigate risk-factor-based asset allocation, concentrating on alternative beta strategies to modify the conventional portfolio. This strategy can contribute to reducing risks or to enhancing returns.

Examining these portfolio strategies in commodity markets is appealing. The S&P GSCI uses the value of global production to weight commodities in the index. Although the index includes different sectors, the energy sector has the most weight in the index. Asset managers choose the weight of commodities in their portfolio, trading off risk and return. The principles behind commodity allocations are based on three pillars: a commodity risk premium, diversification against traditional equity or bond portfolio, and a hedge against inflation risk. As previously mentioned, the average commodity risk premium between 2005 and 2014 was lower (3.67 percent) than between 1959 and 2004 (5.23 percent). The commodity correlations with equities and bonds have become more positive, and the hedge against inflation has been weak because inflation has been low. The following section discusses different alternative allocation strategies to evaluate the investment benefits of commodities: (1) strategic asset allocation (SAA), (2) tactical asset allocation (TAA), and (3) factor-based asset allocation.

STRATEGIC ASSET ALLOCATION

With SAA, investors decide the long-term target asset allocation in relation to the ex ante risk and return objectives. Managers select portfolio weights and use passive products to allocate funds across assets, benchmarking performance to an appropriate commodity index, such as the GSCI index, Dow Jones Commodities Index, or Bloomberg Commodity Index (BCOM). In this context, asset managers use the term *commodity beta* to measure exposure to the index (Kidd 2014). The mentioned commodity indexes have some compositional defects in construction methodologies, based on production and liquidity statistics, which are damaging for investors when selecting a commodity asset class as a component for a long-term strategy (Lincke 2016). These problems include inefficient sector weights (e.g., including iron ore in a commodity portfolio, but not in a commodity benchmark), inappropriate commodity contracts (e.g., using natural gas, which accounts more than 11 percent in BCOM), and a disregard for correlation structures because commodity benchmarks ignore the correlation structure in commodity markets. The S&P GSCI and the BCOM have high volatility (24 and 19 percent, respectively) and include many commodities (between 22 and 24). Investing in fewer commodities may produce similar volatility. In contrast, active managers implement tactical allocation with the aim of altering systematic risk and earning higher risk-adjusted returns.

In an imperfect market, the challenge for asset managers is to select the best opportunities across markets. In a classical approach to portfolio allocation, SAA means deciding long-term asset allocation. These decisions are based on long-term expectations for risk and return benchmarked to one index for each asset class. Since the 1990s, many asset managers have followed the advice of numerous researchers by adding commodities to a SAA-based investment portfolio, so investors must choose the weight and the holding period of commodities. This selection process allows investors to achieve an upward shift in the efficient frontier of the investment set that might include equity, corporate and government bonds, and real estate investment trusts (REITs).

Asset managers must decide the right weight to give to commodity investment vehicles. The value of a commodity can be judged by its contribution toward reducing portfolio risk or to enhancing portfolio returns. Therefore, investors build traditional portfolios with equities and bonds and then add hard or soft commodities, whose weight depends on their risk aversion. Consequently, active managers try to beat the market by investing in commodities with the objective to enhance return or to reduce risk.

When markets are in equilibrium and the price of commodities is efficient, asset managers cannot take advantage of exposure to systematic risk. Assuming markets are in a continuous state of imbalance, asset managers could be inclined to overweight commodities without considering supply and demand for the commodity. Their behavior could push other investors to select commodities to enhance their portfolio returns. If these investors take positions in commodities to enhance portfolio returns, disregarding supply and demand, speculators might exploit the opportunity for their own benefit. Given that speculators cover the gap between the supply and demand of physical assets, they take short positions in overpriced contracts and long positions in undervalued contracts.

Analogous results emerge if portfolio managers select some commodity products linked to alternative beta or to smart beta solutions (Ung and Kang 2013). In this case, asset managers seek to take advantage of relative mispricing between commodities in derivative markets compared to physical commodity markets. In this search for alpha, managers use fundamental analysis to investigate commodity prices and choose the commodities offering a superior trade-off between risk and return. Before a political election, for example, managers can forecast whether the price of gold will increase or decrease and trade accordingly because many consider gold a safe haven.

TACTICAL ASSET ALLOCATION

Asset managers can also improve their performance by varying the commodity exposure over time. These methods involve a tactical approach, taking active positions to gain commodity exposure, and adjusting exposures based on different indicators. Investors can select commodities by using technical analysis to chase alpha. In the short run, active asset managers could analyze the market risk premium or other factor premiums such as momentum, carry, and low-risk factor premiums as described in the next section.

Some studies validate these methods for short-run performance and its effectiveness is highest when applied to high volume and low open interest contracts (Wang and Yu 2004; Hong and Yogo 2010). Fundamentally, TAA is valid in the short term, but contrarian commodity strategies may be unprofitable in the long run.

FACTOR-BASED ASSET ALLOCATION

The financial crisis of 2007–2008 led some asset managers to investigate the application of risk-factors-based asset allocation as a new portfolio selection tool. In this new approach, alternative beta strategies can have a different form with the aim of reducing risk (the risk-factor approach) or enhancing the performance through exposure to systematic factors (the factor-based approach). These strategies contribute to explaining the importance of systematic factors in long-term returns. If asset managers understand the different sources of returns, they can take advantage of each risk premium.

Asset managers select different indexes that use global production and trading liquidity to allocate alternative weights to different sectors and commodities. The factor based approach aims to enhance returns by taking advantage of risk premia linked to systematic factors. In commodity markets, the most common strategies are based on value, contrarian momentum, carry, and monetary policy factors.

Value Investing

Value investing style involves buying undervalued assets and selling overvalued assets. This simple rule is analogous to overweighting equities with good fundamental value and shorting, or underweighting, assets with low fundamental values. This style is primarily linked to equities, but can be extended to commodities by applying other measures of fundamental value such as purchasing power parity or five-year reversal value. For example, in the commodity market, the five-year lagged spot price can be related to the recent price to compute five-year reversal values.

Contrarian Momentum

The *momentum investment* style is based on the tendency of assets to show persistent returns, resulting in a simple rule to buy "winning" assets and to sell "losers." The simplicity of this style allows investors to apply it to commodity markets. Erb and Harvey (2006) and Miffrè and Rallis (2007) find that momentum strategies are profitable for holding periods up to nine months and momentum commodity returns are similar to momentum equity returns. They also note that higher returns are associated with higher standard deviations of returns. In related work indirectly supporting momentum strategies, Wang and Yu (2004) do not find an advantage in following a contrarian strategy in commodity futures, which is a result confirmed in more recent studies (Marshall,

Cahan, and Cahan 2008; Szakmary, Shen, and Sharma 2010; Fuertes, Miffre, and Fernandez-Perez 2014; Neuhierl and Thompson 2014; Zaremba and Koniecka 2014).

Carry

The *carry investment* style is based on selecting higher-yielding markets or assets and financing these positions by shorting lower-yielding markets or assets. Although asset managers often apply this style to currencies and equities based on expected dividend yields, they also apply it to commodity futures using the slope of the futures curve, thereby favoring the most backwardated markets.

Monetary Policy

Tactical commodity allocations can also use monetary policy as a factor. Investors know that the prices of physical commodities are a component of inflation so they can use the commodity index as an inflation proxy. Consequently, changes in monetary policies that concern current and expected inflation could influence the weight of commodities in a portfolio. In this way, asset managers could modify commodity allocations based on changes in the central bank's discount rate. During monetary expansions, asset managers reduce the weight in commodities; while in restrictive policy phases, they increase the weight in commodities. The percentage change in these weights varies between high-risk portfolios (high percentage of commodities) and low-risk portfolios (low percentage of commodities).

Factor models are useful not only in decomposing returns into components, but also in describing the returns covariance structure and in building portfolios with certain characteristics. Three common characteristics include macroeconomic (observable economic or financial series), fundamental (observable asset characteristic), and statistical (unobservable asset characteristic). A commodity multifactor portfolio includes momentum, carry, and a low-volatility premium, which, unlike a commodity factor premium, has a low correlation with the equity market, especially between 1970 and 2006.

The application of factor analysis is common with equities (Roll and Ross 1980; Fama and French 1993, 2015; Carhart 1997), but is now also common with commodities (Erb and Harvey 2006; Kat and Oomen 2007). Recently Bhardwaj and Dunsby (2014) examine a commodity factor model and find that a diversified portfolio of commodity futures represents a good opportunity to reap the benefits of commodity investing. The authors demonstrate that commodity sectors behave differently during the economic expansions and recessions. For example, industrial metals suffer during recessions, but gain during economic expansions. However, the grain sector is insensitive to the economy and performs well during stock market crashes. Energy markets rise during high inflation and unexpected inflation periods. Precious metals exhibit superior performance during periods of high inflation, but do not provide a hedge against economic weakness. In this regard, Bharsdwaj and Dunsby show that a diversified portfolio of commodity futures produces higher risk-adjusted returns.

Blitz and De Groot (2014) also focus on factor premiums in commodity portfolios. They consider general allocations to the commodity market portfolio, but also allocations based on factor premiums. Their commodity risk portfolio consists of a momentum, carry, and low-volatility premium. They show that these compositions improve the risk-return ratio compared to a traditional commodity portfolio. These results demonstrate that commodity allocations using factor premiums can improve portfolio performance.

Summary and Conclusions

The search for improved risk and return results has pushed asset managers into selecting alternative asset classes to overcome the problems linked to the traditional choices of equity and bonds. In this context, the financialization of commodities has supported the new role of commodities as an investment vehicle. Between 1959 and 2004, Gorton and Rouwenhorst (2006) show that investors could select commodities based on (1) forecasts of the commodity's supply and demand that should yield low or negative correlations with equities and bonds; (2) expected inflation (commodity prices are positively correlated with inflation); (3) the business cycle—different commodities are priced in accordance with the state of current economic conditions in the business cycle; and (4) the difference between the historical performance of commodity futures and the return of spot commodities.

The financial crisis of 2007–2008, the global economic expansion in China, and monetary policies that have pushed interest rates close to zero each contributed to changes in historical views toward commodity investment (Bhardwaj et al. 2016). The average risk premium to commodity futures fell to 3.67 percent from the longer-term average of 5.23 percent and correlations between commodities and traditional assets increased to 0.5 during the financial crisis. Only the inflation rate/commodity price relation has remained stable. Consequently, commodities are losing their ability to be an effective alternative asset class for asset managers. According to Erb and Harvey (2016), between December 2004 and June 2015, the total return of the S&P GSCI commodity index was –4.6 percent annually, which was much lower than the +7.4 percent return of S&P 500 Index and the +4.5 percent return of the Barclays U.S. Aggregate Bond Index. The question remains as to whether commodities are still an asset class that provides equity-like returns, diversification toward traditional assets, and protection against inflation.

Discussion Questions

1. Explain the importance of active risk and the meaning of the fundamental law of active management.
2. Identify the main commodity investment vehicles.
3. List three major reasons to include commodities in an investment portfolio.
4. Discuss the effect of economic turbulence on commodity investments.
5. Describe the mechanism of commodity factor premiums.

References

Ang, Andrew. 2012. "Real Assets." Columbia Business School Research Paper.

Asness, Clifford, Antti Ilmanen, Ronen Israel, and Tobias J. Moskowitz. 2015. "Investing with Style." *Journal of Investment Management* 13:1, 27–43.

Bhardwaj, Geetesh, and Adam Dunsby. 2013. "The Business Cycle and the Correlation between Stocks and Commodities." *Journal of Investment Consulting* 14:2, 14–25.

Bhardwaj, Geetesh, and Adam Dunsby. 2014. "How Many Commodity Sectors Are There, and How Do They Behave?" *Journal of Investing* 23:1,107–121.

Bhardwaj, Geetesh, Gary B. Gorton, and K. Geert Rouwenhorst. 2015. "Facts and Fantasies about Commodity Futures Ten Years Later." Yale ICF Working Paper No. 15-18.

Bhardwaj, Geetesh, Gary B. Gorton, and K. Geert Rouwenhorst. 2016. "Investor Interest and the Returns to Commodity Investing." *Journal of Portfolio Management* 42:3, 44–55.

Blitz, David, and Wilma De Groot. 2014. "Strategic Allocation to Commodity Factor Premiums." *Journal of Alternative Investment* 17:2, 103–115.

Buffett, Warren. 2016. "Buffett on Diversification, Risk and Focus." Available at http://rayhightower.com/blog/2016/09/02/buffett-diversification-risk-focus/.

Carhart, Mark M. 1997. "On Persistence in Mutual Fund Performance." *Journal of Finance* 52:1, 57–82.

Clarke, Roger, Harindra Da Silva, and Steven Thorley. 2002. "Portfolio Constraints and the Fundamental Law of Active Management." *Financial Analysts Journal* 58:5, 48–66.

Daskalaki, Charoula, and George Skiadopoulos. 2011. "Should Investors Include Commodities in Their Portfolios After All? New Evidence." *Journal of Banking and Finance* 35:10, 2606–2626.

Domanski, Dietrich, and Alexandra Heath. 2007. "Financial Investors and Commodity Markets." *BIS Quarterly Review*, March, 53–67.

Erb, Claude B., and Campbell R. Harvey. 2006. "The Strategic and Tactical Value of Commodity Futures." *Financial Analysts Journal* 62:2, 69–97.

Erb, Claude B., and Campbell R. Harvey. 2016. "Conquering Misperceptions about Commodity Futures Investing." *Financial Analyst Journal* 72:4, 26–35.

Fama, Eugene F., and Kenneth R. French. 1993. "Common Risk Factors in the Returns on Stocks and Bonds." *Journal of Financial Economics* 33:1, 3–56.

Fama, Eugene F., and Kenneth R. French. 2015. "A Five-Factor Asset Pricing Model." *Journal of Financial Economics* 116:1, 1–22.

Fuertes, Ana-Maria, Joelle Miffre, and Adrian Fernandez-Perez. 2015. "Commodity Strategies Based on Momentum, Term Structure, and Idiosyncratic Volatility." *Journal of Futures Markets* 35:3, 274–297.

Gorton, Gary, and Geert K. Rouwenhorst. 2006. "Facts and Fantasies about Commodity Futures." *Financial Analysts Journal* 62:2, 47–68.

Grinold, Richard C., and Ronald N. Kahn. 1999. *Active Portfolio Management*. 2nd edition. New York: McGraw Hill.

Guedj, Ilan, Guohua Li, and Craigg McCann. 2011. "Futures-Based Commodity ETFs." *Journal of Index Investing* 2:1, 14–24.

Hong, Harrison, and Motohiro Yogo. 2010. "Commodity Market Interest and Asset Return Predictability." Working paper, American Finance Association Meeting, Atlanta, GA.

Idzorek, Thomas M. 2006. "Strategic Asset Allocation and Commodities" Working paper, Ibbotson Associates, commissioned by PIMCO.

Irwin, Scott H., Dwight R. Sanders, and Robert P. Merrin. 2009. "Devil or Angel? The Role of Speculation in the Recent Commodity Price Boom (and Bust)." *Journal of Agricultural and Applied Economics* 41:2, 377–391.

Jensen, Gerald R., and Jeffrey M. Mercer. 2011. "Commodities as an Investment." Working paper, Research Foundation, CFA Institute.

Jensen, Michael J. 1968. "The Performance of Mutual Funds in the Period 1945–1964." *Journal of Finance* 23:2, 389–416.

Kat, Harry M., and Roel C. A. Oomen. 2007. "What Every Investor Should Know about Commodities Part I: Univariate Return Analysis." *Journal of Investment Management* 5:1, 4–28.

Kidd, Deborah. 2014. "Managing the Complexity of Investing in Commodities." *Investment Risk and Performance Newsletter, CFA Institute* 2014:1, 1–4.

Lincke, David M. 2016. "Commodities as an Asset Class: Delivering Beta and Beyond." *CFA Institute Conference Proceedings Quarterly* 33:1, 1–10.

Markowitz, Harry. 1952. "Portfolio Selection." *Journal of Finance* 7:1, 77–91.

Marshall, Ben R., Rochester H. Cahan, and Jared Cahan. 2008. "Technical Analysis around the World: Does It Ever Add Value?" Working paper, Massey University New Zealand.

Miffre, Joelle, and Georgios Rallis. 2007. "Momentum Strategies in Commodity Futures Markets.'" *Journal of Banking & Finance* 31:6, 1863–1886.

Neuhierl, Andreas, and Andrew Thompson. 2014. "Trend Following Strategies in Commodity Markets and the Impact of Financialization." Technical report, Kellogg School of Management, Northwestern University.

Norrish, Kevin. 2015. "Numbers & Nightmares." Working paper, Barclays.

Roll, Richard, and Stephen A. Ross. 1980. "An Empirical Investigation of the Arbitrage Pricing Theory." *Journal of Finance* 35:5, 1073–1103.

Stoll, Hans R., and Robert E. Whaley. 2010. "Commodity Index Investing: Speculation or Diversification?" *Journal of Alternative Investment* 14:1, 50–60.

Szakmary, Andrew C., Qian Shen, and Subhash Sharma. 2010. "Trend-Following Trading Strategies in Commodity Futures: A Re-examination." *Journal of Banking & Finance* 34:2, 409–426.

Tang, Ke, and Xiong Wei. 2012. "Index Investment and the Financialization of Commodities." *Financial Analysts Journal* 68:5, 54–74.

Ung, Daniel, and Xiaowei Kang. 2013. "Alternative Beta Strategies in Commodities." Working paper, S&P Dow Indices McGraw-Hill Financial.

Wang, Changyun, and Min Yu. 2004. "Trading Activity and Price Reversals in Futures Markets." *Journal of Banking & Finance* 28:6, 1337–1361.

Zaremba, Adam, and Przemyslaw Konieczka. 2014. "Value, Size and Momentum across Countries." *Indian Journal of Finance* 8:9, 7–31.

22

Food Prices and Food Price Volatility

DONALD F. LARSON
Affiliated Researcher, Institute for the Theory and Practice of International Relations, College of William and Mary

Introduction

Long-standing policy concerns exist over secular trends in the level and volatility of food prices. The specter of high food prices imperils the welfare of the world's vulnerable, who spend a large share of their incomes on food. Alternatively, policymakers worry that a secular decline in commodity prices, including food prices, coupled with high price volatility will hamper growth in poor countries that depend on commodity exports. At a household level, research suggests that the uncertain prospects of food prices and food-price volatility hamper on-farm investments and encourage the poor to pursue livelihood strategies that keep them poor.

This chapter examines how food prices have evolved since 1900. It explores the interlocking effects of natural resource scarcity, population and income growth, and technical change on price levels, and how storage, speculation, and the financialization of commodities affect the volatility of agricultural prices. The chapter also examines the effects of technological innovations during the Green Revolution, and the potential for sustainable future productivity gains, which are needed to keep food affordable. The chapter reviews how a range of policies meant to alter food price outcomes and volatility failed and prompted a shift to policies intended to lessen harmful effects. The concluding section discusses policies for managing food price risk.

Food Prices, Food-Price Volatility, and Development

Figure 22.1 charts an index that measures the real price of internationally traded food items from 1900 to 2015. The index is a hybrid composed of two parts. Most observations, from 1960 to 2015, are based on an index of food prices updated monthly by the World Bank (2016). Data for earlier years are drawn from a data set of key food prices at the core of the World Bank index constructed by World Bank economists Grilli and Yang (1988). The hybrid is constructed using nominal prices

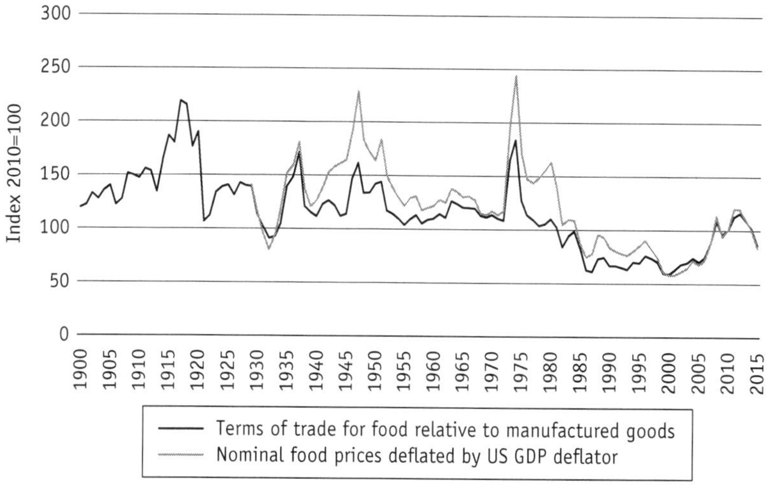

Figure 22.1 Real Food Prices between 1900 and 1916
This figure shows the terms of trade, calculated by dividing the nominal food price index by the Manufactures Unit Value Index (MUV) index, a measure of the price of developing country imports of manufactures in U.S. dollar terms. Source: The MUV and food price index observations from 1960 forward are taken from the World Bank's Global Economic Monitor (GEM) Commodities Database (World Bank 2016); earlier values are based on Grilli and Yang (1988).

and then deflated by the Manufacturers Unit Value (MUV) Index, an index based on the value of manufactured goods imported into developing countries. As with the food price index, values between 1960 and 2016 are calculated by the World Bank, with earlier observations from Grilli and Yang (1988). Because the MUV is based on the price of manufactured goods, the MUV-deflated real price series represents the terms of trade for food exports relative to manufactured imports. For the sake of comparison, the dollar-denominated food price index is also deflated by the GDP deflator for the United States, as reported by the Federal Reserve Bank of St. Louis (2016). As Figure 22.1 shows, the choice of deflator does not affect the food price trajectory overall, although the series deflated by the U.S. deflator shows higher levels from the 1940s through the 1960s and again for a decade starting around the 1975 price spike.

Several episodes stand out: the climb of prices at the start of 1900s and the sharp fall following World War I; the twin peaks for the period around World War II, and the extended subsequent period of decline; the sharp spike in food prices around 1974 and 1975 during the OPEC oil crisis; the extended decline through the end of the millennium, and the more recent climb in prices, including the twin price spikes in 2007–2008 and 2010. As discussed later in this chapter, these collective experiences have influenced commodity and food price policies.

Table 22.1 presents the same data in a different way, reporting MUV-deflated price averages, and high and low values during each decade. The table shows relatively low

Table 22.1 **Real Food Prices, Summary Statistics by Decade**

	Food-Manufacturing Terms of Trade			*Volatility*		
Decade	*Mean*	*Minimum*	*Maximum*	*Terms of Trade*	*Nominal Food Prices*	*MUV*
1900s	132.75	119.62	151.37	0.086	0.067	0.044
1910s	173.26	134.36	219.17	0.132	0.158	0.094
1920s	137.59	106.48	190.31	0.207	0.260	0.068
1930s	119.91	90.95	171.74	0.186	0.245	0.117
1940s	128.49	111.69	162.04	0.120	0.141	0.076
1950s	116.73	103.69	143.84	0.080	0.104	0.068
1960s	116.94	110.03	126.34	0.051	0.048	0.020
1970s	123.97	103.63	183.84	0.193	0.221	0.055
1980s	84.29	61.09	109.93	0.144	0.149	0.062
1990s	68.17	59.91	76.17	0.080	0.086	0.044
2000s	77.06	58.98	108.08	0.095	0.131	0.047
2010s	104.11	86.01	115.70	0.100	0.131	0.039
All Years	115.66	58.98	219.17	0.129	0.161	0.074

Note: This table shows the average, minimum, and maximum value of the food-manufacturing terms of trade by decade. It also includes decade-average volatility measures of the terms of trade and its components, calculated by taking the average year-to-year change, measured in logs.

Source: Food price index (Grilli and Yang 1988); World Bank (2016).

food prices during the 1980s, 1990s, and 2000s. The last three columns report the price volatility for the MUV-deflated food price series and its two components: the nominal food price index and the MUV. For each decade and for the series as a whole, the variation in commodity prices exceeds the volatility of the MUV. Real food prices remained fairly stable in the 1950s and 1960s, and again in the 1990s and 2000s.

Table 22.2 shows episodes when food prices rose sharply or fell steeply. In percentage terms, the sharpest spikes occurred from 1932 to 1937, when food prices rose nearly 89 percent. This period included severe droughts in the United States in 1934 and 1936, and raging dust storms. The second sharpest spike in food prices came in 1972 to 1974 and was linked to an oil embargo against Canada, Japan, the Netherlands, the United Kingdom, and the United States by the Organization of Arab Petroleum Exporting Countries. The third largest run of price increases occurred during a more recent run-up, which culminated in the 2007–2008 price spike. The spike originated in a confluence of events: low initial inventory levels, crop shortfalls, and a contagion of decisions to ban exports (Piesse and Thirtle 2009; Slayton 2009; Headey 2011). Episodes when prices fell sharply sometimes followed periods of sharp price increases, and sometime preceded them. For example, food prices fell by about 44 percent between 1974 and 1987, after climbing by almost 70 percent between 1972 and 1974; food prices dropped 44 percent in 1921, before starting a four-year run of increases.

The tables and figures reveal that price cycles featuring sharp spikes and steep drops have been an enduring feature of international food prices during the last 12 decades. Among these are shifts in long-term average prices that differ markedly from one decade to the next. But do long-term trends exist?

In 1950, two influential economists, Raúl Prebisch (1950) and Hans Singer (1950), argued that, for structural reasons, primary commodities prices tended to trend downward relative to manufactured goods. They further maintained that this trend resulted in declining terms of trade for developing countries, and as a consequence, an enduring inequality among developing primary-producer countries and richer industrial countries. This logic was a departure from the long-dominant view that real commodity prices would rise over time due to the depletion of limited land and mineral resources (Hotelling 1931). The Prebisch-Singer hypothesis helped motivate a series of international agreements among major importers and exporters to manage key commodity markets, which are described later. Researchers have often tested this hypothesis (Diakosavvas and Scandizzo 1991; Cuddington Ludema, and Jayasuriya 2007).

Some empirical studies find support for a secular decline in the price of commodities relative to manufactured goods, while others do not. Despite methodological choices, the period of study seems to be an overriding factor in explaining differences in results, and evidence favoring the Prebisch-Singer hypothesis has declined with time. That said, prices of the individual commodities that comprise the Grilli-Yang index show varying trajectories. Yamada and Yoon (2014) illustrate this point using a filtering technique to search for trending episodes from 1900 to 2010 for each of the commodities included in the Grilli-Yang index and report mixed results. However, they note that several important grain-price series, including the series for rice, wheat, and maize, exhibit negative trends up to roughly 2000, when the trends reversed for rice and wheat.

Volatility is another key feature of commodity prices and ample evidence indicates that it impedes economic development. To start, commodity prices are more volatile

Table 22.2 **Top Dozen Positive and Negative Price Runs**

Decade	*Period*	*Length (Years)*	*Ending Price*	*Percentage Change*
Positive runs				
1930s	1932–1937	5	171.74	88.84
1970s	1972–1974	2	183.84	69.56
2000s	2005–2008	3	108.08	53.58
1940s	1944–1947	3	162.04	44.91
1910s	1913–1915	2	186.83	39.05
1920s	1921–1925	4	140.75	32.18
2000s	2000–2004	4	73.97	25.40
1900s	1906–1908	2	151.37	24.10
1980s	1987–1989	2	74.43	21.82
1910s	1916–1917	1	219.17	21.73
2010s	2009–2012	3	115.70	20.43
1980s	1982–1984	2	98.74	17.20
Negative runs				
1920s	1920–1921	1	106.48	–44.05
1970s	1974–1978	4	103.63	–43.63
1980s	1984–1987	3	61.09	–38.13
1930s	1927–1932	5	90.95	–36.34
1940s	1937–1940	3	111.69	–34.97
1950s	1951–1955	4	103.69	–27.92
2010s	2012–2015	3	86.01	–25.66
1980s	1980–1982	2	84.25	–23.36
2000s	1996–2000	4	58.98	–22.57
1910s	1917–1919	2	176.29	–19.56
1940s	1947–1948	1	133.52	–17.60
1990s	1989–1993	4	63.32	–14.93

Note: This table provides calculations of food-manufacturing terms of trade, also known as real food prices, by dividing the hybrid nominal food price index by the World Bank's Manufactures Unit Value Index (MUV) index. Volatility is calculated as the standard deviation of the logarithmic change in the relevant time series by decade and for the sample. The 2010 numbers are based on data between 2010 and 2015.

Source: Authors calculations based on Hybrid Real Food Price (Terms of Trade) Index.

than the prices of manufactured goods. The last two columns of Table 22.1 illustrate this point, as does research using extended time-series (van der Ploeg and Poelhekke 2009; Jacks, O'Rourke, and Williamson 2011). As a consequence, the terms of trade of commodity exporters as a whole tend to be more volatile than those of countries where exports are more diversified or depend more on manufactured goods. This relation emerges because price rather than volume volatility is the primary source of export revenue volatility among countries that depend on natural resources. Moreover, van der Ploeg and Poelhekke report food prices were as volatile as any commodity group except petroleum between 1970 and 2003. This empirical observation is noteworthy because their study period includes the 1990s, when food prices were stable by historical standards, and excludes the food price spikes of 2007–2008 and 2010.

In turn, ample research shows that terms-of-trade volatility influences economic growth. This relation is particularly true for the economies of small price-taking countries that depend heavily of commodity exports (the so-called periphery). Moreover, growth among periphery countries is slower when price volatility in the commodities they export is greater (Blattman, Hwang, and Williamson 2007; Aghion, Bacchetta, Ranciere, and Rogoff 2009; van der Ploeg and Poelhekke 2009). By slowing economic growth, commodity price volatility is especially harmful to poor households because slowing economic growth tends to slow poverty reduction rates as well (Ravallion 2001; Lopez 2004; Belke and Wernet 2015).

Besides their effects on terms-of-trade volatility, volatile agricultural prices add to a list of risks faced by smallholder farmers. Absent access to formal risk markets and with limited capacity to self-insure, poor rural households adopt risk-mitigating livelihood strategies that can trap them on low-income pathways. Further, risks of all types often result in smallholder households eschewing technologies intended to improve their productivity and incomes (Norman 1974; Morrison 1980; Lipton and Lipton 1993; Rosenzweig and Binswanger 1993; Lipton 2012; Larson, Muraoka, and Otsuka 2016). This relation is important given that 73 percent of all farms worldwide operate on less than a hectare of land (Lowder, Skoet, and Raney 2016). Moreover, the dampening effects of risk on agricultural technology choices and, as a consequence, productivity growth have economy-wide repercussions. Substantial empirical evidence suggests this is because productivity gains in agriculture are a powerful catalyst for pro-poor economic growth, which in turn has an outsized impact on poverty reduction (Irz, Lin, Thirtle, and Wiggins, 2001; Anríquez and López 2007; Bravo-Ortega and Lederman, 2009; de Janvry and Sadoulet, 2010; Diao, Hazell, and Thurlow, 2010; Christiaensen, Demery, and Kuhl, 2011).

Has volatility changed over time? One way to state the question in relative terms is to ask whether commodity price volatility has always exceeded manufacturer price volatility. As discussed previously, the decade-by-decade volatility measures in Table 22.1 suggest that the answer is yes, at least for food commodities since 1900. Further, using other data series, Jacks et al. (2011) conclude that this has been the case for the past three centuries. But have commodity prices become more volatile than historical norms? Here, the data from Table 22.1 are less clear. Simply measured, the 1920s, 1930s, and 1970s were volatile decades for food prices, while the 1960s and 1990s were decades of stability. Despite an upward tick from the 1990s to the 2000s, price volatility has been below historical averages during the last three decades. Still, no clear trend stands out.

Other research has been unable to find clear patterns. For example, after analyzing a broader measure of commodity prices, Jacks et al. (2011) conclude that commodity prices have not become more or less volatile over the longer run, despite extended but intermittent periods of stability and instability. Dehn (2000) finds the same result using quarterly commodity price indices for 113 developing countries. In a review of food price trends and volatility from 1970 to 2010, Gilbert and Morgan (2010) conclude that volatility during the early years of the new millennium was in line with historical experience, but note weak evidence that grain prices may be on the rise.

SHORT-TERM PRICE DETERMINANTS

This section examines several key determinants of food price behavior, looking first at the determinants of the short-run prices and the events that drive them. The roles of storage and of unanticipated events are especially important. The second part of the section contains a discussion of demand, resource scarcity, technical innovation, and supply outcomes, key factors that influence prices over the longer term.

Storage Theory

Figure 22.2 shows two representations of the World Bank's (2016) monthly food price index, deflated by the U.S. consumer price index (Federal Reserve Bank of St. Louis 2016). The data cover January 1960 to October 2016 and are indexed to 2000. The right panel shows the data's distribution ordered from low to high. Most prices fall along the distribution's lower end with a thin tail of peak prices, many from the 1970s. The

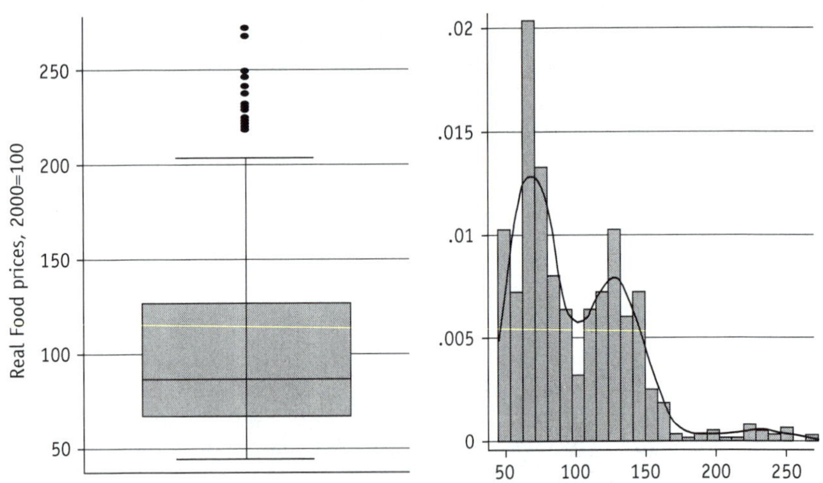

Figure 22.2 Distribution of Monthly Food Prices between 1960 and 2016
This figure shows the calculation of real monthly food prices by deflating the World Bank's nominal monthly food price index by the U.S. consumer price index. Source: World Bank (2016), Federal Reserve Bank of St. Louis (2016), and author's calculations.

median price for the series is 86.65. The peak price of 271.88 occurred in November 1974 and the lowest price, 44.79, occurred in July 2000. The distribution has two peaks on either side of 100, the base-year value of the index. The left panel presents the same data using a box chart. The dark box in the graph represents a range that accounts for the middle half of the observed monthly prices between 1960 and 2016. The line in the box represents the median price. The "whiskers," the lines and demarcations extending from the box, represent an arbitrary but sensible range of data based on the underlying distribution of observations in each quartile. Extreme values tend to fall outside of the whiskers. The panel shows how monthly prices tend to cluster toward the lower end of the observed price range, as does the median price. The remaining prices range upward with extreme values lying above the upper whisker in the uppermost quartile.

Competitive storage is a theoretical construct that accounts for this pattern of sharp-but-brief spikes observed in food prices. The intuition behind the model is that market agents form rational expectations about future prices when deciding how much to store. If sufficiently large, an unanticipated negative shock, such as a series of bad harvests or a suddenly imposed trade embargo, strains current supplies. The shock pushes up current prices and, because inventories are low, increases the probability of higher prices in subsequent periods as well. As supply responds to higher prices, normal stock levels and normal prices are re-established. Unexpected surpluses do not have a symmetric impact on prices because surpluses can be carried forward.

Origins of the storage model can be found in Working (1931) and Kaldor (1939). Although their studies focused on behaviors in futures markets rather than explanations of how short-term commodity prices evolve, the two are related. Specifically, Working and Kaldor explain episodes of "inverse carrying charges" when the spread between spot and futures prices fails to cover the cost of storage, and "backwardation," when the spread turns negative. These episodes are usually associated with periods when inventories are low. Working and Kaldor attribute deviations from calculated returns to risk-free arbitrage to perceived business-related conveniences for inventory holders. Over time, the term *convenience yield* was often used to refer to the residual itself (i.e., the spread between forward and spot prices minus a calculated cost of storage) (Fama and French 1987; Miltersen 2003; Gospodinov and Ng 2013).

Building on Samuelson (1957), Larson (1991, 2007) derives an analytic solution for the optimal storage price that allows for, but does not require, a cost-reducing convenience from inventories. He shows that the optimal market price sits at the cusp of the spatial arbitrage condition and the shadow price of inventories. As such, the expected return to holding inventories, reflected in the spread between spot and forward contract prices, carries a dispersion premium that increases when inventories are drawn down and declines when inventories are flush. This finding is sufficient to explain periods of negative returns to risk-free storage and backwardation.

Gustafson (1958a, 1958b) introduces a numerical competitive storage model, a widely used analytic tool, around the same time that Samuelson (1957) was working on a conceptual formulation. Gardner (1979), Wright and Williams (1982), Lowry, Glauber, Miranda, and Helmberger (1987), and Miranda and Helmberger (1988) offer early extensions. These numerical models are useful in evaluating price stabilization programs based on publicly-held commodity inventories (Williams and Wright 2005; Gouel 2012; Larson, Lampietti, Gouel, Cafiero, and Roberts 2013).

A separate and smaller branch of the literature is concerned with whether time-series models based on competitive storage can replicate correlation patterns observed in Figure 22.1, and the skewed distribution of prices seen in Figure 22.2. After some debate, recent research suggests that they can (Cafiero, Bobenrieth, Bobenrieth, and Wright 2011).

Speculative Fervor and Bubbles

An alternative explanation for commodity price spikes is that episodes of sharp price increases are due, all or in part, to excessive speculative activity. A long discourse exists on the role of speculators, including discussions by Keynes (1930), Working (1931), and Hicks (1946). Current investigations into speculation focus on the role of financial instruments including index funds, hedge funds, and other financial institutions that work across multiple commodity markets and hold commodity positions as part of a larger strategy (Sanders and Irwin 2011; Cheng and Xiong 2013).

Links among individual commodity markets and financial markets are expected because storage is, at the margin, a speculative activity based on expectations about outcomes and conditioned by the value of capital. Kalkuhl, von Braun, and Torero (2016) provide a review of recent empirical studies. All things equal, the deepening of global commodity markets should be a stabilizing force, as information hurdles are lowered and global inventories are made available to respond to changes in local markets. Still, the scale of financialized assets has increased in recent years, and with it, worries that food prices face greater exposure to volatility arising from financial markets. Of special concern is whether financial innovations have introduced more frequent periods of misvaluations or increased volatility in a way that harms producers or consumers.

With this in mind, most studies find little evidence that speculators disrupt agricultural markets in an enduring way. For example, Etienne, Irwin, and Garcia (2014) examine the daily pricing of futures contracts for 12 food commodities between 1970 and 2011. They find multiple episodes of explosive movements among all 12 markets; however, they classify only 2 percent of pricing behaviors as speculative bubbles. They find the bubbles are short-lived, with the vast majority lasting less than 10 days. They reject the notion that bubbles have become more frequent in recent decades. Gilbert (2010) finds that index futures investment contributed to across-the-board increases in food prices during the 2007–2008 price spike, but concludes that erroneous-but-rational expectations about demand from China ultimately drove the investments. Hamilton and Wu (2015) conclude that the activity of CFTC-identified index fund traders did not affect recent food prices. Stoll and Whaley (2010), Sanders and Irwin (2011), and Bruno, Büyükşahin, and Robe (2017) find no links between volatility and index fund activity. Bohl and Stephan (2013) find no causal links between speculation and price volatility in six agricultural and energy markets.

PRICES OVER THE LONGER TERM

Agriculture depends crucially on finite natural resources and systems. Scientists, economists, and the popular press have voiced concerns that resource scarcity would limit food supplies. Malthus (1798) famously described the harsh consequences of rising food prices, and Hotelling (1931) later formalized the impact of scarcity on commodities. Still, despite abundant evidence that the natural resource systems upon which agriculture depends are strained, food prices in 2016 are not so different from prices in 1900. This observation is remarkable, given that the world's population has increased from 1.6 billion to 7.4 billion during that time (Caldwell and Schindlmay 2002; World Bank 2016).

Improvements in incomes have meant that people, on average, consume more calories and more protein than in the past (Popkin 1998). Figure 22.3 shows this relation, which reports the levels and composition of calories and protein for average daily diets between both 1961 and 1963 and 2009 and 2011. Available calories and protein on a per capita basis increased substantially between the two periods. Although grains have been and remain the primary source for many of the calories and much of the protein consumed worldwide, animal products have increased in importance in recent decades.

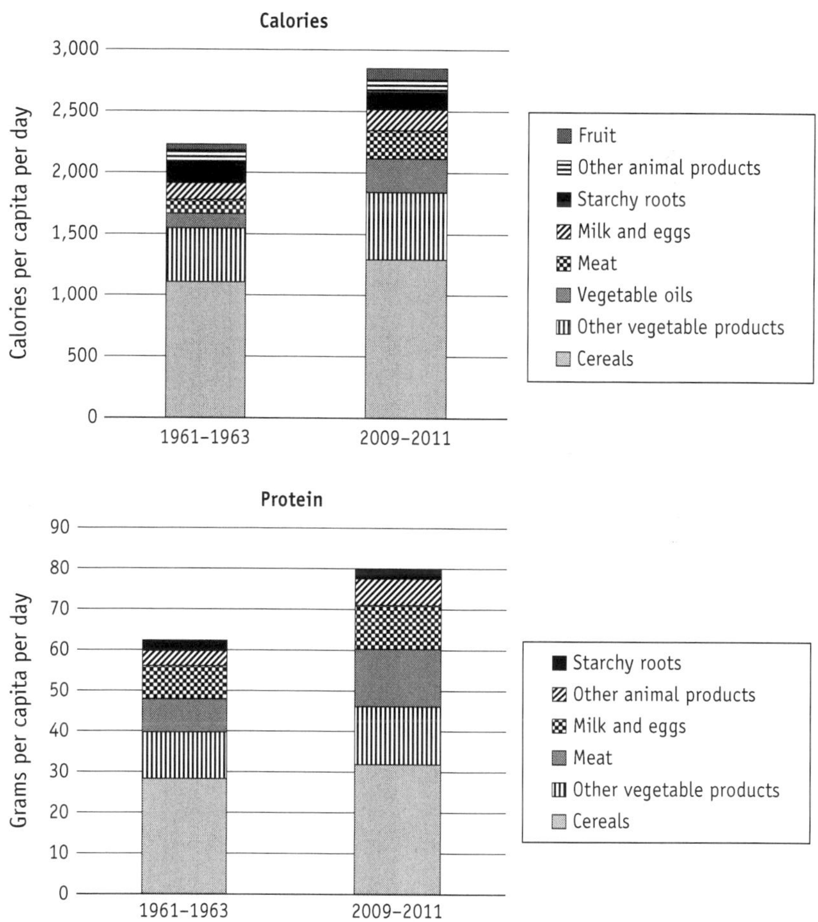

Figure 22.3 Prices, Resources, and Productivity Statistics Based on Decade Averages
This figure expresses available food supplies calories from FAO's Food Balance Sheets. Source: FAOSTAT (2016).

In sum, global food systems are feeding substantially more people more substantive diets than in the past at price levels that are similar to the past.

Table 22.3 lists some key summary statistics by decade between 1961 and 2015. As already noted, real food prices during this period were highest during the 1970s and lowest during the 1990s. Recent price increases since 2010 ended an extended period of relatively low and stable food prices. The global population more than doubled, but the land devoted to agriculture changed slightly, increasing by about 8.5 percent altogether over four-and-a-half decades. Although the global area equipped for irrigation increased markedly, most agricultural lands are rain fed. Rural populations grew in absolute terms, but fell as a share of total population. As a consequence, marketing chains lengthened to reach more urban consumers.

A telling set of numbers from the table reflects productivity gains. Importantly, cereal yields increased by more than 240 percent. This increase is a key development given the dominant role of grains as a source of calories and protein, as previously illustrated in Figure 22.3. Moreover, land productivity gains are apparent. In the 1960s, agricultural

Table 22.3 **Prices, Resource, and Productivity Statistics Based on Decade Averages**

Decade	*1960s*	*1970s*	*1980s*	*1990s*	*2000s*	*2010s*
Real food price index	***118***	***124***	***84***	***68***	*77*	***104***
Population (millions)	3,331	4,023	4,818	5,688	6,483	7,140
Agricultural land (million ha)	4,504	4,609	4,725	4,911	4,930	4,885
Share of land irrigated	3.79	4.36	5.06	5.52	6.21	6.70
Rural share of population (%)	64.72	62.51	59.13	55.51	51.11	47.03
Cereal yields	1.54	1.97	2.43	2.86	3.28	3.72
Nutrients from agricultural land						
Calories per hectare (thousand)	619	766	957	1,122	1,329	1,493
Protein, kg per hectare	17.08	20.71	25.72	30.50	36.75	41.91

Note: This table shows real food price index as the World Bank Food Index divided by the MUV (2010 = 100). Cereals yields are measured in metric tons per hectare of harvested land. Other statistics are calculated from FAOSTAT (2016).

Source: World Bank (2016); FAOSTAT (2016); and author's calculations.

lands produced around 619 thousand calories per hectare per year and slightly more than 17 kilos of protein. By 2010, land productivity had increased by 240 percent, when measured in calories, and 245 percent, when using protein as the metric, so that an average hectare of land produced 1,493 thousand calories and nearly 42 kilos of protein annually.

The statistics in the Table 22.3 are consistent with strong empirical evidence that agricultural productivity grew rapidly worldwide, especially during the closing decades of the twentieth century. Most researchers credit productivity gains with keeping food prices in check despite rapid growth in global demand. Empirical studies consistently report large productivity gains whether productivity is measured across all factors, or measured partially as yields or output-per-worker (Hayami and Ruttan 1970; Mundlak, Larson, and Butzer 1999; Ruttan 2002; Evenson and Gollin 2003b; Fuglie, Wang, and Ball 2012; Mundlak, Butzer, and Larson 2012).

An especially important source of productivity growth in the second half of the twentieth century was a set of technologies based on high-yielding, fertilizer-responsive grain varieties. The new seeds launched a global Green Revolution that began in the 1960s and continued for more than 20 years. Because the breakthroughs largely centered on seeds, not machines, the benefits of the new technologies were available to farms of all sizes. Nevertheless, initial adoption rates were highest on Asia's small and labor-centered farms, which quickly adopted new varieties of wheat and rice (Evenson and Gollin 2003a). Evenson (2003) reports that by 1998, about 82 percent of the area in Asia planted to major crops used improved seeds. The impact on global food supplies was large. From 1961 to 2001, gains from improved crop germplasm boosted global agricultural productivity by 1 percent per year for wheat, 0.8 percent for rice, and 0.7 percent for maize (Evenson and Gollin 2003a; Pingali 2012); world maize, rice, and wheat yields grew annually at 2.1 percent, 1.9 percent, and 2.3 percent, respectively, well above the 1.8 percent growth in population (FAOSTAT 2016). In Asia, rice yields grew by 2 percent annually, and maize and wheat yields grew by more than 3 percent. On balance, productivity gains outpaced demand growth and real food prices fell.

MANAGING RISKS AND INFLUENCING PRICE TRAJECTORIES AS POLICY

By the 1980s, unilateral and multilateral interventions in commodity markets were common as most governments sought to manage commodity prices and price volatility. Marketing boards, public stocks, and stabilization funds were standard policy instruments in both developed and developing economies (Knudsen and Nash1990; Gardner 1992; Gilbert 1996; Larson, Anderson, and Varangis 2004). By the close of the millennium, all international commodity stabilization programs had ended, and most domestic programs had been rolled back as well (Akiyama, Baffes, Larson, and Varangis 2001, 2003). Some stabilization programs failed in spectacular fashion (Anderson and Gilbert 1988; Bardsley 1994). However, many more programs proved ineffective or too costly to maintain during a series of fiscal crises in the 1990s (Akiyama, Baffes, Larson, and Varangis 2001).

Understanding the lessons of this interventionist period requires distinguishing between what motivated the policies of the era and the efficacy of the policy instruments employed. Evidence showing that commodity price volatility is harmful for growth and development was already substantial during the rise of price management as policy, and has since grown. However, with time, evidence accumulated that the instruments implemented to manage food prices were flawed and almost certain to fail. Since then, food policies and agricultural policies have become market-based (Meerman 1997; Larson et al. 2004). Policy goals most frequently focus on improving productivity, managing natural resources, and providing critical services including health, education, and infrastructure to rural communities. Safety nets have emerged as the primary instrument for lessening the impact of spiking food prices, and the chronic problems of malnutrition.

Still, although the goal of managing prices has been largely abandoned, recognition exists that policies do influence food prices over time. As discussed previously, productivity increases have helped stall real food price increases for decades and this situation is due largely to supportive policies. The link is perhaps most obvious in the case of publicly finance agricultural research, which launched the Green Revolution and has consistently paid high dividends (Alston, Beddow, and Pardey 2009; Hurley, Rao, and Pardey 2014). Yet, the institutions that back commodity, capital, land, and risk markets play a role as well, as do policies that promote trade and preserve the natural resources upon which agriculture depends.

Looking to the future, the global population is expected to grow through 2050 and continued income growth is also expected to fuel a continued shift toward diets that include more protein (Godfray, Beddington, Crute, Haddad, Lawrence, Muir, Pretty, Robinson, Thomas, and Toulmin 2010). Because land and water resources are strained, improving the productivity of resources already under production will be a key challenge. As previously discussed, risks of all kinds impede the adoption of technologies designed to improve smallholder productivity, especially in places where formal risk markets are absent and smallholder farmers are too poor to self-insure. For this generation, finding new technologies and other approaches that lower the costs and risk of new technologies, will be important. This is particularly true in sub-Saharan Africa, where the gaps between potential and actual productivity are largest (Larson, Muraoka, and Otsuka 2016).

Less discussed are ways to extend the reach of risk markets, which offer a complementary way of addressing smallholder risks. When compared to the potential for emerging technologies, the scope and benefits of extending risk markets are likely limited. Yet the gains can be important for families and for communities. Additionally, given that risk markets are largely built around private sector activities, the investments governments must make at the margin to develop the necessary institutions and regulatory environments upon which risk markets depend can be small relative to large smallholder development programs. Moreover, many of the types of institutional support needed to support the extension of risk markets fit into the broader goal of most governments to provide an enabling economic environment.

POLICIES TO EXTEND RISK MARKETS

Since the 1990s, the opportunities for hedgers and speculators to trade risk have expanded greatly. For example, around 50 formal exchanges trade agricultural futures and options. And, as previously discussed, a growing number of mechanisms are available for trading commodities as an asset class. The next section reviews three methods of extending price risk markets in another way to allow small farmers to offlay risks. Potentially, these risks work their way through aggregation to the larger ecosystem of traded risk, but this need not be the case.

Warehouse Receipts

Warehouse receipt systems are primarily a mechanism to facilitate credit, using commodity inventories as collateral. However, to do so, warehouse receipt systems introduce a process that certifies commodity standards in a way that lowers transaction costs and facilitates markets. Additionally, warehouses can become a point of sale into spot and forward markets, thereby allowing farmers to address price and counter-party risks.

Most warehouse receipt systems fall into one of two categories: a one-part receipt system based on British common law, and a two-part receipt system that is commonly used in Latin America and most of Europe. However, the two systems are functionally equivalent (Giovannucci, Varangis, and Larson 2000). In both, only certified warehouses are allowed to issue warehouse receipts, sometimes known as warrants. The issuing facilities must show that they are financially sound and have the capacity to safeguard the stored commodity and maintain quality. Usually, the warehouses must be bonded and insured. Governments can license the issuing warehouses, although sometimes commodity exchanges certify the warehouses. When a trader or farmer brings their commodity to the warehouse, the commodity is graded and the owner receives a receipt. The systems allow owners to reassign the receipt to banks as collateral. From the lending bank's perspective, the stored inventories are low risk, regardless of the owner's creditworthiness, because the stored commodity inventories are easy to value, insured, and secured, since the warehouse will only release the inventories against a receipt. Should the original owner default on the loan, the lender has the right to retrieve and sell the inventories immediately, unlike other instances of default in which lenders must seek redress through the court system. Warehouses earn a fee for storage, which covers their costs.

Potentially, the ability to commit or withdraw inventories at any time can help farmers smooth the marketing of their crops (Reddy, Kammar, and Patil 2016). As mentioned previously, warehouse receipt systems can also facilitate forward price markets because the receipt represents a way to deliver ownership of physical quantities against standard contracts. Further, warehouse receipt systems can lead to more competitive internal markets by providing a way for small-scale traders to obtain the working capital needed to purchase grain, coffee, or other commodities from spatially dispersed smallholders.

For these reasons, governments and nongovernmental organizations (NGOs) have frequently promoted warehouse receipt systems and worked to include smallholders. Still, these systems work best in a regulatory environment that is robust, with mature physical and financial markets (Larson 1999). However, warehouse receipt systems can emerge in association with high-valued export crops, like coffee or pepper, which enter into their own specialized marketing chains, expanding to other commodities over time. See, for example, Coulter and Onumah's (2002) discussion of systems in Ghana and

Zambia, and Meijerink, and Bulte, and Alemu (2014) examination of the role of warehouse receipts for sesame in Ethiopia.

Contract Farming

Contract farming is an arrangement whereby farmers agree to supply buyers with an agricultural product at a future time. Some early traditions of contract farming in developing countries are associated with specific crops, and originate in the way the crops are processed. Broadly, in these situations, contract farming serves as alternative to plantation-farm structures. Examples include oil palm and sugarcane, which are crops that must be processed quickly, and where scale and delivery coordination are important. Another example is cotton, which is bulky to transport and store before processing. More recent in developing countries are contracts for crops where exact specifications are important such as fresh flowers or vegetables. The growing role of supermarkets and fast-food restaurants in developing countries has also created the demand for farm-to-fork supply chains that emphasize quality and food safety, where purchases are best arranged in advance. Eaton and Shepherd (2001) provide a good practical guide to contract farming; Bijman (2008) provides a literature review, from which this section draws.

For traditional crops, contract farming solved a processing-management problem, and also provided a way for farmers to obtain inputs on credit, the cost of which would be deducted from sales receipts during processing. Still, conflicts often emerged between producers and processors. For example, in the case of cotton, producers sometimes tried to avoid credit repayment by delivering to other cotton gins. In the case of sugar, producers and monopsonistic processors clashed over sharing sugar revenues (Larson and Borrell 2001).

Generally, researchers see higher benefits associated with contractual arrangements meant to integrate producers into supply chains as a way to ensure product quality or to manage food safety risks. These crops are usually higher valued and the contracts themselves are more detailed, reflecting processing needs, traceability, or end-market standards. Because of the reputational risk associated with subpar quality or the outbreak of food-borne illnesses, buyers often set standards that exceed legal requirements. This action requires contractors to invest in training and in building longer-term partnerships. For these reasons, Little and Watts (1994) describe contract farming as a fundamental restructuring of smallholder agriculture.

Although contract farming often addresses short-term price uncertainty, the effects on smallholder risk are broader. Sophisticated contractual systems allow smallholders to switch to crops that generate more revenue per hectare, which can boost producer welfare, even if price risks remain unchanged. Incentives to build longer-term relationships between buyers and producers also help to reduce transactional risks on both sides. The resolution of transactions risks is important because this class of risk drives the prevalence of cash-based spot markets and informal markets based on personal or kinship-based relationships in developing countries, which in turn, leads to inefficient markets characterized by high transaction costs and limited geographic reach. Like early contractual arrangements for cotton or sugar, contract farming can also solve problems associated with financing and procuring inputs (Key and Runsten 1999).

Studies suggest that smallholders are drawn to contract farming as a way to gain technical knowledge, boost income, and reduce price and marketing risks (Masakure and

Henson 2005; Guo, Jolly, and Zhu 2007). At the same time, not all farmers have equal access to contract farming. In some settings, studies find that buyers prefer larger-scale farmers over smallholders (Key and Runsten 1999; Simmons, Winters, and Patrick 2005; Guo et al. 2007; Bijman 2008). However, this is not always the case and studies in other settings do not find a bias against small-scale farmers (Birthal, Joshi, and Gulati 2005; Miyata, Minot, and Hu 2009). More consistently, research shows that participating farmers benefit from the contract farming, primarily in terms of lower risks, knowledge acquisition (Glover and Kusterer 1990; Little and Watts 1994; Warning and Key 2002; Birthal et al. 2005; Simmons et al. 2005; Miyata et al. 2009).

Nevertheless, researchers argue that a balance of market-power between producers and consumers is critical for producer to benefit from contracts (Dorward, Kydd, and Poulton 1998; Eaton and Shepherd 2001; Bijman 2008). In his review summary, Bijman (2008) concludes that contract farming works best when smallholders have multiple buyers for their crop; when state policies are supportive; when buyer-seller relationships have balanced negotiating power; and when NGOs or producer organizations are present to support farmers.

Insurance for Production Risks

Traditional agricultural insurance can be used to address production risks and many developed and developing countries have done so (Mahul and Stutley 2010; Smith and Glauber 2012). Still, there are two problematic aspects of traditional insurance. To overcome moral hazard risks, traditional programs rely on repeated field visits to confirm reported losses, which make them expensive. Further, farmers know better than insurers the field-specific nature of their risks, leading to adverse selection problems. Consequently, traditional crop insurance is rarely offered without government subsidies (Hazell, Pomareda, and Valdes 1986). Mahul and Stutley report on agricultural insurance programs in 48 developing countries, mostly in middle-income countries in Latin America. Only four countries in sub-Saharan Africa (Mauritius, Nigeria, South Africa, and Sudan) offer agricultural insurance. As a group, the 48 programs are highly subsidized, with public support representing 50 to 150 percent of the premium paid by farmers.

Some policy experts propose index-based insurance programs as a less costly alternative. Conceptually, index insurance is based on a payout trigger that is objectively measured and highly correlated with the losses of the insured, but not influenced by the insured's actions. Because actual losses are not directly insured, loss-verifying field visits are not required and implementation costs are greatly reduced. The most commonly used type of index insurance is based on weather outcomes, although index contracts have been constructed around yields, temperature, humidity, El Niño outcomes, and regional livestock outcomes, to name a few (Miranda and Farrin 2012).

Index insurance has generated much enthusiasm in the development community as a low-cost way to mitigate climate-related risks among smallholder farmers. Various authors provide reviews (Miranda and Farrin 2012; Carter, de Janvry, Sadoulet, and Sarris 2014; Tadesse, Shiferaw, and Erenstein 2014). In their 2010 review, Hazell, Anderson, Balzer, Clemmensen, Hess, and Rispoli (2010) list 30 agricultural index insurance pilot programs in 19 developing countries. Of special interest are several experimental studies suggesting that index insurance can boost technology adoption and investment (Carter, Cheng, and Sarris 2016).

Nevertheless, demand for index insurance products has been low. Few pilots have been scaled up and field experiments have not led to marketed contracts. Analysts suggest that a key obstacle is *basis risk,* which is the potential for insured farmers to experience loss without compensation, due to imperfect correlations between individual farm outcomes and index triggers. Potentially, basis risk can be reduced with improved weather data and better contract design. Still, heterogeneous landscapes and soil conditions can lead to heterogeneous correlations. In this sense, some of the same drivers that generate adverse selection problems in traditional all-peril insurance contracts lead to heterogeneous correlations and greater average basis risk in index insurance contracts.

Binswanger-Mkhize (2012) notes that self-insurance, diversification, and informal forms of insurance can generate greater benefits-for-cost for better-off farmers; however, poorer farmers are cash constrained and therefore cannot pay up-front premiums. In the case of widespread risk events, governments are compelled to intervene, which undercuts the value of purchasing insurance of any kind. As Skees, Varangis, Larson, and Siegel (2005) note, the likely impact of rare and extreme weather events cannot be known well because they are infrequently observed, making them difficult to price under index insurance contracts. This observation suggests a role for government interventions during such times. However, this situation also creates a conundrum for policy. It is during times of severe weather events or a rare sequence of negative events that broadly available informal insurance systems fail, and formal insurance is most valuable. However, these are also the times government and non-government organizations are called upon to intervene. Consequently, a combination of informal group insurance combined with government interventions during disasters may leave little space for formal index insurance.

Summary and Conclusions

Since 1900, average food price levels have shifted from one decade to the next. Yet, there is no evidence of a sustained trend, despite pressures from a growing global population and increasing incomes. Still, since 2010, food prices have averaged higher than in recent decades, raising fears that long-sustained rates of productivity growth in agriculture are slowing.

Wars, trade disruptions, and climate events are clear sources of episodic increases in food price volatility, but there is no evidence of an increase or decrease in volatility over time, despite noteworthy changes in technology, globalization, and the participation of financial institutions in commodity markets. Nevertheless, food prices are among the most volatile of all commodity groups and more volatile than the prices of manufactured goods. This helps drive terms-of-trade volatility in commodity exporting countries. In turn, strong evidence shows that increased terms-of-trade volatility slows both economic growth rates and poverty reduction rates in developing countries. At the household level, episodes of high and volatile food prices can overwhelm the capacity of poor households to cope, with harmful and lasting consequences. For farmers, price-volatility impedes new investments and discourages poor smallholder farmers from adopting technologies designed to improve the productivity of their farms.

To counter these effects, governments have intervened, and some lessons from past policies are clear. Trade policies meant to speed development by favoring manufacturing sectors at the expense of agriculture instead slow overall growth. Further, policies designed to directly manage commodity prices and commodity-price volatility have failed, either because they were structurally flowed or because they proved too expensive to sustain. As a consequence, development policies have shifted away from efforts intended to manage commodity prices to efforts meant to mitigate the harmful effects of food price volatility. One way to do so is by extending the reach of risk markets.

In developed countries, formal markets for crop insurance and price risk are available to transfer risks to those most willing and able to assume risk. Informal mechanisms in developing countries can accomplish the same transfer, but informal systems tend to fail when risks are systemic, frequent, or large. This chapter discusses index insurance, warehouse receipt systems, and contract farming, which are three ways to link smallholder farmers to formal risk markets. Despite compelling conceptual benefits, index insurance experiments have shown limited commercial success. The role of warehouse receipt systems in developing countries is expanding, but the systems are most useful as financial and commodity markets near maturity. Although often limited in scope in many developing countries, contract farming is gaining in scope with urbanization and the associated rise in supermarkets and fast-food restaurants. Research suggests that contract farming can help smallholder farmers manage risk and can boost smallholder incomes.

Discussion Questions

1. Explain why food prices matter for economic development.
2. Discuss whether commodity price volatility matters for economic development.
3. Discuss whether long-term trends exist in food prices.
4. Discuss whether trends exist in food price volatility.
5. Explain whether governments, individually or collectively, can intervene to control commodity price levels and volatility.
6. Discuss possible governmental action to address high food prices and high food price volatility.
7. Identify the mechanisms for extending risk markets.

References

Aghion, Philippe, Philippe Bacchetta, Romain Ranciere, and Kenneth Rogoff. 2009. "Exchange Rate Volatility and Productivity Growth: The Role of Financial Development." *Journal of Monetary Economics* 56:4, 494–513.

Akiyama, Takamasa, John Baffes, Donald F. Larson, and Panos Varangis. 2001. *Commodity Market Reforms: Lessons of Two Decades*. Washington, DC: World Bank.

Akiyama, Takamasa, John Baffes, Donald F. Larson, and Panos Varangis. 2003. "Commodity Market Reform in Africa: Some Recent Experience." *Economic Systems* 27:1, 83–115.

Alston, Julian M., Jason M. Beddow, and Philip G. Pardey. 2009. "Agricultural Research, Productivity, and Food Prices in the Long Run." *Science* 325:5945, 1209–1210.

Anderson, Ronald W., and Christopher L. Gilbert. 1988. "Commodity Agreements and Commodity Markets: Lessons from Tin." *Economic Journal* 98:389, 1–15.

Anríquez, Gustavo, and Ramón López. 2007. "Agricultural Growth and Poverty in an Archetypical Middle Income Country: Chile 1987–2003." *Agricultural Economics* 36:2, 191–202.

Bardsley, Peter. 1994. "The Collapse of the Australian Wool Reserve Price Scheme." *Economic Journal* 104:426, 1087–1105.

Belke, Ansgar, and Andreas Wernet. 2015. "Poverty Reduction through Growth and Redistribution Policies: A Panel Analysis for 59 Developing Countries." *Review of Development Economics* 19:1, 143–162.

Bijman, Jos, 2008. "Contract Farming in Developing Countries: An Overview of the Literature." Working paper, Wageningen University, Department of Business Administration.

Binswanger-Mkhize, Hans P. 2012. "Is There Too Much Hype about Index-Based Agricultural Insurance?" *Journal of Development Studies* 48:2, 187–200.

Birthal, Pratap S., Pramod Kumar Joshi, and Ashok Gulati. 2005. "Vertical Coordination in High-Value Commodities." MTID Discussion Paper No. 85. Washington, DC: International Food Policy Research Institute (IFPRI).

Blattman, Christopher, Jason Hwang, and Jeffrey G. Williamson. 2007. "Winners and Losers in the Commodity Lottery: The Impact of Terms of Trade Growth and Volatility in the Periphery 1870–1939." *Journal of Development Economics* 82:1, 156–179.

Bohl, Martin T., and Patrick M. Stephan. 2013. "Does Futures Speculation Destabilize Spot Prices? New Evidence for Commodity Markets." *Journal of Agricultural and Applied Economics* 45:4, 595–616.

Bravo-Ortega, Claudio, and Daniel Lederman. 2009. "La Agricultura y el Bienestar Nacional en el Mundo." *El Trimestre Economico* 76:3, 577–617.

Bruno, Valentina G., Bahattin Büyükşahin, and Michel A. Robe. 2017. "The Financialization of Food?" *American Journal of Agricultural Economics* 99:1, 243–264.

Cafiero, Carlo, Eugenio S. A. Bobenrieth H., Juan R. A. Bobenrieth H., and Brian D. Wright. 2011. "The Empirical Relevance of the Competitive Storage Model." *Journal of Econometrics* 162:1, 44–54.

Caldwell, John C., and Thomas Schindlmay. 2002. "Historical Population Estimates: Unraveling the Consensus." *Population and Development Review* 28:2, 183–204.

Carter, Michael R., Lan Cheng, and Alexandros Sarris. 2016. "Where and How Index Insurance Can Boost the Adoption of Improved Agricultural Technologies." *Journal of Development Economics* 118:January, 59–71.

Carter, Michael R., Alain de Janvry, Elisabeth Sadoulet, and Alexander Sarris. 2014. "Index-Based Weather Insurance for Developing Countries: A Review of Evidence and a Set of Propositions for Up-Scaling." Development Policies Working Paper 111. Clermont-Ferrand: Fondation pour les Études et Recherches sur le Développement International.

Cheng, Ing-Haw, and Wei Xiong. 2013. "The Financialization of Commodity Markets." NBER Working Paper No. 19642. Cambridge, MA: National Bureau of Economic Research.

Christiaensen, Luc, Lionel Demery, and Jesper Kuhl. 2011. "The (Evolving) Role of Agriculture in Poverty Reduction: An Empirical Perspective." *Journal of Development Economics* 96:2, 239–254.

Coulter, Jonathan, and Gideon Onumah. 2002. "The Role of Warehouse Receipt Systems in Enhanced Commodity Marketing and Rural Livelihoods in Africa." *Food Policy* 27:4, 319–337.

Cuddington, John T., Rodney Ludema, and Shamila A. Jayasuriya. 2007. "Prebisch-Singer Redux." In Daniel Lederman and William F. Maloney (eds.), *Natural Resources, Neither Curse nor Destiny*, 103–140. Washington, DC: World Bank.

de Janvry, Alain, and Elisabeth Sadoulet. 2010. "Agricultural Growth and Poverty Reduction: Additional Evidence." *World Bank Research Observer* 25:1, 1–20.

Dehn, Jan. 2000. "Commodity Price Uncertainty in Developing Countries." World Bank Policy Research Working Paper 2426. Washington, DC: World Bank.

Diakosavvas, Dimitris, and Pasquale L. Scandizzo. 1991. "Trends in the Terms of Trade of Primary Commodities, 1900–1982: The Controversy and Its Origins." *Economic Development and Cultural Change* 39:2, 231–2264.

Diao, Xinshen, Peter Hazell, and James Thurlow. 2010. "The Role of Agriculture in African Development." *World Development* 38:10, 1375–1383.

Dorward, Andrew, Jonathan Kydd, and Colin Poulton. 1998. *Smallholder Cash Crop Production under Market Liberalisation: A New Institutional Economics Perspective*. Wallingford: CAB International.

Eaton, Charles, and Andrew Shepherd. 2001. *Contract Farming: Partnerships for Growth*. Services Bulletin 145. Rome: Food and Agriculture Organization.

Etienne, Xiaoli L., Scott H. Irwin, and Philip Garcia. 2014. "Bubbles in Food Commodity Markets: Four Decades of Evidence." *Journal of International Money and Finance* 42, 129–155.

Evenson, Robert E. 2003. "Production Impacts of Crop Genetic Improvement." In Robert E. Evenson, and Douglas Gollin (eds.), *Crop Variety Improvement and Its Effect on Productivity: The Impact of International Agricultural Research*, 447–472. Cambridge, MA: CABI Publishing.

Evenson, Robert E., and Douglas Gollin. 2003a. "Assessing the Impact of the Green Revolution, 1960–2000." *Science* 300:5620, 758–762.

Evenson, Robert E., and Douglas Gollin, eds. 2003b. *Crop Variety Improvement and Its Effect on Productivity: The Impact of International Agricultural Research*. Cambridge, MA: CABI Publishing.

Fama, Eugene F., and Kenneth R. French. 1987. "Commodity Futures Prices: Some Evidence on Forecast Power, Premiums, and the Theory of Storage." *Journal of Business* 60:1, 55–73.

FAOSTAT. 2016. Food and Agriculture Data. Rome: Food and Agriculture Organization. Available at http://www.fao.org/faostat/en/#data.

Federal Reserve Bank of St. Louis. 2016. Federal Reserve Economic Data. Available at https://fred.stlouisfed.org.

Fuglie, Keith O., Sun Ling Wang, and V. Eldon Ball. 2012. *Productivity Growth in Agriculture: An International Perspective*. Oxfordshire, UK: CAB International.

Gardner, Bruce L. 1979. *Optimal Stockpiling of Grain*. Lexington, MA: Lexington Books.

Gardner, Bruce L. 1992. "Changing Economic Perspectives on the Farm Problem." *Journal of Economic Literature* 30:1, 62–101.

Gilbert, Christopher L. 1996. "International Commodity Agreements: An Obituary Notice." *World Development* 24:1, 1–19.

Gilbert, Christopher L. 2010. "How to Understand High Food Prices." *Journal of Agricultural Economics* 61:2, 398–425.

Gilbert, Christopher L., and C. Wyn Morgan. 2010. "Food Price Volatility." *Philosophical Transactions of the Royal Society B: Biological Sciences* 365:1554, 3023–3034.

Giovannucci, Daniele, Panos Varangis, and Donald F. Larson. 2000. "Warehouse Receipts: Facilitating Credit and Commodity Markets." In Daniele Giovannucci (ed.), *A Guide to Developing Agricultural Markets and Agro-Enterprises*. Washington, DC: World Bank. Available at https://papers.ssrn.com/sol3/papers.cfm?abstract_id=952596.

Glover, David, and Ken Kusterer. 1990. *Small Farmers, Big Business: Contract Farming and Rural Development*. New York, NY: San Martin's Press.

Godfray, H. Charles J., John R. Beddington, Ian R. Crute, Lawrence Haddad, David Lawrence, James F. Muir, Jules Pretty, Sherman Robinson, Sandy M. Thomas, and Camilla Toulmin. 2010. "Food Security: The Challenge of Feeding 9 Billion People." *Science* 327:5967, 812–818.

Gospodinov, Nikolay, and Serena Ng. 2013. "Commodity Prices, Convenience Yields, and Inflation." *Review of Economics and Statistics* 95:1, 206–219.

Gouel, Christophe. 2012. "Agricultural Price Instability: A Survey of Competing Explanations and Remedies." *Journal of Economic Surveys* 26:1, 129–156.

Grilli, Enzo R., and Maw Cheng Yang. 1988. "Primary Commodity Prices, Manufactured Goods Prices, and the Terms of Trade of Developing Countries: What the Long Run Shows." *World Bank Economic Review* 2:1, 1–47.

Guo, Hongdong, Robert W. Jolly, and Jianhua Zhu. 2007. "Contract Farming in China: Perspectives of Farm Households and Agribusiness Firms." *Comparative Economic Studies* 49:2, 285–312.

Gustafson, Robert L. 1958a. "Carryover Levels for Grains: A Method for Determining Amounts That Are Optimal under Specified Conditions." Technical Bulletin 1178. Washington, DC: U.S. Department of Agriculture.

Gustafson, Robert L. 1958b. "Implications of Recent Research on Optimal Storage Rules." *Journal of Farm Economics* 40:2, 290–300.

Hamilton, James D., and Jing Cynthia Wu. 2015. "Effects of Index-Fund Investing on Commodity Futures Prices." *International Economic Review* 56:1, 187–205.

Hayami, Yujiro, and Vernon W. Ruttan. 1970. "Agricultural Productivity Differences among Countries." *American Economic Review* 60:5, 895–911.

Hazell, Peter, Jamie Anderson, Niels Balzer, A. Hastrup Clemmensen, Ulrich Hess, and Francesco Rispoli. 2010. *Potential for Scale and Sustainability in Weather Index Insurance for Agriculture and Rural Livelihoods.* Rome: International Fund for Agricultural Development and World Food Programme.

Hazell, Peter, Carlos Pomareda, and Alberto Valdes. 1986. *Crop Insurance for Agricultural Development: Issues and Experience.* Baltimore, MD: Johns Hopkins Press.

Headey, Derek. 2011. "Rethinking the Global Food Crisis: The Role of Trade Shocks." *Food Policy* 36:2, 136–146.

Hicks, John R. 1946. *Value and Capital.* Oxford: Clarendon Press.

Hotelling, Harold. 1931. "The Economics of Exhaustible Resources." *Journal of Political Economy* 39:2, 137–175.

Hurley, Terrance M., Xudong Rao, and Philip G. Pardey. 2014. "Re-examining the Reported Rates of Return to Food and Agricultural Research and Development." *American Journal of Agricultural Economics* 96:5, 1492–1504.

Irz, Xavier, Lin Lin, Colin Thirtle, and Steve Wiggins. 2001. "Agricultural Productivity Growth and Poverty Alleviation." *Development Policy Review* 19:4, 449–466.

Jacks, David S., Kevin H. O'Rourke, and Jeffrey G. Williamson. 2011. "Commodity Price Volatility and World Market Integration since 1700." *Review of Economics and Statistics* 93:3, 800–813.

Kaldor, Nicholas. 1939. "Speculation and Economic Stability." *Review of Economic Studies* 7:1, 1–27.

Kalkuhl, Matthias, Joachim von Braun, and Maximo Torero. 2016. "Volatile and Extreme Food Prices, Food Security, and Policy: An Overview." In Matthias Kalkuhl, Joachim von Braun, and Maximo Terero (eds.), *Food Price Volatility and Its Implications for Food Security and Policy,* 3–31. Springer Open. Available at http://www.springer.com/us/book/9783319281995.

Key, Nigel, and David Runsten. 1999. "Contract Farming, Smallholders, and Rural Development in Latin America: The Organization of Agroprocessing Firms and the Scale of Outgrower Production." *World Development* 27:2, 381–401.

Keynes, John Maynard. 1930. *A Treatise on Money.* Volume 2. London: Macmillan.

Knudsen, Odin, and John Nash. 1990. "Domestic Price Stabilization Schemes in Developing Countries." *Economic Development and Cultural Change* 38:3, 539–558.

Larson, Donald F. 1991. "Copper and the Negative Price of Storage." Policy Research Working Paper 1282. Washington, DC: World Bank.

Larson, Donald F. 1999. "Alternative Food Security Instruments: The Warehouse Receipts System." In Phil Sawicki (ed.), *Indonesia: Essays on Agricultural Institutions and Policy,* 14–18. Washington, DC: World Bank.

Larson, Donald F. 2007. "On Inverse Carrying Charges and Spatial Arbitrage." *Journal of Futures Markets* 27:4, 305–336.

Larson, Donald F., Jock R. Anderson, and Panos Varangis. 2004. "Policies on Managing Risk in Agricultural Markets." *World Bank Research Observer* 19:2, 199–230.

Larson, Donald F., and Brent Borrell. 2001. "Sugar Policy and Reform." In Takamasa Akiyama, John Baffes, Donald F. Larson, and Panos Varangis (eds.), *Commodity Market Reforms: Lessons of Two Decades,* 121–164. Washington, DC: World Bank.

Larson, Donald F., Julian Lampietti, Christophe Gouel, Carlo Cafiero, and John Roberts. 2013. "Food Security and Storage in the Middle East and North Africa." *World Bank Economic Review* 28:1, 48–73.

Larson, Donald F., Rie Muraoka, and Keijiro Otsuka. 2016. "Why African Rural Development Strategies Must Depend on Small Farms." *Global Food Security* 10:September, 39–51.

Lipton, Michael. 2012. "Learning from Others: Increasing Agricultural Productivity for Human Development in Sub-Saharan Africa." UNDP Regional Bureau for Africa Working Paper 2012-007. New York, NY: United Nations.

Lipton, Michael, and Merle Lipton. 1993. "Creating Rural Livelihoods: Some Lessons for South Africa from Experience Elsewhere." *World Development* 21:9, 1515–1548.

Little, Peter D., and Michael J. Watts. 1994. *Living under Contract: Contract Farming and Agrarian Transformation in Sub-Saharan Africa.* Madison: University of Wisconsin Press.

Lopez, Humberto. 2004. "Pro-growth, Pro-poor: Is There a Tradeoff?" World Bank Policy Research Paper 3378. Washington, DC: World Bank.

Lowder, Sarah K., Jakob Skoet, and Terri Raney. 2016. "The Number, Size, and Distribution of Farms, Smallholder Farms, and Family Farms Worldwide." *World Development* 87:November, 16–29.

Lowry, Mark, Joseph Glauber, Mario Miranda, and Peter Helmberger. 1987. "Pricing and Storage of Field Crops: A Quarterly Model Applied to Soybeans." *American Journal of Agricultural Economics* 69:4, 740–749.

Mahul, Olivier, and Charles J. Stutley. 2010. *Government Support to Agricultural Insurance: Challenges and Options for Developing Countries.* Washington, DC: World Bank.

Malthus, Thomas. 1798. "An Essay on the Principle of Population." Available at http://www.esp.org/books/malthus/population/malthus.pdf.

Masakure, Oliver, and Spencer Henson. 2005. "Why Do Small-scale Producers Choose to Produce under Contract? Lessons from Nontraditional Vegetable Exports from Zimbabwe." *World Development* 33:10, 1721–1733.

Meerman, Jacob. 1997. *Reforming Agriculture: The World Bank Goes to Market.* Washington, DC: World Bank.

Meijerink, Gerdien, Erwin Bulte, and Dawit Alemu. 2014. "Formal Institutions and Social Capital in Value Chains: The Case of the Ethiopian Commodity Exchange." *Food Policy* 49:1, 1–12.

Miltersen, Kristian R. 2003. "Commodity Price Modelling That Matches Current Observables: A New Approach." *Quantitative Finance* 3:1, 51–58.

Miranda, Mario, and Katie Farrin. 2012. "Index Insurance for Developing Countries." *Applied Economic Perspectives and Policy* 34:3, 391–427.

Miranda, Mario J., and Peter G. Helmberger. 1988. "The Effects of Commodity Price Stabilization Programs." *American Economic Review* 78:1, 46–58.

Miyata, Sachiko, Nicholas Minot, and Dinghuan Hu. 2009. "Impact of Contract Farming on Income: Linking Small Farmers, Packers, and Supermarkets in China." *World Development* 37:11, 1781–1790.

Morrison, Barrie M. 1980. "Rural Household Livelihood Strategies in a Sri Lankan Village." *Journal of Development Studies* 16:4, 443–462.

Mundlak, Yair, Rita Butzer, and Donald F. Larson. 2012. "Heterogeneous Technology and Panel Data: The Case of the Agricultural Production Function." *Journal of Development Economics* 99:1, 139–149.

Mundlak, Yair, Donald F. Larson, and Rita Butzer. 1999. "Rethinking within and between Regressions: The Case of Agricultural Production Functions." *Annales d'Economie et de Statistique* 55–56, 475–501.

Norman, David W. 1974. "Rationalising Mixed Cropping under Indigenous Conditions: The Example of Northern Nigeria." *Journal of Development Studies* 11:1, 3–21.

Piesse, Jenifer, and Colin Thirtle. 2009. "Three Bubbles and a Panic: An Explanatory Review of Recent Food Commodity Price Events." *Food Policy* 34:2, 119–129.

Pingali, Prabhu L. 2012. "Green Revolution: Impacts, Limits, and the Path Ahead." *Proceedings of the National Academy of Sciences* 109:31, 12302–12308.

Popkin, Barry M. 1998. "The Nutrition Transition and Its Health Implications in Lower-Income Countries." *Public Health Nutrition* 1:1, 5–21.

Prebisch, Raul. 1950. *The Economic Development of Latin America and Its Principal Problems.* Lake Success, NY: United Nations Department of Economic Affairs.

Ravallion, Martin. 2001. "Growth, Inequality and Poverty: Looking beyond Averages." *World Development* 29:11, 1803–1815.

Reddy, Vijayachandra S., Shivanad K. Kammar, and Chidanand Patil. 2016. "An Economic Analysis on Warehouse Receipts in Hyderabad-Karnataka Region: A Protective Measure Against Distress Sale of Agriculture Produce." *Indian Journal of Economics and Development* 12:1a, 265–270.

Rosenzweig, Mark R., and Hans P. Binswanger. 1993. "Wealth, Weather Risk and the Composition and Profitability of Agricultural Investments." *Economic Journal* 103:416, 56–78.

Ruttan, Vernon W. 2002. "Productivity Growth in World Agriculture: Sources and Constraints." *Journal of Economic Perspectives* 16:4, 161–184.

Samuelson, Paul A. 1957. "Intertemporal Price Equilibrium: A Prologue to the Theory of Speculation." *Weltwirtschaftliches Archiv* 79:2, 181–221.

Sanders, Dwight R., and Scott H. Irwin. 2011. "The Impact of Index Funds in Commodity Futures Markets: A Systems Approach." *Journal of Alternative Investments* 14:1; 40–49.

Simmons, Phil, Paul Winters, and Ian Patrick. 2005. "An Analysis of Contract Farming in East Java, Bali, and Lombok, Indonesia." *Agricultural Economics* 33:s3, 513–525.

Singer, Hans. 1950. "The Distribution of Gains between Investing and Borrowing Countries." *American Economic Review* 40:2, 473–485.

Skees, Jerry, Panayotis N. Varangis, Donald F. Larson, and Paul Siegel. 2005. "Can Financial Markets Be Tapped to Help Poor People Cope with Weather Risks?" In Stefan Dercon (ed.), *Insurance against Poverty*, 422–436. New York, NY: Oxford University Press.

Slayton, Tom. 2009. "Rice Crisis Forensics: How Asian Governments Carelessly set the World Rice Market on Fire." CGD Working Paper 163. Washington, DC: Center for Global Development.

Smith, Vincent H., and Joseph W. Glauber. 2012. "Agricultural Insurance in Developed Countries: Where Have We Been and Where Are We Going?" *Applied Economic Perspectives and Policies* 34:3, 363–390.

Stoll, H. R., and R. E. Whaley. 2010. "Commodity Index Investing and Commodity Futures Prices." *Journal of Applied Finance* 20:1, 7–46.

Tadesse, Getaw, Bernardina, Matthias Kalkuhl, and Joachim von Braun. 2014. "Drivers and Triggers of International Food Price Spikes and Volatility." *Food Policy* 47:August, 117–128.

van der Ploeg, Frederick, and Steven Poelhekke. 2009. "Volatility and the Natural Resource Curse." *Oxford Economic Papers* 61, 727–760.

Warning, Matthew, and Nigel Key. 2002. "The Social Performance and Distributional Consequences of Contract Farming: An Equilibrium Analysis of the Arachide de Bouche Program in Senegal." *World Development* 30:2, 255–263.

Williams, Jeffrey C., and Brian D. Wright. 2005. *Storage and Commodity Markets*. Cambridge: Cambridge University Press.

Working, Holbrook. 1931. "Financial Results of Speculative Holding of Wheat." *Wheat Studies of the Food Research Institute* 7:8, 405–437.

World Bank. 2016. Global Economic Monitor (GEM) Commodities Database. Available at http://www.worldbank.org/en/research/commodity-markets.

Wright, Brian D., and Jeffrey C. Williams. 1982. "The Economic Role of Commodity Storage." *Economic Journal* 92:367, 596–614.

Yamada, Hiroshi, and Gawon Yoon. 2014. "When Grilli and Yang Meet Prebisch and Singer: Piecewise Linear Trends in Primary Commodity Prices." *Journal of International Money and Finance* 42:C, 193–207.

Part Six

ISSUES INVOLVING COMMODITIES

23

High Frequency Trading of Commodities

RAYMOND P. H. FISHE
Patricia A. and George W. Wellde, Jr. Distinguished Professor of Finance, University of Richmond

AARON D. SMITH
Professor of Agricultural and Resource Economics, University of California–Davis

Introduction

In the historical narrative, commodity derivatives markets existed to offer hedging services to holders of underlying commodities, particularly agricultural products. So-called "speculators" or financial firms would take directional positions opposite the hedgers, and expected to earn a risk premium. From the beginning, this story provided a misleading impression of how the markets operate. Natural hedgers trade much more than would be required to maintain a passive hedge, suggesting that they are also speculators (Chen and Xiong 2014). Moreover, daily trading volumes far exceed the daily changes in open interest. This imbalance implies that, even if hedgers were trading for hedging purposes, many more trades were executed than were needed to match new net hedging demand to speculators' positions.

Before the advent of electronic trading platforms, "scalpers" or floor traders were the middlemen who offered temporary liquidity services until a hedger or speculator entered the market willing to hold a position on the other side. These middlemen accounted for the "round-turn" trades that generated high trading volume. To be a middleman in these "pit" markets, one needed to be noticed, so loud and aggressive behavior was dominant, but being quick with a competitive quote was material to win the trade. The influx of high frequency traders (HFTs) over the past decade after the development of fully electronic platforms replaced the noise-driven pits. Because HFTs were faster with quote updates, they supplanted many of the human middlemen positioned intraday between traders who hold overnight positions.

HFTs are the subset of algorithmic traders that seek to profit by messaging order instructions and/or executing trades more quickly than their competitors. Other examples of algorithmic traders include large institutions that use smart order routing (SOR) algorithms to reduce trade impact costs for large orders and proprietary traders using strategies that seek profits through information or technical analysis, but not speed per sé. HFTs monitor losses and risk exposure at greater speed than humans. As a result, information external to these markets is incorporated more rapidly (Hoffmann 2014; Bongaerts and Van Achter 2016). This is not to say that human-entry trading did not enable price discovery or that HFTs improve market quality overall, only that electronic traders reduce the latency involved (Budish, Cramton, and Shim 2015).

This chapter surveys the development of electronic markets in commodities. The focus is on the changes in futures markets and how high frequency trading (HFT) has affected overall market quality, market making, and the role of manual-entry participants. The chapter offers detailed discussions of the research that used exogenous events to isolate HFTs effects and an examination of the research on the flash crash in 2010. It also provides a discussion of problems that may arise with the use of trade data in the new high frequency world and offers information on the speed of trading in selected futures contracts from studies that have access to proprietary account-level data.

Electronic Trading of Commodities

In the United States, the National Association of Securities Dealers (NASD) offered an electronic market "proof of concept" in 1971 when it introduced the NASDAQ (NASD Automated Quotation) system. By linking over-the-counter (OTC) dealers across the country, the NASDAQ system initially offered a timely method of posting and revising quotes. Certainly, it saved time compared to the alternative of calling a dealer on the telephone to request a quote or check for inventory.

Electronic trading of commodities arose for a similar reason. In the late 1980s, the Commodity Mercantile Exchange (CME) and the Chicago Board of Trade (CBOT, now part of the CME group) recognized that global interest in foreign currencies and U.S. Treasury securities created sizable volumes on a 24-hour clock. After-hours trading was introduced to address this market opportunity. An electronic system was seen as an answer to facilitate communications between Asia, Europe, and the United States during these sessions. While one country traded, the other might sleep, but electronic links could prolong the trading day. The CME developed the Globex platform and began service in 1992 for currencies, while the CBOT introduced "Project A" in 1996 for interest rate products. Figure 23.1 offers a view of how futures contract volumes have migrated from the open outcry pits to the Globex system.

Market participants received a clear wake-up call from the future when the Eurex, a new all-electronic derivatives exchange in Europe, opened in 1998. The Eurex exchange took advantage of the opportunities created by the Investment Services Directive (ISD) of 1993. This European Union directive authorized cross-border trade in numerous financial services subject to home country supervision. In particular, it allowed remote access to trading on exchanges for authorized financial institutions. In the same manner that after-hours trade is efficiently conducted on an electronic platform, so are cross-border trades. Eurex offered proof of such gains. Within a year, its contract volumes had surpassed those of the CBOT, validating the effectiveness of an electronic platform for derivatives.

A competitive response initiated by both the CME and CBOT was to allow side-by-side trading, so that their electronic systems could compete directly with human-based open outcry in selected commodities, and not just operate as after-hours

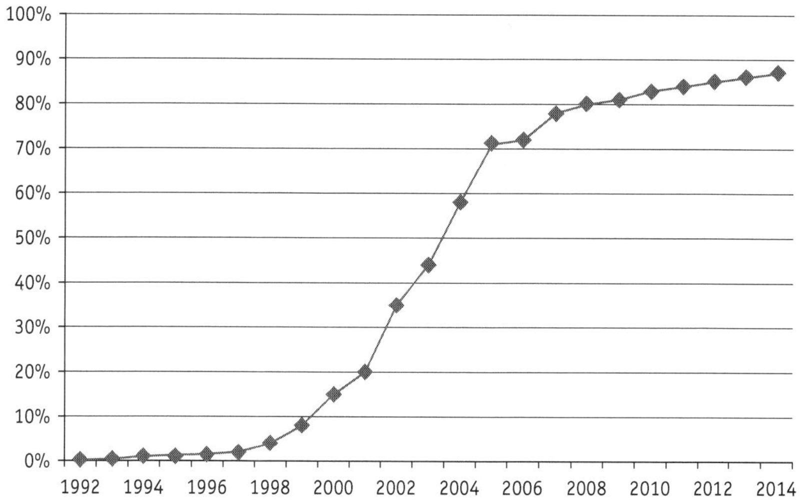

Figure 23.1 Volume of CME Group Contracts Traded on the Globex Platform
The figure shows the percentage of electronic trading volume over all CME Group contracts between the introduction of the Globex electronic platform in 1992 and 2014. Source: Labuszewski and Aldinger (2012) with updates from CME Group news releases.

systems. Numerous academic studies investigated the market quality effects of such side-by-side trading. The German Bund futures contract was a focus of researchers because it was simultaneously traded electronically at the Deutsche Terminbörse (DTB) and through open outcry at the London International Financial Futures Exchange (LIFFE). Both Shyy and Lee (1995) and Kofman and Moser (1997) present Granger causality tests for which platform offered price discovery. The causality results were mixed, but Kofman and Moser suggest information may be incorporated first in the electronic market. Pirrong (1996) finds bid-ask spreads were lower on the DTB's electronic system. He also estimated the effects between volume and price changes to conclude that depth was higher on the DTB's electronic platform. These results suggest that LIFFE was likely at a competitive disadvantage with open outcry.

Indeed, the DTB was an electronic exchange that operated at a lower cost than the LIFFE, which some estimated having two to three times higher labor costs than the DTB (Sarkar and Tozzi 1998). This cost differential made a difference for participants as the DTB grew its market share in Bund futures from less than 25 percent in mid-1997 to nearly 90 percent in early 1998. The Bund futures contract was important for LIFFE's profitability; as such the exchange moved from positive profits in 1997 to recording a loss of nearly £64 million in 1998. To survive, the LIFFE developed an electronic platform called "LIFFE Connect" and by November 2000 had closed all its open outcry pits. Other exchanges also reached this conclusion as the number of exchanges trading future and options on electronic platforms increased from eight in 1990 to 40 in 1997 (Sarkar and Tozzi 1998). Thus, began the so called "arms race" for speed.

POLICY AND NEW PRODUCTS

Policy changes and new products also aided the development of electronic trading. After equity values increased markedly during the 1990s, the CME introduced the E-mini S&P 500 futures contract, which was to trade exclusively on the Globex electronic platform. Each E-mini contract had a notional value one-fifth of the full S&P futures contract. The E-mini became quite popular, particularly after the "open access" policy in late 2000, which allowed customers direct access to Globex as long as they had an account with a futures commission merchant or introducing broker, who in turn had a CME clearing guarantee. This action followed the introduction of side-by-side trading in the Eurodollar futures contract, one of the CME's most popular contracts. The CBOT also introduced side-by-side trading in their agricultural complex in August 2006. As Figure 23.2 shows, the activity of round-turn traders in the corn futures contract increased after the addition of electronic trading in 2006. In effect, more middlemen interactions, on average, occurred after this policy change, lending support to the model of Cartea and Penalva (2012), where HFTs intermediate trades between liquidity and professional traders, and the latter type acts to balance the asynchronous buy-and-sell timing of liquidity traders. Additional volume arises because HFTs strategically extract part of the surplus from asynchronous intermediation.

In October 2006 the CBOT and CME merged to become the CME Group. The merger offered substantial cost savings as the two exchanges could combine research

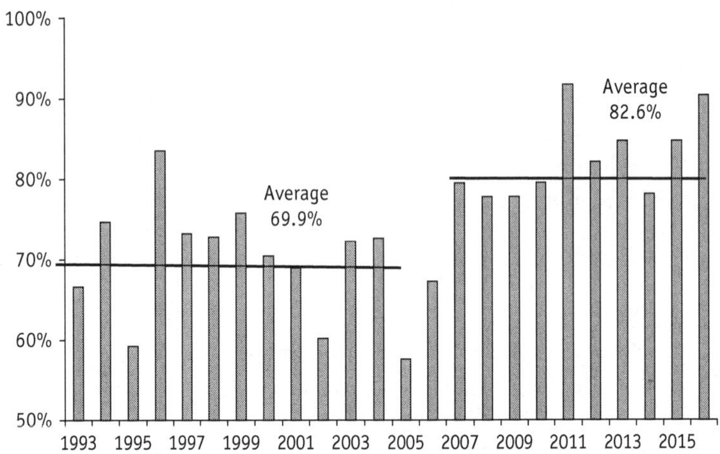

Figure 23.2 Days with Round-Turn Volume More Than 90 Percent of Trades in Corn Futures

The figure shows the percentage of days in which round-turn volume is greater than 90 percent of all trading volume for the CME/CBOT December corn futures contract. The calculation includes only days in which this expiration was the first and second highest volume. The year 2006 introduced side-by-side (pit and Globex) trading for agricultural futures. The solid lines show the data averages for 1993–2005 and 2007–2016, respectively. Source: CME/CBOT market data.

and development efforts for their electronic platforms. Other mergers followed in both commodity and equity markets, driven largely by the goals of reducing technological costs and expanding the market for their listed products.

The ultimate consequence of the mergers and development of electronic trading was the virtual elimination of the open outcry system. Selected pit closures have been announced during the past decade, but perhaps the most significant was the February 2015 announcement by the CME Group that it would close almost all of its pits by July, including the storied agricultural pits. The agricultural pits, particularly for grain futures products, trace their origins to 1865 when the CBOT established new rules to standardize contract terms for quantity, quality, and delivery, as well as requirements for margins. These contract features have lasted to the present day.

PENETRATION BY ELECTRONIC TRADERS

Figure 23.1 shows the overall market share of electronic trading of commodities on the CME. However, the penetration of such trading is slanted toward the higher volume contracts. This relation is most evident in Haynes and Roberts (2015), who use trading data between November 2012 and October 2014 to summarize the fraction of trading conducted by algorithms for a multitude of futures contracts. The CME requires orders to indicate if they are submitted by an Automated Trading System (ATS) or by manual entry. Table 23.1 offers a view of the distribution of trading based on the entry method used by both counterparties. This table is adapted from Table 4 in Haynes and Roberts and excludes foreign exchange (FX) contracts as electronic trading is well established in those commodities.

Table 23.1 ranks commodities by trading volume for the sample period. These data show that an ATS counterparty is dominant, but that the likelihood of trading with an ATS counterparty varies with volume. The financial and energy contracts offer the highest likelihood of meeting an ATS counterparty, while the agricultural and metals contracts offer the lowest likelihoods. One reason for the high proportions in financials may be the presence of electronic platforms for the underlying instruments such as exchange-traded funds (ETFs) for the S&P 500 index and NASDAQ 100, which allow the type of high-speed arbitrage used by algorithms. Another reason may be that relevant information still arrives to the agricultural and metal markets and other lower volume contracts from human-network sources. Additional research is required to sort out the reasons for the differences in ATS penetration for these markets.

ELECTRONIC TRADING: A MIXTURE OF ALGORITHMS

Very fast trading or HFT is a consequence of electronic trading platforms, or in particular the demand for speed. Exchange lore is that when traders rode horses to the NYSE, value resulted in being stabled in the stall closest to the barn door, as that offered the shortest, quickest walk to the floor. However, not all electronic trading is motivated by speed alone. Large institutions use smart order routing (SOR) algorithms to reduce trade impact costs for larger orders, so-called "parent/child" orders.

Table 23.1 **Participation in Trading Volume by Automated Trading Systems (ATS)**

CME Futures Contract	*Total Sample Volume (mm)*	*ATS on One Side of Trade (%)*	*Only ATS Entry Involved (%)*	*Only Manual Entry Involved (%)*	*Likelihood of Manual Trading with ATS (%)*
Eurodollar	1125	85.4	36.1	12.5	79.8
E-Mini S&P 500	866	86.0	43.4	13.8	75.5
10-Year Treasury Note	643	83.7	42.6	11.9	77.5
5-Year Treasury Note	360	83.3	50.5	8.6	79.2
WTI Crude Oil	280	75.7	30.2	19.5	70.0
Natural Gas (Henry Hub)	153	76.5	30.7	19.1	70.6
E-Mini Nasdaq 100	131	93.0	58.2	6.9	83.5
Corn	128	58.7	15.9	34.8	55.2
Soybeans	93	57.7	15.2	36.3	53.9
Gold	85	67.9	24.0	25.5	63.3
Wheat	49	63.4	18.5	33.9	57.0
Copper	31	71.0	27.5	26.0	62.6
Silver	27	64.9	27.9	31.3	54.2

Note: This table shows several of the highest volume contracts traded on the CME between November 2012 and October 2014. The columns show the percent of trades in which an ATS is on one side, both sides, or no sides, with the latter being only manual entry counterparties. The last column shows the likelihood of a manual-entry participant trading with an ATS counterparty. Rounding errors are due to missing entry identifiers.

Source: Adapted from Table 4 in Haynes and Roberts (2015).

O'Hara (2015) suggests that one result of these SOR algorithms is that quotes, not executions, are now providing more information to markets. Shkilko and Sokolov (2016) find that quotes usually contribute more to price discovery than trades, supporting this view.

These SOR algorithms—also called "agency" algorithms—often seek to better a benchmark, such as the volume-weighted average price or the arrival price when the order is submitted. They are generally tuned to adjust to liquidity in the market so that the child orders are resized and their submission timed to reflect normal order flow. Such tuning often disguises the existence of a parent order feeding the order flow and also adjusts for volume impacts; that is, a so-called percentage-of-volume algorithm.

The need for stealth leads these algorithms to use primarily passive orders, but these orders may also become aggressive if liquidity is depleting and the order is near completion. Computers efficiently process executions and update performance relative to SOR goals in milliseconds (ms). Relative to a human-entry alternative, SOR algorithms are faster and make fewer mistakes. Even so, they do not require the fastest, most expensive connection technology available as these systems necessarily pace their activity to the supply of liquidity in the market (Biais and Foucault 2014). For example, the costs of co-location services are likely too high to justify an effectively implemented SOR.

Electronic trading of commodities is thus composed of SOR algorithms, HFTs, and miscellaneous opportunistic or directional traders who use proprietary algorithms to implement their strategies. This chapter focuses on HFTs, but the advent of electronic trading platforms created an environment for all forms of algorithmic trading and the effects of HFTs cannot be understood without considering other forms of algorithmic trading.

High Frequency Traders and Market Quality

Theoretical models show that a speed advantage may affect market quality by impacting adverse selection, inventory, and/or price efficiency for news announcements. Most theoretical models conceive an environment in which slower traders are the incumbents and faster traders are new entrants (Hoffmann 2014; Biais, Foucault, and Moinas 2015). Introducing HFTs creates more aggressive quotes because HFTs can adjust quickly to news events and thereby reduce their own adverse selection costs. However, slower traders know that their quotes may become stale in the new environment, which exposes them to greater adverse selection costs (McInish and Upson 2012). Thus, they place quotes that have a lower probability of execution, which lowers their expected gains from trade. One implication of this framework is that fast traders are more likely to act as market makers, providing as opposed to taking liquidity. Another implication is that slow traders give up some gains from trade relative to the environment without fast traders, so they are worse off (Hoffmann 2014). Similar results on adverse selection costs are also found in the models by Foucault, Kozhan, and Tham (2014) and Biais et al. (2015).

Aït-Sahalia and Saglam (2014) develop a dynamic trading model in which HFTs maximize expected gains from trading at the bid-ask spread subject to inventory costs. They focus on HFTs as market makers. Their model shows that a faster trading or signal acquisition technology offers higher profits by lowering inventory costs and thereby inducing them to offer higher liquidity provision. However, they also derive an adverse result: HFTs provision of liquidity is inversely related to price volatility. High volatility raises the cost of holding inventory, reducing the willingness of HFTs to provide liquidity, which requires holding inventory. However, Hendershott and Menkveld (2014) contend that as an HFT market maker approaches an inventory constraint, asymmetric quote sizes may reduce the likelihood of the constraint being limiting, so the market maker may remain active. The empirical evidence discussed in the following paragraphs appears generally consistent with HFTs withdrawing some liquidity during high volatility events.

Several theoretical papers study informed HFTs (Jovanovic and Menkveld 2015; Bongaerts and Van Achter 2016; Foucault, Hombert, and Roşu 2016) or information effects on market speed (Du and Zhu 2016). When HFTs are informed, welfare improves because of rapid price adjustment resulting in such consequences as adverse selection for uninformed, liquidity, or the slower-to-be-informed traders, which may reduce market liquidity. Du and Zhu suggest that to maximize efficiency in a sequential double auction environment, the speed of trading coincides with the information arrival frequency for scheduled information releases, but may exceed the information arrival frequency for stochastic information arrivals. The intuition for the latter result is that random news arrivals encourage more auctions to reduce delays in responding to new information, implying a need for faster execution platforms. Their calculations suggest that the optimal trading rate for four higher volume futures contracts varies from 0.63 ms for E-mini S&P 500 to 15.2 ms for 10-year Treasury futures. These estimates suggest that avoiding adverse selection effects on manual entry traders may be difficult.

Other theoretical work addresses increased price volatility after HFTs enter markets (Roşu 2015) and the potential for overinvestment in technology—the "arms race" (Biais et al. 2015; Bongaerts, Kong, and Van Achter 2016). Perhaps the finding that gives the greatest pause is the "arms race." Millions of dollars are spent on newer communications networks for only seconds (or milliseconds) of improved price efficiency (Budish et al. 2015). Corporate finance decisions are unlikely to be altered by the additional speed provided to price adjustments from these investments, which suggests that these resources would be better spent elsewhere in the economy unless other sectors are improved from such speed advances.

HFTS AS MARKET MAKERS

The theoretical models create environments in which HFTs come in different shades, almost like the different colored shirts formerly worn by pit traders. However, most models develop an advantage for HFTs in market making versus slower speed incumbents. Classically, market makers supply liquidity to the market, which involves using passive limit orders on both sides of the bid-ask spread and control of inventory levels, possibly with aggressive orders. Empirical findings in equity markets generally support this role for HFTs. That is, the majority (about 70 percent) of HFTs appear to act as market makers (Hagströmer and Nordén 2013).

Even so, the nature of such market making is less passive than the classical theory predicts. Specifically, HFTs are more likely to supply liquidity when the bid-ask spread is wide and take liquidity when it is narrow (Carrion 2013; Hagströmer, Nordén, and Zhang 2014). As Hendershott and Riordan (2013) show, algorithmic traders as a group also act in this manner. Instead of just supplying liquidity, market-making HFTs may be acting to discipline other market participants when spreads appear at inefficiently high or low levels—that is, when the marginal value of market making is high.

A similar phenomenon may also arise in commodity markets. Haynes and Roberts (2015) report aggressive trading percentages for algorithmic versus manual-entry traders averaged over five-minute intervals during the day for selected futures contracts. The algorithmic trades in their sample are dominated by HFTs. Their two-year sample results vary by commodity and show evidence of spikes or trend adjustments at the open and near a session close. They show that the average proportion of trades in which the algorithmic trader was the aggressor was about 70 percent for E-mini S&P 500, 60 percent for WTI crude oil, 65 percent for the 10-year Treasury notes, and nearly 80 percent for Euro FX contracts. These averages are higher than would be expected if these traders are acting only as market makers supplying liquidity in the classic sense.

One characteristic of market making—whether classical or quote-correcting—is that a market maker seeks to be quick to adjust to new information. Thus, a speed advantage arises when market information calls for a quote change. When a quote improves the best bid or ask price, for example, a market maker is not competitive if her quote remains unchanged. The same market maker with a slow technology will place new quote orders behind those with faster technologies, and hence face delays in execution and possibly greater adverse selection costs.

Hasbrouck and Saar (2013) examine reaction times after a quote improvement using order type data for a sample of NASDAQ-listed equities trading during two months in 2007 and 2008. They show estimated differences in latency across traders using a hazard rate model. The *hazard rate* is the instantaneous rate at time *t* for an event conditional on survival until time *t* or later (Kalbfleisch and Prentice 2002). Hasbrouck and Saar show hazard rates for three specific events after a quote improvement occurs: (1) same-side quote submission, (2) same-side quote cancellation, and (3) same side execution against improved quote. They find that the hazard rate peaks between 2 to 3 ms for all three events. Although human response rates vary with specific stimuli, a large sample test—more than 37 million observations—of human mouse clicks concludes that the fastest human reaction times range between 200 and 250 ms (Kosinski 2006).

The Hasbrouck and Saar (2013) results indicate that humans are not competitive with algorithms in quote matching (i.e., same-side quote submission, which is an essential characteristic of both passive and quote-correcting market making). Therefore, the fact that researchers find a majority of HFTs engaged in some type of market-making behavior is unsurprising.

GOOD AND BAD EFFECTS OF HFTS ON MARKET QUALITY

HFTs and algorithms bring a new technology to markets. Arguably, this new technology populated equity before commodity markets, so most analyses of market quality are based on equity market data. Harris (2013), Jones (2013), Biais and Foucault (2014), U.S. Securities and Exchange Commission (2014), O'Hara (2015), Menkveld (2016), and others offer surveys of recent academic findings on how HFTs affect market quality. These surveys document both good and bad effects on markets and other participants.

The most recurring good result is that HFTs are associated with decreasing transaction costs—declining effective spreads, lower commission rates, and reduced implementation short fall for institutional investors—and more efficient prices (Menkveld 2013; Conrad, Wahal, and Xiang 2015). The term "associated" applies because other factors play a role in these results. Specifically, these factors are the reduction of minimum tick sizes accompanied by the onset of decimal pricing; fragmentation of trading across venues, creating more competition in equity markets; and mergers between commodity exchanges, allowing technology costs to be spread across more products. These confounding factors lead researchers to identify exogenous events that may isolate HFT effects. Such events highlight both the good and bad empirical findings, so the discussion defers to those efforts for clarity on HFT effects.

USING EXOGENOUS EVENTS TO IDENTIFY THE EFFECTS OF HFTS

Exogenous events are important to understand how HFTs affect market quality, particularly if such traders are not identified by external methods. Researchers face a "chicken-and-egg" problem without an exogenous event. Jones (2002) documents the long-term decline in spreads for securities, particularly after deregulation of commissions from the mid-1970s to 2000. Menkveld (2016) summarizes related transaction cost information from 2001 to 2011 to show that these declines continued. Because HFT activity has increased in the past decade, any measured improvements in market quality are positively associated with HFT activity. However, that does not mean that HFTs are the cause of such improvements, as they may be part of a longer term trend, other market adjustments, or regulatory actions.

An exogenous event provides a means to sort out "before-and-after" causality. Hendershott, Jones, and Menkveld (2011) use the phase-in of auto-quoting on the New York Stock Exchange (NYSE) in 2003 as an exogenous instrument that is expected to increase algorithmic activity. As HFT is a meaningfully large subset of algorithmic activity, this change is likely to capture the response of HFTs. Before Autoquote, the stock specialist entered the best quotes. Because the NYSE phase-in affected some stocks before others, it created a control group to isolate causal effects. They report that quoted and effective spreads decreased after auto-quoting for larger stocks, but no change occurred for smaller stocks. Apparently, at the time smaller stocks did not attract much algorithmic trading.

Other exogenous events used to study the effects of HFTs include the first availability of co-location facilities (Boehmer, Fong, and Wu 2012; Frino, Mollica, and Webb 2014; Brogaard, Hagströmer, Nordén, and Riordan 2015), the September 2008 ban disallowing most short selling in financial stocks (Brogaard, Hendershott, and Riordan 2016), the scaling of minimum tick sizes based on stock price levels using data from the NASDAQ OMX Stockholm exchange (Hagströmer and Nordén 2013), stress events such as Lehman Brothers in 2008 and the shortage of storage capacity for crude oil at Cushing, Oklahoma during the winter of 2009 (Raman, Robe, and Yadav 2016), and weather events that disrupt electronic communications in microwave networks and thereby temporarily neutralize the advantage of speed traders

(Shkilko and Sokolov 2016). The following subsections provide a review of the results of several of these exogenous event studies.

Co-location Events

The co-location research offers a view of a before and after event targeted directly at electronic trading. In equity markets, Boehmer et al. (2012) examine a large sample of securities from 2001 to 2009, which isolates the beginning of co-location for 39 exchanges around the globe. They use exchanges' co-location announcements as a proxy for an influx of algorithmic trading to find that on average, greater algorithmic trading improves liquidity and price discovery. Brogaard, Hagströmer, Nordén, and Riordan (2015) study an optional speed upgrade at the NASDAQ OMX Stockholm in September 2012. Their results also show improved liquidity, but suggest that the reason is because HFTs can better manage inventory, which translates into lower spreads. This inventory management behavior introduces a greater likelihood for more aggressive trading by HFTs, as noted above.

Boehmer et al. (2012) also report that their "after" results show greater price volatility across exchanges. In contrast, Hagströmer and Nordén (2013) and Hasbrouck and Saar (2013) report that price volatility decreases on average when algorithmic trading increases. However, these two papers are not tied to an exogenous event, so one must give extra weight to the volatility results of Boehmer et al. because their study better identifies causal effects. The benefits of lower transaction costs may thus be measured against the potential for more volatile prices.

In futures markets, Frino et al. (2014) examine liquidity changes on the Australian Securities Exchange (ASX) after the ASX allowed futures traders to co-locate servers in February 2012. They sampled the four most actively traded futures contracts on the ASX—Share Price Index, 90-day Bank Accepted Bills, 3-year and 10-year Government Bonds—for six months before and after the introduction of co-location services. Similar to equity market results, they report evidence of lower bid-ask spreads and an increase in market depth after the introduction of co-location options.

Co-location and the resulting change in algorithmic and/or HFT activity thus appears to lower transaction costs and improve liquidity in markets. However, the change in the mix of participants may also be associated with greater volatility.

Weather Events

Weather is one of the most clearly defined exogenous events available to researchers. Shkilko and Sokolov (2016) exploit this observation to investigate market quality when severe whether events disrupt the microwave communications used by HFTs. They develop a time series of rain and snow events that disrupt microwave communications between data centers near Chicago and New York, so arbitrage traders must then rely on the slower—by approximately 30 percent—fiber-optic technology.

Shkilko and Sokolov (2016) focus on five ETFs closely related to information produced by active futures contracts: SPDR S&P500 (SPY), Financial Select Sector SPDR (XLF), iShares 20+ Year Treasury Bond (TLT), ProShares UltraShort S&P500 (SDS), and SPDR Gold Shares (GLD). Using data from 83 weather stations along the transmission corridor between Chicago and New York, they find that during 2011 and 2012 when precipitation events disrupt communications, price impacts, effective spreads, and realized spreads all decrease, supporting the view that fast traders adversely affect liquidity and adverse selection. Shkilko and Sokolov also report that volatility tends to decrease during weather episodes, consistent with the model by Roşu (2015). They confirmed these various results using a broader sample of 100 ETFs and data from the winter of 2012 and 2013 when a microwave technology provider decided to sell the high-speed price update information by subscription instead of just selling bandwidth. As a result of the subscription plan, the speed advantages previously held by a few select firms were diminished, effectively democratizing these microwave links.

2008 Lehman and 2009 Cushing Crises

Raman et al. (2016) examine whether HFTs reduce participation and liquidity provisions during periods of high volatility. Using detailed transaction data on WTI crude oil futures, they examine market stress events, such as the shortage of storage at the futures delivery site in Cushing, Oklahoma in early 2009 and the uncertainty following the bankruptcy of Lehman Brothers in September 2008. The results here are mixed. The authors find that spreads increased during both periods of high volatility, but that only for Cushing did they find a significant differential between HFT-to-customer versus locals-to-customer spreads. The "locals" here are slower proprietary traders. Their volume results parallel these findings. HFTs tend to decrease participation during the Cushing event, but increase volumes during the Lehman crisis. Raman et al. contend that the difference was that the Cushing event gave locals an information advantage being that storage adjustments at Cushing required site-specific knowledge known to the public only in discrete intervals. Conversely, Lehman was a common shock that generated less asymmetric information than Cushing.

Overall, these exogenous events suggest that HFTs have measurable effects on market liquidity and volatility. However, the precise direction of these effects is less clear in commodity markets. The research suggests that during normal markets HFTs are associated with reduced spreads and higher liquidity, but during more volatile periods or when unexpected events arise, HFT actions may add to volatility and perhaps raise liquidity costs.

FLASH CRASH

A phenomenon that arose since 2010 is the *flash crash,* which is a sudden absence of buy side liquidity and rapid fall of prices—a two to three standard deviation event—to be mostly reversed in a short period, usually minutes. The famous flash crash of May 6, 2010 struck the E-mini S&P 500 futures contract at 2:41 p.m. Eastern Standard Time (EST), with prices declining about 5 percent over the next four and one-half minutes. Prices rebounded rapidly beginning at 2:45:28 p.m., recovering to near pre-crash levels in 23 minutes. Other assets, such as equity ETF produces, were similarly affected. The issue of concern is whether electronic trading or the actions of HFTs caused this event.

Regulators conducted an extensive investigation to uncover the reasons for the May 6 event. The U.S. Commodity and Futures Trading Commission and U.S.

Securities and Exchange Commission (2010) joint report cited events earlier in the day—disturbing political and economic news from Europe concerning the ongoing Greek debt crisis—which led to increased volatility across U.S. markets. Then, the report noted that at 2:32 p.m. a mutual fund complex, subsequently identified as Waddell & Reed, initiated a large sell program for 75,000 E-mini contracts as a hedge to an existing equity position. This seller chose to implement the order using a SOR program, which fed orders into the E-mini market at a rate set to 9 percent of the trading volume calculated over the previous minute. Neither price nor time was a variable used to control this algorithm. The order was executed within 20 minutes. As this order size was substantially greater than the existing buy side liquidity, prices decreased quickly. Thus, an SOR algorithm was involved with the sell program, but a human appears to have made the choice to ignore price and time variables during implementation.

The mutual fund seller was not alone on the sell side at the start of the flash crash. Kirilenko, Kyle, Samadi, and Tuzun (2015) place traders into specific groups based on trading style such as Fundamental, HFT, and Market Maker. They found that Fundamental traders were engaged in selling at the onset of the crash. Importantly, they found that HFTs were initially net buyers for several minutes before switching to being net sellers of the E-mini contract. These HFTs traded more than 1.45 million contracts that day, but they bought and sold so quickly that their inventory rarely exceeded 3,000 contracts on either side of the market. Apparently, HFTs did not change their basic strategy as many bought and sold contacts with each other during the event. However, the need for anonymity with regulatory data prevents Kirilenko et al. from documenting whether all HFTs and Market Makers remained in the market during the crash. Thus, perhaps only a few fast traders retained their in-place trading strategy and interacted with each other.

Although regulators cited several factors that contributed to the flash crash in the joint CFTC-SEC report, they did not identify market manipulation as a cause. That stance changed when the CFTC and U.S. Department of Justice filed suit in 2015 against a London trader, Navinder Singh Sarao, alleging that he engaged in spoofing of May 6, 2010 (United States of America v. Navinder Singh Sarao, 2015). *Spoofing* is bidding or offering with the intent to cancel the bid or offer before execution, and thus possibly distorting the information on the order book. The allegations claim that Sarao layered numerous large sell orders for the near-month E-mini S&P 500 futures contract away from prevailing market prices with no intention of executing such orders. The complaint alleges that Sarao's manipulative activities added to an extreme E-mini futures order book imbalance and contributed to market conditions that led to the May 6 flash crash. After losing a battle to avoid extradition to the United States, Sarao pled guilty to spoofing in federal court in Chicago on November 9, 2016.

Before the guilty plea, Aldrich, Grundfest, and Laughlin (2016) studied the complete order book on May 6 using millisecond timestamps and challenged some of the positions alleged in the complaint. They offer the following explanation, which adds problems with the timeliness of the equity market data feed (Menkveld and Yueshen 2016) to the findings in the CFTC-SEC report (pp. 5–6):

> We present a novel examination of data feeds utilized by algorithmic traders and document an anomaly in the time stamps of trades reported to the Consolidated Tape System. This anomaly suggests that increasingly stale prices for the SPY ETF were disseminated to the market and that the inception and termination of this reporting delay correlates strongly with the inception and termination of the Flash Crash. Unlike the spoofing activity . . . , perceived price oscillations associated with the data feed delay has a statistical impact on futures market returns, which were subsequently transmitted to equities market returns . . .. We also document and measure the withdrawal of liquidity by market participants and further establish that the observed data feed anomalies Granger-cause the withdrawal. This millisecond-level analysis also calls into question the possibility that a 5-second CME trading halt was, alone, a cause of the subsequent market recovery, as suggested by CFTC-SEC (2010) and Kirilenko et al. (2015). We document that prices continued to decline after the CME halt, and began their recovery only after a pause in a market data feed that exhibited extreme price oscillations. The CME halt may therefore have been a necessary but insufficient condition for the recovery if it merely contributed to the correction of the recalcitrant data feed . . .. These analyses support a range of conclusions. In particular, with regard to allegations against Mr. Sarao . . . our analysis further suggests that Sarao's trading was likely not a "but-for" cause of the crash. Instead . . . , we find that the Flash Crash is sufficiently explained as the result of the confluence of the unsettled market conditions that prevailed in the hours leading up to the Flash Crash combined with the size and execution strategy of the Waddell & Reed trades.

What the CFTC-SEC joint report and Aldrich et al. (2016) show is that an unusual negative market news environment, a poorly implemented execution strategy for a large sell order, and timing irregularities in the price feed between linked markets created a "perfect storm" on May 6, 2010. The role of HFT did not appear to be causal in the conclusions. However, what is unsettling about the May 6 event is that it is no longer the anomaly as once presented.

The market data company Nanex LLC has provided ongoing research documenting hundreds of brief episodes of flash or mini-flash crashes dating back to 2009 (http://www.nanex.net/NxResearch/). Some of these events may be due to a "fat finger" on the trade trigger caused when an algorithm goes amiss (Gao, Liu, and Wu 2016). Other events may remain mysteries. One such crash recently affected the U.S. Treasury market and generated another joint staff report from U.S. financial regulators (U.S. Department of the Treasury 2015). A quote from this report states (p. 1):

> On October 15, 2014 . . . the market for U.S. Treasury securities, futures, and other closely related financial markets experienced an unusually high level of volatility and a very rapid round-trip in prices . . .. Moreover, in the narrow window between 9:33 and 9:45 a.m. ET, yields exhibited a significant round-trip without a clear cause, with the 10-year Treasury yield experiencing a 16-basis-point drop and then rebound. For such significant

> volatility and a large round-trip in prices to occur in so short a time with no obvious catalyst is unprecedented in the recent history of the Treasury market.

The U.S. Treasury Joint Staff report did not find a cause for the sudden flash crash and rally in Treasury prices. Theoretical models that predict flash crashes offer only minimal guidance as well. These models focus on external shocks (Weill 2007), the cost of continuous market presence (Huang and Wang 2009), risk-bearing capacity of intermediaries (Nagel 2012), market power with heterogeneous speeds among participants (Du and Zhu 2015), or low cost speedy trading technologies that increase informational efficiency and the occurrence of mini-flash crashes (Dugast and Foucault 2014). Although extant empirical work may be consistent with several of these approaches, no conclusive evidence thus far argues strongly for a particular environment or model of flash crashes and rallies. More importantly, other than the fact that these events are speedy, the causal role played by HFTs has not yet been established.

Empirical Issues

Although many empirical questions arise in HFT research, the most basic has been how HFTs affect market quality. When seeking answers to this question, researchers have made assumptions that might affect the generality of their conclusions. Several of these assumptions address the following questions: Who is an HFT? What conclusions can be made about participants from trade data? How is speed measured? This section addresses these questions.

IDENTIFYING HFTS

The extant literature identifies HFT in one of three ways: (1) the data source says that specific observations involve HFTs, as is the case with the NASDAQ HFT sample between 2008 and 2009; (2) the researcher develops filters to isolate specific trades or traders because activity suggests algorithmic trading at high frequencies, which is the approach used by Kirilenko et al. (2015) to investigate the flash crash; and (3) an indirect measure is developed that is expected to be correlated with HFT activity, which is the case with Hasbrouck and Saar (2013), who develop a method to link order types into same-trader "strategic runs" using publicly available anonymous data. Gomber, Arndt, Lutat, and Uhle (2011) provide summary tables in their appendices that describe the definitions and data used in several previous studies of HFT.

How HFTs are defined may limit the inferences that follow from empirical analysis. Specifically, Fishe, Haynes, and Onur (2016a) seek to examine whether HFTs are engaged in anticipatory trading, which may represent the "front running" of parent orders in special cases. This question calls for an inference about participants. Fishe et al. note that previous researchers use one of the three previously mentioned methods to identify HFTs in their sample, then examine whether they appear to be anticipatory traders (Jiang, Lo, and Valente 2013; Brogaard, Hendershott, and Riordan 2014; Hirschey 2016). However, such pre-censoring does not address the basic question of whether speed is necessary for anticipatory trading.

Using account-level order book data on the WTI crude oil futures contract in 2011, Fishe et al. (2016a) answer this question by identifying all of the accounts that trade early during short-term price paths or trade to anticipate a subsequent price reversal. The authors found that only 308 traders out of more than 7,800 tested were anticipatory at the 2.5 percent control rate used to limit false discoveries. Importantly, those traders who anticipated price direction early in a path were equally divided between manual- and algorithmic-entry methods. These traders acted faster than the sample predicted only during the early part of a price path. Those who anticipated price reversals were more algorithmic, but acted slower than the sample predicted. Fishe et al. concluded that speed of trading was not a defining characteristic of anticipatory trading. Thus, although HFTs may use anticipatory trading strategies, so may manual-entry and slower algorithmic-entry traders. Focusing only on pre-selected HFTs in a sample does generally not reveal this finding.

HFT—WHO IS SPEEDY?

HFT research imbeds the idea that some participants are faster than others, but how is this statement quantified? Specifically, how much faster is one participant versus another? Only a few researchers currently offer any insight into this question (Hasbrouck and Saar 2013; Laughlin, Aguirre, and Grundfest 2014; Budish et al. 2015; Fishe, Haynes, and Onur 2015). Of these, only the efforts of Fishe et al. go beyond futures-equity arbitrage issues.

Fishe et al. (2015) offer the view that speed is measured over fixed time units in the same way that automobile speed is measured as distance traveled per unit of time (miles per hour or kilometers per hour). For financial markets they suggest that messages such as order entry, cancellations, modifications, or executions are equivalent to "distance travelled" and that the time unit is fixed for cross-participant comparisons. Thus, the authors' model messages generated for intervals of 500 ms, 10 seconds (sec), and 100 sec using a negative-binomial model to summarize these data. Their regulatory sample includes futures data for 10 days in October, 2014, for two-, five-, and 10-year Treasury futures, T-Bond futures and the E-mini S&P 500 futures. For comparisons, they group participants by business lines (bank/dealer, futures commission merchant, hedge fund, non-bank dealer, proprietary, and other) and control for whether participants used automated- or manual-entry methods. Fishe et al. find that who is the fastest group depends on the contract and the time interval. For example, hedge funds are fastest in the E-mini contract at 10 sec and 100 sec, but proprietary traders are fastest at 500 ms. The latter group has the most HFTs.

The results of Fishe et al. (2015) also show that manual participants have similar speeds at the 500 ms interval, diverge across business lines at the 10 sec interval, and become more similar again at the 100 sec interval. Speeds for algorithmic entry participants are less similar at the 500 ms interval and continue the show divergence at

10 sec and 100 sec intervals, suggesting more heterogeneity for these electronic traders. These speed estimates also generally reject a possible semi-continuity property of such statistics. That is, intensity of messages at 100 sec for a group is not proportionate to the intensity generated at 10 sec intervals. For example, with proprietary traders in the E-mini, algorithms produce about six messages per 10 sec interval, but only about 30 messages (not 60 messages) per 100 sec interval. This evidence supports the view that messages tend to cluster on the timeline for most groups, except possibly hedge funds in the E-mini futures contract that show the most semi-continuous flow of messages across these three intervals. Such clustering suggests that many trading strategies either begin and end within a short window (< 100 sec) or stretch out well beyond the time units considered by this research.

INFERENCES ABOUT TRADES OR PARTICIPANTS

Market quality research is generally conducted using trade data, although a few researchers have access to order book data and this information helps to expand analyses of liquidity and potential price impacts. However, some claims are made about participants or groups of participants—such as front running behavior, withdrawing liquidity in stressful times, or introducing volatility when entering a market—and these claims may become difficult to establish with trading data. The reason is that trading data oversample the more frequent traders, so coefficient estimates often become skewed toward the strategies followed by HFTs. The effects here may be minimal or meaningful depending on the sample.

Fishe, Haynes, and Onur (2016b) provide a visual presentation of this problem for the E-mini S&P 500 index futures contract using data for August 1, 2014. They seek to understand how long a participant waits after receiving an execution before submitting a new order ("latency gap"). Figure 23.3 shows survival curves for this latency gap using all data for the E-mini S&P 500 futures traded on August 1, 2014. The top panels compute survival curves using latency gaps in all of the data, which imply that HFT data are disproportionately represented. The solid line crossing the top two panels shows that 50 percent of algorithmic-entry proprietary traders resubmitted a new order within 200 ms. Similarly 50 percent of algorithmic-entry agency traders ("trades for customers") resubmitted a new order within 3.25 sec. The manual entry traders are markedly slower by this cutoff measure.

The bottom panels in Figure 23.3 show what happens if each participant receives equal weight in the analysis. For these calculations, latency gap data are sampled once for each participant, with the results averaged over 500 samples. Now, the 50 percent cutoff for algorithmic-entry proprietary traders is a little greater than 5 sec and for algorithmic-entry agency traders it is about 13.6 sec. Even though the curves control for whether a participant is proprietary and using algorithmic entry methods, a large difference exists in new order submission latencies among this group. These new curves are making inferences about participants, not trades, and thus show how frequent trades by specific participants (HFTs) may distort conclusions about the average participant.

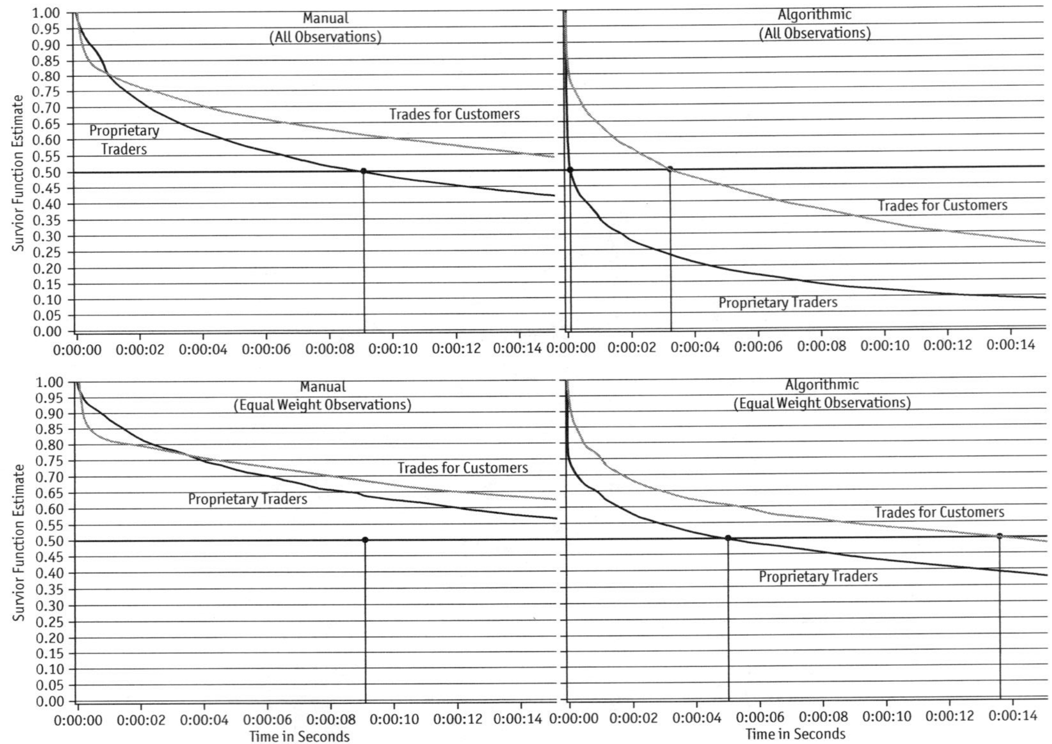

Figure 23.3 Survival Curves for E-mini Futures by Order Entry Method

These panels show survival curves computed for the time between confirmation of the execution of a previous order and the submission of a new order ("latency gap"). These individual account level data are for E-mini futures contracts traded on August 1, 2014. The two panels on the left are for manual-entry accounts and the two on the right are for algorithmic-entry accounts. In each panel, the survival curves are computed for proprietary and agency ("trades for customers") accounts separately. The top two panels use all latency gaps and the bottom show average results for 500 random samples in which each account is sampled only once. The solid lines denote the 50 percent cutoff for these survival curves. Source: Fishe et al. (2016b), Figure 2; available on the CFTC website.

Summary and Conclusions

This chapter summarized how electronic trading arose in commodity markets, which led to increased participation by HFTs. The theoretical and empirical evidence is reviewed, with the latter focused on exogenous events and the flash crash of 2010. Much evidence suggests that HFTs act as market makers and their speed advantage has lowered transaction costs, generally during normal markets. However, they may not be market makers in a classical sense, using more aggressive orders to discipline the market when spreads are not in equilibrium. Evidence also suggests that HFTs may exacerbate volatility by withdrawing liquidity in times of market stress such as during "flash" crashes. However, the evidence on this point is not entirely conclusive on the role of HFT, so more research on a larger sample of those events is needed.

Discussion Questions

1. Explain why U.S. futures markets took several years to become fully electronic trading platforms.
2. Research into the flash crash on May 6, 2010 identified delays in trade reporting as correlated with the beginning and end of the crash. It also suggests that these data feed anomalies may be causally related to the withdrawal of liquidity from the market. Explain why stale prices affect liquidity and whether the expected effect is likely to differ for algorithms versus human traders.
3. A computer algorithm is a set of rules that is followed to make trading decisions. These rules rely on inputs from both market data and external sources, such as economic news announcements. If a trader knew the rules followed by some very active trading algorithms, explain what would limit the trader's ability to take advantage of these participants.
4. Spoofing involves placing orders with the intent to cancel before a trade occurs. Explain why such behavior did not arise in traditional open outcry markets and why spoofing might be disruptive to current electronic markets.

References

Aït-Sahalia, Yacine, and Mehmet Saglam. 2014. "High Frequency Traders: Taking Advantage of Speed." Working paper, Princeton University.

Aldrich, Eric M., Joseph A. Grundfest, and Gregory Laughlin. 2016. "The Flash Crash: A New Deconstruction." Working paper, University of California–Santa Cruz.

Biais, Bruno, and Thierry Foucault. 2014. "HFT and Market Quality." *Bankers, Markets & Investors* 128:January–February, 5–19.

Biais, Bruno, Thierry Foucault, and Sophie Moinas. 2015. "Equilibrium Fast Trading." *Journal of Financial Economics* 116:2, 292–313.

Boehmer, Ekkehart, Kinglsey Fong, and Julie Wu. 2012. "International Evidence on Algorithmic Trading." Working paper, EDHEC Business School.

Bongaerts, Dion, Lingtian Kong, and Mark Van Achter. 2016. "Trading Speed Competition: Can the Arms Race Go Too Far?" Working paper, Rotterdam School of Management, Erasmus University.

Bongaerts, Dion, and Mark Van Achter. 2016. "High-Frequency Trading and Market Stability." Working paper, Rotterdam School of Management, Erasmus University.

Brogaard, Jonathan, Björn Hagströmer, Lars Nordén, and Ryan Riordan. 2015. "Trading Fast and Slow: Colocation and Liquidity." *Review of Financial Studies* 28:12, 3407–3443.

Brogaard, Jonathan, Terrence Hendershott, and Ryan Riordan. 2014. "High Frequency Trading and Price Discovery." *Review of Financial Studies* 27:8, 2267–2306.

Brogaard, Jonathan, Terrence Hendershott, and Ryan Riordan. 2016. "High Frequency Trading and the 2008 Short Sale Ban." Working paper, University of Washington. Forthcoming in the *Journal of Financial Economics.*

Budish, Eric, Peter Cramton, and John Shim. 2015. "The High-Frequency Trading Arms Race: Frequent Batch Auctions as a Market Design Response." *Quarterly Journal of Economics* 130:4, 1547–1621.

Carrion, Allen. 2013. "Very Fast Money: High Frequency Trading on the NASDAQ." *Journal of Financial Markets* 16:4, 680–711.

Cartea, Alvaro, and José Penalva. 2012. "Where Is the Value in High Frequency Trading?" *Quarterly Journal of Finance* 2:3, 1–46.

Chen, Ing-Haw, and Wei Xiong. 2014. "Why Do Hedgers Trade So Much?" *Journal of Legal Studies* 43:S2, S183–S207.

Conrad, Jennifer, Sunil Wahal, and Jin Xiang. 2015. "High-Frequency Quoting, Trading, and the Efficiency of Prices." *Journal of Financial Economics* 116:2, 271–291.

Du, Songzi, and Haoxiang Zhu. 2015. "Welfare and Optimal Trading Frequency in Dynamic Double Auctions." Working paper, Sloan School of Management, MIT.

Du, Songzi, and Haoxiang Zhu. 2016. "What Is the Optimal Trading Frequency in Financial Markets?" Working paper, Sloan School of Management, MIT. Forthcoming in *Review of Financial Studies.*

Dugast, Jerome, and Thierry Foucault. 2014. "False News, Informational Efficiency, and Price Reversals." Working paper, School of Management, HEC.

Fishe, Raymond P. H., Richard Haynes, and Esen Onur. 2015. "Speed and Latency in Treasury and E-mini Futures Contracts—Part 1." White Paper, Office of the Chief Economist, Commodity Futures Trading Commission.

Fishe, Raymond P. H., Richard Haynes, and Esen Onur. 2016a. "Anticipatory Trading and Trading Speed." Working paper, Robins School of Business, University of Richmond.

Fishe, Raymond P. H., Richard Haynes, and Esen Onur. 2016b. "Speed and Latency in Treasury and E-mini Futures Contracts—Part 2." White Paper, Office of the Chief Economist, Commodity Futures Trading Commission.

Foucault, Thierry, Johan Hombert, and Ioanid Roşu. 2016. "News Trading and Speed." *Journal of Finance* 71:1, 335–381.

Foucault, Thierry, Roman Kozhan, and Wing Wah Tham. 2016. "Toxic Arbitrage." Working paper, Department of Finance, HEC. Forthcoming in *Review of Financial Studies.*

Frino, Alex, Vito Mollica, and Robert I. Webb. 2014. "The Impact of Co-location of Securities Exchanges' and Traders' Computer Servers on Market Liquidity." *Journal of Futures Markets* 34:1, 20–33.

Gao, Ming, Yu-Jane Liu, and Weili Wu. 2016. "Fat-Finger Trade and Market Quality: The First Evidence from China." *Journal of Futures Markets* 36:10, 1014–1025.

Gomber, Peter, Björn Arndt, Marco Lutat, and Tim Uhle. 2011. "High Frequency Trading." Working paper, Goethe Universität.

Hagströmer, Björn, and Lars Nordén. 2013. "The Diversity of High Frequency Traders." *Journal of Financial Markets* 16:4, 741–770.

Hagströmer, Björn, Lars Nordén, and Dong Zhang. 2014. "How Aggressive Are High-Frequency Traders?" *Financial Review* 49:2, 395–419.

Harris, Larry. 2013. "What to Do about High-Frequency Trading." *Financial Analysts Journal* 69:2, 6–9.

Hasbrouck, Joel, and Gideon Saar. 2013. "Low-Latency Trading." *Journal of Financial Markets* 16:4, 646–679.

Haynes, Richard, and John Roberts. 2015. "Automated Trading in Futures Markets." White Paper, Office of the Chief Economist, Commodity Futures Trading Commission.

Hendershott, Terrence, Charles Jones, and Albert Menkveld. 2011. "Does Algorithmic Trading Improve Liquidity?" *Journal of Finance* 66:1, 1–33.

Hendershott, Terrence, and Albert Menkveld. 2014. "Price Pressures." *Journal of Financial Economics* 114:3, 405–620.

Hendershott, Terrence, and Ryan Riordan. 2013. "Algorithmic Trading and the Market for Liquidity." *Journal of Financial and Quantitative Analysis* 48:4, 1001–1024.

Hirschey, Nicholas H. 2016. "Do High-frequency Traders Anticipate Buying and Selling Pressure?" IFA Working Paper, London Business School.

Hoffmann, Peter. 2014. "A Dynamic Limit Order Market with Fast and Slow Traders." *Journal of Financial Economics* 113:1, 156–169.

Huang, Jennifer, and Jiang Wang. 2009. "Liquidity and Market Crashes." *Review of Financial Studies*, 22:7, 2607–2643.

Jiang, George J., Ingrid Lo, and Giorgio Valente. 2013. "High-Frequency Trading around Macroeconomic News Announcements: Evidence from the U.S. Treasury Market." Working paper, Bank of Canada, Ottawa, Canada.

Jones, Charles M. 2002. "A Century of Stock Market Liquidity and Trading Costs." Working paper, Columbia Business School, Columbia University.

Jones, Charles M. 2013. "What Do We Know about High-Frequency Trading?" Working paper, Columbia Business School, Columbia University.

Jovanovic, Boyan, and Albert Menkveld. 2015. "Middlemen in Limit-Order Markets." Working paper, VU University, Amsterdam.

Kalbfleisch, John D., and Ross L. Prentice. 2002. *The Statistical Analysis of Failure Time Data*. 2nd edition. Hoboken, NJ: John Wiley & Sons, Inc.

Kirilenko, Andrei, Albert S. Kyle, Mehrdad Samadi, and Tugkan Tuzun. 2015. "The Flash Crash: The Impact of High Frequency Trading on an Electronic Market." Working paper, Commodity Futures Trading Commission. Forthcoming in *Journal of Finance*.

Kofman, Paul, and James T. Moser. 1997. "Spreads, Information Flows, and Transparency across Trading Systems." *Applied Financial Economics* 7:3, 281–94.

Kosinski, Robert J. 2006. "A Literature Review on Reaction Time." Available at http://www.fon.hum.uva.nl/rob/Courses/InformationInSpeech/CDROM/Literature/LOTwinterschool2006/biae.clemson.edu/bpc/bp/Lab/110/reaction.htm.

Labuszewski, John W., and Lori Aldinger. 2012. "Electronic Trading: Twenty Years of CME Globex." Working paper, Research and Product Development, CME Group.

Laughlin, Gregory, Anthony Aguirre, and Joseph Grundfest. 2014. "Information Transmission between Financial Markets in Chicago and New York." *Financial Review* 49:2, 283–312.

McInish, Thomas, and James Upson. 2012. "Strategic Liquidity Supply in a Market with Fast and Slow Traders." Working paper, Department of Finance, University of Memphis.

Menkveld, Albert J. 2013. "High Frequency Trading and the New-Market Makers." *Journal of Financial Markets* 16:4, 712–740.

Menkveld, Albert J. 2016. "The Economics of High-Frequency Trading: Taking Stock." *Annual Review of Financial Economics* 8, 1–24.

Menkveld, Albert J., and Bart Z. Yueshen. 2016. "The Flash Crash: A Cautionary Tale about Highly Fragmented Markets." Working paper, VU University of Amsterdam.

Nagel, Stefan. 2012. "Evaporating Liquidity." *Review of Financial Studies* 25:7, 2005–2039.

O'Hara, Maureen. 2015. "High Frequency Market Microstructure." *Journal of Financial Economics* 116:2, 257–270.

Pirrong, Craig. 1996. "Market Liquidity and Depth on Computerized and Open Outcry Trading Systems: A Comparison of the DTB and LIFFE Bund Contracts." *Journal of Futures Markets* 16:5, 519–543.

Raman, Vikas, Michel A. Robe, and Pradeep K. Yadav. 2016. "Liquidity Provision Under Stress: The Fast, the Slow, and the Dead." Working paper, Kogod School of Business, American University.

Roşu, Ioanid. 2015. "Fast and Slow Informed Trading." Working paper, School of Management, HEC.

Sarkar, Asani, and Michelle Tozzi. 1998. "Electronic Trading on Futures Exchanges." Federal Reserve Bank of New York, *Current Issues in Economics and Finance* 4:1, 1–6.

Shkilko, Andriy, and Konstantin Sokolov. 2016. "Every Cloud Has a Silver Lining: Fast Trading, Microwave Connectivity and Trading Costs." Working paper, Lazaridis School of Business and Economics, Wilfrid Laurier University.

Shyy, Gang, and Jie-Haun Lee. 1995. "Price Transmission and Information Asymmetry in Bund Futures Markets: LIFFE versus DTB." *Journal of Futures Markets* 15:1, 87–99.

United States of America v. Navinder Singh Sarao. 2015. Case 1:15-cr-00075 Document #1, N.D. Ill., Feb 11, 2015, Court Docket.

U.S. Commodity and Futures Trading Commission and U.S. Securities and Exchange Commission. 2010. *Findings Regarding the Market Events of May 6, 2010*. Report of the Staffs of the CFTC and SEC to the Joint Advisory Committee on Emerging Regulatory Issues, September 30. Available at https://www.sec.gov/news/studies/2010/marketevents-report.pdf.

U.S. Department of the Treasury. 2015. *The U.S. Treasury Market on October 15, 2014*. Joint Staff Report with the Board of Governors of the Federal Reserve System, Federal Reserve Bank of New York, U.S. Securities and Exchange Commission, and the U.S. Commodity Futures Trading Commission. July 13. Available at https://www.treasury.gov/press-center/press-releases/Documents/Joint_Staff_Report_Treasury_10-15-2015.pdf.

U. S. Securities and Exchange Commission. 2014. *Equity Market Structure Literature Review—Part II: High Frequency Trading*. Report of the Staff of the Division of Trading and Markets, U.S. Securities and Exchange Commission. March 18. Available at https://www.sec.gov/marketstructure/research/hft_lit_review_march_2014.pdf.

Weill, Pierre-Olivier. 2007. "Leaning against the Wind." *Review of Economic Studies* 74:4, 1329–1354.

24

Energy Risk Management

THOMAS BARKLEY
Professor of Finance Practice, Whitman School of Management, Syracuse University

MINGWEI (MAX) LIANG
Independent Financial Consultant

ANDREW C. SPIELER
Professor of Finance, Frank G. Zarb School of Business, Hofstra University

Introduction

As global population and standard of living increase, energy consumption is expanding with economic growth. Therefore, worldwide energy consumption is expected to rise over the next decade, despite concerns about global energy sustainability, climate protection, and efficiency of energy consumption. According to the IEO2016 (U.S. Energy Information Administration 2016), total world consumption of marketed energy will expand from 549 quadrillion British thermal units (Btu) in 2012 to 815 quadrillion Btu in 2040—a 48 percent increase in the next two decades (U.S. Energy Information Administration 2016). As Figure 24.1 shows, non-OECD countries in Asia, including China and India, account for more than half of the anticipated increase of total energy consumption during this period.

With the swift development of a global oil market in the 1980s, energy became a tradable commodity. The rapid growth in energy consumption led to increased volume and breadth of associated derivative products. Because of a high level of uncertainty of commodity prices, participants in this global integrated energy market, including power plants, oil companies, financial institutions, and even airlines, generally use energy derivatives to hedge against risks related to their energy trading and exposure (Jacque 2010). Those energy derivatives are based on an underlying energy asset, such as natural gas, crude oil, or electricity. Energy derivatives can be classified into exchange-traded contracts (energy futures and options) and over-the-counter (OTC) contracts (energy forwards and swaps).

This chapter focuses on risk management in the energy sector. It begins by introducing commonly used derivatives by energy companies followed by a comprehensive examination of risk and risk management in the energy sector and a general method to identify the primary risk factors for an energy company. The remainder of the chapter is organized as follows. The next section discusses key financial instruments used

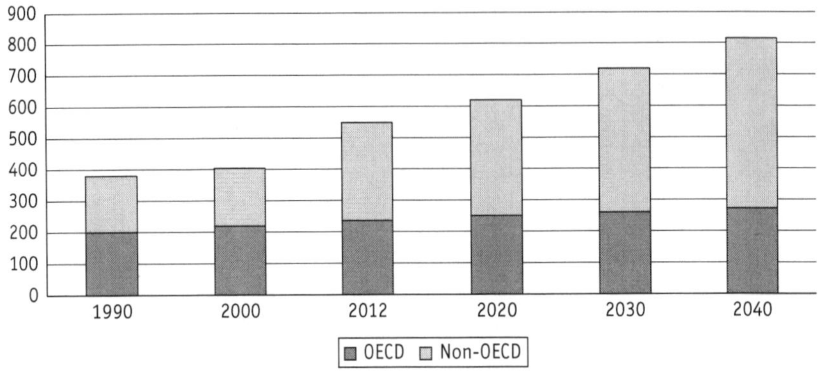

Figure 24.1 World Energy Consumption between 1990 and 2040 (Quadrillion Btu) The figure shows the amount of historical and predicted energy consumption of OECD and non-OECD countries between 1990 and 2040. Source: U.S. Energy Information Administration (2016).

in the energy markets. The third section examines the market risk of an energy portfolio and the risk metrics of measurement, such as Value at Risk (VaR) and related measures. The fourth section provides an overview of credit risk, the external and internal credit rating, and methods applied to mitigate credit risk. The fifth section discusses additional risks, such as liquidity risk, operational risk, and legal risk, that are receiving increased attention within risk management processes. The final section provides a summary and conclusions.

Financial Instruments

Hedgers use different financial instruments, primarily derivatives, in the energy markets. In many instances, business practices in the energy markets require unique features, especially when energy products display particular seasonality or trends. Some important derivatives used include forward and futures contracts, commodity swaps, call and put options on various spreads, and more exotic options.

Futures contracts are traded on different energy products: crude oil, natural gas, refined products (e.g., gasoline, heating oil, and jet fuel), biofuels (e.g., ethanol and biodiesel), coal, electricity, and petrochemicals (e.g., ethane, propane, and butane). These exchange-traded contracts are standardized in terms of price quotes, contract size, maturity dates, delivery periods and procedures, and required margins. Trading futures contracts on an exchange involves very little credit risk because settlement via a clearinghouse takes place on a daily basis. Although some trading in these contracts results in physical delivery of the commodities, the majority of the contracts are closed out before maturity. Two of the largest global exchanges for energy futures are the New York Mercantile Exchange (NYMEX, now part of CME Group) and Intercontinental Exchange (ICE).

Forward contracts, unlike futures, are traded in the OTC markets. As a result, the contracts are tailored to suit the needs of the parties involved in the contract with specific details about the price, contract size, and when and where delivery should take place. Due to the customized nature of forwards, these contracts usually result in delivery of the energy commodity, as exiting the contracts or trading them with a third party is difficult. Credit risks in OTC contracts tend to be higher, as one of the counterparties may default on its payment or delivery obligations.

Commodity swaps are financial instruments similar to interest rate swaps, except cash flows in a plain vanilla swap are based on fixed and floating commodity prices over a set period. Suppose an energy wholesaler enters into a long-term contract to deliver 10,000 MMBtu (millions of British thermal units) of natural gas to one of its clients for the next five years at a fixed price. If the energy wholesaler is concerned that natural gas prices will increase substantially in the next few years, the wholesaler may choose to hedge the position with a plain vanilla natural gas swap. In this instance, the energy firm would pay a fixed price for natural gas each month for the next 60 months, receiving the floating (market) price each month. As long as the fixed price per MMBtu on the swap contract is lower than the fixed delivery price to its client, the energy firm will profit each month because it can buy natural gas at spot prices using the cash flows received from the swap contract.

Hedgers use other types of swap contracts (Kaminsky 2016). Although a standard swap considers the differences between floating and fixed prices, a *differential swap* (or "diff" swap) is based on the difference between a fixed price differential for two energy products and the realized differential over time. For instance, an airline may hedge its jet fuel exposure using gasoline swap contracts. Although returns on the two refined products are correlated, they typically are not perfectly correlated. If the price differential between jet fuel and gasoline narrows, the airline may decide to use a diff swap contract to lock in a particular price differential. In a particular month when the realized price differential exceeds the fixed price differential, the airline would receive the difference; if the realized price differential were to drop below the fixed differential, the airline would pay the difference. Thus, the airline would be hedged against increases in the price differential between these products.

Options that give the buyer the right but not the obligation to enter into a specified swap contract with the issuer on a specified date in the future, at the cost of an option premium, are called *swaptions*. The two different kinds of swaptions are payer swaptions and receiver swaptions. In a *payer swaption*, the holder has the right to enter into a swap agreement in which the holder would pay the fixed price and receive the floating price. Because this instrument gives the holder the right to buy at the fixed price, it is also referred to as a *call swaption*. Similarly, in a *receiver swaption*, the holder has the right to enter into a swap agreement in which the holder would become the fixed-price receiver and the floating-price payer. This instrument is also termed a *put swaption* because it gives the holder the right to sell at the fixed price.

In a *double-up swap*, the swap user can obtain a better fixed price than the prevailing price observed in the market. This situation occurs as long as the swap provider is given an embedded option to double the notional size of the swap before the start of the pricing period if the underlying price drops below a predetermined strike price. The mechanism used to obtain this arrangement is for consumers (who are interested in paying a fixed price) to sell a put swaption, or for producers (who are interested in receiving a fixed price) to sell a call swaption. In either case, the option premium from the sale subsidizes the swap price. Consider a coal mining company that negotiates a swap price of \$50 per ton, but can increase this price to \$54 per ton by selling a call swaption on the same swap to its counterparty. On the exercise date of the swaption, the swap provider will decide whether to double the volume of the swap.

Some embedded options in swaps relate to the *tenor* of the swap (i.e., the amount of time left until the contract expires), rather than the notional size. For instance, an *extendable swap* gives an option to one of the counterparties to extend the swap for a pre-specified period at the end of the initially-agreed period. In a similar manner, a *cancelable swap* gives an option to one of the counterparties to terminate the swap at some future point before the end of the initially-agreed period. The option premium will be incorporated into the fixed price associated with one of these swaps.

Many participants in the energy markets are either natural consumers or producers of energy products. As a result, hedging is important for those wanting to fix either their purchase or selling prices. Some participants, however, are exposed to both purchase prices of input products as well as sale prices of output products, and consequently their interests are to lock in the spreads between their revenues and costs. In particular, oil refineries use the term *crack spread* to mean the price differential between crude oil and a petroleum product such as gasoline. In other words, this price differential represents the profit margin that an oil refinery can obtain through the "cracking" of crude oil. Similarly, power generators use the term *spark spread* to refer to the price differential between electricity produced and the natural gas required to produce it.

Margin swaps allow refiners to either pay or receive the difference between a fixed margin and a realized margin. Alternatively, refiners can choose to trade *spread options*, which derive their value from the difference between two prices. Call options on crack spreads allow holders to enjoy the upside potential of larger spreads, while put options provide upside potential with smaller spreads. If the crack spread increases beyond a certain level, represented by the strike price of the option, call options will be worth more; when the crack spread decreases below a certain level. put options will be worth more. In such cases, the payoffs for the options would be as given in Equations 24.1 and 24.2:

$$c = \text{MAX}\left[\left(G_T - C_T\right) - K,\ 0\right] \tag{24.1}$$

$$p = \text{MAX}\left[K - \left(G_T - C_T\right)0\right] \tag{24.2}$$

where, at time T, c is the payoff for a call option; p is the payoff for a put option; G_T is the price of gasoline; C_T is the price of crude oil; and K is a strike price. In general, a (fixed) conversion parameter may also be included so that both sets of prices are in comparable units such as dollars per gallon or dollars per barrel. These are exotic options because they involve more than one underlying asset price. Such options can be valued using Margrabe's (1978) approach.

Finally, another important, exotic, path-dependent option often used in energy risk management is an Asian option. An *Asian option* is one in which the payoff depends on the arithmetic average of the underlying commodity's price during the option's life, in which sampling may occur on pre-specified dates. Hull (2014) describes average price and average strike options, giving the payoffs for the options in Equations 24.3 through 24.6:

$$\text{Average price call}: c = \text{MAX}\left[S_{ave} - K,\ 0\right] \tag{24.3}$$

$$\text{Average price put}: p = \text{MAX}\left[K - S_{ave,}\ 0\right] \tag{24.4}$$

$$\text{Average strike call}: c = \text{MAX}\left[S_T - S_{ave,}\ 0\right] \tag{24.5}$$

$$\text{Average strike put}: p = \text{MAX}\left[S_{ave} - S_{T,}\ 0\right] \tag{24.6}$$

where at time *T*, *c* is the payoff for a call option; *p* is the payoff for a put option; S_{ave} is the arithmetic average price of the underlying commodity; S_T is the final price of the underlying commodity; and *K* is the (fixed) strike price.

Consider a shipping company that buys diesel fuel on a monthly basis at market prices. The company wants to hedge its diesel fuel purchases by buying a 12-month Asian call option with monthly sampling. If the average price deviates substantially from a pre-specified strike price during the option's life, the company will exercise the option at maturity and receive a payoff that will offset some of the fuel costs. Conversely, if the average price is below the strike price of the option, the company will allow it to expire worthless given that the company has already enjoyed the benefit of cheaper fuel during the course of the year.

Definition of Risk and Risk Management

Every company has a level of uncertainty and systematic risk. Energy companies are no exception because most of the risk comes from the fluctuations of the commodity price of energy products. For an oil exploration and refining company, the main risk is the fluctuation of crude oil prices, which directly relates to its revenues. Therefore, the risk management objective for an oil company is to hedge against negative oil price movements.

To better understand the inherent risks and risk management for energy companies requires defining risk. Referring to ISO 31000 (International Organization for Standardization):

> Risk is defined as the effects of uncertainty on objectives, which will be positive or negative deviations from the expectations. Objectives for risk

can have different aspects, including financial, health and safety, and environmental goals. (ISO 2009)

According to Burger, Graeber, and Schindlmayr (2014), risk management of energy companies is the methodical identification, assessment, and prioritization of risks, as well as coordinated and economical application of resources to minimize, monitor, and control the probability and/or impact of unfortunate events. Risk management is important to energy companies because it not only provides the process and the tools used to evaluate and measure risks in energy supplies and derivatives contracts, but also helps with the management of various risks within a company's physical and financial assets.

Kallman and Maric (2004) point out five steps to establish risk management for common companies, a procedure that is also applicable for energy companies. Those steps are (1) risk identification, (2) risk assessment, (3) solution analysis, (4) decision process, and (5) system administration.

The development of risk management must begin with identifying relevant risk factors. Different methods are available to identify the possible risks. One method is to use surveys or interviews with the potential risk owners to reveal universal risk exposures and factors. After collecting results, an analyst can draw a risk map to help analyze the company's primary identified risk factors. For example, an analyst can use a risk map to draw the primary risk factors. As Figure 24.2 shows, the risk map for an energy company should primarily include risk factors on a basic level.

The next step is risk assessment, which involves evaluating those main risk factors. This assessment should include risk magnitude that combines both likelihood and consequence of the risks. This stage also involves collecting data on the probability, severity, and timing of loss (Kallman and Maric 2004). Some risk metric models, such as VaR and other risk assessment methods, are needed within the process to determine the quantitative and qualitative impacts of different risk factors.

The third step of risk management is solution analysis. Solution analysis consists of three sub-steps: identifying a solution, measuring the solution, and evaluating the solution's stability. The identification of a solution helps to recognize all options available to manage the risks. The fourth step is a decision process that involves selecting

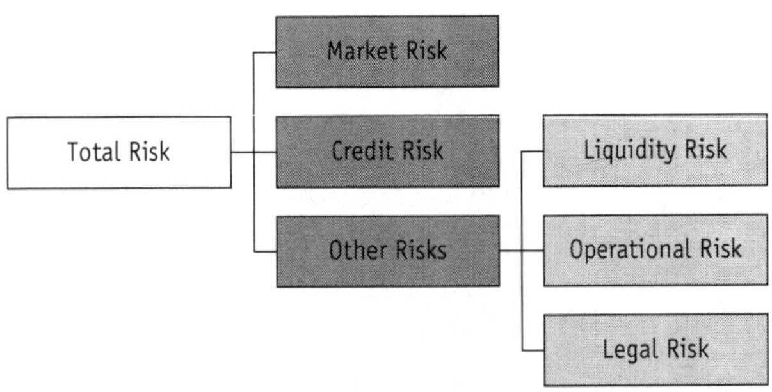

Figure 24.2 Risk Map with Main Risk Factors
This figure depicts the risk map of main risk factors within energy risk management.

the best solution, using decision models to make decisions, and implementing the solutions to migrate risks. The fifth step of the risk management process—system administration—includes three stages: monitoring, judging, and evaluating the entire risk management process. This last step ensures risk management activities are effective in helping the organization achieve its goals (Kallman and Maric 2004).

Market Risk

Market risk is the risk of financial loss resulting from movements in market prices. For an energy company, market risk is the exposure to commodities or energy products. Since the early 2000s, prices for the majority of energy commodities have more than tripled and set record highs. Concurrently, energy markets have become increasingly volatile and risky (Ahmed and Trabelsi 2014). This volatility occurred partly due to the rise of competition and deregulation in power and gas markets, the development of new technologies that increased oil extraction, and the occurrence of political events that caused unstable demand-supply equilibrium in the oil market (Burger et al. 2014). In such an unpredictable, volatile, and risky environment, determining how to bolster the protection against market risk has become an essential issue for energy companies. Generally, market risk management should start from the industry standard VaR, which is one of the most popular tools in quantification of market risk (Ahmed and Trabelsi 2014).

VALUE AT RISK

VaR is a statistical technique to measure and quantify the profit or loss of a given portfolio within a specific time frame with an associated probability (Holton 2009). VaR specifies a "worst case" for a portfolio's value with a probability not to exceed a given risk likelihood over the holding period. Today, comprehensive studies on VaR are available (Jorion 2006; Holton 2009). Hull (2014) introduces applications of the VaR concept.

The term VaR did not enter the financial lexicon until the early 1990s. In 1975, the U.S. Securities and Exchange Commission (SEC) established a Uniform Net Capital Rule (UNCR) that included a system of "haircuts" applied to a firm's different asset classes to determine the liquidity and safe net worth as safeguards against market losses (Sadeghi and Shavvalpour 2006). The popularity of VaR began with the publication of JP Morgan's RiskMetrics Technical Document, which specified a firm-wide VaR system (Guldimann 1995). Since then, VaR has become the most adopted risk measurement metric that is widely used by financial institutions, regulators such as the Basel Committee, fund managers, and corporate treasurers. VaR can be readily applied to the energy sector.

Several reasons help to explain the widespread adoption of VaR. First, VaR concisely communicates the maximum loss for a specific holding period with a prespecified degree of confidence. Hence, the concept of VaR is easier to understand than many other volatility measures because it combines both the probability and magnitude of loss. Finally, VaR is applicable to many asset classes, including stocks,

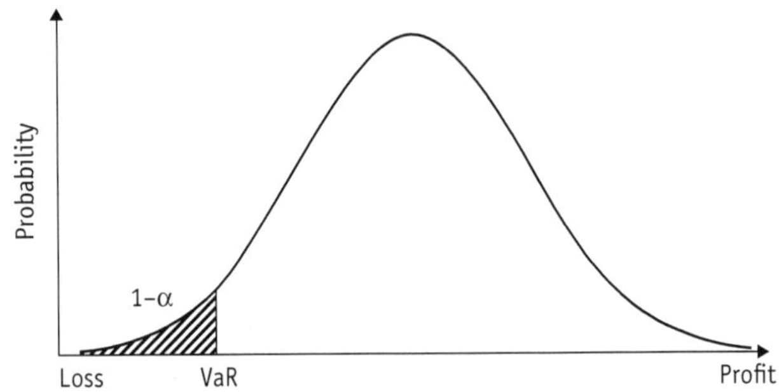

Figure 24.3 Value at Risk
This figure shows the probability distribution associated with VaR, noting the extreme loss in the left tail.

bonds, currencies, and derivatives, making comparisons and risk budget allocations easier. Yet, VaR is not without its limitations particularly for assets with asymmetric or nonlinear payoffs. Additionally, VaR does not indicate the maximum possible loss but rather the probability of exceeding a loss level.

Figure 24.3 illustrates VaR. If $X[t_1,t_2]$ represents the random variable of the market value change of a given portfolio during the time period $[t_1,t_2]$, with the probability distribution P, then $\text{VaR}(\alpha,t_1-t_2)$ with the holding period $[t_1,t_2]$ and confidence level α is defined as:

$$\text{P}(X[t_1,t_2]\leq x)\geq 1-\alpha$$

However, VaR only describes a portfolio's expected loss not exceeded with a given probability of α. It does not address situations when possible losses may exist in the tail, that is, in the remaining probability of $1-\alpha$. For this reason, the conditional VaR (CVaR) is necessary to estimate the expected excess loss given a tail event. More precisely, CVaR serves as an extension of VaR. Figure 24.4 shows that a portfolio has more risk in the tails of the distribution (CVaR) than the portfolio in Figure 24.3, but the VaRs of both portfolios are the same.

PARAMETERS OF VAR

The basic VaR model assumes that market returns are normally distributed or follow a random walk. The two parameters of VaR are the time horizon or holding period and confidence level. Assuming that the changes in portfolio value (i.e., returns) on N successive days are independent identically distributed normal random variables having distributions with mean zero, VaR can be expressed as shown in Equation 24.7:

$$\text{VaR}(\alpha,N)=\sqrt{N}\,\text{VaR}(\alpha,1) \tag{24.7}$$

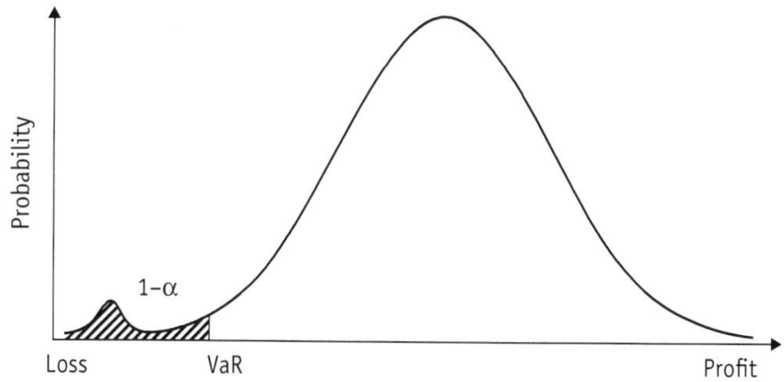

Figure 24.4 Conditional Value-at-Risk
This figure shows the probability distribution associated with CVaR, noting the extreme loss in the left tail.

Therefore, a VaR over a given time horizon can be easily converted to any other time horizon by scaling with $\sqrt{N}$. In light of choosing the time horizon according to the Basel II Accord market risk framework, the calculation of capital for trading uses the VaR measure with a time horizon of 10 days ($N = 10$) and a confidence level of 99 percent (Basel Committee on Banking Supervision 2010). Another common convention for choosing the time horizon is to choose a time horizon that covers the appropriate market liquidity holding period (e.g., a day trader might use a one-day VaR). Confidence levels are typically between 95 and 99 percent for calculating VaR.

VAR METHODS

Three primary methods are available for computing VaR: historical simulation, the variance-covariance (analytical) method, and Monte Carlo simulation. Given that VaR measures the potential future changes in the portfolio's value that depend on certain market variables (Linsmeier and Pearson 2000), a common initial procedure for each method is to identify which market factors affect the portfolio's value. For a large energy portfolio consisting of several different commodities, market risk factors should be commodity price fluctuations of each instrument (Burger et al. 2014). In this case, the holding periods of those commodities should be considered separately because various delivery periods of different contracts may be available, such as daily, weekly, monthly, and annually.

THE HISTORICAL SIMULATION METHOD

The historical simulation method is a non-parametric method that does not require the assumption of normality, or any distribution for that matter, as the analytical method does. In short, the historical approach constructs a distribution of portfolio returns based on the historical changes in market prices. VaR is then computed by taking the loss that exceeds a given confidence level (e.g., for a holding period) (Cabedo and Moya 2003).

Suppose a crude oil producer wants to hedge the price of future crude oil production and keeps rolling contracts to short crude oil futures with a notional amount of $15 million. For simplicity, assume the holding period is a single day ($t = 1$), and the past 100 business days ($N = 100$) are used to compute the VaR (assume a 5 percent confidence level). For this case, the process for computing VaR under the historical simulation approach consists of the following four steps:

1. Identify the basic market factors and express the mark-to-market (MTM) value in terms of these factors. In other words, this step involves computing the futures contract values as a function of the spot market price of crude oil.
2. Obtain the historical values for the last N periods. For this example, this step involves collecting the spot oil contract prices for the last 100 business days (N periods).
3. Calculate the daily profits and losses of the portfolio (i.e., the daily changes of values of the portfolio subject to market risk factors).
4. Rank the MTM returns (potential losses and gains in the preceding step) in ascending order.

Select the loss level that is equal to the fifth percentile from the distribution of the daily returns. In this case, with 100 daily returns and a 5 percent confidence level, the VaR is the fifth percentile of all daily returns multiplied by the portfolio value. In Figure 24.5, the dollar VaR is $390,000. The standard terminology is to quote VaR losses as positive values while a negative VaR would indicate a tail value with a positive return.

The advantages of the historical approach are obvious. First, the VaR is easily calculated based on historical returns derived from historical prices. Second, no distributional assumptions are necessary. Third, the method is very flexible to adapt to changing confidence levels or holding periods. Conversely, the simplicity of the method has drawbacks. First, the historical method assumes each observation has

Percentiles (%)	**Day**	**MTM Returns (%)**	
1	2	−12.1	
2	45	−7.9	
3	71	−4.8	
4	91	−3.7	
5	**22**	**−2.6** ←	VaR = 2.6%($15 million) = $390,000
...	...	....	(positive VaR = loss)
98	3	3.9	
99	56	4.1	
100	78	6.3	

Figure 24.5 An Example of VaR Using the Historical Simulation Method
This figure provides a sample of historical returns over 100 days and the associated VaR (one-day, 5 percent VaR, $N = 100$).

equal weight. Common sense, however, dictates that placing more weight on recent observations is more appropriate when volatility of returns increased in recent periods. Second, the method assumes that the historical distribution will continue into the future (i.e., unbiased expectations). Lastly, the method uses historical prices and so would be inappropriate for securities or commodity prices with limited history or new, inactive, or illiquid instruments.

VARIANCE-COVARIANCE (ANALYTICAL) METHOD

Some consider the variance-covariance method, also known as the *analytical method*, as the simplest and the most common method for calculating VaR. This method requires assuming a probability distribution for portfolio returns with the most common assumption being market returns are normally distributed. The VaR under the variance-covariance method can be determined by applying the mathematical properties of the normal distribution. Intuitively, the portfolio returns are a weighted average of individual asset returns using the linearity property of normal distributions. Calculating the portfolio's variance is more challenging because using a variance-covariance matrix requires factoring in the cross-correlations between assets. A common approach is to assume the cross-correlations are zero to simplify the portfolio VaR calculation. For example, suppose the confidence level is 5 percent and the holding period is N days, then Equation 24.8 shows the VaR equation:

$$\begin{aligned}\text{VaR} = &\text{Current portfolio market value} \times 1.65\\ &\times \text{Standard deviation of returns} \times \sqrt{N}\end{aligned} \tag{24.8}$$

In most cases, the returns of an energy portfolio are not normally distributed, a violation of the basic assumption of the variance-covariance method. Therefore, a large diversified portfolio will yield a more accurate result of VaR than individual products because the returns of the portfolio more closely resemble a normal distribution than the returns of individual products. The variance-covariance method can be further differentiated to two models according to whether the portfolio exposure is linear.

First, the delta-normal method assumes a linear approximation for the change in portfolio value. If the portfolio contains an option, then the changes in the underlying will have a nonlinear impact on the values of the portfolio, and thus distort the results from the delta-normal method. Consequently, the delta-normal method works best for a portfolio containing delta one products such as forwards or futures. Under the assumption that the returns of instruments for a small holding period, such as one day, are approximately normally distributed, the VaR delta-normal method can be expressed as Equation 24.9:

$$\text{VaR}(\alpha, \Delta t) = MV\sigma_{\Delta v} C_{\alpha} \sqrt{\Delta t} \tag{24.9}$$

where α denotes the significance level; Δt represents the holding period; and C_{α} is the associated critical value under the given significance level. Finally, $\sigma_{\Delta v}$ represents the standard deviation of the changes in portfolio value, which are normally distributed with mean zero. Using the same example as for the historical simulation, VaR for the one-day holding period and 5 percent confidence level can be calculated as shown in Equation 24.10:

$$\text{VaR}\left(5\text{ percent, 1 day}\right)=\text{Current market value} \\ \times \text{Standard deviation of change inportfolio value}\times 1.65\times\sqrt{1} \qquad (24.10)$$

In Equation 24.10, for a standard normal distribution, 1.65 corresponds to a one-tail p-value of 5 percent.

The second method is the delta-gamma method, which is appropriate when the portfolio contains a substantial number of nonlinear positions. Gamma is the second-order approximation of changes in portfolio value. In other words, it measures how delta changes as the price of the underlying instrument changes (Linsmeier and Pearson 2000).

MONTE CARLO SIMULATION

Monte Carlo simulation provides an alternative approach to the historical simulation and variance-covariance methods. This method differs from the historical method by using a stochastic model to generate a forward-looking distribution, as opposed to using a static historical distribution. Next, VaR can be determined under a given confidence level based on the distribution of portfolio values.

For example, in the case of an energy forward contract, the Monte Carlo method can generate thousands of changes in spot commodity prices of the energy contracts and the hypothetical profit and loss of this portfolio can be calculated based on those price changes. With a given level of confidence, VaR can be computed from this distribution.

The primary advantage of the Monte Carlo method is that virtually any distribution can be specified to model the portfolio value and so it does not require assuming a normal distribution. However, one drawback of the Monte Carlo method is that simulations require large amounts of computing power because the portfolio has to be revalued many times. Another drawback is that the initial sampling is still dependent on historical data.

VOLATILITY AND CORRELATION

The analytical method for computing VaR requires the volatility of returns of the financial instrument as an input. However, estimating volatility and the covariance matrix are difficult and this process is even more complex for energy derivative contracts. Analysts use two common models to estimate volatility and correlation that can be used with the analytical method: (1) exponentially weighted moving averages (EWMA) and (2) the generalized autoregressive conditional heteroscedasticity model (GARCH) (Eydeland and Wolyniec 2003).

The EWMA model can be used to calculate volatility by adding all the weighted average rates of return during a period, given that the weights on the returns decrease exponentially backward in time and each weight is equal to λ times the preceding weight. This EWMA has the advantage of emphasizing the most recent returns (i.e., more weight in recent data). The *RiskMetrics* database, released by JP Morgan in 1994, uses EWMA with λ equal to 0.94 to refresh daily volatility (Alexander 2013).

Another method for estimating volatilities is the GARCH model introduced by Bollerslev (1986). Given that economic and financial data exhibit more time-varying volatility than constant volatility, the GARCH model is better suited to estimating time-varying volatility. Because financial returns have "heavy-tailed" or "outlier-prone" probability distributions, GARCH can be used to model both the conditional heteroskedasticity and the heavy-tailed distributions of financial market data (Box, Jenkins, Reinsel, and Ljung 2016). A GARCH model can fit a wide range of volatility behavior so modeling volatility in the energy markets seems adequate.

OTHER MARKET RISK MEASURES

Although VaR is the most commonly used method for quantifying risk, other measures address specific issues that are not directly incorporated into the VaR approach, including concerns with the company's ability to make payments (liquidity), and with shareholders' returns (profitability).

A basic assumption of the VaR methodology is that the portfolio position does not turn over during the holding period. As a result, the common VaR model does not perfectly measure market risk for energy companies that typically hold very large positions that would be adversely affected if immediate liquidity is required. Hence, the market risk of holding positions computed by VaR will be overestimated because the positions keep diminishing in size during the holding periods. In such a case, using a Liquidity-adjusted Value at Risk (LVaR) is more appropriate than the traditional VaR to quantify market risk for large portfolios with changing positions (Burger et al. 2014).

Aside from traditional VaR and LVaR, analysts can use Profit at Risk (PaR) to measure downside risk. PaR is used for measuring the market risk of an energy portfolio's profit based on changing spot prices. For a given confidence level, say 95 percent, PaR denotes a 5 percent probability that the profit of a given portfolio will be lower than the normal range for profit at delivery.

Credit Risk

Traditionally, energy companies exhibit a high degree of creditworthiness because they typically hold valuable assets and generate stable cash flows. In fact, some energy companies have implicit and explicit backing from their governments, increasing their perceived creditworthiness. *Credit risk* for energy companies historically referred to the risk that end users fail to make payment for the energy products they consumed. However, as the energy markets become a more liberalized, competitive, and meaningful part of the value chain, understanding credit risk for energy companies becomes increasingly important. In particular, because the contractual agreements between companies have become a very significant part of the business model of energy companies, counterparty risk is a heightened concern. In fact, the bankruptcies of Enron in 2001 and Lehman Brothers in 2008 emphasize the critical role of credit risk management in the successful operation of a complex organization.

Credit risk arises when a counterparty cannot fulfill its contractual obligations, including default on interest or principal payments, or on the physical delivery of short forwards. Theoretically, credit risk can be limited by only conducting exchange-cleared trades, but the trades in the energy sector often occur OTC. The classification of credit risk here includes settlement risk and replacement risk. *Settlement risk* is the possibility that a counterparty fails to deliver benefits or payments at the time of settlement. Settlement risk is common for most businesses and it can be estimated for fixed priced contracts. Similarly, *replacement risk* is the possibility that participants will have to enter a new replacement contract during potentially adverse market conditions. This risk is akin to reinvestment risk in the bond market. Replacement risk is an important risk for an energy trading company and cannot be perfectly forecast.

CREDIT RATING

Counterparty analysis is one of the most important tasks for an energy company when starting a new trading relation because OTC transactions involve default risk of the counterparty. Many ways are available to conduct counterparty analysis. Such an analysis normally evaluates two aspects of risks. Analysts evaluate business risk by the company's competitive position, operational environment, and earnings quality. They also evaluate financial risk using quantitative methods, particularly financial ratios. Conducting counterparty analysis of energy companies also requires examining some special considerations of the entire industry, such as commodity price volatility, cyclicality, capital intensity, or regulatory environment.

Credit rating analysis is an important tool for monitoring a counterparty's creditworthiness. Energy companies can use external and/or internal credit ratings in their evaluation. *External credit ratings* refer to the public credit ratings from an external rating agency or business information service such as Moody's, Standard & Poor's, or Fitch Ratings. These companies among others specialize in assessing creditworthiness based on their broad database and experience in a wide range of industries, and methodologies to identify the key operational and financial credit determinants in a particular industry.

The maturity of the debt affects the credit rating. The short-term rating puts more emphasis on qualifications of short-term instruments, such as commercial paper or any instrument with maturities less than one year. By contrast, the long-term rating focuses on longer-term instruments, such as notes and securities with maturities greater than one year, medium-term notes, or mortgage bonds.

Internal credit ratings can be applied to assess the creditworthiness and default probability of a counterparty when it is not publicly rated by external rating agencies but needs to be evaluated to support counterparty analysis. An *internal credit rating* is a rating procedure that analyzes qualitative and quantitative criteria in a scoring system. Implementing the qualitative criteria requires a strong understanding of the prospective counterparty's business profile including business type, corporate structure, public/private ownership, market position of the counterparty, economic situation of the sector, legal issues, duration of business connections, and turnover on cash flow.

MITIGATION OF CREDIT RISK

Reducing and ideally eliminating credit risk is the goal of credit risk management. Unlike market risk, which is based on the fluctuation of market prices, credit risk is affected not only by the creditworthiness of the counterparty but also by changing market conditions. The credit risk of the counterparty increases when an energy company enters a long forward with the counterparty and the value of the forward contract increases (i.e., the spot price of the underlying asset increases). As a result, credit risk is harder to monitor and mitigate than market risk. Thus, most credit-risk-reducing measures are implemented before establishing contracts with a counterparty (Burger et al. 2014).

Margining Agreements

Margining agreements are the most commonly used instruments to limit credit risk of OTC derivatives transactions. The margin bilateral agreement between two trading parties sets out standard terms of transactions and relevant detailed information including the transaction of collateral, threshold limits, minimum transfer amount (MTA), notification time, rounding amount, and other terms. The legal basis of a margining agreement is some credit support annex, established by the International Swaps and Derivatives Association (ISDA), the European Federation of Energy Traders (EFET), or the North American Energy Standards Board (NAESB). The ISDA master agreement is a standard document that is generally used to govern OTC derivatives transactions, outlining terms to be applied between two parties.

Although the master agreement is often associated with banks and financial institutions, energy companies widely use it. The advantages of a master agreement are trifold. First, it reduces the burdensome renegotiation of the terms of agreements for future transactions and accelerates the time for exchange of contracts. Second, a master agreement aids in reducing disputes between the two parties by providing extensive resources defining terms of the transaction. Finally, the master agreement helps reduce credit risk during the transaction.

Collateral Management

One important method to reduce counterparty credit risk in energy trading is to obtain a financial and/or physical pledge of assets from the counterparty, so that the collateral can be used to offset exposure if the counterparty defaults. The exchange of collateral could raise a host of legal and operational issues that can be addressed in the contracts governed by ISDA. A line of credit is a special form of collateral. Because cash is important for maintaining adequate liquidity for an energy company, a counterparty can require a third party, typically a commercial bank, to issue a line of credit instead of posting cash collateral.

Credit Limits

Credit limits restrict the credit exposure placed on a particular counterparty. The credit limits are assigned based on counterparty analysis that considers total shareholders' equity and a firm's credit rating. Generally, larger companies with better credit ratings will receive higher credit limits if they have a lower risk of default. All else equal, a financial company of the same size and rating as an industrial company will receive a lower credit limit. As time passes and the risk of default increases, the potential credit exposure calculation will include both the actual and potential exposure. By lowering the credit limits extended to a counterparty, a company can reduce its exposure to this counterparty.

Portfolio Compression

Portfolio compression helps to reduce the credit risk of energy trading by replacing many existing trades with large notional amounts with fewer new trades with substantially smaller notional amounts. However, the new portfolio still carries the same risk profile and cash flows as the original portfolio. This portfolio compression also helps to reduce operational risks because of the substantially reduced number of trades. The Dodd-Frank Wall Street Reform and Consumer Protection Act (Dodd-Frank Act) and European Market Infrastructure Regulation (EMIR) consider portfolio compression as a risk management method.

Credit Sleeve

A credit sleeve is another common method to control a counterparty's credit risk for OTC trades via a broker. A *credit sleeve* is a form of credit agreement where the "sleeve provider" (the broker) provides collateral on behalf of one company (the energy company) to another company (the commodity provider), and is also involved in the trades between those two parties. The aim of the credit sleeve is to reduce the credit risk of the trades between those two parties.

Parent Guarantees

For entities that are smaller affiliates or subsidiaries of larger organizations and do not meet the criteria to receive a credit limit from a counterparty, parent guarantees can help to reduce the credit risk of those entities in energy trades. The parent guarantee constitutes a promise of the parent company to pay the obligations of its subsidiary if the subsidiary defaults on its obligations.

Netting

When multiple positions or payments occur between counterparties at the same time, netting allows each participant to reduce the credit risk (settlement risk) with the counterparty. In the event the counterparty defaults, netting prevents large losses in demanding payments from the defaulting party as parts of payments have been collected by netting. Netting is also an important feature of a margining agreement because it reduces overall exposure and simplifies payments (Brigo, Morini, and Pallavicini 2013).

Over-the-Counter Clearing Platforms
For OTC energy trades, using OTC clearing can mitigate counterparty credit exposure. Electronic platforms, such as ICE and CME ClearPort, provide various cleared energy products.

Other Risks

Although market risk and credit risk might be considered risks of first-order importance, they are by no means the only risks that a company faces. Firms should have established risk management policies that cover: (1) its need for access to capital in the short term; (2) internal and external factors that might harm the business; and (3) matters of concern that arise from new regulation, legislation, and litigation. These risks are discussed in the following sections.

LIQUIDITY RISK

Liquidity risk can be classified into market liquidity risk and funding liquidity risk. *Market liquidity risk* is a risk that the lack of marketability of commodities or derivatives causes a loss when those instruments cannot be bought or sold quickly enough. According to Fernandez (1999), market liquidity incorporates key elements of volume, time, and transaction costs and can be defined by three dimensions that incorporate these elements: depth, breadth (or tightness), and resiliency.

In the energy sector, physical delivery and use of commodities are critical. Market liquidity risk includes the risk of timely delivery. For example, a gas pipeline operator is concerned that the total quantity of gas transported through its pipeline system cannot meet the required quantity for the agreed specification. This shortfall of gas supply forces the pipeline operator to pay a higher price in the spot market for buying extra gas from external storage to fulfill its required quantity specification (GARP 2008).

The energy sector must also consider funding liquidity risk. According to the Basel Committee on Banking Supervision (2008), *funding liquidity risk* is the inability of a financial intermediary to service its liabilities as they become due. For an energy company, a major source of funding liquidity risk is collateral requirements from its energy trades. For example, Metallgesellschaft AG used futures contracts to hedge OTC forward sales commitments. A fall in spot prices triggered staggering margin calls for the company, leading to a liquidity crisis to fund the required collateral and forcing the company to close contracts at a huge loss (Mello and Parsons 1995).

OPERATIONAL RISK

According to the Basel II Accord, *operational risk* is the risk of loss resulting from inadequate or failed internal processes, people, or internal systems or from external events (Basel Committee on Banking Supervision 2011). Operational risk may damage a company as much or more than market or credit risk. An important difference is that operational risk does not have the ability to generate profits and can be ideally eliminated.

Unfortunately, countless examples of catastrophic operational risk errors are available. For example, China Aviation Oil Corporation is the Singapore subsidiary of China Aviation Oil and primarily deals in jet fuel procurement for the airports in the People's Republic of China and international oil trading. In 2005, the company incurred a $550 million loss in oil operation trades because of weak operational risk management including poor corporate governance, market monitoring and surveillance, compliance and regulation, as well as inadequate knowledge in risk management (PRMIA 2016).

The principles of sound operational risk management set by the Basel Committee include establishing a strong risk management culture, developing and maintaining a risk management framework, identifying and assessing operational risk, and having monitoring and reporting processes in place. These principles are designed to manage the operational risk of financial institutions, but can also be applied to the energy sector (Burger et al. 2014).

LEGAL RISK

After the implementation of Dodd-Frank Act and other federal and local market regulations, more stringent regulations, as well as the threat of sanctions for lack of compliance, have become challenges for companies in both the financial sector and energy industry. According to the Basel II Accord, legal risk is classified as a subset of operational risk. Specifically, *legal risk* is the risk arising from failure to comply with statutory or regulatory obligations (McCubbrey 2016). Many regulators and much legislation oversee the reporting, compliance, and recording of energy trading, including the Commodity Futures Trading Commission (CFTC), Securities and Exchange Commission (SEC), and Dodd-Frank Act. Additionally, the Federal Energy Regulatory Commission (FERC) and the Department of Justice (DOJ) are now armed with new tools for monitoring and prevention of price manipulation in the U.S. energy and commodity markets, including jurisdiction in swap markets. Furthermore, the Environmental Protection Agency (EPA) and federal, state, and local fracking regulations require energy companies to comply with laws and regulations for the protection of air, water, and waste disposal.

According to the regulation outlook from Deloitte (Campbell and Prokop 2016), six regulatory trends that are likely to affect the energy industry in 2016 and beyond include the following:

- Regulators now assess compliance based on both the adherence to rules and objective and mitigation measures of operational risk.
- Energy companies should focus on the changing legitimations of compliance and should maximize the use of their compliance resources.
- Regulators including FERC, CFTC, and FTC will continue strengthening the enforcement focused on anti-manipulation, disruptive trading practices, and misconduct of individuals.
- More uncertainty will exist in the legislation of energy compliance in the future, such as a Clean Air Act update, possible regulations of financial transmission risks in markets, or limits on other instruments.

- More regulation will emphasize preventing risks and dangers in cyber technology for businesses and operations of physical and financial transactions.
- Energy companies should put more resources into trade surveillance, monitoring, and the creation of comprehensive compliance policies to oversee trading.

Summary and Conclusions

Worldwide energy consumption has been growing rapidly and is expected to increase into the next decade. Not surprisingly, concerns about global energy sustainability, climate protection, and efficient energy consumption continue to increase. In such an energy-demanding era, coupled with increasing uncertainty of commodity prices, energy companies are being forced to use energy derivatives to hedge against risks related to energy trading, leading to a more important role for risk management in the operation of these companies.

The goal of this chapter was to summarize the primary risks related to energy trading and risk management for firms in the energy sector. Given that most risks of energy companies arise from the price fluctuations of energy products, market risk management is the most essential part of energy risk management. Several quantitative methodologies are available to measure market risk with the most well-known being VaR. For portfolios with more tail risk in their return distribution, CVaR is a better measure of market risk. Other variations of VaR include LVaR and PaR. In terms of VaR implementation, three main methods are available for computing VaR: the historical simulation approach, the variance-covariance (analytical) method, and Monte Carlo simulation. EWMA and GARCH models also provide more accurate estimations of return volatility as an input for VaR models.

Credit risk has received much more attention after the bankruptcies of Enron in 2001 and Lehman Brothers in 2008. To evaluate the creditworthiness of counterparties, energy companies mostly rely on credit ratings provided by rating agencies or internal credit ratings. Unlike market risk, a counterparty's credit risk is difficult to quantify and should be mitigated through several measures such as margining agreements, collateral, credit limits, credit sleeves, netting, and other similar procedures. Besides market risk and credit risk, other risks, including operational risk, liquidity risk, and legal risk, are critical components in energy risk management. Energy companies should pay close attention to these other risks related to business operations because they can easily cripple a company. Thus, they require risk management that is adaptive to the changing market and regulatory environments.

Discussion Questions

1. Identify the major financial instruments used in energy risk management.
2. Discuss the principal steps in establishing an energy risk management program.
3. Identify the main assumption underlying the calculation of VaR, discuss its advantages and disadvantages, and explain why CVaR might be a better risk metric than VaR.

4. Identify the various means available to mitigate credit risk in energy trading.
5. List the steps used in the historical simulation method to compute VaR.

References

Ahmed, Ghorbel, and Abdelwahed Trabelsi. 2014. "Energy Portfolio Risk Management Using Time-Varying Extreme Value." *Economic Modelling* 38:C, 470–485.

Alexander, Carol. 2013. "Moving Average Models for Volatility and Correlation, and Covariance Matrices." In J. Frank Fabozzi (ed.), *Encyclopedia of Financial Models*, volume 3, 395–414. Hoboken, NJ: John Wiley & Sons, Inc.

Basel Committee on Banking Supervision. 2008. *Principles for Sound Liquidity Risk Management and Supervision*. September. Available at http://www.bis.org/publ/bcbs144.pdf.

Basel Committee on Banking Supervision. 2010. *Revisions to the Basel II Market Risk Framework*. July. Available at http://www.bis.org/publ/bcbs158.pdf.

Basel Committee on Banking Supervision. 2011. *Principles for the Sound Management of Operational Risk*. June. Available at http://www.bis.org/publ/bcbs195.pdf.

Bollerslev, Tim. 1986. "Generalized Autoregressive Conditional Heteroskedasticity." *Journal of Econometrics* 31:3, 307–327.

Box, George E. P., Gwilym M. Jenkins, Gregory C. Reinsel, and Greta M. Ljung. 2016. *Time Series Analysis: Forecasting and Control*. Hoboken, NJ: John Wiley & Sons, Inc.

Brigo, Damiano, Massimo Morini, and Andrea Pallavicini. 2013. *Counterparty Credit Risk, Collateral and Funding: With Pricing Cases for All Asset Classes*. Hoboken, NJ: John Wiley & Sons, Inc.

Burger, Markus, Bernhard Graeber, and Gero Schindlmayr. 2014. *Managing Energy Risk: An Integrated View on Power and Other Energy Markets*. Hoboken, NJ: John Wiley & Sons, Inc.

Cabedo, David J., and Ismael Moya. 2003. "Estimating Oil Price 'Value at Risk' Using the Historical Simulation Approach." *Energy Economics* 25:3, 239–253.

Campbell, Paul, and Michael Prokop. 2016. "Forward Look Top Regulatory Trends for 2016 in Energy." Deloitte. Available at https://www2.deloitte.com/us/en/pages/regulatory/energy-regulatory-outlook.html.

Eydeland, Alexander, and Krzysztof Wolyniec. 2003. *Energy and Power Risk Management: New Developments in Modeling, Pricing, and Hedging*. Hoboken, NJ: John Wiley & Sons, Inc.

Fernandez, Frank A. 1999. *Liquidity Risk: New Approaches to Measurement and Monitoring*. New York, NY: Securities Industry Association.

Global Association of Risk Professionals (GARP). 2008. *Foundations of Energy Risk Management: An Overview of the Energy Sector and Its Physical and Financial Markets*. Hoboken, NJ: John Wiley & Sons, Inc.

Guldimann, Till. 1995. *RiskMetrics—Technical Document*. Morgan Guaranty Trust Company.

Holton, Glyn A. 2009. *Value at Risk: Theory and Practice*. San Diego, CA: Academic Press.

Hull, John C. 2014. *Options, Futures, and Other Derivatives*. Boston, MA: Pearson Education.

International Organization for Standardization (ISO). 2009. "ISO 31000—Risk Management." Available at http://www.iso.org/iso/home/standards/iso31000.htm.

Jacque, Laurent L. 2010. *Global Derivative Debacles: From Theory to Malpractice*. Singapore: World Scientific Publishing Co.

Jorion, Philippe. 2006. *Value at Risk: The New Benchmark for Managing Financial Risk*. New York, NY: McGraw-Hill Education.

Kallman, James W., and Romy V. Maric. 2004. "A Refined Risk Management Paradigm." *Risk Management* 6:3, 57–68.

Kaminsky, Vincent. 2016. *Managing Energy Price Risk*. London: Risk Books.

Linsmeier, Thomas J., and Neil D. Pearson. 2000. "Value at Risk." *Financial Analysts Journal* 56:2, 47–67.

Margrabe, William. 1978. "The Value of an Option to Exchange One Asset for Another." *Journal of Finance* 33:1, 177–186.

McCubbrey, Don. 2016. "What Is Legal Risk?" Available at https://www.boundless.com/users/235420/textbooks/business-fundamentals/international-business-for-the-entrepreneur-14/political-and-legal-risk-in-international-business-57/what-is-legal-risk-258-15561/.

Mello, Antonio S., and John E. Parsons. 1995. "Maturity Structure of a Hedge Matters: Lessons from the Metallgesellschaft Debacle." *Journal of Applied Corporate Finance* 8:1, 106–121.

Professional Risk Managers' International Association (PRMIA). 2016. "China Aviation Oil Case Study." Available at http://www.prmia.org/sites/default/files/references/China_Aviation_Oil_-_090911_v2.pdf.

Sadeghi, Mehdi, and Saeed Shavvalpour. 2006. "Energy Risk Management and Value at Risk Modeling." *Energy Policy* 34:18, 2267–3373.

U.S. Energy Information Administration. 2016. "International Energy Outlook 2016." May. Available at http://www.eia.gov/outlooks/ieo/.

25

Financialization of Commodity Markets

KYLE J. PUTNAM
Assistant Professor, Linfield College

RAMESH ADHIKARI
Assistant Professor, Humboldt State University

Introduction

Since the turn of the millennium, the composition of the participants in the commodity futures markets has changed dramatically. Traditionally, privy investors dominated the marketplace and would earn a risk premium by taking positions opposite of commodity producers and processors. These specialized investors would effectively provide insurance to commodity producers (processors) who were concerned about potential price decreases (increases) in the market (Keynes 1923; Hicks 1939).

However, the early 2000s saw an unprecedented change in investor type and flows to the commodity futures markets (Cheng and Xiong 2014). Financial investors who historically had never been engaged in the marketplace on such a grand scale began to devote large amounts of capital to the commodity markets, spurring rapid growth. The Commodity Futures Trading Commission (CFTC) estimates that between 1998 and 2008 exchange-traded futures and futures options trading volume grew from about 630 million contracts to 3.8 billion contracts, a nearly sixfold increase. Moreover, 2008 Q2 net investment flows to various commodity futures indexes reached roughly \$200 billion (CFTC 2008). Using data from Barclay's Capital, Irwin and Sanders (2011) find that worldwide commodity index investment boomed from about \$50 billion to \$300 billion between 2004 and 2010.

Leading the surge in investment were commodity index traders (CITs)—institutions, such as insurance companies, pension funds, and endowments, that use strategic asset allocation and long-only policies. Between 2000 and 2009 the number of CITs quintupled and the number of hedge funds trading commodity futures more than tripled. To provide some context, over the same time frame, the number of traders involved in the futures markets to merely hedge commodity price risk only increased by 1.5 times (Cheng, Kirilenko, and Xiong 2015). The birth of CITs emerged after the U.S. equity market collapse in 2001. Commodity futures offered investors exposure to "equity-like" returns and diversification benefits due to their low and even negative return correlations with equities (Erb and Harvey 2006; Gorton and Rouwenhorst 2006). The advent of these new types of investors and their increasing role in the operation of the commodity markets is commonly called the *financialization of commodity markets*. Some contend that this financialization altered the fundamental risk and return features of commodity futures.

The financialization of commodity markets has sparked serious concerns among the world's major policy leaders surrounding its impact on market operations. Increased volatility, price bubbles in the energy and food markets, and questions surrounding the accuracy of prices led many pundits to blame the presence of new traders for such consequences. In 2009, a U.S. Senate subcommittee reported on the effects of *excessive speculation* (i.e., speculation in excess of what is required to satisfy hedging demand) in the wheat market. The findings outlined a growing uneasiness about the importance of index traders and their alleged link to increases in the price of grain (U.S. Senate Permanent Subcommittee on Investigations 2009). Moreover, testimony in 2008 by Michael Masters, chief investment officer of Masters Capital Management, LLC, before the Committee on Homeland Security and Governmental Affairs, advocated the idea that financial investors are "unequivocally" contributing to energy and food price inflation, and that speculation in the futures markets caused the 2007–2008 peak in commodity prices that led to considerably higher consumer energy and food costs across the globe (Masters 2008). In fact, following the financial crisis of 2007–2008, also known as the global financial crisis (GFC), the United States introduced regulatory initiatives through the Wall Street Reform and Consumer Protection (Dodd-Frank) Act to promote market transparency and reduce counterparty and operational risk. The Act regulates over-the-counter (OTC) swaps and directs the CFTC to create a smaller and more homogeneous swap market that limits the activity of financial traders.

Despite the evidence and public policy underscoring a direct link between the financialization of commodity markets and the observed futures market changes, a large strand of literature maintains that little systematic evidence supports such views (Irwin, Sanders, and Merrin 2009; Büyükşahin and Harris 2011; Irwin and Sanders 2011; Bhardwaj, Gorton, and Rouwenhorst 2016). Opponents of the financialization theory contend that the influence of CITs and other speculative capital on commodity futures prices poses no substantial concerns, objecting that the fundamentals of supply and demand and variations in business cycle conditions, particularly episodes of severe economic turmoil, can explain the behavior in commodity prices. According to Irwin and Sanders (2011), the commodity markets are not a place where the probability of a bubble is particularly high. Given that futures contracts by their very nature have a limited investment horizon and involve few restrictions on short sales, the potential for bubbles in most theoretical models is predominantly absent. Any drift in prices should be quickly eliminated because few limits to arbitrage in the futures markets exist. Moreover, some related studies suggest that changes in involvement (i.e., increased investor participation) in the marketplace by CITs and hedge funds, or "speculators," cannot fully explain commodity price changes, but the inverse—price changes precipitating position changes—is seemingly more valid.

The remainder of this chapter is organized as follows. The next section provides an overview of the commodity markets and the evolution of its participants. Following that the sections address how financial investors may affect the risk and return features of commodity futures, and discusses the empirical changes in the marketplace in conjunction with the breadth of research on the impact of financialization. The chapter concludes with a brief summary.

Overview of Commodity Markets and Participants

The unique benefits of commodity-related investments drove financial investors to allocate substantial amounts of capital to the markets beginning in the early 2000s. Exposure to the markets can be achieved with ease through two primary mediums: the spot market and the derivatives market. In general, investment in the spot market is a relatively less popular option because of a lack of centralized clearing prices and most investors have little desire to be involved in the delivery of the underlying commodity. The more popular approach, by far, is to invest in the derivatives market consisting of futures, forwards, options, and swaps. This section explores the growth of the commodity derivatives market and its participants.

THE DERIVATIVES MARKET

Generally, financial investors opt to participate in a commodity fund that mimics a popular commodity index. The fund manager will either directly invest in commodity futures or enter into an OTC swap contract, which can be tailored to meet the needs of the particular fund. The swap dealer on the other side of the transaction will enter the futures markets and take positions in the appropriate contracts offsetting the risk of the OTC derivative. An alternative approach is for institutions to avoid using a fund altogether and deal directly with a swap dealer, where once again the swap dealer will take direct offsetting positions in the futures markets (Irwin and Sanders 2011). The unparalleled growth in OTC commodity derivatives trading that occurred after the turn of the millennium is staggering. The scale of the increased size of the OTC markets gives a prominent impression of one of the hallmark changes to the overall commodity markets.

Panel A of Figure 25.1 presents the worldwide notional outstanding amount of OTC forwards, swaps, and options between 1998 and 2015, normalized to 1998 levels. Growth in the notional value of derivative contracts provides a reasonable indication of how fast a market is expanding. The notional value of all open commodity OTC derivative positions increased an explosive 15 times between mid-1998 and 2008. The rise in outstanding contracts was primarily led by commodities outside of the gold and precious metals sectors, although precious metals saw a relatively modest spike around 2008. After the GFC, volume contracted greatly from its peak, with the size of the market shrinking back to the levels of 2005 by year-end 2015. Panel B shows the evolution of the worldwide market value, similarly normalized to 1998 levels, of the aforementioned OTC derivatives. The market value of the derivatives follows a pattern similar to Panel A, reflecting the rapid increase in demand for the securities beginning in the mid-2000s and peaking at nearly 20 times over in 2008.

The organized exchanges concurrently matched the swift expansion of the OTC derivatives market. Yet, while the volume of OTC derivatives trading greatly

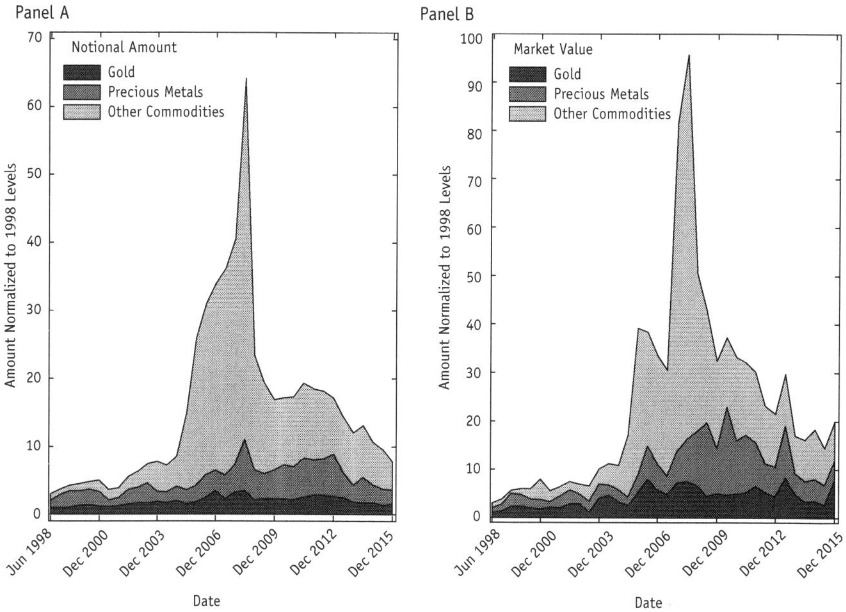

Figure 25.1 Global OTC Derivatives
Panel A shows the notational amount of OTC forwards, swaps, and options outstanding in the world between 1998 and 2015, normalized to 1998 values. Panel B shows the market value of OTC forwards, swaps, and options in the world between 1998 and 2015, normalized to 1998 values. Source: Authors' calculation based on data from Bank for International Settlements.

subsided after the GFC, the trading activity of standardized instruments continued to increase. Zaremba (2015) highlights that after 2000 the commodity derivatives market grew considerably faster than the derivatives market of any other asset class. Figure 25.2 illustrates the weekly trading volume of U.S. commodity futures contracts between 1986 and 2016, normalized to 1986 levels, by commodity sector. The commodity futures within each sector are as follows: foods and fibers (cocoa, coffee, orange juice, sugar #11, cotton #2, and lumber), grains and oilseeds (corn #2, oats, soybeans, soybean meal, soybean oil, and wheat), livestock (feeder cattle, live cattle, lean hogs, and pork bellies), energy (WTI crude oil, heating oil #2, natural gas, unleaded gas, and propane), and precious metals (copper, gold, palladium, platinum, and silver). The disaggregation of overall trading volumes into sectors is of particular interest because it shows which groups exhibited the greatest changes. Overall, each sector displays some degree of growth beginning in either the early or mid-2000s. The energy sector's growth clearly dwarfs that of all other groups, peaking at 45 times its initial level in 2016. The dominance of energy growth is hardly surprising given that crude oil, natural gas, and heating oil are historically some of the most actively traded commodity futures due to their predominant use as resource inputs in the U.S. and other global economies. The grains and oilseeds as well as the foods

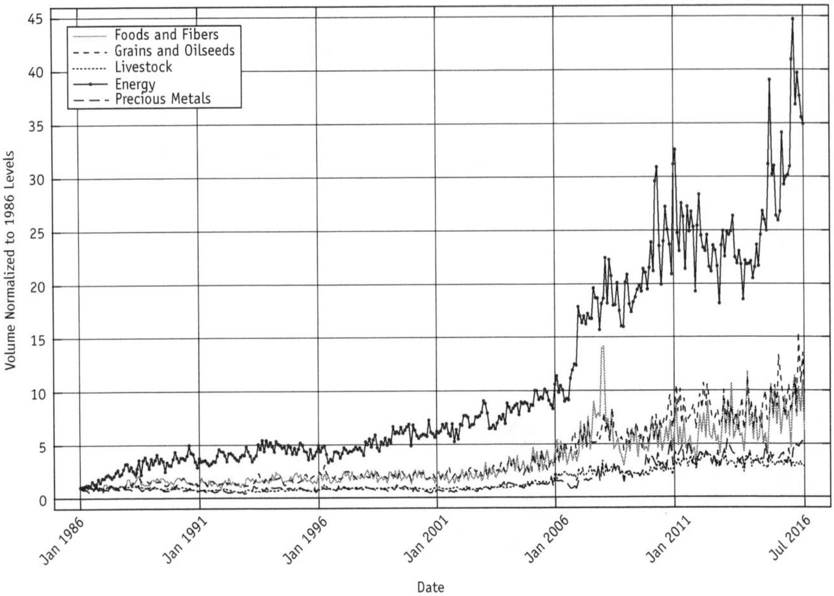

Figure 25.2 Volume by Commodity Sector

This figure shows the aggregate weekly volume for each of the five commodity sectors between 1986 and 2016, normalized to 1986 levels. Source: Authors' calculation based on the data from Commodity Research Bureau (CRB).

and fibers sectors also show a substantial advance in trading volume, although their increase is not nearly the magnitude of energy.

Volume provides a useful gauge of the intensity or pressure behind a particular price trend, but open interest measures the flow of money into a market. Figure 25.3 shows the weekly open interest of U.S. commodity futures contracts between 1986 and 2016, normalized to 1986 levels, by commodity sector. Unsurprisingly, the growth of open interest for the energy sector trumps all other groups once again. A more interesting feature of the energy sector is that it exhibits a clear upward trend since open interest records began in 1986, though the trend becomes much more drastic after 2001. Such a pattern is distinct from the volume data, which have a much more gradual run-up and sharp increase in the mid-2000s. The remaining sectors, excluding precious metals, show a relatively large jump in open interest around year-end 2005 and continue to trend up into 2016, with the exception of livestock, which began to dip in 2014.

COMPOSITION OF MARKET PARTICIPANTS

A rise in involvement by financial investors accompanied the increased activity in the futures markets post-2000. Such investors are colloquially known as *speculators* because their primary objective is to realize investment profits and they are typically

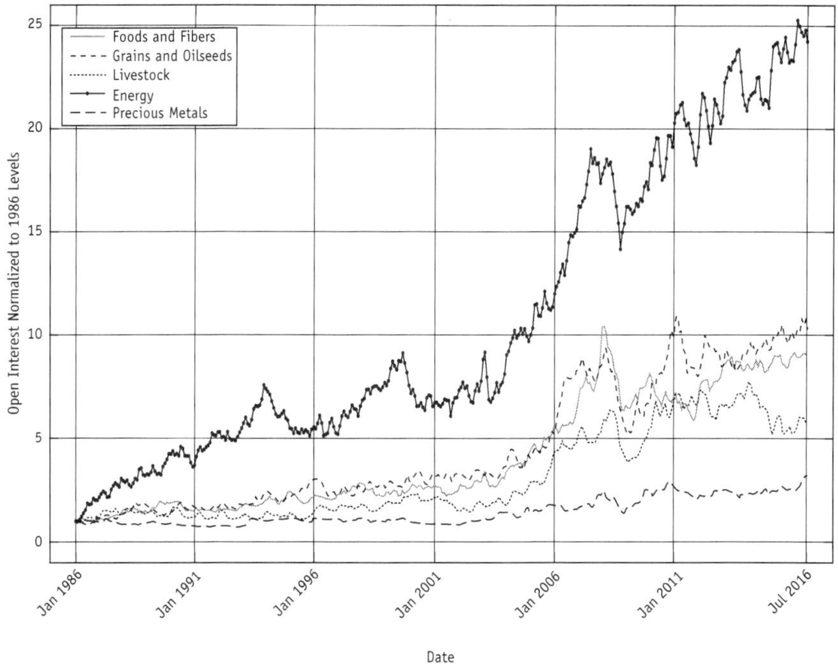

Figure 25.3 Open Interest by Commodity Sector
This figure shows the aggregate weekly open interest for each of the five commodity sectors between 1986 and 2016, normalized to 1986 levels. Source: Authors' calculation based on data from Commodity Research Bureau (CRB).

not engaged in the production or consumption-side business activities associated with the commodities.

The CFTC, as the regulator of the futures and swaps markets, divides large traders into two distinct groups—commercial and noncommercial—and records their positions in the weekly Commitments of Traders (COT) report. Generally, traders are classified as commercial participants if they use futures contracts in a particular commodity for hedging business activities, and are classified as noncommercial participants otherwise. Although one cannot be classified as both a commercial and noncommercial trader in the same commodity, the issue is complicated by the fact that a trader can be classified as commercial in some commodities and noncommercial in others—as is common in multifunctional organizations with numerous trading arms. To further complicate the issue, a third category exists for "non-reportables," which do not meet the position size required by the CFTC for reporting purposes. This category of traders is often referred to as "small speculators," although the number of traders involved and their true classification (commercial vs. noncommercial) is unknown. Though inherently complex, the CFTC's simple division of its market participants provides some intuitive insight into the structure and changes of the commodity futures markets and its investors.

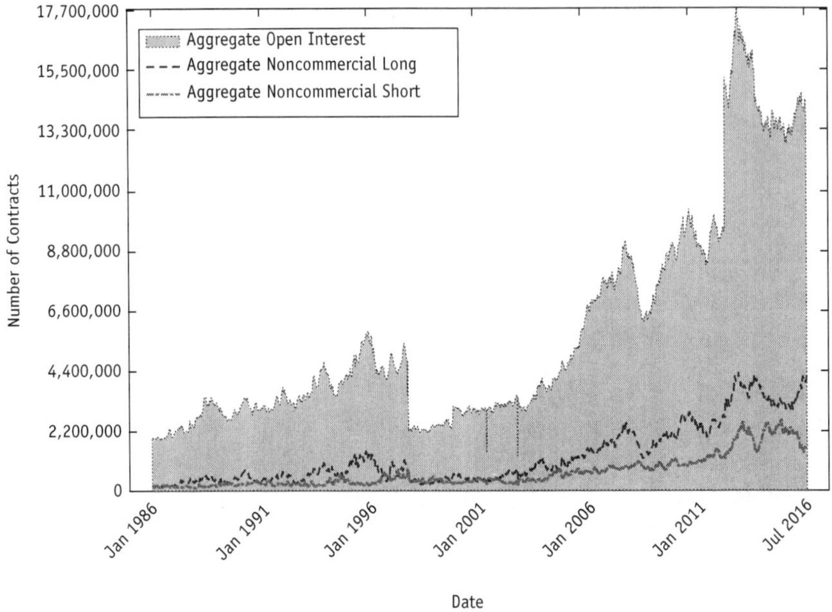

Figure 25.4 Noncommercial Open Interest
This figure shows the aggregate open interest, noncommercial long, and noncommercial short positions across the entire U.S. marketplace between 1986 and 2016. Source: Authors' calculation based on data from Commodity Futures Trading Commission (CFTC).

The growth in noncommercial investors can best be viewed through the lens of open interest because it links the idea of money flow to the positions taken. Figure 25.4 shows the aggregate noncommercial long and short positions plotted against aggregate commodity futures markets open interest in the U.S. marketplace. Post-2000, as open interest growth began to boom, so did aggregate positions in the futures markets for noncommercial participants. This growth is particularly true for the long positions, which generally represent investors such as CITs and to a lesser extent hedge funds. Noncommercial long positions as a percentage of total open interest approximately tripled between 2001 and 2016, when much of the growth took place, increasing from about 11 to 31 percent. Figure 25.5 shows the aggregation of all long and short positions of noncommercial traders for each of the five commodity sectors between 1986 and 2016, normalized to 2001 values. The number of noncommercial large futures traders markedly rose for all sectors beginning in the early 2000s. The energy sector, as alluded to earlier, is admittedly a special case as investor involvement far surpasses that of all other groups. Nevertheless, a clear upward trend is evident in all sectors. In fact, between 1986 and 2013, the aggregate number of open positions held by commercial investors has trended down while the aggregate number of open positions for noncommercial investors has trended up. The net effect

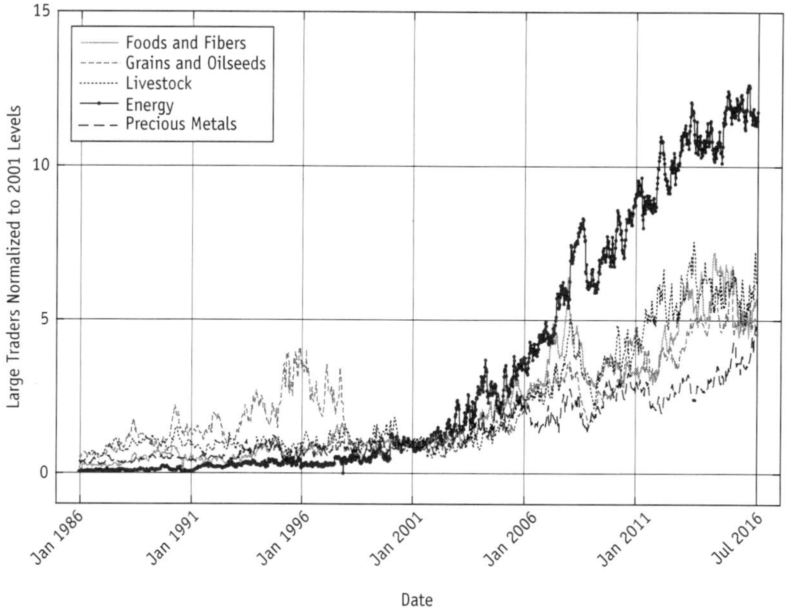

Figure 25.5 Positions of Large Traders by Commodity Sector
This figure shows the aggregate long and short positions of noncommercial participants for each of the five commodity sectors between 1986 and 2016, normalized to 2001 levels. Source: Authors' calculation based on data from Commodity Futures Trading Commission (CFTC).

has been an unprecedented increase in market share of around 22 percent for non-commercial participants (Zaremba 2014).

CITs and Index Fund Investment

CITs are a relatively new and controversial class of investors in the commodity futures markets. Their emergence in the early 2000s brought a whole new set of investment vehicles such as index funds, exchange-traded funds (ETFs), and exchange-traded notes (ETNs) to the world of commodities and provided easy access for investors to the asset class's unique investment properties. One of the primary concerns expressed about CITs is that they represent such a large portion of futures trading that the size of their positions may distort commodity prices and cross-market price linkages. Stoll and Whaley (2010) note that index investors have held almost half of open interest in agricultural commodity futures in recent years. As Sanders, Irwin, and Merrin (2008) report, index traders held more than 20 percent of the open interest in the live cattle, lean hogs, and Chicago Board of Trade (CBOT) wheat markets. Additionally, index fund investment generally holds a disproportionate share of the long side of the commodity markets due to the nature of their investment strategy. Sanders and Irwin (2010) find that the percentage of commodities held by index funds varies widely from one commodity market to the next, documenting a range from 12 percent (cocoa futures) to 47 percent (live cattle futures).

Due to the concerns arising from increasing capital flows to index investment, the CFTC began reporting the positions held by index traders in 2006 as a supplement to its traditional COT reports. Trying to disaggregate the commercial and noncommercial level data into index trader positions is challenging in practice and the CFTC admits that its classification procedure is not completely accurate. The CFTC notes that some traders categorized as "index traders" are concurrently engaged in other futures activity that cannot be disaggregated. Similarly, traders involved in index trading that does not constitute a major portion of their activities will fail to be included in the "index traders" categorization. Panel A of Figure 25.6 presents the aggregate notional value of index investment between 2007 and 2015. Following the GFC, the net long value peaks in mid-2010 at about $255 billion before steadily declining back to 2007 levels. Panels B, C, and D show the CIT open interest, long, and short positions held across the nine U.S. agriculture commodities between 2006 and 2016, respectively. Overall, open interest in the agricultural markets has continued to trend upward following the GFC, reaching about 7 million contracts in 2016. Long positions have been somewhat stable, hovering between $1.2 million and $1.8 million between 2009 and 2016, while short positions have seen about a 50 percent reduction since their 2010 peak.

Cheng et al. (2015) try to get a more accurate view of participant characteristics by exploiting the CFTC's proprietary Large Trader Reporting System (LTRS) database, as traders in the LTRS account for around 70 to 90 percent of open interest in a given commodity futures contract. The authors' classification of traders based on their position-level data reveals several salient features about the evolution of the futures markets and the role of CITs and other participants. After 2004, the median notional net long CIT investment jumped from $352.94 million to a staggering $2.33 billion in 2010. Similarly, traders whose positions classify them as a hybrid of index traders and hedge funds (CIT-HFs) saw a near doubling of median notional net long positions from $388.17 to $725.79 million. Interestingly, the total number of CITs is relatively few despite their large net positions: only four in 2000 and 18 in 2010. The number of CIT-HFs in 2010 is even fewer with only 14. To provide some context, the number of commercial hedgers grew from 810 in 2000 to almost 1,500 in 2010. Despite the relatively large number of entities, the commercial hedgers recorded just a fraction of the median notional net positions of CITs and CIT-HFs, with net short positions of $7.13 million and net long positions of $1.36 million, respectively.

How Financial Investors Affect Risk

The fact that the commodity markets experienced substantial growth in investor participation since 2001 is apparent. Yet, the economic channels through which this growth is presumed to have affected commodity risk and return features are less obvious. This section explores the economic mechanisms through which investor participation can influence the commodity markets in addition to the theoretical impact of financialization on commodity futures characteristics.

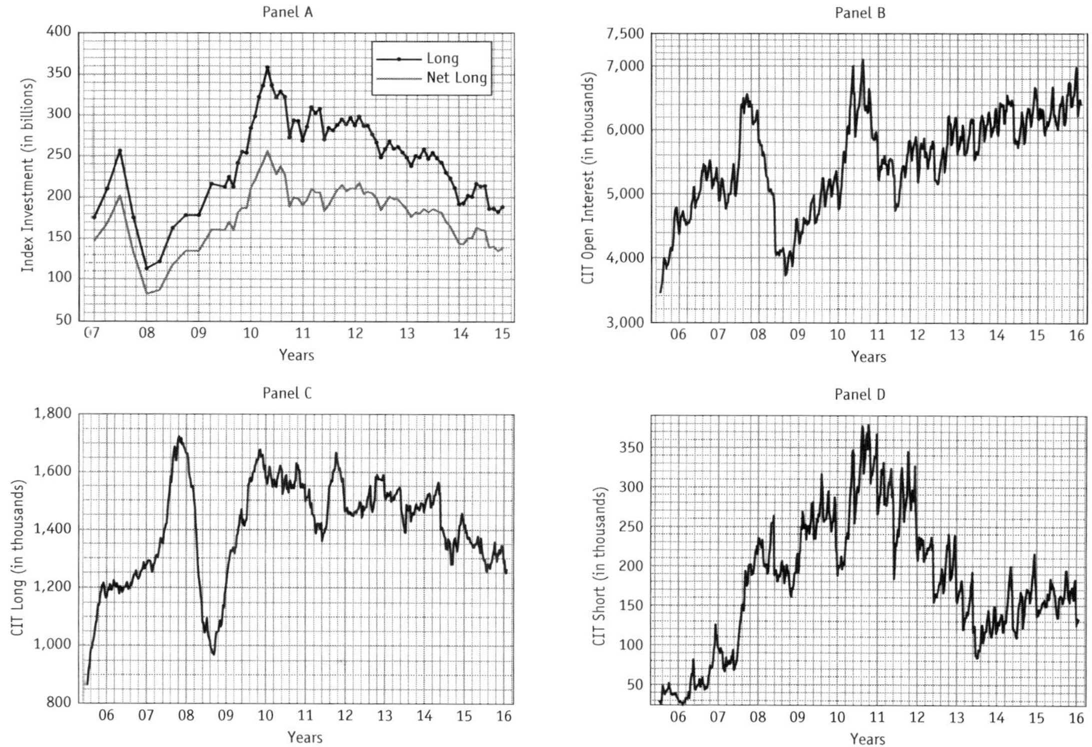

Figure 25.6 Index Investment and Agricultural CIT Positions

Panel A shows the aggregate notional long and net long values of index investments between 2007 and 2015. Panels B, C, and D show the open interest, long, and short positions held by CITs across nine U.S. agriculture commodities between 2006 and 2016, respectively. Source: Authors' calculation based on data from Commodity Futures Trading Commission (CFTC).

ECONOMIC TRANSMISSION MECHANISMS

Cheng and Xiong (2014) explore the underpinning economic mechanisms of storage, risk sharing, and information discovery as the means through which futures markets trading may influence prices. Empirical evidence suggests the latter two functions have been transformed by the financialization of the commodity markets, and these mechanisms are examined in this section. First, the idea of risk sharing is most easily conceptualized through the window of the long-standing hedging pressure theory of Keynes (1923) and Hicks (1939). The theory suggests hedgers are typically short in their futures positions and offer a positive risk premium to attract speculators on the opposite (long) side to mitigate risk. Financial investors can affect the commodity markets through this risk-sharing mechanism by way of dual roles as liquidity providers and consumers. For instance, with many investors naturally being brought to the long side of the transaction, financialization serves to improve the prospects of risk sharing and mitigate hedging pressure as the new market participants act as liquidity providers (Tang and Xiong 2012). However, as put forth by Acharya, Lochstoer, and Ramadorai (2013), these same investors have time-varying risk appetites, which are a byproduct of constraints and financial distress, and thus can also have an inverse effect on liquidity. For instance, financial investors may have to reverse their long commodity positions in order to ease risk exposure because of an unexpected price drop in the equity markets. These market participants then act as consumers of liquidity, and subsequently transmit price shocks to the commodity markets. Such volatility spillovers from outside the commodity markets, resulting from either portfolio changes or rebalancing, can also cause futures prices to become more correlated with each other and with competing asset classes (Tang and Xiong 2012). Cheng et al. (2015) find supporting evidence that CITs and hedge funds react negatively during times of financial distress and transmit the flow of risk away from themselves back toward commercial hedgers. This reallocation of risk, conditional on trades initiated by CITs and hedge funds, confirms the impact of financial investors on the commodity markets. Additionally, the findings motivate a valid extension of the traditional hedging pressure theory that should incorporate the time-varying risk capacities of financial investors.

Second, financialization can affect the information discovery process because of its contribution to frictions in the global supply/demand and inventory information levels. Singleton (2013) emphasizes that the informational frictions associated with "speculative activity" can induce prices to drift from their fundamental values and result in booms and busts. Moreover, in the face of such frictions, heterogeneous beliefs among financial investors may affect expected rates of return as well as inventory responses during associated commodity price booms. As discussed in Cheng and Xiong (2014), an increase in prices accompanied by the typical increase in inventory assumes traders can distinguish between price increases prompted by economic fundamentals and those prompted by speculation. However, in the presence of informational frictions, this assumption may be impractical; speculation may distort the price discovery mechanism and create non-fundamental transitory booms without the typical inventory response. Fattouh, Kilian, and Mahadeva (2013) reach similar conclusions studying oil inventory data.

THEORETICAL PREDICTIONS

The empirical literature on the financialization of commodity markets is replete with evidence contributing to the policy debate on its economic impact. The theoretical literature on the subject is much sparser. Recent research that models the theoretical implications of financialization is discussed below. First, Sockin and Xiong (2015) examine the effects of informational frictions on the commodity markets. They develop a model with a tractable log-linear equilibrium and demonstrate that noise brought on by financial investors trading in the futures markets can feed back into the demand of final goods producers. The producers then cannot accurately differentiate whether prices are moving because of investor trading or changes in global fundamentals. The analysis illuminates the weakness, common to empirical studies, in assuming that different types of shocks are directly observable to all market participants and that the effects of the shocks are homogenous. In fact, the authors show that supply shocks are often understated and demand shocks overstated. The findings also caution against the common empirical practice of using inventory to detect speculative effects, as previously discussed.

Second, Baker (2016) constructs a dynamic equilibrium model with heterogeneous risk-averse agents in an effort to explain how financialization may impact the futures prices of storable commodities. As a consequence of financialization, the modeled transaction costs to the household agents engaged in the futures markets are reduced. The framework implies that financialization significantly reduces both expected excess returns and the frequency of the futures curve in backwardation. The findings also suggest an increased correlation between futures open interest and spot prices, and implies an increased volatility of futures prices.

Third, Basak and Pavlova (2016) develop a robust theoretical framework that models the effects of institutions on all commodity futures prices. They consider a multi-good, multi-asset dynamic model economy comprised of both institutional investors and standard futures market participants. The model posits that institutional financial investors care about performance relative to a commodity index because their investment performance is evaluated relative to such a benchmark. Institutional investors do not like poor performance when their respective benchmark index is performing well, and so have an extra incentive to do well when the benchmark is doing well.

Comparing the model economy with an identical benchmark economy that has no institutional investors captures three potential effects from financialization. First, the prices of all commodity futures increase with financialization. The price increases tend to be higher for commodity futures that are part of an index than for those that are non-indexed. The result occurs because institutions make every effort not to lag behind a well-performing index. Hence, financial institutions value assets that pay off more in high-index states than low-index states. Moreover, a strong positive relation exists between the size of the institutional investors and the pricing effect. Second, the volatilities of indexed and non-indexed commodity futures returns increase with financialization, although the volatilities of indexed futures tend to increase more. In an economy without financial institutions, only two sources of risk are likely to exist: supply and demand. In an economy with institutional investors, participants also face the risk of falling behind the performance of the index. Such risk is reflected in the futures prices and increases the volatilities of returns. Third, equity-commodity correlations and correlations among commodity futures increase with financialization. Benchmarking institutions to a commodity index is argued to lead to the emergence of the index as a common factor in returns for both commodity futures and equities. In equilibrium, all assets load positively on the new factor, and hence increase the covariance and correlations of the asset classes. The commodity futures belonging to the index are generally more sensitive to the common factor and accordingly their covariance and correlations increase more so than for the non-indexed commodity futures.

Impact of Financialization

Numerous empirical studies examine the impact of financialization on commodity markets, but the results are wide ranging and mixed. Haase, Zimmerman, and Zimmerman (2016) review 100 empirical research papers that examine the effects from financialization on commodity markets. They categorize the studies based on six focus variables that financialization is hypothesized to have affected: prices, returns, risk premiums, spreads, volatilities, and spillover effects. In general, they find evidence points toward financialization as having a significantly positive or reinforcing impact on prices; a negative or weakening impact on returns and risk premiums; and a relatively mixed impact on spreads, volatility, and spillovers.

Although the number of studies supporting versus contradicting the effects of financialization are nearly equal, the specification of the speculation variable used in the analyses seems to influence the findings. Specifically, if studies use an indirect or proxy variable for speculation, the majority of evidence shows positive, reinforcing effects from financialization. On the contrary, if studies measure speculation directly, the distribution of weights shifts and many studies document negative, weakening effects from financialization. This section focuses on critically reviewing the findings of major empirical studies both in favor of and against the impact of financialization on commodity markets, while providing an overview of the changes in the marketplace.

PRICES, RETURNS, AND VOLATILITIES

Table 25.1 provides a broad overview of the commodity markets. It reports summary statistics for each of the five commodity sectors over the pre-financialization period (i.e., January 1986–December 2000) and financialization period (i.e., January 2001–July 2016). Interestingly, the financialization literature lacks a complete consensus on when financialization actually began. Many studies use the 2001–2004 time frame as a breakpoint. However, only a general agreement supports that financialization started in the early 2000s. Several interesting features emerge from Table 25.1. For example, average returns for all sectors, except livestock, are higher in the financialization era. Standard deviations for all sectors exhibit a similar pattern. In general, an improvement occurs in risk-adjusted measures (i.e., the adjusted Sharpe ratio and M^2) and the cumulative return measure in the financialization era, where livestock again is the exception.

Table 25.1 **Descriptive Statistics by Commodity Sector**

Descriptive	*Foods and Fibers (%)*	*Grains and Oilseeds (%)*	*Livestock (%)*	*Energy (%)*	*Precious Metals (%)*
Jan. 1986–Dec. 2000					
Arithmetic mean	0.92	−4.02	9.65	1.32	1.06
Geometric mean	0.41	−5.19	8.03	0.43	−0.25
Standard deviation	10.16	15.31	18.08	13.28	16.26
Skewness	29.57	47.41	52.04	−21.59	29.49
Kurtosis	112.65	95.85	256.76	294.84	161.80
Adjusted Sharpe ratio	−1.65	−32.34	48.17	1.72	−0.15
Cumulative return	13.82	−60.47	145.15	19.78	15.98
CAPM alpha	0.83	−3.46	9.12	1.40	1.14
CAPM beta	3.83	−24.92	23.92	−3.78	−3.46
M^2	1.04	0.03	2.58	1.14	1.08
Tracking error	10.61	15.79	18.23	13.68	16.58
Jan. 2001–Jul. 2016					
Arithmetic mean	7.30	8.16	1.79	7.83	5.41
Geometric mean	6.59	6.44	−0.35	6.14	3.15
Standard deviation	11.87	18.54	20.63	18.26	21.33
Skewness	−30.22	−7.04	−17.21	−68.32	25.14
Kurtosis	148.05	106.58	77.19	259.52	82.02
Adjusted Sharpe ratio	56.02	41.91	7.23	38.58	24.21
Cumulative return	114.13	127.59	27.93	122.41	84.62
CAPM alpha	6.76	7.10	0.58	6.67	4.16
CAPM beta	37.49	73.63	83.96	80.73	86.98
M^2	2.52	1.89	0.56	1.85	1.20
Tracking error	12.02	18.35	20.39	18.02	21.08

Note: This table displays the annualized values of five commodity sectors split into two sample periods: (1) pre-financialization (January 1986 to December 2000) and (2) financialization (January 2001 to July 2016).

Source: Authors' calculation based on data from the Commodity Research Bureau (CRB).

A simple plot of normalized average prices by commodity sector, as seen in Figure 25.7, shows a reasonably strong upward trend beginning in the early 2000s for the majority of groups. In fact, prices rose to four times their average pre-2000 levels beginning in 2011, before declining in subsequent years. This observed price increase as a consequence of rising participation by financial investors has empirical support from Singleton (2013), who explores the crude oil futures markets and finds investor flows have a positive and significant effect on prices. The largest impact on the futures prices, owing to informational frictions, comes from money-managed accounts and growth rates of index positions around the 2008 boom and bust cycle in the oil markets. Henderson, Pearson, and Wang (2014) reach a similar conclusion about the impact of financialization on commodity prices through a unique analysis of OTC commodity-linked notes (CLNs) between 2003 and 2014. Generally, financial institutions hedge their CLN obligations by taking long positions in the commodity futures markets or commodity swaps. These trades and their subsequent reversals link the investors' demands for commodity exposure to the futures markets. Evidence indicates that such hedge trades have a significantly positive impact on futures prices around the pricing dates of the CLNs and a significantly negative impact on prices around the determination dates, when the trades are unwound. The findings highlight that the CLNs investment flows, which do not convey information about pricing fundamentals, still affect prices. The multi-faceted analysis by Cheng et al. (2015) also supports such price consequences. They document that substantial price drops in almost all commodity markets accompany negative position responses by CITs and hedge funds to increases in the VIX volatility index beginning September 2008.

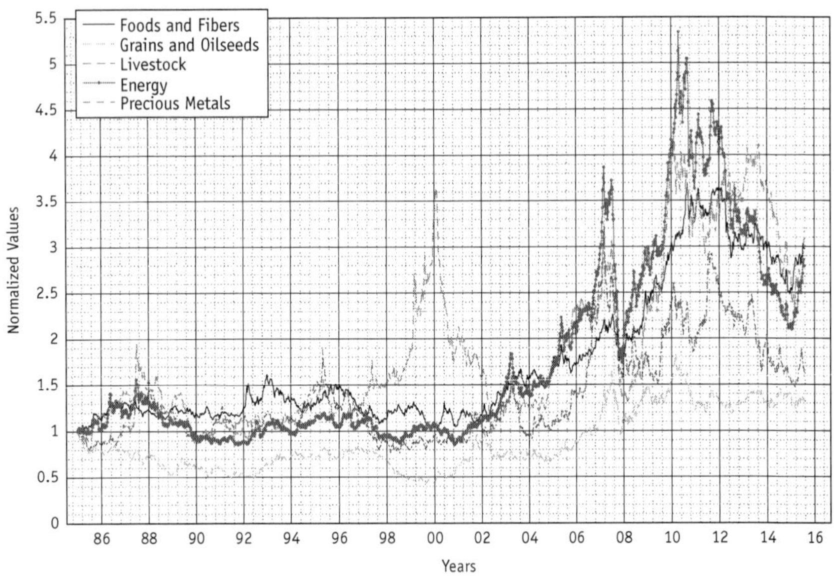

Figure 25.7 Average Prices by Sector

This figure shows the equally-weighted average prices for each of the five commodity sectors between 1986 and 2016, normalized to 1986 prices. Source: Authors' calculation based on data from Commodity Research Bureau (CRB).

Using price information to calculate returns, Figure 25.8 plots the cumulative weekly excess returns of the commodity markets as proxied by the S&P Goldman Sachs Commodity Index (S&P GSCI) and an equally-weighted commodity index. An upward trend is evident beginning in the early 2000s, before a large drop and subsequent recovery after the GFC. Adhikari, Putnam, and Maroney (2016) explicitly analyze commodity futures returns before and after the rise in market participation and note the impact of financialization has been to raise expected returns about 5.5 percent. They find that in the financialization era, returns are quite volatile and have experienced a dramatic shift in exposure to U.S. equity, foreign exchange, and world value, thereby increasing positive loadings on these factors.

Figure 25.9 partitions the excess returns by commodity sector to provide a more in-depth picture of the markets. In the mid-2000s excess returns began to rise rapidly, particularly for the precious metals and energy sectors, and all have remained well above their historical averages into the most recent period.

Figure 25.10 plots the average unconditional (rolling) and conditional (GJR-GARCH) standard deviations of the commodity futures markets. The figure shows a clear volatility spike around 2007, which persists through 2009 before declining to long-run averages. The volatility peak is consistent with the initial run-up in commodity prices viewed in Figure 25.7 and the subsequent GFC.

Silvennoinen and Thorp (2010) analyze commodity bivariate conditional volatility from 1990 to 2009 and find that financial traders' positions influence

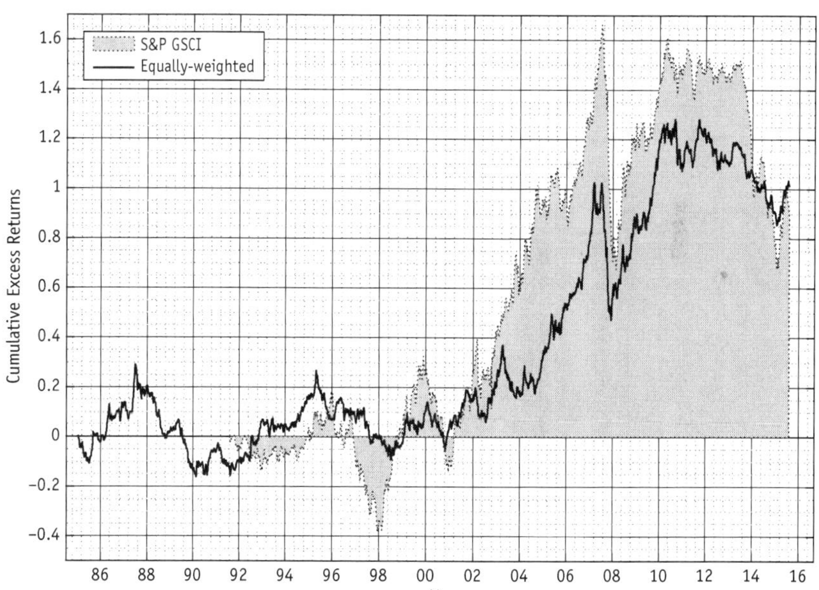

Figure 25.8 Cumulative Weekly Returns

This figure shows the cumulative weekly returns of the commodity markets proxied by the S&P 500 Goldman Sachs Commodity Index (GSCI) and an equally-weighted index of commodity futures between January 1986 and July 2016. Source: Authors' calculation based on data from Commodity Research Bureau (CRB).

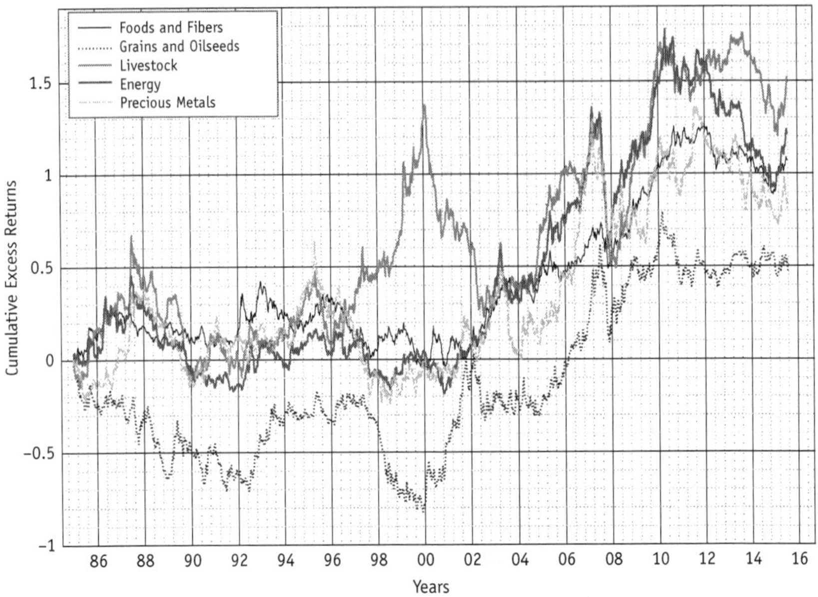

Figure 25.9 Cumulative Weekly Returns by Commodity Sector
This figure shows the cumulative weekly returns for each of the five commodity sectors between January 1986 and July 2016. Source: Authors' calculation based on data from Commodity Research Bureau (CRB).

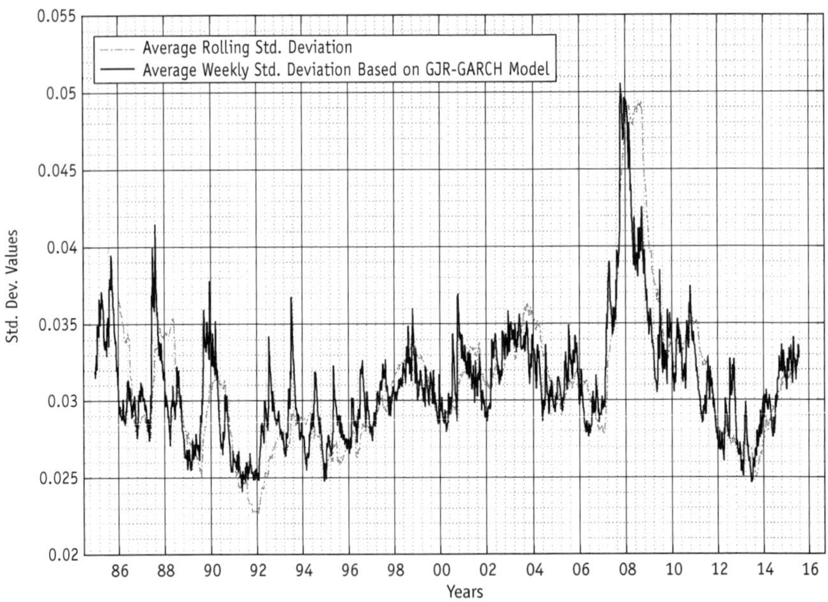

Figure 25.10 Average Standard Deviations of Commodity Futures
This figure shows the average unconditional and conditional standard deviations (volatility) of commodity futures between 1986 and 2016. Source: Authors' calculation based on data from Commodity Research Bureau (CRB).

volatility—specifically, an increase in the percentage of noncommercial short open interest increases futures price volatility. However, the impact of an increase in long open interest on volatility varies between markets. They also confirm significant positive volatility spillovers from a set of common financial factors (e.g., VIX, exchange rate, short sales, and spreads) for commodities that are a part of the S&P GSCI. In a similar vein of work, the findings of Adams and Gluck (2015) suggest the majority of volatility spillovers are attributed to a *style effect*, which is the practice of commodity index traders buying and selling commodities and equities together. The authors note that the spillovers are unidirectional (i.e., stocks affect commodities only) and that stock market shocks did not transmit to the commodity markets before the GFC, but that substantial spillovers occurred after September 2008 due to the increased role of CITs. Notably, Tang and Xiong (2012) find that non-energy-indexed commodities of the S&P GSCI and Dow Jones UBS Commodity Index (DJ-UBSCI) show much greater volatility increases than non-energy non-indexed commodities from 2004 through 2011. Their findings are consistent with a spillover effect by commodity index investors. That is, they find that the spillover of oil price volatility through index investment contributed greatly to the volatility increase of non-energy-indexed commodities, particularly between 2007 and 2008.

CORRELATIONS AND DIVERSIFICATION

Arguably, one of the more prominent effects of financialization has been the increase in intra- and intermarket return correlations. Figure 25.11 plots the average

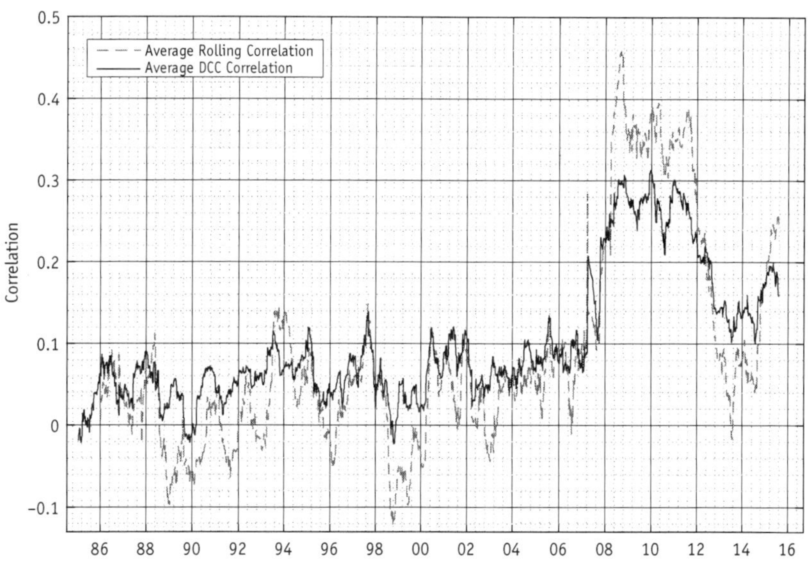

Figure 25.11 Average Return Correlations of Commodity Futures with the S&P 500 Index

This figure shows the average unconditional and conditional return correlations of commodity futures with the equity markets between 1986 and 2016. Source: Authors' calculation based on data from Commodity Research Bureau (CRB).

unconditional (rolling) and conditional (dynamic conditional correlations, DCC) correlations of commodities with the S&P 500 index. The rise in equity-commodity correlations remained at record highs through 2012 before decreasing sharply and flattening out above long-term averages.

Silvennoinen and Thorp (2010) report a general increase in dynamic correlations between 1990 and 2009 for commodity futures and U.S. equity. They document a rise in average correlations from about zero to 0.50, beginning around 2000, favoring the idea of financial market integration. The authors also note an increasing integration between the energy and agricultural futures markets. Extending this line of research, Büyükşahin and Robe (2014) find that correlations between commodity and equity indexes rise amid greater participation by hedge funds that are engaged in both the equity and commodity markets. However, a similar association does not seem to hold for either CITs or swap dealers. Although the results are not fully supportive of the effects of financialization, the findings underscore that who trades in the marketplace matters.

Tang and Xiong (2012) address the pattern of rising co-movement between individual commodity futures between 1998 and 2011. They find that the futures prices of non-energy commodities are much more correlated with oil prices after 2004, and that the increase is more pronounced for indexed commodities than non-indexed commodities. Provided that oil generally carries the greatest weight in a commodity index and that energy and non-energy commodity futures have no economic rationale to strongly comove, Tang and Xiong contend that the pronounced increase in correlations concurrent with the rapid growth of index investment is a reflection of the financialization process.

Figure 25.12 plots the average unconditional (rolling) and conditional (DCC) correlations of commodity futures with crude oil. The steady rise and peak of correlations from 2004 through 2011 is apparent. Of some interest to the financialization debate is the subsequent decrease beginning in 2012 and appearance of a return toward long-run averages thereafter.

The rise in equity-commodity correlations is of central importance because it implies reduced diversification benefits from investing in commodity futures. Adhikari et al. (2016) examine the diversification benefits of commodity portfolios in light of the financialization of the markets. They find the diversification benefits of adding commodity futures to a reference portfolio of assets still persists. In particular, they note that incorporating portfolios of commodity futures into a reference portfolio of U.S. equity and bonds is significantly higher than combining them with a globally diversified reference portfolio, particularly since 2001. The findings underscore the effects of the increased exposure of commodity futures to international factors, such as equity and foreign exchange rates. Similar research by Lundstrom and Visvanathar (2015) examining the addition of non-energy commodity indexes to a portfolio of stocks and bonds in the financialized era provides more varied results. Although mixed, the findings imply that for a minimum variance investor, diversification benefits have declined, but for a Sharpe ratio maximizer, the diversification benefits have increased.

Panels A through D of Figure 25.13 show efficient frontier plots to visualize the potential diversification benefits from sector-wise futures investment. An upward

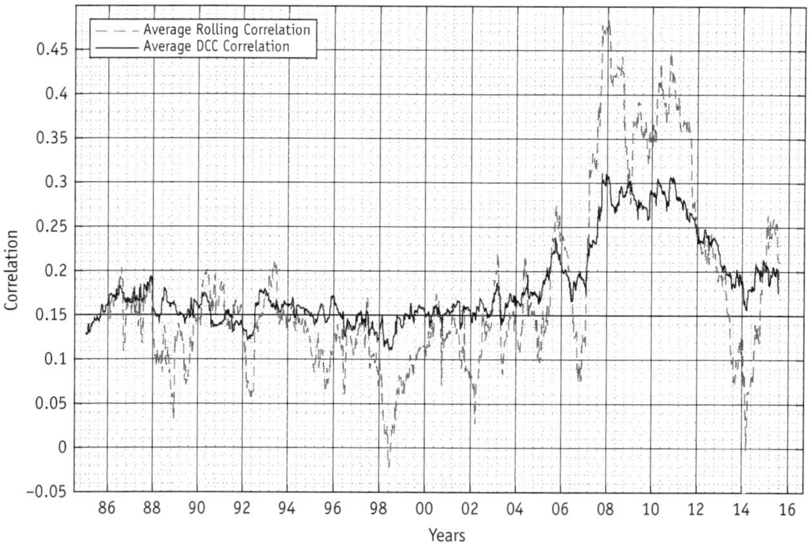

Figure 25.12 Average Return Correlations of Commodity Futures with Crude Oil This figure shows the average unconditional and conditional return correlations of commodity futures with crude oil between 1986 and 2016. Source: Authors' calculation based on data from Commodity Research Bureau (CRB).

shift in the efficient frontier occurs when the addition of a portfolio of commodity futures to a well-diversified portfolio of U.S. and international equity, bonds, and foreign currency provides diversification benefits. Panels A, B, and D of Figure 25.13 show an upward shift from adding the foods and fibers, grains and oilseeds, or energy sectors to the reference portfolio, respectively, despite the financialization of the markets. The livestock sector fails to provide any diversification benefits.

EVIDENCE OPPOSING THE IMPACT OF FINANCIALIZATION

Not all research finds that the aforementioned changes in the commodity markets are a by-product of increased market participation. In fact, Irwin et al. (2009) contend that little systematic evidence is available linking financialization to a change in the risk and return properties of commodity futures. They maintain that arguments favoring such a link are conceptually flawed and reflect a misunderstanding of how the futures markets work. Moreover, the authors highlight the historical pattern of attacks that speculation undergoes during times of extreme market turbulence, such as the GFC. Likewise, Irwin and Sanders (2011) broadly put forth that many of the studies finding a significant impact from financialization are subject to various criticisms about data, methodologies, and assumptions, which call into doubt the validity of the results. They highlight the complexity of the market dynamics, which are difficult to disentangle in the data, noting the assumption that hedgers only engage in the commodity futures markets to avoid risk and

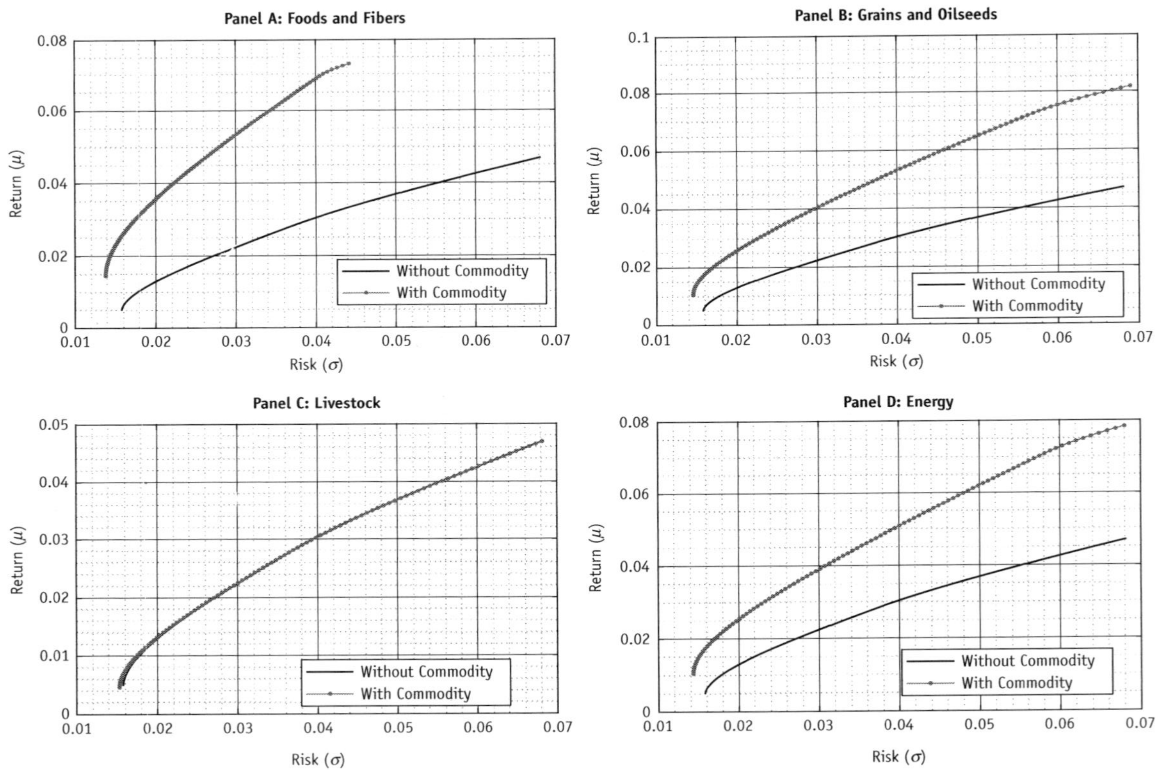

Figure 25.13 Commodity Efficient Frontiers by Sector
This figure shows the shift in the efficient frontier for a portfolio of traditional assets (composed of U.S. equity, world equity, U.S. Treasury bonds, and a dollar index) when combined with a portfolio of sector-wise commodity futures during the financialization period between January 2001 and July 2016. Source: Authors' calculation based on data from Commodity Research Bureau (CRB).

speculators only enter it as pure risk-seekers ignores the multifaceted interplay of the various participants.

Empirically, Sanders and Irwin (2011a) use CFTC data on swap dealers and find little evidence that their net positions aid in predicting weekly returns for a sample of agricultural and energy commodity futures contracts between 2006 and 2009. Similarly, Sanders and Irwin (2011b) explore supplementary CFTC data, which categorizes the net position changes of CITs, and still find that such changes fail to predict weekly returns in the corn and wheat markets. However, they find some predictive evidence for soybeans. Expanding the aforementioned studies, Irwin and Sanders (2012) use quarterly index investment data and apply a cross-sectional approach across position-level data for a range of 19 commodities to examine the impact of CIT investment on commodity prices. Their aggregate findings show little evidence that changes in index positions affect market returns or volatility between 2008 and 2011. The findings of Brunetti, Büyükşahin, and Harris (2016) mirror the aggregate conclusions of Irwin and Sanders (2011, 2012). After examining position level data on merchants, manufacturers, floor brokers, swap dealers, and hedge funds, they find that changes in net positions in all the groups fails to predict changes in futures prices across the crude oil, natural gas, and corn markets since 2005.

Büyükşahin and Harris (2011) employ a series of causality tests that analyze the lead/lag relations between price and positions of noncommercial participants. Interestingly, they find little evidence that hedge funds and other similar-type participants' position changes cause futures price changes, but instead point to results that suggest price changes induce position changes. Along these lines, Irwin et al. (2009) reason that one of the major inconsistencies in explaining why long-only index traders are responsible for futures price increases is that the increase did not occur uniformly across all commodity markets. Their cross-sectional tests of the relative size of index positions against subsequent returns show significant positive correlations in only one of 12 models examined, thus providing meager evidence supporting the impact of index fund positions on returns.

Sanders and Irwin (2013) investigate the accuracy of the mapping algorithm employed in various capacities, such as Masters (2008) and Singleton (2013), that measures index positions and their impact on commodity prices. Analyzing the crude oil futures markets, they conclude that the procedure generates unreliable data. That is, imputed data may contain extremely large absolute errors, which require viewing the results with caution. Yan, Irwin, and Sanders (2016) reach similar conclusions about the data procedure.

More recently, Bhardwaj et al. (2016) take a unique approach to examining the magnitude of the effects on the commodity futures markets over the last decade by benchmarking the experience against its previous 45-year history. They contend that variation in business cycle conditions and not financialization explains the changes observed in commodity prices since 2005. The increase in equity-commodity return correlations are merely an artifact of the business cycle—peaking during periods of severe economic turmoil—and have since returned to their long-run average after the GFC. Although speculative interest has grown since 2000, Bhardwaj et al. note that the proportion between noncommercial and commercial interest has remained relatively stable. Moreover, the calculated annual risk premium of 3.67 percent is both close to its historical average and consistent with the fundamental economic function of the futures markets.

Summary and Conclusions

Commodity market participation and investor flows changed substantially beginning in the early 2000s, but the debate over whether the financialization of commodity markets fundamentally affected the features of the futures markets is still ongoing and seems far from settled. Mixed results largely occur from the various focus and speculation variables used in analyses, sample periods examined, and statistical procedures employed. Interestingly, visual inspection of various plots of prices, volatility, and correlations show a change in behavior beginning around 2012, which seems to be consistent with long-term averages, despite the continued presence of index investors. Regardless of the observed changes the commodity markets have undergone, investment in futures still appears to be a valuable diversification tool for portfolios and has the potential to provide substantial returns.

Discussion Questions

1. Explain the meaning of the financialization of commodity markets.
2. Discuss the major types of participants in the commodity futures markets.
3. Discuss how the rise in investor participation may affect the commodity futures markets.
4. Summarize the empirical evidence on the impact of financialization.

References

Acharya, Viral V., Lars A. Lochstoer, and Tarun Ramadorai. 2013. "Limits to Arbitrage and Hedging: Evidence from Commodity Markets." *Journal of Financial Economics* 109:2, 441–465.

Adams, Zeno, and Thorsten Gluck. 2015. "Financialization in Commodity Markets: A Passing Trend or the New Normal?" *Journal of Banking & Finance* 60:C, 93–111.

Adhikari, Ramesh, Kyle J. Putnam, and Neal Maroney. 2016. "The Impact of Financialization on the Benefits of Commodity Futures Investment." Working paper, Humboldt State University.

Baker, Steven D. 2016. "The Financialization of Storable Commodities." Working paper, University of Virginia.

Basak, Suleyman, and Anna Pavlova. 2016. "A Model of Financialization of Commodities." *Journal of Finance* 71:4, 1511–1555.

Bhardwaj, Geetesh, Gary B. Gorton, and K. Geert Rouwenhorst. 2016. "Investor Interest and the Returns to Commodity Investing." *Journal of Portfolio Management* 42:3, 44–55.

Brunetti, Celso, Bahattin Büyükşahin, and Jeffrey H. Harris. 2016. "Speculators, Prices and Market Volatility." *Journal of Financial and Quantitative Analysis* 51:5, 1545–1574.

Büyükşahin, Bahattin, and Jeffrey H. Harris. 2011. "Do Speculators Drive Crude Oil Futures Prices?" *Energy Journal* 32:2, 167–202.

Büyükşahin, Bahattin, and Michel A. Robe. 2014. "Speculators, Commodities and Cross-Market Linkages." *Journal of International Money and Finance* 42:April, 38–70.

Cheng, Ing-Haw, Andrei Kirilenko, and Wei Xiong. 2015. "Convective Risk Flows in Commodity Futures Markets." *Review of Finance* 19:5, 1733–1781.

Cheng, Ing-Haw, and Wei Xiong. 2014. "Financialization of Commodity Markets." *Annual Review of Financial Economics* 6, 419–441.

Commodity Futures Trading Commission. 2008. "Commodity Swap Dealers & Index Traders with Commission Recommendations." Commodity Futures Trading Commission Staff Report.

Erb, Claude B., and Campbell R. Harvey. 2006. "The Strategic and Tactical Value of Commodity Futures." *Financial Analysts Journal* 62:2, 69–97.

Fattouh, Bassam, Lutz Kilian, and Lavan Mahadeva. 2013. "The Role of Speculation in Oil Markets: What Have We Learned So Far?" *Energy Journal* 34:3, 7–33.

Gorton, Gary, and K. Geert Rouwenhorst. 2006. "Facts and Fantasies about Commodity Futures." *Financial Analysts Journal* 62:2, 47–68.

Haase, Marco, Yvonne S. Zimmermann, and Heinz Zimmermann. 2016. "The Impact of Speculation on Commodity Futures Markets: A Review of the Findings of 100 Empirical Studies." *Journal of Commodity Markets* 1:3, 1–15.

Henderson, Brian J., Neil D. Pearson, and Li Wang. 2014. "New Evidence on the Financialization of Commodity Markets." *Review of Financial Studies* 28:5, 1285–1311.

Hicks, John R. 1939. *Value and Capital: An Inquiry into Some Fundamental Principles of Economic Theory*. Oxford: Clarendon Press.

Irwin, Scott H., and Dwight R. Sanders. 2011. "Index Funds, Financialization, and Commodity Futures Markets." *Applied Economic Perspectives and Policy* 33:1, 1–31.

Irwin, Scott H., and Dwight R. Sanders. 2012. "Testing the Masters Hypothesis in Commodity Futures Markets." *Energy Economics* 34:1, 256–269.

Irwin, Scott H., Dwight R. Sanders, and Robert P. Merrin. 2009. "Devil or Angel? The Role of Speculation in the Recent Commodity Price Boom (and Bust)." *Journal of Agricultural and Applied Economics* 41:2, 377–391.

Keynes, John M. 1923. "Some Aspects of Commodity Markets." *Manchester Guardian Commercial: European Reconstruction Series*, Section 13, March 29, 784–786.

Lundstrom, Elin, and Kevin Visvanathar. 2015. "Commodities as a Diversification Instrument: Implications of the Commodity Financialization." Working paper, Stockholm School of Economics.

Masters, Michael W. 2008. Testimony before Committee on Homeland Security and Governmental Affairs of the United States Senate.

Sanders, Dwight R., and Scott H. Irwin. 2010. "A Speculative Bubble in Commodity Futures Prices? Cross Sectional Evidence." *Agricultural Economics* 41:1, 25–32.

Sanders, Dwight R., and Scott H. Irwin. 2011a. "The Impact of Index Funds in Commodity Futures Markets: A Systems Approach." *Journal of Alternative Investments* 14:1, 40–49.

Sanders, Dwight R., and Scott H. Irwin. 2011b. "New Evidence on the Impact of Index Funds in US Grain Futures Markets." *Canadian Journal of Agricultural Economics* 59:4, 519–532.

Sanders, Dwight R., and Scott H. Irwin. 2013. "Measuring Index Investment in Commodity Futures Markets." *Energy Journal* 34:3, 105–127.

Sanders, Dwight R., Scott H. Irwin, and Robert P. Merrin. 2008. "The Adequacy of Speculation in Agricultural Futures Markets: Too Much of a Good Thing?" *Applied Economic Perspectives and Policy* 32:1, 77–94.

Silvennoinen, Annastiina, and Susan Thorp. 2010. "Financialization, Crisis and Commodity Correlation Dynamics." Research Paper 267, Quantitative Finance Research Centre, University of Technology Sydney.

Singleton, Kenneth J. 2013. "Investor Flows and the 2008 Boom/Bust in Oil Prices." *Management Science* 60:2, 300–318.

Sockin, Michael, and Wei Xiong. 2015. "Informational Frictions and Commodity Markets." *Journal of Finance* 70:5, 2063–2098.

Stoll, Hans R., and Robert E. Whaley. 2010. "Commodity Index Investing and Commodity Futures Prices." *Journal of Applied Finance* 20:1, 7–46.

Tang, Ke, and Wei Xiong. 2012. "Index Investment and the Financialization of Commodities." *Financial Analysts Journal* 68:5, 54–74.

U.S. Senate Permanent Subcommittee on Investigations. 2009. "Excessive Speculation in the Wheat Market." Committee on Homeland Security and Governmental Affairs.

Yan, Lei, Scott H. Irwin, and Dwight R. Sanders. 2016. "The Relationship between Commodity Investment Flows and Crude Oil Futures Prices: Real or Spurious?" Working paper, University of Illinois, Urbana-Champaign.

Zaremba, Adam. 2014. "Strategies Based on Momentum and Term Structure in Financialized Commodity Markets." *Business and Economics Research Journal* 7:1, 31–46.

Zaremba, Adam. 2015. *The Financialization of Commodity Markets*. New York: Palgrave Macmillan.

26

Virtual Currencies as Commodities

LAMIA CHOUROU
Assistant Professor, University of Ottawa

SAMIR SAADI
Associate Professor, University of Ottawa

AZIZAH ALJOHANI
Msc Student, University of Ottawa

Introduction

Virtual currency, also known as cryptocurrency and digital currency, is a medium of exchange not authorized or adopted by a government. Virtual currencies share several properties common to physical currencies or fiat money without being in physical format. Many different digital currencies are being used over the Internet but Bitcoin is the most common cryptocurrency. In fact, according to Coinmarketcap (2017), 722 types of cryptocurrencies exist that are crowding the virtual currency scene and are a rapidly evolving topic of interest for many stakeholders. Virtual currencies such as World of Warcraft Gold and online payments such as Payal are not new and have existed for decades. But what make cryptocurrencies, such as Bitcoin, special is that, unlike online currencies or online payment systems, they are decentralized, peer-to-peer networks that allow for the proof and transfer of ownership of virtual currencies without the need for an intermediary such as a bank. By removing the need for intermediaries, digital currencies can provide a more efficient infrastructure for the transfer of money, allowing cheaper and faster payments.

Cryptocurrencies are widely viewed as a disruptive technology that raise both hopes and fears in the minds of consumers, businesses, investors, charities, and regulators. In fact, virtual currencies offer several potential advantages to different stakeholders and to the wider economy as a method of payment. Moreover, the "distributed ledger" technology that supports virtual currencies has substantial potential for innovative applications of the technology across financial services and beyond. Yet, virtual currencies present some existing and potential risks that could harm consumers, financial systems, and even the national security, which is now an important matter, especially to developed countries facing an enhanced threat of terrorism.

Not surprisingly, several countries, including the United States, are trying to introduce regulations aimed at creating a hostile environment for illicit users of digital currencies, while providing a supportive environment for their legitimate use to flourish. As U.S. senator Tom Carper, the Homeland Security Committee's chairman, notes: "rather than play 'whack-a-mole' with the latest website, currency, or other method criminals are using . . . we need to develop thoughtful, nimble and sensible policies that protect the public without stifling innovation and economic growth" (*Financial Times* 2013).

Despite the potential of virtual currencies, only a relatively small number of consumers and businesses worldwide have currently adopted them. This situation is due to several factors, including the lack of a regulatory framework needed to enhance the credibility and legitimacy of digital currencies. This lack of a regulatory framework continues to cause some uncertainty for businesses. Another factor is the excessive volatility of their value. For instance, investors who believed in Bitcoin when it first emerged made millions of dollars due to the rapid increase of its value. However, those who invested later lost millions of dollars because of its quick decline in value. Bitcoin's volatility proved to be a double-edged sword for investors. Negative media coverage of arrests related to illicit financial activities and the security problems that led to different breaches affected volatility in the dollar-to-Bitcoin exchange rate. For example, a breach involving Mt. Gox occurred in February 2016 that resulted in losses of $500 million. Businesses investing in Bitcoin are also finding difficulties opening bank accounts, as some banks are still treating virtual currencies transactions as fraudulent.

Beyond negative media coverage, other factors can explain the high volatility of Bitcoin. For instance, because both the technology and the industry that has grown up around Bitcoin are still in an early stage, large trades of Bitcoins can substantially affect exchange rates. Additionally, many people still do not know or fully understand what virtual currencies are, which gives rise to noise trading as opposed to informed trading that is based on fundamentals.

On the positive side, virtual currencies have witnessed the emergence of private funds and alternative virtual currencies' investment. Among many things, the creation of hedge funds that encompass strategic trading on virtual currencies' volatility has become a trend. One of those entities, called Global Advisors Bitcoin Investment Funds (GABI), received regulatory approval from the Jersey Financial Services Commission (JFSC) in July 2014, making it the first regulated virtual currencies investment fund. Also on February 25, 2015, the New York Stock Exchange (NYSE) announced that it is investing in the U.S.-based Bitcoin exchange and wallet service called Coinbase. Coinbase Exchange is the first regulated Bitcoin exchange, providing what seems to be a reliable and secure platform for Bitcoin trading that is backed by investors such as the New York Stock Exchange. On March 24, 2015, Noble Markets, a platform for trading Bitcoin, announced that it is adopting the same software used by major securities exchanges around the world, provided by Nasdaq OMX Group Inc. The embrace of Bitcoin by the NYSE and NASDAQ, which are the biggest U.S. stock exchange operators, is a sign that the digital currency is emerging from underground and is here to stay.

This chapter has the following organization. The next section briefly discusses the most common cryptocurrencies (i.e., Bitcoin, Darkcoin, Peercoin, Primecoin, and Dogecoin), followed by a discussion about their nature and classification. The chapter then explains how Bitcoin works and discusses the transaction costs associated with it. Next, the chapter provides a discussion of advantages and disadvantages of digital currencies and how they are regulated. Lastly, the chapter concludes with closing remarks about the future of virtual currencies and in particular Bitcoin.

Most Prominent Digital Currencies

Although hundreds of cryptocurrencies are available for trade in online markets, only 26 have market capitalizations greater than $10 million (Coinmarketcap 2017). The following sections discuss some of the most common cryptocurrencies.

BITCOIN

Created by an anonymous group of developers (Nakamoto 2008), Bitcoin is the most prominent virtual currency. It has been on the market since 2009 and is created through a "mining" process with every transaction saved in the transaction log or blockchain. Like any other currency, Bitcoin is divided in sub-units called milli-Bitcoin, micro-Bitcoin, and Satoshi. Since its inception, the popularity of Bitcoin has increased among both businesses and consumers. In fact, Bitcoin's market capitalization has increased from roughly $144 million on January 4, 2013 to beyond an all-time high of $16 billion on January 4, 2017 (Blockchain.info 2017).

The main differences between Bitcoin and known fiat money are:

- Bitcoins are generated by a unique code and transactions are stored in a public ledger. In other words, transactions are made public and are traceable.
- The whole Bitcoin transaction process is decentralized (i.e., with no central repository or administration) and is not under the control of any bank, state, or country.
- A total of 25 Bitcoins are mined every 10 minutes and an estimated maximum of 21 million Bitcoins will be reached between 2110 and 2140.
- Anyone can participate in the mining process by dedicating processor power to the open-source code. Users who do so are called miners and are rewarded for their efforts with Bitcoins.
- Bitcoin does not have any physical form, and thus its environmental impact is limited to electricity (albeit a high 1.46 terawatt-hours per year, which corresponds approximately to the consumption of 135,000 average American homes) (*Economist* 2015).

LITECOIN

In 2011, a former Google engineer invented Litecoin, the second most popular virtual currency after Bitcoin (Rao 2014). Similar to Bitcoin, Litecoin is a decentralized system that can be generated electronically by anyone around the world who is running a computer. It contains an open source global payment system, which means that it can be owned by anyone, and it does not require any form of monitoring. The key difference between Bitcoin and Litecoin is that Litecoin allows for faster transaction confirmation as it processes a blockchain roughly four times faster than Bitcoin (i.e., 2.5 minutes instead of 10 minutes in the Bitcoin network). Moreover, the Litecoin network produces about four times more currency units than produced by the Bitcoin network. Despite this competitive edge over the Bitcoin, the Litecoin network still has fewer users than the Bitcoin network (Gibbs and Yordchim 2014).

DARKCOIN

Because transactions are traceable in the blockchain, the use of the Bitcoin network can have implications for users' personal privacy. Contrary to Bitcoin, Darkcoin allows its users to maintain a high level of privacy. In fact, Darkcoin is the first privacy-centric cryptographic currency. To anonymize transactions, Darkcoin uses a decentralized implementation protocol, which Duffield and Hagan (2014) name "DarkSend." However, because of the decentralized implementation of DarkSend, the Darkcoin network faces the risk of being hacked by rogue users who can modify the software and prevent transactions from being completed.

PEERCOIN

Peercoin, also known as P2P or PPCoins, started in 2012 and was also inspired by the framework of Bitcoin. It consumes less energy than the Bitcoin network. Moreover, it does not have a fixed upper limit to the coins produced, which makes it an inflationary currency (King and Nadal 2012).

DOGECOIN

Dogecoin is a degenderized peer-to-peer network with an uncapped supply. An advantage of Dogecoin is that it deals with large volume of coins with relatively low individual value. Such a feature makes Dogecoin more accessible to new users.

PRIMECOIN

Introduced in July 2013, Primecoin offers great security and strong monitoring over the network, which makes the mining process quite easy and fast. According to King (2013), the speed of the payment through a Primecoin network is 10 times faster than in the Bitcoin network. Similar to Peercoin, no predefined ultimate number of coins exists for Primecoin.

Are Virtual Currencies Commodities, Currencies, or Both?

Since their inception, cryptocurrencies have been the subject of debate with respect to their nature and classification: Are they currencies, commodities, both, or another class of asset altogether? Yermack (2014) contends that Bitcoin does not qualify as currency but is rather a speculative investment. Moreover, unlike commodities, cryptocurrencies are not tangible and have no inherent value by design given that they are not backed by a government or commodity. Yet they share a number of properties common to currencies and commodities. As Grinberg (2012, p. 201) notes:

> Bitcoin is similar to the dozens of gold-backed digital currencies that already exist, such as Pecunix or GoldMoney, because it is liquid, digital, easy for end users to exchange with one another, generally anonymous, and popular among government-distrusting "gold bugs." However, Bitcoin is different in several key ways: (1) there is no central authority that can issue new currency or defraud holders of the currency (e.g., by holding fractional reserves while promising to hold full reserves), (2) it is fiat money rather than commodity money, and (3) it may be difficult to regulate because there is no centrally controlling authority.

Similar to the vast majority of currencies and commodities, cryptocurrencies provide their holders with the right to use them in any way they want. Holders can also write contracts involving them (Grinberg 2012). As for their perceived lack of inherent value, some contend that cryptocurrencies, such as Bitcoin, do have value given their fixed level of supply and over time rarity. In September 2015, the U.S. Commodity Futures Trading Commission (CFTC) ruled that virtual currencies should be considered as commodities. The slow adoption of virtual currencies as commodities by the CFTC is due to the lack of clarity involving which jurisdiction virtual currencies should fall. The International Monetary Fund (IMF) (2016, p. 24) summarizes the status of virtual currencies (VCs) as follows:

> VCs combine properties of currencies, commodities, and payments systems, and their classification as one or the other will often have implications for their legal and regulatory treatment—in particular, in determining which national agencies should regulate them. Finding a consistent classification for VCs even within the same jurisdiction has proven difficult, as different competent authorities may classify them according to their own policy priorities. For example, the U.S. tax authority, the IRS, has classified VCs as "property" for the purpose of federal taxation, whereas the Treasury Department's FinCEN has classified VCs as "value" for the purpose of AML/CFT obligations. Other jurisdictions have taken a different approach, avoiding a formal classification and focusing instead on the nature or type of transaction being conducted. This disparity of treatment within and among jurisdictions may hamper coordination and may lead to inconsistencies.

To date, the United States is the only country that considers virtual currencies as commodities. In Canada, the Canadian Revenue Agency treats virtual currencies as barter transactions for tax purposes. However, other developed countries may follow the lead of the United States in classifying virtual currencies as commodities just like crude oil or wheat. Because Bitcoin dominates the universe of virtual currencies as reflected in the research output and media coverage on virtual currencies, the rest of the chapter focuses on Bitcoin.

How Does Bitcoin Work?

Unlike traditional currencies, Bitcoin does not rely on central banks but is supported by its users through a peer-to-peer computer network that allows the transfer of Bitcoins between users and the generation of new Bitcoins. Bitcoins are created through a procedure known as *Bitcoin mining*, which is essentially a mathematical execution of difficult number-crunching problems in the Bitcoin network (*Economist* 2013). Bitcoins generators, called *miners*, are compensated with Bitcoin transaction fees. The mathematical tasks used to generate Bitcoins are designed so that they become increasingly difficult over time, while setting a cap on the total number of Bitcoins that can be mined of around 21 million.

Anyone can become a Bitcoin miner by running software with specialized hardware. The Bitcoin software is easily available via Bitcoin's official website (https://bitcoin.org/en/choose-your-wallet). Bitcoin software has many features, including a digital wallet, which stores information, including the user's Bitcoin balance. The wallet creates an address randomly using a combination of letters and numbers that requires using the network (Böhme, Christin, Edelman, and Moor 2015). To enhance privacy, users can delve into the Bitcoin system using nicknames or Bitcoin addresses, so that users do not have to reveal their identity or disclose their place of residence to create their own wallet (Blockchain.info 2017). Users can obtain several unique addresses in which they do not need to provide personal information. Users can transfer Bitcoins to each other for a certain service or goods by scanning the barcode of the address that appears in the digital wallet in any device (Androulaki, Karame, Roeschlin, Scherer, and Capkun 2013). Bitcoin uses a key system that allows users to store and spend Bitcoin money. Each Bitcoin address contains a private key and a public key. The private key unlocks the wallet to allow receiving and sending Bitcoins, while the public key confirms all payment process sent from that address. Anyone can find the inside address, but only the private key can unlock the wallet to allow receiving and sending Bitcoins.

In the Bitcoin network, blockchain records all historical transactions (Fink and Johann 2014). Bitcoin continuously groups all transactions and every new transaction becomes part of this group and is called a *block*. These blocks validate the authority and ensure that no unauthorized transactions occur. The process of confirming transaction is a continuous process that occurs almost every 10 minutes (Böhme et al. 2015).

In the Bitcoin database, each transaction includes the input (sender) address, output (recipient) address, number of Bitcoins sent to the receiver, and time at which the transaction was added to the network. Generally, any transaction may contain one sender (input) or multiple senders; the same situation applies to the receiver (output), in which the receiver can be one or more individuals (Fink and Johann 2014). The number of Bitcoins sent is usually related to the number of Bitcoins received previously by the same client. Assume person A received five Bitcoins from person B, who receives seven Bitcoins from person C. The five and seven Bitcoins are the output in the previous transactions and serves as the input in the following transaction, such as person A sending two Bitcoins to person D. This transaction must have one input (either the five or seven Bitcoins) and three outputs. One of the outputs should be assigned to person D by Bitcoins; the second output should be allocated as a transaction fee by, for example, 0.01 Bitcoins to the miner who verifies the transaction. The last output should be assigned to person A as a charge by 2.99 Bitcoins. Unlike other popular online payment systems, Bitcoin network cannot reverse the payment once it is made, even in case of a wrong transaction (Robleh, Barrdear, Clews, and Southgate 2014a; Böhme et al. 2015).

Transaction Costs of Bitcoin

Bitcoin has three types of transaction costs: (1) search and information costs, (2) bargaining and decision costs, and (3) policing and enforcement costs. Currently, Bitcoin has no formal transaction fees. When a transaction takes place, any portion of the transaction not received by the recipient is considered a fee and is given to the miner who solved that transaction block as a reward. Thus, cryptocurrencies offer a way to exchange money while foregoing the laws involved in ensuring the customer's privacy. From a retailer's' perspective, the main driver of accepting electronic currencies is the promise of lower transaction fees. However, the marginal cost of verifying transactions is actually higher for miners than centralized payment systems. Additionally, the costs of verifying transactions are expected to rise in electronic currencies while remaining constant in traditional payment systems. As Robleh, Barrdear, Clews, and Southgate (2014b, p. 280) state, "The low transaction fees for digital currency payments are largely driven by a subsidy that is paid to transaction verifiers (miners) in the form of new currency. The size of this subsidy depends not only on the current price of the digital currency, but also on miners' beliefs about the future price of the digital currency."

As more people begin to support electronic currencies, demand will increase, allowing miners to continue to accept low transaction fees due to the prospect of future increases in system usage. However, because the supply of electronic currencies is usually fixed, sustaining a subsidy to miners in the long run will be impossible, which will likely result in higher transaction fees.

Benefits and Risks of Digital Currencies

Cryptocurrencies in general and Bitcoin in particular have some unique advantages and disadvantages for the economy, investors, and consumers. Being a peer-to-peer network system, all transactions in the Bitcoin network occur without passing through a third-party such as a bank, state, or government. Thus, Bitcoin is an extremely disruptive technology in the financial sector, which some compare to the advent of personal computers in 1975 or the Internet in 1993. Eliminating the traditional middleman will reduce the total cost of payments and increase the efficiency of the financial world, but will cause enormous losses to banks and governments who are the middlemen. The existence of cryptocurrencies would ultimately lead to more competition among banks and traditional financial players to lower their costs for a share of the market. The increasing competition in the financial sector should also lead to better service for consumers. Moreover, because Bitcoin is not under the control of any central bank or government, no "printing press" entity exists that can create additional Bitcoins and inflate the consumers' saving value, which is another huge benefit to the economy. As discussed later in the chapter, governments are trying to catch-up and regulate the cryptocurrency industry, whereas banks are readying their strategies to deal with cryptocurrencies as soon as the regulation is approved.

The peer-to-peer network system eliminates transaction costs that consumers pay today with credit cards (usually around 3 percent) and will improve the economy overall, with more money in consumers' pockets. According to a report by the British government's Her Majesty's Treasury (2015), the lower transaction costs associated with digital currencies can translate into billions of dollars of savings to businesses. In fact, a peer-to-peer network system enables businesses to monetize very low cost goods and services and accept micro-payments. These savings can be reinvested to create more jobs or can help reduce the price of goods. By removing the need for traditional intermediaries, cryptocurrencies provide a more efficient infrastructure for the transfer of money, allowing for faster payments. The traditional interbank payment systems can take several hours, if not days, to move money between accounts. Faster settlement has cash flow benefits for businesses by allowing corporate capital to be put to more productive use than at present. The lower cost and faster payment associated with cryptocurrencies are even more pronounced in the context of cross-country transactions in which settlement often involves high transaction fees of around 8 percent and payment can easily take several days to be processed. This feature is particularly important for small businesses facing cash flow problems.

Another advantage of cryptocurrencies is their availability. In fact, while conventional payment services are available only during banking hours, cryptocurrencies are available 24 hours a day. Such property is even more desirable in the context of unbanked or under-banked countries where the absence of a traditional banking system deprives people in remote regions of payments and other financial services. Moreover, transactions made using digital currencies prevent the possibility of fraud through using fake payments or double spending of digital currency units. Another major advantage with cryptocurrencies is that their associated technologies have several possible applications beyond retail payment services. In fact, the distributed ledgers based on blockchain can be used, for instance, to record and transfer the ownership of financial instruments such as bonds and shares.

Bitcoin consumers use the cryptocurrency as a peer-to-peer cash system that is more transparent than most other types of payments. The parties involved in the transaction are clearly identified and the transaction details are stored in the Bitcoin ledger. However, those transactions are irreversible. Although consumers might consider this irreversibility a disadvantage, merchants consider it an advantage because it removes the risk of any reversal of payment. Moreover, because cryptocurrency networks allow for lower costs and faster settlement times, they attract both legitimate and illegitimate users. In fact, digital currencies network can be used to trade illicit goods and services, engage in money laundering, or even to finance terrorists. However, in October 2014, the National Crime Agency (NCA) concluded that the risk of criminal use of digital currencies is essentially limited to the sale and purchase of illicit goods and services (Her Majesty's Treasury 2015). The risks that digital currencies pose to a country's monetary and financial stability should be low because of the very low volume of digital currencies circulating at present compared to fiat currencies.

Another risk associated with virtual currency stems from the unsupervised e-currency trading platforms. The issue of arbitrage and trading collusion surfaces when using e-currency trading platforms. Bitcoins, for instance, are traded through an online exchange. From an investor's perspective, these exchanges provide online platforms for transferring cash for the equivalent in virtual currencies and vice versa. Because many of these platforms operate simultaneously, they can arguably create arbitrage opportunities. Given that the same Bitcoin can be bought on one platform and sold on another, sometimes with fees and delays involved, arbitrage opportunities might exist. If two of those exchanges collude, therefore removing a potential barrier of fiat transfer between the two for an exclusive segment of privileged customers or owners, such unethical trading could take place for the exclusive benefit of certain persons.

Volatility of Bitcoin Price

Bitcoin has some unique features that differentiate it from fiat currencies. For instance, Bitcoin is not considered as a payment instrument in the sense of the monetary and financial code because it is issued without a money deposit. Moreover, contrary to fiat currencies, Bitcoin does not endow the trust of central banks, with irreversible transactions that do not explicitly identify the payer or the payee. Another important feature of Bitcoin is its highly volatile value. During the first two years since its creation, the parity of Bitcoin with the U.S. dollars was about 0.10. By February 7, 2011, the price of Bitcoin reached $1. Bitcoin experienced a second surge on June 6, 2011, reaching $22. Following multiple surges, Bitcoin reached a peak of $979 on November 25, 2013. However, the price of Bitcoin decreased sharply in 2014 due to the bankruptcy of a Bitcoin exchange based in Tokyo, named Mt. Gox. After reaching a low of $232 on August 17, 2015, Bitcoin has continued to gain momentum and was priced at $1,069 on January 4, 2017. Figure 26.1 illustrates the high volatility of Bitcoin between 2012 and 2015 compared to the price of gold, two broad stock markets indices (i.e., MSCI Emerging Markets Index and MSCI Global Market Index), and two currencies (the euro and yen).

Table 26.1 provides summary statistics for all the series, along with the Jarque-Bera test for normality. In dollar terms, Bitcoin's realized monthly volatility between May 2012 and May 2015 was 265 percent, which is much higher than gold's 118 percent. This high volatility hinders Bitcoin ability to be used as a medium of exchange. Table 26.1 shows that kurtosis is positive and high for all variables, suggesting presence of fat tails. The uro and Chinese exchange rate for gold and Bitcoin is positively skewed but negatively skewed for stock markets. This leptokurtic excess

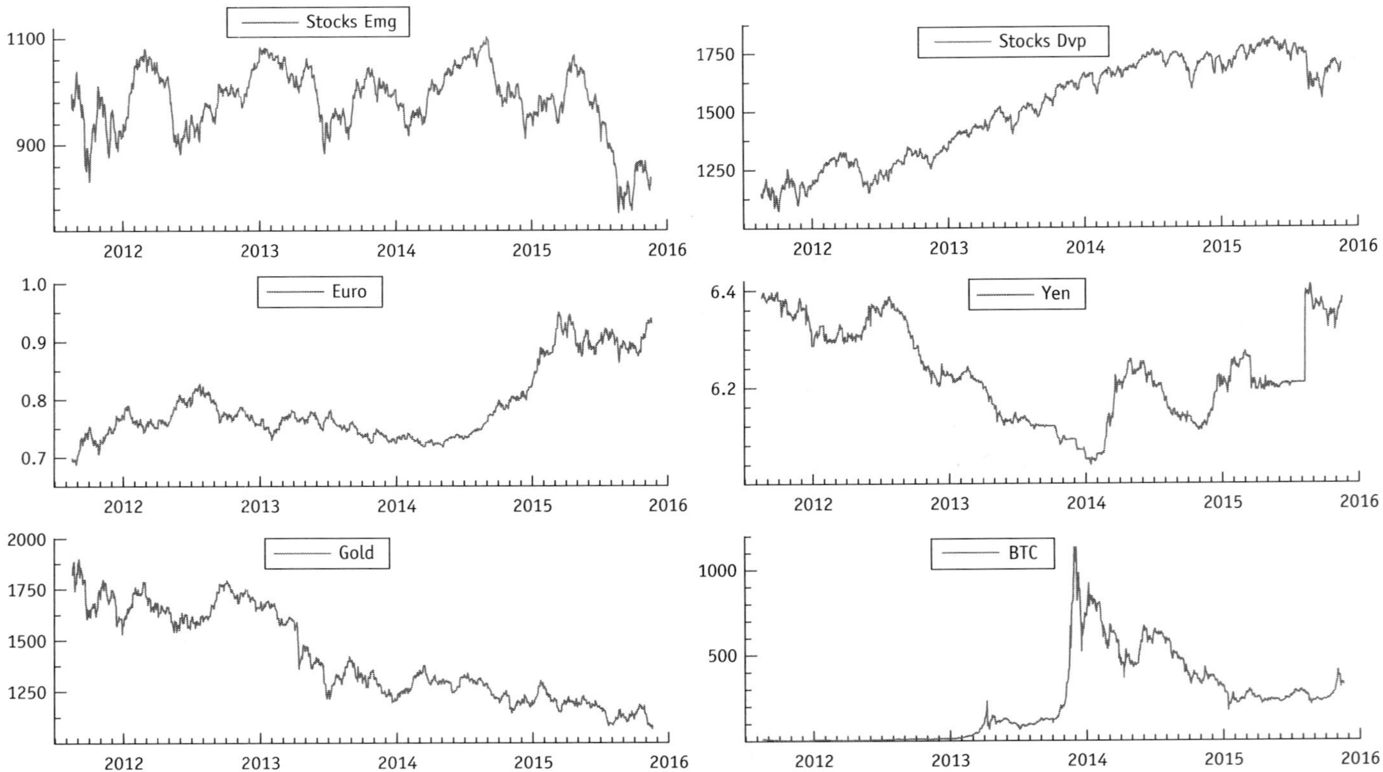

Figure 26.1 Time-Series Depiction of Bitcoin Daily Price and Other Financial Series
This figure depicts the daily price level of the following series between January 9, 2011 and January 11, 2015: MSCI Emerging Markets Index (EMG), MSCI Global Market Index (WRD), the Euro (EURO) and Chinese exchange rate (YEN), gold bullion (GOLD), Bitcoin (BTC). Data are drawn from DataStream, Eurostat, and blockchain.info.

Table 26.1 **Descriptive Statistics of Bitcoin Daily Price and Other Financial Series**

	BTC	*GOLD*	*Stock-EMG*	*Stock-DVP*	*EURO*	*YEN*
Mean	229.59	1455.91	1011.15	1553.96	0.80	6.42
Median	143.99	1359.81	1020.22	1602.17	0.78	6.40
Maximum	1165.96	1944.13	1133.93	1865.12	0.98	6.60
Minimum	2.31	1100.97	794.85	1106.63	0.70	6.21
Standard deviation	242.77	226.50	65.61	217.02	0.06	0.09
Skewness	1.11	0.35	−0.80	−0.32	1.06	0.07
Kurtosis	3.63	1.66	3.65	1.69	2.90	1.99
Jarque-Bera	227.47	109.58	128.29	102.84	199.81	53.31
(P-value)	(0.000)	(0.000)	(0.000)	(0.000)	(0.000)	(0.000)

Note: This table presents descriptive statistics of the daily price level of the following series between January 9, 2001 and January 11, 2015: Bitcoin (BTC), gold bullion (GOLD), MSCI Emerging Markets Index (Stock-EMG), MSCI Global Market Index (Stock-DVP), the euro (EURO), and Chinese exchange rate (YEN). Data are drawn from DataStream, Eurostat, and Blockchain.info.

and asymmetry are consistent with the Jarque-Bera test, justifying the rejection of normality.

As previously discussed, a major difference between Bitcoin and fiat currencies is that no centralized authority regulates Bitcoin. This lack of control both attracts people to and scares them away from Bitcoin. Although the possibility exists for large gains in exchange rates, such rates could also fall dramatically. One way that banks maintain a stable currency is to control the currency supply by increasing or decreasing inflation. Bitcoin, however, cannot employ the same strategy. Every four years, the number of Bitcoins is increased by a half. This increase in the currency supply coupled with a decreasing or stable trade activity results in substantial volatility. Like any currency or commodity, a highly unstable supply of and demand for Bitcoins led to higher volatility of its market value. Because Bitcoins are infrequently traded, large trades can dramatically influence exchange rates.

The fact that this digital currency is still in the infancy of its market evolution further exacerbates the exchange rate volatility of Bitcoin's price. Similarly, relevant news related to Bitcoin can affect its exchange rate. Positive news might dramatically increase the exchange rate, while negative news could send it plummeting. Also, many people still do not know or understand the nature of Bitcoin. Therefore, news introduces them to the currency, inevitably increasing Bitcoin demand and likely helping to stabilize its volatility (*Economist* 2015). What most merchants do not realize about Bitcoin is that it can be used simply as a payment system that enables them to convert customers' payment in Bitcoins to a stable currency. However, the 1 percent transaction fee that companies charge is insufficient to cover the exchange rate risk of Bitcoin. A possible remedy is to engage in a swap or futures contract. The use of derivatives instruments can lessen Bitcoin's volatility and enhance the development of its network's infrastructure (Brito, Shadab, and Castillo 2014).

Due to its finite supply, Bitcoin is more like a commodity than a currency. Given its similarities to commodities, the continuing decline in the rate of supply and a tendency for demand to increase as stability takes hold, can lead to an increase in the exchange rate between Bitcoins and dollars in the long run. However, such an increase assumes that education and awareness of Bitcoin continue to increase and no massive speculative selling by traders occurs.

Academic research dealing with cryptocurrencies has mainly focused on their ability to become an alternative monetary system (Segendorf 2014; Dwyer 2015). A few research studies examine Bitcoin's volatility. Some researchers postulate that demand for Bitcoins heavily influences the volatility (Buchholz, Delaney, Warren, and Parker 2012), while others contend that the Bitcoin's value has nothing to do with economic theories but rather speculation drives its value (Kristoufek 2015). Ciaian, Rajcaniova, and Kancs (2016) suggest that market fundamentals and Bitcoin's attractiveness to investors affect the price formulation of Bitcoin. Users of Bitcoin anticipate that the exchange rate will increase and do not want to sell at a low value. However, they may not realize that by holding Bitcoins they are causing a decrease in the demand for the currency, eventually decreasing its exchange rate.

Few studies examine cryptocurrencies as hedging and diversification tools. Investors look for alternative investment instruments as part of diversified investment portfolios. For example, during the early 2000s, investors considered commodity instruments effective for portfolio diversification because of their lower correlation with stock returns. Today, cryptocurrencies represent such an alternative because of their high average return and low correlation with financial assets (Bouoiyour and Selmi 2014).

Guesmi, Ftiti, Saadi, and Abid (2016) examine the conditional cross effects and volatility spillover between Bitcoin and financial indicators using different multivariate generalized autoregressive onditional heteroskedasticity (GARCH) specifications. They find that a dynamic conditional correlation (DCC)-GARCH is the best-fit model for modeling the joint dynamics of different financial variables and Bitcoin. In particular, they find that unpredicted changes in the returns on different financial indicators significantly affect the conditional volatility of Bitcoin returns. Thus, a shock to financial variables, regardless of their signs, implies an increase in the volatility of Bitcoin returns. Their evidence also shows that a short position in the Bitcoin market allows hedging the risk investment for all different financial assets. Additionally, hedging strategies involving gold, oil, stocks of developing markets, and Bitcoin considerably reduce the portfolio's risk, as measured by variance, compared to the portfolio risk consisting of only gold, oil, and stocks of developing markets.

Regulation of Cryptocurrencies

The gradual acceptance of the electronic currencies is likely to eventually result in their financial product securitization. Considering the perceived risks associated with virtual currencies, notably the hacking risks and the tax/security/money laundering concerns, the next logical step is to enact clear and stringent legislation to enable the full potential of virtual currencies and to reduce undesirable use. Although digital currencies are unregulated in most countries, some major economies have regulation in place and others are studying the potential need to do so (Fuller 2014). As outlined in a comprehensive study of Bitcoin conducted by the Law Library of the U.S. Congress (2014, p. 1), "there is widespread concern about the Bitcoin system's possible impact on national currencies, its potential for criminal misuse, and the implications of its use for taxation."

UNITED STATES

One country that regulates digital currencies is the United States. In November 2013, the U.S. Senate Committee on Homeland Security and Governmental Affairs held two days of hearings on the different risks and potentials of digital currencies (U.S. Senate Committee on Homeland Security and Governmental Affairs 2013). In January 2013, the Financial Crimes Enforcement Network of the U.S. Department of the Treasury published how it will approach individuals and businesses that invest in Bitcoin and other virtual currencies. The goal of creating guidelines for the currency was to enable innovators to explore opportunities with the technology while also following federal law. The agency provided additional guidance in October 2014 when it ruled that custodial Bitcoin exchanges and payment processors may be considered money services businesses under law (Financial Crimes Enforcement Network 2014). In fact, the U.S. government has transacted in Bitcoins when it auctioned off 10 blocks of Bitcoin that it had confiscated when it shut down the online black market Silk Road in 2013 (Coindesk 2014a).

Individual states are also beginning to push forward with regulations related to digital currencies, as evidenced by a recent move toward tougher regulation in New York state that is considered to be more stringent than the regime that pertains to banks (*Forbes* 2014a). Other states, however, such as Utah and New Hampshire, are considering legislation more favorable to digital currencies that would allow taxpayers in those states to pay taxes in Bitcoin (*Bitcoin Magazine* 2015).

On July 17, 2014, the New York Department of Financial Services (NYDFS) proposed a regulatory framework for virtual currency firms, called BitLicence, which includes several requirements that are usually found in securities law (BitLicence 2015).

BRAZIL

In October 2013, Brazil enacted a law facilitating the creation of electronic currencies, including Bitcoin. In April 2014, the government declared that gains in Bitcoins would be considered taxable income and announced that it will require holders of Bitcoins to recognize capital gains similar to requirements for capital gains on securities (*Forbes* 2014b).

CANADA

The Canadian government followed the U.S. government's footsteps and recently established regulatory guidelines classifying Bitcoin as a decentralized virtual currency, and Bitcoin miners as Money Service Businesses (MSBs) that are subject to legal obligations and registration to the Financial Transactions and Reports Analysis Centre of Canada. In 2015, the Québec Autorité des marchés financiers (AMF) amended the Money-Services Businesses Act to force virtual currency automated teller machine owners to obtain a license in conformity to the Act (Autorité des Marchés Financiers 2015).

CHINA

In December 2013, the central bank of China issued the "Notice on Precautions against the Risks of Bitcoins," in which it defined Bitcoin as a "virtual commodity" , as a result, should not be circulated in the market as a currency. The Notice also prohibited banks from dealing in Bitcoins and strengthened oversight of Internet websites related to it (Library of Congress 2017).

RUSSIA

In October 2014, Russia's Finance Ministry proposed fines of up to 1 million rubles for those producing and/or carrying out transactions with digital currencies. This action followed on the Bank of Russia's statement in January 2014 that dealing in Bitcoins would be considered as involvement in suspicious activity according to Russia law related to crime and terrorist financing. Whether this law has been enacted by early 2017 is unclear but at least a de facto ban is in place on the currency (Library of Congress 2017).

UNITED KINGDOM

A comprehensive study of digital currencies in the United Kingdom; during the summer of 2013 raised concerns but ultimately left the currency unregulated at that time (Robleh et al. 2014b). More recently, in November 2014, the Bank of England issued a call for information on the benefits and risks of digital currencies as well as to get the public's views on whether regulation of digital currencies is required. In a discussion paper released in February 2015, the Bank of England raised the question of whether central banks should use such technology to issue digital currencies (Bank of England 2015). In the United Kingdom, Bitcoins have been classified as "single purpose vouchers," meaning that they are subject to a 10 to 20 percent tax.

EUROPEAN UNION

In the European Union (EU), the European Central Bank released reports on virtual currencies in October 2012 and in December 2013, and its regulatory agency, the European Banking Authority, issued a warning on the dangers associated with dealing in virtual currencies (European Central Bank 2012; European Banking Authority 2013). This warning outlined that since Bitcoin is unregulated, consumers are unprotected and may be liable for taxes. However, the EU has not passed legislation related to Bitcoins.

TAXATION AND BITCOINS

Regarding taxation, many countries, including the United States, Japan, Finland, and Germany, currently tax Bitcoins. Ecuador was the first country to issue its own digital currency with a launch date of February 26, 2015. The Ecuador's Central Bank noted at the time that the currency is intended to support the country's dollar-based monetary system and not to replace it.

Alternative Virtual Currencies' Investment

During 2014 and 2015, various entities were created to benefit from the expansion of virtual currencies. For example, some hedge funds now engage in strategic trading on virtual currencies' volatility and private equity firms invest in small portfolios of virtual currencies' companies. One of these entities, called Global Advisors Bitcoin Investment Funds (GABI), received regulatory approval from the Jersey Financial Services Commission (JFSC) in July 2014, making it the first investment fund in virtual currencies to be regulated, albeit regulated in a commonly known tax-heaven jurisdiction (Coindesk 2014b). GABI describes virtual currencies as Internet money, a store of value, a medium of exchange, and a unit of account, all digitized.

On February 25, 2015, the NYSE announced its investment in the U.S.-based Bitcoin exchange and wallet service Coinbase (*Financial Times* 2015). In 2015, major banks such as Goldman Sachs, Morgan Stanley, BNP Paribas, and Société General became involved in a new derivative-trading platform specializing in futures and options tied to the price of Bitcoin. Such derivative-trading platforms provide businesses with additional solutions in managing daily transactions, especially those that encompass an international or a speculative component. The main concerns of Bitcoin merchants are the strong volatility of the currency coupled with tax concerns. Given the functioning of Bitcoin, a merchant can accept a Bitcoin within a 10-minute timeframe and reconvert this Bitcoin within the time frame of 10 minutes. Thus, the daily fluctuation risk is reduced to an overall 20-minute timeframe risk of volatility. Combined with an appropriate system, the use of any electronic currencies as a medium of exchange has the potential to radically cut costs for businesses.

On March 10, 2017, however, the Securities and Exchange Commission (SEC) rejected an application by the stock exchange Bats BZX Exchange to create the first exchange-traded fund (ETF) for Bitcoin (*Washington Post* 2017). The news caused an abrupt decline in Bitcoin price by more than 16 percent. The SEC denied the application because Bitcoin exchanges are not regulated and are susceptible to fraudulent or manipulative acts and practices.

Summary and Conclusions

Virtual currency is a medium of exchange not authorized or adopted by a government. Many are using digital currencies over the Internet with the most common cryptocurrency being Bitcoin. Virtual currencies have several properties common to fiat currencies and commodities. Although virtual currencies and their associated technology offer much potential to investors, consumers, businesses, and government entities, they are also the source of risks and challenges to both users and regulators.

An important question remains: What does the future hold for virtual currencies? Cryptocurrencies have a dark history of mishaps, especially with the Mt. Gox scandal, where hackers stole hundreds of millions of dollars through Bitcoin transactions. However, the future of Bitcoin recently got brighter with the U.S. and Canadian governments leading the way in the early stages of regulation and taxation. For instance, the Bank of Montreal announced that it will accept dealing with cryptocurrencies as soon as these are regulated and reliable. According to Ben Bernanke, the former chairman of the Federal Reserve, "[Virtual currencies] may hold long-term promise, particularly if the innovations promote a faster, more secure and more efficient payment system" (*Forbes* 2014c). In fact, the recent implementation of tokenization in Apple Pay and the endorsement of tokenization by Visa show a clear trend for this new practice, which has been at the heart of every cryptocurrency transaction since inception. This fact reinforces the future of cryptocurrencies and shows the advantages of this cryptographic encryption process.

Another potential future of cryptocurrencies is the advent of smart property. Although still at the conceptual level, smart property is likely to change current ownership concepts. Through smart property, an entity can pay electronically to access a cryptographic key giving access to a property temporarily or permanently. Examples encompass any kind of property, whether non-physical (e.g., rights, patents, and trademarks) or physical (e.g., automobile rental and resort time-sharing). As an example, in the future world of smart cars, a cryptographic key can ensure that the smart property is secure and no theft can occur. Hence, although cryptocurrencies are very volatile and risk extinction, the technology behind them is here to stay and may become a major player in the future smart world. Some contend that the chances of an evolved form of cryptocurrency will replace paper money by 2050 if that form is backed by a solid commodity or a set of commodities. The adoption of the technology behind the cryptocurrencies has the potential to validate any single transaction every person makes on the planet.

In the future, money may be likely to be treated as bits of information. If and when that happens, money exchange will be similar to information exchange. The next generation of developers will create cryptographic breakthroughs that revolutionize financial transactions. Although the current concept of cryptocurrency will evolve over time, the technology and innovation that come with it will open the way to something much bigger—a revolution not only in financial transactions but also in every transaction.

Discussion Questions

1. Discuss at least one type of risk associated with virtual currencies.
2. Discuss the main differences between virtual currencies and fiat money such as the U.S. dollar.
3. Explain why Bitcoin is highly volatile.
4. Discuss other possible uses of the technology associated with virtual currencies beyond retail payment services.
5. Identify the countries that consider virtual currencies as commodities.

References

Androulaki, Elli, Ghassan O. Karame, Marc Roeschlin, Tobias Scherer, and Srdjan Capkun. 2013. "Evaluating User Privacy in Bitcoin." *Proceedings of Financial Cryptography*. Available at http://eprint.iacr.org/2012/596.pdf.

Autorité des Marchés Financiers. 2015. Money-Services Businesses Act. Available at https://www.lautorite.qc.ca/en/act-msb.html.

Bank of England. 2015. "One Bank Research Agenda." Available at http://www.bankofengland.co.uk/research/Documents/onebank/discussion.pdf

Bitcoin Magazine. 2015. "Bitcoin-Friendly Bills Unveiled in Utah, New Hampshire, New York City." February 27. Available at https://bitcoinmagazine.com/19418/bitcoin-friendly-bills-unveiled-utah-new-hampshire-new-york-city/.

BitLicence. 2015. Regulations of the Superintendent of Financial Services. Part 200: Virtual Currencies. Department of Financial Services, New York State. Available at http://www.dfs.ny.gov/legal/regulations/adoptions/dfsp200t.pdf.

Blockchain.info. 2017. "Bitcoin Charts." Available at https://blockchain.info/charts/.

Böhme, Rainer, Nicolas Christin, Benjamin Edelman, and Tyler Moore. 2015. "Bitcoin: Economics, Technology, and Governance." *Journal of Economic Perspectives* 29:2, 213–238.

Bouoiyour, Jamal, and Refk Selmi. 2014. "What Does Crypto-currency Look Like? Gaining Insight into Bitcoin Phenomenon." Working paper, University Library of Munich.

Brito, Jerry, Houman B. Shadab, and Andrea Castillo. 2014. "Bitcoin Financial Regulation: Securities, Derivatives, Prediction Markets, and Gambling." *Columbia Science and Technology Law Review* 6:Fall, 240–297.

Buchholz, Martis, Jess Delaney, Joseph Warren, and Jeff Parker. 2012. "Bits and Bets: Information, Price Volatility, and Demand for Bitcoin." Available at http://www.bitcointrading.com/pdf/bitsandbets.pdf.

Ciaian, Pavel, Miroslava Rajcaniova, and d'Artis Kancs. 2016. "The Economics of Bitcoin Price Formation." *Applied Economics* 48:19, 1799–1815.

Coindesk. 2014a. "How the US Government's Sale of 30,000 BTC Could Impact Bitcoin Prices." June 26. Available at http://www.coindesk.com/us-governments-sale-30000-btc-impact-bitcoin-prices/.

Coindesk. 2014b. "First Regulated Bitcoin Investment Fund to Launch on Island of Jersey." July 10. Available at http://www.coindesk.com/first-regulated-bitcoin-investment-fund-launch-island-jersey/.

Coinmarketcap. 2017. "Crypto-currency Market Capitalizations." Available at https://coinmarketcap.com/all/views/all/.

Duffield, Evan, and Kyle Hagan. 2014. "Darkcoin: Peer to Peer Crypto Currency with Anonymous Blockchain Transactions and an Improved Proof of Work System." Available at https://www.dash.org/wp-content/uploads/2014/09/DarkcoinWhitepaper.pdf.

Dwyer, Gerald P. 2015. "The Economics of Bitcoin and Similar Private Digital Currencies." *Journal of Financial Stability* 17:C, 81–91.

Economist. 2013. "How Does Bitcoin Work?" April 11. Available at http://www.economist.com/bitcoinexplained.

Economist. 2015. "The Magic of Mining." January 10. Available at http://www.economist.com/news/business/21638124-minting-digital-currency-has-become-big-ruthlessly-competitive-business-magic.

European Central Bank. 2012. "Virtual Currency Schemes." Available at https://www.ecb.europa.eu/pub/pdf/other/virtualcurrencyschemes201210en.pdf.

European Banking Authority. 2013. "EBA Warns Consumers on Virtual Currencies." Available at https://www.eba.europa.eu/-/eba-warns-consumers-on-virtual-currencies.

Financial Crimes Enforcement Network. 2014. "Request for Administrative Ruling on the Application of FinCEN's Regulations to a Virtual Currency Payment System." Issued on October 27. Available at https://www.fincen.gov/sites/default/files/shared/FIN-2014-R012.pdf.

Financial Times. 2013. "Bitcoin Hits $785 with a Little Help from Bernanke." November 18. Available at https://www.ft.com/content/6c5b941c-5052-11e3-9f0d-00144feabdc0.

Financial Times. 2015. "Bitcoin Company Coinbase Lands $75m Investment from NYSE and BBVA." January 20. Available at https://www.ft.com/content/b6f63e4c-a0af-11e4-9aee-00144feab7de.

Fink, Christopher, and Thomas Johann. 2014. "Bitcoin Markets." Working paper, University of Mannheim.

Forbes. 2014a. "New York Is Ready with Revision of Bitcoin Regulations." December 18. Available at http://www.forbes.com/sites/tomgroenfeldt/2014/12/18/new-york-is-ready-with-revision-of-bitcoin-regulations/#36ae8cba41a5.

Forbes. 2014b. "Brazil Follows IRS, Declares Bitcoin Gains Taxable." April 7. Available at http://www.forbes.com/sites/kenrapoza/2014/04/07/brazil-follows-irs-declares-bitcoin-gains-taxable/.

Forbes. 2014c. "Is Bitcoin the Future?" December 1. Available at http://www.forbes.com/sites/johnmauldin/2014/12/01/is-bitcoin-the-future/.

Fuller, Cameron. 2014. "Bitcoin around the World: How Virtual Currencies Are Treated in 40 Different Countries." Available at http://www.ibtimes.com/bitcoin-around-world-how-virtual-currencies-are-treated-40-different-countries-1553532.

Gibbs, Toby, and Suwaree Yordchim. 2014. "Thai Perception on Litecoin Value." *International Journal of Social, Behavioral, Educational, Economic, Business and Industrial Engineering* 8:8, 2613–2615.

Grinberg, Reuben. 2012. "Bitcoin: An Innovative Alternative Digital Currency." *Hastings Science and Technology Law Journal* 4:Winter, 160–207.

Guesmi, Khaled, Zied Ftiti, Samir Saadi, and Ilyes Abid. 2016. "Portfolio Diversification with CryptoFinance." Working paper, University of Ottawa.

Her Majesty's Treasury. 2015. "Digital Currencies: Response to the Call for Information." Available at https://www.gov.uk/government/uploads/system/uploads/attachment_data/file/414040/digital_currencies_response_to_call_for_information_final_changes.pdf.

International Monetary Fund. 2016. "Virtual Currencies and Beyond: Initial Considerations." Available at https://www.imf.org/external/pubs/ft/sdn/2016/sdn1603.pdf.

King, Sunny. 2013. "Primecoin: Cryptocurrency with Prime Number Proof-of-Work." Available at http://betouchi.free.fr/doc_et_ebook/cryptocoins/primecoin-paper.pdf.

King, Sunny, and Scott Nadal. 2012. "PPCoin: Peer-to-Peer Crypto-Currency with Proof-of-Stake." Available at http://ppcoin.org/static/ppcoin-paper.pdf.

Kristoufek, Ladislav. 2015. "What Are the Main Drivers of the Bitcoin Price? Evidence from Wavelet Coherence Analysis." *PLoS ONE* 10:4. Available at http://journals.plos.org/plosone/article/file?id=10.1371/journal.pone.0123923&type=printable.

Library of Congress, Law Library. 2014. "Regulation of Bitcoin in Selected Jurisdictions." Available at http://www.loc.gov/law/help/bitcoin-survey/regulation-of-bitcoin.pdf.

Nakamoto, Satoshi. 2008. "Bitcoin: A Peer-to-Peer Electronic Cash System." Available at http://bitcoin.org/bitcoin.pdf.

Rao, Siddharth. 2014. "Turning Bitcoins into the Best-Coins." Working paper, Department of Mathematics and Informatics, University of Tartu.

Robleh, A., John Barrdear, Roger Clews, and James Southgate. 2014a. "Innovations in Payment Technologies and the Emergence of Digital Currencies." *Bank of England Quarterly Bulletin* 54:3, 262–275.

Robleh, A., John Barrdear, Roger Clews, and James Southgate. 2014b. "The Economics of Digital Currencies." *Bank of England Quarterly Bulletin* 54:3, 276–286.

Segendorf, Björn. 2014. "What Is Bitcoin?" *Sveriges Riksbank Economic Review* 2, 71–87. Available at http://www.riksbank.se/Documents/Rapporter/POV/2014/2014 2/rap pov1400918eng.pdf.

U.S. Senate Committee on Homeland Security and Governmental Affairs. 2013. "Beyond Silk Road: Potential Risks, Threats, and Promises of Virtual Currencies." Hearings held November 18–19. Available at https://www.hsgac.senate.gov/hearings/beyond-silk-road-potential-risks-threats-and-promises-of-virtual-currencies.

Washington Post. 2017. "SEC Rejects Bitcoin ETF Application from Winklevoss Twins." March 10. Available at https://www.washingtonpost.com/news/get-there/wp/2017/03/10/sec-rejects-bitcoin-etf-application-from-winklevoss-twins/?utm_term=.497fdae70a91

Yermack, David. 2014. "Is Bitcoin a Real Currency? An Economic Appraisal." Working paper, NBER.

27

Research Issues in Commodities and Commodity Derivatives

SCOTT MIXON
Associate Director, Office of the Chief Economist, U.S. Commodity Futures Trading Commission

Introduction

One of the most intriguing aspects of commodities and commodity derivatives is that they directly link the real economy with financial market activity. Presently, a rich set of connections exists between these two aspects of commodity derivatives, but despite many decades of research into these markets, substantial knowledge gaps remain.

Academics in agricultural and applied economics, as well as financial economics, have made great progress in understanding the functioning of these markets at a deep level, but applying the knowledge to highly specialized, practical applications is challenging. Decision-makers often require robust solutions to problems for which the precise theory is either not developed or meager in nature or no data are available. Moreover, regulators or participants in markets are often constrained by very particular institutional frameworks that have evolved, and these often vary by industry. In some respects, the institutional environment in energy commodities differs from the environment for grain or livestock, for example, and they are all quite specialized when compared to the environment for interest rate swaps or credit default swaps. The financial crisis of 2007–2008 and the subsequent regulatory responses dramatically affect each of these market environments.

Because commodity-related issues are important for many different markets and have potentially substantial policy and real economy implications, many different types of research opportunities are available. This chapter provides an overview of some major themes in commodity research but does not attempt to provide a checklist of all research conducted on all possible topics. Rather, the target is research that links the real economy with the financial economy, with an eye toward framing policy issues appropriately and evenhandedly.

The first goal is to provide an overview of key themes in the current academic literature that would help a decision-maker understand the core issues that should be addressed when interpreting and forming opinions about observed market behavior, the regulatory environment, or potential changes in behavior or the environment.

Research that would be helpful in this respect is likely to be more impactful in the real world. A second goal is to highlight some practical research issues raised by recent regulatory concerns; the discussion provides many open questions. Decision-makers often hear conflicting or selected facts by parties desiring particular outcomes. Regulators must make choices, often on short timelines, guided by the best information that is available at the time. Researchers must therefore prepare the groundwork ahead of time in order to have a voice and help decision-makers separate signal from noise.

Organizing the topics in this way means excluding some intellectually interesting topics. Some very practical issues, such as the ongoing debate over the value added by managed futures funds, are not covered. For the purposes of this overview, managed futures would be directly interesting insofar as they represent active or potential participants in commodity futures markets, but their performance as investment vehicles is less relevant. Similarly, topics such as optimal hedge ratios or price behavior of commodities are covered as they relate to the useful functioning of derivatives markets, but they are not covered in depth on their own.

The chapter is organized as follows. The second section provides a brief discussion of the historical trajectory of commodity market research and regulation in order to provide context. The next section then discusses academic research, with several topics broken out into their own subsections. Finally, the chapter provides examples of the types of topics faced by researchers who consider practical, policy-related issues, many of which are open questions. A final section concludes.

Background: Commodity Research and Regulations

This section provides basic background for the commodity derivatives regulatory environment in the United States. A headline resulting from the discussion is that regulation has been linked to data gathering for many years. Copious amounts of data exist, and, in many cases, such data have been readily provided to the public. This situation has been true for many decades with respect to futures but is still evolving for swaps markets. However, this path has evolved separately from the path for securities market regulation. The comprehensive data on commodity derivatives positions held by various market participants do not have an analog in securities markets.

Disagreements over the social benefits and proper scope of agricultural derivatives trading were a regular feature of public debate during the late nineteenth and early twentieth centuries in the United States. By the early 1920s, the federal government had commenced data intensive investigations by the Federal Trade Commission and had begun constructing a regulatory framework covering futures trading. For the first time, regulations required exchanges to provide transparency via public release of data on open interest and volume of trading, in addition to price information. The Grain Futures Administration (part of the Department of Agriculture), a predecessor of the Commodity Exchange Authority, which was in turn a predecessor of the Commodity Futures Trading Commission (CFTC), was tasked with overseeing the derivatives markets. The implicit motivation of protecting the users of these markets—farmers, ranchers, millers, or other commodity producers and consumers—has been a cornerstone of the regulations since the beginning.

Wheat futures experienced substantial volatility during 1925, and the Senate requested an investigation by the Secretary of Agriculture. The resulting report featured detailed, quantitative information on the trading activities of different classes of traders (e.g., "speculators" and "hedgers") (U.S. Congress 1926). Among the analyses were effectively order flow regressions relating day-to-day net changes in positions of traders to the price change of the futures. Finding a compelling, positive correlation between the position changes of speculators and price changes, researchers suggested policy conclusions, including restrictions on large positions in order to minimize "unwarranted" or disruptive price changes. Collection and public dissemination of such data on trading volume or positions of large traders, grouped into economically meaningful categories in order to retain anonymity of individual participants, have continued since then. The data have formed a core part of many empirical analyses of commodity markets.

Regulation of securities markets followed a separate and somewhat later path, as did the academic work on securities markets. Although some researchers, notably Holbrook Working at the Stanford University Food Research Institute, examined wheat futures activities starting in the 1920s, academic research on securities markets was sporadic until the 1950s and 1960s. This separation led to the research topics evolving separately, although merging of important ideas from both fields is a crucial exercise for modern research.

Table 27.1 provides a summary of publicly available Commitments of Traders (COT) data for select commodities. The CFTC's data are used in many of the studies described in this chapter. The data are for the futures and options positions combined. Therefore, long call positions and short puts are treated as delta-equivalent long futures positions. Similarly, short call and long put positions are treated as delta-equivalent short futures positions. Net positions may not sum to zero because of both rounding and the table excluding non-reportable, typically small trader, positions. The table displays average open interest and average positions for certain participant types between 2006 and 2015. One key observation is that participants generally involved in the handing of commodities ("Producers/Merchants/Processors/Users," often denoted "Commercials") are commonly net short in futures as a hedge against long positions held in the actual commodity. Although some users hedge by being long, the commercial position is often short in aggregate. Because derivatives instruments are in zero net supply (for every long, a short exists), these net short positions must be offset by long positions held by other participants. Table 27.1 illustrates that each of these other types tend to be net long and each type, on average, therefore tends to facilitate hedging by commercial users.

Academic Literature

This section begins by discussing recent literature related to core concepts for commodity markets. What do hedgers do? Who facilitates the positions that commercial

Table 27.1 **Average Reported Net Positions, by Participant Type, in Select Commodities (Thousands of Contracts) between 2006 and 2015**

Future	*Open Interest*	*Producer/ Merchant/ Processor/User*	*Swap Dealers*	*Managed Money*	*Other*
Coffee	202	−33	27	3	2
Corn	1,822	−322	257	127	51
Cotton	251	−86	45	28	10
Crude oil, light sweet	2,455	−81	−232	209	90
Gold	680	−95	−59	100	32
Lean hogs	301	−99	63	39	9
Live cattle	401	−131	81	68	8
Soybean meal	333	−93	33	37	5
Soybeans	884	−154	93	87	14
Sugar No. 11	933	−219	136	39	40
Wheat	551	−110	139	−5	−5

Note: This table displays average open interest for select commodity futures and the average reported net positions for key participant types, as reported in the CFTC's Disaggregated Commitments of Traders report. Positions held by traders with small, nonreportable positions are not displayed.

Source: U.S. Commodity Futures Trading Commission.

hedgers desire, and why? How are position changes, and the associated price changes, facilitated? What is the cost to trade (i.e., what are transaction costs and how do they vary)? Once these general themes are covered, two recent trends in the markets are described that have led to new directions in the literature. The first issue concerns so-called financialization of commodity markets—the dramatically increased participation by financial market participants that do not have commercial commodity activity as their main business. The second issue concerns the financial innovation of commodity index investing and the swap market activity facilitating over-the-counter (OTC) transactions in the indexes and in individual commodities.

HEDGING BEHAVIOR BY COMMERCIALS

The basic fact that most hedgers using derivatives are net short in traditional commodities is obvious from Table 27.1. Industry studies such as Tufano (1996) and Haushalter (2000) provide insight into the details of the hedging demands by firms. Although a prominent theme in the corporate finance literature on hedging has asked

"Does hedging add to firm value?" this question seems somewhat less useful for commodity research.

However, the corporate finance literature provides avenues for understanding how firms desire to hedge and actually hedge. For example, Acharya, Lochstoer, and Ramadorai (2013) use measures of aggregate commodity producer default risk as a proxy for the aggregate level of hedging demand. They motivate this proxy from prior literature suggesting that managerial risk aversion affects hedging strategy and firms hedge more actively when default risk is high. Conversely, Rampini, Sufi, and Viswanathan (2014) recognize that hedging may become prohibitively expensive at times because it requires collateral. When does hedging increase with default risk, and how does that interact with other firm choices? The literature appears to have focused more on interest rate and foreign exchange hedging by corporates, due to historical data availability, but the commodity-related hedging questions remain interesting and do not have obvious answers.

The institutional details appear important in discriminating among various conclusions. Futures contracts are cheaper to trade, but they require collateral, and the requirements for posting variation margin, in case of adverse price moves, is quite inflexible. Many firms prefer to trade OTC because of the flexibility they can gain, particularly with respect to margin (compared to futures margin). Commercial firms do trade futures in some cases and forwards and swaps in other cases, and perhaps the same firms engage in both OTC and listed trading. Although reasons exist that explain cross-sectional variations in commodity hedging activity and commodity hedging instruments, much more research can be done in this area.

An ancillary issue raised by the possibility of firms hedging in either futures or the OTC market is that the extant aggregate data on hedging pressure are invariably based on the CFTC's Commitments of Trader data. Although useful and available, the data may be misleading in some instances if hedgers tend to use the OTC markets more. Researchers should be mindful of this caveat.

Cheng and Xiong (2014b) also frame an important aspect of hedging behavior quite succinctly. They find that the volatility of hedger positions is much higher than the volatility of output, whether measured by ex post output fluctuations or by month-to-month changes in output forecasts. A conclusion that is tempting for some is that they are simply trading "too much," or speculating. Cheng and Xiong also find that between 2007 and 2011 the hedge ratios of futures to aggregate output are 17 percent for corn, 28 percent for wheat, 32 percent for soybeans, and 57 percent for cotton. Casual observation suggests these figures are well below theoretically optimal levels given most models. An interesting question for theoretical models of hedging is whether they can generate the variability of hedge ratios observed in the data and simultaneously generate the low average levels of hedging.

LONG-TERM PROVISION OF LIQUIDITY

The traditional risk premium or hedging pressure theories of Keynes (1923) and Hicks (1939) predict that hedgers are willing to pay to induce financial participants to take the other side of their hedge. If hedgers are long the physical asset and want to short the future, speculators require the equilibrium futures price to be a bit below the expected price at maturity, in order for the speculators to make money on the trade. Bessembinder (1992) and De Roon, Nijman, and Veld (2000) provide modern tests of this theory and offer some support for it.

Gorton, Hayashi, and Rouwenhorst (2013) examine a broad range of commodities using aggregated CFTC Commitments of Traders data and find evidence for a risk premium in futures that varies across commodities and time depending on the level of inventories. Using more finely disaggregated daily data on futures contracts held on crude oil, gasoline, and heating oil, Dewally, Ederington, and Fernando (2013) find that the cross-sectional variation in trading profits across 11 different types of market participants is well-explained by observable differences in their trading strategies or characteristics. Mean hedger profits are negative but mean speculator profits are positive. They find results consistent with hedging pressure theories and conclude that the profits of speculators and particularly hedge funds are due to the risk-bearing capacity they provide hedgers. Market participants who are willing to hold positions opposite hedgers get paid to do so, especially when volatility is high or inventories are low.

Moskowitz, Ooi, and Pedersen (2012) examine monthly data between 1965 and 2009 and also time frames of a year or more. They conclude that noncommercial traders benefit from futures time-series momentum at the expense of commercials. Boyd, Büyükşahin, Haigh, and Harris (2016) provide further information on hedge fund herding behavior. At least a portion of this compensation appears to due to the roll return, which would support the hedging pressure theory.

These studies support the idea that hedgers are willing to pay in order to maintain a hedge over long periods of time (e.g., over a crop year). In other words, hedgers provide compensation to other market participants in order to induce them to provide long-term liquidity. Interestingly, some authors suggest that commercial traders may also provide liquidity in the relatively short term (e.g., day-to-day). Kang, Rouwenhorst, and Tang (2017) suggest that, while hedgers desire a long-term hedge position, they may vary these hedge positions in the short term if they are paid for the immediacy they provide to other participants.

Fishe and Smith (2012) find similar results. They use powerful statistical techniques to identify informed traders and, as a byproduct, identify common characteristics of liquidity providing traders (i.e., those who are uninformed about the next day's price change but trade in the opposite direction to concurrent price changes). Fishe and Smith examine 12 commodities between 2000 and 2009 and conclude that select large managed money traders and hedge funds pay commercial traders, especially commodity dealers and merchants, for immediacy. Such findings could help resolve Cheng and Xiong's (2014b) puzzle regarding the substantial amount of trading in which hedgers engage.

INTRADAY INTERMEDIATION AND PRICE DISCOVERY

The most visible aspect of intermediation in commodity markets, for well over a century, was the trading pit for futures. Human traders on futures exchanges, known as

Table 27.2 **Automated Trading Volume as a Percentage of Total Volume, by Product Group**

Product Group	*11/2012–10/2014*	*11/2014–10/2016*
Agriculture—Grain and Oilseed	39.0	49.0
Agriculture—Livestock	32.4	45.8
Agriculture—Lumber and Pulp	10.5	20.4
Energy—Crude Oil	54.3	63.0
Energy—Electricity	0.0	0.0
Energy—Natural Gas	44.2	56.8
Equities—U.S. Index	66.5	71.5
FX—G10	80.7	83.7
Interest Rates—U.S. Treasury	64.0	68.4
Metals—Precious	45.9	53.5

Note: This table displays the percentage of total trading volume for select groups of commodities, attributable to "Automated Trading." In this context, automated trading refers to trades not submitted manually to the exchange; trades are flagged in the audit trail data if they are not submitted manually. Statistics are shown for the periods November 2012 to October 2014 and November 2012 to October 2016.

Source: Haynes and Roberts (2017).

"locals," provided intraday liquidity to participants who wanted to go long or short futures immediately. Locals traded substantial quantities but went home flat, or with a very modest position, at the end of most trading days. In contrast to the specialists who were obliged to maintain orderly markets in equities, pit locals had no such mandate and acted voluntarily. Electronic order books, once introduced, rapidly displaced trading pits, and most have closed (Gousgounis and Onur 2016).

Table 27.2 displays summary statistics on the fraction of automated trading (i.e., roughly, trades that are not manually entered but rather involve machine processing) in various futures products in recent years. Automated trading in financial instrument futures is higher than for physical commodity futures, but an upward trend appears clear in both types. Some activity, such as trading in products such as electricity or in thinly traded agricultural products or roll activity, appears to have more of a role for human processing (Haynes and Roberts 2017).

Electronic traders interact more anonymously than pit traders, and they can rely on automated programs to trade faster than humans can. Examining physical commodities might offer different insights into electronic trading than examining purely financial assets, which has constituted much of the research. Kofman, Michayluk, and Moser (2009), for example, study trading in natural gas when electronic and pit trading coexisted. Studies such as Raman, Robe, and Yadav (2016) provide direction on how liquidity provision in commodity futures might be different in the modern environment, especially during stressed periods.

MEASURING LIQUIDITY

Studies of transactions costs and liquidity in commodity markets are not as prevalent as in equity and bond markets, but some recent work has begun to fill in the gaps. Wang, Garcia, and Irwin (2014) examine the "top of the book" best bid and offer for corn futures, finding a generally tight market with relatively small bid-ask spreads. Marshall, Nguyen, and Visaltanachoti (2012, 2013) provide estimates of transacting in commodity futures. They find that costs are generally small (i.e., a few basis points) for orders occurring at the top of the order book, but increase sharply as trade size increases. The authors also find that liquidity is quite resilient in that the order book replenishes fairly quickly: 70 percent of the depth is restored five minutes after a large trade. Additionally, they conclude that the Amihud measure, which is easy to compute with daily data, is highly correlated with intraday measures of liquidity that are more difficult to compute. Across markets, Marshall et al. find that common trends in liquidity exist for different commodities, but they are unable to find strong evidence for the drivers of the trends.

Since the October 15, 2014 "flash crash" in the U.S. Treasury market, much discussion has revolved around the measurement of and variation in market liquidity, and to what extent the regulatory environment has contributed to any changes. Previously cited papers include data extending to around 2010, which suggests that more current estimates of transaction costs and order book dynamics may be useful to evaluate claims of reduced liquidity in the post-financial crisis period. In particular, understanding how liquidity varies during normal periods and stressed periods is a challenging but useful topic. Studies exploring activity around regular information events, the actual impact of large sized trades, and the potential capacity of markets to absorb large flows would be worthwhile.

Another issue worth careful consideration is the extent to which liquidity measures can readily be applied to less active instruments. For example, many measures of liquidity work well when the instrument trades at least once a day, or ideally many times per day (e.g., active equities). But derivatives markets feature complications exceeding those in, say, the corporate bond market, which includes many instruments that trade infrequently. Listed futures for long-dated contracts may trade infrequently, but they feature liquidity that is highly related to close substitutes. For example, a November contract expiring in *N* years would have liquidity similar to the December contract expiring in *N* years, even if the November contract did not trade on a given day and the December contract was quite active. Calendar spreads are quite common in commodity markets such as natural gas, and gauging liquidity in the spread markets presents further challenges. Evaluating liquidity for options or more bespoke instruments in the OTC market gives rise to even more complications because they may not trade. Simple computations may be insufficient to gauge liquidity. Furthermore, models must be used to impose enough structure to gain the required answers to simple questions such as "Has liquidity for hedgers in natural gas futures deteriorated in the past few years?"

FINANCIALIZATION

Financialization is a catch-all term that refers to the increased importance of traditionally financial actors in commodity markets, especially since the beginning of the twenty-first century. These participants might be pension funds seeking exposure to commodities as investments, retail investors taking advantage of new financial products to trade commodities, or hedge funds taking positions in commodities. The term is often used in a pejorative sense, with some commentators taking strong positions that commodity markets have been substantially "distorted" by large flows from these investors. Increased and volatile prices of food and crude oil, especially crude oil's sharp price increase and decline between 2007 and 2008, have engendered heated policy debates in recent years. Interestingly, the tone of the literature relating commodities to other financial markets between the 1970s and 1990s was that futures were somewhat segmented from other financial markets (Bessembinder and Chan 1992), which was deemed an undesirable outcome. The debate flipped in the early 2000s, with detractors claiming that the markets were not segmented enough from financial markets.

Two points are worth noting. First, survey papers, such as Cheng and Xiong (2014a), cover a broad spectrum of the financialization literature in detail. This section is necessarily more brief and focused. Second, little use exists in setting forth a false dichotomy suggesting that modern commodity markets are either totally driven by financial actors or totally unaffected by financial actors, much the way that financial research that only seeks to separate markets into "perfectly efficient" versus "not perfectly efficient" groups will gain less traction.

More useful research will aim to highlight the manner and extent to which purely financial actors affect commodity markets. An example is the work by Basak and Pavlova (2016), who model how the introduction of institutional investors may influence futures and spot commodity prices. The finance literature has made substantial progress in recent years by introducing frictions that complicate perfect markets assumptions. Sockin and Xiong (2015), for example, model how the influx of investor money into commodity markets can make distinguishing between price shocks due to physical demand shocks or shocks to investment demand difficult for market participants. Henderson, Pearson, and Wang (2015) find some evidence for this information extraction problem by cleverly using commodity-linked note issuance events to identify investment shocks.

Etula (2013) focuses on constraints for intermediaries and relates commodity returns to time-varying broker-dealer risk appetite. As Acharya et al. (2013) note, a parallel to this "limits to arbitrage" story is a "limits to hedging" story for commodity market participants. In their model, equilibrium hedging results from the interaction of hedgers who want to maximize share value, but are averse to price risk and financial intermediaries who face capital constraints. Because equilibrium hedging is endogenous, futures prices and spot prices are also endogenous. By this mechanism, financial frictions have real effects on spot markets and the real economy.

Traditional ideas about hedging often ascribe exceedingly simple behaviors to hedgers. For example, intuition about traditional hedging pressure stories implicitly assumes that hedgers have an exogenous quantity to hedge, even if financial participants exhibit demand schedules that depend on prices. Relaxing this strong assumption in various ways is likely to bring many rewards. More subtly, empirical analysis without explicit theoretical modeling often embeds strong assumptions on hedging behavior. For example, Working's (1960) T index of speculation embeds this implicit assumption that speculative traders vary quantities based on prices, but hedgers do not. Further studies that revisit the important "adequacy of speculation" debate such as Sanders, Irwin, and Merrin (2010) regarding the effectiveness of commodity markets might benefit from more explicitly acknowledging that hedgers also optimize.

INDEX INVESTING AND SWAPS

Discussions of index investing ignited the debates over the financialization of commodity markets. In particular, Michael Masters, a hedge fund manager, popularized the claim that institutional investors had driven commodity prices far above the prices justified by supply and demand fundamentals (i.e., a "bubble"). Masters (2008, p. 6) testified to the Senate that "Index Speculator Demand is Driving Prices Higher" and "Traditional Speculators provide liquidity by both buying and selling futures. Index Speculators buy futures and then roll their positions by buying calendar spreads. They never sell. Therefore, they consume liquidity and provide zero benefit to the futures markets."

Of course, index investors do sell commodity index products and index managers sell individual commodities included in the index as prices change in the marketplace. For instance, ceteris paribus, if the price of a commodity included in an index rises, the commodity will be overweight in the index and so the fund manager will necessarily sell to keep the index in balance. Other participants in the debate countered that commercial hedgers, who naturally wanted to short commodity exposure, faced a dearth of natural longs that would provide them the liquidity they desired. According to one financial industry executive who testified to the Senate about the introduction of the Goldman Sachs Commodity Index (GSCI), "When we first conceived of the GSCI, we did so with an eye toward improving liquidity in the commodity markets by helping to fill the gap between the large number of commodity producers who wish to hedge their risk, and the more limited number of consumers who are willing to provide those hedges . . . most of these investors are large-scale asset allocators who seek to invest in markets in which capital is in short supply" (Strongin 2009, p. 1).

A Senate committee reviewed the facts, including the testimonies quoted above, about activity in the wheat market and produced a report concluding, "Significant and persuasive evidence that one of the major reasons for the recent market problems is the unusually high level of speculation in the Chicago wheat futures market due to the purchases of futures contracts by index traders offsetting sales of commodity index instruments" (U.S. Senate, Permanent Subcommittee on Investigations 2009, p. 3).

Researchers provide alternative explanations besides index investment in explaining the "market problems" previously noted, in particular convergence issues in wheat futures at expiration. Aulerich, Fishe, and Harris (2011) offer a detailed examination of the delivery process for the relevant contracts and conclude that the details of the contract specifications, which were later modified, provided the most compelling explanation for the lack of convergence. After rigorously modeling the embedded option in the contract, they conclude that it provides a consistent explanation.

Many academic papers search for the alleged effects of the so-called "Masters Hypothesis" that unbridled index speculation wildly inflated the prices of food and other commodities. Many of the empirical papers find exceedingly little support for the hypothesis (Büyükşahin and Harris 2011; Irwin and Sanders 2012; Aulerich, Irwin, and Garcia 2014; Bruno, Büyükşahin, and Robe 2017). Brunetti and Reiffen (2014) provide empirical evidence that index investors reduce the cost of hedging and have become an important supply of price risk insurance.

A difficulty in quantifying the impact of index investing on commodity markets was the unavailability of direct data on commodity swaps activity, despite having a substantial amount of the index investment being executed via swaps. Mostly relying on Commitments of Traders-type data from the CFTC, researchers tried several workarounds (Hamilton and Wu 2014, 2015; Singleton 2014). When the debate began, the CFTC was publishing Commitments of Traders (COT) data classified into two main trader categories: Commercial and Non-Commercial. The "Commercial" grouping commingled the "Producer/Merchant/Processor/User" category and the "Swap Dealer" category broken out separately in Table 27.1. Analysts complained that this aggregation was increasingly misleading as swap dealers grew in importance.

In the interest of transparency, the CFTC began disaggregating the public data as shown in Table 27.1 and backfilled the data to 2006. The CFTC also supplemented its regular COT report with a Commodity Index Trader report and with a monthly survey of index investment, but each of these data sets came with shortcomings (Sanders and Irwin 2013).

Table 27.3 illustrates one of the problems arising with attempts to work around the lack of relevant swap data. This table uses the 2006–2015 COT data used to produce Table 27.1, but it displays the annual values for a single commodity, WTI crude oil, which accounts for roughly 25 percent of the commodity exposure in one of the broad indexes. Assuming the variation in swap dealer positions is due to the dealers facilitating long swap exposure by financial investors, the data in Table 27.3 are hard to interpret. Between 2006 and 2010, swap dealers had long futures positions, which would be a hedge for long exposure desired by index investors, although the positions are relatively small. However, swap dealer positions are short between 2011 and 2015, which makes no sense as a hedge for short index swap exposures.

Mixon, Onur, and Riggs (2017) introduce a new CFTC data set that provides direct evidence on swap positions held by dealers and their counterparties. The authors find that dealers perform a substantial intermediary role in WTI crude oil derivatives markets. That is, dealers stand between financial investors (who generally desire long, implicit exposure to WTI via index swaps) and commercial end-users (who generally desire short, explicit exposure to WTI, often through positions with optionality). In aggregate, dealers have relatively small net positions that they appear to offset in the futures market.

Mixon et al. (2017) also find that commercial end-users, in aggregate, hold even larger positions in swaps than they hold in futures and are net short in both markets. This finding is consistent with the otherwise puzzling results in Table 27.3; the interpretation is that the swap dealer exposure is due more to the large short swap exposure desired by commercials than the long exposure desired by financial investors. The data also suggest that WTI swap exposure via index investments accounts for less

Table 27.3 **Average Reported Net Positions, by Participant Type, in Light Sweet Crude Oil (Thousands of Contracts), Yearly between 2006 and 2015**

Year	*Open Interest*	*Producer/Merchant/ Processor/User*	*Swap Dealers*	*Managed Money*	*Other*
2006	1,856	- 86	35	50	12
2007	2,410	–141	50	88	9
2008	2,887	–115	23	87	14
2009	2,740	–177	53	93	24
2010	2,637	–194	14	138	28
2011	2,706	–182	–83	207	31
2012	2,411	–57	–213	171	85
2013	2,463	37	–367	239	88
2014	2,204	–45	–345	259	111
2015	2,493	–156	–151	171	133

Note: This table displays, for NYMEX Light Sweet Crude Oil—West Texas Intermediate (WTI) futures, average open interest and the average reported net positions for key participant types, as reported in the CFTC's Disaggregated Commitments of Traders report. Positions held by traders with small, non-reportable positions are not displayed.

Source: U.S. Commodity Futures Trading Commission.

than a quarter of the open swap positions. Exploring commodity derivatives markets with a more complete picture including both swaps and futures holds promise to provide substantial insights into the markets.

Practical Questions

This section provides several granular examples of questions on which a social planner or regulator might be asked to opine. In particular, regulators are generally required by their statutes to consider the costs and the benefits of the regulations they promulgate. The particular statutes set the parameters by which the regulators must abide, and the courts act as adjudicators in litigation about a regulator's actions. More broadly, however, the academic community can help develop the research questions and the methodologies by which the detailed analysis for a particular proposal can be framed. Economists in the regulatory sphere will often lean on the rigorous academic work done by others in order to evaluate a proposal. These applied economists can benefit from such groundwork in internal policy discussions that help frame the issues for decision-makers or in providing transparency to the public.

In either case, these applied economists live within the broader community of the economics profession and strive to use the most on-point tools, methodologies, and research in thinking about relevant issues. This section discusses some of the issues that have arisen in commodity derivatives markets in the past few years. The descriptions are intended to provide a broad sense of the open questions, of which some academics may not be aware and could provide substantial public benefits by addressing.

The first broad theme in this section relates to issues that have arisen with respect to swap reporting. The second theme introduces a recent trend in commodity markets, whereby dealers have stepped away from providing liquidity and other commercial trading houses have stepped in to replace them.

TRANSPARENCY AND PRICE DISCOVERY

One person's price discovery is another's harm. Before the passage of the Dodd-Frank Wall Street Reform and Consumer Protection Act of 2010 (Dodd-Frank), the OTC markets were generally opaque. The Bank for International Settlements (BIS) provided semiannual surveys describing the size of the markets, market participants possessed knowledge about their own transactions, and market participants heard market color about transactions that "traded away" with other dealers or had occurred through other dealers. More systematic swap data, comparable to equities, corporate bonds (post-TRACE), or listed futures and options did not exist. TRACE, which stands for Trade Reporting And Compliance Engine, is a program developed by the National Association of Securities Dealers (NASD) that allows for the reporting of over-the-counter (OTC) transactions pertaining to eligible fixed-income securities. Brokers, who are NASD members and deal with specific fixed-income securities, must to report their transactions by Securities and Exchange Commission (SEC) rules. Post-Dodd-Frank, the CFTC's rules implement a framework for real-time public dissemination of swap transactions. Generally, reporting parties must report the transaction data to a Swap Data Repository (SDR) "as soon as technologically practicable." The regulations allow for public prints of large transactions with a dealer to be delayed no more than two hours; large transactions between two commercial end-users are allowed to be delayed 48 hours. This dissemination of trades is colloquially known as a "real-time ticker" for the OTC swaps market. The SDR data are publicly available through the SDRs, vendors such as Bloomberg, and other vendors such as Clarus Financial Technology, which enriches the data with other information and/or processing tools.

Researchers have used these public data, merging them with other data sets, in order to evaluate the changes to markets and, in some cases, the effects of particular regulatory changes. Loon and Zhang (2016), for example, examine credit default swap (CDS) markets and conclude that liquidity improved after the public dissemination of OTC derivatives trades. Moreover, cleared trades, trades executed on exchange-like venues, end-user trades, and bespoke trades exhibited lower trading costs, price impact, and price dispersion. Benos, Payne, and Vasios (2016) conclude that end-user trader costs dropped sharply after centralized trading began for some vanilla contracts, but that markets fragmented geographically as dealers attempted to maintain market power.

However, little work has been done to exploit the public commodity swap data. Peterson (2014) gauges the activity in various agricultural commodity swaps markets. Skarecky (2017) provides some color on the quality of the data for energy swaps. This untapped resource should provide new insights into the previously opaque swaps world, but some work will be required to find the most useful ways to exploit it.

Market participants, however, appear to have been using the data to their advantage as soon as such data were published. This situation was much to the chagrin of other market participants who preferred the anonymity of the pre-Dodd-Frank world. Commercial end-users may desire chunky, sporadic hedging in size trades (e.g., a few times a year), and each tranche may take a dealer days or weeks to lay off the risk with offsetting flow or in the futures market. Virtually instantaneous public prints of the hedger's first trades may have tipped their hands early. On the surface, this situation is appealing because it means that prices can adjust quickly to the demand requested by commercials. However, immediate publication of trades may be undesirable because such publication immediately transmits the private knowledge of commercial traders into public knowledge. Both the change in social welfare and ideas for optimal reporting should be evaluated in future research.

Southwest Airlines Oil Hedges

One example of oil hedges involves Southwest Airlines, which had a large, well-known hedging program that was differentiated from that of its peers by featuring trades in much longer-dated expiries. As one Southwest executive testified to the Senate Agriculture Committee in 2013:

> Following the rule's implementation, Southwest immediately began receiving phone calls from dealer counterparties after reviewing the reported swap trades with statements like, "I see you just did a trade in 2017." That [is] anecdotal evidence that our positions, although not listed by name, are readily identifiable to the market given our unique strategy and large positions, which stand out in illiquid months on the curve. (Ricks 2013, p. 2)

Southwest stated that, due to the difficulty in laying off risk for trades that were publicly disseminated, dealers began to widen their spreads and impose additional costs on hedging transactions. In November 2014, the CFTC granted no-action relief to Southwest Airlines, allowing the dealers a 15-calendar day delay for publicly disseminating Brent and WTI crude oil trades in contracts expiring at least two years out (U.S. Commodity Futures Trading Commission 2014).

Mexico Oil Hedges

Mexico is a large exporter of crude oil and oil industry earnings account for about one-third of government revenues. Each year, Mexico's Ministry of Finance and Public Credit (Secretaría de Hacienda y Crédito Público, or SHCP) engages in hedging operations to purchase crude oil put options in order to reduce short-term revenue volatility and guarantee a minimum price received.

Implementation of the hedge is nontrivial. No liquid derivatives market exists for Mayan crude, the blend used for pricing Mexico's exports. Public sources indicate that SHCP purchases a combination of Asian puts on Mayan crude and Brent crude. The size of the program elevates the importance of liquidity and transparency issues. In 2016, the hedge was for 250 million barrels of oil, with premiums totaling $1,028 million. The program involved seven counterparties and 46 operations between mid-May and the end of August. As a rough gauge of the program's size, consider that the average open interest for NYMEX WTI futures over that interval was roughly 1.75 million contracts; hence, the notional size of the program was a meaningful 14 percent of the notional size of listed WTI futures.

During the 2014 hedging program, the press observed real-time swap ticker transactions from an SDR and speculated they were part of SHCP's hedging program. Asked about the relevance of the press attention, SHCP's head of public debt responded:

> It definitely made it more complex and more challenging to have these new disclosure rules. It is always better for us to go under the radar as much as possible, because that helps our counterparties offload the risk that they assume with the programme. When the market is fully aware of the execution that complicates life for them, and for us as a consequence. (Energy Risk Staff 2015)

The academic literature provides some clues about how to think about transparency, and regulators have been keenly aware of the theoretical and empirical work (Spatt 2006). For example, Friederich and Payne (2014) examine an institutional change on the London Stock Exchange and find that full post-trade anonymity dramatically improves liquidity and reduces execution costs. Specifically, they posit that large traders who trade repeatedly in the same direction bear the cost of order anticipation (OA) facilitated by lack of anonymity. Tipped off to the presence of such a trader, anticipators take liquidity that would have gone to the large trader. In the absence of timely information on such trading, the large traders act more patiently and thus can supply liquidity over time to other participants.

As a counterpoint, Bessembinder, Carrion, Tuttle, and Venkataraman (2016) find that large, predictable trades are not always subject to predatory activity. In particular, they examine the monthly roll trades executed by oil ETFs and find that depth increases around these trades. Liquidity suppliers are attracted to this roll event and provide benefits to the liquidity demander. Theoretical analyses, such as the work by Naik, Neuberger, and Viswanathan (1999), may be helpful in sorting out consequences of various prospective actions. Although the framing of the previous discussion was in terms of swap markets, similar questions also arise in evaluating block trading in futures markets, which allows some large transactions to occur off-exchange.

THE WRONG KIND OF LIQUIDITY

In January 2014, the Federal Reserve Board issued an advance notice of proposed rulemaking about the potential environmental catastrophe and other risks associated with physical commodity activities of financial holding companies (FHCs), which some might interpret as "a bank." The Board received more than 17,000 comments, most of which were form letters. In December 2016, the Board proposed rules that, among other changes, would modify the risk weights applied to physical commodities, which generally would make trading such commodities much more capital intensive. Roughly speaking, the idea is that risk weights should appropriately reflect the risks of, say, an oil spill for which the FHC was liable.

In the proposal, the Board considered the implications of the increased risk weights and other rule changes and noted that

> a significant portion of FHC's physical commodity activity is related to their commodity derivatives trading activity. Based on the CFTC Bank Participation Report, the market share of U.S. banks in derivative contracts involving physical commodities typically ranges from 2 percent to 15 percent.... Thus, any reduction in activity related to financial contracts that may arise from the proposal should not materially impact the overall market for financial commodity contracts. (Regulations Q and Y 2016, pp. 67229–67230)

The existing academic literature appears to provide little guidance on how to gauge questions such as those proposed by the Board. How might the synergies between physical and derivative commodity trading be quantified? How would an FHC optimally allocate capital among the trading of related commodities if one were physical (with environmental risks internalized in some fashion) and one were a derivative? How would price discovery be affected? How might the impacts differ in the cross-section of commodities? For example, physical and natural gas futures for delivery at Henry Hub versus the many regional delivery locations might be differentially affected, and the impact might be very different from the effects on, say, the corn market. How would relationships between existing or prospective clients be affected? At the present time, many FHCs have left the physical commodity business, but how would different regulations impact their future choices? What methods would a regulator or supervisory entity use to calibrate properly risk weights for such activity, especially if it involves rare events?

The larger context for energy commodity derivatives activity is one that pessimistic journalists have described as the "wrong kind of liquidity." Market participants have voiced various complaints about market conditions in recent years, with some complaints alleging that post-financial crisis of 2007–2008 regulations have indirectly harmed commercial end-users of commodity derivatives by reducing liquidity. Although anecdotal reports from the press serve as a basis for creating attention about the concerns, research into each of the underlying issues will take time.

Farrington (2016) neatly summarizes many complaints. She notes a structural shift in OTC liquidity for commodities, with regulations making long-dated hedges more costly to execute. Alleged causal factors include a reduced risk appetite for banks, which means less warehousing of commodity risk and less market making far out in the term structure. Participants specifically complain about higher capital charges. Farrington claims that "the dollar-per-barrel capital charge for a CCC-rated client three years out might be almost a hundred times the charge for a AAA-rated client trading" the contract nearest to expiration. Corporations face different constraints than hedge funds, for example, which will naturally hold a substantial amount of high quality collateral in order to facilitate derivatives trading. According to one banker quoted by Farrington, "Most of the clients we deal with that want to trade [over a year] out are corporates, and they don't have the working capital to post margin." The alleged result is that some commercials have moved toward much more listed trading instead of OTC trading.

While dealers have scaled back liquidity provision, other entities have moved in the opposite direction. For example, Morgan Stanley sold its merchant global oil business to Castleton Commodities International in 2013, and JP Morgan sold its physical commodities business to the trading house Mercuria in 2014. Some claim that these firms tend to provide more liquidity in the front end of the curve and do not provide the same broad relationships that a commercial might find with a regulated FHC. That is, a FHC might offer other services such as lines of credit, margining based on the total portfolio rather than the futures portfolio, or other investment banking services.

These changes offer many new opportunities for analysts. Large FHCs are often regulated by many supervisors: market regulators and banking regulators in multiple jurisdictions. How have the various capital and derivatives regulations affected the market environment for certain end users? Are the changes merely reflecting appropriate pricing of risk in the current environment, or are ways available to modify regulations, with the benefit of ex post data and experience, to achieve different outcomes? Although the prevailing tone of market chatter is negative about the effects of some trends, such as the move toward trading houses providing liquidity, under what conditions would this disintermediation of banks be a good or bad outcome for other commercial end-users? How will trading houses innovate to capture new profit opportunities left untouched by traditional dealers? These trading houses often do not have the balance sheets that the large FHCs had, and they may institutionalize in various ways to adapt (e.g., issuing debt, partnering with deep pocketed backers, or becoming public firms). Because the environment and business model for these nontraditional dealers is still evolving, the topic is unlikely to become stale in the near future.

Summary and Conclusions

Commodity derivatives allow hedgers to smooth wealth across different states of the world. This chapter has described recent research related to core concepts for these products. It covered topics related to hedging behavior, the provision of liquidity in commodity markets, and the "financialization" debate related to the recent inflow of institutional investments into commodities. The chapter also provided insights into the types of topics faced by researchers who consider policy-related issues.

Although key topics in the literature, such as price discovery and liquidity, have been examined for decades, the integration of commodity markets into broader financial market trends highlights new aspects of these topics. For example, the intraday intermediation of futures transactions has moved from a business model with exchange locals who physically transact among themselves to a business model including highly computerized firms transacting via central limit order books. Commodity trading firms that often incorporate physical commodity merchandizing and trading with their derivatives activities may also be important liquidity providers as some traditional, bank-affiliated trading desks step away from that activity due to more restrictive regulations. Such a change blurs the traditional distinction between "commercial" and "noncommercial" firms in futures markets. Also, the increasing relevance of swap market activity has complicated the intermediation of risk among various end users of commodity derivatives. Hence, the evolving regulatory and market environment leads directly to new themes in the commodity literature.

Discussion Questions

1. Describe the CFTC's Commitments of Traders (COT) report and discuss how it can be used in research.
2. Discuss why firms might choose between trading listed futures contracts and trading OTC.
3. Discuss how theories of hedging pressure explain the determination of equilibrium futures prices.
4. Describe the financialization debate for commodities.

Disclaimer

This chapter was written in the author's personal capacity, and not his official capacity as an employee of the Commodity Futures Trading Commission (CFTC). The analyses and conclusions expressed in this chapter are those of Dr. Mixon and do not reflect the views of other employees of the CFTC Office of the Chief Economist, other CFTC staff, the CFTC itself, or the United States Government.

References

Acharya, Viral V., Lars A. Lochstoer, and Tarun Ramadorai. 2013. "Limits to Arbitrage and Hedging: Evidence from Commodity Markets." *Journal of Financial Economics* 109:2, 441–465.

Aulerich, Nicole M., Raymond P. H. Fishe, and Jeffrey Harris. 2011. "Why Do Expiring Futures and Cash Prices Diverge for Grain Markets?" *Journal of Futures Markets* 31:6, 503–533.

Aulerich, Nicole M., Scott H. Irwin, and Philip Garcia. 2014. "Bubbles, Food Prices, and Speculation: Evidence from the CFTC's Large Trader Data Files." In Jean-Paul Chavas, David Hummels, and Brian D. Wright (eds.), *The Economics of Food Price Volatility*, 211–253. Chicago, IL: University of Chicago Press.

Basak, Suleyman, and Anna Pavlova. 2016. "A Model of Financialization of Commodities." *Journal of Finance* 71:4, 1511–1556.

Benos, Evangelos, Richard Payne, and Michalis Vasios. 2016. "Centralized Trading, Transparency and Interest Rate Swap Market Liquidity: Evidence from the Implementation of the Dodd-Frank Act." Bank of England Staff Working Paper No. 580. Available at https://www.banque-france.fr/sites/default/files/18_benos.pdf.

Bessembinder, Hendrik. 1992. "Systematic Risk, Hedging Pressure, and Risk Premiums in Futures Markets." *Review of Financial Studies* 5:4, 637–667.

Bessembinder, Hendrik, Allen Carrion, Laura Tuttle, and Kumar Venkataraman. 2016. "Liquidity, Resiliency and Market Quality around Predictable Trades: Theory and Evidence." *Journal of Financial Economics* 121:1, 142–166.

Bessembinder, Hendrik, and Kalok Chan. 1992. "Time-Varying Risk Premia and Forecastable Returns in Futures Markets." *Journal of Financial Economics* 32:2, 169–193.

Boyd, Naomi, Bahattin Büyükşahin, Michael S. Haigh, and Jeffrey H. Harris. 2016. "The Prevalence, Sources, and Effects of Herding." *Journal of Futures Markets* 36:7, 671–694.

Brunetti, Celso, and David Reiffen. 2014. "Commodity Index Trading and Hedging Costs." *Journal of Financial Markets* 21:November, 153–180.

Bruno, Valentina, Bahattin Büyükşahin, and Michel Robe. 2017. "The Financialization of Food?" *American Journal of Agricultural Economics* 99:1, 243–264.

Büyükşahin, Bahattin, and Jeffrey H. Harris. 2011. "Do Speculators Drive Crude Oil Futures Prices?" *Energy Journal* 32:2, 167–202.

Cheng, Ing-Haw, and Wei Xiong. 2014a. "The Financialization of Commodity Markets." *Annual Review of Financial Markets* 6, 237–256.

Cheng, Ing-Haw, and Wei Xiong. 2014b. "Why Do Hedgers Trade So Much?" *Journal of Legal Studies* 43:52, S183–S207.

De Roon, Frans, Theo E. Nijman, and Chris Veld. 2000. "Hedging Pressure Effects in Futures Markets." *Journal of Finance* 55:3, 437–1456.

Dewally, Michaël, Louis H. Ederington, and Chitru S. Fernando. 2013. "Determinants of Trader Profits in Commodity Futures Markets." *Review of Financial Studies* 26:10, 2648–2683.

Energy Risk Staff. 2015. "Risk Manager of the Year (Sovereign): Mexico's Ministry of Finance and Public Credit." Risk.net, June 9. Available at http://www.risk.net/awards/2407591/risk-manager-year-sovereign-mexicos-ministry-finance-and-public-credit.

Etula, Erkko. 2013. "Broker-Dealer Risk Appetite and Commodity Returns." *Journal of Financial Econometrics* 11:3, 486–521.

Farrington, Stella. 2016. "'Wrong Type of Liquidity' Spells Trouble for Energy Hedges." Risk.net, December 3. Available at http://www.risk.net/commodities/energy/2478927/wrong-type-liquidity-spells-trouble-energy-hedges.

Fishe, Raymond P. H., and Aaron D. Smith. 2012. "Identifying Informed Traders in Futures Markets." *Journal of Financial Markets* 15:3, 329–359.

Friederich, Sylvain, and Richard Payne. 2014. "Trading Anonymity and Order Anticipation." *Journal of Financial Markets* 21:November, 1–24.

Gorton, Gary, Fumio Hayashi, and K. Geert Rouwenhorst. 2013. "The Fundamentals of Commodity Futures Returns." *Review of Finance* 17:1, 35–105.

Gousgounis, Eleni, and Esen Onur. 2016. "The Effect of Pit Closure on Futures Trading." Manuscript, Commodity Futures Trading Commission. Available at http://www.cftc.gov/idc/groups/public/@economicanalysis/documents/file/oce_effectofpitclosure.pdf.

Hamilton, James D., and Jing Cynthia Wu. 2014. "Risk Premia in Crude Oil Futures Prices." *Journal of International Money and Finance* 42:April, 9–37.

Hamilton, James D., and Jing Cynthia Wu. 2015. "Effects of Index Fund Investing on Commodity Futures Prices." *International Economic Review* 56:1, 187–205.

Haushalter, G. David. 2000. "Financing Policy, Basis Risk, and Corporate Hedging: Evidence from Oil and Gas Producers." *Journal of Finance* 55:1, 107–152.

Haynes, Richard, and John Roberts. 2017. "Automated Trading in Futures Markets—Update." Manuscript, Commodity Futures Trading Commission. Available at http://www.cftc.gov/idc/groups/public/@economicanalysis/documents/file/oce_automatedtrading.pdf.

Henderson, Brian J., Neil D. Pearson, and Li Wang. 2015. "New Evidence on the Financialization of Commodity Markets." *Review of Financial Studies* 28:5, 1285–1311.

Hicks, John R. 1939. *Value and Capital*. Oxford: Oxford University Press.

Irwin, Scott, and Dwight Sanders. 2012. "Testing the Masters Hypothesis in Commodity Futures Markets." *Energy Economics* 34:1, 256–269.

Kang, Wenjin, K. Geert Rouwenhorst, and Ke Tang. 2017. "A Tale of Two Premiums: The Role of Hedgers and Speculators in Commodity Futures Markets." Working paper, Yale University. Available at http://finance.uc.cl/docs/conferences/11th/Rouwenhorst-Tale%20of%20two%20premiums.pdf.

Keynes, John Maynard. 1930. *A Treatise on Money*. Volume 2. London: Macmillan.

Kofman, Paul, David Michayluk, and James Moser. 2009. "Reversing the Lead, or a Series of Unfortunate Events? NYMEX, ICE, and Amaranth." *Journal of Futures Markets* 29:12, 1130–1160.

Loon, Y. Cheng, and K. Zhaodong Zhong. 2016. "Does Dodd-Frank Affect OTC Transactions Costs and Liquidity? Evidence from Real-Time CDS Trade Reports." *Journal of Financial Economics* 199:3, 645–672.

Marshall, Ben R., Nhut H. Nguyen, and Nuttawat Visaltanachoti. 2012. "Commodity Liquidity Measurement and Transaction Costs." *Review of Financial Studies* 25:2, 599–638.

Marshall, Ben R., Nhut H. Nguyen, and Nuttawat Visaltanachoti. 2013. "Liquidity Commonality in Commodities." *Journal of Banking and Finance* 37:1, 11–20.

Masters, Michael W. 2008. "Testimony of Michael W. Masters before the Committee on Homeland Security and Governmental Affairs, U.S. Senate. May 28.

Mixon, Scott, Esen Onur, and Lynn Riggs. 2017. "Integrating Swaps and Futures: A New Direction for Commodity Research." *Journal of Commodity Markets*, forthcoming.

Moskowitz, Tobias, Yao Hua Ooi, and Lasse Heje Pedersen. 2012. "Time Series Momentum." *Journal of Financial Economics* 104:2, 228–250.

Naik, Narayan Y., Anthony Neuberger, and S. Viswanathan. 1999. "Trade Disclosure Regulation in Markets with Negotiated Trades." *Review of Financial Studies* 12:4, 873–900.

Peterson, Paul E. 2014. "How Large Is the Agricultural Swaps Market?" Proceedings of the NCCC-134 Conference on Applied Commodity Price Analysis, Forecasting, and Market Risk Management. St. Louis, MO. Available at http://farmdoc.iilinois.edu/nccc134.

Raman, Vikas, Michel A. Robe, and Pradeep K. Yadav. 2016. "Liquidity Provision under Stress: The Fast, the Slow, and the Dead (Evidence from Crude Oil Futures, 2006–2009)." Working paper, American University.

Rampini, Adriano, Amir Sufi, and S. Viswanathan. 2014. "Dynamic Risk Management." *Journal of Financial Economics* 111:2, 271–296.

"Regulations Q and Y; Risk-Based Capital and Other Regulatory Requirements for Activities of Financial Holding Companies Related to Physical Commodities and Risk-Based Capital Requirements for Merchant Banking Investments; Notice of Proposed Rulemaking." 2016. 81 *Federal Register* 190. September 30, 67220–67239.

Ricks, Ron. 2013. Letter to Senate Committee on Agriculture. June 1. Available at https://www.agriculture.senate.gov/imo/media/doc/Southwest%20Airlines.pdf.

Sanders, Dwight, and Scott Irwin. 2013. "Measuring Index Investment in Commodity Futures Markets." *Energy Journal* 34, 105–127.

Sanders, Dwight, Scott Irwin, and Robert Merrin. 2010. "The Adequacy of Speculation in Agricultural Futures Markets: Too Much of a Good Thing?" *Applied Economic Perspectives and Policy* 32:1, 77–94.

Singleton, Kenneth. 2014. "Investor Flows and the 2008 Boom/Bust in Oil Prices." *Management Science* 60:2, 300–318.

Skarecky, Tod. 2017. "Exploring Energy Swaps on the SDR." Clarus Financial Technology. March 1. Available at https://www.clarusft.com/exploring-energy-swaps-on-the-sdr/.

Sockin, Michael, and Wei Xiong. 2015. "Informational Frictions and Commodity Markets." *Journal of Finance* 70:5, 2063–2098.

Spatt, Chester S. 2006. "Discussion: An Overview of Bond Market Transparency." American Finance Association Meetings. January 6. Available at https://www.sec.gov/news/speech/spch010606css.htm.

Strongin, Steven H. 2009. "Testimony of Steven H. Strongin, Managing Director, Goldman, Sachs & Co., Permanent Subcommittee on Investigations, Committee on Homeland Security and Governmental Affairs, U.S. Senate." July 21. Available at https://www.hsgac.senate.gov/download/stmt-strongin-goldmansachjuly-21-09-psi-hrg.

Tufano, Peter. 1996. "Who Manages Risk? An Empirical Examination of Risk Management Practices in the Gold Mining Industry." *Journal of Finance* 51:4, 1097–1137.

U.S. Commodity Futures Trading Commission. 2014. "Time Limited No-Action Relief: Further Time Delay for Public Dissemination of Long-Dated Brent and WTI Crude Oil Swap and Swaption Contracts Executed by or with Southwest Airlines." CFTC Letter No. 14-134.

U.S. Congress. 1926. "Fluctuations in Wheat Futures." Senate Document No. 135, 69th Congress, 1st Session. June 28.

U.S. Senate, Permanent Subcommittee on Investigations. 2009. "Excessive Speculation in the Wheat Markets." Washington, DC.

Wang, Xiaoyang, Philip Garcia, and Scott H. Irwin. 2014. "The Behavior of Bid-Ask Spreads in the Electronically-Traded Corn Futures Market." *American Journal of Agricultural Economics* 96:2, 557–577.

Working, Holbrook. 1960. "Speculation on Hedging Markets." *Food Research Institute Studies* 2:May, 185–220.

28

Future of Commodity Markets and Investments

HUNTER M. HOLZHAUER
UC Foundation Assistant Professor of Finance, University of Tennessee Chattanooga

Introduction

Philip Hopwood, leader of Deloitte's Global Mining group, notes (Deloitte 2016, p. 1):

> Just as, during the super cycle, people imagined prices would go up forever, people now imagine the market will never recover. Neither extreme represents the truth. What is true, however, is that our cycle times are lengthening. That means is could take years to adjust to current market forces—but it's still a cycle.

The commodities market, like most other markets, follows a typical cyclical pattern. However, unlike other markets, commodities markets enjoy two huge advantages. First, they provide a diversification benefit for equity investors looking to decrease their portfolio volatility while also increasing their expected returns. Second, they provide an efficient market for most goods that make the global economy work. In other words, a reason exists for calling the commodity market the world's grocery store. Thus, the commodity market will not only survive in the short term but also thrive in the long term as long as the global economy demands commodities and those underlying assets can be transferred from supply sellers to demand buyers.

How will commodity trading change in the future? The simple answer is that it depends. The future looks vastly different for different commodities and for the market in general. This chapter focuses on important trends and issues in the commodity markets. The chapter begins by providing a summary of the growth in the global and U.S. commodity markets and then focuses on three major topics. The first topic involves excess supply in the commodity markets, including how some traders are changing strategies to adjust to the current imbalance between supply and demand. The steel industry is highlighted, including its impact of the recent slowdown in global demand. Also discussed is how demand may rise in the future as the global population is expected to increase and how climate change is creating new concerns and opportunities for various commodity markets. The second topic concerns how the increased regulatory environment has created several trends in commodity trading, most notably a drastic reduction in the role for investment banks. The third topic involves the growth in algorithmic trading. The penultimate section discusses three different scenarios that could play out for the commodity market in the future. The final section offers a brief conclusion focused primarily on the need for the commodity industry to focus on finding creative solutions to changes in investor demand, regulations, and technology in order to remain relevant.

GLOBAL GROWTH

Globally, the commodity market has grown substantially from 2005 to 2015. In fact, commodity derivatives volumes increased by more than 20 percent between 2005 and 2015. Moreover, trading volume increased by 26 percent in 2015 with more than 4.3 billion contracts traded to pass single stock options as the most traded class of derivative contracts. The driving forces of this growth are China and the broader Asia Pacific region (55 percent) with more modest growth in the Americas (28 percent) and in the Europe, Middle East, and Africa (EMEA) region (16 percent) (WFE/IOMA 2016).

GROWTH IN THE UNITED STATES

The growth of commodity markets may be finally shifting toward other areas outside of Asia. China will likely remain the largest oil importer for some time, but countries such as the United States, which is enjoying a shale oil revolution, are becoming larger oil exporters. For example, during the recession of 2007–2009, the United States was net importing an average of more than 2 million barrels of refined oil products each day with some estimates as high as 3 million barrels a day during the peak. Just five years later the United States became a net exporter of around 1.2 million barrels a day (Bousso and Noueihed 2013). In fact, the United States is trending to be a net exporter of all energy products. According to the Energy Information Administration (EIA 2016), the U.S. energy market is currently balanced as a net exporter of both petroleum products and coal, but a net importer of natural gas and crude oil. The EIA expects the United States to become a net exporter of energy as early as 2019 if energy prices stay high. However, the EIA cautions that the United States could still be a net energy importer in 2040 if energy prices remain low (EIA). Nonetheless, this energy trade swing represents a radical shift for the United States, which has been a steady net importer of energy since the 1950s. This growth trend in the U.S. commodity market is not expected to reverse anytime soon. According to a survey of commodity traders by KMPG (2016), North America received the most votes (20 percent of respondents) as the region with the greatest growth potential for commodity trading in the near future.

One clear sign of growth for commodities in the United States is employment growth in these areas. Although several U.S. commodity industries have recently lost jobs due to the slowing growth of the Chinese economy, a broader view of the commodities market looks more promising. Stebbins and Comen (2015) rank U.S. industries based on their employment growth between 2005 and 2014 and several commodities-related industries are among America's 25 most-thriving industries. Industries in the energy, metals, and recyclables markets include support activities for mining (ranking 8th with 96.8 percent growth); oil and gas pipeline construction (ranking 11th with 89.7 percent growth); copper, nickel, lead, and zinc mining (ranking 14th with 75.8 percent growth); materials recovery facilities (ranking 15th with 74.3 percent growth); mining and oil and gas field machinery manufacturing materials recovery facilities (ranking 16th with 71.5 percent growth); oil and gas extraction (ranking 23rd with 56.3 percent growth); and pipeline transportation of crude oil (ranking 25th with 54.1 percent growth). Several industries in agriculture and livestock ranked even higher, including dry pea and bean farming (ranking 3rd with 117.0 percent growth); soybean farming (ranking 4th with 111.7 percent growth); goat farming (ranking 6th with 100 percent growth); apiculture (ranking 7th with 97.0 percent growth); wineries (ranking 21st with 57.4 percent growth); and corn farming (ranking 24th with 54.5 percent growth). Interestingly, two finance industries with broad ties to commodities also made the list: portfolio management (ranking 18th with 62.2 percent growth) and investment advice (ranking 20th with 57.6 percent growth). Lastly, almost no commodities industries made the list for the 25 dying industries in the United States. The one notable exception was the declining U.S. cotton industry, which has been hurt by the heavy outsourcing of fabrics production, including hosiery and stock mills (ranking 8th with a 61.7 percent reduction); curtain and linen mills (ranking 11th with a 56.9 percent reduction); broad woven fabric mills (ranking 12th with a 54.8 percent reduction); and textile and fabric finishing mills (ranking 15th with a 54.8 percent reduction).

Excess Supply

Although the United States is increasing production of several commodities, the country does not control global demand. Developments in the global economy, especially in emerging economies or transforming economies such as China, will most likely shape the future of the commodities industry. These emerging economies can influence the scale of the industry by changing both supply and demand for various commodities. For example, China's shift to a consumer-led economy has single-handedly decreased the need for infrastructure investments on a global scale, which has created a noticeable reduction in the demand for metals worldwide. This reduced demand has created too much capacity that will need to be drawn down over the long term (KPMG 2016).

Excess capacity definitely hurt profits for commodity trading. Almost every segment of the commodities industry felt the collapse of commodity prices in 2015. Energy trading companies performed well due to higher volatility in prices, but the oversupply of metal and agricultural products continues to create a lag effect on the industry. In a survey of 80 professionals in the global commodities market (KPMG 2016), 70 percent of respondents expressed concern about low commodity prices. Lower prices are the result of either increasing supply or decreasing demand. Of the two options, respondents seemed most concerned about decreasing demand because it signals lower trading volume, which will likely continue, at least in the short term, as large developing countries such as China shift from investment-led to consumption-led economic models. According to KPMG, the two biggest concerns for commodity traders during 2017 and 2018 are low global commodity prices (21 percent of respondents) and weak economic growth (18 percent of respondents). Thus, in the short term, the biggest challenge for the commodities industry will likely be shrinking trading margins due to the slowdown of global economic growth. The oversupply of commodities and shrinking of margins can have cascading effects as traders are encouraged to make deals that have more risk, more complexity, and more capital requirements. As traders abandon less profitable markets, the result is once again less available liquidity and higher probabilities of price spikes. The one positive spin of excess capacity is that, at least in the short term, the energy market will shrug off supply shocks. According to Franke, Frankl, Rechtsteiner, and Sharp (2014), the entire globe from the United States to China to Russia is overstocked with energy commodities, including crude oil, natural gas, and coal.

CHANGING STRATEGIES

Given the global oversupply of almost all commodities, traders are focused on optimizing their investments by securing commodities with stable demand. For example, commodity traders who traditionally borrowed or leased their assets are now purchasing assets to secure demand. These assets range from coal mines to storage terminals to gasoline retail chains. In other words, traders are increasingly trying to lock down stable sources of demand by securing long-term supply contracts. These contracts are commonly referred to as *structural shorts* and represent one of several growing trends in the commodities market (Franke et al. 2014).

EXCESS CAPACITY IN THE STEEL INDUSTRY

As previously stated, excess capacity has hurt almost every area of the commodities sector. Yet excess capacity and volatility in global commodity markets has affected few areas as severely as the mining and metals sector, especially steel. Like other commodity companies, steel companies have focused on cutting costs and increasing efficiency (Deloitte 2016). For example, PWC (2016) reports that more than 45 million tonnes of global steelmaking capacity was shut down or idled in 2015. A *tonne* is a unit of weight equal to 1,000 kilograms (kg) or 2,204.6 pounds. In the short term, the challenges for metal commodities will continue to grow as excess capacity in the global steel industry grows. A primary reason global demand for steel will likely remain low is the declining growth in China. Responsible for roughly 40 percent of global demand, China is a double-edged sword for prices in metal commodities because it is not only lowering its demand but also supplying cheap steel.

Historically, excess capacity is a relatively new story. In the last two decades of the twentieth century, the OECD (2015) reports little growth in the steel industry's steelmaking capacity. However, since the turn of the millennium, steel capacity has essentially doubled. Initially, steel capacity was ramped up in the early 2000s to meet the global demand for growing manufacturing and construction projects, especially the demand for new infrastructure in emerging countries. Yet few investors predicted the recession of 2007–2009, which cooled global demand and increased excess capacity. That gap between capacity and demand has only widened since the recession and excess capacity is one of the main concerns for the future of the global steel sector.

If global demand is falling, investors might ask why the OECD (2015) is projecting steel capacity to continue to increase from 2.16 billion to 2.36 billion tonnes from 2013 to 2017. Another main reason for excess capacity is government interventions. For example, the two most impactful government steel policies include continued subsidies for inefficient steel facilities and approval for new steel facilities. In fact, the OECD reports that, with the exception of the European Union, steelmaking capacity will likely increase in almost every area of the globe. Asia, in particular, will increase steelmaking capacity by 143 million tonnes, almost three times the growth of steelmaking capacity for the rest of the world combined (54 million tonnes). Governments can influence the steel capacity in other ways as well such as by introducing trade related measures, constraints on foreign investment, and specific operating procedures for government financial agencies. The OECD contends that governments need to allow market mechanisms to work properly to reduce activity that artificially contributes to excess steel capacity.

Despite government intervention, steelmakers are trying to address the excess capacity by cutting costs, reducing debt, and improving efficiency. In a survey of 37 chief executive officers (CEOs) in the metals industry from 24 countries, PWC (2016) finds that 84 percent plan to reduce costs in the next year. This percentage is not only higher than the 69 percent reported by CEOs for the overall commodities market but also higher than any other commodities sector besides energy. In particular, more than half of metals CEOs are concerned about high tax rates (compared to only 30 percent overall), which makes sense given that metals have the highest tax rates of any industry. Additionally, nearly half (46 percent) of metals CEOs are extremely worried about both rising energy costs and declining commodity prices, which is more than double the overall commodities market (19 and 21 percent, respectively). Metals CEOs are also uneasy about access to affordable capital (32 percent compared to 17 percent overall) and rising interest rates (30 percent compared to 19 percent overall). These last two concerns are important because continual capital expenditure is required to build new facilities and remain competitive from both a quality and cost perspective. However, securing capital is a challenge. Even when metals companies can find new investors, securing that capital at affordable interest rates can be difficult.

POPULATION GROWTH

One sign for optimism for the commodities industry is the continued rise in the global population. As the population grows, especially in developing countries, the demand for commodities should also grow. According the United Nations (UN) (2015), the global population reached 7.3 billion as of mid-2015 and is expected to increase to 8.5 billion by 2030, 9.7 billion by 2050, and 11.2 billion in 2100. The majority of this growth will occur in Africa and Asia with Europe representing the only continent that is projected to decline in population. Although the United States and Europe represent a substantial bulk of the demand for commodities, these projections suggest that emerging markets may play an even greater role in commodities demand in the future. Population growth can also play a role in the short term as expanding emerging markets have a direct impact on spot and future prices (Uhlfelder 2012). For example, base metals and other raw materials will be needed to build infrastructure, energy resources will be required to provide electricity and transportation, and agricultural products will essential to meet the increased consumption of meat and other commodities (Levitt 2012). These projections are highly dependent on advances in healthcare and the path of fertility behavior in several undeveloped countries. In other words, these UN projections could change, but the population in 2100 should still range between 9 and 13 billion (United Nations).

CLIMATE CHANGE

In sum, the global population is all but guaranteed to grow in both the short and long term. This growth will likely present new opportunities and threats for the global commodities market. Climate change is the perfect example of how population growth has created new opportunities and threats for the global commodities market. As a case in point, natural gas and coal are respective winners and losers of increased regulations due to climate change. Natural gas has been the beneficiary of increasing regulations on the coal industry. Although the U.S. coal industry likely received a temporary reprieve with the election of Donald Trump, concerns about climate change and the increased sustainability of renewable resources will probably continue to put downward pressure on the demand for coal. As the future for coal gets dimmer, the future for natural gas becomes brighter. In fact, many traders are hopeful that natural gas might even be traded more like oil in the near future (KPMG 2016).

In many ways, climate change is leading the way in creating new opportunities for many emerging commodity markets. An example is natural gas. Fracking is a growing but controversial new energy production method, which has not only increased U.S. energy production but also has made fracking beans a new commodity too. Another example includes changing weather patterns, especially large weather phenomena such as El Niño, which not only affect crop yields but also alter energy usage for heating during the winter, cooling during the summer, or even traveling during holidays. Also, recyclable commodities have enjoyed a steady growth as builders have looked to incorporate more sustainable materials into construction projects. Lastly, potable water has become an emerging commodity as the population continues to grow and deplete freshwater sources (Levitt 2012). The scarcity of potable or drinking water may seem odd considering that nearly three-quarters of the world is covered by water. However, fresh water comprises only 2.5 percent of the world's water and more than three-quarters of freshwater is not easily accessible, with most of it trapped in glaciers and snowfields (Mayell 2003). Thus, without serious improvement in desalination technology and infrastructure, potable water is likely to be a major commodity in the future.

Even Wall Street banks are going green. An investment bank, such as Citi, might not seem like the most obvious environmentally friendly company. Citi received the

2015 "Emissions House of the Year" award in part for its unique partnership in 2015 with Facebook. Essentially, Citi provided Facebook with a 13.5-year physical power hedge and renewable energy credits in order to structure a long-term source of clean energy for Facebook. The clean energy came from the Shannon Wind project, a 204-megawatt wind farm 90 miles from where Facebook was planning to build a massive data facility. However, Facebook wanted to assume neither the credit risk nor the construction risk of a wind farm project. Thus, Citi administered the entire deal by providing the hedge to Facebook, offering a $212 million construction loan to the wind farm builders, and participating in the $219 million tax equity financing with Berkshire Hathaway Energy. Like other investment banks, Citi's business deals in green energy are growing, especially in the United States and Europe, and include areas such as solar renewable energy agreements and carbon dioxide credits (Risk.net 2016a).

Increased Regulation and Restrictions to Financing

Climate change segues into discussing growing regulations for the commodity market. Increases in regulation, regardless of the cause, reduce returns for traditional traders by adding an extra layer of costs and by limiting resources. The one regulation change that is most likely to be a massive burden on the industry is a change in capital requirements. Depending on how new regulations are structured, the compliance costs will most likely make trading commodities less profitable. Although the initial purpose of regulation on capital requirements was to address firms that were too big to fail, the traders that may be most affected will be smaller traders lacking the resources to afford their own compliance departments (KPMG 2016).

Nonetheless, KPMG (2016) reports that one-third of all commodity traders expect regulation to have a "medium" impact on their existing operations. Some obvious ways regulation could increase costs for these traders include reconfiguring reporting systems, retraining employees, and hiring new compliance personnel. Interestingly, only 13 percent of traders reported that regulation will have a "significant" impact on their operations. Some obvious costs for these traders include major changes in their business structure/model, reporting systems, and even primary location. Perhaps the reason this number was low is that almost a third of traders (31 percent) reported the impact of regulation on their operations is unclear. Only 23 percent of traders stated that regulation will have a "limited" impact on their operations.

One reason traders may not have made up their mind about regulations is because they are so many regulations for them to track. KPMG (2016) lists the following regulations (in order) based on commodity traders' perceived impact of the regulation on their business activities: Markets in Financial Instruments Directive 2 (MiFID III); European Market Infrastructure Regulation (EMIR); Dodd-Frank Wall Street Reform and Consumer Protection Act; Corporate Tax Reform III (CTR III); Base Erosion and Profit Sharing (BEPS); Financial Markets Infrastructure Act (FMIA/FinfraG); Regulation on Market Integrity and Transparency (REMIT); Securities and Futures Act (SFA); Basel IV; and Extractive Industries Transparency Initiative (EITI).

Given the large number of regulations, commodity traders (21 percent) list "complexity of regulations" as their main regulatory concern followed by 18 percent of traders listing the "increased costs of compliance." KPMG (2016) lists four specific ways regulation can increase compliance costs: (1) consulting external advisors, (2) hiring new legal/compliance personnel, (3) reallocating internal resources toward compliance, and (4) upgrading reporting systems. Another costly issue of increased regulation is the way it restricts access to funding for some traders. In fact, KPMG reports that one-third of commodity traders are experiencing additional financing costs due to fewer funding options. Moreover, 30 percent of traders have begun diversifying their sources of capital to ensure sufficient financing for future endeavors.

BANK EXODUS

A prime example of the impact on regulations on commodity trading is the mass exodus of investment banks from the commodity markets. Although several regulations affect the overall commodities markets, Franke et al. (2014) cite two specific regulations—the Dodd-Frank Act in the United States and the Basel III/CRD IV in the EU—as playing a key role in forcing the banks to exit the commodity markets. Historically, banks played the dominant role in the commodities market by helping producers and consumers hedge through derivatives to manage price volatility. However, the new regulatory environment, along with collapsing price volatility, has ushered in a new era where banks are losing ground to trading houses as banks experience a slowdown in both client flows (Zhdannikov and Milhench 2013) and revenue (Register 2014)—effectively creating a double-edged sword for slashing commodity assets under bank management. As evidence, assets at the top 10 commodities hedge funds, which work in tandem with investment banks, totaled more than $50 billion in 2008. However, due to poor performance and investor withdrawals, these assets dropped more than 80 percent to less than $10 billion by 2015. In 2015 alone, bank revenues from commodities declined by 18 percent (De Sousa 2016). This slide has been even steeper for the first six months of 2016. According to Hume (2016), revenues for trading commodities at top investment banks were down 25 percent compared to the same six-month period in 2015. In other words, the problem is likely to get worse before it gets better.

Banks in commodity trading have other problems besides losing money and clients. They are also losing top talent to non-bank commodity traders such as Noble, Glencore, Cargill, Louis Dreyfus, Vitol, and Trafigura who can offer less red tape (Register 2014). Excessive bureaucracy or adherence to rules and formalities is only getting worse too. In an interview for Nussbaum and Blas (2016), Ross Gregory, an employment specialist in New York for the London-based Commodity Search Partners, states that regulations are pushing more commodity specialists out of bank doors. He vividly explains that top bank talent sees each new regulation as "just more rope around our necks." Gregory estimates that banks are losing about 10 to 20 percent of their commodity specialists to trading houses each year. Other specialists are opting to leave banks to establish their own firms. For example, David Silbert, the original builder of Deutsche Bank's commodities business, left in 2013 to create TrailStone Group. In a similar vein, Ben Freeman left his career as an oil derivatives trader at Goldman Sachs to found HudsonField LLC (Nussbaum and Blas 2016).

In some cases, banks are even selling their top talent. For example, after years of declining commodity-trading revenue and increasing regulation, Morgan Stanley tried to sell its oil division first to Qatar's sovereign-wealth fund in 2012 (Lucchetti and Pleven 2012), then Russia's Rosneft Oil Co. in 2013 (Baer and Mason 2013), and eventually sold it to Castleton Commodities International LLC in 2015 (Berthelsen 2015). Likewise, after years of regulatory pressure, lawsuits, and declining revenue, in 2013 JPMorgan also sold a substantial portion of its physical commodities business to the Swiss trading house Mercuria (Hume 2014). Other large investment banks, including Barclays and Deutsche Bank, have scaled back their commodities business (Hume 2016). In total, nine of the 10 largest Western banks that have been active in physical commodity trading decided to either leave the commodity markets completely or plan to substantially reduce their trading activity (Franke et al. 2014).

CHANGING LANDSCAPE OF COMMODITY TRADERS

In many ways, regulations are effectively closing the door on commodity trading at banks. However, like the famous revolving doors at most banks, one door usually opens when regulations close another. In other words, regulations also have beneficiaries. In this case, as the banks become smaller participants in the market, their absence opens the door for hedge funds and other trading houses to gain market share. For example, Osipovich (2016) reports that non-bank energy companies such as Axpo Trading and BP have performed extremely well in physical markets, especially electricity and natural gas, where bank departures have been most prominent.

Despite increased regulatory angst and declining revenues, some banks have decided to remain in the commodity business hoping the market will return to its more profitable past. Currently, the top three investment banks in commodity trading listed in order of revenue for 2015 are Goldman Sachs, JPMorgan, and Citi (Crowe 2016; Hume 2016). The bright spot for investment banks in commodity trading is that no new surprise exits occurred in 2015, and some banks even reported revenue growth (Osipovich 2016). Whether 2015 represents a turning point and how these investment banks might transform their roles in commodity markets based on regulations will be interesting to observe. As a case in point, the largest bank departures in commodity trading are on the proprietary side, in which regulations increased the difficulty for banks to trade with their own money. One way banks will likely survive is by bundling trading services with other services such as consultation for mergers and the acquisition of capital. For instance, investment banks such as Goldman Sachs are playing key roles in financing the massive investment opportunities into new energy technologies, including hydraulic fracturing, horizontal drilling, and renewable energy sources (Register 2014). Even Barclays, which initially scaled back its commodity trading, has adapted to the changing market and entered supply arrangements with both Hawaiian and British refineries (Zhdannikov and Milhench

2013). However, the real winner of late, at least based on 2016 Energy Risk Awards, is Citigroup. Citi won the coveted "Derivatives House of the Year" award for executing long-dated transactions and structuring complex deals that most investment banks would not even consider. Citi also won "House of the Year" awards in 2015 in both the precious metals and emissions categories—the latter based on Citi's role in creating a unique energy hedge for Facebook, as discussed previously. In a similar fashion, Citi received all three awards in recognition of its efforts in administering some of the largest and most innovative deals in these respective industries (Risk.net 2016b). Thus, despite recent regulatory burdens, banks such as Citi still represent a viable option for commodity deals requiring a higher level of service, creditworthiness, and transparency to provide efficient exchanges between buyers and sellers (Register 2014). In the future, banks will continually recalibrate their exposure to commodities and look to grab market share in profitable niches.

MATURATION OF THE MARKET

A common result of increased regulations and market maturation is increased liquidity and transparency. This maturation of the commodities market will squeeze intermediary commodity traders that previously focused on creating margins by supplying commodities that were inaccessible by open markets. For example, Franke et al. (2014) report that, as recently at 2009, traders using long-term fixed-price contracts to supply thermal coal could earn margins as high as \$3 to \$5 per ton. However, now that thermal coal is widely traded on open markets with transparent pricing, those margins have fallen down to only \$1 to \$3 per ton. Natural gas is another example of a semi-liquid commodity that may soon experience drastic reductions in margins as liquefied natural gas becomes more accessible.

HOMOGENEOUS MARKET STRUCTURE

Another trend in commodity markets related to regulatory change is the evolving structure of several commodity segments. For example, Franke et al. (2014) list key segments of the energy market such as oil, power, and gas as fragmented with many different players. Yet their market share of other segments, including metals and minerals, is concentrated with only a few large participants. Franke et al. predict that in the short term, the structures for different commodity classes will become more homogenous as larger players, especially in the energy and agricultural markets, take advantage of economies of scale. KPMG (2016) agrees that size matters. Larger firms with more financing options will be better positioned to take advantage of the current environment. Unlike smaller firms, larger firms can more effectively negotiate friendlier prices and prepayment structures. Larger firms are also better equipped to create their own sources of financing. For example, large energy producers, such as major oil companies, are restructuring themselves by monetizing their upstream production and gaining more control over their value chains. As a result, the margins for smaller energy producers are being squeezed, forcing these traders to either reduce or discontinue their trading activities (Franke et al. 2014). Others besides small traders are concerned about decreasing margins. According to KPMG (2016), 88 percent of commodity traders are feeling "some" or "strong" pressure on trading margins. Nearly 25 percent of these traders are planning to revise their strategies due to this pressure and 22 percent are planning to exit certain business activities completely.

NEW PERFORMANCE METRICS

Regulations will also affect how performance is measured. For example, Franke et al. (2014) predict that commodity price spikes may increase in the future based on new performance metrics for traders. Traditionally, commodity traders have been evaluated based on the returns on equity. However, traders are now more likely to be evaluated on returns from total capital employed (i.e., returns from equity and debt combined). The additional emphasis on debt is due to the increase in bond issuances by commodity traders looking to secure long-term capital requirements to acquire assets. As the evaluation metrics shift in commodity price, spikes are likely to occur due to supply disruptions. In short, the new evaluation criteria essentially punish independent traders who have traditionally made volumes of inventory readily available in order to smooth out supply and demand imbalances. Assuming these new performance metrics stay in place, the rising capital costs could drastically reduce margins for traditional commodity strategies associated with holding inventory, which could in turn result in less liquidity and unintended price spikes.

Rise of Algorithms

Besides excess supply and regulation, a pressing concern for commodity traders seeking alpha is the ever-increasing speed and efficiency of algorithmic trading. These algorithms are already trading more efficiently than most human traders because computers are both faster and more accurate regarding optimizing market conditions. In fact, nearly three-fourths of traders surveyed by Algofxsolution (2016) report that algorithmic trading is affecting the future of trading.

As the mathematical models for algorithms advance to take better advantage of data-driven fundamental and technical analysis, commodity traders will likely work in an even more specialized capacity than they do today. For example, a large percentage of commodity traders and analysts in the future will likely work for only a handful of large trading companies or large multinational firms that can afford the technical expertise required to tailor specific computer algorithms to the needs of their clients or company. In fact, Algofxsolution (2016) reports that only 22 percent of professional traders rely on external coding for their algorithms compared to 41 percent of amateur traders.

The remaining commodity traders will use more nuanced trading strategies and likely work on complex deals for specific commodities, especially in emerging market or other niche areas where algorithms are scarce. These nuanced trading strategies will be very important for a large percentage of amateur and professional traders. Algofxsolution (2016) reports that nearly half (45 percent) of amateur and professional traders do not plan to use algorithmic trading in the future. Another 27 percent have not made up their mind, which leaves only 29 percent of traders planning to use algorithms in the future. Fortunately, the commodity business will have a large array of job opportunities for traders in the future. For example, some more nuanced traders will probably work for either the supplier that extracts or produces the commodity or the buyer that demands the commodity as an input for their business. Two obvious examples include traders focusing on agricultural products from less developed countries in South America or traders focusing on crude oil derivatives for a company in the Middle East.

In short, algorithmic trading will have the largest impact on amateur traders. According to Algofxsolution (2016), 41 percent of amateur traders (compared to only 32 percent of professional traders) believe that algorithmic trading will have a deleterious effect on profitability and stability of retail traders. On the other side of the spectrum, amateur traders are the most vocal again, with 45 percent (compared to only 38 percent of professional traders) believing that algorithmic trading will improve profitability and stability. In other words, only 14 percent of amateur traders (compared to 30 percent of professional traders) believe algorithmic trading will affect the profitability and stability of retail traders. These statistics show that amateur traders are likely to be more affected—for better or worse—than professional traders.

Scenarios

No one can predict the future, but Franke et al. (2014) provide three scenarios based on new regulations and market reactions to recent trends. The first scenario is the status quo, which essentially means continued low commodity prices and heavy regulation. This is the doomsday scenario for the commodities market because traders, especially smaller traders, will eventually leave the commodities market because they will be able to find more profitable uses for their capital in other markets. As KPMG (2016) reports, only 15 percent of traders expect commodity prices to rise in 2017. More than half of traders (51 percent) expect commodity prices to stay at current low levels for the next few years, and the remaining third (34 percent) foresee prices rising between two and five years.

When adding the exodus of small traders to the overall bank exodus for the commodities market, this doomsday scenario looks even scarier. At least in the short term, this scenario suggests that some less profitable niches would face both liquidity constraints and rising hedging costs for producers and consumers (Franke et al. 2014). No clear way is available to gauge the impact that this illiquidity could have on these niches or the commodity market in general. However, looking at downside risk, a worst-case scenario would include the sudden bankruptcy of another commodities giant such as Enron in 2001. The unexpected collapse of Enron not only shocked the energy markets but also created similar liquidity concerns in energy niches around the world. Fortunately, at that time, the commodities market had a host of major energy trading banks with both the capability and creditworthiness to quickly provide liquidity to exchanges and normalize flows (Register 2014). If the commodities markets see another Enron in the near future, the question remains whether new commodity regulations will have taken away the very liquidity the market will need to survive.

Fortunately, most commodity traders expect prices to increase sometime in the next five years (KPMG 2016). Their views support the second scenario laid out by Franke et al. (2014), which is a return to business as usual. This reversion to normalcy would entail commodity price volatility returning to its long-term averages and rating agencies adopting more trader friendly performance metrics. In this scenario, the bigger traders will still possibly push out the smaller traders but the bigger traders would also be incentivized to provide the structure and stability that the large banks once provided for the commodities market.

The third scenario essentially eases regulations and provides incentives for banks to return to the commodities market. This scenario will provide the best chance for increasing market liquidity and trading activity. Regardless of which scenario plays out, the commodity market is vast and complex. The best traders will be those who specialize in specific niches and can also quickly adapt to changes in investor demand, regulations, technology, and other pressing issues such as political risk and climate change.

Summary and Conclusions

In summary, the commodity market is not going away. Commodities will remain an important option for investors because they offer diversification benefits. In layman terms, commodities tend to zig when other markets zag (Rogers 2013). This correlation is important because Markowitz (1952) shows that diversification within a portfolio can effectively reduce volatility and increase expected returns. In other words, the commodity market, with its array of correlations—or lack of correlations—with other markets, has, for all practical investment purposes, created an almost innate investor demand. Nonetheless, the persistence of the specific trends outlined in this chapter will depend largely on how that innate demand changes over time.

Although much uncertainty exists in the short term about investor demand, the long-term future will likely be more stable for the commodities market as the market becomes more efficient. The increased efficiency will be the result of regulations requiring better transparency, research providing better information, and enhanced technology providing a multitude of benefits. Technology will not only improve the speed and optimization of trades, but also create new demand for specific commodities and improve the production and storage capacity for more volatile commodities such as electricity (Sainsbury 2015).

Although several reasons support the notion of more stable commodity markets in the future, some time may be required for this stability to be realized, especially in transforming economies. For example, the transition of China from a developing economy to a consumer-led economy explains a large percentage of volatility in the commodities market. Although imagining another emerging economy having the same impact in the near future as China is difficult, traders will likely be concerned with large capital investments into transforming economies.

Lastly, even when the commodity market fully recovers, stability is not a sign that commodity traders can afford to be complacent. The rapid pace of changes in investor demand, technology, and even climate and political issues means traders must rely less on long-term trends. In today's commodity markets, traders need to be constantly adapting to the commodity markets of tomorrow. Commodities traders have historically proven extremely proficient in their abilities to adapt strategies to an evolving economy. This combination of creativity and flexibility will prove critical in the future as commodity traders will need to create unique strategies to minimize risk while also developing creative deals to increase leverage and maximize return.

Discussion Questions

1. Identify the global region with the most growth potential for commodity trading in the near future and provide support for this view.
2. Identify two primary causes of the excess supply in commodity markets and the commodity industry most affected by this excess supply.
3. Discuss the primary reason for the mass exodus of banks from the physical commodity trading business and which investment banks represent the three largest remaining participants in the commodity markets.
4. Explain how changes in technology both positively and negatively affect the commodity industry and provide several examples.

References

Algofxsolution. 2016. "Survey of What Traders Think about the Role of Algorithmic Trading." Available at http://algofxsolution.com/blog/survey-of-what-traders-think-about-the-role-of-algorithmic-trading/.

Baer, Justin, and Everdeen Mason. 2013. "Morgan Stanley to Sell Oil Trading, Storage Business to Rosneft: Bank's Commodity-Trading Revenue Has Logged 5 Years of Declines." *Wall Street Journal*, December 20. Available at http://www.wsj.com/articles/SB10001424052702303773704579270753675449452.

Berthelsen, Christian. 2015. "Morgan Stanley to Sell Oil Arm to Castleton: Deal Represents Bank's Third Attempt to Unload Business." *Wall Street Journal*, May 11. Available at http://www.wsj.com/articles/morgan-stanley-to-sell-oil-arm-to-castleton-1431379581.

Bousso, Ron, and Lin Noueihed. 2013. "What China? Energy Traders See Money in the Good Old USA." *Reuters*, November 8. Available at http://www.reuters.com/article/us-commodities-summit-china-idUSBRE9A614J20131108.

Crowe, Portia. 2016. "The Definitive Ranking of Wall Street Investment Banks in Every Business Line." *Business Insider*, March 23. Available at http://www.businessinsider.com/wall-street-banks-ranked-2016-3.

Deloitte. 2016. "Tracking the Trends 2016: The Top 10 Issues Mining Companies Will Face in the Coming Year." Available at https://www2.deloitte.com/content/dam/Deloitte/global/Documents/Energy-and-Resources/gx-er-tracking-the-trends-2016.pdf.

De Sousa, Agnieszka. 2016. "Goldman Still Top for Commodities during Dire Year for Banks." *Bloomberg*, March 23. Available at https://www.bloomberg.com/news/articles/2016-03-24/goldman-still-top-for-commodities-during-dire-year-for-banks.

Franke, Alexander, Ernst Frankl, Roland Rechtsteiner, and Graham Sharp. 2014. "The Dawn of a New Order in Commodity Trading—Act III: Five Megatrends That Will Alter the Industry and Commodity Markets." *Oliver Wyman*. Available at http://www.oliverwyman.de/content/dam/oliver-wyman/global/en/2014/oct/NYC-MKT21401-019_WEB.PDF.

Hume, Neil. 2014. "JPMorgan and Mercuria Scale Down Commodities Deal: Deal with Trading House Cut to $800m from Original $3.5bn." *Financial Times*, October 3. Available at https://www.ft.com/content/84ac84ca-4aea-11e4-839a-00144feab7de.

Hume, Neil. 2016. "Goldman Sachs Remains Top Dog in Commodities." *Financial Times*, September 23. Available at https://www.ft.com/content/15649fbc-ea39-3d1e-9bea-5d0944013098.

KPMG. 2016. "Clarity on Commodities Trading." Available at https://assets.kpmg.com/content/dam/kpmg/pdf/2016/04/ch-2016-clarity-on-commodities-trading-en.pdf.

Levitt, Aaron. 2012. "Commodities of the Future." *Investopedia*. December 24. Available at http://www.investopedia.com/financial-edge/1212/commodities-of-the-future.aspx?lgl=bt1tn-no-widget.

Lucchetti, Aaron, and Liam Pleven. 2012. "Morgan Stanley in Talks to Sell Part of Commodities Unit to Qatar." *Wall Street Journal*, October 4. Available at http://blogs.wsj.com/deals/2012/10/04/morgan-stanley-in-talks-to-sell-part-of-commodities-unit-to-qatar/.

Markowitz, Harry. 1952. "Portfolio Selection." *Journal of Finance* 7:1, 77–91.

Mayell, Hillary. 2003. "UN Highlights World Water Crisis." *National Geographic News*, June 5. Available at http://news.nationalgeographic.com/news/2003/06/0605_030605_watercrisis.html.

Nussbaum, Alex, and Javier Blas. 2016. "Fed Rules Seen Speeding Commodity Trader Exodus from Banks." *Bloomberg*, September 23. Available at https://www.bloomberg.com/news/articles/2016-09-23/fed-commodity-rules-seen-speeding-trader-exodus-from-wall-street.

Organization for Economic Cooperation and Development (OECD). 2015. "Excess Capacity in the Global Steel Industry: The Current Situation and Ways Forward." March 10. Available at http://www.oecd.org/officialdocuments/publicdisplaydocumentpdf/?cote=DSTI/SU/SC(2014)15/FINAL&docLanguage=En.

Osipovich, Alexander. "Energy Risk Commodity Rankings 2016: Risk of the Non-banks—Non-banks Shine in Rankings of the Top Dealers and Brokers in Global Commodity Markets." *Risk.net*. January 25. Available at http://www.risk.net/energy-risk/analysis/2443172/energy-risk-commodity-rankings-2016-rise-of-the-non-banks.

PWC. 2016. "19th Annual Global CEO Survey: Metals Industry Key Findings." Available at https://www.pwc.se/sv/pdf-reports/19th-annual-global-ceo-survey-metals.pdf.

Register, Chip. 2014. "Some Banks Haven't Given Up on Trading Commodities. And That's a Good Thing." *Forbes*, April 29. Available at http://www.forbes.com/sites/chipregister1/2014/04/29/some-banks-havent-given-up-on-trading-commodities-and-thats-a-good-thing/#631924b62020.

Risk.net. 2016a. "Emissions House of the Year: Citi—Facebook Wind-Power Deal Underscores Bank's Strength in Renewables." *Risk.net*. May 31. Available at http://www.risk.net/energy-risk/analysis/2459415/emissions-house-of-the-year-citi.

Risk.net. 2016b. "Energy Risk Awards 2016: The Winners—Rising Commodities Powerhouse Citi Wins Three Awards; Four Nonbank Dealers Also Recognized." May 31. Available at http://www.risk.net/energy-risk/special/2459632/energy-risk-awards-2016-the-winners.

Rogers, Jim. 2013. "Commodities Tend to Zig When the Equities Markets Zag." Jim Rogers Blog. November 6. Available at http://jimrogers1.blogspot.com/2013/11/jim-rogers-commodities-tend-to-zig-when.html.

Sainsbury, Peter. 2015. *Commodities: 50 Things You Really Need to Know*. *Pronoun*.

Stebbins, Samuel, and Evan Comen. 2015. "America's 25 Thriving Industries." *24/7 Wall Street*. December 9. Available at http://247wallst.com/special-report/2015/12/16/25-thriving-industries/.

Uhlfelder, Eric. 2012. "The Future of Commodities." *Financial Advisor*. February 3. Available at http://www.fa-mag.com/news/the-future-of-commodities-9527.html.

United Nations. 2015. "World Population Prospects: 2015 Revision." Available at https://esa.un.org/unpd/wpp/publications/files/key_findings_wpp_2015.pdf.

U.S. Energy Information Administration (EIA). 2016. "Annual Energy Outlook 2016 with Projections to 2040." Available at http://www.eia.gov/outlooks/aeo/pdf/0383(2016).pdf.

World Federation of Exchanges and International Options Market Association (WFE/IOMA). 2016. "WFE/IOMA 2015 Derivatives Market Survey." Available at file:///C:/Users/FVK528/Downloads/2015%20IOMA%20Derivatives%20Market%20Survey.pdf.

Zhdannikov, Dmitry, and Claire Milhench. 2013. "Banks, Traders Morph Roles in Commodity Market Rivalry." Reuters, November 8. Available at http://www.reuters.com/article/us-commodities-summit-banks-idUSBRE9A70LV20131108.

Discussion Questions and Answers

Chapter 2: The Economics of Commodities and Commodity Markets

1. **Discuss two common explanations for the term structure of commodity prices.**
   The term structure of commodities can be either upward sloping ("contangoed") or downward sloping ("backwardated"). Two competing explanations are available for this term structure. According to one theory, called "normal backwardation," commodity futures curves should all be backwardated as producers have a natural tendency to hedge their production stocks, incentivizing speculators to buy commodity futures by yielding them a premium. Empirical evidence shows limited support for this theory. Another theory is the "theory of storage," which states that holding inventories is convenient to commodity producers. To push producers to sell forward their stocks, speculators must propose a selling price that offsets the price of convenience.

2. **Explain the relation between the commodity basis and the expected returns on commodities.**
   The commodity basis is the return an investor would receive by buying a future on commodities and keeping the position until maturity, when the spot price of this commodity does not vary. When holding a buy-and-hold position in commodity futures over a prolonged period, an investor would need to "roll" her position from one futures contract to the next. When distant futures have a lower (respectively higher) price than shorter-term ones, the investor would continuously earn (respectively yield) a premium, as the price of distant futures will rise (respectively decrease) toward the shorter-term one. This "roll yield" is only a portion of the return on investment in commodities. The spot price variations are the other part. Depending on the maturity of the future bought and the steepness of the future curve, this roll yield can dominate the final profit-and-loss of buying commodities. For shorter-term maturities futures and frequent rolls, the spot price variations would historically dominate the evolution of the position's profit.

3. **Identify the main drivers of spot returns of commodities.**
The drivers of commodity spot returns are diverse. One driver is technological change, which impacts both the quantity produced and production cost. Another driver is demand. Some researchers find that global demand affects all commodities and was a strong driver of the commodity price peak in 2008. Commodity-specific demand can also trigger substantial changes in the price of commodities. A third driver is supply-side shocks, which can have brief to long-lasting effects. A sudden supply disruption can shake commodity prices. Finally, the rise of the "financialization" of commodities led some researchers to suspect that speculation affected commodities. Proof of such an impact of speculators is currently limited.

4. **Discuss the typical effects of an oil price shock.**
An oil price shock is an unexpected rise or decrease in oil prices. Many economists view a positive price shock as recessionary. However, a negative price shock has historically left growth unchanged. More recently, by disentangling global demand shocks from commodity specific shocks, empirical evidence reveals that not all price shocks are alike. Global demand shocks are only recessionary in the longer run but are positive for growth in the shorter run. Positive commodity-specific price shocks are recessionary, especially in the case of oil prices. Likewise, a negative oil price shock resulting from a global demand negative shock is negative for growth, partially explaining the asymmetry of the relation between economic growth and oil prices.

Chapter 3: Commodity Exchanges and Regulation

1. **Explain the roles of DCMs, DCOs, FCMs, IBs, APs, CTAs, CPOs, swap dealers, MSPs, MBSPs, FDMs, and RFEDs.**
   - **DCMs** are derivative exchanges regulated by the U.S. Commodity Futures Trading Commission (CFTC). DCMs act as self-regulatory organizations (SROs) that must enforce specified core principles.
   - **DCOs** are clearinghouses that guarantee performance of derivative contracts traded on DCMs. Like DCMs, DCOs are regulated by the CFTC and must enforce specified core principles.
   - **FCMs** are brokers who execute orders and accept funds from customers for the execution of derivatives regulated by the CFTC.
   - **IBs** are brokers who accept orders from customers for the execution of derivatives regulated by the CFTC. IBs cannot accept customer funds.
   - **APs** are employees of FCMs, IBs, CTAs, and CPOs and are required to register with the CFTC. An AP is any salesperson or person who supervises salespersons.
   - **CTAs** are persons who advise others on the values of CFTC regulated instruments.
   - **CPOs** are pools of investor funds that are traded by the pool operator in commodity futures or commodity options. Some describe a commodity pool as the analog to a mutual fund in the securities industry.

- **Swap dealers** are persons who deal in swaps on a regular basis and meet specified statutory tests.
- **MSPs and MBSPs** are entities who are not swap dealers or security-based swap dealers, but who meet any of three statutory tests, including persons that maintain substantial swap positions for their own account.
- **FDMs** are retail foreign exchange (forex) derivative dealers who are required to register with the National Futures Association (NFA).
- **RFEDs** are firms offering retail off-exchange forex transactions to retail customers and are required to register with the CFTC.

2. **Explain the differences between a CPO and a CTA.**
A CPO is the entity operating a commodity pool, while a CTA is someone who provides trading advice.

3. **Discuss how customer funds are protected in bankruptcy if an FCM fails.**
Under the Commodity Exchange Act of 1936 (CEA), customer regulated funds must be kept segregated in specially designated accounts that are given priority in the event of insolvency of futures commission merchants.

4. **Discuss how margin requirements are calculated for futures contracts.**
Initial margin is a good faith deposit by customers seeking to ensure performance of their obligations. Variation margin is the daily marked-to-market change in the value of a customer position. If adverse, the customer must post margin in the amount of the change.

5. **Describe how jurisdiction is allocated among the SEC, CFTC, and bank regulators over swaps and retail forex derivatives.**
The Dodd-Frank Act divided jurisdiction over swaps among the SEC, CFTC, and bank regulators. The CFTC has jurisdiction over "swaps" where the underlying is a commodity. The SEC has jurisdiction over "security-based swaps," which are swaps that have a security as the underlying. The SEC and CFTC have joint jurisdiction over "mixed swaps," which are swaps that have elements of both swaps and securities-based swaps. Bank regulators have jurisdiction over swap transactions by banking institutions. The Dodd-Frank Act allocates jurisdiction over retail forex transactions among the SEC, CFTC, and the federal banking agencies. The Dodd-Frank Act prohibits retail forex transactions unless conducted in accordance with the rules of one of these regulators.

Chapter 4: Behavioral Aspects of Commodity Markets

1. **Discuss how futures markets participants might exhibit psychological biases.**
Research shows that retail investors exhibit many types of psychological biases, including loss aversion, the disposition effect, reliance on reference points, overconfidence, sentiment, the break-even effect, and positive feedback trading. Futures markets participants have the same cognitive processes as retail investors, so they are also likely to succumb to these biases. Additionally, the fast pace and high stakes nature of futures trading is likely to heighten behavioral biases. The literature shows, however, that experience and sophistication somewhat mitigate

these biases. As financial professionals, futures market participants are more likely to be more disciplined. The participants that routinely lose money because of biases do not survive in the investments industry. Thus, the remaining traders learn to overcome their biases.

2. **Explain how loss aversion differs from risk aversion and who is likely to exhibit loss aversion.**
   In traditional expected utility theory, people are risk averse. They only take on risk if they are offered a reward—a risk premium. Risk is typically measured as a function of return volatility. The amount of risk a person assumes depends on his degree of risk aversion and the magnitude of the risk premium. Alternatively, prospect theory states that people react to changes in wealth from internalized reference points. Consider that if risk is measured as volatility, prospect theory predicts that people would not feel bad about making more money than expected. Instead, they fear the regret of losing money. Evidence suggests that individual investors, floor traders, and hedgers exhibit loss aversion.

3. **Explain the disposition effect and indicate who in the commodities and futures markets exhibits this effect.**
   The disposition effect is a derivative of prospect theory. People dislike taking a loss more than they like a gain of equal magnitude. Thus, they are predisposed to holding onto their losers too long and selling their winners too soon. A financial ramification of this behavior is that investors hold onto underperforming positions that continue to underperform and sell overperforming positions that continue to overperform. They also pay more capital gains taxes by holding losers and selling winners. In the Korean stock index futures market, individual investors are much more susceptible to the disposition effect than institutional and foreign investors. Institutions and foreign investors experience the effect, but to a lesser degree than individual investors. Evidence from Finnish and Taiwanese futures market is similar. Other studies find that floor traders, especially locals, exhibit the disposition effect.

4. **Define positive feedback trading and how it might affect futures markets.**
   Positive feedback trading occurs when an investor buys a security that has risen in price and/or sells a security that has fallen in price. Momentum is the phenomenon where prices that rise in value continue to rise in value. Investors who buy stocks because they have risen in price are positive feedback trading on momentum. When many influential market participants conduct positive feedback trading, prices may be driven beyond fundamental values. Researchers attribute various price bubbles to positive feedback trading, including the NASDAQ tech bubble of the late 1990s and the 2008 oil price bubble.

Chapter 5: Commodity Derivatives

1. **Discuss the main features of a "beta" commodity index such as the S&P GSCI.**
   The S&P GSCI index tracks the performance of a basket of short-dated commodity futures. Its aim is to replicate the return of a long-only, non-leveraged position.

The non-leveraged assumption states that a cash deposit equal to the value of the constituent futures is maintained and earns interest at the Treasury bill rate. The index has three main sources of return:

- The spot return measures the profit or loss from the directional movement of the future.
- The roll yield measures any profit or loss from having to maintain an ongoing futures position. When combined with the spot return, the roll yield generates the excess return.
- The total return incorporates the excess return as well as the Treasury bill return on the hypothetical deposit.

As commodity markets have evolved, structuring institutions have offered variations on beta indices. These bespoke indices may incorporate features that differentiate them from the beta indices. For example, the index may reference longer-dated futures; the roll period may take place outside the time frames used by the beta indices; and the index may allow for both short and long futures positions.

2. **Identify and explain some features of commodity futures that differentiate them from traditional financial equivalents.**
Commodity futures exhibit a term structure similar to traditional financial instruments. The commodities market uses the terms "backwardation" and "contango" to describe the circumstances where the forward curve is downward and upward sloping, respectively. Traditional financial futures derive their value from the spot price of the financial asset plus the cost of carrying the underlying asset. Although this relation is true for certain commodities such as gold and specific market conditions (contango), it does not always hold. When a market is in backwardation, the key influences on value are supply bottlenecks, spikes in short-term demand, storage issues, and supply-side constraints. Commodity futures can be cash or physically settled but in the latter circumstance the product can be delivered over the course of the settlement month.

3. **Explain how commodity structured notes differ from popular structures seen in other markets such as equities.**
Many commodity structured notes favor using correlation-dependent structures such as baskets options or outperformance options. Given than different commodities have dissimilar supply chains and demand and supply characteristics, a low price correlation often exists. This low price correlation translates into a lower price for the embedded option, which can result in very attractive participation rates.

4. **Identify the features of commodities structurers can exploit to increase the participation rate of a structured product.**
A low intra-commodity correlation can result in relatively inexpensive products such as baskets and outperformance options. When embedded within capital-protected structures, the low correlation results in very attractive participation rates. If the forward curve for the commodity is downward sloping, an option

struck at-the-money appears to be relatively inexpensive because a European-style option takes its value from the underlying forward. So if the spot market is 100 and the forward is, say, 90, an at-the-money spot European option will actually be out-of-the-money with respect to the forward.

Another aspect is the term structure of volatility. For traditional financial products in normal markets, this volatility term structures slopes upward. However, given that short-dated commodity prices can be exceptionally volatile, the term structure is commonly downward sloping. According to this type of term structure, longer-dated options are valued using a relatively lower volatility value, resulting in a lower option value. This lower option value results in a higher participation rate.

Chapter 6: Fundamentals and Commodity Prices

1. **Explain why a commodity such as lean hogs or cotton is expected to be more fundamentally driven than commodities such as oil or copper.**
   Lean hogs and cotton are primarily farm products with markets that are largely affected by local weather and supply/demand from a limited geographic area. Conversely, oil and copper are largely global markets that are relatively unaffected by local weather patterns or more narrow supply/demand characteristics.

2. **Despite commodity markets being deeply fundamentally driven, explain what could reverse that relation.**
   As commodities have become a financial asset and part of larger portfolios, prices could move beyond fundamentals. Additionally, expected changes in the global economic outlook and indicators such as the Purchasing Manager's Index (PMI) strength or weakness may not be directly related to supply and demand, but may affect commodity prices. Furthermore, changes in expected inflation and monetary events such as quantitative easing and changes in the dollar value may play an important role in commodity price changes at various points in time, and weaken the relation between fundamentals and commodity price changes.

3. **Explain the meaning of the following statement: "The non-fundamentals for commodities are the fundamentals for gold."**
   Gold serves as a store of value and competes with other interest-generating assets. Changes in the U.S. dollar, expectations about inflation, and changes in interest rates, which are items commonly associated with non-fundamentals for other commodities but not related to supply and demand for physical gold, commonly influence gold prices.

4. **Explain why using forward-looking equity prices to proxy supply and demand fundamentals is more appropriate than using fundamental data on supply and demand.**
   Forward-looking equity prices often react to global economic conditions, particularly for businesses that use commodities as inputs or produce commodities as outputs. Given this sensitivity to economic conditions, which proxy for global

growth and therefore commodity demand and supply, equity prices can proxy for commodity demand and supply. Moreover, because equity prices are readily observable at short frequencies, they can produce reliable proxies in a timely manner.

5. **Explain why different asset prices react differently to oil demand and supply shocks.**
   Oil demand and supply shocks have a differential impact on different asset prices for two main reasons. First, oil is a commodity input into many assets such as transportation firms, plastics manufacturers, and the CDSs of oil-consuming countries, so that high oil prices convey bad news to these assets. Second, oil is a commodity output for exploration and production companies, oil drillers, and oil-field services companies, so that high oil prices convey good news to the equities of these firms as well as the CDSs and currencies from oil-producing countries.

Chapter 7: Physical Commodities

1. **Discuss the effects of pairing transactions in commodity spot and futures markets.**
   When trading commodities, pairing transactions in the spot market with futures contracts can help to mitigate the risk of price volatility between the intertemporal prices. This process aids traders looking to capitalize on carrying cost discrepancies and others looking to hedge spot positions or future needs, where the effectiveness of the hedge is contingent on the liquidity and depth of the futures market. Simultaneously participating in both markets creates a new risk, called basis risk, which represents the possibility of deviations between spot prices and futures contract prices. Basis risk relies heavily on how well the futures contract hedges the present transaction.

2. **Discuss the short-term effects of commodity super cycles on the commodity markets.**
   Due to the supply and demand imbalance brought about by the emergence of a commodity super cycle, generally the increase in demand will drive the price of commodities up as suppliers attempt to increase production with a lag. Because many commodities need lead time for production, prices will be relatively inelastic in the short term and this inelasticity will substantially affect commodities most heavily used for construction and expansion. Industrial booms have driven many past super cycles.

3. **Explain how the need for transportation and storage for physical commodities affects commodity prices.**
   The need for transportation and storage for physical commodities necessary to facilitate production and consumption over time adds a layer of complexity that heavily influences commodity prices. For example, the proximity of commodity production locales to places of storage and terminals for transportation, such as ports for maritime transportation, may result in different prices between

commodities of similar quality, but available at different locales. Increased distance leads to lower prices in anticipation of greater carrying costs. In addition, buyers in the futures market are generally expected to compensate sellers for carrying costs.

4. **Discuss the interconnection between market interest and lease rates within the physical commodity markets.**
   Market interest rates often have an inverse relation with commodity prices, in which rising interest rates lead to downward pressure on commodity prices because commodities would be less appealing as an investment opportunity and more expensive to hold as inventory over time. Prices would have to fall to a level that would present an appealing potential yield for investing to increase demand for commodity and thus stabilize the price. Changing lease rates, conversely, are the result of changing supply and demand trends and are also contingent on changing trends in other investment opportunities. As investors compare other investment possibilities, they may want to borrow commodities, such as precious metals such as gold, to hedge against a market downturn. This demand for borrowing increases lease rates and vice versa if other investment possibilities are more appealing than borrowing commodities.

5. **Identify the largest participants within the physical commodity markets.**
   Because physical commodity transactions require large sums of capital and the necessary means to handle carry costs such as transportation, storage, and insurance, smaller investors are far less likely than larger investors to participate. As a result, physical commodity market participants are larger in scale. These participants include commodity producers and manufacturers who seek to moderate supply and demand necessary for operations using the spot and futures markets; commodity trading firms (CTFs) who seek to capitalize on their expertise of using different transformations of commodities; and financial firms (perhaps connected to bank or financial holding companies) that can handle large transactions.

Chapter 8: Agricultural

1. **Discuss the various ways to settle futures contracts.**
   Agricultural futures contracts can be settled in several ways. One of the most common ways is through physical delivery. If the contract is held through expiration, the holder of the contract will receive a shipping certificate that allows the commodity to be physically delivered by the seller of the contract. Additionally, negotiable warehouse receipts allow the buyer to gain ownership of the commodity without physically delivering the commodity. Another means of settlement, often used for dairy products, is through cash settlement. In this case, the contract's ultimate value is equal to the quantity of the product times the final settlement price.

2. **Discuss the use of subsidies in the agriculture industry.**
   Agricultural commodities are particularly susceptible to supply and demand shocks because of their cyclical nature, the necessity of gradual consumption,

and their unique storage needs. To mitigate those effects and smooth out variation in profitability, the U.S. government provides subsidies for agricultural production. The main goal of these subsidies is to ensure a constant supply of food to the United States as well as the countries to which the United States exports. The main agricultural products that benefit from these subsidies include corn, soybeans, wheat, cotton, sugar, and rice. An example of one such subsidy is the agricultural insurance subsidy. The federal government pays for crop insurance for farmers to insure against potential natural disasters that could have a severe impact on a farmer's income.

3. **Explain some common ways to invest in agricultural commodities.**
   One way to invest in agricultural commodities is through buying either the physical product or various nonphysical financial investments. Alternatives to buying the physical product include investing in exchange-traded futures and options, or in other financial markets. Investment opportunities in the securities market include exchange-traded funds (ETFs) and stocks related to companies in the business of agricultural commodities.

4. **Define basis and its importance in agricultural commodities.**
   Basis is the difference between a futures price and specified cash price for a given agricultural commodity. In a basis contract for any given commodity, the price is based on the spread between the cash price and futures price. Investors easily hedge the exposure to a futures market price on an exchange, but exposure to the local cash price is more difficult to hedge and represents risk in the transaction.

Chapter 9: Energy

1. **Briefly explain why energy markets are important.**
   Energy markets are vitally important to the world economy and fluctuations in energy prices can markedly affect consumers, manufacturers, airlines, and other energy users.

2. **Describe some common features of energy markets.**
   Energy markets generally are characterized by inelastic short- and medium-term demand curves whereby demand decreases rather slowly as prices increase and short- and medium-term supply curves that are relatively flat until storage and production capacity constraints start to bind, at which point supply curves steepen or become vertical. Another common feature of energy markets is periods of peak and off-peak demand, either seasonal as with natural gas and gasoline, or intraday as with electricity. Energy markets also tend to feature illiquid spot markets, so price discovery occurs in futures markets and long-term contracts with prices based on benchmarks.

3. **Explain why supply and demand in energy markets are more elastic in the long run than in the short to medium term.**
   In the long run, technological innovation such as fracking of natural gas or the enhanced ability to extract crude oil from shale can increase supply, while demand

can be adjusted by acquiring and using energy-efficient products when prices are high or by switching to alternative energy sources such as solar or wind power. Because energy commodities must be drilled, fracked, pumped, and transported, supplies cannot always adjust immediately to increased demand. Thus, short- and medium-term elasticities are higher than long-term elasticities in the energy markets.

4. **Explain how energy futures markets typically differ from other commodity futures markets such as agricultural markets.**
   Agricultural futures contracts currently provide for delivery of a wide variety of grades and locations, typically under a system of fixed differentials. The result of this contract structure is that while more users can conveniently deliver against the futures contract, futures prices typically reflect the "cheapest-to-deliver" grade and location, which may vary over time. In contrast, energy futures contracts are structured to reflect the price of a single location, grade, and variety. Thus, futures prices can consistently comprise widely used benchmarks for energy prices across the industry. This situation also means that greater varieties of derivative products are available in the energy industry to provide more precise hedges for end users.

5. **Explain how and why the structure of energy derivative markets has changed over the last 30 years.**
   Bilateral and uncleared OTC energy swaps arose along with futures contracts during the late twentieth century. In 1999, the energy trading company Enron created a single-dealer electronic trading platform called EnronOnline, which listed an enormous variety of energy swaps with Enron as a counterparty to every trade. Enron's 2001 bankruptcy led to a collapse in OTC energy swaps trading but the market revived when both ICE's electronic trading platform and NYMEX's (now CME) ClearPort later introduced swap clearing. Following implementation of the 2010 Dodd-Frank Act, both ICE and CME converted energy swaps to otherwise identical futures contracts so market participants could avoid certain swap regulations such as swap dealer registration.

6. **Describe two major legislative changes since 2000 that affected energy derivatives markets.**
   One major legislative change was the Commodity Futures Modernization Act (CFMA) in 2000. The CFMA was hailed as providing legal certainty for the OTC derivatives markets and allowed for electronic trading of energy OTC derivatives. The Dodd-Frank Act enacted in 2010 was a second major legislative change. Before Dodd-Frank, OTC swap transactions were generally unregulated, although certain natural gas and electricity swaps, known as significant price discovery contracts were brought under limited CFTC oversight in 2008. Dodd-Frank brought these OTC energy derivatives fully under the regulation of the CFTC.

Chapter 10: Livestock

1. **Jameson Meatpackers is a large buyer of live cattle. Jameson purchases its live cattle from various feedlots and engages in grid pricing using the current spot price for**

its base price, adjusting for premiums and discounts depending on the quality of the live cattle. Jameson is concerned that over the next few months, spot prices for live cattle are likely to increase. As a hedging measure, Jameson enters a short position on 100 live cattle futures contracts. Explain whether this strategy is appropriate for Jameson in order to hedge an increase in the spot prices of live cattle.
Jameson Meatpackers is a buyer, not a seller, of live cattle. Live cattle are an input that Jameson turns into various final products. Increasing prices of live cattle negatively affect Jameson's profits. Because Jameson is concerned with live cattle prices increasing (i.e., the cost of its inputs increasing), Jameson should enter a long futures position on live cattle, locking in the price the position will pay in the future to hedge against price increases. Jameson also could have entered a forward agreement locking in a price at which it could purchase live cattle.

2. **Jameson Meatpackers purchases hogs in two cash markets located in the western Corn Belt. John Jameson oversees basis calculations and record-keeping. He receives a lean hog futures quote for next month for $0.5025 per pound. He also knows that all week he can buy hogs in the two cash markets in which Jameson transacts, in Market A for $0.50 per pound and in Market B for $0.505 per pound. Describe how many and what type of bases Jameson must calculate. Explain what Jameson can infer from these calculations. Explain what basis changes Jameson is expecting if he entered a long position on a lean hogs futures contract at $0.5025 per pound.**
Jameson must calculate two current bases (Spot price – Futures price),
$0.50 – $0.5025 = -$0.0025 per pound
$0.505 – $0.5025 = $0.0025 cents per pound
As a buyer of livestock, Jameson prefers a weaker basis, which results in weaker cash markets. An inference is that Jameson is better off buying hogs in cash Market A quoted at $0.50 per pound rather than in Market B for $0.505 per pound. If Jameson enters into a long futures position at $0.5025 per pound, Jameson would prefer the basis for both markets to weaken or become more negative. This scenario could occur if spot prices decreased more than futures prices or futures prices increased more than spot prices.

3. **Describe the differences between live cattle and feeder cattle futures contracts.**
The major differences between live cattle and feeder cattle futures contracts are the number of pounds the contract represents, daily price limits, and settlement type. Live cattle futures represent 40,000 pounds of cattle, while feeder cattle futures represent 50,000 pounds of cattle. Daily price fluctuation limits on feeder cattle futures are $0.045 per pound and $0.03 per pound for live cattle futures. Feeder cattle futures are cash-settled contracts, while live cattle futures are subject to physical delivery if the contract is not offset.

4. **Before the delisting of pork belly futures contracts, a trader wanted to speculate on pork belly pricings using options. Explain whether and why the trader would have been better off placing his trade on Globex or in an open outcry.**
All else equal, the trader would have been better off placing a trade for pork belly options in an open outcry relative to placing it on Globex because before the

delisting of pork belly futures trading, volume was relatively low, resulting in high volatility. The illiquid market for pork belly options would have been difficult to combat on Globex, where any modification to an order causes the order to lose its time priority in the limit order book.

5. **Explain how changes in the quantity supplied and demanded for livestock differ from changes in supply/demand.**
   Changes in quantity supplied and demanded result from movements along the current supply and demand curve. These types of changes are normally observed in the short term and result from factors such as sudden harsh weather conditions or disease outbreaks. Changes in supply and demand reflect shifts of the supply/demand curves. These types of changes are normally observed over the long term and result from an array of factors, including changes in aggregate income and resource prices.

Chapter 11: Metals

1. **Discuss how metals are related to each other in sourcing and use.**
   Metal ore often contains several metals mixed together, such as lead and zinc, platinum and palladium, or gold and silver. Metals are also often used together, such as nickel and iron in stainless steel, or copper, steel, aluminum, and platinum in cars.
2. **Explain how gold fundamentals differ from other metals.**
   More than any other metal, gold is used as a store of value. Other metals are more likely to be used as an industrial input. As a store of value, gold is often traded as a currency, is less likely than other metals to have supply shocks, and is rarely in backwardation.
3. **Explain how the process for setting precious metal spot prices has changed.**
   Since 2013, all precious metal auctions that once set a reference spot price have moved to more transparent electronic platforms. This change allows nonmember traders to submit bid or sell orders through a member without sharing real-time knowledge of their orders with the trader of the member placing proprietary orders for the member.
4. **Explain how price discovery around iron ore and steel has changed.**
   Since 2008, iron ore and steel trading has moved onto exchanges, with most of the trading volume in Singapore and China. Before that, iron ore prices were set through annual negotiations between the largest iron ore producers and the largest steel producers.
5. **Discuss the market changes that resulted from long LME load-out wait times.**
   Long LME load-out wait times between 2011 and 2013 led to changes in LME rules and the rise of regional aluminum premium contracts on both the CME and the LME. Long load-out wait times may also have contributed to increased trading volume on competing exchanges such as the CME and the SHFE.

Chapter 12: Commodity Trading Advisors and Managed Futures

1. **Discuss the differences between managed futures and commodity trading advisors.**
   Managed futures are the set of active trading strategies that use futures and related derivative securities in global capital markets. *Commodity trading advisors* (CTAs) are individuals or organizations that help investors manage their investments in these strategies either directly through separate accounts or indirectly via commodity pool operators (CPOs). CTA is also a regulatory term defined by the U.S. Commodity Futures Trading Commission (CFTC) and requires those performing such roles to register in that status. The CFTC formally defines a CTA as an entity that, for compensation or profit, advises others as to the value of or the advisability of buying or selling futures contracts, options on futures, or retail off-exchange forex contracts or swaps.

2. **Identify various types of managed futures strategies and summarize their important characteristics.**
   Managed futures strategies implemented by CTAs can be classified according to their trading styles and markets. The two major types are discretionary and systematic. Discretionary CTAs base their trading on their fundamental analysis of economic data, such as macroeconomic news and global supply/demand imbalances, and adopt a fully active management style. Systematic CTAs base their trading on rules and algorithms that are based on quantitative models. They do not apply sentiment or judgment. Some CTAs employ both fundamental and systematic trading strategies to deal with a potential failure of an algorithmic trading rule even without being diversified in the markets in which they trade. Most systematic CTAs are trend-following because they base their trading decisions on quantitative measures of trends, such as a moving average and exponential smoothing, and try to exploit momentum in futures prices. Furthermore, they tend to trade long and short positions diversified across multiple futures contracts. A smaller subcategory of systematic CTAs is counter-trend-followers, who employ quantitative mean-reversion models and technical analysis indicators to detect price reversals, a common phenomenon in commodity markets.

   Regarding the futures markets in which CTAs trade, CTAs are classified as either fully diversified or focused on a specific set of markets. For example, fully diversified CTAs trade many contracts and could systematically weight them equally or based on measures such as volatility. Specialized CTAs could trade in a single market such as currencies, agricultural commodities, metals, energy, and equities. They could also operate in larger sets such as financials that encompass currencies and equities or physicals that cover all commodities.

3. **Discuss the stylized facts about managed futures returns.**
   Two major stylized facts about managed futures returns are low correlation with other asset classes and positive performance during equity market downturns. CTAs enjoy very desirable (close to zero and negative) correlation characteristics

with major asset classes. For example, the long-short trend-following nature of the CTAs is underscored by the almost zero correlation with the long-only commodity index. The summary statistics provided in the chapter also demonstrate that managed futures perform positively, both in absolute and in relative terms, during periods in which equity markets experience large losses.

4. **Discuss the research findings about the stand-alone performance of CTAs.**
Studies in the 1980s had mixed results, possibly due to the limited availability of data and various biases. Lintner (1983) finds favorable results for the CTAs, whereas Elton, Gruber, and Rentzler (1987, 1989, 1990) and Irwin, Krukemyer, and Zulauf (1993) conclude that these funds provide returns less than the risk-free rate. Using Sharpe ratios, Edwards and Liew (1999) report evidence for superior risk-adjusted performance.

In the 1990s, several studies attempted to explain CTA returns with factor models and documenting the performance of these funds through their alphas. For example, Fung and Hsieh (2001), Kazemi and Li (2009), and Gregoriou, Hübner, and Kooli (2010) develop models with option-based factors, whereas Hurst, Ooi, and Pedersen (2013) use time-series momentum strategies to explain CTA returns. They show that alphas disappear at the individual level, but survive at the index level even when option-based factors are considered to explain more than 50 percent of the variation in returns. Gregoriou et al. also find performance persistence and confirm its presence based on the median alpha cutoff. However, their tests fail to pass quartile-based measures.

More recent studies also offer mixed findings. Abrams, Bhaduri, and Flores (2014) provide evidence to confirm the findings of Lintner (1983) with a much-extended data set. Bhardwaj, Gorton, and Rouwenhorst (2014) find that CTAs do not provide significant alpha net of fees, despite gross performance being significantly positive.

Most recently, Miffre (2016) provides an extensive literature review on the long-short commodity investing, an approach commonly adopted by CTAs and managed futures mutual funds. She concludes that most recent academic studies confirm the superiority of this strategy over long-only commodity futures portfolios.

Chapter 13: Commodity Exchange-Traded Funds

1. **Differentiate between an exchange-traded note (ETN) and an exchange-traded fund (ETF).**
An ETN is a senior, unsecured debt security issued by a financial institution with the stated objective of tracking an underlying index. Unlike an ETF, an ETN does not hold the underlying securities but rather is a promissory note whose value increases or decreases with the value of the underlying index.

2. **Describe the benefits of including an ETC in a diversified portfolio of stocks and bonds.**
Commodities typically have an imperfect correlation with both stocks and bonds. The benefits of including an ETC in a diversified portfolio is a reduction in overall risk as defined by standard deviation while maintaining a stable Sharpe ratio.

3. **Explain the types of commodities investors can access through ETCs.**
Through an ETC, investors can invest in broad or narrow baskets of commodities and individual commodities. An example of a broad basket would include a fund that delivers exposure to energy, agricultural products, and precious and industrial metals. A narrow basket might consist of multiple energy commodities such as heating oil, crude oil, and natural gas. Individual commodities accessed through an ETC include gold, silver, soy, and wheat.

4. **Aside from the ETN, identify what types of regulatory structures under which an ETC might file.**
An ETC can file with the SEC under the Investment Company Act of 1940 as a grantor trust, or with the CFTC as a commodity pool or partnership ETF.

5. **Describe two possible effects that the growth in ETCs might have on the futures markets.**
Since the debut of ETCs, research reports that cross-asset correlations have risen across commodity futures. Another effect has been an increase in market depth and liquidity that these funds provide by increasing capital committed to the futures market.

Chapter 14: Commodity Mutual Funds

1. **Discuss whether commodity mutual funds (CMFs) are feasible instruments to take advantage of short-term swings in commodity prices.**
CMFs are not feasible instruments for at least three reasons. First, CMFs do not generally invest directly in commodities but rather in the equity of firms involved in various commodities markets. The returns of those firms are correlated with commodity price changes over the long run but are subject to tracking error in the short run. Second, CMFs discourage in-and-out trading with exit fees and restrictions on short-term trading. Third, like other mutual funds, investors buy CMFs at a single price that is determined by the fund's NAV at the end of the business day, which makes CMFs inappropriate investments for taking advantage of intraday price movements.

2. **State whether a commodity price index would be expected to have a higher correlation with a CMF or with a commodity ETF and explain why.**
ETF returns would generally be expected to have a higher correlation with the changes in a commodity price index because ETFs often directly invest in commodities, while CMFs frequently invest in equity of companies involved in the commodities business.

3. **Discuss the long-run trends in CMF expense ratios.**
Between 1996 and 2016, CMF expense ratios declined and converged across fund types. Small funds tend to have higher expense ratios.

4. **Discuss whether CMF managers have generated alpha, on average, relative to the Fama-French factors and momentum between 1996 and 2016.**
Estimated alphas for CMFs between 1996 and 2016 have been, on average, negative or not statistically significantly different from zero using most measures, with

the exception of large funds based on AUM, which have generated positive alphas on average. Hence, CMF managers have not generated alpha, on average, relative to the Fama-French factors and momentum between 1996 and 2016.

Chapter 15: Pricing of Futures Contracts

1. **A stock index currently stands at 2,170. The risk-free interest rate is 1 percent a year with continuous compounding and the dividend yield on the index is 2 percent a year. Calculate the futures price for a six-month contract.**
   The "fair value" of the futures contract is $2{,}170e^{(r-dy)t} = 2{,}170e^{(0.01-0.02)(.5)} = 2{,}159.18$.

2. **If the stock index futures price in the market in question 1 were 2,150, explain what an arbitrageur would do to make a risk-free profit from the situation, and the amount that the arbitrageur would theoretically make per contract. Assume the "unit" or "tick" value of the futures contract in this example is $50.**
   Because the futures price is undervalued relative to the index in the market, the optimal strategy is to buy the futures contract, short the stocks in the index at 2,170, and invest the cash proceeds at a 1 percent rate of interest, while paying the dividend yield of 2 percent. At expiration, however, the investor will collect cash of $2{,}170e^{(r-dy)t} = 2{,}159.18$ less the long futures price of 2,150 and collect a net profit of $9.18 per contract, or $9.18*($50/tick) = $459 per contract in total.

3. **Identify the cost of carry for (a) non-dividend-paying stock, (b) dividend-paying stock, (c) stock index, (d) a commodity with storage costs, and (e) a foreign currency.**
   (a) The cost of carry is the risk-free rate.
   (b) The cost of carry is the risk-free rate minus the present value of dividends.
   (c) The cost of carry is the risk-free rate minus the dividend yield of the index.
   (d) The cost of carry is the risk-free rate plus storage costs.
   (e) The cost of carry is the domestic risk-free rate minus the foreign currency risk-free rate.

4. **Assume that silver is currently trading for $20 per ounce in the spot market, interest rates are 2 percent a year for a one-year maturity, and there is a cost of 3 percent a year to store a large quantity of silver bullion. Calculate the futures price of silver for delivery in one year.**
   The "fair value" of the futures contract is $Se^{(r+u)t} = 20e^{(0.02+0.03)(1)} = \$21.025$.

Chapter 16: Return Characteristics of Commodities

1. **Explain the primary disadvantage of owning physical commodities.**
   The primary disadvantage of owning physical commodities is the cost of carry. Investors who buy physical commodities must transport them, store them, and, in the case of agricultural commodities, contend with spoilage. The cost of insuring the physical commodity can also be part of the cost of carry. These costs can erode the potential return of investing in physical commodities.

2. **Explain the concept of a convenience yield.**
The *convenience yield* is the non-monetary benefit received from physically holding a commodity. It is an implied return. The convenience yield is inversely related to the level of inventory of the commodity. As inventory falls, a greater benefit exists to holding and having access to the physical commodity. In times when supply is high, fewer benefits exist to holding the physical commodity.

3. **Describe three sources of commodity futures returns.**
Three sources of commodity futures returns are the collateral return, spot return, and roll yield.

    - The *collateral return*, also called the Treasury-bill return, the cash return, or the collateral yield, is the return generated from the futures collateral position. Because commodity futures are leveraged, investors can have a large amount of cash tied up in collateral, which gets invested in other assets, usually risk-free assets such as Treasury bills.
    - The *spot price* of a commodity is the current price. The spot return reflects changes in the underlying commodity price.
    - The *roll yield* results when a commodities investor wants to hold a long position in futures over a long period of time. The investor must sell or "close out" positions in futures contracts that are expiring and reinvest in longer-term contracts. The roll return is the gain or loss associated with rolling a futures contract forward. Whether the market is in contango or backwardation determines whether the roll yield is positive or negative.

4. **Describe three advantages of adding commodities to a diversified portfolio.**
Adding commodities to a diversified portfolio has several advantages. First, some studies indicate commodities have historically earned equity-like returns with similar volatility. Second, commodities have a low or negative correlation with stock and bond returns, making them good diversifiers in a traditional portfolio. Third, commodities are positively correlated with inflation and changes in inflation, making them a good hedge against inflation.

Chapter 17: Issues in Benchmarking Commodity Performance

1. **Define a futures curve and discuss what it means for such a curve to be in "contango" or "backwardation."**
The *futures curve* is a graphic representation, called the term structure, which plots current (spot) and expected future (futures) prices of commodity investments. "Contango" and "backwardation" are terms used to describe the relation between spot and futures prices. When the term structure is in *contango*, the futures curve is upward sloping, resulting in the futures price being above the current spot price. Subsequently, a futures curve is in *backwardation* when the term structure of the futures curve is downward sloping and the futures price is lower than the current spot price.

2. **Discuss the major differences between the three generations of commodity indexes and how each generation generally addresses the issues of contango on a futures curve.**
   The most important difference between the three major commodity generations is how each deals with market contango. The first generation of indices is long only and does not account for the fundamentals of backwardation or contango. The second generation is also long only, but takes a more active approach by attempting to smooth the negative effects of contango and take advantage of backwardation. The third generation considers both long and short positions to take advantage of positive price appreciation during backwardation and negative price appreciation during contango markets, respectively.

3. **Discuss the concept of "financialization," including the arguments Masters (2008) and Irwin and Sanders (2012) make about its effect on commodity futures markets.**
   Financialization describes a growing presence and reliance on financial professionals in a market. Between 2003 and 2008, assets in passive commodity investments increased by 300 percent. Masters (2008) contends that these institutional investors are a root cause of the commodity bubble and subsequent crash in the mid-2000s. Conversely, Irwin and Sanders (2012) find increased correlations between commodity and capital markets, but increased correlations do not necessarily equate to a bubble. In fact, they maintain that lowering of transaction fees and barriers to entry into commodity markets has made these markets more efficient.

4. **Define "co-integration" and discuss its applicability to the association between commodity futures markets and public equity markets.**
   Co-integration is the statistical relation between asset price movements over time. Büyüksahin, Haigh, and Robe (2010) observe that correlations between the two first-generation commodity and equity indices rose dramatically during the financial crisis of 2007–2008, when equity markets rose and eventually fell. This finding suggests that electronically traded commodity markets cannot provide proper diversification benefits when they are most needed. It also suggests that index performance may deviate from true fundamentals in favor of investor behavior during times of extreme market events.

5. **Discuss the claim that commodity indexes are not truly passive indexes.**
   Unlike a publicly traded equity or bond index, which may weight index constituents by market capitalization, commodities do not have a market capitalization due to the netting principles of futures markets. Instead, commodity indexes are based on alternative weighting methodologies, such as worldwide production or liquidity, which can be subjective. For example, the GSCI weights its constituents by "worldwide production," which skews the performance of the index toward energy commodities. This index should outperform others if energy commodity prices surge. Additionally, commodity indexes are comprised of futures contracts, which require contracts to be rolled forward into new contracts before expiration. This process suggests that index construction must subjectively decide the tenure

of each commodity contract, as well as the strategy to mitigate the effects of contango and backwardation when contracts are rolled forward. These decisions are more active in nature, supporting the argument that commodity indexes have an active component to them.

Chapter 18: Volatility Transmission across Commodity Futures Markets

1. **Identify the three major classes of commodities.**
   The three major classes of commodities are agricultural products, energy, and metals.

2. **Explain the term "financialization of commodity markets."**
   Financialization of commodity markets refers to the phenomenon that a large inflow of investment capital to commodity futures markets occurred starting in the early 2000s.

3. **Identify three main reasons for the boom and bust in commodity prices.**
   The causes of boom and bust in commodity prices include (1) the growing demand from emerging economies, especially China, (2) low interest rates and effective dollar depreciation, and (3) improved liquidity attributable to the growing interest of institutional investors, including hedge funds and exchange-traded funds (ETFs).

4. **Identify which commodity futures markets are the largest contributors (recipients) of volatility spillovers to (from) others between 1990 and 2016.**
   The largest contributors and recipients of global commodity price volatility are energy and precious metals.

Chapter 19: Commodities in International and Emerging Markets

1. **Discuss several conventional facts about global commodity markets and how they relate to the movement of both equity and bond returns.**
   Past studies show that many benefits exist to investing in commodities' futures because their returns exhibit a fairly stable negative correlation with both equity and bond returns resulting from different commodity futures' behavior over a business cycle. By tracking the peaks and troughs of the business cycle and analyzing the performance of commodity futures, studies document that, on average, stocks and commodity futures behave similarly during expansions and recessions. Yet, the diversification benefits sought by investors are not only observable during early stages of recessions but also during late expansions, when returns on stocks and bonds are below their overall average. Thus, commodity futures serve to diversify cyclical variation in stock and bond returns.

Historically, commodity futures contribute relatively low risk (less downside risk) to a portfolio of stocks and bonds, but they perform better during periods of unexpected inflation and assist in the diversification of the cyclical movement in stock and bond markets.

2. **Explain some benefits of international diversification in equity and bond markets, including the emerging markets.**
Investors seek international diversification to reduce the overall risk of their portfolios and to potentially improve returns from this wide-spectrum strategy, notably in the emerging equity and bond markets. Studies make strong arguments favoring international stock and/or bond diversification. Although capital market integration has decreased some benefits of international portfolio diversification, the correlation coefficients between markets are still far from being perfectly positive. Thus, international assets provide risk-reduction opportunities for many investors. For instance, some emerging markets exhibit a low level of integration with the world market, while others are constrained by liquidity problems or have firms concentrated in a few industries. For instance, oil and construction companies dominate the economies of Saudi Arabia and its Persian Gulf neighbors. The economies of Brazil and Indonesia are similarly dependent on natural resources. Stock markets in these countries and hence the fortunes of the local economy reflect international commodity prices. Various ex post studies look at the gains of international diversification in equity and bond markets, including emerging markets. Some stress the importance of including corporate securities of less developed countries in international portfolios and building various investment strategies to profit from changes in emerging economies.

3. **Define an emerging market and discuss how the inclusion of global commodity futures could enhance investment strategies in emerging markets.**
An emerging market generally includes countries that are ready to emerge and be poised to grow more rapidly than the developed world. The World Bank defines "emerging economies" as nations with a per capita GDP below a certain level that are on the path from a less developed to a developed status. Emerging markets have experienced major transformations recently, representing countries with rapidly growing national economies in which industries have undergone and are continuing to undergo dramatic structural changes, and that hold promise despite generally having volatile and weak legal systems. Additionally, investors may adopt some emerging market-based strategies employed by hedge funds, typically using a top-down approach to identify investment opportunities across a broad range of countries, and then participating in all equity, bond, and commodity markets. Thus, investing in appropriate positions in some relevant global commodity futures connected to those emerging markets is another effective strategy to enhance emerging market bond and/or equity portfolios. This strategy can improve the overall returns and hedge potential exposures on a situational basis.

4. **Discuss the importance and role of the open interest of commodity futures in guiding investment decisions of global investors, notably those considering the emerging markets.**
   An important feature of the futures markets is *open interest*, which is the total number of outstanding contracts. A high open interest indicates that more trades will occur in the future and has a positive impact on trading volume. Open interest can be used to guide trades. Yet, open interest of commodity futures is indicative and informative about economic activity and inflation expectations as well. For instance, participants who are trying to roll their positions will adjust their bids or offers over time based on the amount of open interest remaining in the expiring month, using their previous experience of pricing patterns during a roll. In the futures markets, open interest is arguably a suitable measure of participant activity, because it represents the total demand for futures contracts. Moreover, open interest is also partly related to the market size of the underlying product. Institutional investors who implement various hedging or speculative strategies in commodity futures markets need to consider the size of a commodity market and how open interest influences market depth to be assured of adequate liquidity for buying and selling large numbers of contracts.

5. **Explain the nature of the relation between global commodity movement and business cycle of the emerging markets.**
   Evidence shows that while other macro and market variables may create a better understanding of the dynamics of emerging economies, the global commodity movement has a direct effect on GDP growth of many emerging markets. Metals, for instance, followed by agricultural and then energy futures market performances, contain much information about the business cycle of selected emerging market countries. Furthermore, commodities tend to move in an orderly fashion over the business cycle: when inflation pressures start to develop, commodities in general boom, but they peak when the inflation starts to decline.

6. **Identify and discuss a possible channel that links the state of global commodities and the overall outlook for emerging bond markets.**
   Empirical studies show that the dynamic relations between emerging nation bond markets and the state of global commodity markets is ubiquitous. Yet, differences exist in terms of economic significance, persistence, and magnitude across emerging nations and specific commodities. For instance, as energy products (e.g., oil and its refined fuels) perform well, energy-exporting countries, energy-dependent countries, and energy companies also do well in their debt obligations. However, during energy market downturns, these countries and firms often need to raise further capital (external debt or domestic bonds), thus offering other investors borrowing and investment opportunities. For some emerging countries, investment projects increase the need for diverse sources of funding with long-term maturities in order to balance books or maintain expansive plans. For instance, a drop in international oil prices usually puts considerable pressure on the fiscal and external debt positions of some countries and energy companies. This pressure

may prompt government officials to avoid issuing bonds if prices of energy products (or relevant commodities to that specific nation) remain above a comfortable level to the point that a national budget deficit may be eradicated and thus the need for issuing new bonds is reduced.

Chapter 20: Commodity Trading Strategies, Common Mistakes, and Catastrophic Blowups

1. **Discuss distinguishing features among trend-following CTAs.**
A successful trend-follower will curb losses on losing trades and let the winners ride. That is, trend followers quickly exit false trends and pursue real trends. Good managers will quickly cut losses and increase their exposures to winning trades, appropriately applying dynamic leverage.

2. **Define a futures calendar spread.**
A *futures calendar spread* is the spread between two or more of a commodity futures contract's delivery months. In all commodity futures markets, a different price exists for a commodity, depending on the commodity's delivery date. For example, with natural gas, a futures contract with an October delivery has a different price than a contract whose delivery is in December. Accordingly, a futures trader may trade the spread between the October versus December futures contracts, which would be termed the October-December calendar spread.

3. **Discuss three common mistakes that occur in carrying out commodity trading strategies.**
Commodity trading strategies involve three common trading mistakes. The first mistake is targeting absolute returns rather than risk metrics. Although traders should not target returns because trading strategies are ephemeral, they can target risk. In doing so, when a trading strategy inevitably loses its potency, a trader's results will not be catastrophic if the trader carefully manages risk.

A second common mistake is pursuing inappropriate sizing. Traders should be careful with trade sizing because commodity markets do not have natural two-sided flow. The commodity markets have *nodal liquidity*. If a commercial market participant needs to initiate or lift hedges, the timing may not come at a speculator's convenience. Before initiating a position, particularly one that is large compared to the size of the marketplace, traders should have a clear understanding of what flow or catalyst allows them to exit the position. Otherwise, the results can be catastrophic.

A third mistake is treating trading as an "intellectual challenge" rather than an exercise in "self-mastery and endurance." If novice traders believe that futures trading, particularly leveraged futures trading, is an "intellectual exercise," they may be psychologically unprepared for the periodic large-scale losses that are inevitable with this activity. Futures trading is a sustainable business activity for those who understand their own risk tolerance and adopt trading strategies that are consistent with their psychological profiles.

4. **Discuss key lessons learned from the Amaranth debacle.**
   Although one can justify the economic rationale for Amaranth's trading strategy, both trade sizing *and* value matter even more so. Amaranth's trade sizing was massive relative to the natural gas futures market's daily trading volume and open interest at the time. The fund had also entered into spread positions at levels that were far beyond typical levels for those spreads.
   Two possible conclusions can be drawn about Amaranth's risk managers. First, they should have been concerned about their fund being such a large fraction of the natural gas futures market. Second, they should have been concerned that large-scale losses would result if the valuation of the fund's spread positions reverted to past spread levels. The Amaranth case study also provides an example showing that a commodity market does not have natural two-sided flow, so that before initiating a large-scale position, traders should always have a clear exit plan in mind so as to avoid massive losses from a distressed liquidation.

5. **Discuss key lessons learned for FCM clients from the MF Global bankruptcy.**
   A key lesson from the MF Global (MFG) collapse is to pay more attention to the full scope of an FCM's business activities. Futures customers need to perform rigorous due diligence in choosing agents and counterparties. Another lesson is that the customer business of MFG and the institutional face—the proprietary business of MFG—differed substantially. Because MFG's FCM customers were apparently unaware of this fact, they did not understand the enhanced risks of using MFG as a steward of their futures margin funds. A third lesson involving the MFG bankruptcy is that FCM customers had to become more skeptical about the effectiveness of customer protections and therefore become more careful about the level of excess margin left at FCMs.

Chapter 21: Asset Allocation Strategies and Commodities

1. **Explain the importance of active risk and the meaning of the fundamental law of active management.**
   Active risk is the standard deviation of active returns and it indicates how much additional risk investors took to generate active returns. The fundamental law of active management helps to assess the value of active management, as expressed by the information ratio, which uses only breadth and skill. Breadth indicates the number of independent investment opportunities, while skill reflects an asset manager's ability to convert every forecast into a success.

2. **Identify the main commodity investment vehicles.**
   The main commodity investment vehicles include physical commodities, equities of commodity companies, derivative contracts, mutual funds, and ETFs. The proliferation of derivative contracts and ETFs has prompted the term "financialization of commodity markets."

3. **List the three major reasons to include commodities in an investment portfolio.**
Academics and practitioners agree upon the standard reasons to invest in commodities: (1) better diversification than a traditional portfolio composed of equity and bonds, (2) a hedge against inflation risk, and (3) the capture a commodity risk premium.

4. **Discuss the effect of economic turbulence on commodity investment.**
The financial crisis of 2007–2008, global economic expansion in China, and monetary policies drove interest rates nearly to zero and contributed to changing the previous rules in investing in commodities. The average risk premium to commodity futures between 2005 and 2014 was 3.67 percent compared to 5.23 percent previously with an increase in the correlation with traditional assets to 0.5 during the financial crisis. Only inflation has maintained a positive correlation with commodities. The consequence is that commodities may be losing their capacity to be an alternative asset class for asset managers.

5. **Describe the mechanism of commodity factor premiums.**
Factor-based approaches aim to enhance returns by taking advantage of risk premia linked to systematic factors. In commodity markets, the most widely used factors are value, contrarian momentum, carry, and monetary policy. *Value investing* style involves buying undervalued assets and selling overvalued assets. The *momentum investment* style is based on the simple rule to buy "winning" assets and to sell "losers." The *carry investment* style is based on selecting higher-yielding markets or assets and financing these positions by shorting lower-yielding markets or assets. Monetary policy, as a factor, is based on changes in monetary policies that could influence the weight of commodities in a portfolio.

Chapter 22: Food Prices and Food Price Volatility

1. **Explain why food prices matter for economic development.**
In developing countries, poor and near-poor households spend a large share of their incomes on food. Food prices matter for economic development because global poverty rates fall (rise) when food prices fall (rise).

2. **Discuss whether commodity price volatility matters for economic development.**
At a macroeconomic level, high commodity price volatility is the primary source of terms-of-trade volatility for developing countries that rely heavily on commodity exports. In turn, high rates of terms-of-trade volatility are associated with slow economic growth. At the farm level, price volatility discourages investment and the adoption of new technologies that improve on-farm productivity. In developing countries, commodity price risk adds to a large set of risks faced by poor smallholder farmers. Without access to formal risk markets and with limited capacity to self-insure, poor households adopt livelihood strategies that help them survive but keep them poor. An important consequence of poor-household livelihood strategies is that poor households are reluctant to adopt technologies designed to boost their incomes.

3. **Discuss whether long-term trends exist in food prices.**
Since 1900, traded food commodity prices have experienced trending sub-periods but no trend is apparent over the entire period. Studies using longer time series find the same result. Sustained increases in agricultural productivity have offset large increases in global food demand, forestalling price gains. Still, prices in the 2010s are high relative to recent history.

4. **Discuss whether trends exist in food price volatility.**
Surprisingly, trends do not exist in food price volatility, especially given major changes in technology and globalization since 1900, and the increased use of commodities as an asset class. Evidence shows that commodity prices are generally more closely linked to financial market events but this relation has not led to an increase in volatility. Commodity prices have not become more or less volatile relative to manufactured goods. In other words, no trend appears in developing countries' terms of trade. At the same time, many middle-income countries have managed to diversify their exports, thereby lessening the negative impact of volatile commodity prices on economic growth.

5. **Explain whether governments, individually or collectively, can intervene to control commodity price levels and volatility.**
History and economic theory suggest that governments are unable to intervene to control commodity price levels and volatility. International commodity agreements and domestic interventions meant to control commodity prices were commonplace in the second half of the twentieth century, but were largely abandoned as ineffective or too costly. During the same period, policies meant to speed economic development by favoring the manufacturing sector over agriculture slowed overall economic growth instead.

6. **Discuss possible governmental action to address high food prices and high food price volatility.**
Governments can provide targeted assistance to help chronically poor families and families affected by emergencies. Governments can also invest in people and communities to prepare household members for better jobs as well as in agricultural research and extension to improve productivity and influence food prices in the long term. Finally, governments can help extend the reach of risk markets to benefit developing country households.

7. **Identify mechanisms for extending risk markets.**
Important mechanisms for extending risk markets include warehouse receipt systems, index insurance, and contract farming. Warehouse receipt systems allow farmers and traders to use commodity inventories as collateral. However, these systems work best when commodity and financial markets are mature. Index insurance uses an easily observed indicator, like rainfall or average area yield, to trigger payouts. Index insurance is conceptually attractive, and experimental evidence shows that it encourages the adoption of better technologies, but index insurance has not been widely adopted outside of pilot programs. Contract farming reduces price and marketing risks for farmers. In settings where bargaining power is shared between buyers and sellers, evidence shows contract farming

can improve smallholder incomes. Contract farming has worked well in many countries.

Chapter 23: High Frequency Trading of Commodities

1. **Explain why U.S. futures markets took several years to become fully electronic trading platforms.**
   The U.S. exchanges were primarily mutual associations owned and governed by their members. Members traded for themselves or leased their seat to others who traded. Electronic trading was a form of direct competition that required new investments in capital for members. Many members were aging, so such investments were undesirable. They chose instead to limit electronic trading to non-pit hours, thereby continuing to earn returns on their (depreciating) human capital. By demutualizing, exchanges allowed many members to cash out, which opened the door for side-by-side electronic trading and the advent of high frequency traders (HFTs).

2. **Research into the flash crash on May 6, 2010 identified delays in trade reporting as correlated with the beginning and end of the crash. It also suggests that these data feed anomalies may be causally related to the withdrawal of liquidity from the market. Explain why stale prices affect liquidity and whether the expected effect is likely to differ for algorithms versus human traders.**
   Liquidity is the willingness to accept the other side of an incoming trade. The incoming trade is commonly a market order, so it seeks to clear order size at the prevailing price. However, with stale trade prices, liquidity providers are unclear as to what price to charge for supplying liquidity, so the market begins to fail as suppliers withdraw standing orders until prices are current. Whether algorithms or humans react differently depends on how participants determine that prices are stale. During the flash crash, prices diverged between futures and exchange-traded fund (ETF) markets that trade the underlying index. Algorithms are likely to see these divergent results first, as they are milliseconds apart. Some algorithms may have sought to arbitrage the differences only to find that they could not execute at the prices they thought had been quoted, which would confirm a delay in the data feed. Human traders are likely to take seconds or minutes, not milliseconds, to realize this problem.

3. **A computer algorithm is a set of rules that is programmed to make trading decisions. These rules rely on inputs from both market data and external sources, such as economic news announcements. If a trader knew the rules followed by some very active trading algorithms, explain what would limit the trader's ability to take advantage of these participants.**
   Knowing the rules is only the first step in developing a strategy to "front run" an algorithm. The system must also be faster than the target algorithm and to do that it must receive inputs, process information, and/or transmit messages faster. This type of speed advantage is costly, so front running an incumbent algorithm, whose in-place technology investments are sunk costs, may be unprofitable.

4. **Spoofing involves placing orders with the intent to cancel before a trade occurs. Explain why such behavior did not arise in traditional open outcry markets and why spoofing might be disruptive to current electronic markets.**
Traditional open outcry markets did not maintain order books with information available to all participants to enable spoofing. Canceling oral quotes was implicit in these markets as the quote was considered "good" only as long as the participant's breath was "warm." Participants were limited to quotes near the current market price. Other participants or pit managers sanctioned those who did not honor immediate responses to a quote. Present-day electronic markets reveal aggregate data on order sizes at different quote levels. A spoofer who places a large order may affect the actions of smart order routing (SOR) algorithms, leading to mistakes in the optimal size of child orders, which creates price impacts that may have been avoided with accurate information.

Chapter 24: Energy Risk Management

1. **Identify the major financial instruments used in energy risk management.**
The more important derivatives used in energy risk management include forward and futures contracts, commodity swaps, differential swaps on energy products, call and put options on various spreads, swaptions, and more exotic options.

2. **Discuss the principal steps in establishing an energy risk management program.**
Establishing a risk management program at an energy company involves five steps. The first step is to identify primary risk factors that can be used to draw a risk map to help with risk analysis. The second step is to use quantitative methods, such as risk metric models, to assess those key risk factors. The third step is solution analysis, which includes identifying, measuring, and evaluating the solution. The fourth step is the decision process that involves selecting the best solution, using decision models to make decisions, and implementing the solutions to migrate risks. The final step is system administration that monitors, judges, and evaluates the entire risk management process.

3. **Identify the main assumption underlying the calculation of VaR, discuss its advantages and disadvantages, and explain why CVaR might be a better risk metric than VaR.**
The basic analytic VaR model assumes that market variable returns are normally distributed. VaR has several advantages: (1) VaR reflects the maximum loss for a specific holding period with a given degree of confidence; (2) the concept of VaR is relatively easy to understand; and (3) VaR can be applied to different asset classes. VaR's main disadvantages are (1) the VaR measure is inaccurate for assets with asymmetric or nonlinear payoffs; and (2) the VaR measure does not indicate the maximum possible loss. CVaR may be better than VaR because it estimates the expected excess loss given a tail event.

4. **Identify the various means available to mitigate credit risk in energy trading.**
Mitigating credit risk in energy trading involves:

- Using margining agreements between the two trading parties to set transaction standards.
- Obtaining collateral from the counterparty.
- Establishing a credit limit for the counterparty.
- Reducing the total number of trades between the two parties by portfolio compression.
- Using a credit sleeve by trading with a broker (intermediary).
- Requesting guarantees from a parent company when the counterparty is one of its subsidiaries.
- Netting the payments or transactions between the counterparties.
- Using OTC clearing platforms.

5. **List the steps used in the historical simulation method to compute VaR.**
   Using the example provided in the chapter, the steps include:

   - Identifying the market factor as the spot market price of crude oil and computing future values based on the historical spot market price.
   - Obtaining the historical marked-to-market values for the last 100 days.
   - Calculating the daily returns of the marked-to-market values.
   - Ranking the 100 daily returns (potential gains and losses in the preceding step) in ascending order.
   - Selecting the loss equal to the fifth percentile of all the daily returns and multiplying this amount by the portfolio's value.

Chapter 25: Financialization of Commodity Markets

1. **Explain the meaning of the financialization of commodity markets.**
   The financialization of commodity markets refers to the increased market participation of financial investors in the commodity futures markets. These investors have no interest in the underlying commodity and only invest in the marketplace to improve the risk-return trade-off of their portfolios.

2. **Discuss the major types of participants in the commodity futures markets.**
   The two major types of participants in the commodity futures markets are commercial and noncommercial traders. Commercial traders are typically called hedgers and largely consist of commodity producers and processors who engage the futures markets to limit losses as prices change. Noncommercial traders are colloquially referred to as speculators and typically consist of institutional investors and other large traders such as hedge funds and money managers. These investors do not engage in commodity production or consumption activities, but use futures contracts for investment purposes.

3. **Discuss how the rise in investor participation may affect the commodity futures markets.**
   Financial investors can affect the futures markets through risk sharing by way of their role as liquidity providers and consumers. They can also affect the

information discovery process through their contribution to informational frictions associated with "speculative activity." In theory, investor involvement makes futures market prices, volatility, and intra- and intermarket return correlations rise. Other factors beyond the well-understood fundamental effects of supply and demand affect prices.

4. **Summarize the empirical evidence on the impact of financialization.**
   The empirical evidence is mixed given that the number of studies supporting and contradicting the impact of financialization on commodity futures markets is similar. The specification of the speculation variable seems to influence the findings. Studies using a proxy variable generally find evidence of reinforcing effects from financialization, whereas studies directly measuring speculation find weakening or no effects from financialization. Overall, evidence points toward financialization as having a reinforcing impact on prices, a weakening impact on returns and risk premiums, and a mixed impact on volatility and spillovers.

Chapter 26: Virtual Currencies as Commodities

1. **Discuss at least one type of risk associated with virtual currencies.**
   Virtual currencies have risks to both their users and regulators. For instance, the irreversibility of transactions on virtual currencies poses a major risk to consumers who may lack legal recourse for reversing contested transactions. Moreover, because cryptocurrency networks allow for lower costs and faster settlement times, they sometimes attract illegitimate activities. In fact, digital currency networks can be used to trade illicit goods and services, engage in money laundering, or even to finance terrorists.

2. **Discuss the main differences between virtual currencies and fiat money such as the U.S. dollar.**
   Several key features distinguish virtual currencies from fiat currencies. First, unlike fiat money, virtual currencies have no physical shape or form. Second, virtual currencies are decentralized (i.e., have no central repository or administration) and lack backing by a commodity or any legal entities. Third, virtual currencies cannot be reproduced easily because they are generated by unique codes. Fourth, most virtual currencies enjoy the property of being scarce because of their finite/capped supply.

3. **Explain why Bitcoin is highly volatile.**
   Several reasons can explain the excessive volatility of Bitcoin. One factor is the highly unstable supply and demand of Bitcoin. Because of infrequent trading, large trades of Bitcoins can materially affect exchange rates. The high volatility of Bitcoin is also due to the lack of endorsement by regulatory bodies, which decreases investors' confidence in its value, making Bitcoin rather attractive to speculators. The finite supply of Bitcoin is another important reason for it excessive volatility. In fact, the maximum supply of 21 million Bitcoins is expected to be reached between 2110 and 2140.

4. **Discuss other possible uses of the technology associated with virtual currencies beyond retail payment services.**
The technology associated with cryptocurrencies has several possible applications beyond retail payment services. For example, the distributed ledgers based on a blockchain can be used to record and transfer the ownership of financial instruments such as bonds and equity shares. Though blockchain technology is largely associated with the financial sector, its applications can extend to other industries such as media, consumer products, industrial products, automobiles, travel, hospitality, retail, life sciences, healthcare, government, and energy. For instance, the distributed ledger applications of blockchain can be extended to travel and hospitality sector through the simplification of settlement process, real-time updating of points balances, and improved points management across franchised operations.

5. **Identify the countries that consider virtual currencies as commodities.**
Whether cryptocurrencies should be classified as a commodity is still the subject of debate. To date, only the U.S. government, through the CFTC actions in September 2015, has classified cryptocurrencies as a commodity.

Chapter 27: Research Issues in Commodities and Commodity Derivatives

1. **Describe the CFTC's Commitments of Traders (COT) report and discuss how it can be used in research.**
The Commitments of Traders (COT) report provides a breakdown of each Tuesday's open interest for markets in which 20 or more traders hold positions greater than or equal to the reporting levels established by the CFTC. Reports are available in both a short and a long format. The short report shows open interest separately by reportable and nonreportable positions. For reportable positions, additional data are provided for commercial and noncommercial holdings, spreading, changes from the previous report, percentages of open interest by category, and numbers of traders. Besides the information in the short report, the long report groups the data by crop year, where appropriate, and shows the concentration of positions held by the largest four and eight traders. Supplemental reports show aggregate futures and option positions of Noncommercial, Commercial, and Index Traders in 12 selected agricultural commodities. The CFTC also makes available more than three years of history of disaggregated data included in the weekly COT reports. The data included in the COT reports can be used to conduct numerous studies involving commodities.

2. **Discuss why firms might choose between trading listed futures contracts and trading OTC.**
Firms might choose between trading listed futures contracts and trading OTC due to structural differences that exist between them. For example, futures contracts are standardized and typically more liquid and regulated than OTC

markets. However, exchanges require collateral, and the requirements for posting variation margin are inflexible. Many firms prefer to trade OTC because of the flexibility they offer, particularly with respect to margin. Historically, the OTC marketplace was less regulated, lacked price transparency, and was void of central clearing. Another issue is that aggregate data on hedging pressure are based on the CFTC's COT data, which can be misleading if hedgers tend to use the OTC markets more.

3. **Discuss how theories of hedging pressure explain the determination of equilibrium futures prices.**
An academic debate started in the 1930s over the existence and source of a commodity futures risk premium. The first hypothesis for the source of a commodity futures risk premium was the risk transfer or hedging pressure hypothesis of Keynes (1930) and Hicks (1939), in which a risk premium accrued to speculators as a reward for accepting the price risk that hedgers sought to transfer. In other words, hedging pressure theory for futures states that if demand for short hedging exceeds long speculation, long speculators require compensation in the form of a risk premium. Simply stated, if the balance of hedging positions is net short, speculators must be enticed to offset the imbalance by going net long, demanding more return (i.e., a risk premium) for taking more risk.

In the original normal backwardation theory of Keynes and Hicks, producers take short positions in the futures market to hedge their initial long positions in the commodity. Their supply of futures contracts, or hedging pressure, tends to drive down the futures price relative to the expected value of the later spot price, to generate a downward bias (normal backwardation) in the futures price. Speculators who enter on the long side of futures contracts bear a risk. Being risk-averse, they are therefore compensated by a positive expected profit on their positions. The hedging pressure models are "partial equilibrium" in the sense that they do not model the consumption choice between the futures-traded and other commodities.

Several researchers extended this theory, culminating in the equilibrium-based generalized hedging pressure hypothesis in which due to nonparticipation effects, hedging pressure influences the risk premium of commodity futures. These theories link backwardation, the mainstay of the Keynesian theory, to lower levels of hedgers' hedging pressure, and contango, to higher levels of hedgers' hedging pressure.

4. **Describe the financialization debate for commodities.**
Over the past decade or so, commodity futures have become a popular asset class in investor portfolios. The large inflow of investment capital to commodity futures markets during this period, a phenomenon called financialization, has generated a heated debate about whether financialization distorts commodity prices. Opposing views concern whether investment flows from financial investors have affected commodity prices. Some contend that the dramatically increased participation by financial market participants that do not have commercial commodity activity as their main business distorts commodity prices. The "bubble view" contends that commodity index investors caused a gigantic bubble in energy and

agricultural commodities in 2007 and 2008. The "business-as-usual view" maintains that no bubble existed. Rejecting one extreme view does not justify the other because the truth might be more nuanced. In all likelihood, financialization has transformed commodity markets in subtle ways—some of are good, while others are bad.

Others contend that financialization has changed the behavior and dependence structure between commodities and the general stock market. A common perception is that the increase in co-movements resulted from distressed investors selling both assets during the recent financial crisis. Some evidence suggests that financial distress alone cannot explain the size and persistence of co-movements. One argument is that commodities have become an investment style for institutional investors. Given that institutional investors continue to target funds into commodities, spillovers between commodities and the stock market are likely to remain high in the future. In conclusion, the same economic mechanisms for financial markets—information aggregation and risk sharing—may also affect commodity markets.

Chapter 28: Future of Commodity Markets and Investments

1. **Identify the global region with the most growth potential for commodity trading in the near future and provide support for this view.**
According to commodity traders, North America has the most growth potential. The United States has increased its oil production via the shale oil boom. In fact, the United States could become a net exporter of all energy products as soon as 2019 if energy prices remain high. Another clear sign of growth for U.S. commodities is the large swing in employment growth in several specific industries across the various commodity markets, including energy, metals, recyclables, agriculture, livestock, and even industries in financial markets related to commodity trading.

2. **Identify two primary causes of the excess supply in commodity markets and the commodity industry most affected by this excess supply.**
Two primary causes of excess supply in commodity markets are China and government interventions. China's shift to a consumer-led economy from a manufacturing-based economy has created a global slowdown in the demand for commodities, especially metals such as steel. China not only represents about 40 percent of global demand for metal commodities, but it also is lowering its demand of foreign steel and increasing its supply of cheap steel. Like other commodities, steel companies have been forced to make drastic cuts to increase operating efficiency. These cuts included shutting down or idling more than 45 million tonnes of global steelmaking capacity. Besides China, government interventions are another large reason for excess steel capacity. These interventions include subsidies for inefficient steel facilities and approval for new steel facilities, mandated

trade measures, constraints on foreign investment, and specific operating policies for government financial agencies.

3. **Discuss the primary reason for the mass exodus of banks from the physical commodity trading business and which investment banks represent the three largest remaining participants in the commodity markets.**
   Regulations are squeezing the margins on banks in commodity trading, making the situation difficult for banks to find profitable areas for business, especially in those areas where they have to physically hold the commodities. Although several regulations affect the overall commodities markets, the Dodd-Frank Act in the United States and the Basel III/CRD IV in the European Union are arguably two of the major reasons banks are leaving the commodity markets. Banks are not only losing revenue and clients, but top talent is also leaving to join trading houses or to start their own firms. In some cases, banks are even selling their top talent to non-bank competitors. Currently, the top three investment banks in commodity trading listed in order of revenue for 2015 are Goldman Sachs, JPMorgan, and Citi.

4. **Explain how changes in technology both positively and negatively affect the commodity industry and provide several examples.**
   On the positive side, several obvious changes in technology such as fracking have led to increased commodity production, and better batteries have resulted in increased energy storage. However, on the negative side, the one change in technology that worries many commodity traders is the rise of algorithmic trading. As the mathematical models for algorithms advance to take better advantage of data-driven fundamental and technical analysis, commodity traders will probably be forced to leave the industry or work in an even more specialized capacity than they already do. For example, a large percentage of future commodity traders will likely either work for a large multinational firm that can afford employees that can create and manage algorithms or work on complex deals in niche areas where algorithms are scarce.

Index

Note: Page numbers in italics refer to tables (*t*) and figures (*f*) within the text.)

Printed in the USA/Agawam, MA
September 4, 2019

737459.002